Issues in Education

Keepers of the Dream

Becoming A TEACHER

Becoming A TEACHER

Fourth Edition

Forrest W. Parkay
Washington State University

Beverly Hardcastle Stanford
Azusa Pacific University

Allyn and Bacon

Boston / London / Toronto / Sydney / Tokyo / Singapore

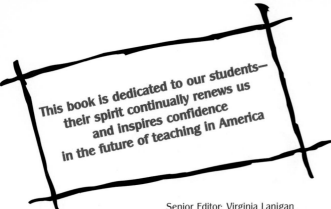

This book is dedicated to our students—their spirit continually renews us and inspires confidence in the future of teaching in America

Senior Editor: Virginia Lanigan
Developmental Editor: Mary Ellen Lepíonka
Editorial Assistant: Kris Lamarre
Senior Marketing Manager: Kathy Hunter
Editorial-Production Administrator: Rob Lawson
Editorial-Production Service: Colophon
Copyeditor: Susan Bonthron
Photo Researcher: Susan Duane
Composition Buyer: Linda Cox
Manufacturing Buyer: Suzanne Lareau
Cover Administrator: Linda Knowles
Text Designer: Melinda Grosser

Library of Congress Cataloging-in-Publication Data

Parkay, Forrest W.
    Becoming a teacher / Forrest W. Parkay, Beverly Hardcastle
  Stanford. — 4th ed.
      p.   cm.
    Includes bibliographical references and indexes.
    ISBN 0-205-26861-7
      1. Teaching—Vocational guidance.   2. Education—Study and
  teaching—United States.   3. Teachers—United States—Attitudes.
  4. Teaching—Computer network resources.   I. Stanford, Beverly
  Hardcastle, 1938–   . II. Title.
  LB1775.P28   1997
  371.1′0023′73—DC21   97-11802
                                                              CIP

Printed in the United States of America
10 9 8 7 6 5 4 3 2   01 00 99 98

Contents

3 HISTORICAL FOUNDATIONS OF AMERICAN EDUCATION 63

7 LEGAL CONCERNS IN AMERICAN EDUCATION   199

8 TEACHING DIVERSE LEARNERS   237

9 ADDRESSING LEARNERS' INDIVIDUAL NEEDS 275

12 TEACHERS AS EDUCATIONAL LEADERS 379

Preface

The fourth edition of *Becoming a Teacher* introduces you to the stimulating and complex world of teaching at the threshold of the 21st century. To help you begin your journey toward becoming a professional teacher, we highlight the concept of **mentoring** throughout the book. For example, the **"Dear Mentor"** feature gives you an opportunity to be advised by outstanding teachers from around the country. These high-performing teachers will provide you with practical advice for meeting the complex challenges of teaching. The book also highlights **teacher leadership,** since today's teachers are assuming diverse leadership roles beyond the classroom. For instance, **a new chapter, "Teachers as Educational Leaders,"** describes how teachers are playing a vital role in educational reform.

In addition, the book includes in its chapter-ending material a **new "Teacher's Database"** feature with **online activities** for using the vast resources of the World Wide Web and the Internet to facilitate your professional growth. Cyberspace has transformed teaching and learning in many schools and classrooms; and advanced telecommunications will continue to change the way teachers teach and assess students' learning.

In addition, the book continues the popular **"Professional Portfolio"** feature that will enable you to document your growth and accomplishments over time. Each chapter includes guidelines for creating a portfolio entry you can actually use when you begin teaching; in addition, you may wish to use selected portfolio entries during the process of applying for your first teaching position.

HOW THIS BOOK IS ORGANIZED

The first two chapters of the book are on the theme of teachers and teaching. After reading these chapters you will be better able to determine if teaching is a good career choice for you. Among the topics we address are: why people choose to teach, the challenges and realities of teaching, the knowledge and skills you will need to become a teacher, and how to establish mentoring relationships.

Chapters 3 through 7 take up the foundations of education, which every professional teacher needs to know. These foundational areas include the historical, social, cultural, philosophical, political, financial, and legal dimensions of American education.

In chapters 8, 9, 10, and 11, we explore student characteristics and the worlds of the classroom and the school. We examine characteristics of students at different stages of development, students as learners, the dynamics of classroom life, and the curricula that are taught in schools.

Finally, in the last three chapters we consider issues and trends that will impact your quest to become an effective teacher, especially the expanding leadership role of teachers, the use of educational technology and cyberspace, planning for a successful first year of teaching, international education in a changing world, and your role in shaping the future of education. Included in *Becoming a Teacher* are many features we believe will help you prepare for a rewarding future as a professional teacher.

FEATURES AND LEARNING AIDS THROUGHOUT THIS BOOK

Opening scenarios present decision-making or problem-solving situations for you to reflect upon and resolve. These situations are referred to again in the chapter and give you an opportunity to apply your new learning in specific problem-solving contexts.

So that you may be inspired by outstanding teachers, a **Keepers of the Dream** feature in each chapter profiles an individual in education whose philosophies and professional contributions reflect a commitment to touching others' lives through teaching.

A **Professional Reflection** feature in each chapter gives you an opportunity to reflect on your beliefs and values and on issues teachers face. This feature is designed to give you practice in the applied reflective inquiry that should characterize your professional life.

So that you will be aware of contemporary issues in becoming a teacher, **Issues in Education** in each chapter use a cartoon format to present interesting developments or controversies in education that have aroused public opinion and attracted media attention.

Dear Mentor is a popular feature in each chapter that presents an actual exchange of letters between preservice teachers, such as yourself, and experienced mentor teachers. In their letters the novices raise questions or concerns they have about teaching. In the replies, expert practicing teachers, including many award-winning teachers and Teachers of the Year, provide practical and wise advice.

To guide your study, **Focus Questions** at the beginning of each chapter reflect the questions posed in the main headings of the text. As a further study aid, **Key Terms and Concepts** are boldfaced in the text and listed with page cross-references at the end of chapters. An expanded **Glossary** at the end of the book helps you quickly locate the definitions of key terms and concepts and the text pages on which they appear. **Professional Portfolio** is a popular end-of-chapter feature that gives you the opportunity to begin preparing a professional portfolio.

Other end-of-chapter learning aids in this edition include a concise **Summary** and suggested **Applications and Activities.** Applications and activities include journal-writing opportunities in "Teacher's Journal," guidelines for finding educational resources on the World Wide Web and Internet in "Teacher's Database," and field experiences in "Observations and Interviews." In the **Teacher's Journal,** we continue a feature that has proved useful and popular with readers. The short, optional journal-writing activities are based on the

"writing-to-learn" and "writing-across-the-curriculum" concepts. Your instructor may ask you to keep a teacher's journal to encourage you to actively reflect as you learn about teaching.

An updated and expanded **Teacher's Resource Guide** at the end of the book provides a rich and varied array of materials, sources, strategies, contacts, and data you can rely on for support as you enter the teaching profession. Students who have used previous editions of this book report that the Teacher's Resource Guide has proven extremely valuable as they prepare for, and begin, their first teaching position.

TELL US WHAT YOU THINK IS IMPORTANT!

So that we may serve you better, this edition of *Becoming a Teacher* provides you with opportunities to become directly involved in the development of the next edition. Information that you supply on the **Reader Feedback Form** (see last page of this book) helps to guide us in the revision process, and we encourage you to respond when you complete your course. You may also contact the authors directly by e-mail:

Forrest Parkay: fwparkay@wsu.edu

Beverly Stanford: stanford@apu.edu

In addition, check out the Allyn and Bacon homepage on the web to locate more information and activities relating specifically to the fourth edition of *Becoming a Teacher:*

http://www.abacon.com

Allyn and Bacon invites you to participate in their ongoing **Novice-Mentor Correspondence Program,** in which selected student letters on chapter-related topics are answered by master teachers and considered for publication. Send your letter, addressed "Dear Mentor," to the following address:

"Novice Letter"
c/o V. Lanigan
Allyn and Bacon
160 Gould Street
Needham Heights, MA 02194-2310

Or send your letter by e-mail to the following address:

VLaniganAB@aol.com

We congratulate you on accepting the challenge of becoming a professional teacher. We hope this text will serve you well as you begin your quest. Best wishes!

ACKNOWLEDGMENTS

Many members of the Allyn and Bacon team provided us with expert assistance during the preparation of the fourth edition of *Becoming a Teacher*. Without a doubt, Mary Ellen Lepionka, our developmental editor, heads this list. Her suggested chapter revision outlines, expert feedback on draft manuscripts, and skillful orchestration of the revision process, from beginning to end, are deeply appreciated. As with the previous two editions, the authors benefited from Mary Ellen's broad knowledge of education and textbook publishing and her superb talent as a writer and editor. The strengths of the final text reflect, in no small measure, Mary Ellen's input. Lastly, during the final months of the revision process, Mary Ellen provided Forrest W. Parkay with unwavering support as he completed the remaining revision tasks while adjusting to his role as Visiting Fulbright Scholar at Kasetsart University's Center for Research on Teaching and Teacher Education in Bangkok, Thailand. He is deeply grateful for her patience, encouragement, and understanding, as well as her willingness to devote additional hours to bring the project to completion.

The authors extend a very special thanks to Nancy Forsyth, Editor-in-Chief; Virginia Lanigan, Series Editor; Kathy Hunter, Marketing Manager; and Rob Lawson, Production Administrator; as well as Peg Latham, Production Coordinator; Susan Bonthron, copyeditor; and Lisa Turowsky, indexer, all of whom were steadfast in their support of the fourth edition.

The authors extend a special thanks to Kate Steffens of Bemidji State University. A gifted teacher with a keen understanding of how students learn, Kate prepared an outstanding Test Bank for the fourth edition.

We are also grateful to the many people throughout the United States who have used the previous edition and provided suggestions and materials for this edition, including our students. We extend thanks to Thomas Gougeon of the University of Calgary, Alberta, for his input and for expanding the usefulness of this book for Canadian readers by preparing *Becoming a Teacher*, [*Canadian Edition*] (Prentice Hall, Canada, 1996). We also wish to thank the following reviewers, who provided concise, helpful suggestions during the developmental stages of this book:

Clinton Collins, University of Kentucky

Augustine Garcia, California State University, Bakersfield

Jeffrey Glanz, Kean College of New Jersey

Mildred L. Rice Jordan, Rider University

Van D. Mueller, University of Minnesota

Betty Jo Simmons, Longwood College

Peter H. Yaun, College of Charleston

Ronald L. Zigler, Penn State, Abington-Ogontz

Forrest W. Parkay appreciates the support of his family, friends, and colleagues during the intensive, months-long revision process. In particular, Bernard Oliver, Dean of the College of Education at Washington State University; Walter H. Gmelch, Associate Dean and Acting Chair of Kinesiology and Leisure Studies; Larry Bruya, Assistant Dean; Donald Reed, Chair of the Department of Educational Leadership and Counseling Psychology; and the faculty, teaching assistants, and research assistants in the Department of Educational Leadership and Counseling Psychology gave him much-appreciated encouragement and support. During the final months of the revision process, the following individuals at Kasetsart University in Bangkok, Thailand, were understanding and supportive: Supitr Samahito, Dean, Faculty of Education; Pranee Potisook, Director, Center for Research on Teaching and Teacher Education; and Center staff members Putachard Chansakorn, Pontip Chaiso, Apa Chantrarasakul, Pawinee Srisukvatananun, Mantmart Leesatayakul, Saowaporn Muangkoe, and Yupa Viravaidhaya.

In addition, the following colleagues provided Forrest W. Parkay with ideas, resources, and suggestions for this edition: Jacki Erickson, Gisela

Ernst-Slavit, Tim Gadson, Mary Gardiner, Fumie Hashimoto, Etta Hollins, Karen Michaelis, Darcy Miller, Merrill M. Oaks, Nils Peterson, Toby Schwartz, and Chris Sodorff, all of Washington State University; Sandra Damico, Emory University; Robert Leahy, Stetson University; Judith McBride, McGill University; Cynthia Dillard, Ohio State University; Ralph Karst, Northeastern Louisiana University; James Monroe, Dade County School System; Sandi MacQuinn, Rogers High School; and Kristi Rennebohm-Franz, Sunnyside Elementary School. And, for demonstrating the power of professional inquiry, he owes a profound debt to a great teacher, mentor, and friend, Herbert A. Thelen, Professor Emeritus, University of Chicago.

Finally, the personal support Forrest W. Parkay received from his family was invaluable. During the revision process, the moments he spent with his daughters Anna, Catherine, and Rebecca were very special and brought much-needed balance back into his life. To Arlene, his wife, friend, and helper, he gives a deep thanks. She was always there to provide the support that made the fourth edition possible. Moreover, she made many valuable contributions to the project, from obtaining letters of permission, to selecting cartoons, to cross-checking references and hundreds of revision-related details while her husband was overseas. Since the first edition of *Becoming a Teacher,* Arlene's encouragement, patience, and understanding have been remarkable.

Beverly Hardcastle Stanford thanks the many individuals who provided inspiration and assistance in the preparation of this fourth edition. At Azusa Pacific University, the supportive spirits of President Richard Felix, Provost Patricia Anderson, and Alice Watkins, Dean of Education and Behavioral Studies, brighten the way for faculty to dream and toil on projects such as this. Additional thanks go to Dean Watkins for connecting the author with several dynamic teachers who are "experts" in this volume. Stanford also appreciates the support of all her colleagues in the Education Department. She thanks especially, Maria Pacino, for her ready assistance with relevant research, and pays tribute to her colleagues who teach so creatively with this book: Nancy Brashear, Director of Secondary Teacher Education; Marti Garlett, Director of Elementary Teacher Education; Marilyn Lewis, Dennis Jacobsen,

Margaret Albertson, Mimi Zamary, and Jim Eagon. Special recognition is always due to the department assistants who lighten loads and lift spirits, and for this project in particular, Donna Kappe and Chris Zeilenga. Stanford is grateful to librarians Jacquelyn Swinney of Azusa Pacific University and Arlene Sapp of Johns Hopkins University who provided expert assistance as she worked on this endeavor at her home university and during her sabbatical in Maryland.

For their inspiration as passionate educators and their generosity in sharing time in their busy careers, Stanford is grateful to the Keepers of the Dream: James Banks, Nel Noddings, Kristi Rennebohm Franz, Matty Rodriquez-Walling, Sandra Dylan MacQuinn, Caroline Bitterwolf, Kay Toliver, Marion Wright Edelman, and Vito Perrone. In memory of the late Ernest Boyer, who thanked us for our profile on him in the last edition and to whom we pay tribute as a Keeper in this, we say we are forever indebted to his shining example of a compassionate educator and unrelenting advocate for improving the quality of life and education for our children and young people.

Beverly Hardcastle Stanford also thanks the students with whom she has been privileged to work, beginning teachers and veterans alike. Their questions and insights continue to teach her. For this book, she is especially thankful to those who contributed questions and concerns as novices in the "Novice and Expert Teachers on Teaching" feature: Stephanie Pine, Erwin Obdam, Allison Jones, Mari Cortes, Tricia Wahlstrom, Brad Mack, Danae Martinez, Moya Lyttle, Lori Iwamoto, Connie Dougherty, John Gage, Kevin Glaspy, Eddie Franco, and Pam Schnelbach.

In addition, she expresses a special thanks to the expert teachers who offered their wisdom so generously in the same feature: Mary Beth Blegen, Rosamond Welchman, Glen Green, Rodney D. Smith, Michael Morales, Mary Harrell, Stacy DeKnikker, Masako Kawase, Paul Flores, Moyra Contreras, Elizabeth Haden, Elizabeth Ann Lyles, Paul Liner, and Carol Gilkinson.

For their personal encouragement and support, Beverly Hardcastle Stanford thanks her friends and family. To Kaoru Yamamoto, professor and mentor, she extends deep gratitude once more for his friendship and the high standards he sets for caring as

Forrest Parkay with his daughters Catherine and Rebecca and family pet Shadow.

Beverly Hardcastle Stanford with her grandsons Parker Daniel Smith and Emerson Lewis Smith.

well as scholarship. She thanks her son, Daniel Clayton Lewis, daughter-in-law, Monica DeMott, and sister, Valerie Schamel, for their steady interest in this work. To her daughter, Jennifer Lewis Smith, and son-in-law, Douglas Smith, she gives heartfelt thanks for being such wonderful hosts for her sabbatical fall. The daily assistance, healthy dinners, and beautiful memories contributed richly to the final days of this project. Grandsons Parker Daniel Smith and Emerson Lewis Smith were no small part of that golden time. Their delightful natures, energetic curiosity, and intent attention to the world around them brought home once more how important a teacher's work is.

Finally, her greatest thanks goes to Dick Stanford, her husband, partner, and friend. His expertise in educational technology was generously tapped in the development of the Teacher's Resource Guide. His ongoing able assistance, unrelenting encouragement, and joyful spirit have made her work on each edition of this text possible and continue to enrich her life.

F.W.P.
B.H.S.

Becoming
A TEACHER

"Why do I [teach]? It's the way I am!"
—Mary V. Bicouvaris
1989 National Teacher of the Year

Teaching: Your Chosen Profession

You began to take courses to become a teacher just two years ago—it hardly seems possible that today you're going to have your first job interview. "Am I ready? Do I have what it takes to be a good teacher? Can I handle the stress?" These and other questions about your readiness for teaching fill your mind while walking from the faculty parking lot toward the school, a three-story brick building in a residential area of a medium-sized city.

Approaching the main entrance, you look at the dozens of students playing on the open field next to the building. Their joyful, exuberant sounds this warm late-August morning remind you of your own school days. Some children are moving constantly, running in tight circles and zig-zags as they yell and motion to friends who are also on the move. Others stand near the entrance in groups of two or three, talking and milling about as they wait for the bell signaling the start of the first day of school.

At the bottom of the long stairs leading up to a row of green metal doors, you overhear the conversation of three students.

"It's a great movie. What time should we meet?" the taller of two girls asks. Before her friends can respond, she adds, "My aunt's going to pick me up at four o'clock, so I should be home by four-thirty."

"Let's meet at five o'clock," the other girl says. "I can be ready by then."

"Si, pero no creo que pueda hacerlo para las cinco," the boy says. "Tengo que llevar a mi hermanita a la clinica. ¿Podermos hacerlo después?"

"Bueno, pero no muy tarde," the tall girl says, switching effortlessly to Spanish. "Tenemos que reunirnos con los otros chicos."

"Si, además no quiero perder el comienzo de la película," says the other girl.

Reaching the top of the stairs, you open a door and walk through the vestibule out into a brightly lit hallway. The main office is directly in front of you. To the right of the office door is a bulletin board proclaiming in large red block letters, "Welcome back, students!" Beneath that greeting, in smaller black letters, is another message: "It's going to be a great year!"

Inside the office, you approach the counter on which sits a plastic sign that says "Welcome" in five languages: English, Spanish, Swahili, Chinese, and Russian. You introduce yourself to the school's head secretary. He remains seated behind a gray steel desk covered with loose papers.

"I have an appointment with Mrs. Wojtkowski," you inform him. "It's about a replacement for Mr. Medina."

"Good. She's expecting you. Why don't you have a seat over there?" He motions for you to sit on the couch across from the teachers' mailboxes. "She's working with some teachers on setting up a meeting of our Site-Based Council. She ought to be finished in just a few minutes."

While waiting for Mrs. Wojtkowski, you think about questions you might be asked. Why did you choose to become a teacher? What is your philosophy of education? How would you use technology in your classroom? What is your approach to classroom management? How would you meet the needs of students from different cultural and linguistic backgrounds? How would you set up a program in your major teaching area? How would you involve parents in the classroom? What are your strengths? Why should the district hire you?

Reflecting on these questions, you admit they are actually quite difficult. Your answers, you realize, could determine whether or not you get the job.

■

Though predictable, the interview questions just posed are surprisingly challenging. Why *did* you decide to become a teacher? How *will* you meet the needs of all students? What *do* you have to offer students? The answers to these and similar questions are dependent on the personality and experiences of the person responding. However, they are questions that professional teachers recognize as important and worthy of careful consideration.

The primary purpose of this book is to orient you to the world of education and to help you begin to formulate answers to such questions. In addition, this book will help you answer *your own* questions about the career you have chosen. What is teaching really like? What are the trends and issues in the profession? What problems can you expect to encounter in the classroom? What kind of rewards do teachers experience?

We begin this book by asking you to examine why you want to become a teacher because we believe that "good teachers select themselves" (Carmichael, 1981, 113). They know why they want to teach and what subjects and ages they want to teach. They are active in the choosing process, aware of the options, informed about the attractions and obstacles in the field, and anxious to make their contributions to the profession.

WHY DO YOU WANT TO TEACH ?

People are drawn to teaching for many reasons. For some, the desire to teach emerges early and is nurtured by positive experiences with teachers during the formative years of childhood. For others, teaching is seen as a way of making a significant contribution to the world and experiencing the joy of helping others grow and develop. And for others, life as a teacher is attractive because it is exciting, varied, and stimulating.

DESIRE TO WORK WITH CHILDREN AND YOUNG PEOPLE

Figure 1.1, based on a national survey of more than 1,000 teachers, shows that what teachers like most about their jobs is the opportunity to work with children or young people and to contribute to their growth and development. Though the conditions under which teachers work may be challenging, their salaries modest, and segments of their communities unsupportive, most teach simply because they care about students.

The day-to-day interactions between teachers and students build strong bonds. Daily contact also enables teachers to become familiar with the personal as well as the academic needs of their students, and this concern for students' welfare and growth outweighs the difficulties and frustrations of teaching. Like the following teachers, they know they can make a difference in students' lives:

> When I was struggling as a kid, one of my teachers was really there for me. She listened to me and supported me when nobody else believed in me. I want to pay her back by helping others like me (Zehm and Kottler 1993, 35).

> [Students] need someone to recognize their uniqueness and specialness and respect it and nurture it (Hansen 1995, 132).

Others, no doubt, love students because they appreciate the unique qualities of youth. They enjoy the liveliness, curiosity, freshness, openness, and trust of young children or the abilities, wit, spirit, independence, and idealism of adolescents. Like the following teacher, they want to be connected to their students: ". . . I now know that I teach so I can be involved in my students' lives, in their real life stories" (Henry et al. 1995, 69).

Teachers also derive significant rewards from meeting the needs of diverse learners. While students from our nation's more than one hundred racial and ethnic groups and students with special needs are increasing in number, effective teachers recognize that their classrooms are enriched by the varied backgrounds of students. To enable you to

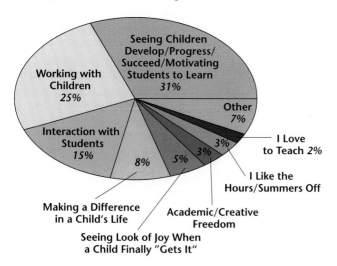

FIGURE 1.1 What teachers like most about their jobs (Source: *The Metropolitan Life Survey of the American Teacher, 1984–1995: Old Problems, New Challenges.* New York: Louis Harris and Associates, Inc., 1995, 13. Based on a survey of 1,011 randomly selected public school teachers throughout the U.S.)

Keepers of the Dream

Anne Sullivan Macy
"Teacher" to Helen Keller

Helen Keller told the world that Anne Sullivan Macy had created her "out of a clod of silence," and throughout their nearly half century of teacher-student companionship, she called her "Teacher."

Anne overcame formidable hardships of her own before she became Helen's teacher. Two of her siblings died in infancy; she lost much of her eyesight because of untreated trachoma when she was five; and her mother died when she was eight. She and her youngest brother were taken to the state poorhouse, a dismal, death-filled place where she lived for the next six years. While there, her little brother died, devastating Anne. She escaped from the poorhouse when she begged the chairman of a commission investigating the facility to let her go to school. She was sent to the Perkins Institute for the Blind in Boston in 1880. She had studied there six years when she was selected to be Helen Keller's teacher.

The story that followed is a celebrated one. Helen, seven, was deaf and mute as a consequence of an illness

"She created me out of a clod of silence."

contracted when she was nineteen months old. Frustrated and given to tantrums because of her inability to communicate, Helen was a handful. Anne undertook a program to firmly and patiently correct her charge's misbehavior.

She also persistently guided Helen toward the discovery of language. After weeks of signing the names of things into Helen's palm, Anne combined the signing of the word *water* with the flow of water from a pump and Helen realized the connection. She would one day speak five languages, graduate cum laude from Radcliffe College, and write fourteen books, including the classic *The Story of My Life* (Keller 1954).

While revered as Helen Keller's intellectual and spiritual teacher, Anne is also recognized for her contributions to pedagogy (Brooks 1956, 12). Her beliefs are still relevant today:

> Every teacher must learn, that only through freedom can individuals develop self-control, self-dependence, will power and initiative. There is no education except through self-education. There is no effective discipline except self-discipline. All that parents and teachers can do for the (children) is to surround (them) with right conditions. (They) will do the rest . . . the things (they) will do for (themselves) are the only things that really count in (their) education (Lash 1980, 443).

experience the satisfaction of helping *all* students learn, significant portions of this book are devoted to **student variability** (differences among students in regard to their developmental needs, interests, abilities, and disabilities) and **student diversity** (differences among students in regard to gender, race, ethnicity, culture, and socioeconomic status). An appreciation for such diversity, then, will help you to experience the rewards that come from enabling each student to make his or her unique contribution to classroom life.

The opportunity to work with young people, whatever their stage of development and whatever their life circumstances, is a key reason people are drawn to teaching and remain in the profession.

LOVE OF TEACHING

The *Metropolitan Life Survey of the American Teacher, 1984–1995: Old Problems, New Challenges* includes the following observation: ". . . teachers overwhelmingly agree with the statement, 'I love to teach.' This is true for teachers in urban as well as sub-urban and rural schools" (Louis Harris and Associates 1995). The survey, based on a nationally representative sample of 1,011 public school teachers interviewed in 1995, goes on to report that teachers express a great deal more personal satisfaction with teaching than they did in 1984, and they are more likely to say they would recommend teaching as a profession. Why do teachers find teaching so satisfying? What does it mean to *love* teaching?

LOVE OF SUBJECT   Some teachers who expressed a love of teaching may have meant that they love teaching in their discipline. The opportunity to continually learn more in one's profession and to share that knowledge with students is a definite attraction. Most of us can recall teachers who were so excited about their subjects that they were surprised when students were not equally enthusiastic. The affinity of such teachers toward their subjects was so great that we tended to see the two as inseparable—for instance, "Miss Gilbert the French teacher" or "Mr. Montgomery the math teacher." Though other factors may draw teachers to their work, a love of subject is clearly one of them.

LOVE OF THE TEACHING LIFE   For those teachers who always enjoyed school, it is often the life of a teacher that has appeal—to be in an environment that encourages a high regard for education and the life of the mind. John Barth, novelist and English professor, wrote eloquently of his love of the teaching life: "There is chalkdust on the sleeve of my soul. In the half-century since my kindergarten days, I have never been away from classrooms for longer than a few months. I am as at home among blackboards, half-desks, lecterns, and seminar tables as among the furniture of my writing-room; both are the furniture of my head" (Barth 1987, 166).

LOVE OF THE TEACHING–LEARNING PROCESS   To love teaching can also mean to love the act of teaching and the learning that can follow. Many teachers, like the following high school special education teacher, focus on the *process* rather than on the subject or even the students: "I enjoy what I do. . . . I've been teaching long enough that when the fun stops . . . I'll get out. But it hasn't stopped yet, after thirty-four years. Every day is different. Every day is interesting" (Godar 1990, 244). Persons with this orientation are attracted by the live, spontaneous aspects of teaching and are invigorated by the need to think on their feet and to capitalize on teachable moments when they occur. They relish the "simultaneity" of teaching (Wigginton 1985), the times when several learning opportunities occur at once, and they constantly work to identify the full array of chesslike moves they can make in leading students to new insights. For them, the teaching–learning process is fascinating.

INFLUENCE OF TEACHERS

It seems reasonable to assume that the process of becoming a teacher begins early in life. In fact, a Metropolitan Life Survey of 1,002 graduates who began teaching in a public school in 1990–91 reported that 52 percent decided to become teachers before college (Louis Harris and Associates 1990). Although it is not true that some people are born teachers, their early life experiences often encourage them to move in that direction. A teacher's influence during his or her formative years may have been the catalyst. In most cases, the adults who have the greatest influence on children—beyond their parents or guardians—are their teachers. For example, two University of Chicago researchers reported that 58 percent of the teenagers they interviewed said one or more teachers influenced them to become the kind of people they are (Csikszentmihalyi and McCormack 1986, 414–419).

Evidence also suggests that those who become teachers were often more influenced by their teachers *as people* than as subject-matter experts. "It is the human dimension that gives all teachers . . . their power as professional influencers" (Zehm and Kottler 1993, 2). Behind the decision to become a teacher is often the inspirational memory of earlier teachers to whom one continues to feel connected in a way that goes beyond the subjects they taught.

DESIRE TO SERVE

Many choose to teach because they want to serve others; they want the results of their labor to extend beyond themselves and their families. Some decide to select another major or leave teaching in order to earn more money elsewhere, only to return to teaching, confiding that they found the other major or work lacking in meaning or significance. Being involved in a service profession is their draw to the field.

For many teachers, the decision to serve through teaching was influenced by their experiences as volunteers. Nearly half of the teachers surveyed by the New York City School Volunteer Program, for example, reported that they had served as volunteers in an educational setting before deciding to become a teacher, and 70 percent of these teachers reported that this experience contributed to their decision to become a teacher (Educational Testing Service 1995). As one New York teacher said, "I always wanted to be a teacher, and all of my volunteer experiences contributed to this career choice" (p. 8).

The desire to serve others and give something back to society is a key attraction of the **Teach for America** program developed by Wendy Kopp as an outgrowth of her senior thesis at Princeton University. Teach for America volunteers, recent graduates from some of America's best colleges and universities, are assigned to teach for a minimum of two years in urban and rural school districts with severe shortages of science, math, and language arts teachers. Volunteers complete five weeks of intensive training at the Teach for America Institute in Houston. After two years of teaching, being monitored by state and school authorities, and taking professional development courses, Teach for America teachers can earn regular certification. Upon completion of their two-year assignment, volunteers then return to their chosen careers in other fields, though 60 percent stay past the two-year commitment (*Seattle Post Intelligencer* 1994, B1, B3).

Explore more deeply your reasons for becoming a teacher. The following Professional Reflection feature focuses on several characteristics that may indicate your probable satisfaction with teaching as a career.

Assessing Your Reasons for Choosing to Teach

For each of the following characteristics, indicate on a scale from 1 to 5 the extent to which it applies to you.

	Very applicable				Not at all applicable
1. Love of learning	1	2	3	4	5
2. Success as a student	1	2	3	4	5

3. Good sense of humor	1	2	3	4	5
4. Positive attitudes toward students	1	2	3	4	5
5. Tolerance toward others	1	2	3	4	5
6. Patience	1	2	3	4	5
7. Good verbal and writing skills	1	2	3	4	5
8. Appreciation for the arts	1	2	3	4	5
9. Experiences working with children (camp, church, tutoring, etc.)	1	2	3	4	5
10. Other teachers in family	1	2	3	4	5
11. Encouragement from family to enter teaching	1	2	3	4	5
12. Desire to serve	1	2	3	4	5

Total score _____

Now that you have completed the self-assessment, calculate your total score; the highest score = 60, the lowest = 12. Interpret the results of your self-assessment with caution. A high score does not necessarily mean that you will be dissatisfied as a teacher, nor does a low score mean that you will be highly satisfied.

PRACTICAL BENEFITS OF TEACHING

Not to be overlooked as attractions to teaching are its practical benefits. Teachers' hours and vacations are widely recognized as benefits. Though the number of hours most teachers devote to their work goes far beyond the number of hours they actually spend at school, their schedules do afford them a measure of flexibility not found in other professions. For example, teachers with school-age children can often be at home when their children are not in school, and all teachers, regardless of their years of experience, receive the same generous vacation time: holiday breaks and a long summer vacation.

SALARIES AND BENEFITS Although intangible rewards represent a significant attraction to teaching, teachers are demanding that the public acknowledge the value and professional standing of teaching by supporting higher salaries. As a result, teacher earnings have increased steadily (50 percent of teachers' households reported incomes of $50,000 or more in 1995), and today's teachers are much more pleased with their salaries than they were a decade ago. Figure 1.2 on page 10 shows that only 37 percent of teachers in 1984 agreed with the statement, "My job allows me the opportunity to earn a decent salary," and 63 percent agreed in 1995. Similarly, 62 percent of teachers in 1985 said an inadequate salary was the main reason they considered leaving teaching; in 1995, however, this percentage had dropped to 41 percent (Louis Harris and Associates 1995, 60).

The National Center for Education Statistics reported that the 1994–95 average salary of public school teachers ($36,933) gave them a purchasing power that was at or near a record high; and the American Federation of Teachers reported that in 1993 teachers had increases in earnings that exceeded the rate of inflation, as they had for eleven of the previous twelve years (American Federation of Teachers 1993). Table 1.1 on page 11 shows a state-by-state comparison of average teacher salaries for 1994–95.

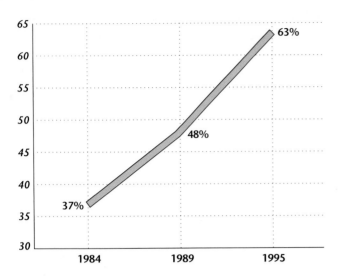

FIGURE 1.2 Teachers' satisfaction with salaries. Percentage of teachers who agree with the statement: "My job allows me the opportunity to earn a decent salary." (Source: *The Metropolitan Life Survey of the American Teacher, 1984–1995: Old Problems, New Challenges.* New York: Louis Harris and Associates, Inc., 1995, 15.)

When comparing teacher salaries state-by-state, it is important to remember that higher salaries are frequently linked to a higher **cost of living,** a more experienced teaching force, and a more desirable location. For example, the National Center for Education Statistics found a $23,000 difference between the highest and lowest average state teachers' salaries in 1995; after using a regional cost-of-living index, however, the difference narrowed to about $14,000 (National Center for Education Statistics 1995). Another study by economists at North Carolina State University found that New Hampshire, which ranked 25th among states in actual salaries for 1995, jumped to ninth in the ranking adjusted for cost of living, while Indiana dropped from 16th to 38th (*Education Week* 1996, 16).

Teachers' salaries are typically determined by years of experience and advanced training as evidenced by graduate credit hours or advanced degrees. Additional duties, such as coaching an athletic team, producing the yearbook and school newspaper, sponsoring clubs, or directing the band, bring extra pay for many teachers. Most districts offer at least limited summer employment for teachers who wish to teach summer school or develop curriculum materials. Additionally, about one-fourth of the nation's two million public school teachers **"moonlight"** (i.e., hold a second job) to increase their earnings.

Teachers also receive various **fringe benefits,** such as medical insurance and retirement plans, which are usually given in addition to base salary. These benefits vary from district to district and are determined during collective bargaining sessions. When considering a school district for your first position, carefully examine the fringe benefits package as well as the salary schedule and opportunities for extra pay.

JOB SECURITY AND STATUS Compared to workers in other sectors of American society who experienced increasing layoffs during the first half of the 1990s, teachers enjoyed a higher level of job security during the same period. Technological advances, corporate mergers and breakups, and a need to cut costs to remain competitive in a global economy led to huge layoffs in the 1990s. Not surprisingly, 77 percent of teachers surveyed in 1995 rated job security as better in teaching than in other occupations they had considered (Louis Harris and Associates 1995). In light of projected increases in the number of elementary and secondary students through the 1990s and a gradually increasing demand for teachers (Applegate and Andrews 1991, 52–55; Gerard and Hussar 1991), it is highly unlikely that the nation's two million public school teachers will face extensive layoffs like workers in other occupations. The widespread practice of **tenure** (job security granted to teachers after satisfactory performance for a specified period, usually two to five years) contributes to job security for teachers.

TABLE 1.1

Estimated average annual salary of teachers in public elementary and secondary schools, by state: 1994–95

State	1994–95	State	1994–95
United States	$36,933	Missouri	31,217
Alababma	31,144	Montana	28,785
Alaska	47,951	Nebraska	30,822
Arizona	32,090	Nevada	34,836
Arkansas	28,409	New Hampshire	34,974
California	40,667	New Jersey	46,801
Colorado	34,571	New Mexico	28,865
Connecticut	51,300	New York	47,250
Delaware	39,076	North Carolina	31,079
District of Columbia	42,959	North Dakota	26,327
Florida	32,588	Ohio	36,685
Georgia	32,828	Oklahoma	27,971
Hawaii	38,518	Oregon	38,700
Idaho	29,783	Pennsylvania	44,489
Illinois	41,041	Rhode Island	40,729
Indiana	36,516	South Carolina	30,341
Iowa	31,511	South Dakota	26,017
Kansas	34,936	Tennessee	31,270
Kentucky	32,257	Texas	31,310
Louisiana	26,574	Utah	28,676
Maine	31,856	Vermont	36,311
Maryland	40,636	Virginia	33,753
Massachusetts	42,078	Washington	36,120
Michigan	47,412	West Virginia	31,923
Minnesota	37,412	Wisconsin	37,349
Mississippi	26,910	Wyoming	31,300

(Source: National Center for Education Statistics (1995, October). *Digest of education statistics, 1995.* Washington, D.C.: U.S. Department of Education, Office of Educational Research and Improvement, p. 85.)

Perhaps the most accurate view of the status accorded teachers comes from the teachers themselves. In 1984, 47 percent of the 1,981 teachers responding to *The Metropolitan Life Survey of the American Teacher* agreed with the statement, "As a teacher, I feel respected in today's society." According to the 1995 survey of 1,011 teachers, the number of teachers agreeing with the statement had increased to 53 percent (Louis Harris and Associates 1995, 16). These results may reflect the fact that teachers' status is partially defined by their students; "successful, high-status students reflect and reinforce the perceptions of status that attach to their teachers" (Hargreaves 1995, 85), while teachers of lower-ability students may believe they have less status.

WHAT ARE THE CHALLENGES OF TEACHING ❓

Like all professions, teaching has undesirable or difficult aspects. As one high school social studies teacher put it: "Teaching is not terrible. It's great. I love it. It just feels terrible sometimes" (Henry et al. 1995, 119).

Prospective teachers need to consider the problems as well as the pleasures they are likely to encounter. You need to be informed about what to expect if you are to make the most of your professional preparation program. With greater awareness of the realities of teaching, you can more purposefully and meaningfully (1) reflect on and refine your personal philosophy of education, (2) acquire teaching strategies and leadership techniques, and (3) develop a knowledge base of research and theory to guide your actions. In this manner, you can become a true professional—free to savor the joys and satisfactions of teaching and confident of your ability to deal with its frustrations and challenges. Table 1.2 shows that teachers must deal with a variety of problems in the schools.

CLASSROOM MANAGEMENT

For fifteen of the twenty-seven years between 1969 and 1993, the public ranked lack of discipline as the most important problem facing the schools in the annual Gallup Polls of the Public's Attitudes Toward the Public Schools. Not surprisingly, discipline and increased crime and violence among youth are strong concerns for education majors. Before teachers can teach they must manage their classrooms effectively. Even when parents and the school community are supportive and problems are relatively minor, dealing with discipline can be a disturbing, emotionally draining aspect of teaching.

In addition, many schools have high **teacher–student ratios,** which can make classroom management more difficult. Feeling the press of overcrowding and valiantly resisting the realization that they cannot meet the needs of all their students, teachers may try to work faster and longer to give their students the best possible education. All too often, however, they learn to put off, overlook, or otherwise attend inadequately to many students each day. The problem of high teacher–student ratios becomes even more acute when complicated by the high **student-mobility rates** in many schools. In such situations, teachers have trouble not only in meeting students' needs but also in recognizing students and remembering their names! As you will see, developing a leadership plan, a learning environment, and communication skills will help you face the challenges of classroom management.

SOCIAL PROBLEMS THAT IMPACT STUDENTS

Many social problems affect the lives and learning of many children and youth, such as substance abuse, teen pregnancy, homelessness, poverty, family distress, child abuse and neglect, violence and crime, suicide, and health problems such as HIV/AIDS and fetal alcohol syndrome. The social problems that place students at risk are not always easy to detect. Students' low productivity, learning difficulties, and attitude problems demand teacher attention; yet teachers may be unaware of the source of those difficulties. Even when teachers do recognize the source of a problem, they may lack the resources or expertise to offer help. Teachers feel frustrated by the wasted potential they observe in their students. In addition, when the public calls for schools to curb or correct social problems, that expectation can increase the stress teachers experience.

TABLE 1.2

Teacher's perceptions of "very serious" or "somewhat serious" problems in the schools:
By size of place (in percent)

| | Total Teachers | | Size of Place | | | | | | | | | |
| | | | Inner City | | Other Urban | | Suburb | | Small Town | | Rural | |
	'95	'85	'95	'85	'95	'85	'95	'85	'95	'85	'95	'85
Teachers of Grades 7–12												
The amount of drinking by students	76	66	61	60	69	68	77	71	80	60	80	67
The number of students who lack basic skills	74	80	87	83	79	90	68	76	72	81	74	79
The number of students using drugs	64	58	73	63	73	66	59	68	67	55	55	49
The number of teenage pregnancies	59	49	81	57	71	62	43	32	58	54	62	47
The number of dropouts	44	40	69	49	52	48	29	30	40	44	47	36
Incidence of violence in and around schools	41	n/a	72	n/a	54	n/a	41	n/a	28	n/a	30	n/a
The number of students carrying handguns, knives, and weapons to school	25	n/a	46	n/a	31	n/a	20	n/a	18	n/a	24	n/a
The number of teenage suicides	14	18	18	10	21	30	15	21	10	10	13	21
Number of Teachers	518	820	67	93	52	102	137	251	141	216	119	156
Teachers of Grades K–6												
Overcrowded classes	53	49	66	60	55	44	53	50	52	48	46	50
Students' lack of interest in their classes	50	n/a	65	n/a	57	n/a	35	n/a	49	n/a	56	n/a
Inadequate programs for remedial students	41	n/a	48	n/a	60	n/a	35	n/a	44	n/a	35	n/a
Absenteeism	34	28	50	42	40	31	20	18	37	26	36	31
Incidence of violence in and around schools	26	n/a	51	n/a	34	n/a	20	n/a	25	n/a	16	n/a
Number of Teachers	523	1124	82	182	47	134	142	300	142	284	109	220

(Source: *The Metropolitan Life Survey of the American Teacher 1984–1995: Old Problems, New Challenges.* New York: Louis Harris and Associates, Inc., 1995, 29.)

NEED FOR FAMILY AND COMMUNITY SUPPORT

Support from parents and the community can make a significant difference in the teacher's effectiveness in the classroom. Increasingly, there has been a realization that school, parents, and community must work together so that children and youth develop to their maximum potential academically, socially, emotionally, and physically. For example, parents who talk with their children, help with homework, read to them, monitor their television viewing, and attend meetings of the Parent Teacher Organization (PTO) and school open houses can enhance their children's ability to succeed in school (Henry 1996; Moore 1992; Fuligni and Stevenson 1995). Similarly, communities can support schools by providing essential social, vocational, recreational, and health support services to students and their families. While teachers in suburban and rural schools believe that parental and community support has increased since 1984 (see Figure 1.3), teachers in urban schools have seen an alarming *decrease* in support. Also, among teachers who seriously considered leaving teaching in 1995, "lack of respect/support from parents" was identified by 14 percent as a major factor (Louis Harris and Associates 1995, 60).

A low rate of parental participation in their children's schooling is reflected in the 1994 Gallup Poll of the Public's Attitudes Toward the Public Schools, which reported that less than 50 percent of the parents of public school students attended a PTA (Parent-Teacher Association) meeting during the academic year. Nevertheless, the 1992 Gallup Poll revealed that 59 percent of the public would be willing to help in their local schools without pay if needed. According to the poll, public school par-

Issues in Education

- What points does this cartoon make about public expectations that teachers and schools will take steps to address social problems?
- What societal ills are identified?
- What is suggested about constraints on teachers and schools as solvers of social problems?
- To what extent do you agree or disagree with the cartoonist's point of view? Why?
- What might be some realistic expectations for teacher and school involvement in improving society?
- How might you change the cartoon captioning to best reflect your view?

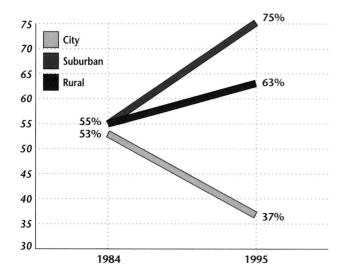

FIGURE 1.3 Percentage of teachers who believe parental and community support is "excellent or good": 1984 and 1995 (Source: *The Metropolitan Life Survey of the American Teacher, 1984-1995: Old Problems, New Challenges.* New York: Louis Harris and Associates, Inc., 1995, 20.)

ents were more willing to serve as unpaid volunteers (72 percent willing) than those with no children in school (51 percent willing) or with children in private schools (49 percent willing).

LONG WORKING HOURS AND JOB STRESS

The official working hours for teachers are attractive, but the real working hours are another matter. Not built into contracts are the after-hours or extra assignments found at all levels of teaching—from recess duty and parent conferences to high school club sponsorships and coaching. Also not obvious are the hours of preparation that occur before and after school—frequently late into the night and over the weekend. As Table 1.3 shows, over 90 percent of teachers work more than forty hours per week, with the largest percentage working more than fifty-five hours per week.

The need to complete copious amounts of paperwork, including record keeping, may be the most burdensome of the teacher's nonteaching tasks. On average, teachers spend ten hours per week on school-related responsibilities not directly related to teaching (Louis Harris and Associates 1995, 68). Other nonteaching tasks include

TABLE 1.3

Number of hours per week spent on school-related responsibilities (in percent)

	Total	Years of Teaching Experience		Type of School			Size of Place		
	Total	Less Than 10	10 or More	Elementary	Junior High	High School	Urban	Suburban	Rural
Less than 40	9	8	12	12	8	9	10	10	8
41–45	12	10	12	11	15	9	17	10	11
46–50	30	30	30	31	28	29	30	28	32
51–55	14	15	13	16	9	14	13	15	11
More than 55	35	38	34	30	40	39	29	37	38
Median	50	54	50	51	51	55	50	55	51
Base	1011	254	757	523	240	309	246	271	216

(Source: *The Metropolitan Life Survey of the American Teacher, 1984-1995: Old Problems, New Challenges.* New York: Louis Harris and Associates, Inc., 1995, 67. Based on a survey of 1,011 randomly selected public school teachers throughout the U.S.)

supervising student behavior on the playground, at extracurricular events, and in the halls, study halls, and lunchrooms; attending faculty meetings, parent conferences, and open houses; and taking tickets or selling at concessions for athletic events. Individually, such assignments and responsibilities may be enjoyable; too many of them at once, however, become a burden and consume the teacher's valuable time.

In addition to long working hours, factors such as students' lack of interest, conflicts with administrators, public criticism, overcrowded classrooms, lack of resources, and isolation from other adults cause some teachers to experience high levels of stress. Unchecked, acute levels of stress can lead to job dissatisfaction, emotional and physical exhaustion, and an inability to cope effectively—all classic symptoms of teacher **burnout.** To cope with stress and avoid burnout, teachers report that activities in seven areas are beneficial: social support, physical fitness, intellectual stimulation, entertainment, personal hobbies, self-management, and supportive attitudes (Gmelch and Parkay 1995, 46–65).

GAINING PROFESSIONAL EMPOWERMENT

In an interview with journalist Bill Moyers, noted Harvard educator Sara Lawrence Lightfoot eloquently describes why teachers desire **professional empowerment**:

> [Teachers are] saying, "I haven't had the opportunity to participate fully in this enterprise." Some teachers are speaking about the politics of teachers' voice. They're saying, "We want more control over our lives in this school." Some of them are making an even more subtle point—they're talking about voice as knowledge. "We know things about this enterprise that researchers and policy makers can never know. We have engaged in this intimate experience, and we have things to tell you if you'd only learn how to ask, and if you'd only learn how to listen"(Moyers 1989, 161).

Although some teachers may experience frustration in their efforts to gain professional empowerment, efforts to empower teachers and to "professionalize" teaching are leading to unprecedented opportunities for today's teachers to extend their leadership roles beyond the classroom. As pointed out in *Teachers as Leaders: Evolving Roles,* "[T]here have been calls for expanded and qualitatively different leadership opportunities for teachers. . . . [T]he nation is come to realize a need for more authentic forms of school reform or restructuring to meet the needs of an increasingly diverse student population and our rapidly changing society" (Livingston 1992, 10).

WHAT IS TEACHING REALLY LIKE ?

In this section we examine six basic **realities of teaching** that illustrate why teaching is so demanding *and* why it can be so exciting, rewarding, and uplifting. And when we say that teaching is demanding, we mean more than the fact that Mr. Smith's third-period plane geometry students just can't seem to learn how to compute the area of a triangle; or that Miss Ellis's sixth-grade composition class can't remember whether to use *there* or *their;* or even that 35 percent of teachers in 1995 reported they were "under great stress" almost every day or several days a week (Louis Harris and Associates 1995, 55). While there are many frustrating, stressful events with which teachers must cope, the difficulty of teaching goes much further, or deeper, than these examples suggest.

REALITY 1: THE UNPREDICTABILITY OF OUTCOMES

The outcomes of teaching, even in the best of circumstances, are neither predictable nor consistent. Any teacher, beginner or veteran, can give countless examples of how the outcomes of teaching are often unpredictable and inconsistent. Life in most classrooms usually proceeds on a fairly even keel—with teachers able to predict, fairly accurately, how their students will respond to lessons. Adherence to the best laid lesson plans, however, may be accompanied by students' blank stares, yawns of boredom, hostile acting out, or expressions of befuddlement. On the other hand, lack of preparation on the teacher's part does not necessarily rule out the possibility of a thoroughly exciting class discussion, a real breakthrough in understanding for an individual student or the entire class, or simply a good, fast-paced review of previously learned material. In short, teachers are often surprised at students' reactions to classroom activities.

STUDENTS' RESPONSES   Contrary to the popular notion that teaching consists entirely of a specific number of competencies or observable behaviors, the reactions of students to any given activity cannot be guaranteed. Furthermore, teachers, unlike other professionals, cannot control all the results of their efforts.

One example of the unpredictability of teaching is given in a teacher intern's description of setting up an independent reading program in his middle-school classroom. Here we see how careful room arrangement and organization of materials do not ensure desired outcomes and how a teacher learned to adjust to one reality of teaching.

> I wanted everything looking perfect. For two more hours, I placed this here and stuffed that in there. . . . There were stacks of brand-new books sitting on three odd shelves and a metal display rack. . . . I coded the books and arranged them neatly on the shelves. I displayed their glossy covers as if the room was a B. Dalton store.

A few weeks after setting up the reading program, however, this teacher observes that

> The orderly environment I thought I had conceived was fraught with complications. For example, the back rows of the classroom were inaccessible regions from which paper and pencil pieces were hurled at vulnerable victims, and there were zones where, apparently, no teacher's voice could be heard. . . . The books . . . remained in chaos. Novels turned up behind shelves, on the sidewalks outside, and in the trash can. And still, at least once a week, I dutifully arranged them until I was satisfied. But something was happening. It was taking less and less for me to be satisfied. . . . [I] loosened up (Henry et al. 1995, 73–76).

Contrary to the preceding example, unpredictability in the classroom is not always bad. Another teacher intern describes her unexpected success at setting up a writing workshop at an urban middle school with a large population of at-risk students. One day she began by telling her students that

> "We're going to be starting something new these six weeks. . . . We will be transforming this classroom into a writing workshop." What was I trying to do here? They're not writers. . . . Raymond stared down at *Where's Waldo*. Michael was engrossed in an elaborate pencil drum solo. Edwina powdered her nose and under her eyes.

> "Listen to me, you guys," I said, trying not to lose it before we even started. "We're starting something completely different, something you never get a chance to do in your other classes."

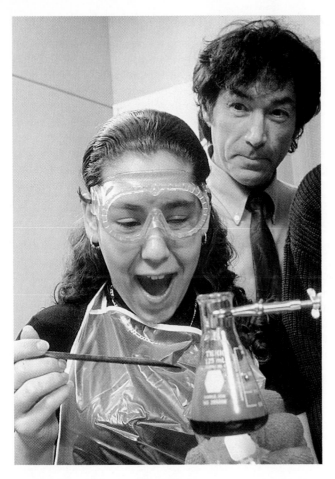

A few heads turned to face me. Veronica slugged Edwina, and Edwina slid her compact into her back pocket.

"What, Miss . . . chew gum?"

In spite of her initial reservations, this teacher made the following observations the next day—the first day of the writing workshop.

> Today, it's all clicking.
>
> "Aw, man, I told you I don't understand that part. Why does that guy in your story . . . Chris . . . say that it's too early to rob the store?" David pleads. "It doesn't make sense."
>
> Raymond tips his desk forward and smiles. "It's too early because they want to wait until the store's almost closed."
>
> "Well, then, you've got to say that. Right, Miss?"
>
> I lean against the door frame and try not to laugh. I listen to the conversations around me. Yes, they're loud and they're talking and they're laughing. But they're learning. My students are involved in their writing, I say to myself and shake my head (Henry et al. 1995, 54–55).

Philip Jackson describes the unpredictability of teaching in his well-known book *Life in Classrooms*: "[As] typically conducted, teaching is an opportunistic process. . . . Neither teacher nor students can predict with any certainty exactly what will happen next. Plans are forever going awry and unexpected opportunities for the attainment of educational goals are constantly emerging" (Jackson 1990, 166).

In what ways must this classroom teacher face the reality of unpredictable outcomes? What are five other basic realities that all teachers face in their work?

RESULTS IN THE FUTURE   Teachers strive to effect changes in their students for the future as well as for the here and now. In *Life in Classrooms*, Jackson labels this the preparatory aspect of teaching. In addition to having students perform better on next Monday's unit exam or on a criterion-referenced test mandated by the state, teachers expect students to apply their newly acquired skills and knowledge at some indeterminate, usually distant, point in the future. Thus, as an English teacher points out, it may take some time for students to display what they have learned from teachers:

> English particularly is so much a business of increasing [students'] ability to think for themselves, to write their thoughts, get them down on paper, that sometimes you don't know until they're seniors whether what you have taught them as sophomores has penetrated at all. . . . Sometimes it doesn't work until they're in college (Lortie 1975, 146).

Just as months or years may pass before the results of teaching become manifest, teachers may wait a long time before receiving positive feedback from students. The following comment by a kindergarten teacher illustrates the delayed satisfaction that can characterize teaching:

About a month ago I had a 22-year-old boy knock on the door. He said, "Miss R?" I said, "Yes." He is now in England, an architect; he's married and has a little girl. I thought, "This is not happening to me. I had you in kindergarten." If you teach high school and a kid comes back and he's married in two or three years, that's expected, but 16 years or 18 years—first year in kindergarten. It's rewarding . . . be it one year, or ten years down the road. . . . There are daily satisfactions—"She got it!"—that's a reward in itself, but I think it's a little bit down the road that you get your satisfaction (Cohn and Kottkamp 1983, 42–43).

REALITY 2: THE DIFFICULTY OF MEASUREMENT

It is difficult to measure what students learn as a result of being taught. The ultimate purpose of teaching is to lead the student to a greater understanding of the things and ideas of this world. But, as even the most casual appraisal of human nature will confirm, it is very difficult, perhaps impossible, to determine precisely what another human being does or does not understand. Although the aims or intentions of teaching may be specified with exacting detail, one of the realities of teaching, as the following junior high school teacher points out, is that some of what students learn may be indeterminate and beyond direct measurement:

> There is no clear end result. . . . That frustrates me. I want so badly for my joy [of teaching] to be neatly tied up so that I can look at it admiringly. . . . I want so badly to *see* my successes—I don't know, give me certificates or badges or jelly beans. Then I can stack them up, count them, and rate myself as a teacher (Henry et al. 1995, 68–69).

In spite of state-by-state efforts to institute standardized tests of basic skills and thereby hold teachers accountable, the conventional wisdom among teachers is that they are often uncertain about just what their students learn. We have miles of computer printouts with test data, but very little knowledge of what lies behind a child's written response, little understanding of how the child experiences the curriculum. As one educational researcher concludes: "The inaccessibility of data is similar both in science and in learning. We cannot directly 'see' subatomic particles, nor can we 'see' the inner-workings of the mind and emotions of the child. Both are inferential: both are subject to human interpretation" (Costa 1984, 202).

On the one hand, then, teachers must recognize their limited ability to determine what students actually learn; on the other, they must continuously work to become more sensitive to what students learn. To reduce uncertainties about students' learning, Philip Jackson (1986) suggests four basic approaches available to teachers, outlined in Figure 1.4 on page 20.

REALITY 3: THE NEED FOR TEACHER–STUDENT PARTNERSHIP

The teacher's ability to influence student behavior is actually quite limited. The very fact that we refer to the *teaching–learning process* indicates the extent to which classroom events are "jointly produced" (Doyle 1986, 395) and depend upon a teacher–student partnership. According to Arthur Combs (1979, 234–235) in a book aptly titled *Myths in Education: Beliefs That Hinder Progress and Their Alternatives*:

> A teacher's influence on all but the simplest, most primitive forms of student behavior, even in that teacher's own classroom, cannot be clearly established. The older children get, the less teachers can influence even those few, primitive forms of behavior. The attempt to hold teachers responsible for what students do is, for all practical purposes, well nigh impossible.

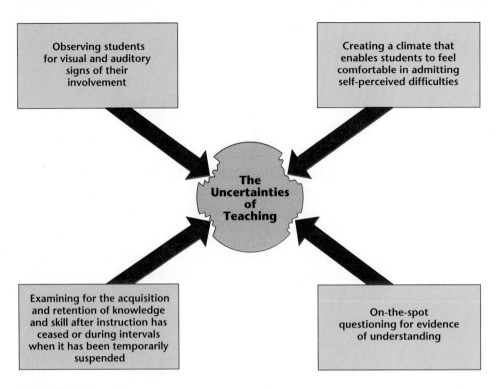

FIGURE 1.4 Reducing the uncertainties of teaching: four strategies (Source: Reprinted by permission of the publisher from Jackson, Philip W., *The Practice of Teaching* (New York: Teachers College Press, © 1986 by Teachers College, Columbia University. All rights reserved.)

At best, a teacher tries to influence students so that they make internal decisions to behave in the desired manner—whether it be reading the first chapter of *The Pearl* by Friday or solving ten addition problems during a mathematics lesson. Teaching is a uniquely demanding profession, therefore, because the work of teachers is evaluated not in terms of what teachers do but in terms of their ability "to help the students become more effective as learners," to "become active seekers after new development" (Joyce and Weil 1996, 387, 396). This reality underscores the need for a partnership between teacher and learners, including learners who are culturally diverse.

REALITY 4: THE IMPACT OF TEACHERS' ATTITUDES

With the role of teacher also comes the power to influence others by example. Albert Bandura (1977, 12) writes that "virtually all learning phenomena resulting from direct experience occur on a vicarious basis by observing other people's behavior and its consequences for them." Clearly, students learn much by imitation, and teachers are models for students. In the primary grades, teachers are idolized by their young students. At the high school level, teachers have the potential to inspire students' emulation and establish the classroom tone by modeling expected attitudes and behaviors.

In *The Tact of Teaching: The Meaning of Pedagogical Thoughtfulness*, Max van Manen (1991, 167) states the importance of teachers' attitudes toward students:

> An educator needs to believe in children. Specifically he or she needs to believe in the possibilities and goodness of the particular children for whom he or she has responsi-

bility. My belief in a child strengthens that child—provided of course that the child experiences my trust as something real and as something positive.

A high school social studies teacher expresses the same idea in this manner: "[The] relationship between teachers and students is becoming one of the most important aspects of teaching. [In] a world of broken homes and violence, the encouragement of their teachers may be the only thing students can hold onto that makes them feel good about themselves" (Henry et al. 1995, 127).

Teachers also model attitudes toward the subjects they teach and show students through their example that learning is an ongoing, life-enriching process that does not end with diplomas and graduations. Their example confirms the timeless message of Sir Rabindranath Tagore that is inscribed above the doorway of a public building in India: "A teacher can never truly teach unless he is still learning himself. A lamp can never light another lamp unless it continues to burn its own flame."

REALITY 5: THE DRAMA AND IMMEDIACY OF TEACHING

Interactive teaching is characterized by events that are rapid-changing, multidimensional, and irregular. We have already discussed how the outcomes of teaching are unpredictable and inconsistent. Yet the challenges of teaching go beyond this. The face-to-face interactions teachers have with students—what Jackson (1990, 152) has termed **interactive teaching**—are themselves rapid-changing, multidimensional, and irregular. "Day in and day out, teachers spend much of their lives 'on stage' before audiences that are not always receptive . . . teachers must orchestrate a daunting array of interpersonal interactions and build a cohesive, positive climate for learning" (Gmelch and Parkay 1995, 47).

When teachers are in the **preactive teaching** stages of their work—preparing to teach or reflecting on previous teaching—they can afford to be consistently deliberate and rational. Planning for lessons, grading papers, reflecting on the misbehavior of a student—such activities are usually done alone and lack the immediacy and sense of urgency that characterize interactive teaching. While actually working with students, however, you must be able to think on your feet and respond appropriately to complex, ever-changing situations. You must be flexible and ready to deal with the unexpected. During a discussion, for example, you must operate on at least two levels. On one level, you respond appropriately to students' comments, monitor other students for signs of confusion or comprehension, formulate the next comment or question, and be alert for signs of misbehavior. On another level, you ensure that participation is evenly distributed among students, evaluate the content and quality of students' contributions, keep the discussion focused and moving ahead, and emphasize major content areas.

How do teachers' attitudes affect students' learning? In what ways are teachers significant role models for students?

During interactive teaching, the awareness that you are responsible for the forward movement of the group never lets up. Teachers are the only professionals who practice their craft almost exclusively under the direct, continuous gaze of up to thirty or forty clients. Jackson (1990, 119) sums up the experience: "The *immediacy* of classroom events is something that anyone who has ever been in charge of a roomful of students can never forget."

REALITY 6: THE UNIQUENESS OF THE TEACHING EXPERIENCE

Teaching involves a unique mode of being between teacher and student—a mode of being that can be experienced but not fully defined or described. On your journey to become a teacher, you will gradually develop your capacity to listen to students and to convey an authentic sense of concern for their learning. Unfortunately, there is no precise, easy-to-follow formula for demonstrating this to students. You will have to take into account your personality and special gifts to discover your own best way for showing this concern.

One reason it is difficult to describe teaching is that an important domain of teaching, **teachers' thought processes,** including professional reflection, cannot be observed directly. Figure 1.5 shows how this unobservable domain interacts with and is influenced by the observable domain of teachers' actions and the effects of these actions on student learning and the learning environment. Teachers' thought processes include their theories and beliefs about students and how they learn, their plans for teaching, and the decisions they make while teaching. Thought processes and actions can be constrained by the physical setting of the classroom or external

FIGURE 1.5 A model of teacher thought and action (Source: From "Teachers' Thought Processes" by Christopher M. Clark and Penelope L. Peterson. Reprinted by permission of Macmillan Publishing Company from *Handbook of Research on Teaching,* Third Ed. Edited by Merlin C. Wittrock. Copyright © 1986 by the American Educational Research Association.)

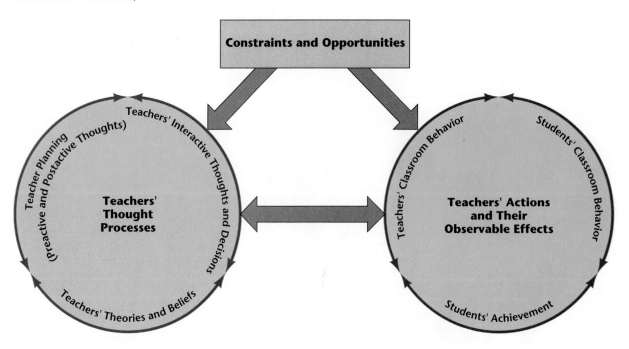

factors such as the curriculum, the principal, or the community. On the other hand, teachers' thought processes and actions may be influenced by unique opportunities, such as the chance to engage in curriculum reform or school governance. The model also illustrates a further complexity of teaching—namely, that the relationships between teacher behavior, student behavior, and student achievement are reciprocal. What teachers do is influenced not only by their thought processes before, during, and after teaching but also by student behavior and student achievement. This complexity contributes to the uniqueness of the teaching experience.

WHAT DOES SOCIETY EXPECT OF TEACHERS ?

The prevailing view within our society is that teachers are public servants accountable to the people. As a result, society has high expectations of teachers—some would say too high. Entrusted with our nation's most precious resource, its children and youth, today's teachers are expected to have advanced knowledge and skills and high academic and ethical standards. While promoting students' academic progress has always been their primary responsibility, teachers are also expected to further students' social, emotional, and moral development and to safeguard students' health and well-being. Increasingly, the public calls on teachers and schools to address social problems and risk factors that affect student success.

THE PUBLIC TRUST

Teaching is subject to a high degree of public scrutiny and control. The level of trust that the public extends to teachers as professionals varies greatly. On the one hand, the public appears to have great confidence in the work that teachers do. Because of its faith in the teaching profession, the public invests teachers with considerable power over its children. For the most part, parents willingly allow their children to be influenced by teachers and expect their children to obey and respect teachers. However, the public trust increases and decreases in response to social and political changes that lead to waves of educational reform.

In the 1970s, for example, teachers were portrayed as incompetent, unprofessional, unintelligent, and generally unable to live up to the public's expectations. Calls for higher standards and minimum competency testing were an expression of diminished public trust. Further professionalization of teaching has been the response. During the 1980s, the image of teachers was battered by ominous sounding commission reports, a negative press, and public outcries for better schools. National reports, such as *A Nation at Risk,* declared that American education was shockingly inadequate, if not a failure.

In the 1990s, however, deliberate efforts were made to restore dignity to the profession of teaching. To highlight the important work of teachers, public and commercial television stations aired programs with titles such as "Learning in America: Schools That Work," "America's Toughest Assignment: Solving the Education Crisis," "The Truth about Teachers," "Why Do These Kids Love School?", "Liberating America's Schools," and "America's Education Revolution: A Report from the Front." The Learning Channel began to air *Teacher TV,* a news-style program that explores education trends and issues and features teachers, schools, and communities around the country. Many national corporations initiated award programs to recognize excellence among teachers. Disney Studios, for example, initiated Disney's American Teacher Awards in 1991. As a tribute to countless outstanding teachers, a major media campaign to recruit new teachers in the early 1990s was formed around the

TABLE 1.4

Ratings given the local public schools (in percent)

	1995	1993	1991	1989	1987	1985	1983
A & B	41	47	42	43	43	43	31
A	8	10	10	8	12	9	6
B	33	37	32	35	31	34	25
C	37	31	33	33	30	30	32
D	12	11	10	11	9	10	13
Fail	5	4	5	4	4	4	7
Don't know	5	7	10	9	14	13	17

(Source: Alec M. Gallup, Lowell C. Rose, and Stanley M. Elan, "The 24th Annual Gallup Poll of the Public's Attitudes Toward the Public Schools," *Phi Delta Kappan,* (September 1992), 45; and Stanley M. Elam and Lowell C. Rose, "The 27th Annual Phi Delta Kappa/Gallup Poll of the Public's Attitudes Toward the Public Schools," *Phi Delta Kappan,* (September 1995), 42.)

slogan, "Be a Teacher. Be a Hero." Table 1.4 shows how people rated their public schools in selected years between 1983, just after the release of *A Nation at Risk,* and 1995.

TEACHER COMPETENCY AND EFFECTIVENESS

Society believes that competent, effective teachers are important keys to a strong system of education. Accordingly, teachers are expected to be proficient in the use of instructional strategies, curriculum materials, advanced educational technologies, and classroom management techniques. They are also expected to have a thorough understanding of the developmental levels of their students and a solid grasp of the content they teach. To maintain and extend this high level of skill, teachers are expected to be informed of exemplary practices and to demonstrate a desire for professional development.

Teacher competency and effectiveness includes the responsibility to help all learners succeed. Though today's students come from a diverse array of backgrounds, society expects teachers to hold strong beliefs about the potential for all children. Regardless of their students' ethnicity, language, gender, socioeconomic status, family backgrounds and living conditions, abilities, or disabilities, teachers have a responsibility to ensure that all students develop to their fullest potential. To accomplish this, teachers are expected to have a repertoire of instructional strategies and resources to create meaningful learning experiences that promote students' growth and development.

TEACHER ACCOUNTABILITY

Teachers must "be mindful of the social ethic—their public duties and obligations—embodied in the practice of teaching . . ." (Hansen 1995, 143). Society agrees that teachers are primarily responsible for promoting students' learning, though it is not always in agreement about *what* students should learn. In any case, society expects teachers to understand how factors such as student backgrounds, attitudes, and learning styles can affect achievement; and it expects that teachers will create safe and effective learning environments. Society also believes that teachers and schools should be accountable for equalizing educational opportunity and maintaining high professional standards.

Teacher accountability also means meeting high standards of conduct. Teachers are no longer required to sign statements such as the following, taken from a 1927 contract: "I promise to sleep at least eight hours a night, to eat carefully, and to take every precaution to keep in the best of health and spirits, in order that I may be better able to render efficient service to my pupils" (Waller 1932, 43). Nevertheless, society does expect teachers to hold high standards of professional ethics and personal morality and to model behaviors that match those standards.

HOW DO GOOD TEACHERS VIEW THEIR WORK

Teachers' overall satisfaction with their careers has increased significantly since the 1980s. Figure 1.6 shows that more than 50 percent of teachers report high satisfaction with their careers—a proportion that compares favorably to the level of satisfaction reported by members of other professions.

Good teachers derive greatest satisfaction when they are effective in promoting students' learning—when they "make a difference" in students' lives. When you recall your most effective teachers, you probably think of particular individuals, not idealizations of the teacher's many roles. What good teachers do can be described in terms of five **modes of teaching,** which are more general and significant than a discussion of roles. You may recognize these modes in your observations of teachers and in the writings of gifted teachers when they reflect on their work. You may even acknowledge these modes of teaching as deeper reasons for becoming a teacher.

FIGURE 1.6 Teachers' satisfaction with career, 1984–1995 (Source: *The Metropolitan Life Survey of the American Teacher, 1984–1995: Old Problems, New Challenges.* New York: Louis Harris and Associates, Inc., 1995, 9.)

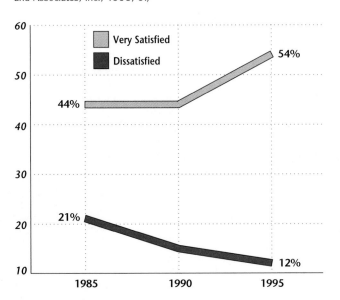

A WAY OF BEING

In becoming a teacher, you take on the role and let it become a part of you. Increasingly, the learning of facts can be achieved easily with good books, good TV, CD-ROMs, and an on-line computer service. What cannot be done in these ways is teaching styles of life, teaching what it means to be, to grow, to become actualized, to become complete. The only way a teacher can teach these qualities is to possess them. "They become living examples for their students, showing that what they say is important enough for them to apply to their own lives. They are attractive models who advertise, by their very being, that learning does produce wondrous results" (Zehm and Kottler 1993, 16).

Dear Mentor

NOVICE AND EXPERT TEACHERS ON CHARACTERISTICS OF A GREAT TEACHER

Dear Stephanie,

What a wonderful question you asked! I have been a teacher for 30 years and your question has me thinking. I will try to explain to you what I believe it takes to be a good teacher. I don't believe you "just know." I do believe that as you go through school and have opportunities to be in classrooms you will begin to understand what does happen and whether or not you want to give it a try. I also believe that it is very important to visit with teachers and ask good questions.

Teaching is a very complex and important job in today's world. Teachers have the opportunity to make a difference with kids, but to make that difference something has to happen between student and teacher. I believe that the best teachers have a deep love for kids, all kinds of kids. The love teachers feel for kids allows them to overlook some of the difficulties and frustrations that can sometimes fill school days. A good teacher looks at kids and senses the potential despite what the surface says. A good teacher looks first at kids and then at subject material. Teachers do so much for kids in addition to teaching. They look at kids as important individuals who deserve so much. They put kids first.

I also believe that a good teacher loves and understands learning. In today's world we are realizing that students learn best when they are actively engaged in the classroom. The teacher who senses and is willing to find out when kids are really learning has an advantage. One of the most important things a teacher can do is to allow the child to begin to discover his or her own voice, whether it is in the first readings and writings of a kindergarten child or in the more complicated writings and readings of seniors in high school. In allowing students to find and develop their own voices, we are encouraging them to understand their own learning process and we are acting as a facilitator to that process.

A good teacher must be willing to work toward positive change. Education will always be a very dynamic process and the teacher who can adapt to change and even institute change will be one who can make a difference, not only for kids but also for other teachers.

Stephanie, I will leave you with a couple of quotes, which are written on a worn sheet of paper and are stuck to my desk. They are two questions that I believe a teacher must think about every day: "What are we doing in this room that the students will take into their world?" and "What are the students going to do with what we are doing in this class?"

I am very proud to be a teacher. I must say that I have worked hard and have always thought I could do more. But I do know that teachers can make a difference in kids' lives. Good teaching changes lives. Thank you, Stephanie, for asking.

Mary Beth Blegen
1996 National Teacher of the Year

> **Dear Mentor,**
>
> I am now realizing that to be a good teacher takes a lot of hard work and effort. It is not an easy job. I would like to know if there are some specific personality traits and characteristics that are necessary for being a good teacher–a great teacher. I have heard that "you will just know" if you want to be a teacher. But I do not "just know," and that concerns me.
>
> Stephanie Pine

A CREATIVE ENDEAVOR

Teaching is a creative endeavor in which teachers are continually shaping and re-shaping the lessons, events, and experiences of their students. In *The Call to Teach*, David Hansen (1995, 13) describes the creative dimensions of teaching this way: "In metaphorical terms, teaching is . . . more than carrying brick, mortar, and shovel. Rather, it implies being the architect of one's classroom world."

With careful attention to the details of classroom life, effective teachers artistically develop educative relationships with their students; they "read" the myriad events that emerge while teaching and respond appropriately. The following high school teacher, identified as highly successful by her principal, reported: "I have to grab the kids that don't want to do math at all and somehow make them want to do this work. I'm not sure how I do it, but kids just want to do well in my class. For some mysterious reason, and I don't care why, they really want to do well."

A LIVE PERFORMANCE

Teaching is a live performance with each class period, each day, containing the unpredictable. Further, teachers are engaged in live dialogues with their classes and individual students. The experience of teaching is thus an intense, attention-demanding endeavor—an interactive one that provides minute-to-minute challenges.

Some teachers embrace the live performance aspect of teaching more than others, believing that within it lies true learning. They recognize that teaching ". . . is full of surprises; classroom lessons that lead to unexpected questions and insights; lessons that fail despite elaborate planning; spur-of-the-moment activities that work beautifully and that may change the direction of a course; students who grow and learn; students who seem to regress or grow distant" (Hansen 1995, 12).

What are five modes of teaching that define the essence of good teaching and distinguish gifted teachers? Which mode of teaching might this photo represent?

A FORM OF EMPOWERMENT

Power is the dimension of teaching most immediately evident to the new teacher. It is recognized in the first-grader's awed "Teacher, is this good?" on through the high school senior's "How much will this paper count?" Customarily, teachers get respect, at least initially; the deference derives from their power to enhance or diminish their students' academic status and welfare.

Even in the most democratic classrooms, teachers have more influence than students because they are responsible for what happens when students are with them, establishing the goals, selecting the methods, setting the pace, evaluating the progress, and deciding whether students should pass or fail. How you use this power is critical. As you know, students at any level can be humiliated by teachers who misuse their power. For example, a high school student quoted in *Tales Out of School* (Welsh 1987, 153) complained:

> Last year the highest grade given on a test in my advanced modern language course was my C. Most of the other grades were D's and F's. This teacher treated us like dirt. She told one boy who was struggling, "You're stupid—what are you doing here?"

AN OPPORTUNITY TO SERVE

To become a teacher is to serve others professionally—students, the school, the community, and the country, depending on how broad the perspective is. Most who come to teaching do so for altruistic reasons. The altruistic dimension of teaching is at the heart of the motivation to teach. The paycheck, the public regard, and the vacations have little holding power compared to the opportunity to serve. As the authors of *On Being a Teacher* observe:

> Very few people go into education in the first place to become rich or famous. On some level, every teacher gets a special thrill out of helping others. . . . [The] teachers who flourish, those who are loved by their students and revered by their colleagues, are those who feel tremendous dedication and concern for others—not just because they are paid to do so, but because it is their nature and their ethical responsibility (Zehm and Kottler 1993, 8–9).

Whatever form the altruistic rewards of teaching take, they ennoble the profession and remind teachers of the human significance of their work.

AS KEEPERS OF THE DREAM

Many of our country's most talented youth and dedicated veterans in the teaching field retain the desire to teach. In part, the desire endures because teachers have been positively influenced by one or more teachers of their own, who enriched, redirected, or significantly changed their lives. The desire also endures because teachers recognize the many joys and rewards the profession offers.

Reflecting on dedicated teachers and their contributions to our lives, we are guided to teaching for the benefit it brings to others. In doing so, we become keepers of a part of the American dream—the belief that education can improve the quality of life. That dream, more powerful than all our images of teachers, is alive throughout the country in classrooms where outstanding teachers work. This textbook acknowledges these teachers in every chapter in a special feature called *Keepers of the Dream*.

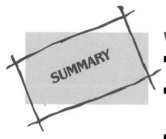

SUMMARY

Why Do You Want to Teach?

- An important reason for becoming a teacher is a desire to work with children and young people.
- Other reasons include a passion for teaching based on a love of subject, the teaching life, or the teaching–learning process; the influence of teachers in one's past; and a desire to serve others and society.
- Practical benefits of teaching include on-the-job hours at school, vacations, increasing salaries and benefits, job security, and a feeling of respect in society.

What Are the Challenges of Teaching?

- Working conditions for teachers can be difficult and stressful; however, for most teachers satisfactions outweigh dissatisfactions.

- Though problems in schools vary according to size of community, location, and other factors, teachers in most schools face five challenges: classroom management, social problems that impact students, need for family and community support, long working hours and job stress, and need for professional empowerment.
- Maintaining discipline and avoiding school-based violence are major concerns among preservice teachers.
- Social problems that impact the lives of many children and youth include substance abuse, teen pregnancies, homelessness, poverty, family distress, child abuse, violence and crime, suicide, and health problems such as HIV/AIDS and fetal alcohol syndrome.
- Since the 1980s, teachers in suburban and rural schools have seen a steady increase in essential support from families and communities, while teachers in urban schools have seen an alarming decrease.
- Though hours in the teacher's work day may appear attractive, over 90 percent of teachers work more than forty hours per week and spend an average ten hours per week on work not directly related to teaching assignments.
- Though job-related factors cause some teachers to experience high levels of stress, stress-reduction activities can help teachers cope and avoid burnout.
- As a consequence of nationwide efforts to improve schools, teachers are assuming new leadership roles and experiencing higher levels of professional empowerment.

What Is Teaching Really Like?

- The outcomes of teaching, even in the best of circumstances, are neither predictable nor consistent.
- It is difficult to measure what students learn as a result of being taught.
- The teacher's ability to influence student behavior is actually quite limited.
- With the role of teacher also comes the power to influence others by example.
- Interactive teaching is characterized by events that are rapid-changing, multi-dimensional, and irregular.
- Teaching involves a unique mode of being between teacher and student—a mode of being that can be experienced but not fully defined or described.

What Does Society Expect of Teachers?

- Society has high expectations of the teachers to whom it entrusts its children and youth.
- The public's image of teachers and its attitudes toward schools have improved since the 1980s.
- Society expects teachers to be competent and effective, and it holds teachers accountable for student achievement, for helping all learners succeed, and for maintaining high standards of conduct.

How Do Good Teachers View Their Work?

- Teachers' overall satisfaction has increased significantly since the 1980s.
- Helping students learn and making a difference in students' lives provide teachers with their greatest satisfaction.
- The essence of good teaching can be described in terms of modes of teaching illustrating what good teachers do.

- Five modes of teaching are teaching as a way of being, a creative endeavor, a live performance, a form of empowerment, and an opportunity to serve.

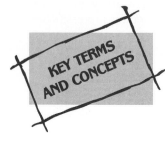

KEY TERMS AND CONCEPTS

burnout, 16
cost of living, 10
fringe benefits, 10
interactive teaching, 21
modes of teaching, 25
moonlight, 10
A Nation at Risk, 23

preactive teaching, 21
professional empowerment, 16
professional portfolio, 31
realities of teaching, 16
student diversity, 6
student-mobility rates, 12

student variability, 6
Teach for America, 8
teacher accountability, 25
teacher–student ratios, 12
teachers' thought processes, 22
tenure, 10

APPLICATIONS AND ACTIVITIES

Teacher's Journal

1. Consider your reasons for deciding to become a teacher. How do they compare with those described in this chapter?

2. Describe a former teacher who has had a positive influence on your decision to teach. In what ways would you like to become like that teacher?

3. What is your impression of the public's image of teachers in your state or community today? What factors might be contributing to the kind of attention or lack of attention teachers are receiving?

4. Think about a time when a teacher truly motivated you to learn. What did that teacher do to motivate you? Do you believe other students in the class had the same reaction to this teacher? Why or why not?

5. Recall and describe specific experiences you had with teachers in elementary school, middle school or junior high school, or high school. Were you ever made uncomfortable because of a teacher's power over you? Were you ever ridiculed or diminished by a teacher? Or have you experienced the opposite—being elevated by a teacher's regard for you?

Teacher's Database

1. Make a list of recent portrayals of teachers in the movies, television, and other media. Analyze the portrayals in terms of the type of teacher image they present—positive, neutral, or negative.

2. Clip articles in a major newspaper that relate to one of the focus questions in this chapter. Analyze the clippings as sources of information and examples you can use to develop an answer to that question.

3. On the World Wide Web, visit the home page of Allyn and Bacon Textbooks in Education. From there you will find many resources specifically designed to help you get the most out of *Becoming a Teacher,* succeed in the course you are taking, and advance your career planning. Features include general and text-specific data-bases, opportunities to communicate directly with the authors and with other students and faculty using *Becoming a Teacher,* information about scheduled on-line events relating to your course, and invitations to contribute your essay, portfolio idea, or written case for possible publication in a future edition of *Becoming a*

Teacher. Download all the information you need to participate fully in the on-line programs that have been developed for your course.

Allyn and Bacon Web Site: **http://www.abacon.com**

4. While you are on the Web, explore Ed Web (http://k12.cnidr.org:90/), which is sponsored by the Corporation for Public Broadcasting. Note information about on-line resources that you can use in this course and in other education courses you will be taking. Search for information by key words or topics such as: teacher burnout, cost of living, moonlighting, Teach for America, accountability, teacher–student ratios, and tenure.

Observations and Interviews

1. As a collaborative project with classmates, visit a local school and interview teachers to learn about their perceptions of the rewards and challenges of teaching. Share your findings with other groups in your class.

2. Arrange to observe a teacher's class. During your observation, note evidence of the five modes of teaching discussed in this chapter. Ask your instructor for handout master 1.1, "Observing Modes of Teaching," that has been developed for this activity.

3. Ask your instructor to arrange group interviews between students in your class and students at the local elementary, middle, junior, and senior high schools. At each interview session, ask the students what characterizes good and not so good teachers. Also, ask the students what advice they would give to beginning teachers.

4. During an observation of a teacher's class, note evidence of the six realities of teaching discussed in this chapter. How many realities are evident during your observation? Which reality is most prevalent? Least prevalent? To help you record your observations, ask your instructor for handout master 1.2, "Observing Realities of Teaching."

5. Visit a first-year teacher (possibly a graduate from your institution) and ask about his or her first impressions of becoming a teacher. What aspects of teaching were difficult? Which easy? What surprises did this first-year teacher encounter? How would this person have prepared differently?

Professional Portfolio

To help you in your journey toward becoming a teacher, each chapter in this textbook includes suggestions for developing your **professional portfolio,** a collection of evidence documenting your growth and development while learning to become a teacher. At the end of this course you will be well on your way toward a portfolio that documents your knowledge, skills, and attitudes for teaching and contains valuable resources for your first teaching position.

For your first portfolio entry, expand on Teacher's Journal entry #1, which asks you to consider your reasons for becoming a teacher. In your entry (or videotaped version), identify the rewards of teaching for you. Identify the satisfactions. Also, describe the aspects of teaching that you will find challenging.

Teaching ultimately requires judgment, improvisation, and conversation about means and ends. Human qualities, expert knowledge and skill, and professional commitment together compose excellence in this craft.

—National Board for Professional Teaching Standards

chapter

2

Learning to Teach

F O C U S
Q U E S T I O N S

1. What essential knowledge do you need to teach?
2. What are five ways of viewing the teacher knowledge base?
3. How do reforms in teacher education affect you?
4. How can you gain practical experience for becoming a teacher?
5. How can you develop your teaching portfolio?
6. How can you establish mentoring relationships?
7. What opportunities for continuing professional development will you have?

I experience the tension between the rolled-up-sleeves feeling of teaching in action and the higher philosophical aims I formulate about what I do. It's as if there are two opposing worlds for education, one seething with organic activity, the other a pristine latticework of ideas and beliefs. When I started my internship at Twain (Middle School), experienced teachers laughed knowingly as I told them about the theories we were studying in our night classes. "All that philosophical thinking about education is interesting," they would say, "but you'll find it isn't worth squat in the classroom. That's teaching."

Meanwhile, in the seminar rooms at (the university), I was being told to challenge that opinion. I needed to bring my philosophical beliefs into the classroom and act upon them as I taught. "That's professionalism," my professors said.

"Okay," I thought, smart-aleck just out of college and full of ideas. "I'll try it."

Very quickly I found out for myself that action and reflection in teaching can be worlds apart. The smell of a middle school, the whirlwind appearance of the classroom, the things there that have been touched, chewed, stepped on by adolescents—these things drive clean, well-crafted, long-prepared ideas from the building screaming in terror. Oh, you could probably heavily Scotch-Guard the ideals and smuggle them in, but don't expect miracles. "Be pessimistic," I hear teachers say in their hesitant suggestions about my grand ideas. "That way, you won't be disappointed when they don't work."

Do I dare put my emotional and intellectual foundations on the line every day by attempting to reflect on my deepest beliefs in the daily tempest of middle school? Is self-preservation a good enough excuse to answer, "No"?

I don't think I'm ready. . . . But don't count me out yet. I still take great pleasure in returning to the safety of my home, where I can face the things I believe at the bottom of my heart. . . . I tell myself, "I am a teacher." My ideals intact . . . I sit and reflect upon the day that, once the laughter and the tears have been wiped away, becomes a tool with which I may better myself. For now, it's the most professional thing I can do (Henry et al. 1995, 106–107).

■

In the preceding excerpt from *To Be a Teacher: Voices From the Classroom,* Jeff Huntley reflects upon his year-long internship at an urban middle school. Now a sixth-, seventh-, and eighth-grade reading teacher, Huntley recognized that applying what he learned in education classes would not be easy, "that action and reflection in teaching can be worlds apart." Much to his credit, though, he also recognized that the hallmark of a professional teacher is the ability to reflect upon one's experiences in the classroom. He learned that teaching is a complex act—one that requires thoughtfulness, insight into the motivations of others, and good judgment.

Among the factors that enabled Huntley to have a constructive, meaningful internship were his ability to draw from what he learned in the fifth-year M.A.T. program he began three days after graduating with a B.A. in English, and the support, guidance, and encouragement he received from a mentor teacher at the school. Thus, by the end of his internship, Huntley had acquired much of the knowledge teachers need to enter the classroom confidently and proficiently.

WHAT ESSENTIAL KNOWLEDGE DO YOU NEED TO TEACH

Students preparing to become teachers must have three kinds of knowledge before they can manage effectively the complexities of teaching: knowledge of self and students, knowledge of subject, and knowledge of educational theory and research. It is to this essential knowledge that we now turn.

SELF-KNOWLEDGE

Effective teachers are aware of themselves and sensitive to the needs of their students. Although it is evident that teachers should understand their students as fully and deeply as possible, it is less evident that this understanding depends on their level of self-knowledge. If teachers are knowledgeable about their needs (and, most importantly, able to take care of those needs), they are better able to help their students. As Arthur Jersild (1955, 3), one of the first educators to focus attention on the connection between the teacher's personal insight and professional effectiveness, pointed out, a teacher's self-understanding and self-acceptance are prerequisites for helping students to know and accept themselves.

Teachers' self-evaluations often are influenced by emotions that teachers may experience when they teach, such as anxiety or loneliness. Promoting anxiety are the realities of teaching outlined in Chapter 1. For example, three conditions that cloud teachers' efforts are (1) the interminable nature of teaching (i.e., their work is never completed), (2) the intangible and often unpredictable characteristics of teaching results, and (3) the inability to attribute learning results to specific teachers' instruction. Unlike architects, lawyers, and doctors, teachers can never stand back and admire *their* work. If a student does well, that success rightfully belongs to the student.

Teachers thus need to develop the ability to tolerate ambiguities and to reduce their anxieties about being observably effective. Without this ability, a teacher "can feel that one is 'wrong,' 'missing something,' a 'bad fit' with students and with teaching itself. One can feel that one's circumstances are unfair, that one is giving but not receiving. One can feel helpless, not knowing what to do, not even knowing how to get the frustration out of mind let alone how to resolve it in practice" (Hansen 1995, 60).

Teachers can also experience loneliness or psychological isolation, since most of their time is spent interacting with children and youth, not adults. Though increased opportunities for professional collaboration and networking are reducing teacher isolation, teachers are behind classroom doors most of the day, immersed in the complexities of teaching and trying to meet the diverse needs of their students. Most teachers would welcome more interaction with their colleagues. As Roland Barth (1990, 33) puts it: "I do not think that teachers and principals really like to work the greater part of each day swamped by students and isolated from adults, secluded in what one teacher called 'our adjoining caves.'"

KNOWLEDGE OF STUDENTS

Knowledge of students is also important. Student characteristics such as their aptitudes, talents, learning styles, stage of development, and their readiness to learn new material are among the essential knowledge teachers must have. The importance of this knowledge is evident in comments made by an intern at the middle school referenced in this chapter's opening scenario: "To teach a kid well you have to know a kid well. . . . teaching middle school takes a special breed of teachers who understand the unique abilities and inabilities . . . [of] those undergoing their own metamorphosis into teenagers" (Henry et al. 1995, 124–125). Teachers gain this kind of knowledge through study, observation, and constant interaction. Without considerable understanding of children and youth, teachers' efforts to help students learn and grow can be inappropriate and, in some cases, counterproductive. Teachers' expectations of students directly affect student achievement. The following Professional Reflection activity is designed to guide you in reflecting on opportunities you have already had to acquire knowledge about learners.

Inventorying Your Teaching Experiences

You probably have had more experience with some of the teacher's roles than you realize. Maybe you took charge of a group such as scouts, 4-H, summer camp, or a club in high school. If you were responsible for what the group learned from the experience, you were a teacher. Maybe you tried to tutor someone. Or perhaps your friend, brother, or sister needed something explained or demonstrated. Even as a baby-sitter you might have had to explain or demonstrate something occasionally. The subject matter might have ranged from algebra to tying shoes. Completing the following should result in a greater awareness of your previous teaching experience. Use a form similar to the one below to list your teaching experiences.

Inventory of Teaching Experiences

Experience	Subject Matter	Learner's Age or Grade Level	Context (e.g., school, camp, youth group)	Ways Different from You (e.g., racial, cultural socioeconomic)
0	Swimming	Age 7–9	Summer camp	City kids
1				
2				
3				
4				
5				

(Source: From *Field Experience* by George J. Posner. Copyright © 1996 by Longman Publishers. Reprinted by permission.)

KNOWLEDGE OF SUBJECT

With the title of teacher comes an assumption of knowledge. Those outside the field of education expect a teacher to be a ready reference for all sorts of information: How do you spell *esophagus?* When should *mother* be capitalized? What is the plot of *King Lear?* Which countries border the Mediterranean? Who is the prime minister of Israel? What is the significance of the Monroe Doctrine? Teachers are expected to be informed and to hold defensible positions on a full range of issues, from local politics to English literature to American history to world geography.

Teachers who have extensive knowledge of their subjects are also better equipped to help their students learn. These teachers, as the National Board for Professional Teaching Standards (1991, 13–14) puts it, "have a rich understanding of the subject(s) they teach and appreciate how knowledge in their subject is created, organized, linked to other disciplines and applied to real-world settings." To describe how knowledgeable teachers modify their instructional strategies based on student perceptions of the subject, the Board goes on to say that these teachers

> are aware of the preconceptions and background knowledge that students typically bring to each subject and of strategies and instructional materials that can be of assistance. They understand where difficulties are likely to arise and modify their practice accord-

ingly. Their instructional repertoire allows them to create multiple paths to the subjects they teach, and they are adept at teaching students how to pose and solve their own problems (p. 14).

KNOWLEDGE OF METHODS FOR APPLYING EDUCATIONAL THEORY AND RESEARCH

Theories about learners and learning guide the decision making of professional teachers. Not only do such teachers know that a certain strategy works, but they also know *why* it works. Because they recognize the importance of theories, they have at their disposal a greater range of options for problem solving than teachers who have not developed their repertoire of theories. Your ultimate goal as a professional is to apply theoretical knowledge to the practical problems of teaching.

To illustrate the usefulness of research on students' learning, we present six teaching functions that educational researcher Barak Rosenshine (1988, 75–92) found enhance students' learning of the basic skills. The effectiveness of each function is supported by carefully designed research studies in actual classrooms.

1. Daily review, homework check, and, if necessary, reteaching
2. Rapid presentation of new content and skills in small steps
3. Guided student practice with close monitoring by teachers
4. Corrective feedback and instructional reinforcement
5. Independent practice in seatwork and homework with a success rate greater than 90 percent
6. Weekly and monthly review

For teaching higher-level thinking skills, Rosenshine and a colleague, Carla Meister (1992, 27), found that effective teachers use the following steps:

What kinds of basic knowledge and skills do teachers need to do their jobs well? How will you acquire and develop knowledge and skills in these areas?

1. Present the new cognitive strategies (i.e., higher-level thinking skills)
2. Regulate difficulty during guided practice
3. Provide varying contexts for student practice
4. Provide feedback
5. Increase student responsibility
6. Provide independent practice

It may be helpful to think of educational research as providing teachers with rules of thumb to guide their practice. Rosenshine and Meister, in cautioning teachers about how to implement their research findings for teaching higher-order thinking strategies, put it this way:

"The teaching of cognitive strategies is a higher-level operation itself; there is no specific, predetermined, or guaranteed path of instructional procedures to follow. Rather, there are sets of procedures [and] suggestions . . . that a teacher selects, develops, presents, attempts, modifies, and even abandons in order to help students learn the cognitive strategy" (p. 33).

WHAT ARE FIVE WAYS OF VIEWING THE TEACHER KNOWLEDGE BASE

Just as people hold different expectations for schools and teachers, there are different views on the knowledge and abilities teachers need to teach well. The complexities of teaching make it difficult to describe in exact detail the **knowledge base** on which teaching as a profession rests. This difficulty results, in part, because there is no universally accepted definition of what good teaching is. Educational researchers are still learning *what* good teachers know and *how* they use that knowledge. Five widespread views of teachers' knowledge and abilities are portrayed in Figure 2.1.

A PERSONAL DEVELOPMENT VIEW

One view of what teachers need to know and be able to do places primary emphasis on who the teacher is as a person. According to this view, teachers should be concerned with developing themselves as persons so that they may learn to use

FIGURE 2.1 Five views of the teacher knowledge base

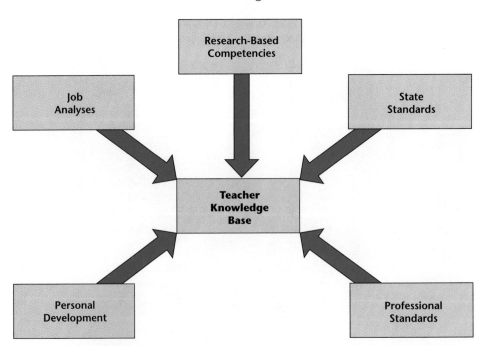

themselves more effectively. The importance of personal development is described as follows by the authors of *On Being a Teacher:* ". . . teachers who appear in charge of their own lives, who radiate power, tranquility, and grace in their actions, are going to command attention and respect. People will follow them anywhere. . . . What we are saying is that you have not only the option, but also the imperative, to develop the personal dimensions of your functioning, as well as your professional skills" (Zehm and Kottler 1993, 15).

What this approach requires, then, is that teachers continually develop their powers of observation and reflection so that they can most effectively respond to the needs of students. Teaching becomes an authentic, growth-oriented encounter between teacher and students. An important dimension of this **personal development view** is the teacher's need for self-knowledge, particularly in regard to oneself as a learner.

RESEARCH-BASED COMPETENCIES

Since the late 1980s, several states and a few large cities have developed their own lists of **research-based competencies** that beginning teachers must demonstrate. These competencies are derived from educational research that has identified what effective teachers do. Typically, the states have developed *behavioral indicators* for each competency, which trained observers from universities and school districts use to determine to what extent teachers actually exhibit the target behaviors in the classroom.

Florida, Texas, Georgia, Louisiana, and North Carolina are among the states that have developed research-based performance appraisal systems. The Texas Teacher Appraisal System (TTAS), for example, has sixty-five behavioral indicators for five domains: instructional strategy, classroom management and organization, presentation of subject matter, learning environment, and professional growth and responsibilities.

STATE STANDARDS

In addition to sets of research-based competencies for evaluating practicing teachers, several states have developed performance-based standards for what new teachers should know and be able to do. Known as **outcome-based** or **performance-based teacher education,** the new approach is based on several assumptions:

- Outcomes are demonstrations of learning rather than a list of teaching specializations, college courses completed, or concepts studied.
- Outcomes are performances that reflect the richness and complexity of the teacher's role in today's classrooms—not discrete, single behaviors.
- Demonstrations of learning must occur in authentic settings—that is, settings similar to those within which the teacher will teach.
- Outcomes are culminating demonstrations of what beginning teachers do in real classrooms.

Typically, outcome-based standards are developed with input from teachers, teacher educators, state department of education personnel, and various professional associations. To illustrate state standards for teacher preparation, we present standards from Kentucky and Colorado on pages 513–515 in the Teacher's Resource Guide.

A JOB-ANALYSIS APPROACH

Another view of what teachers need to know and be able to do is based on the job analyses that some school districts conduct. Typically, a **job analysis** begins with a review of existing job descriptions and then proceeds to interviews with those currently assigned to the job and their supervisors regarding the activities and responsibilities associated with the job. These data are then analyzed to identify the dimensions of the job. Finally, interview questions based on the dimensions are developed and used by district personnel responsible for hiring.

To illustrate the job-analysis view of the knowledge, skills, and attitudes needed by teachers, we present the thirteen dimensions used for selecting "star" urban teachers. By comparing the behaviors and beliefs of outstanding urban teachers with those of quitters and failures, Martin Haberman (1995, 779–780) and his colleagues at the University of Wisconsin, Milwaukee, identified thirteen characteristics of successful teachers of low-income urban students. These characteristics, identified by principals, supervisors, other teachers, parents, and the teachers themselves, include the following:

- *Persistence.*
- *Protecting learners and learning.* Star teachers see protecting and enhancing students' involvement in learning activities as their highest priority. . . .
- *Application of generalizations.* [Stars are] able to take principles and concepts from a variety of sources (i.e., courses, workshops, books, and research) and translate them into practice.
- *Approach to "at-risk" students.* Star teachers believe that, regardless of the life conditions their students face, they as teachers bear a primary responsibility for sparking their students' desire to learn.
- *Professional versus personal orientation to students.* [Stars] use such terms as *caring, respect,* and *concern,* and they enjoy the love and affection of students when it occurs naturally. But they do not regard it as a prerequisite for learning.
- *Burnout: its causes and cures.* [Star teachers] recognize that even good teachers will eventually burn out if they are subjected to constant stress, so they learn how to protect themselves. . . .
- *Fallibility.* [Stars] can accept their own mistakes.

The remaining six dimensions are *organizational ability, physical/emotional stamina, teaching style* modeled on coaching, *explanation of success* based on students' effort rather than ability, *rapport* with students, and *readiness* to believe that education will provide students with the best chance of "making it" in American society.

PROFESSIONAL VIEWS

Various professional associations have outlined what teachers should know and be able to do. The **National Board for Professional Teaching Standards (NBPTS),** established in 1987 as an outgrowth of the Carnegie Forum report *A Nation Prepared: Teachers for the 21st Century,* has developed the following five general standards on which voluntary national teacher certification will be based; specific standards are also being developed in more than thirty certification areas.

- Teachers are committed to students and their learning.
- Teachers know the subjects they teach and how to teach those subjects to students.
- Teachers are responsible for managing and monitoring student learning.
- Teachers think systematically about their practice and learn from experience.

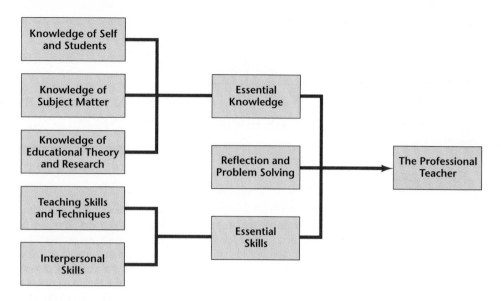

FIGURE 2.2 Essential knowledge and skills for the professional teacher

■ Teachers are members of learning communities (National Board for Professional Teaching Standards 1991, 13–14).

Standards proposed by the **Interstate New Teacher Assessment and Support Consortium (INTASC),** also established in 1987, reflect a trend toward performance-based or outcome-based assessment of essential knowledge and abilities for teachers. In other words, such standards describe what teachers should know and be able to do rather than listing courses that teachers need in order to receive a license to teach. To enhance collaboration among states for the initial licensing of teachers, INTASC proposed in early 1993 ten principles that are compatible with the standards proposed by the NBPTS (see page 516 in the Teacher's Resource Guide). Specific statements for essential "knowledge," "dispositions," and "performances" were also developed for each principle.

In light of the five differing views of what teachers ought to know and be able to do, it seems clear that becoming a teacher is complex and demanding. We believe that effective teachers use five kinds of knowledge and skills to meet the challenges of the profession. As Figure 2.2 shows, effective teachers are guided by **reflection** and a **problem-solving orientation.** On the basis of reflection and problem solving, they use knowledge of self and students (including cultural differences), knowledge of subject matter, and knowledge of educational theory and research to create optimum conditions.

HOW DO REFORMS IN TEACHER EDUCATION AFFECT YOU 🔲

Since the publication in 1983 of *A Nation at Risk: The Imperative for Educational Reform,* the United States has experienced an unprecedented push for reform in education. During that time, numerous commissions were established and scores of

Dear Mentor

NOVICE AND EXPERT TEACHERS
ON TEACHING AS A PROFESSION

Dear Erwin,

Some benefits that you might expect from a profession are the ability to be creative and responsible, to make informed choices based on expertise, and to have a profound impact on many others. Teaching will provide you with all of these.

I would like to talk to you about professional preparation from my own perspective, as one concerned with the preparation of K–12 teachers of mathematics. I believe that you would hear the same viewpoint from specialists in all other curriculum areas.

If you became a teacher of mathematics, you would be able to trace your knowledge of teaching mathematics to your own schooling in the subject, your professional training in how to teach, and your experiences as a beginning teacher. However, teachers who will be able to meet the challenges of teaching mathematics for the next century will require a carefully coordinated professional development program.

Let's first consider your own schooling. Perhaps you were taught mathematics in ways that are not in accord with current curriculum reform. While college classes might broaden your understanding at an adult level, they might not help you to learn the variety of ways in which you can think about and communicate the subject. I would not like to rely on school and college experiences to prepare a teacher to teach in any subject area. Remembering and analyzing our own adult learning does not help us to understand differences in the ways that children learn.

Perhaps you can learn to be a great teacher through experience in the school where you get your first job. In reality, new teachers who lack professional preparation are lucky to get jobs in good schools at the forefront of educational reform, with top-notch teachers and resources for staff development. You may be able to learn about new ways to learn and teach content areas such as mathematics on your own, through extensive reading of professional journals and attendance at professional meetings, such as those of the National Council of Teachers of Mathematics.

What you don't learn from your own experiences as a student or from your work as a teacher, you might learn from courses in Education, including methods courses. Students at my college report that these courses are chock full of material that is intellectually challenging, exciting, fun to share with peers, and relevant to new teachers. Our students also have varied field experiences in which master teachers and college faculty familiar with new curriculum materials support them as they begin interacting with children.

Finally, students have a right to professional teaching practice. I believe you are most likely to acquire the knowledge and skills for professional practice in a program leading to teacher certification, in which academic classes, education classes, field placements, and initial teaching experiences are all coordinated to help you in becoming a teacher.

> ### Dear Mentor,
>
> Do you think that teaching has all the benefits of a profession? In Los Angeles, teacher certification is not even needed to begin a career as a public school teacher. What professional knowledge and skills do certified teachers have beyond those of nonteachers?
>
> Erwin Obdam

Rosamond Welchman
Professor, Mathematics Education,
    Brooklyn College of City University of New York
Director, New York Collaborative for
    Excellence in Teacher Preparation

reports were written outlining what should be done to improve America's schools. Most of these reports called for changes in the education of teachers. In fact, the preparation program you are now involved in probably has been influenced by this **educational reform movement.** Calls for reform in teacher education have emphasized increased academic preparation, an expanded role for schools, and a national board for teacher certification.

INCREASED ACADEMIC PREPARATION

One call for the reform of teacher education was made by the **Holmes Group,** named after Henry W. Holmes, dean of the Harvard Graduate School of Education during the 1920s. The Holmes Group was initially made up of ninety-six major universities. In *Tomorrow's Teachers,* a 1986 report written by thirteen deans of education and one college president, the Holmes Group recommended that all teachers have a bachelor's degree in an academic field and a master's degree in education. Although the Holmes Group viewed additional academic preparation as a means of enhancing the professional status of teachers, critics maintained that students' education would be delayed and be more expensive, with no assurance that students who spent five years obtaining a teaching certificate would be paid more.

The Holmes Group held an action summit in 1993 to develop a comprehensive plan for redesigning the schools of education at Holmes Group member institutions. The plan outlined steps for creating Tomorrow's School of Education (TSE)—an institution that has put into practice the Holmes Group agenda for the reform of teacher education. In early 1995, the Holmes Group released the TSE plan, which recommended that teacher educators become more involved with schools and that students move through a five-year program in cohorts. The report also urged colleges of education to establish **professional development schools** (PDSs) that are linked to colleges or universities and operate on the same principle as teaching hospitals. Students act as intern teachers, and college faculty and school staff develop new teaching methods and collaborate on educational research projects.

EXPANDED ROLE FOR SCHOOLS

Based on his comprehensive, on-site study of twenty-nine teacher education programs in eight states, noted educator John Goodlad set forth a detailed blueprint for transforming teacher preparation in his 1990 book, *Teachers for Our Nation's Schools.* To improve teacher preparation, Goodlad recommended the creation of Centers of Pedagogy that would operate according to a specific set of principles. These centers would take the place of current teacher education departments, and they would be staffed by a team of teacher educators, liberal arts professors, and educators from local schools. In addition, Goodlad recommended that school districts and universities create jointly operated partner schools. Selected teachers at the partner school would divide their time between teaching students at the school and supervising beginning teachers. Partner schools would thus become centers for the renewal of education as well as laboratory schools for the professional development of beginning teachers.

NATIONAL CERTIFICATION

The National Board for Professional Teaching Standards (NBPTS) was created to issue certificates to teachers who meet the Board's high standards. The NBPTS is

Keepers of the Dream

Caroline Bitterwolf

**National Board
Certified Teacher**

Caroline Bitterwolf remembers sitting at her typewriter, completing her application for national certification, with a fellow teacher helping her assemble the final materials. They just made the 9:00 a.m. deadline. At least 100 hours of preparation preceded that moment, and, according to Bitterwolf, she could not have done it without the support of family, friends, her school colleagues, students, and their parents. Later, with the rigorous evaluation behind her, she would become the first Idaho teacher and one of the first 81 (of 289) national candidates to be certified by the National Board for Professional Teaching Standards (NBPTS).

Bitterwolf's telephone inquiry to the NBPTS in Detroit marked what she describes as "the beginning of a wonderful relationship." The staff's friendliness encouraged her, but when the Board's directions and standards arrived, she found them daunting. "I'll never do it. The expectations are so high. No way I'll measure up," she thought, and she put the box of information on a back shelf.

She tried to forget the box but couldn't. So she began working through the materials, and discovered that nothing was required that she was not already doing. The directions guided the seventh-grade study skills teacher to constantly reflect on and write about what she was doing, why, and how it fit her students. She also needed to document her practices with lesson plans, videotapes of her teaching, and written analyses. The time-consuming effort proved to be of real value. "I was amazed at what I found. Who I was, why I was teaching, what my goals were—it consolidated everything for me."

"I was amazed at what I found."

For the final phase of the review, the Moscow, Idaho, teacher traveled to the Vancouver, Washington, assessment center where she participated in two twelve-hour days of activities, developing curriculum, evaluating materials, responding to videos of others teaching, writing essays, and being interviewed. She regards the overall application and assessment process as "the best professional development activity I have ever experienced."

Bitterwolf's involvement in national certification did not stop with her achieving national certification. She also participated in a video promoting the national standards and was elected to the National Board for Professional Teaching Standards.

That she came so far she attributes to the wonderful teachers she knew and met along the way. In addition to the teachers in her family and in her own schooling experience, Bitterwolf gives credit to a woman she regards as her professional mentor, Sally Borghart, "a four-foot ten-inch English lady who wore wedgies," who helped her teach 9th grade inner city remedial reading in Annapolis, Maryland. It was the only job Bitterwolf was able to get—a teaching assistantship through CETA (Comprehensive Employment Training Act). The transition from a southern church preschool to the tough vocabulary of inner city youths caused the young teacher to spend most of the first semester in tears. "But Sally had a way with these young adults and through her I learned, really learned, how to communicate with my students—to empathize with them. She literally taught me how to diagnose student problems and set up programs to meet their individual needs, how to set up thematic units. She was way ahead of her time."

For a teacher, who moved from "no way, I'll never measure up," to being a nationally certified teacher and member of the National Board for Professional Teaching Standards, Bitterwolf's words of advice for teachers fit well: "Constantly strive to keep learning . . . do not be afraid to try new things," and be active in your profession so that we "can be the best we can be."

governed by a sixty-three member board of directors, the majority of whom are active classroom teachers. In 1995, five nationally certified teachers were elected to the board.

The NBPTS encourages school districts and states to pay its certification fee ($2,000 for 1997–98) on behalf of teachers who seek board certification. Candidates first submit portfolios documenting their performance over several months; then they complete a series of exercises at an assessment center. Examples of NBPTS portfolio activities and assessment center activities for the early adolescence English/language arts and generalist certificates are included in the Teacher's Resource Guide. In 1994 eighty-one of the 289 teachers who took the first national certification test passed.

HOW CAN YOU GAIN PRACTICAL EXPERIENCE FOR BECOMING A TEACHER ?

A primary aim of teacher education programs is to give students opportunities to experience, to the extent possible, the real world of the teacher. Through field experiences and carefully structured experiential activities, preservice teachers are given limited exposure to various aspects of teaching. Observing, tutoring, instructing small groups, analyzing video cases, operating instructional media, performing student teaching, and completing various noninstructional tasks are among the most common experiential activities.

CLASSROOM OBSERVATIONS

Classroom observations are a vital element of many **field experiences.** Students report that these experiences aid them greatly in making a final decision about entering the teaching field. Most become more enthusiastic about teaching and more motivated to learn the needed skills; a few decide that teaching is not for them. Recognizing the value of observations, a number of universities are attempting to incorporate such fieldwork earlier in their teacher education programs.

Currently, many universities and school districts are cooperating on the use of two-way interactive compressed video technology to enable preservice teachers on campus to observe live coverage in school classrooms off campus. Compressed video can be transmitted over existing telephone lines or the Internet in a relatively inexpensive, unobtrusive, and time-efficient way. **Distance learning** enables teacher education programs to use the power of models for learning how to teach. For example, distance learning enables students at Texas A & M University and the University of Memphis to observe inner-city classrooms and afterwards to discuss their observations with the teachers. One of the designers of the interactive video program at Memphis comments on its benefits: "Previously everyone visited different schools and saw very different things. [This] shared clinical experience will lead to a more focused discussion of teaching methods" (The University of Memphis 1994/95, 2).

Observations are more meaningful when they are focused and conducted with clear purposes. Observers may focus on the students, the teacher, the interactions between the two, the structure of the lesson, or the setting. More specifically, for example, observers may note differences between the ways boys and girls or members of different ethnic groups communicate and behave in the classroom. They may note student interests and ability levels, study student responses to a particular teaching strategy, or analyze the question and response patterns in a class discussion. Much of what observers will notice will be determined by the questions that have been raised before they enter the classroom.

With reform efforts to improve education in the United States has come the development of instruments to facilitate the evaluation of teacher performance, a task now widely required of school administrators. Students preparing to teach can benefit by using these evaluative instruments in their observations, such as the "Formative Observation of Effective Teaching Practices Instrument." This instrument is included in the Teacher's Resource Guide at the back of this textbook.

CLASSROOM EXPERIENCES

Because of the need to provide opportunities to put theory into practice before student teaching, many teacher education programs enable students to participate in microteaching, teaching simulations, analyses of video cases, field-based practica and clinical experiences, and classroom aide programs.

MICROTEACHING   Introduced in the 1960s, **microteaching** was received enthusiastically and remains a popular practice. The process calls for students to teach brief, single-concept lessons to a small group of students (five to ten) while concurrently practicing a specific teaching skill, such as positive reinforcement. Often the microteaching is videotaped for later study.

As originally developed, microteaching includes the following six steps.

1. Identify a specific teaching skill to learn about and practice.
2. Read about the skill in one of several pamphlets.
3. Observe a master teacher demonstrate the skill in a short movie or on videotape.
4. Prepare a three- to five-minute lesson to demonstrate the skill.
5. Teach the lesson, which is videotaped, to a small group of peers.
6. Critique, along with the instructor and student peers, the videotaped lesson.

SIMULATIONS   As an element of teacher training, **teaching simulations** provide opportunities for vicarious practice of a wide range of teaching skills. In simulations, students analyze teaching situations that are presented in writing, on audiotape, in short films, or on videotape. Typically, students are given background information about a hypothetical school or classroom and the pupils they must prepare to teach. After this orientation, students role-play the student teacher or the teacher who is confronted with the problem situation. Following the simulation, participants discuss the appropriateness of solutions and work to increase their problem-solving skills and their understanding of the teacher's multifaceted role as a decision maker.

With recent advances in computer technology, some teacher education programs now use computer-based simulations that enable students to hone their classroom planning and decision-making skills. Students at Nova Southwestern University in Florida, for example, learn to diagnose learning disabilities among children and youth by analyzing computer-simulated cases (Brown 1994). In addition, continuing progress in the development of virtual reality technology suggests that preservice teachers soon will be able to practice their skills with computer-simulated students (Van Lehn et al. 1994, 135–175).

VIDEO CASES   Teacher education students who view, analyze, and then write about video cases have an additional opportunity to appreciate the ambiguities and complexities of real-life classrooms, to learn that "there are no clear-cut, simple answers to the complex issues teachers face" (Wasserman 1994, 606). Viewing authentic video cases enables students to see how "teaching tradeoffs and dilemmas emerge in the video 'text' as do the strategies teachers use, the frustrations they experience, the brilliant and less-brilliant decisions they make" (Grant, Richard, and Parkay 1996, 5).

PRACTICA   A **practicum** is a short-term field-based experience (usually about two weeks long) that allows teacher education students to spend time observing and assisting in classrooms. Though practica vary in length and purpose, students are often able to begin instructional work with individuals or small groups. For example, a cooperating teacher may allow a practicum student to tutor a small group of students, read a story to the whole class, conduct a spelling lesson, monitor recess, help students with their homework, or teach students a song or game.

CLASSROOM AIDES   Serving as a teacher's aide is another popular means of providing field experience before student teaching. A teacher aide's role depends primarily on the unique needs of the schools and its students. Generally, aides work under the supervision of a certified teacher and perform duties that support the teacher's instruction. Assisting teachers in classrooms familiarizes college students with class schedules, record-keeping procedures, and students' performance levels, and provides ample opportunity for observations. In exchange, the classroom teacher receives much needed assistance.

STUDENT TEACHING

The most extensive and memorable field experience in teacher preparation programs is the period of student teaching. The purpose of student teaching, according to the following excerpt from *The Student Teacher's Handbook,* "is to contribute to your socialization into the teaching profession, to prepare you for your regular job by having you experience how real-life (i.e., not textbook) teachers behave in class, in school, and in relationships with students, other teachers, the principals, and parents" (Schwebel et al. 1992, 5). States require students to have a five-week to semester-long student teaching experience in the schools before certifying them as teachers. The nature of student teaching varies considerably among teacher education programs. Typically, a student is assigned to a cooperating (or master) teacher in the school, and a university supervisor makes periodic visits to observe the student teacher. Some programs even pay student teachers during the student teaching experience.

Student teaching is a time of responsibility. As one student teacher put it, "I don't want to mess up [my students'] education!" It is also an opportunity for growth, a chance to master critical skills. According to data gathered from 902 teacher education institutions in the United States, about 60 percent of the student teacher's time is actually spent teaching (Johnson and Yates 1982). The remaining time is devoted to observing and participating in classroom activities. The amount of time one actually spends teaching, however, is not as important as one's willingness to reflect carefully on the student teaching experience. Two excellent ways to promote reflection during student teaching are journal writing and maintaining a reflective teaching log.

What strategies can you use to make your student teaching experience truly valuable to you in becoming a teacher? In what sense will you remain a student teacher throughout your career?

STUDENT TEACHER JOURNAL WRITING   Many supervisors require student teachers to keep a journal of their classroom experiences so that they can engage in reflective teaching and begin the process of criticizing and guiding themselves. The following entry was written by a student teaching in a third-grade classroom.

February 3

If there is one thing that *really* drives me crazy about these kids, it's how they don't listen to directions. Today in my language lesson all they had to do was rewrite a paragraph—not make corrections, just rewrite. We are working on paragraph form. I explained the directions once and had one of the students read it out loud again. Then I asked for any questions—none. Then as soon as I said "begin" the questions started flying. But what really got me was that they were all questions I had already explained or that were in the directions right there on their papers. I finally said they would have to ask their neighbors for the answer. It was *so* frustrating. Mrs. B. said for me to tell them next time that I would explain the directions once and ask for questions, then that was it. They would have to ask someone else! What a day!

Relatively unstructured, open-ended journals, such as the one from which this entry was selected, provide student teachers with a medium for subjectively exploring the practicum experience.

REFLECTIVE TEACHING LOGS   To promote the practice of reflecting more analytically, some supervisors ask their student teachers to use a more directed and structured form of journal keeping, the **reflective teaching log.** In this form a student lists and briefly describes the daily sequence of activities, selects a single episode to expand on, analyzes the reason for selecting it and what was learned from it, and considers the possible future application of that knowledge.

To illustrate the reflective teaching approach to keeping a log, we share here a partial entry for one episode that was recounted and critiqued by a college student tutoring a student in Spanish. The entry is of particular interest because it provides us with a glimpse of a college student's first experience with a pupil's difficulty in understanding subject matter.

Log #1: February 14, 1991 (10:00–10:30AM)

Sequence of Events: Worked with Richy on his Spanish

Episode: Because I wasn't sure of Richy's level, I asked him a few questions to see what he knew. His homework exercises involved work like reflexives, irregular verbs, and vocabulary. But when he and I started reviewing, he didn't remember the very basics of conjugation. He said, "I know this stuff, I just need review." We reviewed the conjugation of regular verbs. I set up a chart of *ar, er* and *ir* endings and had him fill in the correct forms. He kept saying, "I just don't remember," or "Oh yeah, I knew that." His facial expressions reflected concentration and perhaps frustration. At times, he would just stare at the page until I gave him a hint. His forehead was scrunched up and he fidgeted a bit with his hands and legs. After working on the regular endings, he wanted to get a drink. I told him to go ahead. . . .

Analysis: I guess that I was just shocked at how little Richy knew. What we went over was the most simple form of Spanish grammar and in a way he was acting as if he had no idea what we were doing. I was surprised, like I said, but only on the inside. I just helped him along, showing him *why* the concepts made sense. I had no idea how we were going to do his homework assignments since they were considerably more difficult . . . (Posner 1993, 116–117). (From *Field Experience* by George J. Posner. Copyright © 1996 by Longman Publishers. Reprinted by permission.)

Though student teaching will be the capstone experience of your teacher education program, the experience should be regarded as an *initial* rather than a *terminal* learning opportunity—your first chance to engage in reflection and self-evaluation for a prolonged period.

INDUCTION AND INTERNSHIP PROGRAMS

In response to widespread efforts to improve education, many states and local school districts, often in collaboration with colleges and universities, have begun teacher induction and/or internship programs. Among the programs that have received national attention are the Florida Beginning Teacher Program, the California Mentor Teacher Program, the Virginia Beginning Teacher Assistance Program, and the Kentucky Beginning Teacher Internship Program.

Induction programs provide beginning teachers with continued assistance at least during the first year. **Internship programs** also provide participants with support, but they are usually designed primarily to provide training for those who have not gone through a teacher education program. In some instances, however, the terms *induction* and *internship* are used interchangeably.

Most induction and internship programs serve a variety of purposes:

1. To improve teaching performance
2. To increase the retention of promising beginning teachers during the induction years

3. To promote the personal and professional well-being of beginning teachers by improving teachers' attitudes toward themselves and the profession
4. To satisfy mandated requirements related to induction and certification
5. To transmit the culture of the system of beginning teachers (Huling-Austin 1990, 539).

To accomplish these purposes, induction programs offer resources such as workshops based on teacher-identified needs, observations by and follow-up conferences with individuals not in a supervisory role, support from mentor (or buddy) teachers, and support group meetings for beginning teachers.

SCHOOL-BASED TEACHER EDUCATION

A new model of teacher preparation that provides students with extensive practical field experiences is known as **school-based teacher education.** In most instances, school-based programs are designed for students who have received a bachelor's degree and then wish to obtain teacher certification. Two examples are the school-based teacher education programs in Texas and the Teachers for Chicago plan.

Since 1985, completion of a school-based program has been one path to teacher certification in Texas. Candidates complete a year-long paid internship at a school, during which they undertake intensive practical study of teaching. Interns are mentored by the supervisor of the district's teacher education program, the district's curriculum specialist, the principal, the assistant principal, and, in some cases, a university supervisor. Area universities deliver courses specifically designed for the interns. At the end of the year, interns take district- and/or state-adopted tests of content and pedagogy to become eligible for standard certification.

To select, train, and retain effective teachers for Chicago's schools, a group of schools, the Chicago Teachers Union, deans of education at area universities, and the Golden Apple Foundation for Excellence in Teaching created the Teachers for Chicago Program. Candidates, selected through a rigorous interview process, enroll in a graduate education program at one of nine area colleges and universities. After a summer of coursework, they begin a two-year paid internship under the guidance of a mentor teacher. Interns fill vacant teacher positions in the schools and are responsible for the academic progress of their students. Upon completion of the program, interns have earned a master's degree and have met state certification requirements.

SUBSTITUTE TEACHING

Upon completion of a teacher education program and prior to securing a full-time teaching assignment, many students choose to gain additional practical experience in classrooms by **substitute teaching.** Others, unable to locate full-time positions, decide to substitute, knowing that many districts prefer to hire from their pool of substitutes when full-time positions become available. Substitute teachers replace regular teachers who are absent due to illness, family responsibilities, personal reasons, or professional workshops and conferences.

Each day, thousands of substitutes are employed in our nation's schools. For example, during 1992–93 at the fifteen high schools in a large urban district, the total number of absences for 1,200 regular teachers equaled 14,229 days. Multiplying

Advantages and Disadvantages of Substitute Teaching

Advantages

- **Gain experience without all the nightly work and preparation.**
- **Compare and contrast different schools and their environments.**
- **Be better prepared for interviews by meeting administrators and teachers.**
- **Teach and learn a variety of material.**
- **Get to know people—network.**
- **See job postings and hear about possible vacancies.**
- **Gain confidence in your abilities to teach.**
- **Practice classroom management techniques.**
- **Learn about school and district politics—get the "inside scoop."**
- **Choose which days to work—flexible schedule.**

Disadvantages

- **Pay is not as good as full-time teaching.**
- **No benefits such as medical coverage, retirement plans or sick days.**
- **Lack of organized representation to improve wages or working conditions.**
- **May receive a cool reception in some schools.**
- **Must adapt quickly to different school philosophies.**
- **Lack of continuity—may be teaching whole language one day; phonetics the next.**

FIGURE 2.3 Advantages and disadvantages of substitute teaching (Source: John F. Snyder, "The Alternative of Substitute Teaching." In *The Job Search Handbook for Educators: 1996 ASCUS Annual.* Evanston, IL: Association for School, College and University Staffing, Inc., p. 32.)

this figure by five (the number of classes per day for most high school teachers) yields 71,145 class periods taught by substitutes that year (St. Michel 1995).

Qualifications for substitutes vary from state to state and district to district. An area with a critical need for subs will often relax its requirements to provide classroom coverage. In many districts, it is possible to substitute teach without regular certification. Some districts have less stringent qualifications for short-term, day-to-day subtitutes and more stringent ones for long-term, full-time ones. In many districts, the application process for substitutes is the same as that for full-time applicants; in others, the process may be somewhat briefer. Often, substitutes are not limited to working in their area of certification; however, schools try to avoid making out-of-field assignments. If you decide to substitute teach, contact the schools in your area to learn about the qualifications and procedures for hiring substitutes.

In spite of the significant role substitutes play in the day-to-day operation of schools, " . . . research tells us that they receive very little support, no specialized training, and are rarely evaluated. . . . In short, the substitute will be expected to show up to each class on time, maintain order, take roll, carry out the lesson, and leave a note for the regular teacher about the classes and events of the day without support, encouragement, or acknowledgement" (St. Michel 1995, 6–7). While working conditions such as these are certainly challenging, substitute teaching can be a rewarding, professionally fulfilling experience. Figure 2.3 presents several advantages and disadvantages of substitute teaching.

HOW CAN YOU DEVELOP YOUR TEACHING PORTFOLIO

Now that you have begun your journey toward becoming a teacher, you should acquire the habit of assessing your growth in knowledge, skills, and attitudes. Toward this end, you may wish to collect the results of your reflections and self-assessment in a professional portfolio. A **professional portfolio** is a collection of work that documents an individual's accomplishments in an area of professional practice. An artist's portfolio, for example, might consist of a résumé, sketches, paintings, slides and photographs of exhibits, critiques of the artist's work, awards, and other documentation of achievement. Recently, new approaches to teacher evaluation have included the professional portfolio. The National Board for Professional Teaching Standards, for example, uses "portfolios [and] other evidence of performance prepared by the

How Can You Develop Your Teaching Portfolio? **51**

What characteristics and qualities will you look for in a mentor teacher? What might you ask a mentor about developing your professional portfolio?

candidate" (National Board for Professional Teaching Standards 1991, 55) as one way of assessing whether teachers have met the high standards for Board certification. Teacher education programs at several universities now use portfolios as one means of assessing the competencies of candidates for teacher certification. Also, many school districts are beginning to ask applicants to submit portfolios that document their effectiveness as teachers.

PORTFOLIO CONTENTS

What will your portfolio contain? Written materials might include the following: lesson plans and curriculum materials, reflections on your development as a teacher, journal entries, writing assignments made by your instructor, sample tests you have prepared, critiques of textbooks, evaluations of students' work at the level for which you are preparing to teach, sample letters to parents, and a résumé. Nonprint materials might include video- and audiotapes featuring you in simulated teaching and role-playing activities, audiovisual materials (transparencies, charts, or other teaching aids), photographs of bulletin boards, charts depicting room arrangements for cooperative learning or other instructional strategies, sample grade book, certificates of membership in professional organizations, and awards.

Your portfolio should represent your *best work* and give you an opportunity to become an advocate of *who you are* as a teacher. Because a primary purpose of the professional portfolio is to stimulate reflection and dialogue, you may wish to discuss what entries to make in your portfolio with your instructor or other teacher education students. In addition, the following questions from *How to Develop a Professional Portfolio: A Manual for Teachers* (Campbell et al. 1996) can help you select appropriate portfolio contents:

> Would I be proud to have my future employer and peer group see this? Is this an example of what my future professional work might look like? Does this represent what I stand for as a professional educator? If not, what can I revise or rearrange so that it represents my best efforts? (p. 5).

USING A PORTFOLIO

In addition to providing teacher education programs with a way to assess their effectiveness, portfolios can be used by students for a variety of purposes. Campbell et al. (1996, 7–8) suggest that a portfolio may be used as

1. A way to establish a record of quantitative and qualitative performance and growth over time.
2. A tool for reflection and goal setting as well as a way to present evidence of your ability to solve problems and achieve goals.
3. A way to synthesize many separate experiences; in other words, a way to get the "big picture."
4. A vehicle for you to use to collaborate with professors and advisors in individualizing instruction.
5. A vehicle for demonstrating knowledge and skills gained through out-of-class experiences, such as volunteer experiences.
6. A way to share control and responsibility for your own learning.
7. An alternative assessment measure within the professional education program.
8. A potential preparation for national, regional, and state accreditation.
9. An interview tool in the professional hiring process.
10. An expanded résumé to be used as an introduction during the student teaching experience.

HOW CAN YOU ESTABLISH MENTORING RELATIONSHIPS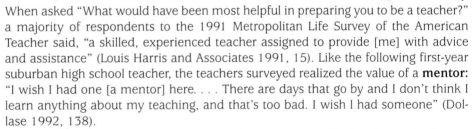

When asked "What would have been most helpful in preparing you to be a teacher?" a majority of respondents to the 1991 Metropolitan Life Survey of the American Teacher said, "a skilled, experienced teacher assigned to provide [me] with advice and assistance" (Louis Harris and Associates 1991, 15). Like the following first-year suburban high school teacher, the teachers surveyed realized the value of a **mentor**: "I wish I had one [a mentor] here. . . . There are days that go by and I don't think I learn anything about my teaching, and that's too bad. I wish I had someone" (Dollase 1992, 138).

In reflecting on how a mentor contributed to his professional growth, Forrest Parkay defined **mentoring** as

> . . . an intensive, one-to-one form of teaching in which the wise and experienced mentor inducts the aspiring protégé [one who is mentored] into a particular, usually professional, way of life. . . . [T]he protégé learns from the mentor not only the objective, manifest content of professional knowledge and skills but also a subjective, nondiscursive appreciation for *how* and *when* to employ these learnings in the arena of professional practice. In short, the mentor helps the protégé to "learn the ropes," to become socialized into the profession (Parkay 1988, 196).

An example of "learning the ropes" is contained in an urban middle school intern's description of how his mentor helped him develop effective classroom management techniques: " 'You've got to develop your own sense of personal power,' [my mentor] kept saying. 'It's not something I can teach you. I can show you what to do. I can model it. But I don't know, it's just something that's got to come from within you' " (Henry et al. 1995, 114).

Those who have become highly accomplished teachers frequently point out the importance of mentors in their preparation for teaching. A mentor can provide moral support, guidance, and feedback to students at various stages of professional preparation. The following comments by two beginning middle school teachers highlight the benefits of having a mentor.

I have two mentors. They're infinite in their ability to help me because I can always bounce ideas off them, and I can always get myself redirected and refocused. More important, these teachers are helping me to develop my own theories on education. Helping me to see the big picture of pedagogy and methodology.

My informal mentor was most valuable to me as a role model. I like the way she interacted with the students and her underlying positive attitude. She's just a very positive person. . . . I just felt comfortable going in and saying, "Oh, I had the worst time with so-and-so." She'd say, "Well, maybe you could try this, and, hey, don't worry about it, it happens" (Dollase 1992, 137–139, with permission of Teachers College Press).

WHAT OPPORTUNITIES FOR CONTINUING PROFESSIONAL DEVELOPMENT WILL YOU HAVE 🔲

Professional development is a life-long process; any teacher, at any stage of development, has room for improvement. Many school systems and universities have programs in place for the continuing professional development of teachers. Indeed, teachers are members of a profession that provides them with a ". . . continuous opportunity to grow, learn, and become more expert in their work" (Lieberman 1990, viii).

SELF-ASSESSMENT FOR PROFESSIONAL GROWTH **Self-assessment** is a necessary first step in pursuing opportunities for professional growth. A teacher comments on the importance of self-assessment after being certified by the National Board for Professional Teaching Standards: "Serious reflection and self-examination [were necessary] as I gauge[d] my skills and knowledge against objective, peer-developed, national standards in specific teaching areas" (National Board for Professional Teaching Standards 1995, 13).

Several questions can help you make appropriate choices as a teacher: In which areas am I already competent? In which areas do I need further development? How will I acquire the knowledge and skills I need? How will I apply new knowledge and practice new skills? Answers to such questions will lead you to a variety of sources for professional growth: teacher workshops, teacher centers, professional development schools, the opportunity to supervise and mentor student teachers, and graduate programs. Figure 2.4 illustrates the relationship of these professional development experiences to your teacher education program.

TEACHER WORKSHOPS The quality of **inservice workshops** is uneven, varying with the size of school district budgets and the imagination and knowledge of the administrators and teachers who arrange them. It is significant that the most effective inservice programs tend to be the ones that teachers request—and often design and conduct.

Some workshops focus on topics that all teachers (regardless of subject or level) can benefit from: classroom management, writing-across-the-curriculum, multicultural education, or strategies for teaching students with learning disabilities in the general education classroom, for example. Other workshops have a sharper focus and are intended for teachers of a subject at a certain level—for example, whole-language techniques for middle school students, discovery learning for high school science students, or student-centered approaches to teaching literature in the high school classroom.

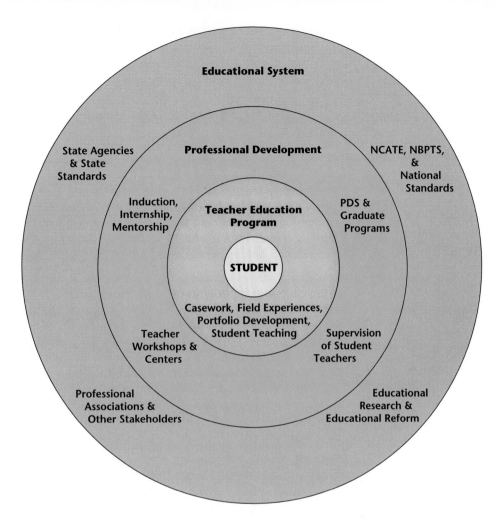

FIGURE 2.4 Professional development: From teacher education student to practitioner

TEACHER CENTERS **Teacher centers** are "places where teachers can come together with other teachers, and perhaps with other useful persons . . . to do things that will help them teach better" (Gage 1978, 57). In contrast to inservice programs, these are more clearly initiated and directed by teachers. Some centers cooperate with a local or neighboring college of education and include members of the faculty on their planning committees.

Many teachers find teacher centers stimulating because they offer opportunities for collegial interaction in a quiet, professionally-oriented setting. The busy, hectic pace of life in many schools, teachers often find, provides little time for professional dialogue with peers. Furthermore, in the teacher center, teachers are often more willing to discuss openly areas of weakness in their performance. As one teacher put it:

> At the teacher center I can ask for help. I won't be judged. The teachers who have helped me the most have had the same problems. I respect them, and I'm willing to learn from them. They have credibility with me.

PROFESSIONAL DEVELOPMENT SCHOOLS   Professional development schools (PDSs) have emerged recently as a way to link school restructuring and the reform of teacher education in America. These school–university partnerships offer teachers the following opportunities:

- Fine learning programs for diverse students
- Practical, thought-provoking preparation for novice teachers
- New understanding and professional responsibilities for experienced educators
- Research projects that add to all educators' knowledge about how to make schools more productive (The Holmes Group, n.d., 1).

For example, a teacher at a PDS might team with a teacher education professor and teach a university-level course, participate in a collaborative research project, offer a professional development seminar for other teachers, arrange for the teacher educator to demonstrate instructional strategies in his or her classroom, or jointly develop relevant field experiences for prospective teachers.

SUPERVISION AND MENTORING OF STUDENT TEACHERS   After several years in the classroom, teachers may be ready to stretch themselves further by supervising student teachers. Some of the less obvious benefits of doing so are that teachers must rethink what they are doing so that they can explain and sometimes justify their behaviors to someone else, learning about themselves in the process. Furthermore, because they become a model for their student teachers, they continually strive to offer the best example. In exchange, they gain an assistant in the classroom—another pair of eyes, an aid with record keeping—and more than occasionally, fresh ideas and a spirit of enthusiasm.

GRADUATE STUDY   A more traditional form of professional development is to do graduate study. With the recent reforms, most states now require teachers to take some graduate courses to keep their certifications and knowledge up to date. Some teachers take only courses that are of immediate use to them; others use their graduate study to prepare for new teaching or administrative positions; and still others pursue doctoral work in order to teach prospective teachers or others in their discipline at the college level.

STUDY ON THE INTERNET   If you have access to the **Internet,** a set of more than 10,000 interconnected computer networks around the world, you can locate many possibilities for continuing professional development. Teachers use the Internet to exchange ideas and experiences and to acquire additional expertise in teaching or to share their expertise with others. One source of professional development opportunities available on the Internet is Teacher's Edition Online (http://www.teachnet.com/) which provides a current listing of teacher workshops and innovative educational materials. The National Education Association (NEA) provides peer mentoring opportunities through its 21st Century Teachers program (http://www.ustc.org/21stcentury/). Launched in 1996, 21st Century Teachers is a voluntary corps of teachers who develop innovative ways to use information-age technology in schools. Various professional associations and colleges and universities will train, mentor, and offer one-on-one support to 21st Century Teachers as they learn new skills.

Issues in Education

- In what ways and to what extent is the Internet affecting what children learn?
- In what ways and to what extent is the Internet changing teacher education?
- According to this cartoonist, what might be an unintended consequence of these changes?
- Are you concerned for your future students? For yourself? Why or why not?

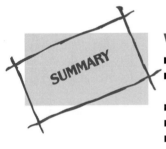

SUMMARY

What Essential Knowledge Do You Need to Teach?

- Professional teachers reflect upon their classroom experiences.
- Teachers need three kinds of knowledge: knowledge of self and students, knowledge of subject, and knowledge of educational theory and research.
- Teachers' self-knowledge influences their ability to understand students.
- The ambiguities of teaching can cause teachers to experience anxiety.
- Elementary teachers can experience loneliness because they are isolated from adults; secondary teachers because of departmentalization.
- Teachers must know their students' aptitudes, talents, learning styles, stage of development, and readiness to learn new material.
- Teachers must understand their subjects deeply so they can modify instructional strategies based on students' perception of content.
- Knowledge of educational theory enables professional teachers to know *why* certain strategies work.
- Educational research provides teachers with rules of thumb for practice.

What Are Five Ways of Viewing the Teacher Knowledge Base?

- There is no universally accepted definition of "good" teaching.
- The teacher knowledge base (essential knowledge and abilities) can place primary emphasis on personal development, research-based competencies, state standards, job analyses, or the views of professional organizations.

- Many states have developed standards for outcome-based or performance-based teacher education. Outcomes are based on what beginning teachers do in real classrooms.
- The job-analysis view of teaching is based on identifying job dimensions—the knowledge, skills, and attitudes teachers need.
- The National Board for Professional Teaching Standards (NBPTS) has developed standards for voluntary national certification.
- Effective teachers are guided by reflection and a problem-solving orientation.

How Do Reforms in Teacher Education Affect You?

- As part of the educational reform movement, the Holmes Group recommends that teachers obtain a bachelor's degree in an academic field and a master's degree in education.
- The Holmes Group recommends establishing professional development schools linked to colleges of education.
- In *Teachers for Our Nation's Schools,* John Goodlad recommends the creation of Centers of Pedagogy.
- The National Board for Professional Teaching Standards (NBPTS) is developing standards in more than 30 areas across six student age levels.

How Can You Gain Practical Experience for Becoming a Teacher?

- Teacher education students can gain practical experience through focused classroom observations, microteaching, teaching simulations, analyses of video cases, field-based practica and clinical experiences, and classroom aide programs.
- Distance-learning classrooms, using compressed video, link teacher education programs to schools off-campus.
- In microteaching, students practice specific skills by teaching brief lessons that are later analyzed.
- Computer simulations and virtual reality—as well as written, videotaped, and audiotaped cases—are being used for teaching simulations.
- Journal writing and reflective teaching logs increase the benefits of the student teaching experience.
- Induction programs provide assistance to beginning teachers. Internship programs and school-based teacher education programs provide extensive practical experiences.
- Substitute teaching provides additional practical experience after completing a teacher education program.

How Can You Develop Your Teaching Portfolio?

- A portfolio documents professional growth and development over time.
- A portfolio can be organized around specific outcomes or standards.
- Portfolio contents should represent one's best work.
- Professional portfolios can be used in teacher evaluation, self-evaluation, and hiring.

How Can You Establish Mentoring Relationships?

- Ask for advice from teachers you admire.
- Mentoring can be a source of professional growth for experienced teachers.
- Mentoring enables the protégé to "learn the ropes."

What Opportunities for Continuing Professional Development Will You Have?

- Self-assessment is necessary to select appropriate professional development experiences.
- Opportunities for professional development include teacher workshops, teacher centers, professional development schools, supervision and mentoring of student teachers, graduate study, and the Internet.

distance learning, 45

educational reform movement, 43

field experiences, 45

Holmes Group, 43

induction programs, 49

inservice workshops, 54

Internet, 56

internship programs, 49

Interstate New Teacher Assessment and Support Consortium (INTASC), 41

job analysis, 40

knowledge base, 38

mentor, 53

mentoring, 53

microteaching, 46

National Board for Professional Teaching Standards (NBPTS), 40

observations, 45

outcome-based teacher education, 39

performance-based teacher education, 39

personal development view, 39

practicum, 47

problem-solving orientation, 41

professional development schools (PDS), 43

professional portfolio, 51

reflection, 41

reflective teaching log, 48

research-based competencies, 39

school-based teacher education, 50

self-assessment, 54

substitute teaching, 50

teacher centers, 55

teaching simulations, 46

Teacher's Journal

1. What does self-knowledge mean to you? Why is self-knowledge important in teaching? What steps can you take to achieve greater self-knowledge?

2. As a teacher, you will encounter challenges related to student variability (differences in developmental needs, interests, abilities, and disabilities) and student diversity (differences in gender, race, ethnicity, culture, and socioeconomic status). To begin thinking about how you will acquire and use knowledge about your students, write a brief profile of yourself as a student in elementary school, in middle school or junior high school, and in high school.

3. Reflect on your education as a teacher. What are your primary concerns about the preparation you are receiving? What experiences do you think will be most helpful to you as you move toward becoming a teacher? What qualities would you look for in a mentor?

4. On the basis of your field experiences to date and the information in Chapters 1 and 2, ask yourself these questions and respond in your journal: Do I have the aptitude to become a good teacher? Am I willing to acquire the essential knowledge and skills teachers need? Do I really want to become a teacher?

Teacher's Database

1. If possible, access the education resources on America Online (AOL), which gives you free hours to explore this service before deciding whether or not to subscribe for a monthly fee. AOL hosts Allyn and Bacon's College Online (COL), where, for example, you can download a free 14-page document, *Internet Resources for Teacher Educators and K–12 Educators* by Susan McIntyre of the University of Wisconsin. You can also access online support for *Becoming a Teacher* directly at URL http://www.abacon.com. The authors also invite you to contact them directly at any time through E-mail.

fwparkay@wsu.edu
stanford@apu.edu

2. AOL's College Online invites users to contribute an essay to TEACHERS ON TEACHING—essays by actual classroom teachers on their experiences, including observations of novice teachers and advice from experienced teachers. Your essay could even appear in the next edition of *Becoming a Teacher!* Topics for teacher essays, information about participating, guidelines for writing essays, and a data/release form are provided both on College Online and at Allyn & Bacon's web site. Begin now by brainstorming ideas for an essay on one of the following topics. Also consider developing a collaborative essay with a group of classmates.

- a teacher preparation field experience or learning experience you have had and what you gained from it
- a teacher who inspired you to become a teacher or is a model for you of what a good teacher should be
- your experience as a K–12 student in terms of any specific topic in *Becoming a Teacher*
- your philosophy of education and teaching philosophy

Observations and Interviews

1. Think about areas for focused observations of teaching, such as classroom management, student involvement, questioning techniques, evaluation, or teacher–student rapport. For one or more areas, brainstorm and order in logical sequence a set of questions you could use to guide your next observations. Include a list of questions to ask the teacher whom you will observe.

2. As a collaborative project with classmates, interview students who have completed student teaching at your college or university. What tips do they have for developing a positive relationship with a cooperating teacher? For establishing rapport with students? For developing confidence in presenting lessons?

3. Arrange to interview a school administrator about the knowledge, skills, and aptitude he or she thinks teachers must have. To help you plan for the interview, ask your instructor for handout master M2.2, "Interviewing School Administrators about Teachers' Knowledge and Skills." Which of the knowledge and skills discussed in this chapter does the administrator mention? Does he or she mention knowledge and skills not discussed in this chapter?

4. Observe a teacher in the classroom for the purpose of identifying examples that help to answer the following questions. How does the teacher demonstrate or use knowledge of self and students? Knowledge of subject matter? Knowledge of educational theory and research?

5. Observe a classroom in which there is likely to be some teacher–student interaction (for example, questions and answers, discussion, or oral review and feedback). On the basis of the data you collect, what conclusions can you draw about life in this classroom? To help record your observations, ask your instructor for handout master M2.1, "Recording Classroom Interactions."

Professional Portfolio

1. Create a plan for developing your portfolio. What specific outcomes or standards will you use to organize your portfolio entries? What artifacts will you use to demonstrate your professional growth and development?

2. Evaluate the products of your studies in education so far in your preparation for becoming a teacher. Identify a few examples of your best work to include in your portfolio. Also, evaluate your Teacher's Journal, Teacher's Database, and Observations and Interviews for possible inclusions in your portfolio.

. . . we shall see the day when [the kindergarten] will have grown into a mighty tree, and I am more than ever anxious to see the system introduced into our Public schools.

—Susan Blow, 1873
Founder of first successful public kindergarten

chapter 3

Historical Foundations of American Education

**F O C U S
Q U E S T I O N S**

1. What were the European Antecedents of American education?

2. What were teaching and schools like in the American colonies (1620–1750)?

3. What were the goals of education during the Revolutionary Period (1750–1820)?

4. How was the struggle won for state-supported common schools (1820–1865)?

5. How did compulsory education change the schools and the teaching profession (1865–1920)?

6. What were the aims of education during the Progressive Era (1920–1945)?

7. How did the goal of equal educational opportunity for all Americans develop?

8. How did education change during the modern postwar era (1945–1990)?

During your first year of teaching you are talking in the teacher's lounge with three colleagues, Mary, John, and Hal, about educational reform and the changes sweeping across America's schools. The discussion was sparked by a television special everyone watched last night about restructuring schools for the twenty-first century.

"I was really glad to see teachers portrayed in a professional light," you say. "The message to viewers seemed to be 'Let's get behind teachers and help them reform our schools. Effective schools are important to our nation's well-being.'"

"I think it's just a case of schools trying to jump on the band-wagon," Hal says. "All this talk about restructuring schools and developing partnerships with the community—it's just taking time away from what we should be doing, and that's teaching kids. If we don't get back to what really matters, our country won't be able to solve the problems it faces."

"But times have changed; the world is a different place," Mary says. "Today's kids have different needs. Teaching has changed. We can't return to the 'good old days.' "

"Besides, I don't think the 'good old days' ever were," John adds. "We can't return to the past."

"Right, that's a nostalgia trap," Mary says. "History shows us that the United States has always had to grapple with problems, and education has always been part of the solution."

"Well, all I know is that when I started teaching thirty years ago, we taught the basics," Hal says. "It was as simple as that. We were there to teach, and the kids, believe it or not, were there to learn."

Before continuing, Hal's attention turns to you. "Then in the 1980s and 1990s, we got involved in all this reform stuff . . . restructuring schools, empowering teachers, developing partnerships—I don't know where it's all going. What do you think?"

What do you say?

Mary is correct when she says we cannot return to the past, to the "good old days." On the other hand, we shouldn't ignore the past; we should learn from it. We cannot understand schools today without a look at what they were yesterday. Our current system of public and private education is an ongoing reflection of its historical foundations and of the aspirations and values brought to this country by its founders and generations of settlers. It is an important part of your education as a professional to develop an appreciation for this tradition.

Still, you may wonder, what is the value of knowing about the history of American education? Will that knowledge help you to be a better teacher? First, a knowledge of this history will help you evaluate more effectively current proposals for change. You will be in a better position to evaluate changes if you understand how schools have developed and how current proposals might relate to previous change efforts. Second, awareness of the historical development of schools and teaching is a hallmark of professionalism in education.

WHAT WERE THE EUROPEAN ANTECEDENTS OF AMERICAN EDUCATION ?

Many of the practices found in today's schools had their origins in much earlier societies throughout the world. Non–Western civilizations in ancient Egypt, China, and India, for example, emphasized the need for practical education in mathematics, astronomy, medicine, engineering, agriculture, and geography. Similarly, early Western civilizations emphasized the role of education in preparing children and youth for their roles as adults in society. The timeline in Figure 3.1 depicts some of the major events and individuals in Europe that had an impact on the development of education in seventeenth-century colonial America. This section first presents an overview of education in Greece and Rome, a brief glimpse of the kaleidoscope of European history from the fall of Rome to the start of the eighteenth century, and a

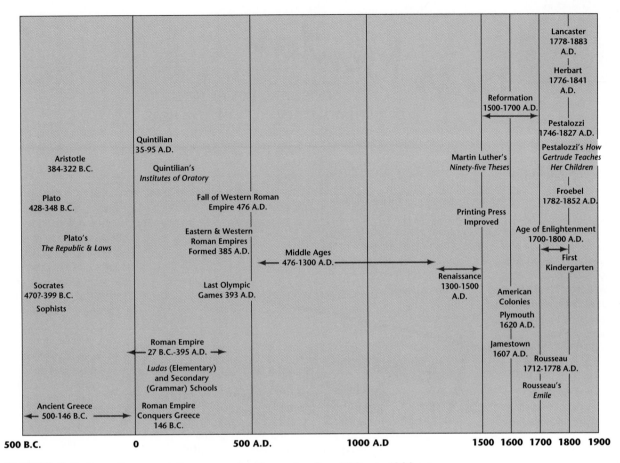

FIGURE 3.1 Some European influences on American education, 500 B.C.–1900 A.D.

review of the influence of four eighteenth-century European thinkers on education in colonial America.

EDUCATION IN ANCIENT GREECE

Education in ancient Greece (500–146 B.C.) has had an enduring impact on today's schools. The Greeks believed that people should use leisure time to reflect on the practical and aesthetic values of life. Based on principles of moderation and balance, the goal of Greek education was the well-rounded development of mind and body. The Olympic games, first celebrated in 776 B.C. and held every four years until A.D. 393, included contests of choral poetry and dance as well as athletic events. While the pursuit of knowledge by the ancient Greeks is worthy of imitation, other facets of this ancient civilization are antithetical to the values and goals of today's society—for example, the leisure enjoyed by the small middle and upper classes in ancient Greece was made possible by a vast population of slaves, and women were not eligible to become citizens.

Numerous philosophers in ancient Greece shaped ideas about the relationship between education and life. Perhaps the greatest contributions were made by Socrates (ca. 470–399 B.C.), Plato (428–348 B.C.), and Aristotle (384–322 B.C.).

Dear Mentor

NOVICE AND EXPERT TEACHERS ON HISTORY'S RELEVANCE FOR TEACHERS

Dear Allison,

Each year for the past eighteen years I have reached into my (now huge) bag of tricks to find some way of getting 13-year-olds interested in United States History. I try to convince them of the value of looking to the past for insight into the present and guidance into the future. "Old folks are boring," they exclaim. I resurrect President Woodrow Wilson who said, "A nation which does not remember what it was yesterday, does not know what it is today. . . . We are trying to do a futile thing if we do not know where we came from or what we have been about." I call upon the genius of Albert Einstein: "Politics are for the moment, but an equation is for eternity." It is finding these "equations," the great contributions and wisdom of the ages, that makes history so valuable.

History, at its core, is simply the study of people. If we "treasure" people, we will always "discover treasure" in the contemplation of history. "Did you know that the founders of this nation had you in mind when they wrote the Constitution?" I ask. "No way!" "Get out of town!" they respond. "It's true," I coolly explain. "The Preamble clearly states their goal . . . 'to secure the blessings of liberty for ourselves and our posterity' . . . "

Dear Mentor,

Do we really look at our past to see what has worked and not worked and learn from mistakes and build on accomplishments? Or do we always just keep trying the newest ideas? How did history affect what you were taught as opposed to what you teach now? How does your classroom reflect changes and continuities in teaching practice?

Allison Jones

I apply the same thinking to the role of history in education and the relevance of the history of education for teachers. As we as educators keep up on the latest trends, fads, and buzz words, we would do well to have a healthy respect for generations past and a clear perspective on the forces that cause changes and continuity in what and how we teach. My work in the classroom reflects my commitment to the idea that we need to be open to new ideas and innovations while at the same time preserving teaching's most effective traditions and time-honored goals. I believe that developments in education are of even greater significance when we understand that they often are created "on the shoulders of giants."

Best wishes to you in your pursuit of the high calling of teaching.

Glen Green
8th Grade U.S. history teacher
Arcadia, California

Socrates

SOCRATES What little we know about Socrates comes to us from his portrayal in the *Dialogues* written by his student, Plato. Socrates's questioning strategies, his emphasis on discussion to promote inquiry, and his quest for virtue are reflected in today's curricular and instructional practices. Socrates questioned his pupils in a manner that led them to see errors and inconsistencies in their thinking. By using an inductive approach, Socrates believed that the truth could be discovered. **Socratic questioning,** according to contemporary educational philosopher Mortimer Adler (1981), is essential for the study of six great ideas: truth, beauty, goodness, liberty, equality, and justice. Through his method of questioning students repeatedly, Socrates led his students to these eternal truths.

Socrates was critical of the **sophists,** traveling Greek educators who taught the practical skills of grammar, logic, and rhetoric to citizens to prepare them to become legislators. Sophists often commercialized their teaching and accepted large fees from an enthralled public. Critics like Socrates charged that behind the sophists' claim to educate "lay the presumption that success in public life, to be defined in terms of power, was more or less the supreme achievement possible to man" (Barrow 1976, 14). Knowledge, according to Socrates, was virtue; and a society was only as good as its schools.

Aristotle

PLATO AND ARISTOTLE A student and disciple of Socrates, Plato believed that the individual's abilities should be developed through education for the good of society. To promote his views among Athenians, Plato founded the free, coeducational Academy, often referred to as the world's first university. Plato believed that boys and girls should be educated from age six to eighteen, with music, mathematics, and gymnastics the main areas of study. Music, a source of noble emotions, included the study of literature and history; mathematics linked the powers of reason with the processes of nature and enabled one to influence the environment; and gymnastics, which emphasized physical and mental well-being, included the study of dance, rhythm, athletics, and military arts. Taken together, the aim of this three-part curriculum was to improve the soul and enable the individual to achieve moral excellence and to realize the ultimate good. Plato's belief that reality consists of ideas and thoughts has earned him the title of the "father of idealism," a school of philosophical thought based on the belief that ideas are the only reality.

Plato's educational theories are most clearly expressed in *The Republic* and the *Laws*. In *The Republic*, Plato confirms Socrates' belief that "knowledge is virtue" and then sets forth a framework for a state-run system of education. The purpose of education was to help the individual develop his or her abilities, find the truth that is within each of us, and to assume a productive role in society.

Aristotle, Plato's most famous student, studied and taught at the Academy for twenty years. While Plato was an idealist and believed that ideas are the ultimate reality, Aristotle was a realist and believed that reality, knowledge, and value exist in the physical world independent of the mind. Goodness and virtue depend upon deeds, not knowledge. Unlike Plato, Aristotle saw ". . . mere intellectual ponderings as insufficient to the advancement of knowledge. What was needed in addition was a diligent and unsparing scrutiny of all observable phenomena" (Meyer 1972, 32). Aristotle, recognized as the founder of the scientific method, believed that all knowledge could be objectively organized, and he was the first to teach logic as a formal discipline. He maintained that ". . . the exercise of rational principle and thought is the ultimate end of man's nature . . ." and education should be developed ". . . with a view to the exercise of these faculties" (Barker 1980, 317–323).

Like Plato, Aristotle believed that society, to function effectively, needed a strong system of education. Aristotle supported education for all Athenian citizens; however, the majority of Athens' inhabitants were not citizens. Women, for example, were ineligible for citizenship because it was felt they lacked the rational capacities for citizenship and wisdom.

EDUCATION IN ANCIENT ROME

In 146 B.C., Greece was conquered by the Roman Empire, which Augustus established in 27 B.C. The Roman Empire continued until A.D. 395, when it was divided into the Western Roman Empire, with the capital at Rome, and the Eastern Roman Empire, with the capital at Constantinople. In A.D. 476, the Roman empire fell.

Roman education was heavily influenced by Greek education. The Roman school system consisted of the *ludus,* or elementary school, and a secondary or grammar school. Boys and girls aged seven to twelve attended the ludi where they learned to read, write, and compute. The education of girls seldom went beyond the ludus. Upper-class boys aged twelve to sixteen attended grammar schools where they studied Greek or Latin grammar and literature. Boys aged sixteen to twenty attended a school of rhetoric where they studied grammar, rhetoric, dialectic, music, arithmetic, geometry, and astronomy.

One of the most noted Roman educators was Marcus Fabius Quintilian (35–95 A.D.). His *Institutes of Oratory* (*Institutio Oratoria*) published upon his death set forth his educational ideas. The aim of education, he believed, should be the development of a moral individual equipped with practical skills for living.

Quintilian

Quintilian's educational ideas are quite contemporary. He believed, for example, that corporal punishment was "a disgrace . . . and in reality . . . an affront" (Monroe 1939, 466). He also advocated school holidays because "relaxation brings greater energy to study" (Castle 1967, 138). His approach to early childhood education reflects an understanding of human growth and development: "Let his instruction be an amusement to him; let him be questioned and praised; and let him never feel pleased that he does not know a thing . . . let his powers be called forth by rewards, such as that age prizes" (Monroe 1939, 455). He also believed that new material should not be taught to students until they were able to master it, and he urged teachers to develop curricula based on students' individual differences.

FROM THE MIDDLE AGES TO THE AGE OF ENLIGHTENMENT

The period from the fall of the Roman Empire to the fourteenth century is known as the Middle Ages. During the medieval period, the Roman Catholic Church came to have the greatest influence on education in Europe. For the most part, the prevailing class structure based on feudalism was not fertile ground for the growth of schools during the Middle Ages, though the clergy received instruction in the monasteries and at cathedral schools, and medieval universities were established in Spain, France, and England.

Thomas Aquinas

Education in the Middle Ages was greatly influenced by Thomas Aquinas (1255–1274), an Italian monk and theologian, who wrote *Summa Theologica;* this set forth the tenets of scholasticism—the logical, philosophical study of Church doctrine according to Aristotle's ideas. Aquinas' theological and philosophical views, later known as Thomism, maintained that God is pure reason, and through the use of reason, one could know God and the truth of reality.

A European *renaissance* or rebirth of interest in Greco-Roman traditions of art, literature, and learning began in the fourteenth century and reached a peak in the fifteenth century. This period, known as the Renaissance, began in northern Europe and Italy and spread throughout Europe. The ideal educated individual during the Renaissance was based on the classical Roman ideals described by Quintilian in his *Institutes of Oratory.*

The key to improving the human condition, according to Renaissance humanists, was to transfer wealth and power from the Church to the populace. In addition, humanists believed that an educational system similar to that of ancient Rome should be created and that instruction should consist of the study of ancient classical literature, particularly the work of Plato and Aristotle. The ideal curriculum of the time was based on the seven liberal arts (dialectic, rhetoric, grammar, astronomy, arithmetic, geometry, and music), Greek and Latin, history, and fine arts.

Martin Luther

When Martin Luther, a monk and professor of religion, challenged the authority of the Catholic Church in 1517 by nailing his *Ninety-five Theses* to the door of a church in Wittenberg, Germany, a century of religious revolution began. Those who protested the authority of the Catholic Church came to be known as Protestants. The Protestants founded new religions based on principles of self-determination and individual reading and interpretation of the Bible. The invention of the printing press by Johann Gutenberg (ca. 1400–1468) aided in the communication of protests against the Church and led to the mass production of printed books and the development of literacy.

EDUCATIONAL THOUGHT IN EIGHTEENTH-CENTURY EUROPE

The Reformation, with its questioning of religious doctrines, revived interest in the scientific understanding of nature. The eighteenth century came to be known as the Age of Enlightenment or the Age of Reason because of the role that reason and scientific inquiry came to play in improving society. European thinkers of the 1700s have had a lasting impact on education in America.

Jeans-Jacques Rousseau (1712–1778), considered by some to be the "father of modern child psychology" (Mayer 1973), believed that children progressed through stages of growth and development that should guide the development of instructional strategies. Rousseau also believed in the innate goodness of children—a natural goodness that society corrupts. Rousseau's child-centered educational theories influenced many educators in France and beyond; for example, John Dewey, whose educational philosophy shaped the progressive education movement in the United States from 1920–1945, was influenced by Rousseau.

Jeans-Jacques
Rousseau

In his novel *Emile,* Rousseau set forth the ideal education for a youth named Emile. During the first five years of life, the child should be allowed to play freely in natural settings, and adults should "not treat the child to discourses which he cannot understand. No descriptions, no eloquence, no figures of speech. Be content to present to him appropriate objects" (Compayre 1888, 299). The next seven years should focus on concrete learning experiences, with abstract concepts and ideas emphasized between ages twelve and fifteen. These ideas match the principles of developmentally appropriate education that are observed today.

Johann Heinrich Pestalozzi (1746–1827) was a Swiss educator who implemented many of Rousseau's ideas. Noted educators worldwide, including Horace Mann from the United States, traveled to Pestalozzi's experimental school in Yverdun, Switzerland, to observe his methods and learn from him. His 1826 book, *How Gertrude Teaches Her Children,* contributed greatly to the development of elementary schools.

What ideas stemming from the Age of Enlightenment permanently affected the development of elementary education in the United States? How did Pestalozzi's philosophy of education reflect those ideas?

Like Rousseau, Pestalozzi believed that the innate goodness of children was corrupted by society, and that instructional practices and curriculum materials should be selected in light of students' natural abilities and readiness to learn. Effective instruction, Pestalozzi believed, moved from concrete experiences to abstract concepts, from the simple to the complex. He also recognized that children's learning was enhanced by a healthy self-esteem and feelings of emotional security. He was particularly concerned about poor children whom he believed needed to feel loved by their teachers, as Ulich (1950, 264) points out: "In the studies of Old Swiss and German schoolmasters one could often find a reproduction of a painting of Pestalozzi, in which we see him, with a profound expression of love on his ugly and wrinkled face, embracing the children of peasants who, clad in rags, enter the simple schoolroom."

Johann Friedrich Herbart (1776–1841) was a student of Pestalozzi's and became known as the father of the science of education and of modern psychology (Schubert 1986). Herbart believed that education should focus primarily on developing moral character. His five-step systematic approach for presenting new material to students is still in use today:

1. Preparation: helping students make connections between what they know and what they are about to learn.
2. Presentation: introducing material in a manner that is appropriate for the psychological development of the student.
3. Association: combining new and previously learned material.
4. Generalization: moving from concrete examples to abstract principles.
5. Application: using recently acquired knowledge to learn more.

The development of schools in the eighteenth and nineteenth centuries was related to European industrialization, urbanization, and population growth. For example, in England, Joseph Lancaster (1778–1838) developed a **monitorial system** for crowded schools in which older students taught younger students. According to the Lancasterian system, one teacher instructed hundreds of pupils through the use of student monitors—older students selected for their academic abilities. Lancaster eventually emigrated to America where monitorial schools spread rapidly in urban areas after the first school opened in New York City in 1806.

Monitorial schools were seen as an inexpensive way to educate the children of workers and to teach them the obedience, neatness, and industriousness they would need to take their places in the factories, shops, and mines. New York governor De Witt Clinton declared that monitorial schools were "a blessing sent down from heaven to redeem the poor" (Spring 1990, 56). The monitorial system was also used to assimilate waves of immigrants.

WHAT WERE TEACHING AND SCHOOLS LIKE IN THE AMERICAN COLONIES (1620–1750) ⟨?⟩

As you have seen, education in colonial America had its primary roots in English culture. The settlers of our country tried initially to develop a system of schooling that paralleled the British two-track system. If students from the lower classes attended school at all it was at the elementary level for the purpose of learning the basics of reading, writing, and computation and receiving religious instruction. Students from the upper classes had the opportunity to attend Latin grammar schools, where they were given a higher education that focused on Latin and Greek classics, in preparation for college.

Above all, the colonial curriculum stressed religious objectives. Generally, no distinction was made between secular and religious life in the colonies. The religious motives that impelled the Puritans to endure the hardships of settling in a new land were reflected in the schools' curricula. The primary objective of elementary schooling was to learn to read so that one might read the Bible and religious catechisms and thereby receive salvation.

THE STATUS OF TEACHERS

"Special but shadowed" is the way noted educator Dan Lortie describes the image of colonial teachers (1975). They were "special" because they, along with the clergy, were the only members of the community to have some education, and they were expected to have superior moral character. Teachers were "shadowed" because they were subordinate to the clergy, the main power of the community. Teachers' extra duties reflected their image: "Teachers rang the church bells, . . . swept up, . . . taught Bible lessons, and occasionally substituted for the ailing pastor. Those who wished to teach had to accept stern inspection of their moral behavior" (Lortie 1975, 11).

Teaching was also shadowed by what was regarded as the real work of the community. According to one source, "Farming was the vital preoccupation. And though males were preferred as teachers, in the summer months, when men were needed to work the land, women were recruited to take their places" (Lightfoot 1978, 47).

COLONIAL SCHOOLS

In the New England Colonies (Massachusetts Bay, New Hampshire, and Connecticut), there was a general consensus that church, state, and schools were interrelated. As a result, town schools were created throughout these colonies to teach children the basics of reading and writing so they could learn the Scriptures. The Puritan view of the child included the belief that people are inherently sinful. Even natural childhood play was seen as devil-inspired idleness. The path to redemption lay in learning to curb one's natural instincts and behave like an adult as quickly as possible.

The Middle Colonies (New York, New Jersey, Pennsylvania, and Delaware) were more diverse, and groups such as the Irish, Scottish, Swedish, Danish, Dutch, and Germans established **parochial schools** based on their religious beliefs. Anglicans, Lutherans, Quakers, Jews, Catholics, Presbyterians, and Mennonites in the Middle Colonies tended to establish their own schools. In the largely Protestant Southern Colonies (Virginia, Maryland, Georgia, and North and South Carolina), wealthy plantation owners believed the primary purpose of education was to promote religion and to prepare their children to attend colleges and universities in Europe. The vast majority of small farmers received no formal schooling and the children of African slaves received only the training they needed to serve their masters.

No one type of schooling was common to all the colonies. The most common types, however, were the dame schools, the reading and writing schools, and the Latin grammar schools. **Dame schools** provided initial instruction for boys and, often, the only schooling for girls. These schools were run by widows or housewives in their homes and supported by modest fees from parents. Classes were usually held in the kitchen where children learned only the barest essentials of reading, writing, and arithmetic during instruction lasting for a few weeks to one year. Females might also be taught sewing and basic homemaking skills. Students often began by learning the alphabet from a **horn book.** Developed in medieval Europe, the horn book was a copy of the alphabet covered by a thin transparent sheet made from a cow's horn. The alphabet and the horn covering were attached to a paddle-shaped piece of wood. Students often hung their hornbooks around their necks with a leather cord threaded through a hole in the paddle.

Reading and writing schools offered boys an education that went beyond what their parents could teach them at home or what they could learn at a dame school. Reading lessons were based on the Bible, various religious catechisms, and the *New England Primer,* first printed in 1690. The **Primer** introduced children to the letters of the alphabet through the use of illustrative woodcuts and rhymed couplets. The first couplet began with the pronouncement that

> In Adam's fall
> We sinned all.

And the final one noted that

> Zaccheus he
> Did climb the Tree
> His Lord to see.

The *Primer* also presented children with large doses of stern religious warnings about the proper conduct of life.

What textbooks might students have used in this early American classroom? What educational beliefs and values were reflected in the curriculum and instruction of this period?

The **Latin grammar school,** comparable to today's secondary school, was patterned after the classical schools of Europe. Boys enrolled in the Latin grammar schools at the age of seven or eight, whereupon they began to prepare to enter Harvard College (established in 1636). Following graduation from Harvard, they would assume leadership roles in the church. The Boston Latin School was founded first in 1635 to provide a precollege education for the new country's future leaders. At a mass meeting that April, the residents of Boston decided that "our brother Philemon Pormont shall be entreated to become schoolmaster, for the teaching and nurturing of children with us" (Button and Provenzo 1983, 17).

The quality of teaching in the Latin grammar schools was higher than that found in the dame schools or reading and writing schools. Latin and Greek were the principal studies, though arithmetic was introduced in 1745. Students were required to read Latin authors and to speak Latin in poetry and prose as well as conjugate Greek verbs. The mode of instruction was rigorous:

> In most of the Latin schools, the course of study lasted for seven years. Apparently school was in session six days a week and continued throughout the winter and summer. The school day was usually from six to eleven o'clock in the morning and from one to four or five o'clock in the afternoon. The boys sat on benches for long hours. Great faith was placed in the *memoriter* method of drill and rote learning. Through repeated recitations the students were conditioned to respond with a definite answer to a particular question. Class discussions were not permitted.

THE ORIGINS OF MANDATED EDUCATION

In the United States today compulsory education laws require that parents, or those who have custody of children between certain ages, send their children to school. Universal compulsory education had its origins in the **Massachusetts Act of 1642.** Prior to this date, parents could decide whether they wished their children to be educated at home or at a school. Church and civil leaders in the colonies, however, decided that education could no longer remain voluntary. They saw that many children were receiving inadequate training. Moreover, they realized that organized schools would serve to strengthen and preserve Puritan religious beliefs.

The Puritans decided to make education a civil responsibility of the state. The Massachusetts General Court passed a law in 1642 that required each town to determine whether young people could read and write. Parents and apprentices' masters whose children were unable "to read and understand the principles of religion and the capital laws of the country" (Rippa 1984, 45) could be fined and, possibly, lose custody of their children.

Although the Act of 1642 did not mandate the establishment of schools, it did make it clear that the education of children was a direct concern of the local citizenry. In 1648, the Court revised the 1642 law, reminding town leaders that "the good education of children is of singular behoof and benefit to any commonwealth" and that some parents and masters were still "too indulgent and negligent of their duty" (Cohen 1974, 394–95). As the first educational law in this country, the Massachusetts Act of 1642 was a landmark.

The **Massachusetts Act of 1647,** often referred to as the Old Deluder Satan Act (because education was seen as the best protection against the wiles of the devil), mandated the establishment and support of schools. In particular, towns of fifty households or more were to appoint a person to instruct "all such children as shall resort to him to write and read." Teachers were to "be paid either by the parents or masters of such children, or by the inhabitants in general" (Rippa 1984, 45). This act furthermore required towns of 100 households or more to establish a Latin grammar school to prepare students for Harvard College. A town that failed to satisfy this law could be assessed a fine of five pounds.

Support for mandated education was later expanded by passage of the Northwest Ordinance in 1785 which gave federal land to the states for educational purposes. The

Between the seventeenth and twentieth centuries, how did educational policies and practices reflect the American social system that had developed? How do educational policies and practices reflect the American social system today?

Ordinance divided the Northwest Territories (now Illinois, Indiana, Michigan, Ohio, Wisconsin, and part of Minnesota) into 36-square-mile sections, with the 16th square mile designated for public schools.

EDUCATION FOR AFRICANS AND INDIANS

At the close of the American Revolution, nearly all of the half million African Americans were slaves who could neither read nor write (Button and Provenzo 1983). In most cases, those who were literate had been taught by their masters or through small, church-affiliated programs. Literate Native Americans and Mexican Americans usually received their training at the hands of missionaries. One of the first schools for African Americans was started by Elias Neau in New York City in 1704. Sponsored by the Church of England, Neau's school taught African and Native Americans how to read as part of the Church's efforts to convert students.

Other schools for African and Native Americans were started by the Quakers who regarded slavery as a moral evil. Though Quaker schools for African Americans existed as early as 1700, one of the best known was founded in Philadelphia in 1770 by Anthony Benezet, who believed that African Americans were ". . . generously sensible, humane, and sociable, and that their capacity is as good, and as capable of improvement as that of white people" (Button and Provenzo 1983, 45). Schools modeled on the Philadelphia African School opened elsewhere in the Northeast, and "Indian Schools" also were founded as philanthropic enterprises. In 1819 federal funds for reservation schools were first granted through the newly created Office of Indian Affairs. Federal involvement brought little improvement in programs and enrollments, however. In 1901, for instance, only 300 of the four to five thousand school-age Navajos attended school (Button and Provenzo 1983, 153).

From the seventeenth to the late-twentieth centuries, schools were segregated by race. The first recorded official ground for school segregation dates back to a decision of the Massachusetts Supreme Court in 1850. When the Roberts family sought to send their daughter Sarah to a white school in Boston, the court ruled that "equal, but separate" schools were being provided and that the Roberts therefore could not claim an injustice (*Roberts v. City of Boston,* 1850). From the beginning, however, schools were not equal, and students did not have equal educational opportunity.

As the nation moved toward civil war, positions on the institution of slavery and the education of slaves hardened. While abolitionists established schools for free and escaped blacks, some southern states made the teaching of reading and writing to slaves a crime. After emancipation and the Civil War, schools for former slaves were opened throughout the South through the **Freedman's Bureau,** but racial segregation and discrimination remained as a central feature of the American way of life.

WHAT WERE THE GOALS OF EDUCATION DURING THE REVOLUTIONARY PERIOD (1750–1820)

Education in America during the revolutionary period was characterized by a general waning of European influences on schools. Though religious traditions that had their origins in Europe continued to affect the curriculum, the young country's need to develop agriculture, shipping, and commerce also exerted its influence on the curriculum. By this time, the original settlers who had emigrated from Europe had been replaced by a new generation whose most immediate roots were in the new soil of America. This new, exclusively American, identity was also enhanced by the rise of civil town governments, the great increase in books and newspapers that addressed life in the new country, and a turning away from Europe toward the unsettled west. America's break with Europe was most potently demonstrated in the American Revolution of 1776, which freed the thirteen colonies of British rule.

Following Independence, many leaders were concerned that new disturbances from within could threaten the well-being of the new nation. To preserve the freedoms that had been fought for, a system of education became essential. Through education, citizens would learn how to become intelligent, participating citizens of a constitutional democracy. Among these leaders were Benjamin Franklin, Thomas Jefferson, and Noah Webster.

BENJAMIN FRANKLIN'S ACADEMY

Benjamin Franklin

Benjamin Franklin (1706–1790) designed and promoted the Philadelphia Academy, a private secondary school, which opened in 1751. This school, which replaced the old Latin grammar school, had a curriculum that was broader and more practical and also focused on the English language rather than Latin. The academy was also a more democratically run institution than previous schools had been. Though **academies** were largely privately controlled and privately financed, they were secular and often supported by public funds. Most academies were public in that anyone who could pay tuition could attend, regardless of church affiliation (Button and Provenzo 1983, 38).

In his *Proposals Relating to the Education of Youth in Pennsylvania,* written in 1749, Franklin noted that "the good Education of youth has been esteemed by wise men in all ages, as the surest foundation of the happiness both of private families and of commonwealths" (Franklin 1931, 151).

Franklin's proposals for educating youth called for a wide range of subjects: English grammar, composition, and literature; classical and modern foreign languages; science; writing and drawing; rhetoric and oratory; geography; various kinds of history; agriculture and gardening; arithmetic and accounting; and mechanics.

EDUCATION FOR WOMEN

English academies multiplied across the country, reaching a peak of about 6,000 in 1850 (Butts and Cremin 1953, 260). Usually, these academies served male students only; a notable exception was Sarah Pierce's Litchfield Female Academy in Litchfield, Connecticut. Pierce began her academy in the dining room of her home with two students; eventually, the academy grew to 140 female students from nearly every state and from Canada (Button and Provenzo 1983, 87).

For the most part, however, girls received little formal education in the seventeenth and eighteenth centuries and were educated for entirely different purposes than were boys, as the following mission statement for Pierce's Academy suggests:

> Our object has been, not to make learned ladies, or skillful metaphysical reasoners, or deep read scholars in physical science: there is a more useful, tho' less exalted and less brilliant station that woman must occupy, there are duties of incalculable importance that she must perform: that station is home; these duties, are the alleviation of the trials of her parents; the soothing of the labours & fatigues of her partner; & the education for time and eternity of the next generation of immortal beings . . . (Button and Provenzo 1983, 88).

Female seminaries were first established in the early nineteenth century to train women for higher education and public service outside of the home. Educational opportunities for women expanded in conjunction with social reform movements that gradually led to greater political equality for women, including the right to vote.

THOMAS JEFFERSON'S PHILOSOPHY

Thomas Jefferson

Thomas Jefferson (1743–1826), author of the Declaration of Independence, viewed the education of common people as the most effective means of preserving liberty. As historian S. Alexander Rippa put it, "Few statesmen in American history have so vigorously striven for an ideal; perhaps none has so consistently viewed public education as the indispensable cornerstone of freedom" (1984, 68).

For a society to remain free, Jefferson felt, it must support a continuous system of public education. He proposed to the Virginia legislature in 1779 his Bill for the More General Diffusion of Knowledge. This plan called for state-controlled elementary schools that would teach, with no cost to parents, three years of reading, writing, and arithmetic to all white children. In addition, twenty state grammar schools would be created in which selected poor students would be taught free for a maximum period of six years.

Jefferson was unsuccessful in his attempt to convince the Virginia House of Burgesses of the need for a uniform system of public schools as outlined in his bill. Jefferson was, however, able to implement many of his educational ideas through his efforts to found the University of Virginia. He devoted the last years of his life to developing the university, and he lived to see the university open with forty students in March 1824, one month before his eighty-first birthday.

NOAH WEBSTER'S SPELLER

In the years following the Revolution, several textbooks were printed in the United States. Writers and publishers saw the textbook as an appropriate vehicle for promoting democratic ideals and cultural independence from England. Toward this end, U.S. textbooks were filled with patriotic and moralistic maxims. Among the most widely circulated books of this type were Noah Webster's *Elementary Spelling Book* and *The American Dictionary*.

Noah Webster

Webster (1758–1843) first introduced his speller in 1783 under the cumbersome title, *A Grammatical Institute of the English Language*. Later versions were titled the *American Spelling Book* and the *Elementary Spelling Book*. Webster's speller earned the nickname "the old blue-back" because early copies of the book were covered in light blue paper and later editions covered with bright blue paper.

In the introduction to his speller, Webster declared that its purpose was to help teachers instill in students "the first rudiments of the language, some just ideas of religion, morals and domestic economy" (Button and Provenzo 1983, 57). Throughout, the little book emphasized patriotic and moralistic virtues. Short, easy-to-remember maxims, taught pupils to be content with their lot in life, to work hard, and to respect the property of others.

Webster's speller was so popular that it eventually sold over twenty-four million copies. Historian Henry Steele Commager said of the book, "The demand was insatiable. . . . No other secular book had ever spread so wide, penetrated so deep, lasted so long" (1958, 12). It has been estimated that more than one billion people have read Webster's book.

HOW WAS THE STRUGGLE WON FOR STATE-SUPPORTED COMMON SCHOOLS (1820–1865)

The first state-supported high school in the United States was the Boston English Classical School, established in 1821. The opening of this school, renamed English High School in 1824, marked the beginning of a long, slow struggle for state-supported **common schools** in this country. Those in favor of free common schools tended to be city residents and nontaxpayers, democratic leaders, philanthropists and humanitarians, members of various school societies, and working persons. Those opposed were rural residents and taxpayers, members of old aristocratic and conservative groups, owners of private schools, members of conservative religious sects, and Southerners and non-English-speaking residents. By far the most eloquent and effective spokesperson for the common school was Horace Mann.

HORACE MANN'S CONTRIBUTIONS

Horace Mann

Horace Mann (1796–1859) was a lawyer, Massachusetts senator, and the first secretary of a state board of education. He is best known as the champion of the common school movement, which has led to the free, public, locally controlled elementary schools we know today. Mann worked tirelessly to convince people that their interests would be well served by a system of universal free schools for all:

> It [a free school system] knows no distinction of rich and poor, of bond and free, or between those, who, in the imperfect light of this world, are seeking, through different avenues, to reach the gate of heaven. Without money and without price, it throws open its doors, and spreads the table of its bounty, for all the children of the State (Mann 1868, 754).

THE REFORMED SCHOOL   In 1837, Mann accepted the position of Secretary of the Massachusetts State Board of Education, a position he held for twelve years. At the time, conditions in Massachusetts schools were deplorable, and Mann immediately began to use his new post to improve the quality of schools. Through the twelve annual reports he submitted while secretary and through *The Common School Journal*, which he founded and edited, Mann's educational ideas became widely known in this country and abroad.

In his widely publicized *Fifth Report* (1841), Mann told the moneyed conservative classes that support of common public schools would provide them "the cheapest means of self-protection and insurance." Where could they find, Mann asked, "any police so vigilant and effective, for the protection of all the rights of person, property and character, as such a sound and comprehensive education and training, as our system of Common Schools could be made to impart?" (Rippa 1984, 119).

In his *Seventh Report* (1843), Mann extolled the virtues of schools he had visited in Prussia that implemented the humane approaches of Pestalozzi. "I heard no child ridiculed, sneered at, or scolded, for making a mistake," Mann wrote (Rippa 1984, 121).

THE NORMAL SCHOOL During the late 1830s, Mann put forth a proposal that today we take for granted. Teachers, he felt, needed more than a high school education to teach; they should be trained in professional programs. The French had established the *école normale* for preparing teachers, and Mann and other influential educators of the period, such as Catherine Beecher, whose sister, Harriet Beecher Stowe, wrote *Uncle Tom's Cabin,* believed that a similar program was needed in the United States. Through her campaign to ensure that women had access to an education equal to that of men and her drive to recruit women into the teaching profession, Beecher contributed significantly to the development of teacher training programs and the professionalization of teaching (Tyack and Hansot 1982).

The first public **normal school** in the United States opened in Lexington, Massachusetts, on July 3, 1839. The curriculum consisted of general knowledge courses plus courses in pedagogy (or teaching) and practice teaching in a model school affiliated with the normal school. Many normal schools later became state teachers' colleges and state universities.

When Mann resigned as secretary in 1848, his imprint on American education was broad and deep. As a result of his unflagging belief that education was the "great equalizer of the conditions of men—the balance wheel of the social machinery" (Mann 1957, 87), Massachusetts had a firmly established system of common schools and led the way for other states to establish free public schools.

REVEREND MCGUFFEY'S READERS

William Holmes McGuffey

Reverend William Holmes McGuffey had perhaps the greatest impact on what children learned in the new school. Far exceeding Noah Webster's speller in sales were the famous **McGuffey readers**. It has been estimated that 122 million copies of the six-volume series were sold after 1836. The six readers ranged in difficulty from the first-grade level to the sixth grade. Through such stories as "The Wolf," "Meddlesome Matty," and "A Kind Brother," the readers emphasized virtues such as hard work, honesty, truth, charity, and obedience.

Absent from the McGuffey readers were the dour, pessimistic views of childhood so characteristic of earlier primers. Nevertheless, they had a religious, moral, and ethical influence over millions of American readers. Through their reading of the "Dignity of Labor," "The Village Blacksmith," and "The Rich Man's Son," for example, readers learned that contentment outweighs riches in this world. In addition to providing explicit instructions on right living, the McGuffey readers also taught countless children and adults how to read and study.

What did children learn from typical lessons in nineteenth-century textbooks like this one, the story of "The Wolf" from McGuffey's *Third Reader*?

JUSTIN MORRILL'S LAND-GRANT SCHOOLS

The common school movement and the continuing settlement of the West stimulated the development of public higher education. In 1862, the **Morrill Land-Grant Act,** sponsored by Congressman Justin S. Morrill of Vermont, provided federal land for states either to sell or to rent in order to raise funds for the establishment of colleges of agriculture and mechanical arts. Each state was given a land subsidy of 30,000 acres for each representative and senator in its congressional delegation. Eventually, seven and a half million dollars from the sale of over seventeen million acres was given to land-grant colleges and state universities. The Morrill Act of 1862 set a precedent for the federal government to take an active role in shaping higher education in America. A second Morrill Act in 1890 provided even more federal funds for land-grant colleges.

HOW DID COMPULSORY EDUCATION CHANGE THE SCHOOLS AND THE TEACHING PROFESSION (1865–1920) ⟨?⟩

From the end of the Civil War to the end of World War I, publicly supported common schools steadily spread westward and southward from New England and the middle Atlantic states. Beginning with Massachusetts in 1852, compulsory education laws were passed in thirty-two states by 1900 and in all states by 1930.

Because of compulsory attendance laws, an ever-increasing proportion of children attended school. In 1870–71, only 64.7 percent of 5- to 17-year-olds attended public school. By 1919–20, this proportion had risen to 78.3 percent; and in 1992–93, it was 91.7 percent (National Center for Education Statistics 1995, 50). The growth in enrollment on the high school level was exceptional. Between 1880 and 1920, the general population in the United States increased 110.8 percent, and high school enrollment increased 1,894.4 percent (Thompson 1951, 90)!

As common schools spread, school systems began to take on organizational features associated with today's schools: centralized control; increasing authority for state, county, and city superintendencies; and a division of labor among teachers and administrators at the individual school site. In part, the trend toward modern operating procedures in schools reflected the accelerating pace of industrialization and urbanization during this period, especially in the northeast where immigrants and rural farmers flocked to the cities to work in factories. New "scientific" systems of management in industry, based on studies of efficiency and productivity, were applied to schools. Influenced by the work of Frederick W. Taylor, an engineer and the founder of **scientific management,** school officials undertook reforms based on management principles and techniques from big business. For example, they believed that top-down management techniques should be applied to schools as well as factories.

HIGHER EDUCATION FOR AFRICAN AMERICANS

Booker T. Washington

In *Up From Slavery,* Booker T. Washington (1856–1915) recounts how he walked part of the 500 miles from his home in West Virginia to attend the Hampton Normal and Agricultural Institute of Virginia, one of the country's first institutions of higher education for African Americans. Four years after graduating from Hampton, Washington returned to be the school's first African-American instructor.

Washington had a steadfast belief that education could improve the lives of African Americans and equip them to ". . . live friendly and peaceably with [their] white neighbors both socially and politically" (Button and Provenzo 1983, 145). In 1880, Washington helped to found the Tuskegee Institute, an industrial school for African Americans in rural Alabama. According to Washington, the Institute would play a key role in bringing about racial equality:

> The Tuskegee idea is that correct education begins at the bottom, and expands naturally as the necessities of the people expand. As the race grows in knowledge, experience, culture, taste, and wealth, its wants are bound to become more and more diverse; and to satisfy these wants there will be gradually developed within our ranks—as already has been true of the whites—a constantly increasing variety of professional and business men and women (Button and Provenzo 1983, 145).

W. E. B. DuBois

Not all African Americans shared Washington's philosophy and goals. William E. Burghardt DuBois (1868–1963), the first African American to be awarded a Ph.D. and one of the founders of the National Association for the Advancement of Colored People (NAACP), challenged Booker T. Washington's views on education. In his book *The Souls of Black Folks,* DuBois criticized educational programs that seemed to imply that African Americans should accept inferior status and develop manual skills. DuBois called for the education of the most "talented tenth" of the African-American population to equip them for leadership positions in society as a whole (Button and Provenzo, 1983).

THE KINDERGARTEN

Early childhood education also spread following the Civil War. Patterned after the theories of the German educator, Friedrich Froebel (1782–1852), the **kindergarten,** or "garden where children grow," stressed the motor development and self-activity of children before they began formal schooling at the elementary level. Froebel believed the aim of education should be self-development through self-expression and that schools should help children explore their surroundings and learn by doing. Through play, games, stories, music, and language activities, a foundation beneficial to the child's later educational and social development would be laid. After founding the first kindergarten in 1837, Froebel developed child-centered curriculum materials that were used in American kindergartens and throughout the world.

Margarethe Schutz, a student of Froebel, opened the first U.S. kindergarten in her home at Watertown, Wisconsin, in 1855. Her small neighborhood class was conducted in German. In 1860, Elizabeth Palmer Peabody, sister-in-law of Horace Mann and the great American writer Nathaniel Hawthorne, opened the first private English-speaking kindergarten in this country in Boston. Initially, kindergartens were privately supported, but in St. Louis in 1873, Susan Blow established what is commonly recognized as the first successful public kindergarten in the United States. She patterned her kindergarten after one she visited while in Germany. So successful was her kindergarten that by 1879, a total of 131 teachers were working in fifty-three kindergarten classes (Button and Provenzo 1983, 169). The United States Bureau of Education recorded a total of twelve kindergartens in the country in 1873, with seventy-two teachers and 1,252 students. By 1994, enrollments had mushroomed to 2,601,000 in public kindergartens and 442,000 in private kindergartens (National Center for Education Statistics 1995, 61).

THE PROFESSIONALIZATION OF TEACHING

During the later 1800s, professional teacher organizations began to have a great influence on the development of schools in America. The National Education Association (NEA), founded in 1857, and the American Federation of Teachers (AFT), founded in 1916, labored diligently to professionalize teaching and to increase teachers' salaries and benefits. The NEA appointed a Committee of Ten in 1892 and a Committee of Fifteen in 1893 to make recommendations for secondary and elementary curricula, respectively. In 1913, the NEA appointed the Commission on the Reorganization of Secondary Education to reexamine the secondary curriculum in regard to students' individual differences.

By the early 1900s, the demand for teachers had grown dramatically. An increasing number of women entered the teaching field at this time, beginning a trend often referred to as the "feminization of teaching." Female teachers were given less respect from the community than their male predecessors, though they were still more highly regarded than women who worked in factories or as domestics. Women nevertheless became influential in shaping educational policies during the early 1900s, in part through the women's suffrage movement that led to the right to vote. Women such as Ella Flagg Young, Catherine Goggin, and Margaret Haley played important roles in the Chicago Teachers Federation and the governance of Chicago schools (Button and Provenzo 1983). Another Chicagoan and visionary educational leader, Jane Addams (1860–1935), founded Hull House, a social and educational center for poor immigrants. In *Democracy and Social Ethics* (1902), Addams drew from her training as a social worker and developed a philosophy of

Margaret Haley

socialized education that linked schools with other social service agencies and institutions in the city (Gutek 1986).

As in the past, teachers during the early 1900s were expected to be of high moral character. They were subjected to a level of public scrutiny hard to imagine today, as illustrated by the following Professional Reflection.

Reflecting on Changes in the Image of Teachers

The following is a public school contract that teachers were required to sign in 1927. Analyze the contract and then write a one-paragraph description of the image of teachers and teaching reflected in the contract. How does this image differ from the current image of teachers and teaching?

Teacher Contract

I promise to take vital interest in all phases of Sunday-school work, donating of my time, service, and money without stint for the uplift and benefit of the community.

I promise to abstain from all dancing, immodest dressing, and any other conduct unbecoming a teacher and a lady.

I promise not to go out with any young men except in so far as it may be necessary to stimulate Sunday-school work.

I promise not to fall in love, to become engaged or secretly married.

I promise not to encourage or tolerate the least familiarity on the part of any of my boy pupils.

I promise to sleep at least eight hours a night, to eat carefully, and to take every precaution to keep in the best of health and spirits, in order that I may be better able to render efficient service to my pupils.

I promise to remember that I owe a duty to the townspeople who are paying me my wages, that I owe respect to the school board and the superintendent that hired me, and that I shall consider myself at all times the willing servant of the school board and the townspeople.

(Source: Willard Waller, *The Sociology of Teaching* [New York: John Wiley, 1932] p. 43. Copyright 1932 by John Wiley. Reprinted with permission of John Wiley & Sons, Inc.)

Because of greater demand for teachers, greater job mobility, and more and more women becoming teachers, the character of teaching changed. Both respected and regarded with suspicion, teachers became distanced from the communities they served. In his classic book *The Sociology of Teaching,* Willard Waller (1932) refers to this distancing as an "impenetrable veil" between the teacher and the rest of the community. Even in the 1930s, "teachers were kept humble and socially isolated from the seats of power. This was more easily done because teaching, since the turn of the century, had been dominated by women, a group that had its own stigma of second-class citizenship" (Andrews, Sherman, and Webb 1983, 53).

WHAT WERE THE AIMS OF EDUCATION DURING THE PROGRESSIVE ERA (1920–1945) ?

From the end of World War I to the end of World War II, the character of American education was profoundly influenced by the **progressive movement** in American society. During the late nineteenth and early twentieth centuries, supporters of progressive ideals were intent on social reform to improve the quality of American life. Educational progressives believed that the child's interests and practical needs should determine the focus of schooling. In 1919, the Progressive Education Association was founded and went on to devote the next two decades to implementing progressive theories in the classroom that they believed would lead to the improvement of society.

Progressives were not united by a single, overarching educational philosophy. For the most part, they were opposed to autocratic teaching methods; teaching styles that relied almost exclusively on textbooks, recitations, and rote memorization; the relative isolation of the classroom from the real world; and classroom discipline based on fear or physical punishment.

Teachers in progressive schools functioned as guides rather than taskmasters. They first engaged students through providing activities related to their natural interests, and then they moved students to higher levels of understanding. To teach in this manner was demanding: "Teachers in a progressive school had to be extraordinarily talented and well educated; they needed both a perceptive understanding of children and a wide knowledge of the disciplines in order to recognize when the child was ready to move through an experience to a new understanding, be it in history or science or mathematics or the arts" (Ravitch 1983, 47).

John Dewey

JOHN DEWEY'S LABORATORY SCHOOL

Progressive educational theories were synthesized most effectively and eloquently by John Dewey (1859–1952). Born in the year that Darwin's *Origin of Species* was published, Dewey graduated when he was twenty from the University of Vermont. He later earned a doctorate at Johns Hopkins University, where his thinking was strongly influenced by the great psychologist William James.

From 1894 to 1904, Dewey served as head of the departments of philosophy, psychology, and pedagogy at the University of Chicago. From 1904 until he retired in 1930, Dewey was a professor of philosophy at Columbia University. Dewey's numerous writings have had a profound impact on U.S. schools. In his best known works, *The School and Society* (1900) and *The Child and the Curriculum* (1902), Dewey states that school and society are connected and that teachers must begin with an understanding of the child's world, the psychological dimension, and then progress to the logical dimension represented by the accumulated knowledge of the human race (Cremin 1961).

While at the University of Chicago, Dewey and his wife Alice established a Laboratory School for testing progressive principles in the classroom. The school opened in 1896 with two instructors and sixteen students and by 1902 had grown to 140 students with twenty-three teachers and ten university graduate students as assistants. The children, four to fourteen years old, learned traditional subjects by working cooperatively in small groups of eight to ten on projects such as cooking, weaving, carpentry, sewing, and metalwork (Cremin 1961).

Maria Montessori

MARIA MONTESSORI'S METHOD

While Dewey's ideas provided the basis for the development of progressive education in the United States, progressive educators in Europe were similarly developing new approaches that would also impact American education. Chief among these was Maria Montessori (1870–1952), an Italian physician who was influenced by Rousseau and believed that children's mental, physical, and spiritual development could be enhanced by providing them with developmentally appropriate educational activities.

At Montessori's school for poor preschool-age children in Rome, teachers created learning environments based on students' levels of development and readiness to learn new material. According to the **Montessori Method,** prescribed sets of materials and physical exercises are used to develop students' knowledge and skills, and students are allowed to use or not use the materials as they see fit. The materials arouse students' interest, and the interest motivates them to learn. Through highly individualized instruction, students develop self-discipline and self-confidence. Montessori's ideas spread throughout the world; by 1915, almost 100 Montessori schools were operating in the United States (Webb, Metha, and Jordan 1996). Today, Montessorian materials and activities are a standard part of the early childhood and elementary curricula in public schools throughout the nation.

EDUCATION OF IMMIGRANTS AND MINORITIES

The diversity of America's school population increased dramatically during the late nineteenth and early twentieth centuries. Latin Americans, Eastern Europeans, and Southern Europeans followed earlier waves of Western- and Northern-European immigrants such as the Irish and Germans. As with Native Americans, the goal of immigrant education was rapid assimilation into an English-speaking Anglo-European society that did not welcome racially or ethnically different newcomers.

Also at stake was the preservation or loss of traditional culture. In some areas, school policies included the punishment of Cuban and Puerto Rican children, for example, for speaking Spanish in school, and children learned to mock their unassimilated parents. In other areas, efforts were made to exclude certain groups, such as Asians, and ethnic enclaves established separate schools for the purpose of preserving, for example, Chinese traditional culture.

By the time Native Americans were granted citizenship in 1924, confinement on reservations and decades of forced assimilation had devastated Native-American cultures and provided few successful educational programs. In 1928, a landmark report titled *The Problem of Indian Administration* recommended that Native-American education be restructured. Among the recommendations were the building of day schools in Native-American communities and the reform of boarding schools for Native-American children. In addition, the report recommended that school curricula be revised to reflect Indian cultures and the needs of local Indian communities. Another 50 years passed before the recommendations began to be implemented.

HOW DID EDUCATION CHANGE DURING THE MODERN POSTWAR ERA (1945–1990)

Throughout the twentieth century, many long-standing trends in American education continued. These trends may be grouped and summarized in terms of three general patterns, shown in Figure 3.2.

Three General Patterns of Trends in American Education

Americanization

- Americanizing of European educational institutions and instructional models
- Americanizing of English language textbooks and curriculum
- Cultural assimilation of immigrants and others through education
- Aims of education based on moral didacticism and pragmatism
- Aims of education relating to child development and child welfare
- Aims of education relating to success in a society based on capitalism
- Aims of education relating to citizenship in a democracy

Democratization

- Steady growth of compulsory, free, secular, publicly funded education
- Preservation of state, local, and parental control of schooling and schools
- Protection of teachers' and students' rights under the U.S. Constitution
- Shifts in educational reform initiatives that reflect a two-party electoral system
- Continual expansion of early childhood education
- Continual expansion of opportunities for higher education and adult education
- Traumatic periodic extensions of educational opportunity to "other" Americans (women; racial, ethnic, and language minorities; people with disabilities)

Professionalization

- Professionalizing of teaching as an occupation
- Professionalizing of teacher organizations and associations
- Growth in scientific and bureaucratic models for the management of schools
- Rising standards for qualifications to teach
- Continual development of institutions and programs for teacher education
- Greater application of theory and research on teaching and learning
- Generally rising status and salaries for teachers as members of a profession

FIGURE 3.2 Three general patterns of trends in American education

At the same time, the decades since the end of World War II have seen a series of profound changes in American education. These changes have addressed three as yet unanswered questions: (1) How can full and equal educational opportunity be extended to all groups in our culturally pluralistic society? (2) What knowledge and skills should be taught in our nation's schools? and (3) How should knowledge and skills be taught?

THE 1950S: DEFENSE EDUCATION AND SCHOOL DESEGREGATION

Teachers and education were put in the spotlight in 1957 when Russia launched the first satellite, named Sputnik, into space. Stunned American leaders immediately pointed an accusing finger at the schools and blamed the space lag on inadequacies in the education system. The Soviet Union was first into space, vocal critics told the public, because of the poor quality of U.S. public schools. Progressive approaches to schooling had so undermined academic rigor that students were taught less science, mathematics, and foreign language than their European counterparts. Americans, asserted Vice Admiral H. G. Rickover in his 1959 book *Education and Freedom,* needed to recognize that "education is our first line of defense."

The federal government appropriated millions of dollars over the next decade for educational reform. Through provisions of the **National Defense Education Act**

Keepers of the Dream

Mary McLeod Bethune

Teacher and Activist for African-American Education

"I cannot rest . . ."

Born as the fifteenth child of former slaves in South Carolina, Mary McLeod Bethune went on to become one of our country's most outstanding educational leaders and a champion of the educational rights of African Americans.

Bethune attended a school operated by the Presbyterian Board of Missions for Freedmen and Barber-Scotia College in Concord, North Carolina. She then went on to study at the Moody Bible Institute in Chicago. One of the first teaching positions she held was at Haines Institute in Augusta, Georgia. She went to Daytona Beach in 1904 where, with only $1.50 in savings, she founded a school for girls. The school was called the Daytona Normal and Industrial School for Training Negro Girls.

The school was in a run-down building Bethune rented. At first, she had only six students, including her son. To keep the school open, Bethune and her students sold sweet potato pies and fried fish and gave concerts in nearby resort hotels. In 1923, the school merged with a boys' school in Jacksonville, Florida, and became Bethune-Cookman College a year later.

Mary McLeod Bethune was an eloquent spokesperson for the educational rights of African-American youth. In 1935 during the Great Depression she was appointed to the Advisory Board of the National Youth Administration (NYA). That year almost 24 percent of the twenty-one million youths between sixteen and twenty-four years of age were out of school and jobless. When Bethune spoke eloquently and passionately on behalf of the educational needs of African-American youths, President Franklin Roosevelt added an office of minority affairs to the NYA and asked Bethune to direct it. As director of the Office of Minority Affairs, she developed a friendship with Eleanor Roosevelt, who personally supported Bethune's campaigns to improve the quality of life for African Americans.

The level of Bethune's commitment to education is reflected in a comment of hers that appeared in the *Journal of Negro Education* (Summer 1982: 290): "I cannot rest while there is a single Negro boy or girl lacking a chance to prove his worth." As director of the NYA, she made it possible for 150,000 African-American young people to attend high school and for 60,000 to graduate from college.

Mary McLeod Bethune received many honors during her lifetime in an era when racial segregation and discrimination were commonplace. For her courage, determination, and achievements, she is remembered today as an inspiration to all teachers.

of 1958, the United States Office of Education sponsored research and innovation in science, mathematics, modern foreign languages, and guidance. Out of their work came the new math; new science programs; an integration of anthropology, economics, political science, and sociology into new social studies programs; and renewed interest and innovations in foreign language instruction. Teachers were trained in the use of new methods and materials at summer workshops, schools were given funds for new equipment, and research centers were established. In 1964, Congress extended the act for three years and expanded Title III of the act to include money for improving instruction in reading, English, geography, history, and civics.

The end of World War II also saw the beginning of school **desegregation.** On May 17, 1954, the United States Supreme Court rejected the "separate but equal" doctrine that had been used since 1850 as a justification for excluding African Americans from attending school with whites. In response to a suit filed by the National Association for the Advancement of Colored People (NAACP) on behalf of a Kansas family, Chief Justice Earl Warren declared that to segregate school children "from others of similar age and qualifications solely because of their race generates a feeling of inferiority as to their status in the community that may affect their hearts and minds in a way unlikely ever to be undone" (***Brown v. Board of Education of Topeka,*** 1954).

The Supreme Court's decision did not bring an immediate end to segregated schools. Though the Court one year later ordered that desegregation proceed with "all deliberate speed," opposition to school integration arose in school districts across the country. Some districts, whose leaders modeled restraint and a spirit of cooperation, desegregated peacefully. Other districts became battlegrounds, characterized by boycotts, rallies, and violence.

THE 1960S: WAR ON POVERTY AND THE GREAT SOCIETY

The 1960s, hallmarked by the Kennedy administration's spirit of action and high hopes, provided a climate supportive of change. Classrooms were often places of pedagogical experimentation and creativity reminiscent of the progressive era. The open-education movement, team teaching, individualized instruction, the integrated-day concept, flexible scheduling, and nongraded schools were some of the innovations that teachers were asked to implement. Implied in these structural, methodological, and curricular changes was the belief that teachers were capable professionals.

The image of teachers and the significance of education was enhanced by the publication and warm reception of a number of books written by educators in the 1960s. A. S. Neill's *Summerhill* (1960), Sylvia Ashton-Warner's *Teacher* (1963), John Holt's *How Children Fail* (1964), Herbert Kohl's *36 Children* (1967), James Herndon's *The Way It Spozed to Be* (1969), and Jonathan Kozol's *Death at an Early Age* (1967)—a few of the classics that appeared at the time—gave readers inside views of teachers at work and teachers' perceptions of how students learn.

Presidents Kennedy and Johnson were instrumental in funneling massive amounts of money into a War on Poverty. Education was seen as the key to breaking the transmission of poverty from generation to generation. The strategy was to develop methods, materials, and programs such as subsidized breakfast and lunch programs, Head Start, Upward Bound, and the Job Corps that would be appropriate to children who had been disadvantaged due to poverty.

The War on Poverty has proved much more difficult to win than imagined, and the present results of such programs have been mixed. The three- to six-year-olds who participated in Head Start did much better when they entered the public schools; however, academic gains appeared to dissolve over time. Although the Job Corps enabled scores of youth to avoid a lifetime of unemployment, many graduates returned to the streets where they eventually became statistics in unemployment and crime records.

The education of low-income children received a boost in April 1965 when Congress passed the **Elementary and Secondary Education Act.** As part of President Lyndon B. Johnson's Great Society program, the act allocated funds on the basis of the number of poor children in school districts. Thus, schools in poverty areas that frequently had to cope with such problems as low achievement, poor discipline, truancy, and high teacher turnover rates received much needed assistance in addressing their problems.

In 1968, the Elementary and Secondary Education Act was amended with Title VII, the Bilingual Education Act. This act provided federal aid to low-income children "of limited English-speaking ability." The act did not spell out clearly what bilingual education might mean other than to say that it provided money for local school districts to "develop and carry out new and imaginative elementary and secondary school programs" to meet the needs of non-English-speaking children. Since the passing of Title VII, debate over the ultimate goal of bilingual education has been intense: Should it help students to make the *transition* to regular English-speaking classrooms, or should it help such students *maintain* their non-English language and culture?

THE 1970S: ACCOUNTABILITY AND EQUAL OPPORTUNITY

The curriculum reform movement of the 1960s did not bear the positive results that its supporters hoped for. The benefits of the new federally funded programs reached only a small percentage of teachers. In regard to some of the new materials—those related to the new math, for example—teachers complained that the recommended approaches failed to take into account the realities of classroom life. Many of the materials, it turned out, were developed by persons who had little or no classroom experience.

The 1970s was a mixed decade for American education, marked by drops in enrollment, test scores, and public confidence, as well as progressive policy changes that promoted a more equal education for all Americans. Calls for "back to basics" and teacher accountability drives initiated by parents, citizens groups, and politicians who were unhappy with the low academic performance level of many students were also prominent during this troubled decade at the height of the Viet Nam War era. For the first time in polling history, more than half of the American adults polled in 1979 reported that they regarded themselves as better educated than the younger generation (Gallup 1975).

Financial difficulties also confronted the schools. Instead of increasing as it had since 1940, the enrollment of children in grades 1–8 in public and private schools declined by nearly five-and-one-half-million during the seventies (Bureau of Census 1982–83, 135). Schools found themselves with a reduction in state aid, which was determined on the basis of pupil attendance figures. Financial problems were exacerbated by reduced support from local taxpayers, who resisted tax increases for the schools because they were stressed by their own economic problems, or had lost confidence in the schools, or because fewer of them had children in school. Consequently, the ability to meet the needs of students was further reduced.

Many parents responded to the crisis by becoming education activists, seeking or establishing alternative schools, or joining the home education movement led by John Holt, who by then had given up on reforming the schools. For these parents, the image of teachers and schools was quite poor; they believed that they could provide a better education for their children than public school teachers could. Those who kept their children in the public schools demanded teacher **accountability,** with the consequence that teachers' instructional flexibility was limited and their evaluation paperwork extended. Basal readers and teacher-proof curricular packages descended on teachers, spelling out with their cookbook directions the deeper message that teachers were not to be trusted to teach on their own. Confidence in teachers reached a low point.

In addition, during the late 1960s and early 1970s increasing numbers of young people questioned what the schools were teaching and how they were teaching it.

Thousands of young people mobilized in protest against an establishment they viewed as in support of an immoral, undeclared war in Vietnam and unconcerned with the oppression of minorities at home. In their search for reasons why these and other social injustices were allowed to exist, many militant youth groups singled out the schools' curricula. From their perspective, the schools were teaching subjects that were not relevant to finding solutions to pressing problems.

Responding in good faith to their critics' accusations, schools greatly expanded their curricular offerings and instituted a wide variety of instructional strategies. In making these changes, however, school personnel gradually realized that they were alienating other groups: taxpayers who accused schools of extravagant spending; religious sects who questioned the values that children were being taught; back-to-basics advocates who charged that students were not learning how to read, write, and compute; and citizens who were alarmed at steadily rising school crime, drugs, and violence.

Despite the siege on teachers and schools, however, the reforms of the 1960s and 1970s did result in a number of improvements that have lasted into the present. More young people graduate from high school now than in previous decades, more teachers have advanced training, school buildings are more adequate, and instructional methods and materials are both more relevant to learners and more diverse.

For those people who had been marginalized by the educational system, the federal acts that were passed in the 1970s brought success and encouragement: the Title IX Education Amendment prohibiting sex discrimination (1972), the Indian Education Act (1972), the Education for All Handicapped Children Act (1975), and the Indochina Migration and Refugee Assistance Act (1975).

Title IX of the Education Amendments Act, which took effect in 1975, stated that "no person in the United States shall, on the basis of sex, be excluded from participation in, be denied the benefits of, or be subjected to discrimination under any education program or activity receiving Federal financial assistance."

The **Education for All Handicapped Children Act** (Public Law 94-142), passed by Congress in 1975, extended greater educational opportunities to children with disabilities. This act (often referred to as the **mainstreaming** law) specifies extensive due process procedures to guarantee that children with special needs will receive a free, appropriate education in the least restrictive educational environment. Through the act's provisions, parents are involved in planning educational programs for their children.

THE 1980S: A GREAT DEBATE

The first half of the 1980s saw a continuation, perhaps even an escalation, of the criticisms aimed at the schools during the two previous decades. With the publication in 1983 of the report by the National Commission on Excellence in Education, *A Nation at Risk: The Imperative for Educational Reform,* a great national debate was begun on how to improve the quality of schools. Education even became a major campaign issue in the presidential election of 1984.

A Nation at Risk and the dozens of other national reports on American schools were interpreted by some as evidence that the schools were failing miserably to achieve their goals. The report claimed that "if an unfriendly foreign power had attempted to impose on America the mediocre educational performance that exists today, we might well have viewed it as an act of war" (National Commission on Excellence in Education 1983).

Responses included more proposals for curriculum reform. Mortimer Adler's *Paideia Proposal* (1982) called for a rigorous core curriculum based on the Great

Books. *High School: A Report on Secondary Education in America* (1983), written by Ernest Boyer for the Carnegie Foundation for the Advancement of Teaching, suggested strengthening the academic core curriculum in high schools, a recommendation that was widely adopted. In 1986, former Secretary of the U.S. Department of Education William Bennett advocated an ideal high-school curriculum that he described in *James Madison High* (1987). Educators at the middle-school level began to create small learning communities, eliminate tracking, and develop new ways to enhance student self-esteem as a result of the Carnegie Foundation's report by its Task Force on Education of Young Adolescents, *Turning Points: Preparing American Youth for the 21st Century* (1989).

These and other reform reports that swept the nation during the 1980s made a lasting imprint on education in the United States.

THE 1990S: TEACHER LEADERSHIP

The push to reform schools begun in the 1980s has continued into the 1990s, and teaching is being transformed in dramatic ways. In response to challenges such as greater diversity, greater international competition, less support for public education, and decentralization and deregulation of schools, innovative approaches to teaching and learning are being developed throughout our country (see Figure 3.3). Teachers are going beyond the classroom and assuming a leadership role in school restructuring and educational reform—a role that we examine more fully in Chap-

Issues in Education

- How and to what extent do the mass media influence public opinion about teachers and schools?
- In print and broadcast media, to what extent does coverage of issues and events in education reflect broader political trends?
- To what extent *should* education policy be influenced by public media?
- What were some positive and negative consequences of media coverage of education issues during the 1980s and early 1990s?

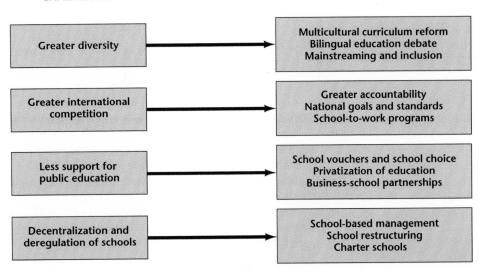

CHALLENGES	RESPONSES
Greater diversity	Multicultural curriculum reform Bilingual education debate Mainstreaming and inclusion
Greater international competition	Greater accountability National goals and standards School-to-work programs
Less support for public education	School vouchers and school choice Privatization of education Business-school partnerships
Decentralization and deregulation of schools	School-based management School restructuring Charter schools

FIGURE 3.3 The 1990s: A sampler of trends in education

ters 12 and 13. Through collaborative relationships with students, principals, parents, and the private sector, teachers are changing the nature of their profession. As Ann Lieberman (1995, 9) points out, for example, "the 'effective schools' of the 1980s placed the principal at the head of school improvement efforts. . . . The 1990s view of leadership . . . [has] principals acting as partners with teachers, involved in a collaborative quest to examine school practices to see how they can improve what the school is doing for all of its students."

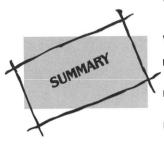

What Were the European Antecedents of American Education?

- Many practices in today's schools had their origins in Europe where the role of education was to prepare children and youth for adulthood.
- Ancient Greeks believed that leisure should be used to reflect on practical and aesthetic values and to develop a well-rounded mind and body.
- Socrates questioned pupils to reveal errors in their thinking and to lead them to eternal truths. He criticized the sophists who received pay for their teaching.
- Plato, a student of Socrates, founded the Academy, often called the world's first university, and expressed his idealism and educational theories in *The Republic* and *Laws.*
- Aristotle, a student of Plato, was a realist who believed that reality, knowledge, and value exist independent of the mind; he expressed the principles of the scientific method.
- Roman education, patterned after Greek education, consisted of the *ludus,* or elementary school, and a secondary or grammar school. Quintilian believed that the education of children should be based on their growth and development.
- Education in the European Middle Ages was mediated through the Roman Catholic Church. The Renaissance marked a rebirth of interest in Greco-Roman art, literature, secular learning, and humanism. The Protestant Reformation contributed to the spread of literacy and the idea of free public education.

- Four eighteenth-century European thinkers who influenced American education are Rousseau, Pestalozzi, Herbart, and Lancaster.

What Were Teaching and Schools Like in the American Colonies (1620–1750)?

- Colonial education was patterned after the British two-track system and its primary objective was to promote religion.
- Colonial teachers had low status, though respect increased with grade level.
- Puritans believed children were naturally corrupt and sinful and should be disciplined sternly at the dame schools, reading and writing schools, and Latin grammar schools common to the colonies.
- Mandated education in the United States had its origins in two colonial laws: the Massachusetts Acts of 1642 and 1647.
- At the end of the American Revolution, the few African and Native Americans who were literate were taught at church-sponsored schools that were segregated by race.

What Were the Goals of Education During the Revolutionary Period (1750–1820)?

- During the Revolutionary Period, characterized by a declining European influence on American education, education in the new democracy was shaped by the ideas of Benjamin Franklin, Thomas Jefferson, and Noah Webster.
- Educational opportunities for women were often limited to preparing them for family life.

How Was the Struggle Won for State-Supported Common Schools (1820–1865)?

- Horace Mann, a strong advocate for state-supported, free common schools, believed that teachers should receive post-secondary training in normal schools.
- The six-volume McGuffey reader, with its moral lessons and emphasis on virtue, determined much of what children learned at school.
- The Morrill Land-Grant Act, passed in 1862, provided federal land for colleges and set a precedent for federal involvement in education.

How Did Compulsory Education Change the Schools and the Teaching Profession (1865–1920)?

- The spread of common schools and dramatic increases in their enrollments led to the use of scientific management techniques for their operation.
- Booker T. Washington, founder of the Tuskegee Institute, believed education could prepare African Americans to live peaceably with whites, while W. E. B. DuBois believed African Americans should educate themselves for leadership positions and not accept inferior status.
- Kindergartens became common and used child-centered curricula patterned after German educator Friedrich Froebel's ideas.
- The National Education Association (NEA) and the American Federation of Teachers (AFT) were founded to professionalize teaching and increase teachers' salaries and benefits.

What Were the Aims of Education During the Progressive Era (1920–1945)?

- John Dewey's Laboratory School at the University of Chicago, a model of progressive education, offered a curriculum based on children's interests and needs.
- Progressive educator Maria Montessori developed age-appropriate materials and teaching strategies that were implemented in the United States and throughout the world.
- Public criticism of progressive education led to its decline at the start of World War II.
- School enrollments became increasingly diverse as a result of immigration, and a goal of education was the rapid assimilation of all groups into an English-speaking Anglo-European culture.

How Did Education Change During the Modern Post-War Era (1945–1990)?

- Russia's launching of Sputnik in 1957 sparked educational reform, particularly in science, mathematics, and foreign languages. Schools were ordered to desegregate with "all deliberate speed" as a result of a 1954 decision by the Supreme Court in *Brown v. Board of Education of Topeka*.
- Innovative curricula and instructional strategies were used in many classrooms of the 1960s. The Elementary and Secondary Education Act of 1965, part of President Johnson's Great Society and War on Poverty programs, provided federal money to improve the education of poor children.
- Alarmed by declining test scores, the public became critical of schools during the 1970s and demanded accountability. An array of federal legislation was passed to provide equal educational opportunity for all students.
- *A Nation at Risk* and other reports during the 1980s addressed weaknesses in America's schools and sparked a "Great Debate" on how to improve American education.
- In response to continuing challenges to education, teachers in the 1990s are taking leadership roles in school restructuring, school governance, curriculum change, and other aspects of educational reform.

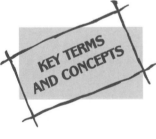

KEY TERMS AND CONCEPTS

Teacher's Journal

1. Based on what you have read in this chapter, identify several broad or long-term trends in the development of American education that continue even today. How are those trends reflected in educational policies and practices through the decades? For example, you might identify the professionalization of teaching as a long-term trend. How is this trend evident at different points in the past and now? How might this trend be manifested in the future?

2. Using the information in this chapter, trace the history of Western education in terms of beliefs and values about the nature of the child or learner. For example, how are teachers' views of children today similar to or different from those of ancient Greece and Rome or the American colonies?

3. What does the history of textbooks tell us about education in America? What values and priorities do textbooks today seem to reflect in comparison to textbooks of the seventeenth, eighteenth, and nineteenth centuries?

4. Develop a proposal for researching an impact of the past on teaching today and record it in your teacher's journal. For suggestions on choosing a specific topic, locating information, and conducting the research, ask your instructor for handout master 3.1, "Researching Impacts of the Past on Teaching Today."

Teacher's Database

1. Explore encyclopedias, bibliographies, periodicals, news sources, and other on-line reference works to research in greater detail the contributions of a pioneer in education or a historical development described in Chapter 3. Search by names and by key words or titles, such as:

W. E. B DuBois	Socratic method	Socrates
Noah Webster	Horace Mann	Plato
Progressivism	William H. McGuffey	Aristotle
John Dewey	Women in education	Maria Montessori
Tuskegee Institute	Desegregation	Margarethe Schurz
Benjamin Franklin	Thomas Jefferson	

As part of your search, check the Library of Congress and your municipal or state public library system. As you search, also explore the databases of libraries and online reference services especially designed for students. For example, try:

> **Gopher:** library.calpoly.edu
> **Select:** Cal Poly Library Services or Online-Reference Resources

2. Research your topic in the ERIC Resources in Education (RIE), which contains the Current Index to Journals in Education (CIJE), which, in turn, contains more than 700,000 records from 1983 to the present. This database is housed in the University of Saskatchewan Library System. To access it, ASKERIC by E-mail or use the following Telnet address:

> Telnet: sklib.usask.ca
> > USERNAME: Enter "sonia"
> > MAIN MENU: Select Education Databases
> > EDUCATION DATABASES: Select 1 CIJE plus RIE: 1983 to Present

Observations and Interviews

1. Interview veteran teachers and administrators at a local school and ask them to comment on the changes in education that they have observed and experienced during their careers. In particular, compare their remarks to this chapter's discussion of education during the post–World War II era, using this chapter's descriptions of the era to guide your questions. What events do respondents identify as having had the greatest impact on their teaching? Tape record, videotape, or transcribe respondents' stories to share with classmates.

2. As a collaborative project with classmates, conduct on-site interviews and observations for the purpose of researching the history of a particular school and its culture or way of life. You might also collaborate with teachers and students of history or social studies at the school to help you in your investigation. For more specific guidelines, ask your instructor for handout master 3.2, "Researching the History of a School."

Professional Portfolio

1. Prepare a video- or audiotaped oral history of the school experiences of older members of the community. Focus on a topic or issue of special interest to you and prepare some questions and probes in advance. For instance, you might be interested in an aspect of curriculum or student relations. Analyze the oral histories in relation to the development of education in the United States and videotape or tape-record your analysis.

2. Write a personal history of your experience as a student, focusing on the age or grade level of the students you plan to teach. Conclude with an analysis of how you expect your experience as a student will influence you as a teacher.

"The primary purpose of education is to prepare students to flourish in a democratic society and to work successfully in a global economy."

—National Education Summit Policy Statement
March 26–27, 1996
Palisades, New York

chapter 4

Schools and Society

F O C U S
Q U E S T I O N S

1. What are the aims of education today?

2. How can schools be described?

3. What are schools like as social institutions?

4. What characteristics distinguish successful schools?

5. What social problems affect schools and place students at risk?

6. What are schools doing to address societal problems?

Carla Watkins is in her tenth year as a social studies teacher at Metropolitan High School. Metro is located in a large industrial city in the Midwest. The school, in the center of a low- to middle-income area known as Uptown, has an enrollment of almost 2,300 students. About 75 percent of these are African Americans, with the remaining 25 percent about evenly divided between Mexican Americans and Anglo European Americans. Metro has a reputation for being a "difficult" school—a label that the school has been unable to shed.

Carla lives with her twelve-year-old son in a condominium on the edge of the Uptown area. Carla believes that teachers have an obligation to their society to address social issues. Several months ago, for example, Carla was the center of controversy when she began a two-week unit on AIDS education and the impact the disease has had on different segments of the American population. She had two persons with AIDS visit her classes, and her students participated in role plays and debates that focused on how to slow down the spread of AIDS.

Many of Carla's colleagues are skeptical about her methods. On the one hand, they believe that she does her students a disservice by reducing the amount of time spent on "academics." These teachers also point out that Metro parents want their children to learn the traditional basics, and they want the freedom to decide how, if at all, they will address the issue of AIDS within their individual families.

On the other hand, a small group of teachers is very supportive of Carla. They remind her detractors that students are highly involved in her classroom and that several potential dropouts have decided to remain in school because of Carla's willingness to address contemporary social issues in the classroom.

Today in the teachers' lounge Carla and two other teachers are talking about the results of a school-wide survey Carla's third-period class did on students' knowledge about AIDS. "My kids are really disturbed about the lack of students' knowledge about AIDS and the high-risk behavior of a lot of our students," Carla says. "We're thinking about starting a major school-wide AIDS awareness campaign."

"That's all well and good," says one teacher. "But I don't see where all of this is going to lead. Our responsibility as teachers is to give our kids the knowledge they need to get a better job. We need to give them the basics so they have a chance of getting out of Uptown. That's what their parents want—they don't want us teaching what should be taught in the privacy of the home. Besides, a host of other agencies, like neighborhood health clinics and family planning centers, are addressing AIDS."

What is the role of the teacher as America prepares to enter the twenty-first century? Should teachers focus on social issues in the classroom? If you were Carla, what would you say to this teacher?

The conflict between Carla and her fellow teacher highlights the expectation of much of the public that schools (and teachers) have a responsibility to address problems that confront modern American society. Those who disagree with Carla's approach to teaching social studies tend to believe that she should teach only content to students. Carla and her supporters, however, believe that teachers have an obligation to address domestic social problems. Underlying both positions are conflicting views on the aims of education.

WHAT ARE THE AIMS OF EDUCATION TODAY ?

Americans agree that the purpose of schools is to educate. Unlike other institutions in society, schools have been developed exclusively to carry out that very important purpose. That we are not always in agreement about what the aims of education should be, however, is illustrated by the fact that we disagree about what it means to *be educated*. Is a person with a college degree educated? Is the person who has overcome, with dignity and grace, extreme hardships in life educated?

Debate about the **aims of education** is not new. Aristotle, for example, expressed the dilemma this way: "The existing practice [of education] is perplexing; no one knows on what principle we should proceed—should the useful in life, or should virtue, or should the higher knowledge, be the aim of our training; all three opinions have been entertained" (1941, 1306). Definitive answers to Aristotle's questions have not been achieved; instead, each generation has developed its own response to what the aims of education should be.

EDUCATION FOR NATIONAL GOALS

In 1994, President Clinton signed into law the **Goals 2000: Educate America Act,** a comprehensive funding program to help schools achieve a set of eight national goals (see following), six of which were developed at a 1989 educational summit meeting convened by President Bush for the fifty state governors. Goals 2000 places a high priority on increasing student achievement in English, mathematics, science, history, and geography; creating more effective learning environments in our nation's schools; providing for teachers' professional development; and increasing parental involvement.

By the year 2000, the following goals are to be accomplished:

1. *School Readiness:* All children in America will start school ready to learn.
2. *School Completion:* The high school graduation rate will increase to at least 90 percent.
3. *Student Achievement and Citizenship:* All students will leave grades 4, 8, and 12 having demonstrated competency in challenging subject matter including English, mathematics, science, foreign languages, civics and government, economics, arts, history, and geography; and every school in America will ensure that all students learn to use their minds well, so they may be prepared for responsible citizenship, further learning, and productive employment in our nation's modern economy.
4. *Mathematics and Science:* United States students will be first in the world in mathematics and science achievement.
5. *Adult Literacy and Lifelong Learning:* Every adult American will be literate and will possess the knowledge and skills necessary to compete in a global economy and to exercise the rights and responsibilities of citizenship.
6. *Safe, Disciplined, and Alcohol- and Drug-Free Schools:* Every school in the United States will be free of drugs, violence, and the unauthorized presence of firearms and alcohol and will offer a disciplined environment conducive to learning.
7. *Teacher Education and Professional Development:* The nation's teaching force will have access to programs for the continued improvement of their professional skills and the opportunity to acquire the knowledge and skills needed to instruct and prepare all American students for the next century.
8. *Parental Participation:* Every school will promote partnerships that will increase parental involvement and participation in promoting the social, emotional, and academic growth of children.

Public approval of the national goals was initially high. As the year 2000 approached, however, doubts about the schools' ability to achieve the goals increased. Conservative groups became increasingly vocal about the possibility that Goals 2000 could lead to a national school board, federal officials evaluating parents' ability to raise children, or the provision of social services through the schools, particularly school-based health clinics that would dispense contraceptives (*Education Week,* May 8, 1996, p. 16).

In April 1996, Congress passed several amendments to Goals 2000, including provisions that would allow school districts in states that were not participating in Goals 2000 to receive funding. (In 1996, Alabama, California, Oklahoma, Virginia, Montana, and New Hampshire were considered nonparticipants.) The amendments also specified that no district, state, or school "shall be required . . . to provide outcomes-based education or school-based health clinics" and that Goals 2000 would not "require or permit any state or federal official to inspect a home, judge how parents raise their children, or remove children from their parents."

EDUCATION FOR PROSOCIAL VALUES

While there is widespread debate about what academic content the schools should teach, the public agrees that schools should teach **prosocial values** such as honesty, patriotism, fairness, and civility. The well-being of any society requires support of such values; they enable people from diverse backgrounds to live together peacefully. Table 4.1 shows the percentage of the public in 1993 and 1994 who advocated teaching specified values in the schools. The strong support for these prosocial values reflects the public's belief that the schools should play a key role in promoting the democratic ideal of equality for all.

EDUCATION FOR SOCIALIZATION

Schools are places where the young become socialized—where they learn to participate intelligently and constructively in American society. This purpose is contained in the national educational goal that calls for schools to prepare students for "responsible citizenship, further learning, and productive employment in our nation's modern economy."

Additionally, schools, more than any other institution in our society, assimilate persons from different ethnic, racial, religious, and cultural backgrounds and pass on the values and customs of the majority. The Los Angeles Unified School District, for example, recently reported that its students represented nine major language groups and 171 languages. It is through the schools that persons from such diverse backgrounds learn English and learn about the importance Americans attach to the Fourth of July or Veterans Day; about the contributions of George Washington, Abraham Lincoln, or Dr. Martin Luther King, Jr.; and about the basic workings of capitalism and democracy.

EDUCATION FOR ACHIEVEMENT

Of the various aims that the schools have, achievement is the most universally agreed on. For most people, the primary purpose of schools is to impart to students the academic knowledge and skills that will prepare them either for additional schooling or for the world of work. Regardless of political ideology, religious beliefs, and cultural values, Americans want their schools to teach academic content. When asked if they favor setting higher standards for what students should know in basic subjects—mathematics, history, English, and science—87 percent of respondents in a public poll said students should meet higher standards for promotion from grade to grade, and 84 percent said that higher standards should be mastered in order to graduate from high school (Elam and Rose 1995, 47).

EDUCATION FOR PERSONAL GROWTH

Our society places great value on the dignity and worth of the individual. Accordingly, one aim of our schools is to enable the young to become all that they are capable of becoming. Unlike socialization or achievement, the emphasis on personal growth puts the individual first, society second. As Vito Perrone states in *A Letter to Teachers,* "education . . . always [begins] with children and young people and their intentions and needs" (1991, 1). According to this view, the desired outcomes of education go beyond achievement to include the development of a positive self-concept and interpersonal skills. Thus equipped, students are able to live independently and to seek out the "good" life according to their own values, needs, and wants. The knowledge and skills students acquire at schools are seen as enabling them to achieve personal growth and self-actualization.

TABLE 4.1

Should values be taught in the public schools?

Should Be Taught	National Totals %	No Children in School %	Public School Parents %	Nonpublic School Parents %
1993				
Honesty	97	97	97	95
Democracy	93	92	93	96
Acceptance of people of different races and ethnic backgrounds	93	92	96	92
Patriotism, love of country	91	91	93	89
Caring for friends and family members	91	90	93	90
Moral courage	91	91	94	83
The golden rule	90	90	89	88
Acceptance of people who hold different religious beliefs	87	87	87	86
Acceptance of people who hold unpopular or controversial political or social views	73	73	75	70
Sexual abstinence outside of marriage	66	66	67	69
Acceptance of the right of a woman to choose abortion	56	56	57	38
Acceptance of people with different sexual orientation: that is, homosexuals or bisexuals	51	52	50	43
1994				
Respect for others	94	94	93	91
Industry or hard work	93	93	93	95
Persistence or the ability to follow through	93	92	94	94
Fairness in dealing with others	92	93	92	90
Compassion for others	91	91	91	89
Civility, politeness	91	91	90	91
Self-esteem	90	90	92	80
High expectations for oneself	87	87	88	82
Thrift	74	73	74	71

(Source: Stanley M. Elam, Lowell C. Rose, and Alec M. Gallup, "The 25th Annual Phi Delta Kappan/Gallup Poll of the Public's Attitudes Toward the Public Schools," [*Phi Delta Kappan,* October 1993], p. 145; and "The 26th Annual Phi Delta Kappan/Gallup Poll of the Public's Attitudes Toward the Public Schools," [*Phi Delta Kappan,* September 1994], p. 50.)

EDUCATION FOR SOCIAL CHANGE

Schools also provide students with the knowledge and skills to improve society and the quality of life and to adapt to rapid social change. Naturally, there exists a wide range of opinion about how society might be improved. Some teachers, like Carla, believe that one purpose of schooling is to raise the awareness of students about social problems and thereby make the world a better place. Less controversial have been efforts to prepare students to serve others through volunteerism and to participate actively in the political life of the nation. During the early 1990s, some high schools began to require every student to complete a service requirement to help students see that they are not only autonomous individuals but also members of a larger community to which they are accountable. Other schools began to introduce service-learning activities into their curricula. **Service learning** provides students with opportunities to deliver service to their communities while engaging in reflection and study on the meaning of those experiences. Service learning brings young people into contact with the elderly, the sick, the poor, and the homeless, as well as acquainting them with neighborhood and governmental issues.

Issues in Education

- In what ways can socio-economic status be a barrier to equal educational opportunity?
- What advantages and disadvantages can you identify in this cartoon?
- According to the cartoonist, how do test scores for academic achievement relate to school districts' per pupil expenditures?
- What are likely educational outcomes for the chidren portrayed?
- In your opinion, how can the American society achieve the aims of equity and excellence in the education of children and youth?
- What more might you need to know to answer this question?

EDUCATION FOR EQUAL EDUCATIONAL OPPORTUNITY

Ample evidence exists that certain groups in American society are denied equality of opportunity economically, socially, and educationally. For example, if we look at the percentage of children three to four years old who are enrolled in preschool—an experience that helps children from less advantaged backgrounds start elementary school on an equal footing with other children—we find that children who are low income are less likely to have such opportunities (see Figure 4.1). In fact, the enrollment rate for children from low-income families compared to those from high-income families widened between 1970 and 1993.

Extensive programs at the federal, state, and local levels have been developed to provide equity for all Americans—regardless of race, ethnicity, language, gender, or religion. Our country has always derived strength from the diversity of its people, and *all* students should receive a quality education so that they may make their unique contributions to our society.

The goal of providing equal educational opportunity for all has long distinguished American education from that found in most other countries. Since the

FIGURE 4.1 Percentage of children 3 to 4 years old enrolled in preschool NOTE: Low income is the bottom 20 percent of all family incomes; high income is the top 20 percent of all family incomes; and middle income is the 60 percent in-between. For 1990, comparable data were not available due to a change in survey procedures (Source: U.S. Department of Commerce, Bureau of the Census. October Current Population Surveys. Reported in *The Condition of Education 1995* (Washington, DC: National Center for Education Statistics, 1995), p. 29).

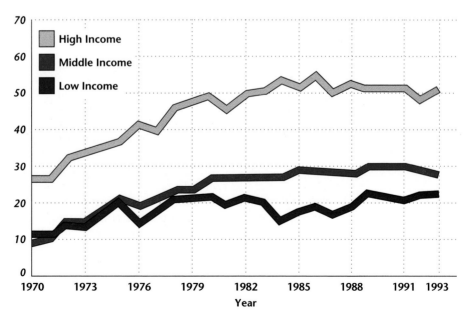

1850s, American schools have been particularly concerned with providing children from diverse backgrounds the education they need to succeed in our society. As James Banks (1994, 290) suggests, schools "incorporate the ethnic diversity that is an integral part of the democratic commitment to human dignity. . . . The schools' goal [is] to help attain a delicate balance of diversity and unity—one nation that respects the cultural rights and freedoms of its many peoples."

HOW CAN SCHOOLS BE DESCRIBED ?

Given the wide variation in schools and their cultures, many models have been proposed for describing the distinguishing characteristics of schools. Schools can be categorized according to the focus of their curricula; for example, high schools may be college prep, vocational, or general. Another way to view schools is according to their organizational structure; for example, open schools or magnet schools. A **magnet school** allows students from an entire district to attend a school's specialized program. Some magnet schools are organized around specific academic disciplines such as science, mathematics, or the basic skills; others focus on the performing and visual arts, health professions, computers, or international studies and languages.

METAPHORS FOR SCHOOLS

Other models view schools metaphorically; that is, what is a school like? Some schools, for example, have been compared to factories; students enter the school as raw material, move through the curriculum in a systematic way, and exit the school as finished products. Arthur Powell and his colleagues (1985) have suggested that high schools are like shopping malls; there is something for everyone, and students are consumers looking for the best value. Others have suggested that schools are like banks, gardens, prisons, mental hospitals, homes, churches, families, and teams.

In the school-as-family metaphor, for example, the effective school is a caring community of adults who attend to the academic, emotional, and social needs of the children and youth entrusted to their care.

SCHOOLS AND SOCIAL CLASS

In spite of a general consensus that schools should promote social change and equal opportunity, some individuals believe that schools "reproduce" the existing society by presenting different curricula and educational experiences to students from different socioeconomic classes. Students at a school in an affluent suburb, for example, may study chemistry in a well-equipped lab and take a field trip to a high-tech industry to see the latest application of chemical research, while students at a school in an impoverished inner-city neighborhood learn chemistry from out-of-date texts, have no lab in which to conduct experiments, and take no field trips because the school district has no funds. Schools, in effect, preserve the stratification within society and maintain the differences between the "haves" and the "have-nots." As Joel Spring puts it: "the affluent members of U.S. society can protect the educational advantages and, consequently, economic advantages, of their children by living in affluent school districts or by using private schools. [T]heir children will attend the elite institutions of higher education, and their privileged educational background will make it easy for them to follow in the footsteps of their parent's financial success" (Spring 1996, 290–291).

A useful way to talk about the relationship between schooling and social class in America is suggested by the four categories of schools Jean Anyon (1996) found in her study of several elementary schools in urban and suburban New Jersey. Anyon maintains that schools reproduce the existing society by presenting different curricula and educational experiences to students from different socioeconomic classes.

Anyon studied a small group of schools in one metropolitan area and her criteria are linked almost exclusively to socioeconomic status. Few schools actually fit the categories in all ways.

The first kind of school she calls the *working-class school*. In this school, the primary emphasis is on having students follow directions as they work at rote, mechanical activities such as completing dittoed worksheets. Students are given little opportunity to exercise their initiative or to make choices. Teachers may make negative, disparaging comments about students' abilities and, through subtle and not-so-subtle means, convey low expectations to students. Additionally, teachers at working-class schools may spend much of their time focusing on classroom management, dealing with absenteeism, and keeping extensive records.

The *middle-class school* is the second type identified by Anyon. Here, teachers emphasize to students the importance of getting right answers, usually in the form of words, sentences, numbers, or facts and dates. Students have slightly more opportunity to make decisions, but not much. Most lessons are textbook based. Anyon points out that "while the teachers spend a lot of time explaining and expanding on what the textbooks say, there is little attempt to analyze how or why things happen. . . . On the occasions when creativity or self-expression is requested, it is peripheral to the main activity or it is 'enrichment' or 'for fun' " (Anyon 1996, 191).

The *affluent professional school,* unlike the previous two types of schools, gives students the opportunity to express their individuality and to make a variety of choices. Fewer rules govern the behavior of students in affluent professional schools, and teacher and student are likely to negotiate about the work the student will do.

Anyon provides the following definition of the fourth type of school she identified, the *executive elite school*:

> In the executive elite school, work is developing one's analytical intellectual powers. Children are continually asked to reason through a problem, to produce intellectual products that are both logically sound and of top academic quality (Anyon 1996, 196).

In the affluent professional and executive elite schools, teacher-student relationships are more positive than those in the working-class and middle-class schools. Teachers are polite to their students, seldom give direct orders, and almost never make sarcastic or nasty remarks. However schools are categorized, it seems clear that they reflect the socioeconomic status of the communities they serve.

WHAT ARE SCHOOLS LIKE AS SOCIAL INSTITUTIONS 🔲

Schools are social institutions. An **institution** is an organization established by society to maintain and improve its way of life. Schools are the institutions our society has established for the purpose of educating the young. For the last 200 years, American schools have developed complex structures, policies, and curricula to accomplish this mission. "The Institutional Structure of Education in the United States" is shown in Figure 4.2 on page 106.

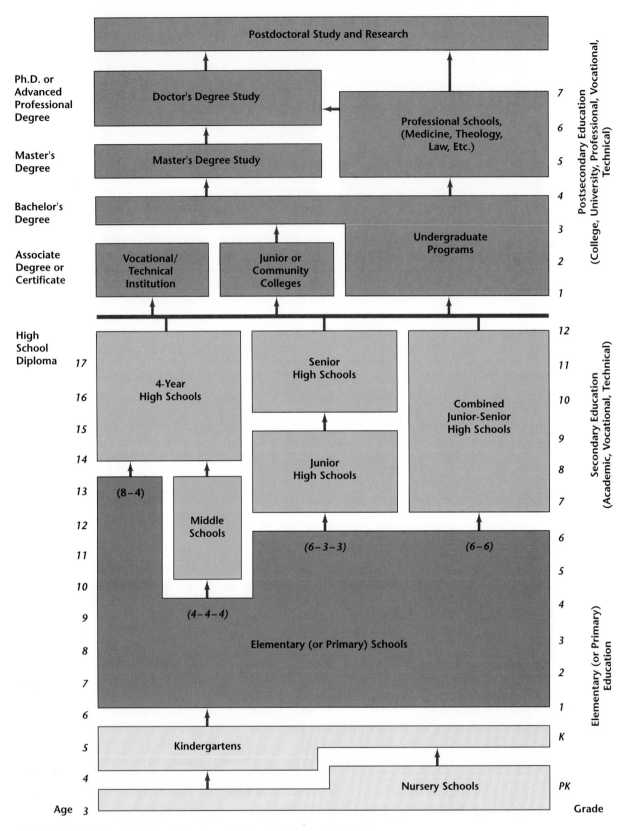

FIGURE 4.2 The institutional structure of education in the United States

THE SCHOOL AS A REFLECTION OF SOCIETY

As you might expect, schools mirror the national American culture and the surrounding local culture and other special interests. Private, parochial, and religious schools, for example, are often maintained by groups that see the school as a means of perpetuating their preferred way of life. One example of how schools reflect contemporary priorities in American life is the growing number of public schools that are located in shopping malls. In commenting on his experiences at a school located in the Landmark Shopping Mall in Northern Virginia, a student is able to say that the goal of countless students around the country is his reality: "As well as getting an education, I get a job" (Spring 1996, 4). Nevertheless, as Mary Henry (1993, 29) points out, "Schools are . . . not simply puppets of the dominant mainstream society. They have their own unique concerns and their own 'poetry' of people and events. Whether public or private, all schools are not the same."

RURAL, SUBURBAN, AND URBAN SCHOOLS   Schools also reflect their location. Schools in rural, urban, and suburban settings often have significantly different cultures. Rural schools are often the focal point for community life and reflect values and beliefs that tend to be more conservative than those associated with urban and suburban schools. While the small size of a rural school may contribute to the development of a family-like culture, its small size may also make it difficult to provide students with an array of curricular experiences equal to that found at larger schools in more populated areas. In contrast, large suburban or urban schools may provide students with more varied learning experiences, but these schools may lack the cohesiveness and community focus of rural schools.

SCHOOLS AND COMMUNITY ENVIRONMENTS   The differences among the environments that surround schools can be enormous. Urban schools found in or near decaying centers of large cities often reflect the social problems of the surrounding area, such as drug abuse, crime, and poverty. One of the most serious problems confronting American education is the quality of such schools. Across the country—in Chicago, New York, Los Angeles, St. Louis, Detroit, and Cleveland—middle-class families who can afford to, move away from urban centers or place their children in private schools. As a result, students in urban school districts are increasingly from low-income backgrounds.

In *Savage Inequalities,* Jonathon Kozol documents the startling contrast between the neighborhoods that surround impoverished

In what ways do schools reflect their communities and the wider American society? What difference might the community make for this school? for the students who attend it? for the teachers who work there?

inner-city schools and those that surround affluent suburban schools. In comparing New Trier High School in affluent Winnetka, Illinois, and Chicago's DuSable High School, an inner-city school at which the first author of this textbook taught for eight years, Kozol points out that New Trier is in a neighborhood of "circular driveways, chirping birds and white-columned homes" (1991, 62). In contrast, DuSable's surroundings are "almost indescribably despairing"; across the street from the school is "a line of uniform and ugly 16-story buildings, the Robert Taylor Homes, which constitute . . . the city's second-poorest neighborhood" (1991; 68, 71).

Though some communities may impact their schools in undesirable ways, many teachers at such schools find their work professionally stimulating and growth-enhancing. As one teacher said:

> I taught in two different environments—middle school in an inner city and high school in a more rural area. I think that combination was the experience that made me become a teacher. When I did my student teaching, I enjoyed it so much, and I realized I had a knack for it. When recruiters looked at my résumé, they were impressed that I had two different experiences I could draw from and elaborate on. I know that's how I got my job (Sallie Mae Corporation 1995, 8).

THE CULTURE OF THE SCHOOL

While schools are very much alike, each school is unique. Each has a culture of its own—a network of beliefs, values and traditions, and ways of thinking and behaving that distinguishes it from other schools.

Much like a community, a school has a distinctive culture—a collective way of life. Terms that have been used to describe **school culture** include *climate, ethos, atmosphere,* and *character*. Some schools may be characterized as community-like places where there is a shared sense of purpose and commitment to providing the best education possible for all students. Other schools lack a unified sense of purpose or direction and drift, rudderless, from year to year. Still others are characterized by internal conflict and divisiveness; students, teachers, administrators, and parents may feel that the school is not sufficiently meeting their needs. Gerald Grant defines a school with a "strong positive ethos" (or culture) as follows:

> A school with a strong positive ethos is one that affirms the ideals and imparts the intellectual and moral virtues proper to the functioning of an educational community in a democracy. It attempts to commit its members to those ideals and virtues in at least a provisional way through the espousal of goals, exemplary actions and practices, ritual, celebrations and observance of norms (1988, 188–189).

THE PHYSICAL ENVIRONMENT   The physical environment of the school both reflects and helps to create the school's overall culture. "Whether school buildings are squeezed between other buildings or located on sprawling campuses, their fenced-in area or other physical separation distinguishes them from the community-at-large" (Ballantine 1993, 235). Some schools are dreary places or, at best, aesthetically bland. The tile floors, concrete block walls, long, straight corridors, and rows of fluorescent lights often found in these schools contribute little to their inhabitants' sense of beauty, concern for others, or personal comfort.

Other schools are much more attractive. They are clean, pleasant, and inviting; and teachers and students take pride in their building. Overall, the physical environment has a positive impact on those who spend time in the school; it encourages learning and a spirit of cohesiveness.

What dimensions of culture might distinguish these students? What dimensions of culture might they all share? These children are participating in the culture of the school. What behaviors, formal practices, and school traditions are probably a part of their school culture?

FORMAL PRACTICES OF SCHOOLS   The formal practices of schools are well known to anyone who has been educated in American schools. With few exceptions, students attend school from six years of age through sixteen at least, and usually to eighteen, Monday through Friday, September through May, for twelve years. For the most part, students are assigned to grade level on the basis of age rather than ability or interest. Assignment to individual classes or teachers at a given grade level, however, may be made on the basis of ability or interest.

Teachers and students are grouped in several ways in the elementary school and in one dominant pattern in junior and senior high school. At the elementary school level, the **self-contained classroom** is the most traditional and prevalent arrangement. In this type of classroom, one teacher teaches all or nearly all subjects to a group of about twenty-five children, with the teacher and students remaining in the same classroom for the entire day. Often art, music, physical education, and computer skills are taught in other parts of the school, so students may leave the classroom for scheduled periods. Individual students may also attend special classes for remedial or advanced instruction, speech therapy, or instrumental music and band lessons.

In **open-space schools,** students are free to move among various activities and learning centers. Instead of self-contained classrooms, open-space schools have large instructional areas with movable walls and furniture that can be rearranged easily. Grouping for instruction is much more fluid and varied. Students do much of their work independently, with a number of teachers providing individual guidance as needed.

In middle schools and junior and senior high schools, students typically study four or five academic subjects taught by teachers who specialize in them. In this organizational arrangement, called **departmentalization,** students move from classroom to classroom for their lessons. High school teachers often share their classrooms with other teachers and use their rooms only during scheduled class periods.

SCHOOL TRADITIONS   **School traditions** are those elements of a school's culture that are handed down from year to year. The traditions of a school reflect what students, teachers, administrators, parents, and the surrounding community believe is important and valuable about the school. One school, for example, may have developed a tradition of excellence in academic programs; another school's traditions may emphasize the performing arts; and yet another may focus on athletic programs. Whatever a school's traditions, they are usually a source of pride for members of the school community.

Ideally, traditions are the glue that holds together the diverse elements of a school's culture. They combine to create a sense of community, identity, and trust among people affiliated with a school. Traditions are maintained through stories that are handed down, rituals and ceremonial activities, student productions, and trophies and artifacts that have been collected over the years.

THE CULTURE OF THE CLASSROOM

Just as schools develop their unique cultures, each classroom develops its own culture or way of life. The culture of a classroom is determined in large measure by the manner in which teacher and students participate in common activities. In addition, "the environment of the classroom and the inhabitants of that environment—students and teachers—are constantly interacting. Each aspect of the system affects all others" (Woolfolk 1995, 400).

The quality of teacher-student interactions is influenced by the physical characteristics of the setting (classroom, use of space, materials, resources, etc.) and the social dimensions of the group (norms, rules, expectations, cohesiveness, distribution of power and influence). These elements interact to shape **classroom culture.** Teachers who appreciate the importance of these salient elements of classroom culture are more likely to create environments that they and their students find satisfying and growth-promoting. For example, a physical science teacher of under-achieving students at an urban high school expresses her image of the classroom culture she wants to create and how students would benefit from that culture:

> I tell students that school should be a place where you can leave your problems behind, where you can find good, regular activity, a structured place. . . . I would like them to really become interested in their grade, in their work, what they can do. . . . They shouldn't have to dwell on their problems all the time. I like to give them a place where they can *work*. Kids need rules and structure or else they jump all over me and each other (Hensen 1993, 22).

In contrast, a beginning teacher at an experimental school describes the classroom culture she wants to create: "What I'm trying to get to in my classroom is that they have power. I'm trying to allow students to have power—to know what their knowledge is and to learn to create their own ideas as opposed to my being the one who is the only holder of ideas in the universe. I want to transfer the authority back to them" (Dollase 1992, 101). The efforts of this teacher to create an empowering classroom culture were supported by the culture of the school itself: "Because her comments reflect the prevailing view of this small, neo-progressive public school, she is able to implement her philosophy in her upper-level middle school classroom. [T]he structure of the school and the organization of the school day, which permits more personalization and more time with each class, are school variables that allow her a chance to succeed in redefining the authority relationships in her class" (Dollase 1992, 101).

WHAT CHARACTERISTICS DISTINGUISH SUCCESSFUL SCHOOLS ⟦?⟧

The challenge of developing a positive classroom climate at a school may seem daunting at this point in your professional education. However, a great many schools in all settings and with all kinds of students are highly successful, including inner-city and isolated rural schools and schools that serve pupils of all socioeconomic, racial, and ethnic backgrounds. What are the characteristics of these schools? Do they have commonalities that account for their success?

MEASURES OF SUCCESS

First, we must define what we mean by a *successful school.* One measure of success, naturally, is that students at these schools achieve at a high level and complete requirements for graduation. Whether reflected in scores on standardized tests or other

Keepers of the Dream

Kay Toliver

Disney's 1992 "Outstanding Teacher for Mathematics Instruction"

Her East Harlem students praise her:

"Miss Toliver, she doesn't teach like the textbook."

"She makes the class want to learn math."

"She keeps on and keeps on until we get it."

"She has to be tough. Lots and lots of homework."

"Their brilliance is almost buried . . ."

These students appear with their award-winning teacher in the video, "Good Morning, Miss Toliver," a lively account of the instructional and motivational strategies Kay Toliver uses to make her students enthusiastic about math and learning in her classroom in the poorest school district in New York City.

Toliver has taught magically for over twenty-eight years in the school where she first student taught. She won Disney's 1992 "Outstanding Teacher for Mathematics Instruction" and a Presidential Award for Excellence in Science and Mathematics Teaching from the National Science Foundation. PBS aired the Foundation for Advancements in Science and Education (FASE) production "Good Morning, Miss Toliver" to launch the 1993 school year.

In Toliver's classroom, small group interaction, hands-on activities, and friendly but vigorous Socratic teacher-student exchanges are woven amply with teacher-planned surprises, and teacher-led student recognition—"Let's give a hand to Miguel, the man!"

Dressed as a box of Sunkist raisins, dancing to the rhythms of "Heard it on the Grapevine," Toliver distributes small boxes of raisins to her students and introduces a lesson on estimating. Not only will the students estimate and count the raisins in their boxes, but they will have to describe in complete sentences the basis of their thinking. Toliver sees communication arts as a key companion to mathematics learning and problem solving in general. She reinforces this idea by having students keep daily math journals in which they summarize what they learned from the day's lesson.

Toliver's care for her students and her belief in them lie at the heart of her successful teaching. Her caring takes many forms, the first of which is the giving of her time. Recognizing and nurturing the student whose "brilliance is almost buried under the problems they are having in their environments and at home" is another form of caring (Toliver 1993, 36). Having high expectations for her students is probably Toliver's most significant form of caring. She believes that her East Harlem students who are "regularly told they are 'disadvantaged'" need this especially.

---

documentation of academic learning gains, students at these schools are learning. They are achieving literacy in reading, writing, computation, and computer skills. They are learning to solve problems, think creatively and analytically, and, most importantly, they are learning to learn.

Another valid measure of success for a school is that it achieves results that surpass those expected from comparable schools in comparable settings. The achievement of students goes beyond what one would expect. In spite of surrounding social, economic, and political forces that impede the educative process at other schools, these schools are achieving results.

Finally, **successful schools** are those that are improving, rather than getting worse. School improvement is a slow process, and schools that are improving—moving in the right direction rather than declining—are also successful.

RESEARCH ON SCHOOL EFFECTIVENESS

During the 1980s and early 1990s, much research was conducted to identify the characteristics of successful (or effective) schools. The characteristics of successful schools were described in different ways in several research projects. The following is a synthesis of those findings.

- *Strong leadership*—Successful schools have strong leaders—individuals who value education and see themselves as educational leaders, not just as managers or bureaucrats. They monitor the performance of everyone at the school—teachers, staff, students, and themselves. These leaders have a vision of the school as a more effective learning environment, and they take decisive steps to bring that about.
- *High Expectations*—Teachers at successful schools have high expectations of students. These teachers believe that all students, rich or poor, can learn, and they communicate this to students through realistic, yet high, expectations.
- *Emphasis on Basic Skills*—Teachers at successful schools emphasize student achievement in the basic skills of reading, writing, and mathematical computation.
- *Orderly School Environment*—The environments of successful schools are orderly, safe, and conducive to learning. Discipline problems are at a minimum, and teachers are able to devote greater amounts of time to teaching.
- *Frequent, Systematic Evaluation of Student Learning*—The learning of students in successful schools is monitored closely. When difficulties are noticed, appropriate remediation is provided quickly.
- *Sense of Purpose*—Those who teach and those who learn at successful schools have a strong sense of purpose. From the principal to the students, everyone at the school is guided by a vision of excellence.
- *Collegiality and a Sense of Community*—Teachers, administrators, and staff at successful schools work well together. They are dedicated to creating an environment that promotes not only student learning but also their own professional growth and development.

Research has also focused on strategies for making schools more effective. Since the early 1990s, school districts across the nation have been participating in **school restructuring** that changes the way students are grouped, uses of classroom time and space, instructional methods, and decision making. A synthesis of research (Newmann and Wehlage, 1995) conducted between 1990 and 1995 on restructuring schools identified four characteristics of successful schools:

- *Focus on student learning*—Planning, implementation, and evaluation focus on enhancing the intellectual quality of student learning. All students are expected to achieve academic excellence.
- *Emphasis on authentic pedagogy*—Students are required to think, to develop in-depth understanding, and to apply academic learning to important, realistic problems. Students might, for example, conduct a survey on an issue of local concern, analyze the results, and then present their findings at a town council meeting.
- *Greater school organizational capacity*—The ability of the school to strive for continuous improvement through professional collaboration is enhanced. For example, teachers exchange ideas to improve their teaching; they seek feedback from students, parents, and community members; and they attend conferences and workshops to acquire new materials and strategies.

- *Greater external support*—The school receives critical financial, technical, and political support from outside sources.

In short, the cultures of effective schools encourage teachers to grow and develop in the practice of their profession.

WHAT SOCIAL PROBLEMS AFFECT SCHOOLS AND PLACE STUDENTS AT RISK ?

A complex and varied array of social issues impact the schools. These problems often detract from the schools' ability to educate students according to the seven aims discussed at the beginning of this chapter: national goals, prosocial values, socialization, achievement, personal growth, social change, and equal opportunity. Furthermore, the schools are often charged with the difficult (if not impossible) task of providing a front-line defense against such problems.

One of the most vocal advocates of the schools' role in solving social problems was George S. Counts, who said in his 1932 book *Dare the School Build a New Social Order?* that "If schools are to be really effective, they must become centers for the building, and not merely the contemplation, of our civilization" (p. 12). Many people, however, believe that schools should not try to build a new social order. They should be concerned only with the academic and social development of students—not with solving society's problems. Nevertheless, the debate over the role of schools in regard to social problems will continue to be vigorous. For some time, schools have served in the battle against social problems by offering an array of health, education, and social service programs. Schools provide breakfasts, nutritional counseling, diagnostic services related to health and family planning, after-school child care, job placement, and sex and drug education, to name a few. In the following sections we examine several societal problems that directly influence schools, teachers, and students.

IDENTIFYING STUDENTS AT RISK

An increasing number of young people live under conditions characterized by extreme stress, chronic poverty, crime, and lack of adult guidance. Frustrated and feeling powerless, many youths escape into music, video games, cults, movies, television, or cruising shopping malls. Others turn also to crime, gang violence, sex, or substance abuse. Not surprisingly, these activities place many young people at risk of dropping out of school. In fact, according to an analysis of research on four areas of behavior associated with at-risk youth (delinquent acts, unprotected sexual intercourse, poor academic achievement, and drug use), the following percentages of 10- to 17-year-olds are likely to experience serious negative outcomes as a result of their behavior: 50 percent at low risk; 25 percent at moderate risk; 15 percent at high risk; and 10 percent at very high risk (Dryfoos 1990).

Among ethnic groups, dropout rates vary considerably. Figure 4.3 on page 114, for example, shows that the high school completion rate for Hispanic Americans has remained consistently lower than the rates for other groups. It has been estimated that one out of every four teenagers will drop out of school before graduating (Oaks, Worthy, and Remaley 1993). **Students at risk** of dropping out tend to get low grades, perform below grade level academically, are older than the average student at their grade level because of previous retention, and have behavior problems in school.

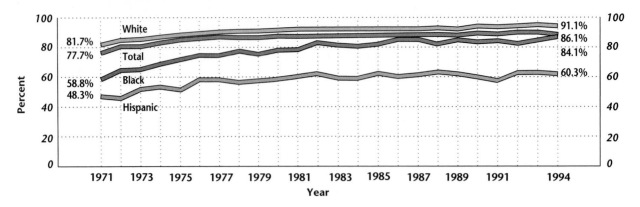

FIGURE 4.3 High school graduation rate (Source: National Center for Education Statistics, *The Condition of Education 1995*. U.S. Department of Education. Washington, DC: Office of Educational Research and Improvement, p. 73.)

Many children in the United States live in families that help them grow up healthy, confident, and skilled, but many do not. Instead, their life settings are characterized by problems of alcoholism or other substance abuse, family or gang violence, unemployment, poverty, poor nutrition, teenage parenthood, and a history of school failure. According to a 1992 survey conducted by the National PTA and the American Academy of Pediatrics, an alarming number of elementary-age children come to school sick, disturbed, or abused (see Table 4.2). Such children live in communities and families that have many problems and frequently become dysfunctional, unable to provide their children with the support and guidance they need. With their futures dimmed by such conditions, these young people are at risk of dropping out of school.

Children at risk are from families of all ethnic and racial groups and all socioeconomic levels. As Marian Wright Edelman of the Children's Defense Fund said:

> Millions of children are not safe physically, educationally, economically, or spiritually. . . . The poor black youths who shoot up drugs on street corners and the rich white youths who do the same thing in their mansions share a common disconnectedness from any hope or purpose (1990, 5).

The life experiences of students who are at risk of dropping out can be difficult for teachers to imagine; and, as an elementary teacher points out, it may be hard to admit that one can do little to help a student: "I have dealt with many students who are affected by social problems. . . . I try to help them any way I can, but as a teacher you

TABLE 4.2

Student problems

Percent of elementary school teachers saying these problems are experienced by students at their school.

Psychological/emotional	92
Unhealthy life-style habits	78
Family violence or abuse	78
Poor nutrition	71
Violent behavior	63
Lack of regular health care	58
Untreated illnesses	45
Untreated hearing/vision	45
Drugs/alcohol abuse	36
Lack of immunizations	11
AIDS	5

(Source: *Health Care and a Child's Ability to Learn*. Chicago, IL, and Elk Grove Village, IL: National PTA and the American Academy of Pediatrics, September 1992. Used with permission of the American Academy of Pediatrics.)

have to realize that you did not create the problem and you probably can't solve it. This is a difficult concept for most educators to confront" (Julie A. Addison, quoted in Parkay and Stanford, 2nd ed., 1992, p. 160).

CHILDREN AND POVERTY

Although the United States is one of the richest countries in the world, it has by no means achieved an enviable record in regard to poverty among children. According to *Five Million Children: 1991 Update* issued by Columbia University's National Center for Children in Poverty, 23 percent of children under six years of age—or five million young children—lived below the poverty line in 1991. In 1993, almost 21 percent of 5- to 17-year-olds—or more than ten million children and youth—lived below the poverty level. In the District of Columbia, almost 50 percent lived in poverty, and more than 30 percent of children and youth in Louisiana, Mississippi, Texas, and West Virginia lived in poverty (National Center for Education Statistics 1995, 27). In addition, Table 4.3 shows that 9 percent of children, or about 6.1 million, live in extreme poverty (families with incomes below 50 percent of the poverty level).

The economic recession of the 1980s and early 1990s contributed to an increase in our nation's homeless population, many of whom are children. In 1991, for example, it was estimated that 50,000 to 200,000 American children are homeless each night (Bassuk 1991). And, not surprisingly, the incidence of child abuse, poor health, underachievement in school, and attendance problems is higher among these children than it is among children with homes.

FAMILY STRESS

The stress placed on families in our complex society is extensive and not easily handled. For some families, such stress can be overwhelming. The structure of families who are experiencing the effects of financial problems, substance abuse, or violence, for example, can easily begin to crumble.

TABLE 4.3

Children at risk

All children under age 18 in 1994	68,018,100
Percent of families with children headed by a single parent in 1993	26%
Percent of mother-headed families receiving child support or alimony in 1993	32%
Percent of children in poverty in 1993	21%
Percent of children in extreme poverty (income below 50% of poverty level in 1993)	9%
Percent of children without health insurance in 1993	13%
Percent of 2-year-olds immunized in 1994	75%

(Source: *Kids Count Data Book, 1996.* Baltimore, MD: Annie E. Casey Foundation, 1996.)

Dear Mentor

NOVICE AND EXPERT TEACHERS
ON TEACHERS AS PARENTS

Dear Mari,

For many students, teachers represent the one adult in their lives with whom they have a stable, reliable, and nurturing relationship. This is what makes teaching so crucial nowadays. Furthermore, this heightened significance in our students' lives also brings with it the need for teachers to model responsible adult behavior in the classroom. Students might not be able to count on much from their parents, but they can rely on us to be there for them—day in and day out—with a challenging lesson plan, respect, and concern.

An invigorating, thought-provoking, student-centered lesson is the most potent way for teachers to reach students of all races, abilities, and needs. Teach a curriculum that truly engages your students—and this requires enormous time and effort—and you will meet your students' various needs.

In addition, set limits/rules in the classroom and back them up in a thoughtful and constructive manner. Kids hunger for structure, especially if they aren't getting it at home. But always remember, the key to classroom discipline is focusing on the student's behavior, not the student.

Positive reinforcement! Reward students, give them positive strokes, applaud their smallest achievements and build on those successes. All kids need to feel successful, so look for that success, no matter how small, and celebrate it.

Dear Mentor,

The breakdown of the family structure affects my role as a teacher. Do you ever find yourself playing parent as well as teacher? Many children today have working parents who don't spend quality time with them. These children are practically raising themselves or being controlled by the TV. What happens when a child is so malnourished emotionally that mentally he or she is not prepared for learning?

Mari Cortes

Successful teachers go well beyond curriculum and classroom management to reach their students. Making yourself personally available, as much as you feel comfortable, also opens another avenue for students. Greet students individually at the door; keep your room open during lunch, before and after school; meet students during your preparation period. The more teacher-student contact you can manage, the better off your students will be. Don't forget that you are not alone; learn to utilize the support services around you. Many schools have counselors and special administrators who provide excellent support for special students. Peer counseling groups, conflict resolution managers, visiting counselors, and teachers whom you respect and can send your student to for help oftentimes save a child from slipping through the cracks. Above all, remember that your students are young people who want what you want: self respect, appreciation, concern, stimulation, and kindness.

Rodney D. Smith
9th Grade English Teacher

In 1996, the National Clearinghouse on Child Abuse and Neglect (NCCAN) reported that state Child Protective Service agencies received two million reports of alleged child maltreatment, involving 2.9 million children. Moreover, over the previous five years, reports of child maltreatment grew by 14 percent, while the number of substantiated cases grew by 27 percent. Clearly, the burden of having to cope with such abuse in the home environment does not prepare a child to come to school to learn.

Stress within the family can have a significant negative effect on students and their ability to focus on learning while at school. Such stress is often associated with health and emotional problems, failure to achieve, behavioral problems at school, and dropping out of school.

With the high rise in divorce and women's entry into the workforce, family constellations have changed dramatically. No longer is a working father, a mother who stays at home, and two or three children the only kind of family in America. The number of single-parent families, stepparent families, blended families, and extended families has increased dramatically during the last decade. Table 4.3 shows that one in four families with children was headed by a single parent in 1993.

Just as there is diversity in the composition of today's families, so, too, there is diversity in the styles with which children are raised in families. As a result of increases in the employment of women and the fact that almost one half of current marriages will eventually end in divorce, an alarming number of children are unsupervised during much of the day. Often referred to as **latchkey children,** it has been estimated that there may be as many as ten million such children between the ages of five and thirteen (U.S. Government Printing Office, 1990). To meet the needs of latchkey children, many schools offer before- and after-school programs.

In addition, many middle-class couples are waiting longer to have children. Although children of such couples may have more material advantages, they may be "impoverished" in regard to the reduced time they spend with their parents. To maintain their life-style, these parents are often driven to spend more time developing their careers. In *When the Bough Breaks: The Cost of Neglecting Our Children,* for example, Sylvia Ann Hewlett points out that the "total contact time" between parents and children has declined as much as 40 percent during the last few decades (1991).

As a result of dramatic changes that have occurred in today's families, the "natural transfer of authority from home to school" (Comer 1989, 5) is not as strong as it has been in the past, and schools and teachers are being called on to play an increased role in the socialization of young people.

SUBSTANCE ABUSE

One of the most pressing social problems confronting today's schools is the abuse of illegal drugs, tobacco, and alcohol. Between 1986 and 1992, drug abuse by students was the most frequently mentioned problem in the Gallup Poll of the public's attitudes toward the public schools. The National Education Goals Panel reported in late 1993 that the nation had made little progress toward attaining the goal of drug-free schools by the year 2000; according to the panel, a third of all students in 1993 had seen a classmate drunk or high on drugs. Table 4.4 on page 118 shows the percentages of 12- to 17-year-olds who reported using illegal drugs, alcohol, and tobacco for selected years between 1979 and 1993. Although substance abuse declined since the late 1970s, the problem is still serious.

TABLE 4.4

Percent of 12- to 17-year-olds reporting drug use during the past year: 1979 to 1993

Type of Drug and Frequency of Use	1979	1982	1985	1988	1991	1993
Any illicit use	26.0	22.0	23.3	16.8	14.8	13.6
Marijuana	24.1	20.6	19.4	12.6	10.1	10.1
Hallucinogens	4.7	3.6	2.6	2.8	2.1	2.1
Cocaine	4.2	4.1	3.9	2.9	1.5	0.8
Heroin	—	—	0.3	0.4	0.2	0.1
Nonmedical use of:						
Stimulants	2.9	5.6	4.1	2.8	1.9	1.6
Sedatives	2.2	3.7	2.8	1.7	1.3	0.8
Tranquilizers	2.7	3.3	3.4	1.5	1.3	0.7
Analgesics	2.2	3.7	4.0	3.0	3.3	2.2
Alcohol	53.6	52.4	51.6	44.5	40.3	35.2
Cigarettes	—	24.8	25.5	22.8	20.1	19.1

—Data not available.

(Source: U.S. Department of Health and Human Services, Substance Abuse and Mental Health Services Administration, *Preliminary Estimates from the 1993 National Household Survey on Drug Abuse.* [This table was prepared August 1994.] Table taken from *Digest of Education Statistics 1995,* National Center for Education Statistics, p 140.)

The use of drugs among young people varies from community to community and from year to year, but overall it is disturbingly high. Mind-altering substances used by young people include the easily acquired glue, white correction fluid, and felt marker, as well as marijuana, amphetamines, and cocaine. The abuse of drugs not only poses the risks of addiction and overdosing, but is also related to problems such as HIV/AIDS, teenage pregnancy, depression, suicide, automobile accidents, criminal activity, and dropping out of school.

For an alarming number of young people, drugs are seen as a way of coping with life's problems.

VIOLENCE AND CRIME

As acts of terrorism, street crime, gang violence, hate crimes, and organized crime attest, ours is a violent, crime-ridden world. Widespread erosion of concern for the rights and property of others increased as a result of child abuse, television and movie violence, drug abuse, welfare and tax fraud, and corruption in business and government. Not surprisingly, violence and vandalism have also become more commonplace in our schools. As the National Education Goals Panel reported in late 1993, the goal of creating schools that are free of violence by the year 2000 seemed far off; according to the panel, 50 percent of tenth graders reported that they feel unsafe at school, and 10 percent had brought a weapon to school during the last month. Also, as a 1993 poll of 2,500 youth indicated, almost 60 percent said they could get a handgun if they wanted one, and more than one in three said they knew someone who had been killed or hurt by gunfire (see Figure 4.4).

More than $600 million are spent each year on school vandalism, according to a report by the U.S. Senate Committee on Delinquency—a figure that the National Parent-Teacher Association pointed out exceeds the amount spent on textbooks for our nation's schools! The National Association of School Security Directors gives the following estimates of crimes committed each year in schools:

- 12,000 armed robberies
- 270,000 burglaries
- 204,000 aggravated assaults
- 9,000 rapes

In addition, the U.S. Department of Justice estimated that there are more than 25,000 youth gangs in the United States, with a total of more than 652,000 members. Moreover, 48 percent of the local law enforcement agencies responding to the first nationwide survey of gang activity reported that gang problems in their communities were getting worse (U.S. Department of Justice 1996). One study of gang-impacted schools found that violence is the primary socializing factor among certain youths, and that the school's culture competes with the gang subculture for the allegiance of these youths (Matlen 1993). Though it has been estimated that

FIGURE 4.4 What youth think about guns (Source: ALH Research, Inc., poll for Harvard School of Public Health of 2,508 youths age 10 to 19, April 19 to May 21, 1993.)

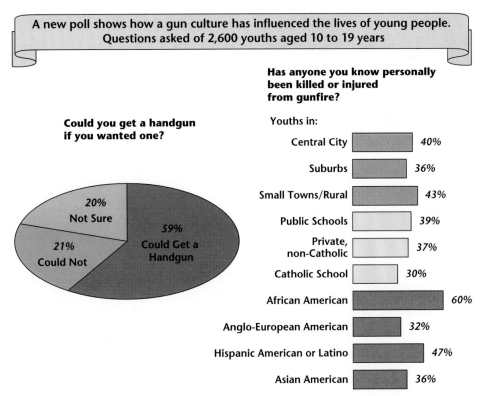

less than 1 percent of students are gang members, this small proportion of students can "undermine the order of a school, create physical and psychological concerns for the people in it, and disrupt the learning process" (Schwartz and Stallings 1987, 315). Strategies for reducing the affect of gang activities on schools include the identification of gang members, implementing dress codes that ban styles of dress that are identified with gangs, and removing gang graffiti from the school (Lal 1991).

Analyzing Risk Factors Relating to Student Violence

The following is a summary of risk factors research has shown to be related to youth violence. After reading the list, consider the following questions: What steps can teachers and other adults take to reduce the influence of these factors on individual youth? What kinds of academic and counseling services might be helpful for students prone to violence? How should schools involve the parents and/or guardians of violence-prone youth?

- economic and social deprivation
- family history of substance abuse and/or crime
- parenting factors and parent-child attachment (e.g., lack of effective parenting and parental rejection)
- victimization by physical or sexual abuse
- observation of domestic violence
- early conduct problems
- academic failure
- substance abuse
- gang affiliation
- possession of guns

(Source: *Youth Violence and Associated Risk Factors: An Epidemiological View of the Literature.* Washington State Department of Health, Non-Infectious Disease and Conditions Epidemiology Section. Olympia, WA, 1994.)

TEEN PREGNANCY

Since 1970, there has been an epidemic in teenage pregnancies. The Alan Guttmacher Institute, a nonprofit research foundation affiliated with Planned Parenthood, estimates that approximately 1 million teenagers become pregnant every year, most of them unintentionally (1994). These figures include about 19 percent of all African American women ages 15 to 19, 13 percent of Hispanic American women, and 8 percent of Anglo-European American women (Alan Guttmacher Institute 1994). Indeed, most teachers of adolescents today may expect to have at least some students who are, or have been, pregnant.

Because the physical development of girls in adolescence may not be complete, complications can occur during pregnancy and in the birthing process. Also, adolescents are less likely to receive prenatal care in the crucial first trimester; they tend not to eat well-balanced diets; and are not free of harmful substances such as alcohol, tobacco, and drugs, which are known to be detrimental to a baby's development. These young mothers "are at risk for chronic educational, occupational, and financial difficulties, and their offspring are also at risk for medical, educational, and behavioral problems" (Durlak 1995, 66). Because most teen mothers drop out of school, forfeiting their high school diplomas and limiting their access to decent, higher-paying job opportunities, they and their children stay at the bottom of the economic ladder.

STUDENTS WITH HIV/AIDS

One of the most challenging social problems confronting the schools is providing for the education of children who have HIV/AIDS (human immunodeficiency virus/acquired immune deficiency syndrome). With AIDS, nearly always fatal, the body is no longer able to defend itself against disease. Many school districts have been involved in litigation over the right of children with HIV/AIDS to attend school, and the condom-distribution programs that a few school systems have initiated to stem the spread of the HIV virus have been challenged in the courts.

According to the Centers for Disease Control (CDC), the number of AIDS cases is increasing at an alarming rate. The cumulative number of AIDS cases reported to the CDC was 513,486 as of 1996, with 319,849 of these resulting in death. In 1996, the World Health Organization (WHO) reported that 18 million adults and adolescents and 1.5 million children were infected with HIV, and 4.5 million of these had developed AIDS. WHO also reported that 6,000 new cases of HIV infection occur every day and predicted that by the year 2000 between thirty and forty million people, worldwide, will be infected with the HIV virus; between four and five million of these will be Americans.

Increasingly, states are beginning to require that schools provide information on HIV/AIDS and how to avoid the disease. In 1993, however, only twenty-seven states required health or sex education of any kind.

SUICIDE AMONG CHILDREN AND YOUTHS

The increase in individual and multiple suicides is alarming. The National Institute of Mental Health reported in 1996 that suicide is the third leading cause of death among youth ages fifteen to twenty-four and accounts for more than 5,000 deaths yearly for this group. Among 5- to 14-year-olds, suicide is the sixth leading cause of death. Moreover, it is estimated that for each completed suicide there may be 300 attempts (Lawton 1991, April 10). According to the Centers for Disease Control and Prevention (1992), 8 percent of high school students attempted suicide, 16 percent planned to do it, and 27 percent seriously contemplated it. Since many suicide attempts are unreported or undetected, these numbers may be higher.

Data also reveal that boys are more likely to *complete* suicide, while girls are nine times more likely to *attempt* it (Kalafat 1990). White youth are five times more likely to commit suicide than African American youth, and Native American youth are ten times more likely than their white peers to do so (Frymier 1988). Also, lesbian and gay youth are two to three times more likely to attempt suicide than their heterosexual peers, and they account for up to 30 percent of all completed suicides among youth (Besner and Spungin 1995).

WHAT ARE SCHOOLS DOING TO ADDRESS SOCIETAL PROBLEMS ?

Responding to the needs of at-risk students is a crucial challenge for schools, families, and communities as we enter the twenty-first century. Since most children attend school, it is logical that this pre-existing system be used for reaching large numbers of at-risk children (and, through them, their families). During the last decade, many school districts have taken innovative steps to address societal problems that impact students' lives.

Though programs that address social problems are costly, the public believes that schools should be used for the delivery of health and social services to students and their families. According to the 1995 Gallup Poll of the Public's Attitudes Toward the Public Schools, for example, 91 percent of respondents said that "serving the emotional and health needs of students" is "very important" or "somewhat important" (Elam and Rose 1995, 44). Similarly, respondents to the 1993 Gallup Poll approved the following services for students: sight and hearing examinations (92 percent), free or low-cost lunches (87 percent), inoculations (84 percent), free or low-cost breakfasts (74 percent), and after-school care for children of working parents (62 percent) (Elam, Rose, and Gallup 1993, 144). According to that same poll, support for condom distribution in public schools was favored by 60 percent of respondents, though 19 percent of those would require parental consent (p. 152).

INTERVENTION PROGRAMS

Under pressure to find solutions to increasing social problems among children and adolescents, educators have developed an array of intervention programs. In general, the aim of these programs is to address the behavioral, social, and academic adjustment of at-risk children and adolescents so they can receive maximum benefit from their school experiences.

In the following sections, we briefly review several comprehensive strategies that have proven effective in addressing academic, social, and behavioral problems among children and adolescents; these approaches to *intervention* are: peer counseling, full-service schools, and school-based interprofessional case management. Chapter 14 presents additional information about recent, innovative steps schools are taking for the *prevention* of the effects of social problems on students. Also see the Teacher's Resource Guide for "Selected Resources for Teaching Students at Risk"—a list of publications, organizations, and online locations that are good sources of information on the problems children and youth may encounter.

PEER COUNSELING   To address the social problems that affect students, some schools have initiated student-to-student **peer counseling** programs—usually monitored by a school counselor or other specially trained adult. In peer counseling programs, students can address problems and issues such as low academic achievement, interpersonal problems at home and at school, substance abuse, and career planning. Evidence indicates that both peer counselors and students experience increased self-esteem and greater ability to deal with problems.

When peer counseling is combined with cross-age tutoring, younger students can learn about drugs, alcohol, premarital pregnancy, delinquency, dropping out, HIV/AIDS, suicide, and other relevant issues. Here the groups are often college-age students meeting with those in high school, or high school students meeting with

What approach to the education of students at risk does the scene in this photograph represent? What other risk factors affect children and youths? What are some other effective approaches for helping students at risk to succeed in school?

those in junior high school or middle school. In these preventative programs, older students sometimes perform dramatic episodes that portray students confronting problems and model strategies for handling the situations presented.

FULL-SERVICE SCHOOLS   In response to the increasing number of at-risk students, many schools are serving their communities by integrating educational, medical, social and/or human services. **Full-service schools** tend to be in low-income urban areas and involve collaborative partnerships among school districts, departments of public health, hospitals, and various nonprofit organizations. At full-service schools, students and their families can receive health screening, psychological counseling, drug prevention counseling, parent education, and family planning information.

One example of a full-service school is Salome Urena Middle Academies (SUMA), a middle school serving a Dominican community in Washington Heights, New York. At SUMA, a family institute offers English as a Second Language, Spanish, aerobics, and entrepreneurial skills. At a family resource center, open from 8:30 A.M. to 8:30 P.M., social workers, paraprofessionals, parents, and other volunteers offer help with immigration and citizenship, housing, and employment. Next to the family resource center, a clinic provides dental, medical, and mental health services. In 1994, the school's 1,200 students, their parents, and siblings were served at a total cost of less than $1,000 per student—significantly less than the per-pupil expenditures in most suburban schools (Dryfoos 1994).

SCHOOL-BASED INTERPROFESSIONAL CASE MANAGEMENT   In responding to the needs of at-risk students, it has been suggested that schools "will need to reconceptualize the networks of community organizations and public services that might assist, and they will need to draw on those community resources" (Edwards and Young 1992, 78). One such approach to forming new home/school/community partnerships is known as **school-based interprofessional case management.** The approach uses professionally trained case managers who work directly with teachers, the community, and the family to coordinate and deliver appropriate services to at-risk students and their families. The case management approach is based on a comprehensive service delivery network of teachers, social agencies, and health service agencies.

One of the first case-management programs in the country is operated by the Center for the Study and Teaching of At-Risk Students (C-STARS) and serves 20 school districts in the Pacific Northwest. Center members include Washington State University, the University of Washington, a community-based organization, and Washington State's Department of Social and Health Services. Working with teachers and other school personnel, an interprofessional case management team fulfills seven functions to meet the needs of at-risk students: assessment, development of a service plan, brokering with other agencies, service implementation and coordination, advocacy, monitoring and evaluation, and mentoring. Program evaluation data have shown significant measurable improvements in student's attendance, academic performance, and school behavior.

COMPENSATORY EDUCATION

To meet the learning needs of at-risk students, several federally funded **compensatory education programs** for elementary and secondary students have been developed, the largest of which is Title I. Launched in 1965 as part of the Elementary and Secondary Education Act (ESEA) and President Lyndon Johnson's Great Society education program, Title I (called Chapter I between 1981 and 1994) was designed to improve the basic skills (reading, writing, and mathematics) of low-ability students from low-income families. Since 1965, more than 5 million students in nearly all school districts have benefited from Title I/Chapter 1 programs. For 1994–95, $7 billion was appropriated for Title 1 programs, with 13.1 percent of all students participating (National Center for Education Statistics, 1995).

Students who participate in Title I programs are usually taught through "pullout" programs, in which they leave the regular classroom to receive additional instruction individually or in small groups. Title I teachers, sometimes assisted by an aide, often have curriculum materials and equipment not available to regular classroom teachers.

Research on the effectiveness of Title I programs has been inconclusive, with some studies reporting achievement gains not found in other studies. Recent research has found positive effects on students' achievement in the early grades, but these gains tend to dissipate during the middle grades. The pattern of short-lived gains is strongest for students attending urban schools that serve a high proportion of families in poverty (Levine and Levine, 1996). Some critics of Title I and other compensatory education programs such as Head Start for preschool children, Success for All for preschool and elementary children, and Upward Bound for high school students argue that they are stop-gap measures at best. Instead, they maintain, social problems such as poverty, the breakdown of families, drug abuse, and crime that contribute to poor school performance should be reduced.

ALTERNATIVE SCHOOLS AND CURRICULA

To meet the needs of students whom social problems place at risk, many school districts have developed alternative schools and curricula. Usually, an **alternative school** is a small, highly individualized school separate from the regular school; in other cases, the alternative school is organized as a **school-within-a-school.** Alternative school programs usually provide remedial instruction, some vocational training, and individualized counseling. Since they usually have much smaller class sizes, alternative school teachers can monitor students' progress more closely and, when problems do arise, respond more quickly and with greater understanding of student needs.

One exemplary alternative school is the Buffalo Alternative High School serving at-risk 7th–12th grade students in the Buffalo, New York, Public School District. To reach students who are not successful at regular schools, the Buffalo program offers individualized instruction, small class sizes, and various enrichment programs delivered in what school staff describe as a "supportive, noncoercive, nontraditional setting." Most students are expected to return to their regular schools after a minimum of four weeks. Students must earn 600 "points" (based on attendance, punctuality, attitude, behavior, and performance) to return to their regular school.

In addition, the Buffalo Alternative High School operates eight satellite schools in nonschool buildings throughout Buffalo. Among these programs are:

- SAVe (Suspension Avoidance Vehicle)—a two-week program students complete before returning to their sending school or enrolling in the Alternative High School
- City-As-School—students serve as interns in the public and private sectors and earn academic credit
- SMART (Students Moving Ahead Through Remediation Testing)—7th and 8th-grade students held behind can qualify for promotion to the appropriate grade
- Bilingual Satellite—educational services provided to Spanish-speaking students

While they don't work in alternative school settings, many highly effective regular teachers have developed alternative curricula to meet the unique learning needs of students at risk. Many teachers, for example, link students' learning to the business, civic, cultural, and political segments of their communities. The rationale is that connecting at-risk students to the world beyond their schools will enable them to see the relevance of education.

SUMMARY

What Are the Aims of Education Today?

- Though debate about the aims of education continues, the public believes that schools have a responsibility to address problems confronting American society.
- One perspective on the aims of education is Goals 2000, a set of national goals in the following areas: school readiness; school completion; student achievement and citizenship; achievement in mathematics and science; adult literacy and lifelong learning; safe, disciplined, and alcohol- and drug-free schools; teacher education and professional development; and parental participation.

- Agreement exists regarding six additional broad educational aims—education for prosocial values, socialization, achievement, personal growth, social change, and equal opportunity.

How Can Schools Be Described?

- Schools can be categorized according to the focus of their curricula and according to their organizational structures.
- Metaphors for schools have suggested that schools are like families, banks, gardens, prisons, and so on, with the school-as-family metaphor often describing schools that are successful.
- Some people believe that schools reproduce the existing social class structure, that they maintain the differences between the "haves" and "have-nots." For example, Anyon's four categories of schools—working-class schools, middle-class schools, affluent professional schools, and executive elite schools—illustrate the relationship between schooling and social class.

What Are Schools Like as Social Institutions?

- As social institutions that contribute to the maintenance and improvement of society, schools mirror the national American culture and the surrounding local culture.
- Schools develop their own unique cultures, and the community environment that surrounds a school can impact it positively or negatively.
- Elements of a school's physical environment such as self-contained classrooms, open-space arrangements, and departmentalization contribute to a school's character and culture. Similarly, each classroom develops its own culture, which is influenced by the physical setting and the social dimensions of the group.

What Characteristics Distinguish Successful Schools?

- Three aspects of successful schools have been suggested: (1) their students manifest a high level of learning; (2) their results surpass those for comparable schools; and (3) they are improving rather than getting worse.
- Research has identified seven characteristics of effective schools: strong leadership, high expectations, emphasis on basic skills, orderly school environment, frequent and systematic evaluation of student learning, sense of purpose, and collegiality and a sense of community.
- Research indicates that successfully restructured schools emphasize student learning, authentic pedagogy, building organizational capacity, and external support.

What Social Problems Affect Schools and Place Students at Risk?

- Among the many social problems that impact the school's ability to educate students are poverty, family stress, substance abuse, violence and crime, teen pregnancy, HIV/AIDS, and suicide.
- Children at risk, who represent all ethnic and racial groups and all socioeconomic levels, tend to get low grades, underachieve, be older than other students at the same grade level, and have behavior problems at school.

What Are Schools Doing to Address Social Problems?

- Schools have developed *intervention* and *prevention* programs to address social problems. Three effective intervention programs are peer counseling, full-service schools, and school-based interprofessional case management.

- Since 1965, an array of federally funded compensatory education programs has provided educational services to improve the basic skills of low-ability students from low-income families.

- Many school districts have developed alternative schools or schools-within-a-school that provide highly individualized instructional and support services for students who have not been successful in regular schools. Also, highly effective teachers modify their techniques and develop alternative curricula to meet the needs of students at risk.

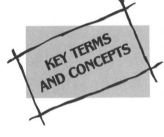

KEY TERMS AND CONCEPTS

aims of education, 98
alternative school, 125
classroom culture, 110
compensatory education programs, 124
departmentalization, 109
full-service schools, 123
Goals 2000: Educate America Act, 99

institution, 105
latchkey children, 117
magnet school, 104
open-space schools, 109
peer counseling, 122
prosocial values, 100
school-based interprofessional case management, 124

school culture, 108
school restructuring, 112
school traditions, 109
school-within-a-school, 125
self-contained classroom, 109
service learning, 102
students at risk, 113
successful schools, 111

APPLICATIONS AND ACTIVITIES

Teacher's Journal

1. Collect and summarize several newspaper and magazine articles that contain references to the public's expectations of education and the schools. To what extent do the articles address the four aims discussed in this chapter? To what extent do they identify social problems that schools are expected to address?

2. Identify and then defend your choice of school reforms that you consider most important for improving the quality of education in the United States. What aims of education do your choices reflect?

3. Reflect on your experiences with the impact of social problems on teaching and learning at the elementary, middle, or high school levels. Select one of the social issues or problems discussed in this chapter and describe its influences on you or your peers.

Teacher's Database

1. Join or start an interactive online discussion on one or more of the following topics discussed in this chapter. You might join a newsgroup already in progress or request discussion partners via an E-mail mailing list or via any one of the message board opportunities that are offered at many of the sites you have already explored. You might also establish a communication link among your classmates or with students in other schools who are taking a similar course.

Goals 2000	HIV/AIDS
teen pregnancies	effective schools
at-risk students	family stress
substance abuse	latchkey children
crime and violence in schools	youth suicide
school restructuring	school-based clinics
children in poverty	alternative schools

Formulate a research question concerning demographic aspects of students and their families, and go online to gather current national and state statistics on topics related to your question. For example, your question might relate to one or more of the above topics.

2. Develop a collaborative project with classmates to investigate and report on issues in drug abuse prevention, at-risk intervention, or violence prevention. Begin by exploring the U.S. government's Children Youth Family Research Network (CYFer-net). CYFer-net includes many databases and services, such as a Food and Nutrition Information Center and information about the Partnerships Against Violence program.

CYFer-net: Gopher: ace.esusda.gov

The CYFer-net also gives you access to information about the Office of Human Development Services; the Administration for Children, Youth, and Families; the Magnet Schools Assistance Program (MSAP); and the Head Start Bureau.

Observations and Interviews

1. Visit a school in your community recognized as successful or effective. What evidence do you find of the characteristics of successful schools (or successfully restructured schools) discussed in this chapter? Are there other characteristics you would add to the list based on your observations? To guide your observations and collaborate with classmates, ask your instructor for handout M4.1, "Observing Characteristics of Effective Schools."

2. Reflect on your experiences relating to social problems at the elementary, middle, or high school levels. Then gather statistics and information about how a local school or local school district is responding to the social problems discussed in this chapter. To help you identify the kind of information to gather, ask your instructor for handout M4.2, "Analyzing Impacts of Social Problems on Schools."

3. Obtain at least one statement of philosophy, or mission statement, from a school with which you are familiar. Analyze the statement(s), identifying and highlighting portions that refer to the major aims of education discussed in this chapter (national goals, prosocial values, socialization, achievement, personal growth, social change, and equal educational opportunity).

4. Write an essay describing the characteristics of an ideal school in which you would like to teach.

1. Analyze a school as a social institution. How is the school organized in terms of roles and statuses? How does the school's organization and functioning reflect the wider society as well as the community in which it is located? What characteristics of the school and its people relate to the urban, rural, or suburban nature of the school environment? Does the school match one of the four categories of schools identified by Jean Anyon on the basis of social class?

2. Develop a case study of a school's culture. Visit a local school or base your study on a school you have attended. Organize your case in terms of the following categories of information:

Environment: How would you describe the school facility or physical plant and its material and human resources? How is space organized? What is the climate of the school?

Formal Practices: What grades are included at the school? How is the school year organized? How is time structured? How are students and teachers grouped for instruction?

Traditions: What events and activities and products seem important to students, teachers, and administrators? What symbols, slogans, and ceremonies identify membership in the school? How do community members view and relate to the school?

Draw conclusions from your case study: What aspects of the school culture seem to support learning and academic achievement? On the basis of your case study, draft a position statement on the kind of culture you would like to create or promote in your classroom.

As a practical discipline, philosophy of education is an attempt to find the most rationally defensible reasons for doing education one way rather than some other.

—Foster McMurray
Concepts of Mind and Intelligence
in Educational Theory

chapter 5

Philosophical Foundations of American Education

F O C U S
Q U E S T I O N S

1. What determines your educational philosophy?

2. What are the branches of philosophy?

3. What are five modern philosophical orientations to teaching?

4. What psychological orientations have influenced teaching philosophies?

5. How can you develop your educational philosophy?

Eastside High School has ranked highest among the city's four high schools on the annual standardized test of basic skills for the last three years. Eastside is in a middle-income area of the city and has an enrollment of about 2,000 students.

Roberta Smith has been teaching English at Eastside for eight years. Roberta takes what she calls a critical approach to teaching—that is, she wants her students to learn the important role they can play in improving the world. To raise her students' level of awareness, Roberta has her students consider the role that race, socioeconomic status, and gender play in political events and in societal inequities. From time to time, Roberta organizes her students to take action to address social problems. Last week, for example, as part of a unit on the homeless in the city, her students spent a weekend helping at a neighborhood soup kitchen.

In the classroom, Roberta uses creative, occasionally risk-taking, strategies. Students often participate in small group projects, simulations, role-plays, and classroom debates on societal issues.

Many of Roberta's colleagues are skeptical about her methods. They believe her teaching is too political and that she does her students a disservice by making them believe that they can change the world. These teachers also point out that Eastside parents want their children to learn the traditional basics rather than learn how to become social activists.

Today in the teachers' lunchroom, Roberta and two other English teachers are discussing how they teach writing. "My kids really got involved in the unit on the homeless," Roberta says. "Now they're working hard to express in writing what they experienced last week at the soup kitchen. They believe they have something to say. Two of my kids even plan to send their papers to the editorial page of the newspaper."

"Well, I think that's pretty unrealistic," says the teacher seated across the table from Roberta. "That's not what our kids need to be doing—firing off letters to the editor, getting involved in all of these causes. We should just be teaching them how to write—period. Then if they want to focus on eliminating poverty, crime, or whatever, that should be their decision."

Do you agree or disagree with Roberta's approach to teaching? What do you think the purposes of education ought to be?

WHAT DETERMINES YOUR EDUCATIONAL PHILOSOPHY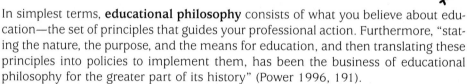

In simplest terms, **educational philosophy** consists of what you believe about education—the set of principles that guides your professional action. Furthermore, "stating the nature, the purpose, and the means for education, and then translating these principles into policies to implement them, has been the business of educational philosophy for the greater part of its history" (Power 1996, 191).

Every teacher, whether he or she recognizes it, has a philosophy of education—a set of beliefs about how human beings learn and grow and what one should learn in order to live the good life. Teachers differ, of course, in regard to the amount of effort they devote to the development of their personal philosophy or educational platform. Some feel that philosophical reflections have nothing to contribute to the actual act of teaching (this stance, of course, is itself a philosophy of education). Other teachers recognize that teaching, because it is concerned with *what ought to be,* is basically a philosophical enterprise. As the great educational philosopher John Dewey put it, to be concerned with education is to be concerned with philosophy: "If we are willing to conceive education as the process of forming fundamental dispositions, intellectual and emotional, toward nature and fellow men, philosophy may even be defined as *the general theory of education*" (1916, 383).

Educational philosophy is also vitally concerned with improving all aspects of teaching. By putting into practice their educational philosophy, teachers can discover the solutions to many educational problems. Five purposes that have been identified for educational philosophy clarify how it can contribute to these solutions:

1. Educational philosophy is committed to laying down a plan for what is considered to be the best education absolutely.
2. Educational philosophy undertakes to give directions with respect to the kind of education that is best in a certain political, social, and economic context.

3. Educational philosophy is preoccupied with correcting violations of educational principle and policy.
4. Educational philosophy centers attention on those issues in educational policy and practice that require resolution either by empirical research or rational re-examination.
5. Educational philosophy conducts an inquiry into the whole of the educational enterprise with a view toward assessing, justifying, and reforming the body of experience essential to superior learning (Power 1982, 15–16).

There is a strong connection between your behavior as a teacher and your beliefs about teaching and learning, students, knowledge, and what is worth knowing (see Figure 5.1). Regardless of where you stand in regard to these five dimensions of teaching, you should be aware of the need to reflect continually on *what* you do believe and *why* you believe it.

BELIEFS ABOUT TEACHING AND LEARNING

One of the most important components of your educational philosophy is how you view teaching and learning. In other words, what is the teacher's primary role? Is the teacher a subject matter expert who can efficiently and effectively impart knowledge to students? Is the teacher a helpful adult who establishes caring relationships with students and nurtures their growth in needed areas? Or is the teacher a skilled technician who can manage the learning of many students at once?

How each of us views the role of the teacher says a lot about our basic conception of teaching. Some people view teaching as a science—a complex activity that is, nevertheless, reducible to a specified set of discrete, objectively determined behaviors. For others, teaching is viewed as an art—a spontaneous, unrehearsed, and creative encounter between teacher and student. And for others, teaching is an activity that is both science and art; it requires the artistic (or intuitive) implementation of scientifically determined procedures.

In regard to learning, some teachers emphasize the individual student's experiences and cognitions. Others stress the student's behavior. Learning, according to the first viewpoint, is seen as the changes in thoughts or actions that result from personal experience; that is, learning is largely the result of internal forces within the individual. In contrast, the other view defines learning as the associations between

FIGURE 5.1 The influence of the teacher's educational beliefs on teaching behavior

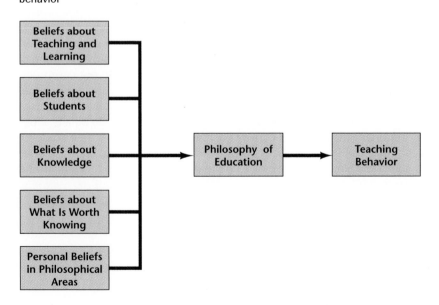

TABLE 5.1

New teachers' expectations of themselves and their students (in percent)

	Total Agree	Total Disagree
All children can learn	99	1
I can really make a difference in the lives of my students	99	1
If I do my job well, my students will benefit regardless of how the rest of the school functions	89	10
Many children come to school with so many problems that it's very difficult for them to be good students	75	25
Even the best teachers will find it difficult to really teach more than two-thirds of their students	45	54

*Less than 0.5%

(Source: Louis Harris and Associates. *The Metropolitan Life Survey of the American Teacher 1990: New Teachers: Expectations and Ideals, Part I: Entering the Classroom.* New York: Louis Harris and Associates, 1990, p. 1. Used with permission.)

various stimuli and responses. Here, learning results from forces that are external to the individual.

BELIEFS ABOUT STUDENTS

Your beliefs about students will have a great influence on how you teach. Every teacher formulates an image in his or her mind about what students are like—their dispositions, skills, motivation levels, and expectations. What you believe students are like is based on your unique life experiences, particularly your observations of young people and your knowledge of human growth and development.

Negative views of students may promote teacher-student relationships based on fear and coercion rather than on trust and helpfulness. Extremely positive views may risk not providing students with sufficient structure and direction and not communicating sufficiently high expectations. In the final analysis, the truly professional teacher—the one who has a carefully thought-out educational philosophy—recognizes that children differ in their predispositions to learn and grow. In regard to beliefs about students, it is important that teachers convey positive attitudes toward their students and a belief that they *can* learn. To assess your beliefs about students, compare your expectations about teaching with those of 1,002 teachers who began teaching in the fall of 1990 (see Table 5.1).

BELIEFS ABOUT KNOWLEDGE

Though it may not seem immediately obvious, how a teacher views knowledge is directly related to how he or she goes about teaching. If knowledge is viewed as the sum total of small bits of subject matter or discrete facts, students will most likely spend a great deal of time learning that information in a straightforward, rote manner. As students, we have all, at one time or another, been directed to memorize certain information: the capitals of the fifty states, definitions for the eight parts of speech, the periodic table in chemistry, and so on.

Other teachers view knowledge more conceptually, that is, as consisting of the big ideas that enable us to understand and influence our environment. Such a teacher would want students to be able to explain how legislative decisions are made in the state capital, how an understanding of the eight parts of speech can empower the writer and vitalize one's writing, and how chemical elements are grouped according to their atomic numbers.

Finally, teachers differ in their beliefs as to whether students' increased understanding of their own experiences is a legitimate form of knowledge. Knowledge of self and one's experiences in the world is not the same as knowledge about a particular subject, yet personal knowledge is essential for a full, satisfying life. Teachers who primarily view knowledge as that which enables the individual to confront and interpret the meaning of experience will present students with opportunities to develop that ability.

BELIEFS ABOUT WHAT IS WORTH KNOWING

Teachers want students to learn as a result of their efforts, though teachers differ in regard to what they believe should be taught. Teacher A feels that it is most important that students learn the basic skills of reading, writing, computation, and oral communication. These are the skills they will need to be successful in their chosen occupations, and it is the school's responsibility to prepare students for the world of work. Teacher B believes that the most worthwhile content is to be found in the classics or the Great Books. Through mastering the great ideas from the sciences, mathematics, literature, and history, students will be well prepared to deal with the world of the future. Teacher C is most concerned with students learning how to reason, communicate effectively, and solve problems. Students who master these cognitive processes will have learned how to learn—and this is the most realistic preparation for an unknown future. Teacher D is concerned with developing the whole child, teaching students to become self-actualizing persons. Thus, the content of the curriculum should be meaningful to the student, contributing as much as possible to the student's efforts to become a mature, well-integrated person. As Roberta and her colleagues illustrated in this chapter's opening scenario, there are no easy answers to the question "What knowledge is of most worth?" Your beliefs about teaching and learning, students, knowledge, and what knowledge is worth knowing, then, are the foundation of your educational philosophy.

WHAT ARE THE BRANCHES OF PHILOSOPHY ?

To provide you with further tools to use in formulating and clarifying your educational philosophy, this section presents brief overviews of six areas of philosophy that are of central concern to teachers: metaphysics, epistemology, axiology, ethics, aesthetics, and logic. Each of these areas focuses on one of the questions that have concerned the world's greatest philosophers for centuries: What is the nature of reality? What is the nature of knowledge and is truth ever attainable? According to what values should one live life? What is good and what is evil? What is the nature of beauty and excellence? and finally, What processes of reasoning will yield consistently valid results?

METAPHYSICS

Metaphysics is concerned with explaining, as rationally and as comprehensively as possible, the nature of reality (in contrast to how reality appears). What is reality? What is the world made of? These are metaphysical questions. Metaphysics also is concerned with the nature of being and explores questions such as, What does it mean to exist? What is humankind's place in the scheme of things? Metaphysical questions such as these are at the very heart of educational philosophy. As one educational philosopher put it, "nothing short of the fullest awareness possible of 'man's place in the cosmos' is the constant problem of the philosopher of education" (Bertocci 1956, 158). Or, as others put it: "Our ultimate preoccupation in edu-

Issues in Education

- What are some sources of teachers' educational philosophies in their personal backgrounds and educational experiences?
- How might teachers' personal philosophies influence teachers' beliefs about teaching and learning and beliefs about students?
- How might teachers' backgrounds and education influence their beliefs about what knowledge is and what is worth knowing?
- How can personal and professional beliefs and values from diverse sources be reconciled or integrated to create a coherent teaching philosophy?

cational theory is with the most primary of all philosophic problems: metaphysics, the study of ultimate reality" (Morris and Pai 1976, 28).

Metaphysics has important implications for education because the school curriculum is based on what we know about reality. And what we know about reality is driven by the kinds of questions we ask about the world. In fact, any position regarding what the schools should teach has behind it a particular view of reality, a particular set of responses to metaphysical questions.

EPISTEMOLOGY

The next major set of philosophical questions that concerns teachers is called **epistemology**. These questions all focus on knowledge: What knowledge is true? How does knowing take place? How do we know that we know? How do we decide between opposing views of knowledge? Is truth constant, or does it change from situation to situation? and finally, What knowledge is of most worth?

How you answer the epistemological questions that confront all teachers will have significant implications for your approach to curriculum and instruction. First, you will need to determine what is true about the content you will teach, then you must decide on the most appropriate means of conveying this content to students. Even a casual consideration of epistemological questions reveals that there are many ways of knowing about the world. We believe that there are at least five different ways of knowing that are of interest to teachers.

1. *Knowing based on authority:* People acquire knowledge from the sage, the poet, the priest, or the ruler. In schools, the textbook, the teacher, the administrator are the sources of authority for students. In everyday conversations, we refer to unnamed experts as sources of authoritative knowledge: *They* say we'll have a manned flight to Mars by the turn of the century.
2. *Knowing based on divine revelation:* Throughout human history, supernatural revelations have been a major source of knowledge about the world. Whether it be the sun god of early man, the many gods of the ancient Greeks, or the Judeo-Christian god, divine revelations have provided humans with knowledge about life.
3. *Knowing based on empiricism (experience):* The term *empirical* refers to knowledge acquired through the senses. When we state that experience is the best teacher, we refer to this mode of knowing. Informally gathered empirical data direct most of our daily behavior.
4. *Knowing based on reason:* We can also come to know things as a result of our ability to reason and use logical analysis. In schools, students learn to apply rational thought to such tasks as solving mathematical problems, distinguishing facts from opinions, or defending or refuting a particular argument. Many students also learn a method of reasoning and analyzing empirical data known as the scientific method. Through this method a problem is identified, relevant data are gathered, a hypothesis is formulated based on these data, and the hypothesis is empirically tested.
5. *Knowing based on intuition:* Just about everyone has at some time acquired knowledge through intuition, a nondiscursive (beyond reason) form of knowing. Intuition draws from our prior knowledge and experience and gives us an immediate understanding of the situation at hand. Our intuition convinces us that we know something, but we don't know how we know. Our intuitive sense would seem to be a mixture of instinct, emotion, and imagination.

AXIOLOGY

The next set of philosophical problems concerns values. Teachers are concerned with values because school is not a neutral activity. There is no school that is value-free; the very essence of school expresses a set of values. The social and individual decisions to provide and to undertake education are based on a set of values, and the daily activity of education is a value-laden one. We educate for some purpose we consider to be good, and what we teach is what we think is a good thing (Nelson, Carlson, and Palonsky 1996, 270).

Among the axiological questions teachers must answer for themselves are: What values should teachers encourage students to adopt? What values raise humanity to our highest expressions of humaneness? What values does a truly educated person hold?

In essence, **axiology** highlights the fact that the teacher has an interest not only in the *quantity* of knowledge that students acquire but also in the *quality* of life that becomes possible because of that knowledge. Extensive knowledge may not benefit the individual if he or she is unable to put that knowledge to good use. This point raises additional questions: How do we define quality of life? What curricular experiences contribute most to that quality of life? All teachers must deal with the issues raised by these questions.

ETHICS   Although axiology addresses the question "What is valuable?," **ethics** focuses on "What is good and evil, right and wrong, just and unjust?

A knowledge of ethics can help the teacher solve many of the dilemmas that arise in the classroom. Frequently, teachers must take action in situations where they are unable to gather all of the relevant facts and where no single course of action is totally right or wrong. For example, a student whose previous work was above average plagiarizes a term paper: Should the teacher fail the student for the course if the example of swift, decisive punishment will likely prevent other students from plagiarizing? Or should the teacher, following her hunches about what would be in the student's long-term interest, have the student redo the term paper and risk the possibility that other students might get the mistaken notion that plagiarism has no negative consequences? Another ethical dilemma: Is an elementary mathematics teacher justified in trying to increase achievement for the whole class by separating two disruptive girls and placing one in a mathematics group beneath her level of ability?

Ethics can provide the teacher with ways of thinking about problems where it is difficult to determine the right course of action. This branch of philosophy also helps the teacher to understand that "ethical thinking and decision making are not just following the rules" (Strike and Soltis 1985, 3).

AESTHETICS   The branch of axiology known as **aesthetics** is concerned with values related to beauty and art. Although we expect that teachers of music, art, drama, literature, and writing regularly have students make judgments about the quality of works of art, we can easily overlook the role that aesthetics ought to play in *all* areas of the curriculum. Harry Broudy, a well-known educational philosopher, said that the arts are necessary, not "just nice" (1979, 347–350). Through the heightening of their aesthetic perceptions, students can find increased meaning in all aspects of life.

Aesthetics can also help the teacher increase his or her effectiveness. Teaching, because it may be viewed as a form of artistic expression, can be judged accord-

- **Treat all thoughts as in need of development.**
- **Respond to all answers with a further question (that calls upon the respondent to develop his thinking in a fuller and deeper way).**
- **Treat all assertions as a connecting point to further thoughts.**
- **Recognize that any thought can only exist fully in a network of connected thoughts. Stimulate students—by your questions—to pursue those connections.**
- **Seek to understand—where possible—the ultimate foundations for what is said or believed.**
- **Recognize that all questions presuppose prior questions and all thinking presupposes prior thinking. When raising questions, be open to the questions they presuppose.**

FIGURE 5.2 The spirit and principles of Socratic questioning (Source: Richard Paul and Linda Elder, "The Art of Socratic Questioning," *Critical Thinking*, Fall 1995, 16.)

ing to artistic standards of beauty and quality (Parkay 1983, April). In this regard, the teacher is an artist and continually tries to improve the quality of his or her work.

LOGIC

If all the parties who have a genuine interest in education were to decide on a single goal that schools ought to strive for, it would most likely be to teach students how to think. Our extensive ability for various kinds of thinking is, after all, one of the major differences between us and other forms of animal life. **Logic** is the area of philosophy that deals with the process of reasoning and identifies rules that will enable the thinker to reach valid conclusions.

The two kinds of logical thinking processes that teachers most frequently have students master are *deductive* and *inductive* thinking. The deductive approach requires the thinker to move from a general principle or proposition to a specific conclusion that is valid. Inductive reasoning moves from the particular to the general rather than from the general to the particular. Here, the student begins by examining particular examples that eventually lead to the acceptance of a general proposition. Inductive teaching is often referred to as discovery teaching—where students discover, or create, their own knowledge of a topic.

Perhaps the best-known teacher to use the inductive approach to teaching was the Greek philosopher Socrates. His method of teaching, known today as the Socratic method, consisted of holding philosophical conversations (dialectics) with his pupils. The legacy of Socrates lives in all teachers who use his questioning strategies to encourage students to think for themselves. Figure 5.2 presents guidelines for using Socratic questioning techniques in the classroom.

The six areas of philosophy that we have examined briefly in the preceding pages—metaphysics, epistemology, axiology, ethics, aesthetics, and logic—represent the mental tools that teachers can use for thinking about various aspects of teaching.

WHAT ARE FIVE MODERN PHILOSOPHICAL ORIENTATIONS TO TEACHING ⟨?⟩

Five major coherent philosophical orientations to teaching have been developed in response to the questions concerning metaphysics, epistemology, axiology, ethics, aesthetics, and logic, with which all teachers must grapple. These orientations, or schools of thought, are progressivism, perennialism, essentialism, social reconstructionism, and existentialism (see Figure 5.3 on page 140). A brief description of each of these orientations is presented in the following sections. At the end of each description, we present a sample portrait of a teacher whose behavior illustrates that philosophical orientation in action.

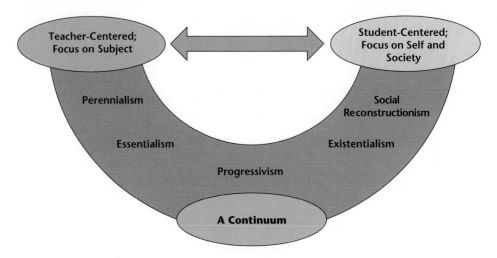

FIGURE 5.3 Five philosophical orientations to teaching

PROGRESSIVISM

Progressivism is based on the belief that education should be child-centered rather than focused on the teacher or the content area. As we learned in Chapter 3, John Dewey's writings in the 1920s and 1930s contributed a great deal to the spread of progressive ideas. Briefly, Deweyan progressivism is based on the following six assumptions:

1. The content of the curriculum ought to be derived from students' interests rather than from the academic disciplines.
2. Effective teaching takes into account the whole child and his or her interests and needs in relation to cognitive, affective, and psychomotor areas.
3. Learning is essentially active rather than passive. Effective teachers provide students with experiences that enable them to learn by doing.
4. The aim of education is to teach students to think rationally so that they may become intelligent, contributing members of society.
5. At school, students learn personal, as well as social, values.
6. Humankind is in a constant state of change, and education makes possible a future that is better than the past.

PROGRESSIVE STRATEGIES   The progressive philosophy also contends that knowledge that is true in the present may not be true in the future. Hence, the best way to prepare students for an unknown future is to equip them with problem-solving strategies that will enable them to cope with new challenges in life and to discover what truths are relevant to the present. Through continual self-analysis and reflection, the individual can identify values that are appropriate for the immediate moment.

Progressives feel that life is evolving in a positive direction and that human beings, young as well as adult, are good and may be trusted to act in their own best interests. In this regard, educators with a progressive orientation give students a considerable amount of freedom in determining their school experiences. Contrary to the perceptions of many, though, progressive education does not mean that teachers do not provide structure or that students are free to do whatever they wish. Progressive teachers begin with where students are and, through the daily give-and-take of the classroom, lead students to see that the subject to be learned can enhance their lives.

The teacher's role in a progressively oriented classroom is to serve as a guide or resource person whose primary responsibility is to facilitate student learning. The teacher is concerned with helping students learn what is important to them rather than passing on a set of so-called enduring truths. Toward this end, the progressive teacher tries to provide students with experiences that replicate everyday life as much as possible. Students are given many opportunities to work cooperatively in groups, often solving problems that the group, not the teacher, has identified as important.

PORTRAIT OF A PROGRESSIVE TEACHER   Mr. Barkan teaches social studies at a middle school in a well-to-do part of the city. Boyishly handsome and in his mid-thirties, Mr. Barkan usually works in casual attire—khaki pants, soft-soled shoes, and a sports shirt. He seems to get along well with students. Mr. Barkan likes to give students as much freedom of choice in the classroom as possible. Accordingly, his room is divided up into interest and activity centers, and much of the time students are free to choose where they want to spend their time. One corner at the back of the room has a library collection of paperback and hardcover books, an easy chair, and an area rug; the other back corner of the room is set up as a project area and has a worktable on which are several globes, maps, large sheets of newsprint, and assorted drawing materials. At the front of the room in one corner is a small media center with three cassette tape recorders with headphones, a CD player, television with VCR, and a computer.

Mr. Barkan makes it a point to establish warm, supportive relationships with his students. He is proud of the fact that he is a friend to his students. "I really like the kids I teach," he says in a soft, gentle voice. "They're basically good kids, and they really want to learn if we— teachers, I mean—can just keep their curiosity alive and not try to force them to learn. It's up to us as teachers to capitalize on their interests."

The visitor to Mr. Barkan's class today can sense his obvious regard for students. He

What hallmarks of progressive education are evident in this photograph of one of the first classrooms in the country operated according to Dewey's philosophy? How would a progressive classroom look today?

is genuinely concerned about the growth and nurturance of each one. As his students spend most of their time working in small groups at the various activity centers in the room, Mr. Barkan divides his time among the groups. He moves from group to group and seems to immerse himself as an equal participant in each group's task. One group, for example, has been working on making a papier-mâché globe. Several students are explaining animatedly to him how they plan to transfer the flat map of the world they have drawn to the smooth sphere they have fashioned out of the papier-mâché. Mr. Barkan listens carefully to what his students have to say and then congratulates the group on how cleverly they have engineered the project. When he speaks to his students he does so in a matter-of-fact, conversational tone, as though speaking to other adults.

As much as possible he likes to bring textbook knowledge to life by providing his students with appropriate experiences—field trips, small-group projects, simulation activities, role-playing, internet explorations, and so on. Mr. Barkan believes that his primary function as a teacher is to prepare his students for an unknown future. Learning to solve problems at an early age is the best preparation for this future, he feels.

> The increase in the amount of knowledge each decade is absolutely astounding. What we teach students as true today will most likely not be true tomorrow. Therefore, students have to learn how to learn and become active problem solvers. In addition, students need to learn how to identify problems that are meaningful to them. It doesn't make much sense to learn to solve problems that belong to someone else.

> To accomplish these things in the classroom, teachers have to be willing to take the lead from the students themselves—to use their lives as a point of departure for learning about the subject. What this requires of the teacher is that he or she be willing to set up the classroom along the lines of a democracy, a close community of learners whose major purpose for being there is to learn. You can't create that kind of classroom atmosphere by being a taskmaster and trying to force kids to learn. If you can trust them and let them set their own directions, they'll respond.

PERENNIALISM

Perennialism, as the term implies, views truth as constant, or perennial. The aim of education, according to perennialist thinking, is to ensure that students acquire knowledge of these unchanging principles or great ideas. Perennialists also believe that the natural world and human nature have remained basically unchanged over the centuries; thus, the great ideas continue to have the most potential for solving the problems of any era. Furthermore, the perennialist philosophy emphasizes the rational thinking abilities of human beings; it is the cultivation of the intellect that makes human beings truly human and differentiates them from other animals.

The curriculum, according to the perennialists, should stress students' intellectual growth in the arts and sciences. To become "culturally literate," students should encounter in these areas the best, most significant works that humans have created. In regard to any area of the curriculum, only one question needs to be asked: Are students acquiring content that represents the human race's most lofty accomplishments in that area? Thus, a high school English teacher would require students to read Melville's *Moby Dick* or any of Shakespeare's plays rather than a novel on the current best-seller list. Similarly, science students would learn about the three laws of motion or the three laws of thermodynamics rather than build a model of the space shuttle.

Robert Maynard
Hutchins

PERENNIALIST EDUCATIONAL PHILOSOPHERS   Two of the best known advocates of the perennialist philosophy have been Robert Maynard Hutchins and, more recently, Mortimer Adler. As president of the University of Chicago, Hutchins (1963) developed an undergraduate curriculum based on the study of the Great Books and discussions of these classics in small seminars. Hutchins's perennialist curriculum was based on three assumptions about education:

1. Education must promote humankind's continuing search for truth. Whatever is true will always, and everywhere, be true; in short, truth is universal and timeless.
2. Because the mind's work is intellectual and focuses on ideas, education must also focus on ideas. The cultivation of human rationality is the essential function of education.
3. Education should stimulate students to think thoughtfully about significant ideas. Teachers should use correct and critical thinking as their primary method, and they should require the same of students.

Noted educational philosopher Mortimer Adler, along with Hutchins, was instrumental in organizing the Great Books of the Western World curriculum. Through the study of over 100 enduring classics, from Plato to Einstein, the Great Books approach aims at the major perennialist goal of teaching students to become independent and critical thinkers. It is a demanding curriculum, and it focuses on the enduring disciplines of knowledge rather than on current events or student interests.

PORTRAIT OF A PERENNIALIST TEACHER   Mrs. Bernstein has been teaching English at the high school since the mid-1960s. Among students and teachers as well, she has a reputation for demanding a lot. As one student put it, "You don't waste time in Mrs. Bernstein's classes."

During the early 1970s, she had a difficult time dealing with students who aggressively insisted on being taught subjects that were "relevant." As a graduate of a top-notch university in the East where she received a classical, liberal education, Mrs. Bernstein refused to lessen the emphasis in her classes on great works of literature that she felt students needed to know, such as Beowulf, Chaucer, Dickens, and Shakespeare.

As far as her approach to classroom management is concerned, one student sums it up this way: "She doesn't let you get by with a thing; she never slacks off on the pressure. She lets you know that she's there to teach and you're there to learn." Mrs. Bernstein believes that hard work and effort are necessary if one is to get a good education. As a result, she gives students very few opportunities to misbehave, and she appears to be immune to the grumblings of students who do complain openly about the workload.

She becomes very animated when she talks about the value of the classics to students who are preparing to live as adults in the twenty-first century:

> The classics are unequaled in terms of the insights they can give students into the major problems that they will have to deal with during their lifetimes. Though our civilization has made impressive technological advances during the last two centuries, we have not really progressed that much in terms of improving the quality of our lives as human beings. The observations of a Shakespeare or a Dickens on the human condition are just as relevant today as they were when they were alive.

Perennialist teachers often inspire students to seek truth, discover universalities in human experience, and celebrate the achievements of human civilizations. How might this music lesson reflect perennialist ideas? How might the lesson be different if it were based on the educational philosophy of essentialism?

ESSENTIALISM

William C. Bagley

Essentialism is a conservative philosophy of education that was originally formulated as a criticism of progressive trends in schools. William C. Bagley (1874–1946), a professor of education at Teachers College, Columbia University, was the founder of the Essentialistic Education Society. To promote the essentialist philosophy, he founded the educational journal, *School and Society.*

Bagley and several other like-minded educators had become very critical of progressive educational practices, contending that the movement had damaged intellectual and moral standards among young people (Bagley 1934). Following World War II, criticism of progressive education became even more widespread and seemed to point to one conclusion: Schools were failing in their task of transmitting the country's social and intellectual heritage.

Essentialism, which has some similarities to perennialism, holds that our culture has a core of common knowledge that the schools are obligated to transmit to students in a systematic, disciplined way. Unlike perennialism, which emphasizes a set of external truths, essentialism stresses what advocates believe to be the essential knowledge and skills that productive members of our society need to know. Several books have been written that lament the decline of rigorous schooling in the United States and call for an essentialist approach to schooling. Among them have been James D. Koerner's *The Case for Basic Education* (1959), H. G. Rickover's *Education and Freedom* (1959), and Paul Copperman's *The Literacy Hoax: The Decline of Reading, Writing, and Learning in the Public Schools and What We Can Do about It* (1978).

According to essentialist philosophy, schooling should be practical and provide children with sound instruction that prepares them to live life; schools should not try to influence or set social policies. Critics of essentialism, however, charge that such a tradition-bound orientation to schooling will indoctrinate students and rule out the possibility of change. Essentialists respond that, without an essentialist approach, students will be indoctrinated in humanistic and/or behavioral curricula that run counter to society's accepted standards and need for order.

THE BACK-TO-BASICS MOVEMENT The **back-to-basics movement** that began in the mid-1970s is the most recent large-scale push to install essentialist programs in the schools. Above all else, the essentialists contend, the schools must train students to communicate clearly and logically. The core skills in the curriculum should be reading, writing, speaking, and computation, and the school has the responsibility for seeing that all students master these skills.

The essentialist curriculum emphasizes the teaching of facts; it has little patience with the indirect, introspective approaches promoted by progressivism. Some essentialists even view the arts and humanities as frills and feel that the hard sciences and technical and vocational courses are the true essentials that students need in order to contribute to society.

Though the essentialist educator does not view the child as evil, neither does he or she view the child as naturally good. Unless children are actively and vigorously taught the value of discipline, hard work, and respect for authority, they will not become valuable members of society. The teacher's role, then, is to shape children, to hold their natural, nonproductive instincts (e.g., aggression, mindless gratification of the senses, etc.) in check until their education has been completed.

PORTRAIT OF AN ESSENTIALIST TEACHER Mr. Samuels teaches mathematics at a junior high school in a poor section of a major urban area. Prior to coming to this school six years ago, he taught at a rural elementary school.

Middle-aged and highly energetic, Mr. Samuels is known around the school as a hardworking, dedicated teacher. His commitment to children is especially evident when he talks about preparing "his" children for life in high school and beyond. "A lot of teachers nowadays have given up on kids," he says with a touch of sadness to his voice. "They don't demand much of them. If we don't push kids now to get the knowledge and skills they're going to need later in life, we've failed them. My main purpose here is to see that my kids get the basics they're going to need."

Mr. Samuels has made it known that he does not approve of the methods used by some of the younger, more humanistically oriented teachers in the school. At a recent faculty meeting, for example, he was openly critical of some teachers' tendency to let students do their own thing and spend time expressing their feelings. He called for all teachers to focus their energies on getting students to master subject-matter content, "the things kids will need to know," rather than on helping students adjust to the interpersonal aspects of school life. He also reminded everyone that "kids come to school to learn." All students would learn, he pointed out, if "teachers based their methods on good, sound approaches that have always worked—not on the so-called innovative approaches that are based on fads and frills."

Mr. Samuels's students have accepted his no-nonsense approach to teaching. With few exceptions, his classes are orderly, business-like operations. Each class period follows a standard routine. Students enter the room quietly and take their seats with a minimum of the foolishness and horseplay that mark the start of many other classes in the school. As the first order of business, the previous day's homework is returned and reviewed. Following this, Mr. Samuels presents the day's lesson, usually a fifteen- to twenty-minute explanation of how to solve a particular kind of math problem. His mini-lectures are lively, and his wide-ranging tone of voice and animated, spontaneous delivery convey his excitement about the material and his belief that students can learn. During large-group instruction, Mr. Samuels also makes ample use of the blackboard, overhead transparencies, and various manipulatives such as a large abacus and colored blocks of different sizes and shapes.

SOCIAL RECONSTRUCTIONISM

As the name implies, **social reconstructionism** holds that schools should take the lead in changing or reconstructing the current social order. Theodore Brameld (1904–1987), acknowledged as the founder of social reconstructionism, bases his philosophy on two fundamental premises about the post-World War II era: (1) We live in a period of great crisis, most evident in the fact that humans now have the capability of destroying civilization overnight, and (2) Humankind also has the intellectual, technological, and moral potential to create a world civilization of "abundance, health, and humane capacity" (Brameld 1959, 19). In this time of great need, then, the schools should become the primary agent for planning and directing social change. As Caroline Pratt, an influential social reconstructionist of the period, stated: "a school's greatest value must be to turn out human beings who could think effectively and work constructively, who could in time make a better world than this for living in" (1948, 17). In short, schools should not only *transmit* knowledge about the existing social order; they should seek to *reconstruct* it as well.

SOCIAL RECONSTRUCTIONISM AND PROGRESSIVISM Social reconstructionism has clear ties to progressive educational philosophy. Both attach primary importance to the kind of experiences students have. Pratt's work, for example, illustrated the union of social reconstructionism and progressivism. In her book, *I Learn From Children,* she stated that the City and Country School she founded in New York City in 1914 would "try to fit the school to the child, rather than as we were doing with indifferent success—fitting the child to the school" (1948, 8). The classroom should be characterized by extensive interactions between teacher and students and among students themselves. Furthermore, both social reconstructionism and progressivism place a premium on bringing the community, if not the entire world, into the classroom. Student experiences often include field trips, community-based projects of various sorts, and opportunities to interact with persons beyond the four walls of the classroom.

Through a social reconstructionist approach to education, students learn appropriate methods for dealing with the significant crises that confront the world: war, economic depression, international terrorism, hunger, inflation, and ever-accelerating technological advances. The curriculum is arranged to highlight the need for various social reforms and, whenever possible, allow students to have firsthand experiences in reform activities. Teachers realize that they can play a significant role in the control and resolution of these problems, that they and their students need not be buffeted about like pawns by these crises.

According to Brameld and social reconstructionists such as George Counts, the educative process should be based on a continuous quest for a better society. The logical outcome of this quest would be the eventual realization of a world-wide democracy (Brameld 1956). Unless we actively seek to create this kind of world through the intelligent application of present knowledge, we run the risk that the destructive forces of the world will determine the conditions under which humans will live in the future.

George S. Counts

Keepers of the Dream

Paulo Freire (1921–1997)

Educational and Political Philosopher

Paulo Freire first expressed his dream to free people trapped in poverty when he was eleven. The famous educational and political philosopher's first years were spent in the comfort of the Brazilian middle class. He encountered poverty when his father lost his job as a military officer during the economic crisis of 1929 (Smith and Smith 1994). Then, as one of his biographers, Richard Shaull, reports, "He came to know the gnawing pangs of hunger and fell behind in school because of the listlessness it produced; it also led him to make a vow, at age eleven, to dedicate his life to the struggle against hunger, so that other children would not have to know the agony he was then experiencing" (Freire 1970, 10).

The experience of living in poverty helped Freire to understand and later write about what he described as "'the culture of silence' of the dispossessed" (Freire 1970, 10). The poor's lack of voice and effort to better themselves he attributed to the physical conditions of poverty and to a deep sense that they were not entitled to move beyond their plight. Freire also believed that the political powers, with the help of the education system, used paternalism to perpetuate the inequality of opportunity. "Rather than being encouraged and equipped to know and respond to the concrete realities of their world, they (poor students) were kept 'submerged' in a situation in which such critical awareness and response were practically impossible" (Freire 1970, 11).

Freire regarded education, and particularly literacy, as the best means of changing the system. He began by extending his own education, studying the thoughts of an international array of philosophers, psychologists, and political thinkers, including Jean-Paul Sartre, Eric Fromm,

"Knowledge emerges only through invention and re-invention. . . ."

and Martin Luther King, Jr. As he did so he created and developed a philosophy of education, which he presented in his University of Recife doctoral dissertation in 1959 and more fully in his now internationally famous book, *Pedagogy of the Oppressed*.

The key premise of his *Pedagogy of the Oppressed* is that "human interaction rarely escapes oppression of one kind or another; by reason of class, race, or gender, people tend to be victims and/or perpetrators of oppression" (Torres 1994, 181). Freire proposed to resist this human tendency in order to improve the human condition for both oppressors and the oppressed and to do so through education. His educational approach "calls for dialogue and ultimately conscientization—critical consciousness or awareness—as a way to overcome relationships of domination and oppression" (Torres 1994, 187).

Freire stressed the significance of dialogue in his pedagogy and contrasted it with the traditional teacher–student relationship, which he described using a banking concept of education, in which teachers deposit their expertise into empty accounts (their students). Freire recognized that "projecting an absolute ignorance onto others, a characteristic of the ideology of oppression, negates education and knowledge as processes of inquiry" (Freire 1970, 58). Freire's pedagogy instead affirmed what Piaget, Vygotsky, and the current advocates of constructionism support, that "knowledge emerges only through invention and re-invention, through the restless, impatient, continuing, hopeful inquiry (people) pursue in the world, with the world, and with each other" (Freire 1970, 58).

The effectiveness of this pedagogy when it was first applied to poor and illiterate adults in Northern Brazil was so great that Freire was regarded as a threat to the existing political order. He was imprisoned and then exiled. Today his ideas have spread far beyond Brazil, and "his new analyses about the role of liberatory pedagogy in advanced industrial societies are important subjects for debate and pedagogical thinking" (Torres 1994, 186).

PORTRAIT OF A SOCIAL RECONSTRUCTIONIST TEACHER At the urban high school where she teaches social studies and history, Martha Perkins has the reputation for being a social activist. On first meeting her, she presents a casual and laid-back demeanor. Her soft voice and warm smile belie the intensity of her convictions about pressing world issues, from international terrorism and hunger to peaceful uses of space and the need for all humans to work toward a global community.

During the early 1970s, Martha participated as a high school student in several protests against the war in Vietnam. This also marked the beginning of her increased awareness of social injustice in general. Like many young people of that era, Martha vigorously supported a curriculum that focused on students understanding these inequities and identifying resources that might eliminate them from society. Before she graduated from high school, Martha had formulated a vision of a healthier, more just society, and she vowed to do what she could to make that vision become a reality during her lifetime.

Martha feels strongly about the importance of having students learn about social problems as well as discovering what they can *do* about them. "It's really almost immoral if I confront my students with a social problem and then we fail to do anything about it," she says. "Part of my responsibility as a teacher is to raise the consciousness level of my students in regard to the problems that confront all human beings. I want them to leave my class with the realization that they *can* make a difference when it comes to making the world a more humane place."

For Martha to achieve her goals as a teacher, she frequently has to tackle controversial issues—issues that many of her colleagues avoid in the classroom. She feels that students would not learn how to cope with problems or controversy if she were to avoid them.

> I'm not afraid of controversy. When confronted with controversy, some teachers do retreat to the safety of the more "neutral" academic discipline. However, I try to get my students to see how they can use the knowledge of the discipline to attack the problem. So far, I've gotten good support from the principal. She's backed me up on several controversial issues that we've looked at in class: the nuclear energy plant that was to be built here in this county, the right to die, and absentee landlords who own property in the poorer sections of the city.

EXISTENTIALISM

Existential philosophy is unique in that it focuses on the experiences of the individual. Other philosophies are concerned with developing systems of thought for identifying and understanding what is common to *all* reality, human existence, and values. **Existentialism**, on the other hand, offers the individual a way of thinking about *my* life, what has meaning for *me*, what is true for *me*. In general, existentialism emphasizes creative choice, the subjectivity of human experiences, and concrete acts of human existence over any rational scheme for human nature or reality.

The writings of Jean-Paul Sartre (1905–1980), well-known French philosopher, novelist, and playwright, have been most responsible for the widespread dissemination of existential ideas. According to Sartre, every individual first exists and then he or she must decide what that existence is to mean. The task of assigning meaning to that existence is the individual's alone; no preformulated philosophical belief system can tell one who one is. It is up to each of us to decide who we are. According to Sartre, "Existence precedes essence. . . .First of all, man exists, turns up, appears on the scene, and, only afterwards, defines himself" (1972, 98).

Jean-Paul Sartre

TWO EXISTENTIALIST VIEWS   There are two schools of existential thought—one *theistic,* the other *atheistic.* Most of those belonging to the first school refer to themselves as Christian Existentialists and point out that humankind has a longing for an ultimate being, for God. Though this longing does not prove the existence of God, people can freely choose to live their lives as if there is a God (Morris and Pai 1976, 259–260). The Spanish philosopher Miguel de Unamuno expresses this position well: "Let life be lived in such a way, with such dedication to goodness and the highest values, that if, after all, it is annihilation which finally awaits us, that will be an injustice" (quoted in Morris and Pai 1976, 260).

Most existentialists, however, point out that it is demeaning to the human condition to say that we must entertain a fantasy in order to live a life of moral responsibility. Such a stance absolves humans of the responsibility for dealing with the complete freedom of choice that we all have. It also causes them to avoid the inescapable fact that "we are alone, with no excuses," and that "we are condemned to be free" (Sarte 1972, 101).

Life, according to existential thought, has no meaning, and the universe is indifferent to the situation humankind finds itself in. With the freedom that we have, however, each of us must commit ourselves to assign meaning to *our* life. As Maxine Greene, an eminent philosopher of education whose work is based on existentialism, states: "We have to know about our lives, clarify our situations if we are to understand the world from our shared standpoints . . . " (1995, 21). The human enterprise that can be most helpful in promoting this personal quest for meaning is the educative process. Teachers, therefore, must allow students freedom of choice and provide them with experiences that will help them find the meaning of their lives. This approach, contrary to the belief of many, does not mean that students may do whatever they please; logic indicates that freedom has rules, and respect for the freedom of others is essential.

Existentialists judge the curriculum according to whether or not it contributes to the individual's quest for meaning and results in a level of personal awareness that Greene terms "wide-awakeness." The ideal curriculum is one that provides students with extensive individual freedom and requires them to ask their own questions, conduct their own inquiries, and draw their own conclusions.

PORTRAIT OF AN EXISTENTIALIST TEACHER   Right after he first started teaching English eight years ago at a suburban high school, Fred Winston began to have doubts about the value of what he was teaching students. Although he could see a limited, practical use for the knowledge and skills he was teaching, he felt he was doing little to help his students answer the most pressing questions of their lives. Also, Fred had to admit to himself that he had grown somewhat bored with following the narrow, unimaginative Board of Education curriculum guides.

During the next eight years Fred gradually developed a style of teaching that placed emphasis on students finding out who they are. He continued to teach the knowledge and skills he was required to teach, but he made it clear that what students learned from him they should use to answer questions that were important to them. Now, for example, he often gives writing assignments that encourage students to look within in order to develop greater self-knowledge. He often uses assigned literature as a springboard for values clarification discussions. And, whenever possible, he gives his students the freedom to pursue individual reading and writing projects. His only requirement is that students be meaningfully involved in whatever they do.

Fred is also keenly aware of how the questions his students are just beginning to grapple with are questions that he is still, even in his mid-thirties, trying to answer for himself. Thoughtfully and with obvious care for selecting the correct words, he sums up the goals that he has for his students:

> I think kids should realize that the really important questions in life are beyond definitive answers, and they should be very suspicious of anyone—teacher, philosopher, or member of organized religion—who purports to have the answers. As human beings, each of us faces the central task of finding *our own* answers to such questions. My students know that I'm wrestling with the same questions they're working on. But I think I've taught them well enough so that they know that my answers can't be their answers.

Fred's approach to teaching is perhaps summed up by the bumper sticker on the sports car he drives: "Question authority." Unlike many of his fellow teachers, he wants his students to react critically and skeptically to what he teaches them. He also presses them to think thoughtfully and courageously about the meaning of life, beauty, love, and death. He judges his effectiveness by the extent to which students are able and willing to become more aware of the choices that are open to them.

WHAT PSYCHOLOGICAL ORIENTATIONS HAVE INFLUENCED TEACHING PHILOSOPHIES ?

In addition to the five philosophical orientations to teaching described in previous sections of this chapter, several schools of psychological thought have formed the basis for teaching philosophies. These psychological theories are comprehensive world views that serve as the basis for the way many teachers approach teaching practice. Psychological orientations to teaching are concerned primarily with understanding the conditions that are associated with effective learning. In other words, what motivates students to learn? What environments are most conducive to learning? Chief among the psychological orientations that have influenced teaching philosophies are humanistic psychology, behaviorism, and constructivism.

HUMANISTIC PSYCHOLOGY

Humanistic psychology emphasizes personal freedom, choice, awareness, and personal responsibility. As the term implies, it also focuses on the achievements, motivation, feelings, actions, and needs of human beings. The goal of education, according to this orientation, is individual self-actualization.

Humanistic psychology is derived from the philosophy of **humanism,** which developed during the European Renaissance and Protestant Reformation and is based on the belief that individuals control their own destinies through the application of their intelligence and learning. People "make themselves." The term "secular humanism" refers to the closely related belief that the conditions of human existence relate to human nature and human actions rather than to predestination or divine intervention. Later expressions of humanism included Jean Jacques Rousseau's child-centered educational theories, in which children were to be viewed as naturally good individuals who learn best in nurturing environments (see Chapter 3).

In the 1950s and 1960s, humanistic psychology became the basis of educational reforms that sought to enhance students' achievement of their full potential through self-actualization (Maslow, 1954, 1962; Rogers, 1961). According to this psychological orientation, teachers should not force students to learn; instead, they should create a climate of trust and respect that allows students to decide what and how they learn, to question authority, and to take initiative in "making themselves."

Teachers should be what noted psychologist Carl Rogers calls "facilitators," and the classroom should be a place "in which curiosity and the natural desire to learn can be nourished and enhanced" (1982, p. 31). Through their nonjudgmental understanding of students, humanistic teachers encourage students to learn and grow.

As an example of a humanist teacher, consider Carol Alexander, who ten years ago began teaching at a small rural middle school—a position she enjoys because the school's small size enables her to develop close relationships with her students and their families. Her teaching style is based on humane, open interpersonal relationships with her students, and she takes pride in the fact that students trust her and frequently ask her advice on problems common to children in early adolescence. The positive rapport Carol has developed with her students is reflected in the regularity with which former students return to visit or to seek her advice.

Carol is also committed to empowering her students, to giving them opportunities to shape their learning experiences. As she puts it: "I encourage students to give me feedback about how they feel in my classroom. They have to feel good about themselves before they can learn. Also, I've come to realize that students should help us (teachers) plan. I've learned to ask them what they're interested in. 'What do you want to do?' 'How do you want to do it?' "

Much of Carol's teaching is based on classroom discussions in which she encourages students to share openly their ideas and feelings about the subject at hand. Carol's interactions with students reveal her skill at creating a conversational environment that makes students feel safe and willing to contribute. During discussions, Carol listens attentively to students and frequently paraphrases their ideas in a way that acknowledges their contributions. She frequently responds with short phrases that indicate support and encourage the student to continue the discussion such as the following: "I see . . . " "Would you say more about that?" "That is an interesting idea, tell us more."

When Carol is not facilitating a whole-group discussion, she is more than likely moving among the small cooperative-learning groups she has set up. Each group decided how to organize itself to accomplish a particular learning task—developing a strategy for responding to a threat to the environment or analyzing a poem about brotherhood, for example. "I think it's important for students to learn to work together, to help one another, and to accept different points of view," says Carol.

BEHAVIORISM

Behaviorism is based on the principle that desirable human behavior can be the product of design rather than accident. According to behaviorists, it is an illusion to say that humans have a free will. Although we may act as if we are free, our behavior is really *determined* by forces in the environment that shape our behavior. "We are what we are and we do what we do, not because of any mysterious power of human volition, but because outside forces over which we lack any semblance of control have us caught in an inflexible web. Whatever else we may be, we are not the captains of our fate or the masters of our soul" (Power 1982, 168).

B. F. Skinner

FOUNDERS OF BEHAVIORISTIC PSYCHOLOGY   John B. Watson (1878–1958) was the principal originator of behavioristic psychology and B. F. Skinner (1904–1990) its best-known promoter. Watson first claimed that human behavior consisted of specific stimuli that resulted in certain responses. In part, he based this new conception of learning on the classic experiment conducted by Russian psychologist Ivan Pavlov (1849–1936). Pavlov had noticed that a dog he was working with would salivate when

How might you explain what is happening in this classroom from the perspective of humanistic psychology? from the perspective of behavioral psychology? from the perspective of cognitive constructivism?

it was about to be given food. By introducing the sound of a bell when food was offered and repeating this several times, Pavlov discovered that the sound of the bell alone (a conditioned stimulus) would make the dog salivate (a conditioned response). Watson was so confident that all learning conformed to this basic stimulus-response model (now termed classical or type S conditioning) that he once boasted, "Give me a dozen healthy infants, well-formed, and my own specified world to bring them up in, and I'll guarantee to take any one at random and train him to become any type of specialist I might select—doctor, lawyer, artist, merchant-chief and, yes, even beggar-man and thief, regardless of his talents, penchants, tendencies, abilities, vocations, and race of his ancestors" (1925, 82).

Skinner went beyond Watson's basic stimulus-response model and developed a more comprehensive view of conditioning known as operant (or type R) conditioning. Operant conditioning is based on the idea that satisfying responses are conditioned, unsatisfying ones are not. In other words, "The things we call pleasant have an energizing or strengthening effect on our behaviour" (Skinner 1972, 74). For the teacher, this means that desired student behavior should be reinforced, undesired behavior should not. Also, the teacher should be concerned with changing students' behavior rather than trying to alter their mental states.

In his novel *Walden Two* (1962), Skinner portrayed how "behavioral engineering" could lead to the creation of a utopian society. The book describes how a community with a desirable social order was created by design rather than by accident. In much the same way, educators can create learners who exhibit desired behaviors by carefully and scientifically controlling the educative process. The teacher need merely recognize that all learning is conditioning and adhere to the following four steps:

1. Identify desired behaviors in concrete (observable and measurable) terms.
2. Establish a procedure for recording specific behaviors and counting their frequencies.
3. For each behavior, identify an appropriate reinforcer.
4. Ensure that students receive the reinforcer as soon as possible after displaying a desired behavior.

PORTRAIT OF A BEHAVIORIST TEACHER   Jane Day teaches fourth grade at a school with an enrollment of about 500 in a small Midwestern town. Now in her fifth year at the school, Jane has spent the last three years developing and refining a systematic approach to teaching. Last year, the success of her methods was confirmed when her students received the highest scores on the state's annual basic skills test.

Her primary method is individualized instruction wherein students proceed at their own pace through modules she has put together. The modules cover five major areas: reading, writing, mathematics, general science, and spelling. She is working on a sixth module, geography, but it won't be ready until next year. She has developed a complex point system to keep track of students' progress and to motivate them to higher levels of achievement. The points students accumulate entitle them to participate in various in-class activities: free reading, playing with the many games and puzzles in the room, drawing or painting in the art corner, or playing video games on one of the two personal computers in the room.

Jane has tried to convert several other teachers at the school to her behavioristic approach, and she is eager to talk to anyone who will listen about the effectiveness of her systematic approach to instruction. When addressing this topic, her exuberance is truly exceptional:

> "It's really quite simple. Students just do much better if you tell them exactly what you want them to know and then reward them for learning it."

In regard to the methods employed by some of her colleagues, Jane can be rather critical. She knows some teachers in the school who teach by a trial-and-error method and "aren't clear about where they're going." She is also impatient with those who talk about the "art" of teaching; in contrast, everything that she does as a teacher is done with precision and a clear sense of purpose. "Through careful design and management of the learning environment," she says, "a teacher can get the results that he or she wants."

CONSTRUCTIVISM

In contrast to behaviorism, constructivism focuses on processes of learning rather than on learning behavior. Since the mid-1980s, researchers have worked at identifying how students construct their understanding of the material they are to learn. According to **constructivism,** through cognitive processes

> learners create or construct their own knowledge through acting on and interacting with the world. Social constructivist approaches also consider the social context in which learning occurs and emphasize the importance of social interaction and negotiation in learning (Woolfolk 1995, 277).

In terms of classroom practice, constructivist approaches therefore support student-centered rather than teacher-centered curriculum and instruction. The student is the key to learning.

Thus, unlike behaviorists who concentrate on directly observable behavior, constructivists focus on the mental processes and strategies that students use to learn. Our understanding of learning has been extended as a result of advances in **cognitive science**—the study of the mental processes students use in thinking and remembering. By drawing from research in linguistics, psychology, anthropology, neurophysiology, and computer science, cognitive scientists are developing new models for how people think and learn.

Teachers who base classroom activities on constructivism know that learning is an active, meaning-making process, that learners are not passive recipients of information. In fact, students are continually involved in making sense out of activities around them. Thus, the teacher must understand students' understanding and realize that students' learning is influenced by prior knowledge, experience, attitudes, and social interactions.

In *Models of Teaching,* Bruce Joyce and Marsha Weil provide the following description of a constructivist teacher.

Jack Wilson is a first-grade teacher in Lincoln, Nebraska. He meets daily for reading instruction with a group of children who are progressing quite well. He is concerned, however, that they have no trouble attacking new words unless they are unable to figure out the meaning from context. If they are able to figure out what the word means from the rest of the sentence, they seem to have no difficulty using principles they have learned to sound the words out. He has concluded that they don't have full control over phonetic and structural analysis concepts and principles. He plans the following activity, which is designed to help them develop concepts of how words are structured and to use that knowledge in attacking words unknown to them.

Jack prepares a deck of cards with one word on each card. He selects words with particular prefixes and suffixes, and he deliberately puts in words that have the same root words but different prefixes and suffixes. He picks prefixes and suffixes because they are prominent structural characteristics of words—easy to identify. (He will later proceed to more subtle phonetic and structural features.) Jack plans a series of learning activities over the next several weeks using the deck of cards as a database. Here are some of the words:

| set | reset | heat | preheat | plant | replant |
| run | rerun | set | preset | plan | preplan |

When the group of students convenes on Monday morning, Jack gives several cards to each student. He keeps the remainder, counting on gradually increasing the amount of information students get. Jack has each student read a word on one of the cards and describe something about the word. Other students can add to the description. In this way the structural properties of the word are brought to the students' attention. The discussion brings out features like initial consonants (begins with an "s"), vowels, pairs of consonants ("pl"), and so on.

After the students have familiarized themselves with the assortment of words, Jack asks them to put the words into groups. "Put the words that go together in piles," he instructs. The students begin studying their cards, passing them back and forth as they sort out the commonalities. At first the students' card groups reflected only the initial letters or the meanings of the words, such as whether they referred to motion or warmth. Gradually, they noticed the prefixes, found out how they were spelled, and looked up their meanings in the dictionary, discovering how the addition of the prefixes affected the meanings of the root words.

When the students finished sorting the words, Jack asked them to talk about each category, telling what the cards had in common. Gradually, because of the way Jack had selected the data, the students could discover the major prefixes and suffixes and reflect on their meaning. Then he gave them sentences in which words not in their deck began and ended with those prefixes and suffixes and asked them to figure out the meanings of those words, applying the concepts they had formed to help them unlock these meanings.

The inductive activity was continued many times as, by selecting different sets of words, Jack led the students through the categories of consonant and vowel sounds and structure they would need to attack unfamiliar words (1996, 146–147).

HOW CAN YOU DEVELOP YOUR EDUCATIONAL PHILOSOPHY ?

As you read the preceding brief descriptions of five educational philosophies and three psychological orientations to teaching, perhaps you felt that no single philosophy fit perfectly with your idea of the kind of teacher you want to become. Or, there may have been some element of each approach that seemed compatible with your own emerging philosophy of education. In either case, don't feel that you need to identify a single educational philosophy around which you will build your teaching career. In reality, few teachers follow only one educational philosophy, and your educational philosophy is only one determinant of the professional decisions you will make as a teacher. As Figure 5.4 suggests, many factors influence philosophical determinants. The educational goals a teacher sets, for example, are influenced by factors such as political dynamics, social forces, the expectations of one's immediate family or community, and economic conditions.

Most teachers develop a somewhat *eclectic* philosophy of education, which means they develop their own unique blending of two or more philosophies. As you will recall from Chapter 2, one characteristic of the professional teacher is that he or she continually tries to arrive at clearer, more comprehensive answers to basic philosophical questions: Why do I teach the way I do? Is my teaching practice consistent

FIGURE 5.4 The relationship of philosophy to educational practice (Source: George R. Knight, *Issues and Alternatives in Educational Philosophy,* 2d ed. (Berrien Springs, MI: Andrews University Press, 1990), p. 33.)

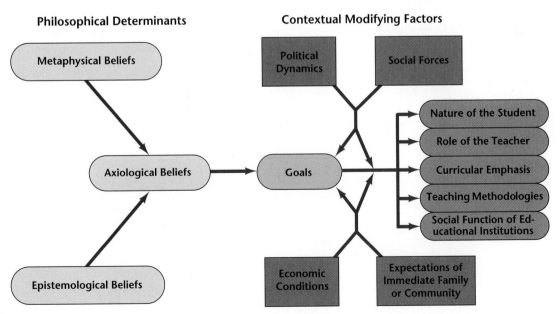

with my beliefs and values about educational goals, curriculum, and teachers' and students' roles in learning? To help you prepare to answer these questions, complete the following Philosophic Inventory.

Using a Philosophic Inventory

The following inventory is to help identify your educational philosophy. Respond to the statements on the scale from 5 "Strongly Agree" to 1 "Strongly Disagree" by circling the number that most closely fits your perspective.

Strongly agree   Strongly disagree

5 4 3 2 1   1. The curriculum should emphasize essential knowledge, *not* students' personal interests.

5 4 3 2 1   2. All learning results from rewards controlled by the external environment.

5 4 3 2 1   3. Teachers should emphasize interdisciplinary subject matter that encourages project-oriented, democratic classrooms.

5 4 3 2 1   4. Education should emphasize the search for personal meaning, *not* a fixed body of knowledge.

5 4 3 2 1   5. The ultimate aim of education is constant, absolute, and universal: to develop the rational person and cultivate the intellect.

5 4 3 2 1   6. Schools should actively involve students in social change to reform society.

5 4 3 2 1   7. Schools should teach basic skills, *not* humanistic ideals.

5 4 3 2 1   8. Eventually, human behavior will be explained by scientific laws, proving there is no free will.

5 4 3 2 1   9. Teachers should be facilitators and resources who guide student inquiry, *not* managers of behavior.

5 4 3 2 1   10. The best teachers encourage personal responses and develop self-awareness in their students.

5 4 3 2 1   11. The curriculum should be the same for everyone: the collective wisdom of Western culture delivered through lecture and discussion.

5 4 3 2 1   12. Schools should lead society toward radical social change, *not* transmit traditional values.

5 4 3 2 1   13. The purpose of schools is to ensure practical preparation for life and work, *not* to encourage personal development.

5 4 3 2 1   14. Good teaching establishes an environment to control student behavior and to measure learning of prescribed objectives.

5 4 3 2 1   15. Curriculum should emerge from students' needs and interests; therefore, it *should not* be prescribed in advance.

5 4 3 2 1   16. Helping students develop personal values is more important than transmitting traditional values.

5 4 3 2 1   17. The best education consists primarily of exposure to great works in the humanities.

5 4 3 2 1   18. It is more important for teachers to involve students in activities to criticize and transform society than to teach the Great Books.

5 4 3 2 1   19. Schools should emphasize discipline, hard work, and respect for authority, *not* encourage free choice.

5 4 3 2 1   20. Human learning can be controlled: Anyone can be taught to be a scientist or a thief; therefore, personal choice is a myth.

5 4 3 2 1   21. Education should enhance personal growth through problem solving in the present, *not* emphasize preparation for a distant future.

5 4 3 2 1   22. Because we are born with an unformed personality, personal growth should be the focus of education.

5 4 3 2 1   23. Human nature is constant—its most distinctive quality is the ability to reason; therefore, the intellect should be the focus of education.

5 4 3 2 1   24. Schools perpetuate racism and sexism camouflaged as traditional values.

5 4 3 2 1   25. Teachers should efficiently transmit a common core of knowledge, *not* experiment with curriculum.

5 4 3 2 1   26. Teaching is primarily management of student behavior to achieve the teacher's objectives.

5 4 3 2 1   27. Education should involve students in democratic activities and reflective thinking.

5 4 3 2 1   28. Students should have significant involvement in choosing what and how they learn.

5 4 3 2 1   29. Teachers should promote the permanency of the classics.

5 4 3 2 1   30. Learning should lead students to involvement in social reform.

5 4 3 2 1   31. On the whole, school should and must indoctrinate students with traditional values.

5 4 3 2 1   32. If ideas cannot be proved by science, they should be ignored as superstition and nonsense.

5 4 3 2 1   33. The major goal for teachers is to create an environment where students can learn on their own by guided reflection on their experiences.

5 4 3 2 1   34. Teachers should create opportunities for students to make personal choices, *not* shape their behavior.

5 4 3 2 1   35. The aim of education should be the same in every age and society, *not* differ from teacher to teacher.

5 4 3 2 1   36. Education should lead society toward social betterment, *not* confine itself to essential skills.

PHILOSOPHIC INVENTORY SCORE SHEET

In the space available, record the number you circled for each statement (1–36) from the inventory. Total the number horizontally and record it in the space on the far right of the score sheet. The highest total indicates your educational philosophy.

Essentialism

Essentialism was a response to progressivism and advocates a conservative philosophic perspective. The emphasis is on intellectual and moral standards that should be transmitted by the schools. The core of the curriculum should be essential knowledge and skills. Schooling should be practical and not influence social policy. It is a back-to-basics movement that emphasizes facts. Students should be taught discipline, hard work, and respect for authority. Influential essentialists include William C. Bagley, H. G. Rickover, Arthur Bestor, and William Bennett; E. D. Hirsch's *Cultural Literacy* could fit this category.

_____ + _____ + _____ + _____ + _____ + _____ = _____
 1   7   13   19   25   31   Total

Behaviorism

Behaviorism denies free will and maintains that behavior is the result of external forces that cause humans to behave in predictable ways. It is linked with empiricism, which stresses scientific experiment and observation; behaviorists are skeptical about metaphysical claims. Behaviorists look for laws governing human behavior the way natural scientists look for empirical laws governing natural events. The role of the teacher is to identify behavioral goals and establish reinforcers to achieve goals. Influential behaviorists include B. F. Skinner, Ivan Pavlov, J. B. Watson, and Benjamin Bloom.

_____ + _____ + _____ + _____ + _____ + _____ = _____
 2   8   14   20   26   32   Total

Progressivism

Progressivism focuses on the child rather than the subject matter. The students' interests are important; integrating thinking, feeling, and doing is important. Learners should be active and learn to solve problems by reflecting on their experience. The school should help students develop personal and social values. Because society is always changing, new ideas are important to make the future better than the past. Influential progressivists include John Dewey and Francis Parker.

_____ + _____ + _____ + _____ + _____ + _____ = _____
  3   9   15   21   27   33   Total

Existentialism

Existentialism is a highly subjective philosophy that stresses the importance of the individual and emotional commitment to living authentically. It emphasizes individual choice over the importance of rational theories. Jean Paul Sartre, the French philosopher, claimed that "existence precedes essence." People are born, and each person must define him- or herself through choices in life. Influential existentialists include Jean Paul Sartre, Soren Kierkegaard, Martin Heidegger, Gabriel Marcel, Albert Camus, Carl Rogers, A. S. Neill, and Maxine Greene.

_____ + _____ + _____ + _____ + _____ + _____ = _____
  4   10   16   22   28   34   Total

Perennialism

The aim of education is to ensure that students acquire knowledge about the great ideas of Western culture. Human beings are rational, and it is this capacity that needs to be developed. Cultivation of the intellect is the highest priority of an education worth having. The highest level of knowledge in each field should be the focus of curriculum. Influential perennialists include Robert Maynard Hutchins, Mortimer Adler, and Allan Bloom.

_____ + _____ + _____ + _____ + _____ + _____ = _____
  5   11   17   23   29   35   Total

Reconstructionism

Reconstructionists advocate that schools should take the lead to reconstruct society. Schools have more than a responsibility to transmit knowledge, they have the mission to transform society as well. Reconstructionists go beyond progressivists in advocating social activism. Influential reconstructionists include Theodore Brameld, Paulo Friere, and Henry Giroux.

_____ + _____ + _____ + _____ + _____ + _____ = _____
  6   12   18   24   30   36   Total

(Source: Prepared by Robert Leahy for *Becoming a Teacher: Accepting the Challenge of a Profession,* 3d ed., 1995. Used by permission of the author.)

Dear Mentor

NOVICE AND EXPERT TEACHERS ON DEVELOPING AN EDUCATIONAL PHILOSOPHY

Dear Tricia,

I have been an educator for twenty-one years. In those twenty-one years the one concern that has always remained constant and close to my heart is the welfare of the children. My personal philosophy on the welfare of children was not something that evolved; it was the source of my motivation to become a teacher. What did evolve was my finding ways to act on my philosophy in relation to educational philosophy and teaching practice.

Our children come from a wide variety of cultures and backgrounds. All children are eager to learn and to do their very best. There are so many outside forces that contribute to a student's ability to learn. For many students the challenge of school is secondary to the challenges they must face outside of school. The current trend of our society has made it more difficult in many instances for children to have the freedom to learn. Negative images in society also make an educator's job increasingly difficult. Moreover, the obstacles are strenuous for our children. For many of the students school is the one place where they can feel confident about themselves and their future.

Dear Mentor,

An educational philosophy must affect every aspect of a teacher's working day. What is your own personal educational philosophy? Was this something that evolved as you gained experience, or was it something that you consciously thought out? On a day-to-day basis how does your educational philosophy affect the way you run your classroom and interact with your students?

Tricia Wahlstrom

As educators we can also be educated by our students if we take the time to walk in their shoes. Using their shoes gives us the opportunity to excel in serving the needs of our students. You should greet your students in the morning and make them feel welcome. Talk to them throughout the day. Each and every student should feel valued and important. Look into their eyes with sincerity.

Tricia, I know you will find your own personal and professional philosophies that best suit you and your classroom. You have already begun your journey by choosing this great profession of teaching. Good luck, Tricia! I wish you the very best.

Michael Morales
History and ESL Teacher, Grades 7–8

SUMMARY

What Determines Your Educational Philosophy?

- An educational philosophy is a set of beliefs about education, a set of principles to guide professional action.
- A teacher's educational philosophy is made up of personal beliefs about teaching and learning, students, knowledge, and what is worth knowing.

What Are the Branches of Philosophy?

- The branches of philosophy and the questions they address are (1) metaphysics (What is the nature of reality?), (2) epistemology (What is the nature of knowledge and is truth attainable?), (3) axiology (What values should one live by?), (4) ethics (What is good and evil, right and wrong?), (5) aesthetics (What is beautiful?), and (6) logic (What reasoning processes yield valid conclusions?).

What Are Five Modern Philosophical Orientations to Teaching?

- Progressivism—The aim of education should be based on the needs and interests of students.
- Perennialism—Students should acquire knowledge of enduring great ideas.
- Essentialism—Schools should teach students, in a disciplined and systematic way, a core of "essential" knowledge and skills.
- Social reconstructionism—In response to the significant social problems of the day, schools should take the lead in creating a new social order.
- Existentialism—In the face of an indifferent universe, students should acquire an education that will enable them to assign meaning to their lives.

What Psychological Orientations Have Influenced Teaching Philosophies?

- Humanism—Children are innately good, and education should focus on individual needs, personal freedom, and self-actualization.
- Behaviorism—By careful control of the educational environment and with appropriate reinforcement techniques, teachers can cause students to exhibit desired behaviors.
- Constructivism—Teachers should "understand students' understanding" and view learning as an active process in which learners construct meaning.

How Can You Develop Your Educational Philosophy?

- Instead of basing their teaching on only one educational philosophy, most teachers develop an eclectic educational philosophy.
- Professional teachers continually strive for a clearer, more comprehensive answer to basic philosophical questions.

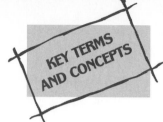

KEY TERMS AND CONCEPTS

aesthetics, 138
axiology, 138
back-to-basics movement, 145
behaviorism, 151
cognitive science, 154
constructivism, 153

educational philosophy, 132
epistemology, 137
essentialism, 144
ethics, 138
existentialism, 148
humanism, 150

humanistic psychology, 150
logic, 139
metaphysics, 136
perennialism, 142
progressivism, 140
social reconstructionism, 146

APPLICATIONS AND ACTIVITIES

Teacher's Journal

1. This chapter refers to the work of several educational philosophers. After researching further, select one of them and write a journal entry in which you discuss how that person's work has influenced your educational philosophy.

2. Imagine that you are a colleague of Roberta Smith who was profiled in this chapter's opening scenario. Write a memo to her in which you react to her philosophical orientation to teaching.

3. Recall one of your favorite teachers in grades K-12. Which of the educational philosophies or psychological orientations to teaching described in this chapter best captures that teacher's approach to teaching? Write your own "portrait" of that teacher.

Teacher's Database

1. Numerous organizations influence educational policy and practice in the United States. Visit the Web sites of two or more of the following organizations and compare the educational philosophies that are reflected in their goals, position statements, and political activities with regard to education.

Alternative Public Schools Inc. (APS)
American Federation of Teachers (AFT)
National Education Association (NEA)
Goals 2000
Chicago Teachers Union (or other municipal teachers' organization)

National Congress of Parents and Teachers (PTA)
Parents as Teachers (PAT)
Texas State Teachers Association (or other state teachers' organization)

2. Beginning at the home page of the American Philosophical Association (APA) (http://www.oxy.edu/apa/apa.html) or the home page for Philosophy in Cyberspace (http://www.monash.edu.au/cc/staff/phi/dey/www/phil/html), compile a list of online publications, associations, and reference materials that you could use in developing further your educational philosophy.

Observations and Interviews

1. Interview a teacher for the purpose of clarifying his or her educational philosophy. Formulate your interview questions in light of the philosophical concepts discussed in this chapter. Discuss your findings with classmates.

2. Administer a philosophical inventory like the one in this chapter to a group of teachers at a local school. Analyze the results and compare your findings with classmates. To guide you in this school-based activity, ask your instructor for handout M6.1, "Administering an Educational Philosophy Inventory."

3. Observe the class of a teacher at the level at which you plan to teach. Which of the five philosophies or three psychological orientations to teaching discussed in this chapter most characterizes this teacher? To help you with this activity, ask your instructor for handout 6.2, "Identifying Educational Philosophies in Action."

4. Visit a school and interview the principal about the school's educational philosophy. Ask him or her to comment on what is expected of teachers in regard to achieving the goals contained in the statement of philosophy.

Professional Portfolio

Prepare a written (or videotaped) statement in which you describe a key element of your educational philosophy. To organize your thoughts, focus on *one* of the following dimensions of educational philosophy:

- Beliefs about teaching and learning
- Beliefs about students
- Beliefs about knowledge
- Beliefs about what is worth knowing
- Personal beliefs about the six branches of philosophy

Develop your statement of philosophy throughout the course, covering all dimensions. On completion of your teacher education program, review your portfolio entry and make any appropriate revisions. Being able to articulate your philosophy of education and your teaching philosophy will be an important part of finding your first job as a teacher.

Politicians compete among themselves for political positions, and workers and business people compete for higher wages and profits. Schools supply the arena for such competition.

—Joel Spring
Conflict of Interests: The Politics of American Education

Governance and Support of American Education

You've just entered the teachers' lounge on your planning period. It's obvious that the four teachers in the room have been having a heated discussion.

"Look at Goals 2000. That's another example of how the federal government is a pawn of big business," says Alex, a physical education teacher who came to the school two years ago. "Might as well say big business controls the schools."

"I don't see how you can say that," says Cheng-Yi, a science teacher.

"Look, high tech industries are concerned about international competition," Alex continues. "So, they exert tremendous political pressure on the feds. Then, the feds lean on us to promote the skills industry needs to be competitive."

"That sounds far-fetched, almost like a conspiracy," says Cheng-Yi, slowing breaking into smile.

"Yeah, what does Goals 2000 have to do with big business?" asks

Kim, an English teacher, before taking a sip of her diet soda.

"Well, Goals 2000 says we're to be first in math and science," Alex continues. "It doesn't say art and music, does it? What about literature and history? Those subjects won't make us economically competitive."

"Alex's got a point," adds Anita, one of the school's master teachers and chair of the school's site-based council. "Big business has a lot of economic and political clout when it comes to schools. Believe me, when someone from business who's on the site-based council talks, we listen."

"That's the way it is," says Alex, nodding his head.

"Remember this September at our first inservice when the president of the chamber of commerce talked about how the schools produce a product?" asks Anita. "In her eyes, the 'product' we produce is workers with basic skills."

"Exactly," Alex says with enthusiasm. "Education in this country is really controlled by big business."

"Come on," Kim sighs. "You two have got to politicize everything when it comes to education. Chen-Yi's right, there's no corporate-sector agenda that's being played out in the schools."

"Right." Chen-Yi says. "Remember, Goals 2000 also talks about responsible citizenship—that sounds pretty democratic to me. I mean . . . we the people control the schools."

"Wait a minute," Alex says. "The Goals just pay lip service to citizenship."

"Plus, whose definition of citizenship do we use?" Anita interjects. "It's being a good worker, a good consumer—someone who strengthens the economy."

"Right," Alex says.

"Well, I still think you're stretching things," says Kim. "Why don't we ask the new teacher here. What do you think?"

The four teachers look at you, awaiting your response. What do you say?

HOW DO POLITICAL EVENTS INFLUENCE EDUCATION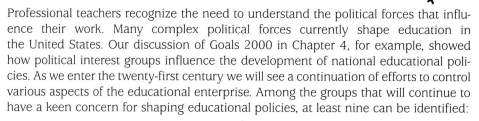

Professional teachers recognize the need to understand the political forces that influence their work. Many complex political forces currently shape education in the United States. Our discussion of Goals 2000 in Chapter 4, for example, showed how political interest groups influence the development of national educational policies. As we enter the twenty-first century we will see a continuation of efforts to control various aspects of the educational enterprise. Among the groups that will continue to have a keen concern for shaping educational policies, at least nine can be identified:

1. *Parents*—Concerned with controlling local schools so that quality educational programs are available to their children
2. *Students*—Concerned with policies related to freedom of expression, dress, behavior, and curricular offerings
3. *Teachers*—Concerned with their role in school reform, improving working conditions, terms of employment, and other professional issues
4. *Administrators*—Concerned with providing leadership so that various interest groups, including teachers, participate in the shared governance of schools and the development of quality educational programs
5. *Taxpayers*—Concerned with maintaining an appropriate formula for determining local, state, and federal financial support of schools
6. *State and federal authorities*—Concerned with the implementation of court orders, guidelines, and legislative mandates related to the operation of schools
7. *Minorities and women*—Concerned with the availability of equal educational opportunity for all and with legal issues surrounding administrative certification, terms of employment, and evaluation

8. *Educational theorists and researchers*—Concerned with using theoretical and research-based insights as the bases for improving schools at all levels
9. *Businesses and corporations*—Concerned with receiving from the schools graduates who have the knowledge, skills, attitudes, and values to help an organization realize its goals

Out of the complex and often turbulent interactions of these groups, school policies are developed. And, as strange as it may seem, no one of these groups can be said to control today's schools. In fact, some observers suggest that the period since 1960 might be characterized as the "era of nobody in charge" (Wirt and Kirst 1989, 20). Those who we might imagine control schools—principals, superintendents, and boards of education—are in reality responding to shifting sets of conditions created by those who have an interest in the schools. In addition, schools are influenced by several out-of-school factors—what sociologists have termed *environmental press*. Because schools are a reflection of the society they serve, they are influenced directly and indirectly by an almost infinite number of factors. The following are some of the more obvious factors that exert their press on the schools:

mass media	political climate	religion
legislative mandates	educational research	technology
growth of minorities	international events	economics
demographic shifts	community attitudes	social issues

Clearly, it is difficult to untangle the web of political forces that influence schools. Figure 6.1 on page 168 shows graphically how school authorities are confronted with the difficult task of funneling the input from various sources into unified, coherent school programs. In the next four sections of this chapter, we examine the many political forces that impinge on the schools by looking at how they are influenced at the local, state, federal, and regional levels.

WHAT IS THE ROLE OF THE LOCAL COMMUNITY IN SCHOOL GOVERNANCE ?

The Constitution does not address the issue of public education, but the Tenth Amendment is used as the basis for giving states the responsibility for the governance of education, that is, the legal authority to create and manage school systems. In addition, as seen in Figure 6.1, various individuals and groups, though not legally empowered, do exercise local control over schools by trying to influence those legally entitled to operate the schools.

The Tenth Amendment gives to the states all powers not reserved for the federal government and not prohibited to the states. The states have, in turn, created local school districts, giving them responsibility for the daily operation of public schools. As a result of efforts to consolidate districts, the number of local public school districts has declined from 127,531 in 1931–32 to 14,881 in 1993–94 (National Center for Education Statistics 1989, 1995).

LOCAL SCHOOL DISTRICT

Local school districts vary greatly in regard to demographics such as number of school-age children; educational, occupational, and income levels of parents; operating budget; number of teachers; economic resources; and number of school buildings. Some serve ultrawealthy communities, others impoverished ghetto neighborhoods or

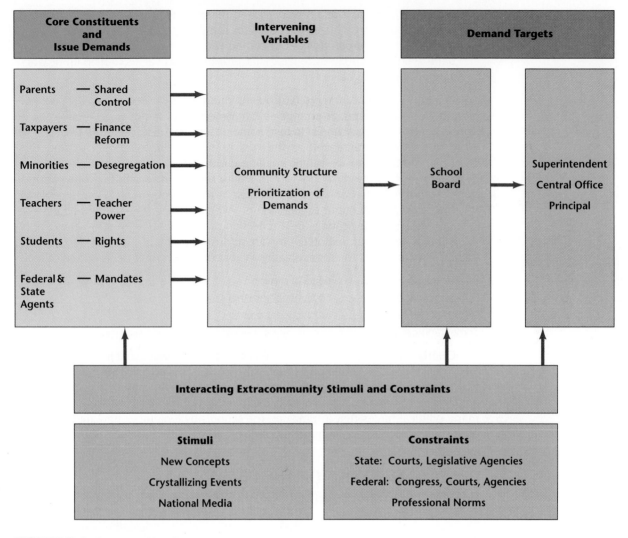

FIGURE 6.1 School politics (Adapted from Frederick M. Wirt and Michael W. Kirst, *Schools in Conflict,* 2d ed. (Berkeley, CA: McCutchan, 1989), p. 13. Used with permission.)

rural areas. Their operations include 442 one-teacher elementary schools in this country (National Center for Education Statistics 1995a, 96) as well as scores of modern, multibuilding campuses in heavily populated areas. The largest school districts are exceedingly complex operations with multimillion-dollar-a-year operating budgets (see Table 6.1 on page 170). The largest—the New York City school system—has more than a million pupils, more than 55,000 teachers, 1,000 schools, and total annual expenditures of more than $7.3 billion.

School districts also differ in regard to their organizational structures. Large urban districts tend to have a more complex distribution of roles and responsibilities than do smaller districts (see Figure 6.2 on page 171).

SCHOOL BOARD

A **school board,** acting as a state agent, is responsible for the following important activities: approving the teachers, administrators, and other school personnel hired

Keepers of the Dream

Ernest Boyer (1928–1996)

"I've never accepted the notion that our schools are failing, and I'm offended when they are described that way. This blanket condemnation goes unchallenged and successes unreported," Ernest Boyer said in 1995, and he added, "It's difficult for schools to be an island of excellence in a sea of societal problems" (Boyer 1995, 54). Boyer's high regard for America's teachers and his leadership in education reform are part of the legacy he left when he died in 1996.

President Jimmy Carter, who appointed Boyer to be U.S. Commissioner of Education during his administration, praised him for winning the respect of educators at all levels, "from preschool to graduate school," and took pride in their shared accomplishments:

> We more than doubled federal support for schools, providing special funds to districts with large numbers of disadvantaged students, and making available grants and loans that made it possible for every qualified student to have the opportunity to attend college (*The Messiah College Bridge*, Special Edition 1996, 11).

Boyer's personal wisdom and ability to communicate memorably made his voice a powerful one in the movement to improve education in this country. He observed that Japan, in contrast to the U.S., celebrates the beginning of school rather than the ending. He urged requiring a service component in the education of all high school students and proposed that reform efforts "confront candidly the moral obligations of education." Boyer also admonished education researchers for overlooking parochial schools in their studies of effective practices. As president

"Now it's time to stop condemning the present system."

of the Carnegie Foundation for the Advancement of Teaching, Boyer directed extensive studies of America's schools and consulted with nations facing education challenges throughout the world.

Boyer's voice and contributions to education at all levels are preserved in his reports, including *Ready to Learn: A Mandate for the Nation* (1991), a prescription for ensuring school readiness for all of America's children; *High School: A Report on Secondary Education in America* (1983); *College: The Undergraduate Experience in America* (1988); *Scholarship Reconsidered: Priorities of the Professorate* (1990); and *The Basic School: A Community for Learning* (1995).

Boyer advised, "Now it's time to stop condemning the present system and pretending that there's some magic innovation we have yet to discover, and start concentrating on what good teachers already know and do" (1995b, 56). In *The Basic School*, the result of an extensive study of America's elementary schools, Boyer proposes that schools become just, caring, disciplined, and celebratory learning communities committed to building character as well as providing a curriculum with coherence. He called for restructuring the traditional curriculum around "eight integrative themes called the Core Commonalities . . . universal human experiences that are shared by all people, those essential conditions that give meaning to our lives" (1995b, 57). "To increase test scores or to be world class in math and science without empowering students or affirming the dignity of human life is to lose the essence of what we and education are presumably all about," he told an educational journalist in 1995 (Goldberg 1995, 48).

In an address at Azusa Pacific University, Boyer observed that we "can live a life that is busy rather than purposeful" and warned that "the tragedy is to die with our convictions undeclared and service unfulfilled." Boyer's life of service to education reflects the power and consequences of such a belief.

TABLE 6.1

Selected data for the ten largest public school systems, 1993–1994

School System	Total Enrollment	Number of Teachers	Pupils per Teacher	Number of Schools	Total Expenditures*	Expenditure per Pupil**
New York City	1,005,521	55,353	18.2	1,064	$7,589,571	$7,420
Los Angeles Unified	639,129	24,933	25.6	640	$3,700,377	$5,706
City of Chicago	409,499	21,722	18.9	609	$2,333,374	$5,551
Dade County, FL	308,465	15,271	20.2	314	$1,802,305	$5,698
Philadelphia	207,667	10,489	19.8	259	$1,340,118	$6,470
Houston Independent School District	200,445	11,410	17.6	256	$946,762	$4,029
Broward County, FL	189,862	9,546	19.9	184	$1,026,532	$5,228
Hawaii Public Schools	180,529	—	—	241	$1,016,323	$5,526
Detroit Public Schools	172,295	7,799	22.2	262	$1,020,968	$5,748
Clark County, Nev.	145,327	7,189	20.2	193	$671,517	$4,526

*Expenditures for 1992–93. Excludes expenditures by state education agencies for local school districts.

**Based on 1992–93 enrollments.

—Data not available.

(Source: Adapted from *Digest of Education Statistics 1995* [Washington, DC: National Center for Education Statistics, U.S. Department of Education], pp. 98–103.)

by the superintendent; developing organizational and educational policies; and determining procedures for the evaluation of programs and personnel.

In most communities, school board members are elected in general elections. In some urban areas, however, board members are selected by the mayor. Board members typically serve a minimum of three to five years, and their terms of office are usually staggered. School boards usually range in size from five to fifteen members, with five or seven frequently suggested as the optimum size. Board members in urban areas usually are paid, but in most other areas are not.

In their 1996 national survey of school board members, *The American School Board Journal* and Virginia Tech reported that women on school boards constituted 43.2 percent and men 53.5 percent (non-responses and rounding account for the other 3.3 percent). The survey also revealed that minority membership on school boards was 9.3 percent. School board members are somewhat atypical of the general population in other ways: They are older (46.9 percent were between forty-one and fifty years old, with another 21.5 percent between fifty-one and sixty), and they are more affluent—the family income of 40 percent of 1996 board members was over $70,000, and over $100,000 for 20.3 percent (Upperman, et al. 1996).

Nearly all school board meetings are open to the public; in fact, many communities even provide radio and television coverage. Open meetings allow parents and interested citizens an opportunity to express their concerns and to get more information about problems in the district.

Criticism of school boards has increased since 1990, and "the argument has been made that systemic reform in public schooling will not be accomplished without a

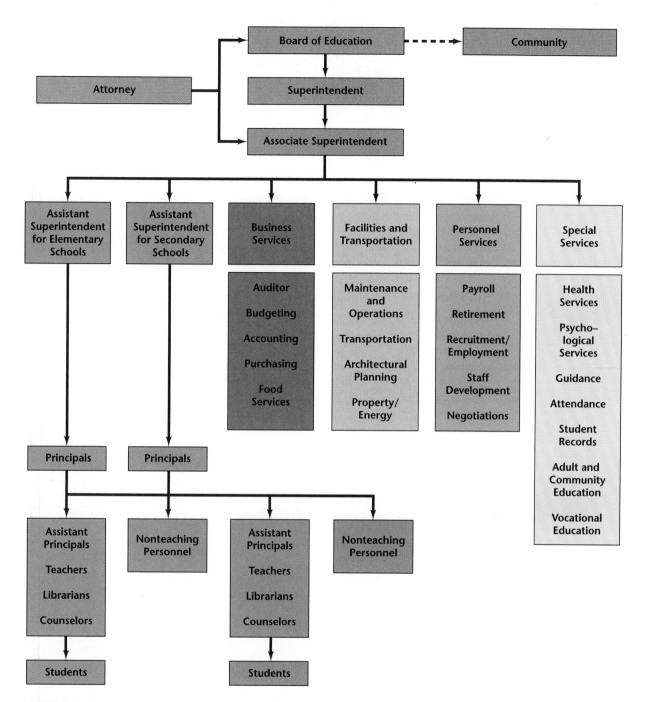

FIGURE 6.2 Typical organizational structure for a medium-sized school district (20,000 pupils)

corresponding restructuring of school boards" (Danzberger 1994a, 371). Critics have pointed out that school boards often

- fail to provide far-reaching or politically risky leadership for reform;
- have become another level of administration, often micromanaging districts;
- are so splintered by members' attempts to represent special interests or meet their individual political needs that boards cannot govern effectively;
- are not spending enough time on educating themselves about issues or about education policy making; and
- exhibit serious problems in their capacity to develop positive and productive, lasting relationships with superintendents (Danzberger 1994b, 369).

Some states have taken steps to reform school boards. For example, West Virginia implemented legislation in 1994 to restructure school boards "so that they become well-informed, responsive, policy-making bodies." Board members now serve for four years rather than six, and they must complete training focused on "boardsmanship and governing effectiveness" (Danzberger 1994a, 394).

SUPERINTENDENT OF SCHOOLS

Though school boards operate very differently, the **superintendent** is invariably the key figure in determining a district's educational policy. The superintendent is the chief administrator of the school district, the person charged with the responsibility of seeing to it that schools operate in accord with federal and state guidelines as well as policies set by the local school board. Though the board of education delegates broad powers to the superintendent, his or her policies require board approval.

The specific responsibilities of the superintendent are many. Among the most important are the following:

1. To serve as professional adviser to the board of education and to make policy recommendations for improving curricular and instructional programs
2. To act as employer and supervisor of professional and nonteaching personnel (janitors, cafeteria workers, etc.)
3. To represent the schools in their relations with the community and to explain board of education policies to the community
4. To develop policies for the placement and transportation of students within the district
5. To prepare an annual school budget and adhere to the budget adopted by the school board

How the superintendent and his or her board work together appears to be related to the size of the school district, with superintendents and school boards in larger districts more likely to be in conflict. Schools boards in smaller districts, however, are more effective when they do oppose the superintendent. In large districts, the board's own divisiveness makes it less likely that the board will successfully oppose the superintendent (Wirt and Kirst 1989). Superintendents have also observed how widely the political climate of school districts can vary. "In some schools, changing the location of a bicycle rack will cause parents to call the principal. In other schools, we can cut the school day from seven periods to six periods without neighborhood reaction." (Wirt and Kirst 1989, 145).

Superintendents must have great skill to respond appropriately to the many external political forces that demand their attention. As Larry Cuban (1985, 28–30) put it, "Conflict is the DNA of the superintendency." Effective superintendents demonstrate that they are able to play three roles simultaneously: politician, manager, and teacher. It is a demanding position, and turnover is high. City superintendents stay in their jobs an average of less than three years, and many vacancies in city super-intendencies attract few candidates (McCloud and McKenzie 1994, 384–385). In an environment characterized by political turbulence and demands from competing in-terest groups, the superintendent cannot be an omnipotent, insensitive figure; he or she must be a "negotiator-statesman" (Wirt and Kirst 1989, 144).

THE ROLE OF PARENTS

Parents may not be involved legally in the governance of schools, but they do play an important role in American education. One characteristic of successful schools is that they have developed close working relationships with parents. Additionally, chil-dren whose parents or guardians support and encourage school activities have a def-inite advantage in school.

Through participation on school advisory councils, parents are making an im-portant contribution to school reform efforts around the country. In addition, groups such as the Parent-Teacher Association (PTA), Parent-Teacher Organization (PTO), or Parent Advisory Council (PAC) give parents the opportunity to communicate with teachers on matters of interest and importance to them. Through these groups, par-ents can become involved in the life of the school in a variety of ways—from mak-ing recommendations regarding school policies to providing much-needed volunteer services, or to initiating school-improvement activities such as fund-raising drives.

The National PTA—the National Congress of Parents and Teachers—is the na-tion's largest parent-teacher organization. Founded in 1897, the PTA now has more than 6.1 million members, and sponsors many activities and publications to support schools, protect children, and help parents learn to be better parents. Ann P. Kahn, past president of the National Congress of Parents and Teachers, points out, for ex-ample, that the PTA has played a key role in

> supporting compulsory public education, including kindergarten; establishing the juvenile-justice system; starting hot lunch programs in schools in order that all children would have at least one nutritious meal a day; field testing the Salk polio vaccine; leading the fight against drug and alcohol abuse by young people; speaking out for adequate funding for public education; and challenging the use of public funds for nonpublic schools (1988, 189).

Many parents are also influencing the character of American education through their involvement with the growing number of private, parochial, for-profit, and charter schools. In addition, many parents are activists in promoting school choice, voucher systems, and the home schooling movement. Parents are also involved in school restructuring.

SCHOOL RESTRUCTURING

At many schools across the country exciting changes are taking place in regard to how schools are controlled locally. To improve the performance of schools, to decen-tralize the system of governance, and to enhance the professional status of teachers, some districts are **restructuring** their school systems. Restructuring goes by several names: shared governance, administrative decentralization, teacher empowerment, professionalization, bottom-up policy-making, school-based planning, school-based management, and shared decision making. What all these approaches to school gov-ernance have in common is allowing those who know students best—teachers, prin-cipals, aides, custodians, librarians, secretaries, and parents—the freedom to decide how to meet students' needs.

In a survey of the extent of school restructuring, the Center on Organization and Restructuring of Schools at the University of Wisconsin (1992) found that restructured schools reflect changes in four areas: (1) student experiences, (2) the professional life of teachers, (3) school governance, and (4) collaboration between school and community. Within these four areas, restructured schools have implemented a wide variety of changes. For example, Table 6.2, based on a 1992 survey of 377 public, Catholic, and independent middle schools, shows the percent of schools that had implemented various approaches to restructuring.

SCHOOL-BASED MANAGEMENT

One of the most frequently used approaches to restructuring schools is **school-based management (SBM).** Most SBM programs have three components in common:

1. Power and decisions formerly made by the superintendent and school board are delegated to teachers, principals, parents, community members, and students at local schools. At SBM schools, teachers can become directly involved in making decisions about curriculum, textbooks, standards for student behavior, staff development, promotion and retention policies, teacher evaluation, school budgets, and the selection of teachers and administrators.

TABLE 6.2

Percent of middle schools with restructuring features

Restructuring Features	Percent of Schools
No homogeneously grouped classes	17
Flexible time scheduling	21
Team teaching in eighth grade	40
Students have same homeroom teacher all middle grade years	24
Scheduled common planning time for department members or teaching teams	36
Staff development program available	57
Semi-departmentalization or self-contained classes	12
Eighth-graders keep same classmates for all classes	18
Students from different grade levels are in the same classroom	37
Eighth-graders are not retained	12
Interdisciplinary teachers share the same students	51
More than 40 percent of students not academically grouped	11
Has schools within the school	14
Eighth-grade classes are organized for cooperative learning	31
Eighth-graders have exploratory classes	50
Eighth-graders do special projects regularly in their curriculum	64

(Source: V. Lee, and J. B. Smith, *Effects of School Restructuring on the Achievement and Engagement of Middle-Grade Students* [Madison: University of Wisconsin, Center on Organization and Restructuring of Schools, 1992]. Presented in *Brief to Policymakers*. Madison: University of Wisconsin, Center on Organization and Restructuring of Schools, *Brief* no. 4, Fall 1992, p. 4.)

What are the goals of school restructuring? In school-based management, who participates in the governance and management of schools? How is school-based management different from the school board model of local governance?

2. At each school, a decision-making body (known as a board, cabinet, site-based team, or council)—made up of teachers, the principal, and parents—implements the SBM plan.
3. SBM programs operate with the whole-hearted endorsement of the superintendent of schools.

A pioneer in school-based management has been the City of Chicago Public Schools. For years, the Chicago Public School System has been beset by an array of problems: low student achievement, periodic teacher strikes, budget crises, a top-heavy central bureaucracy, and schools in the decaying inner city that seemed beyond most improvement efforts. In response to these problems, the late Mayor Harold Washington appointed a fifty-five-member committee of business, education, and community leaders to develop a school reform proposal. Among the group's recommendations was the creation of a **local school council (LSC)** for each of the city's 616 schools, with the majority of council members being parents of schoolchildren.

In December 1988, the Illinois state legislature passed the Chicago School Reform Act, believed by some to be "the most fundamental restructuring since the early part of the twentieth century" (Moore 1992, 153–198). Among the provisions of the act were the following:

- School budgets would be controlled by a local school council made up of six parents, two community members, two school employees, and the principal.
- The council had the authority to hire and fire the principal.
- The council, with input from teachers and the principal, had the authority to develop an improvement plan for the local school.
- New teachers would be hired on the basis of merit, not seniority.
- Principals could remove teachers forty-five days after serving them official notice of unsatisfactory performance.
- A Professional Personnel Advisory Committee of teachers would have advisory responsibility for curriculum and instruction.

To date, the overall effectiveness of the Chicago program has been mixed. While the Reform Act called for all Chicago schools to reach national norms within five years, this goal was not reached (Bryk et al. 1994, 306–319; Walberg and Niemiec 1994, 713–715; 1996, 339). However, "of the schools most in need of change—schools where student achievement had been well below national norms—one-third had developed strong democratic support and participation within their school communities [and] were following a systemic approach toward reform. Another third displayed some of these characteristics but were not as far along in implementing change" (Hess 1995, 111). Though it has yet to result in increased student achievement, the Chicago experiment is clearly one of the more dramatic efforts to empower parents and make them full partners in the educative process.

WHAT POWERS AND INFLUENCE DO STATES HAVE IN GOVERNING SCHOOLS ?

Above the level of local control, states have a great influence on the governance of schools. Throughout the seventies and eighties, the influence of the state on educational policy increased steadily. Sparked by numerous national reports critical of American education in the early 1980s, many states took extensive initiatives to improve education, such as the following:

■ Tougher requirements for graduation from high school
■ Longer school days and years
■ Career ladders for teachers and master teacher programs
■ Higher expectations for students, including testing of basic skills
■ Testing graduates of teacher education programs prior to certification

As mentioned previously, the Tenth Amendment to the Constitution allows the states to organize and to administer education within their boundaries. To meet the responsibility of maintaining and supporting schools, the states have assumed several powers:

■ The power to levy taxes for the support of schools and to determine state aid to local school districts
■ The power to set the curriculum and, in some states, to identify approved textbooks
■ The power to determine minimum standards for teacher certification
■ The power to establish standards for accrediting schools
■ The power to pass legislation necessary for the proper maintenance and support of schools

To carry out the tasks implied by these powers, the states have adopted a number of different organizational structures. Most states, however, have adopted a hierarchical structure similar to that shown in Figure 6.3.

THE ROLES OF STATE GOVERNMENT IN EDUCATION

Various persons and agencies within each state government play a role in operating the educational system within that state. Though state governments differ in many respects, the state legislature, the state courts, and the governor have a direct, critical impact on education in their state.

THE LEGISLATURE   In nearly every state, the legislature is responsible for establishing and maintaining public schools and for determining basic educational policies within the state. To accomplish these ends, the legislature has the power to enact laws related to education. Among the policies that the state legislature may determine are the following:

FIGURE 6.3 Organizational structure of a typical state school system

- How the state boards of education will be selected and what their responsibilities will be
- How the chief state school officer will be selected and what his or her duties will be
- How the state department of education will function
- How the state will be divided into local and regional districts
- How higher education will be organized and financed
- How local school boards will be selected and what their powers will be

In addition, the legislature may determine how taxes will be used to support schools, what will or will not be taught, the length of the school day and school year, how many years of compulsory education will be required, and whether or not the state will have community colleges and/or vocational/technical schools. Legislatures may also make policies that apply to such matters as pupil attendance, admission, promotion, teacher certification, teacher tenure and retirement, and collective bargaining.

THE COURTS   From time to time, state courts are called on to uphold the power of the legislature to develop laws that apply to schools. The state courts must determine, however, that this power does not conflict with the state or federal constitution. It is important to remember, too, that the role of state courts is not to develop laws but to rule on the reasonableness of laws that apply to specific educational situations.

Perhaps no state court had a greater impact on education during the first half of the 1990s than the Kentucky Supreme Court. In 1989, the Court ruled that the state's entire school system was "inadequate." Naming the state superintendent and the state education agency as part of the problem and pointing out that Kentucky schools were ineffective and inequitable, the Court labeled the school system "unconstitutional." The Court called on the governor and the legislature to develop an entirely new system of education for the state. A twenty-two-member task force, appointed by the governor and the legislature, then developed the 906-page **Kentucky Education Reform Act (KERA)** passed in 1990. KERA required each school to form a school-based management council by 1996 with authority to set policy in eight areas: curriculum, staff time, student assignment, schedule, school space, instructional issues, discipline, and extracurricular activities. Three teachers, two parents (elected by their peers), and the principal comprised each council.

THE GOVERNOR   Though the powers of governors vary greatly from state to state, a governor can, if he or she chooses, have a far-reaching impact on education within the state. The governor may appoint and/or remove educators at the state level, and in some states the governor may even appoint the chief state school officer. Furthermore, in every state except North Carolina, the governor may use his or her veto power to influence the legislature to pass certain laws related to education. Governors are also extremely influential because they make educational budget recommendations to legislatures, and, in many states, they may elect to use any accumulated balances in the state treasury for education. The **National Governors' Association (NGA)** is active in teacher education and school reforms.

STATE BOARD OF EDUCATION

The **state board of education,** acting under the authority of the state legislature, is the highest educational agency in a state. Every state, with the exception of Wisconsin, has a state board of education. In most states there are two separate boards, one responsible for elementary through secondary education, the other for higher education.

The method of determining board members varies from state to state. In some states, the governor appoints members of the state board; in other states, members are selected through general elections. Two states have *ex officio* members who, by virtue of the positions they hold, automatically serve on the board. Most states have either seven- or nine-member boards.

People disagree on which is better: electing or appointing board members. Some believe that election to the state board may cause members to be more concerned with politics than with education. Others argue that elected board members are more aware of the wishes of the public whom the schools are supposed to serve. People in favor of appointing members to the state board suggest that appointment increases the likelihood that individuals will be chosen on the basis of merit rather than politics.

The regulatory and advisory functions generally held by state boards are as follows:

- Ensuring that local school districts adhere to legislation concerning educational policies, rules, and regulations
- Setting standards for issuing and revoking teaching and administrative certificates
- Establishing standards for accrediting schools
- Managing state monies appropriated for education
- Developing and implementing a system for collecting educational data needed for reporting and program evaluation
- Advising the governor and/or the state legislature on educational issues
- Identifying both short- and long-range educational needs in the state and developing plans to meet those needs
- Hearing all disputes arising from the implementation of its educational policies

STATE DEPARTMENT OF EDUCATION

The educational program of each state is implemented by the state's department of education, under the leadership of the chief state school officer. State departments of education have a broad set of responsibilities, and they affect literally every school, school district, and teacher education program in a state. In general, the state board of education is concerned with policy making, the **state department of education** with the day-to-day implementation of those policies. Perhaps the greatest boost for the development of state departments of education came with the federal government's Elementary and Secondary Education Act of 1965 (see Chapter 3). This act and its subsequent amendments required that local applications for federal funds to be used for innovative programs and for the education of disadvantaged, disabled, bilingual, and migrant students first receive approval from state departments of education.

Today, the responsibilities of state departments of education include (1) certifying teachers, (2) distributing state and federal funds to school districts, (3) reporting to the public the condition of education within the state, (4) ensuring that school districts adhere to state and federal guidelines, (5) accrediting schools, (6) monitoring student transportation and safety, and (7) sponsoring research and evaluation projects to improve education within the state.

Perhaps the most significant index of the steady increase in state control since the 1980s is the fact that the states now supply the majority of funding for schools. As we enter the twenty-first century, the power and influence of state departments of education will continue to be extensive.

CHIEF STATE SCHOOL OFFICER

The **chief state school officer** (known as the commissioner of education or superintendent of public instruction in many states) is the chief administrator of the state department of education and the head of the state board of education. In twenty-seven states, the state board of education appoints the chief state school officer; in fifteen, the office is filled through a general election; and in the remaining eight, the governor appoints an individual to that position (Council of Chief State School Officers 1996).

Though the specific responsibilities of the chief state school officer vary from state to state, most persons in this position hold several responsibilities in common:

1. Serving as chief administrator of the state department of education and state board of education
2. Selecting state department of education personnel
3. Recommending educational policies and budgets to the state board
4. Interpreting state school laws and state board of education policies
5. Ensuring compliance with state school laws and policies
6. Mediating controversies involving the operation of schools within the state
7. Arranging for studies, committees, and task forces to address educational problems and recommend solutions
8. Reporting on the status of education to the governor, legislature, state board, and public

STATE STANDARDS BOARDS

To regulate and improve the professional practice of teachers, administrators, and other education personnel, states have established **professional standards boards.** In some states, standards boards have the authority to implement standards; in others, they serve in an advisory capacity to educational policymakers. In Washington state, for example, the Washington Advisory Board for Professional Teaching Standards recently made a recommendation to the State Board of Education calling for a three-level teacher certification system. Candidates, upon completion of an approved program, would receive a Residency Certificate. With demonstration of successful teaching and a recommendation from the employing school district, a candidate then would be eligible for a renewable, five-year Professional Certificate. Finally, persons who hold national certification from the National Board for Professional Teaching Standards or who hold a combination of advanced degrees, experience, and proficiency in performance-based standards would be eligible for the optional Professional Career Certificate.

In California, the state Commission on Teacher Credentialing (CTC) recently launched an extensive review of teacher certification standards. Among the issues being addressed by the CTC is whether education students' subject matter preparation should continue to be separate from professional preparation and whether alternative routes to certification such as school district-controlled internship programs should be encouraged.

WHAT ASSISTANCE DO REGIONAL EDUCATION AGENCIES PROVIDE ?

When we think of how schools are governed and the sources of political pressure applied to them, we typically think of influences originating at three levels: local, state, and federal. There is, however, an additional source of control—the regional, or intermediate, unit. The intermediate unit of educational administration, or the **Regional Educational Service Agency (RESA)**, is the least understood branch of the state public school system. The intermediate unit "provides certain administrative and supervisory functions as well as supplementary educational programs and services to a cluster of two or more local school districts. . . . It is the middle echelon in a state system of education that includes the local school district and the state education agency as well" (Knezevich 1984, 198). Through the intermediate unit, local school districts can receive supportive services that, economically and logistically, they could not provide for themselves.

Presently, about half of the states have some form of intermediate or regional unit. The average unit is made up of twenty to thirty local school districts and covers a fifty-square-mile area. The intermediate or regional unit has many different names: educational service district (in Washington), county education office (in California), education service center (in Texas), intermediate school district (in Michigan), multicounty educational service unit (in Nebraska), and board of cooperative educational services (in New York).

The primary role of the intermediate unit is to provide assistance directly to districts in the areas of staff development, curriculum development, instructional media, and program evaluation. Intermediate or regional units also help school districts with their school improvement efforts by providing help in targeted areas such as bilingual education, vocational education, computer education, and the education of gifted and talented students and students with disabilities. Although intermediate units do monitor local school districts to see that they follow state educational guidelines, "local districts [actually] exert more influence over the intermediate unit and often specify what services shall or shall not be rendered by the regional unit" (Knezevich 1984, 190).

HOW DOES THE FEDERAL GOVERNMENT INFLUENCE EDUCATION?

Since the birth of our nation, the federal government has played a major role in shaping the character of our schools. This branch of government has always recognized that the strength and well-being of our country are directly related to the quality of our schools. The importance of a quality education, for example, has been highlighted by many U.S. Supreme Court rulings supporting the free speech rights of teachers and students under the First Amendment and the right of all citizens to equal educational opportunity under the Fourteenth Amendment. As we enter the twenty-first century it is clear that as a nation we face unprecedented levels of both global competition and the need for greater international cooperation. Our rapidly changing, increasingly complex society will require a better-educated workforce if we are to compete and cooperate successfully.

The federal government has taken aggressive initiatives to influence education at several points in our history, such as the allocation of federal money to improve science, mathematics, and foreign language education after Russia launched the world's first satellite. During World War II, the federal government funded several new educational programs. One of these, the Lanham Act (1941), provided funding for (1) the training of workers in war plants by U.S. Office of Education personnel, (2) the construction of schools in areas where military personnel and workers on federal projects resided, and (3) the provision of childcare for the children of working parents.

Another influential and extensive federal program in support of education was the Servicemen's Readjustment Act, popularly known as the **G.I. Bill of Rights.** Signed into law by President Franklin D. Roosevelt in 1944, the G.I. Bill has provided millions of veterans with payments for tuition and room and board at colleges and universities and at technical schools. Similar legislation was later passed to grant educational benefits to veterans of the Korean and Vietnam conflicts. Not only did the G.I. Bill stimulate the growth of American colleges and universities, it also opened higher education to an older and nontraditional student population.

Frederick M. Wirt and Michael W. Kirst (1989, 278–279) have identified six ways in which the executive, legislative, and judicial branches of the federal government influence education:

1. *General aid*—Provide no-strings aid to state and local education agencies or minimal earmarks such as teacher salaries
2. *Stimulate through differential funding*—Earmark categories of aid, provide financial incentives through matching grants, fund demonstration projects, and purchase specific services
3. *Regulate*—Legally specify behavior, impose standards, certify and license, enforce accountability procedures
4. *Discover knowledge and make it available*—Have research performed; gather and make other statistical data available (for example, ERIC)
5. *Provide services*—Furnish technical assistance and consultants in specialized areas or subjects (For example, the Office of Civil Rights will advise school districts that wish to design voluntary desegregation plans.)
6. *Exert moral suasion*—Develop vision and question assumptions through publications, speeches by top officials

"I challenge every community, every school, and every state to adopt national standards of excellence, to measure whether schools are meeting those standards, to cut bureaucratic red tape so that schools and teachers have more flexibility for grassroots reform, and to hold them accountable for results" (*Education Week,* January 31, 1996, 21).

Federal expenditures for elementary-through secondary-level education for the 1995 fiscal year topped $35 billion (National Center for Education Statistics 1995, 378). In some cases, the federal government provides funding for successful programs—for example, the Head Start program which was refunded in 1993. In others, different branches of the federal government operate various schools and educational programs. For example, the Department of Labor operates Job Corps training programs for youth. Over 200 **Department of Defense (DOD) overseas dependents schools** provide education for about 100,000 children of U.S. military personnel and federal employees on overseas assignments. In 1995, the budget for DOD schools was $845 million (National Center for Education Statistics 1995, 380). Also, the Department of the Interior provides education for Native American children through **Bureau of Indian Affairs (BIA) schools,** which had a 1995 budget of $411 million (National Center for Education Statistics 1995, 380). Lastly, the federal government provides funding to disseminate research results and descriptions of exemplary educational programs through sixteen Educational Resources Information Centers (ERIC).

THE IMPACT OF PRESIDENTIAL POLICIES

Presidential platforms on education often have a profound effect on education. Ronald Reagan's two terms of office (1980–1988) and George Bush's term (1988–1992), for example, saw a significant shift in the federal government's role in education. In general, these two administrations sought to scale back what some viewed as excessive federal involvement in education. During the 1990s, many hoped that the federal government would assume a more active role in ensuring equal educational opportunity. As Bill Clinton (1992, 134) put it:

> Within our country there are wide gaps in children's levels of readiness to start school. Many lack the basic building blocks of knowledge and thinking without which learning simply cannot occur. There are huge gaps in how much we spend on different students and in what kind of courses and other opportunities they have. . . . Most important, there are massive performance gaps among our schools that cross economic and social lines.

U.S. DEPARTMENT OF EDUCATION

In 1979 President Carter signed a law creating the Department of Education. This new cabinet-level department assumed the responsibilities of the U.S. Office of Education, which had been formed in 1953 as a branch of the Department of Health, Education, and Welfare. Shirley Hufstedler, a state Supreme Court judge, became the first Secretary of Education when the new department opened in mid-1980. In 1983 President Reagan suggested that the Department of Education be dismantled and replaced with a Foundation for Education Assistance. However, public response to the reform report *A Nation at Risk* convinced the President that education was too important an issue not to be represented at the cabinet level. A proposal to eliminate the Department of Education was soundly defeated at the 1984 Republican National Convention. So solid was the rejection of the proposal to eliminate the department that former secretary of education Terrel H. Bell was moved to comment that "dissolution of the department will not, in my opinion, ever again be a serious issue. . . . The Education Department is here to stay" (Bell 1986, 492).

In addition to supporting educational research, disseminating the results of research, and administering federal grants, the U.S. Department of Education advises the President on stating a platform for his educational agenda. For example, Secretary of Education Richard Riley was a spokesman for the following components of President Clinton's educational platform:

- Continued support of the national goals for education set during President Bush's administration
- National standards for what children should know, including the creation of a national examination system
- A safe schools initiative that would give violence-ridden schools funds for security
- Increased funding for programs to help all children prepare to enter school ready to learn
- Funding for programs such as a Youth Opportunity Corps to reduce the dropout rate among students
- Increased parental choice in education

Taking Perspectives on Federal versus State Roles in Education

At times, the roles of the federal and state governments in education are in conflict. As the trend continues toward increased state control over educational policies, teachers and students may be increasingly affected by partisan politics. For example, in 1996, legislators in one state were unable to override the governor's veto of the state's participation in the Goals 2000 program. The governor, claiming that Goals 2000 would give the federal government too much control over education in the state, said "Our children's future is more important than a few pennies per child in federal funding accompanied by dictates. Now is no time to turn control of our reforms over to federal bureaucrats and politicians . . ." (*Education Week* April 24, 1996, 14).

In your teacher's journal, identify some issues of state versus federal control that might affect you as a prospective teacher and later as a professional educator. For each issue you identify, do you support greater states' rights or greater federal involvement? Explain your reasons.

HOW ARE SCHOOLS FINANCED IN THE UNITED STATES

To provide free public education to all school-age children in our nation is a costly undertaking. Schools must provide services and facilities to students from a wide range of ethnic, racial, social, cultural, linguistic and individual backgrounds. Expenditures for these services and facilities have been rising rapidly. In 1994–95, the total **expenditure per pupil** was $6,084 (in constant 1994–95 dollars). After adjusting for inflation, this figure represented an increase of 23 percent since 1984–85 (see Figure 6.4).

FIGURE 6.4 Current expenditure per pupil in average daily attendance in public elementary and secondary schools: 1970–71 to 1994–95 (Source: U.S. Department of Education, National Center for Education Statistics, *Statistics of the State School Systems; Revenues and Expenditures for Public Elementary and Secondary Education;* and Common Core of Data surveys. Reprinted from *Digest of Education Statistics 1995* (Washington, DC: U.S. Department of Education, National Center for Education Statistics), p. 49.)

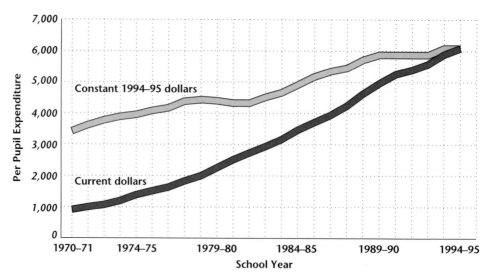

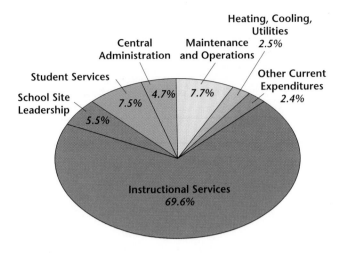

FIGURE 6.5 Average allocation of 1993–94 school district operating budgets (Source: G. E. Robinson and N. Protheroe, "Local School Budget Profiles Study." *School Business Affairs*, September 1994, p. 32.)

Furthermore, it is estimated that expenditures per pupil will increase by 24.3 percent between 1992–93 and 2005–2006 (*Projection of Education Statistics to 2006*, 76). The total estimated expenditure for public elementary through secondary schools in the United States for the year ending 1996 was over $250 billion (*Projection of Education Statistics to 2006*, 84). Figure 6.5 shows how the budget for a typical school district is allocated.

Financing an enterprise as vast and ambitious as our system of free public schools has not been easy. It has proved difficult both to devise a system that equitably distributes the tax burden for supporting schools and to provide equal educational services and facilities for all students. Moreover, there has been a tendency for the financial support of schools to be outpaced by factors that continually increase the cost of operating schools, such as inflation, rising enrollments, and the need to update aging facilities. According to the 1996 Gallup Poll of the public's attitudes toward the public schools, "lack of proper financial support" was seen as the number four problem (after "drug abuse," "lack of discipline," and "fighting/violence/gangs") confronting local schools.

A combination of revenues from local, state, and federal sources is used to finance public elementary and secondary schools in the United States. As Table 6.3 shows, schools received almost half of their 1993 funding from local and other sources, 45.6 percent from the state, and 6.9 percent from the federal government. Since 1980, schools have received almost equal funding from local and state sources; prior to that date, however, schools received most of their revenues from local sources, and early in the twentieth century, nearly all school revenues were generated from local property taxes.

Revenues for education are influenced by many factors, including the apportionment of taxes among the local, state, and federal levels; the size of the tax base at each level; and competing demands for allocating funds at each level. In addition, funding for education is influenced by the following factors:

- The rate of inflation
- The health of the national economy
- The size of the national budget deficit
- Taxpayer revolts to limit the use of property taxes to raise money, such as Proposition 13 in California and Oregon's property tax limitation
- Changes in the size and distribution of the population
- Legislation for equalizing educational opportunity and increasing the accountability of schools

LOCAL FUNDING

At the local level, most funding for schools comes from **property taxes** that are determined by the value of property in the school district. Property taxes are assessed

TABLE 6.3

Public elementary and secondary school revenues as a percentage of gross domestic product (GDP) and revenue sources: Selected school years ending 1920–93

School Year Ending	Public Elementary/ Secondary School Revenues as a Percentage of GDP[1]	Revenue Source (Percent of total public school revenues)		
		Local[2]	State	Federal
1920	—	83.2	16.5	0.3
1930	2.0	82.7	16.9	0.4
1940	2.5	68.0	30.3	1.8
1950	2.1	57.3	39.8	2.9
1960	3.0	56.5	39.1	4.4
1970	4.2	52.1	39.9	8.0
1980	3.9	43.4	46.8	9.8
1990	4.0	46.6	47.3	6.1
1993	4.1	47.4	45.6	6.9

—Not available.

[1]Gross Domestic Product (GDP) is Gross National Product (GNP) less net property income from abroad for the calendar year in which the school year began.

[2]Includes intermediate sources and a relatively small amount from nongovernmental sources (gifts, and tuition and transportation fees from patrons). Nongovernmental sources accounted for 0.4 percent of total revenues in school year 1967–68.

Note: Beginning in school year 1980–81, revenues for state education agencies are excluded. Data for school years 1988–93 reflect new survey collection procedures and may not be entirely comparable to figures for earlier years.

(Source: U.S. Department of Education, National Center for Education Statistics, *Digest of Education Statistics, 1994,* tables 31 and 157 [based on Common Core of Data]; Executive Office of the President, *Economic Report to the President,* February 1994, table B-114. Reprinted from National Center for Education Statistics, *The Condition of Education 1995* [Washington, DC: U.S. Department of Education], p. 387.)

against real estate and, in some districts, also against personal property such as cars, household furniture and appliances, and stocks and bonds. Increasing taxes to meet the rising costs of operating local schools or to fund needed improvements is often a heated issue in many communities. The public is about evenly divided between those who favor spending more money on local schools, even if it means higher taxes, and those who oppose spending more (*Business Week* 1992).

Although property taxes provide a steady source of revenue for local school districts, there are inequities in the ways in which taxes are determined. By locating in areas where taxes are lowest, for example, businesses and industries often avoid paying higher taxes while continuing to draw on local resources and services. In addition, the fair market value of property is often difficult to assess, and groups within a community sometimes pressure assessors to keep taxes on their property as low as possible. Most states specify by law the minimum property tax rate for local school districts to set. In many districts, an increase in the tax rate must have the approval of voters. Some states place no cap, or upper limit, on tax rates, and other states set a maximum limit.

STATE FUNDING

Most state revenues for education come from sales taxes and income taxes. Sales taxes are added to the cost of items such as general goods, gasoline, amusements, alcohol, and insurance. Income taxes are placed on individuals (in many states) and on business and industry.

As mentioned previously, states contribute nearly 50 percent of the resources needed to operate the public schools. The money that a state gives to its cities and towns is known as **state aid.** Table 6.4 compares selected states on the percent of education funds received from federal, state, local and intermediate, and private sources in relation to total expenditures for 1992–93. The table also shows how total expenditures may vary widely from state to state. Between 1984–85 and 1994–95, for example, New Jersey's per pupil expenditures (using constant 1992–93 dollars) increased by 29 percent, while Colorado's declined by more than 1 percent (National Center for Education Statistics 1995a, 165).

FEDERAL FUNDING

The role of the federal government in providing resources for education has been limited. From 1950 to 1980, however, the federal contribution to education rose from less than 4 percent of the gross national product (GNP) to almost 10 percent. Prior to 1980 the federal government had in effect bypassed the states and provided funding for local programs that were administered through various federal agencies, such as the Office of Economic Opportunity (Head Start, migrant education, and Follow Through)

TABLE 6.4

Total expenditures for public elementary and secondary schools and revenues by source for selected states and the District of Columbia

| State | 1992–93 Expenditures | Percent of Total Revenues 1992–93 | | | |
		Federal	State	Local & Intermediate	Private[1]
Alaska	$967,765,000	14.6	64.9	18.3	2.2
California	$24,219,792,000	8.0	62.2	28.6	1.2
Colorado	$2,919,916,000	4.9	42.0	49.7	3.4
District of Columbia	$670,654,000	10.4	—	89.1	0.5
Florida	$9,661,012,000	8.3	48.5	39.1	4.1
Mississippi	$1,600,752,000	17.1	53.7	25.4	3.8
New Jersey	$9,915,429,000	4.2	41.4	52.1	2.3
New York	$20,898,267,000	6.0	39.2	53.3	1.5
Texas	$15,121,655,000	7.5	40.4	49.6	2.9
Washington	$4,679,873,000	5.6	71.3	20.1	3.0

[1]Includes revenues from gifts, and tuition and fees from patrons.

Note: Excludes revenues for state education agencies. Because of rounding, details may not add to totals.

(Source: National Center for Education Statistics, *Digest of Education Statistics 1995,* [Washington, DC: U.S. Department of Education], pp. 152, 157.)

and the Department of Labor (Job Corps and the Comprehensive Employment Training Act [CETA]). Since 1980, the federal contribution to education has declined to 5.4 percent of the gross domestic product (GDP) (National Center for Education Statistics, 1995b, 399). Federal aid has increasingly been given directly to the states in the form of **block grants,** which a state or local education agency may spend as it wishes with few limitations. The 1981 **Education Consolidation and Improvement Act (ECIA)** gave the states a broad range of choices in spending federal money. The ECIA significantly reduced federal aid to education, however, thus making state aid to education even more critical.

Though a small proportion of the funds for schools comes from the federal level, the federal government has enacted supplemental programs to help meet the educational needs of special student populations. Such programs are often referred to collectively as **entitlements.** The most significant is the Elementary and Secondary Education Act of 1965. Title I of the act allocates a billion dollars annually to school districts with large numbers of students from low-income families. Among the other funded entitlement programs are the Vocational Education Act (1963), the Manpower Development and Training Act (1963), the Economic Opportunity Act (1964), the Bilingual Education Act (1968), the Indian Education Act (1972), and the Education for All Handicapped Children Act (1975).

The federal government also provides funding for preschool programs such as Project Head Start. Originally started under the Economic Opportunity Act of 1964 to provide preschool experiences to poor children, Head Start was later made available to children whose parents were above the poverty level. Currently, it is estimated that Head Start and similar programs serve fewer than half of the nation's three- and four-year-olds living in poverty (Elam, Rose, and Gallup 1992, 48). While some research studies concluded that the benefits of Head Start disappeared as children progressed through school, others concluded that the program was effective and provided a $3 return for every dollar spent (Elam, Rose, and Gallup 1993, 143). Although the cost of providing preschool programs to all children would be great—an estimated $30 billion annually (Elam, Rose, and Gallup 1992, 143)—the public believes that preschool experiences are important. Three-fourths believe that preschool programs for children from poverty-level households would help them perform better in school during their teenage years, and a slight majority (49 percent versus 42 percent) say they would be "willing" to pay increased taxes to fund such programs.

How are schools funded in the United States at the local, state, and federal levels? How does the system of school funding contribute to inequities? What are some solutions to the problem of funding inequity?

WHAT ARE SOME TRENDS IN
FUNDING FOR EQUITY AND EXCELLENCE [?]

The fact that schools have had to rely heavily on property taxes for support has resulted in fiscal inequities for schools. Districts with a high level of property wealth are able to generate more money per pupil than districts with less. The degree of inequity between the wealthiest and the poorest districts, therefore, can be quite large. In some states, for example, the ability of one district to generate local property tax revenues may be as much as seven times greater than another district's (Odden 1988, 121).

In *Savage Inequalities: Children in America's Schools,* noted educator Jonathan Kozol (1991) presents a compelling analysis of the inequities in school funding. Some affluent suburban districts, for example, spend more than twice as much per pupil as schools in the nearby inner city. Disputing those who claim that parental values, not high spending on education, determines how much children learn, Kozol points out that high spending on education in affluent districts *does* coincide with high achievement.

TAX REFORM AND REDISTRICTING

To correct funding inequities, several court suits were initiated during the 1970s. In the 1971 *Serrano v. Priest* case in California, it was successfully argued that the relationship between spending and property wealth violated the state's obligation to provide equal protection and education. The California Supreme Court ruled in a six-to-one decision that the quality of a child's education should not be dependent on the "wealth of his parents and neighbors." The court also recognized that communities with a poor tax base could not be expected to generate the revenues of more affluent districts. Nevertheless, the Court did not forbid the use of property taxes to fund education.

Then, in 1973, the U.S. Supreme Court decided in *San Antonio Independent School District v. Rodriguez* that fiscal inequities stemming from unequal tax bases did not violate the Constitution. That court's decision reversed a lower court's ruling claiming that school financing on the basis of local property taxes was unconstitutional.

Regardless of the mixed outcomes of court challenges, many state legislatures have enacted school finance equity reforms during the last fifteen years. A few states (California, Hawaii, New Mexico, Washington, and West Virginia, for example) have led the way by developing programs to ensure statewide financial equality. These states have **full-funding programs** in which the state sets the same per-pupil expenditure level for all schools and districts. This trend toward equal funding was supported by a 1993 Gallup Poll of the public's attitudes toward the public schools, which revealed that 85 percent of the public supported equal funding, even if it meant taking funds from wealthy districts and giving it to poor districts (Elam, Rose, and Gallup 1993, 142).

Other states have adopted new funding formulas to try to broaden their revenue base. Level funding augmented by sales taxes, cigarette taxes, state lottery revenues, property taxes on second homes, and school-choice plans are among the solutions tried. One of the most dramatic changes in educational funding occurred in Michigan in 1993 with the passage of Proposal A, a plan that greatly reduced school funding from local property taxes and increased funding from the state's sales tax.

Since each state has been free to determine the number of districts within its boundaries—the number varied from 1,046 in Texas to 1 in Hawaii in 1993–94 (National Center for Education Statistics 1995a, 97)—a common approach to achieving equal funding is **redistricting,** redrawing school district boundaries to reduce the range of variation in the ability of school districts to finance education. Redistricting not only equalizes funding; it can reduce the cost of maintaining and operating schools if smaller districts are combined. The per-pupil cost of instruction, supplies, and equipment is usually lower in large districts. In addition, greater resources often allow larger districts to offer a broader curriculum and higher salaries to attract more qualified teachers.

VERTICAL EQUITY

Other states have developed various mechanisms for providing **vertical equity**, that is, for allocating funds according to legitimate educational needs. Thus, additional support is given to programs that serve students from low-income backgrounds; those with limited English proficiency, or special gifts and talents; and those who need special education or vocational programs.

Additional state-appropriated funds to cover the costs of educating students with special needs are known as **categorical aid.** Funding adjustments are also made to compensate for differences in costs within a state—higher expenses due to rural isolation or the higher cost of living in urban areas, for example. Some states even conduct periodic regional cost-of-living analyses, which are then used to determine adjustments in per-pupil funding.

SCHOOL CHOICE

Interest has grown in proposals that would allow students to attend schools based on **school choice,** especially after former president Bush made parental choice a part of his educational platform. According to the 1995 Phi Delta Kappan/Gallup Poll of the public's attitudes toward the public schools, 65 percent were in favor of allowing students and their parents to choose among public schools; however, only 33 percent favored allowing them to choose a private school to attend at public expense (Elam and Rose 1995, 46). Currently, more than half of the states have adopted some form of parental choice programs, and many others are considering them.

Nevertheless, heated debate continues about whether school choice programs promote equity and excellence. Choice programs are often criticized because it is believed that more affluent, better-educated, Anglo families take advantage of the programs. In addition, *School Choice,* a report released by the Carnegie Foundation for the Advancement of Teaching in 1992, concluded that choice programs do not necessarily improve students' achievement, require additional money, and may serve to widen the gap between rich and poor districts. On the other hand, proponents point to research data and testimonials in support of choice programs. For example, survey results from 126 principals in Minnesota, a state with strong support for choice, indicated that choice

> increased competition and collaboration between school districts; stimulated improvements to school curricula and support services; promoted greater parent and teacher involvement in school planning and decision making; fostered a more equitable distribution of school resources and student access to educational services; and increased the ethnic and cultural diversity of schools (Tenbusch and Michael 1993, 1).

Dear Mentor

Dear Brad,

Whenever newly trained teachers enter the classroom, they are frequently concerned with curriculum and classroom management, but rather quickly they see the need for a better understanding of allocation of monies and resources. You are to be commended for expressing an interest in school finance early in your career.

Historically, the funding of American schools has come from taxation of its citizens. That tradition has continued, but has taken on some rather complex features in regard to how the collected taxes are to be dispersed. Almost half of the financial support for public schools comes from state coffers. In most states, legislators have established a modified foundation program or have enacted equalization formulas.

Other sources of funding, which directly impact the classroom, are federal grants, challenge grants (such as the Annenberg), entitlements, state lotteries, and technology grants from businesses. Some businesses adopt schools and assist those schools in the acquisition of computers and other instructional materials. School improvement funds are available in some states, providing resources for the purchase of computers and for staff development.

As a classroom teacher, I have taken advantage of several resources to enhance my instructional program, including small grants from service clubs such as Rotary International, the National Endowment for the Humanities, and the American Red Cross. At my school the Parent–Teacher Association recently purchased new television sets and VCRs for nine classrooms. The PTA also reimburses teachers for instructional materials purchased by teachers.

Low-cost and free materials are listed in national and state educational publications. I recently purchased 100 paperbacks for $99.00, an offer that was extended through one of several publishing companies serving junior high students. I also make the rounds of libraries, seeking cast-off books. Having personal library cards from three city libraries helps to supplement my classroom resources. Then, after Christmas, large and small retail stores offer materials at reduced prices. I may find inexpensive bolts of fabric, lace and yarn, and artificial flowers to assist me in art projects. Last year I found big tubs of sidewalk chalk on sale at a local drug store. That chalk was used in combination with other materials to produce art work relating to our study of a South American Spanish poem.

Seeking out sources of funding remains a challenging task, but individual teachers can be very resourceful and successful in providing enriching resources for their students.

Mary Rose Harrell
Junior High School Teacher

> ### Dear Mentor,
>
> Are all the resources you feel your students need available to you? I have heard stories of teachers conducting fundraisers for more supplies or even getting materials out of their own pockets. What are your thoughts? Which schemes for increasing funding for schools do you support?
>
> Brad Mack

VOUCHER SYSTEMS

One approach to providing educational equity that has generated considerable controversy is the **voucher system** of distributing educational funds. Although various plans have been proposed, one of the most common would give states the freedom to distribute money directly to parents in the form of vouchers. Parents would then use the vouchers to enroll their children in schools of their choice. Some voucher proposals would allow parents to choose from among public as well as private (secular, parochial, for-profit, and charter) schools; others would limit parents' choice to public schools. The public opposed the voucher idea by a 54 percent to 45 percent majority, according to the 1994 Gallup Poll of the Public's Attitudes Toward the Public Schools; and voucher referendums were solidly rejected in Oregon, Colorado, and California during the early 1990s.

People in favor of the voucher system of distributing funds say that it would make available to students from low socioeconomic backgrounds the same educational opportunities available to students from more advantaged backgrounds. Furthermore, the voucher system would be a direct, powerful way to make schools accountable to local citizens. In open competition, schools that were not excellent and did not possess the factors parents consider important in choosing a school would not survive.

Issues in Education

- In your opinion, what is the likelihood that vouchers would improve equity and excellence in education? What are your reasons?
- On what side of the issue does this cartoonist stand?
- What is the cartoonist's implicit claim about opponents of the voucher idea?
- In your opinion, should publicly funded school choice and voucher systems include the option of parents enrolling their children in private schools? Why or why not?

Opponents of the voucher system point out that allowing parents to choose where to send their children to school will not necessarily improve education, nor will it promote educational equity:

> No evidence supports the conclusion that massive institutional decentralization and reliance on the marketplace will improve education. [R]esearch . . . leads to the conclusion that school choice theorists have misidentified the problems with the education system and that their proposed cures are likely to reduce equity without improving performance. Public choice in education simply does not work (Smith and Meier 1995, 121).

> Since poor parents lack the supplemental resources that rich people have for helping their children, it is foolish to argue that voucher programs would help to equalize educational opportunities. (For example, rich parents can afford the extra costs for transportation, clothing, and educational supplies when they send their children to a distant, private school; poor parents cannot) (Berliner and Biddle 1995, 175).

Other critics contend that vouchers could lead to the creation of segregated schools and schools that would be more committed to competing for education dollars and the most able, manageable students. Still others point out that, while voucher systems are offered as a solution to America's education crisis (Chubb and Moe 1990), our nation's school system is *not* failing, it is *perceived* as failing. As David Berliner and Bruce Biddle (1995, 4) point out in *The Manufactured Crisis: Myths, Fraud, and the Attack on America's Public Schools,* "When one actually *looks* at the evidence [for a failing school system], one discovers that most of the claims of the Manufactured Crisis are, indeed, myths, half-truths, and sometimes outright lies."

CORPORATE-EDUCATION PARTNERSHIPS

To develop additional sources of funding for equity and excellence, many local school districts have established partnerships with the private sector. Businesses may contribute funds or materials needed by a school, sponsor sports teams, award scholarships, provide cash grants for pilot projects and teacher development, and even construct school buildings. One example of a corporate-education partnership is Thomas Jefferson High School for Science and Technology, a college preparatory magnet school in Alexandria, Virginia. Twenty-five local and multinational businesses, including AT&T, Mobil, Boeing, Honeywell, and Exxon, raised almost a million dollars for the school. State-of-the-art facilities include a $600,000 telecommunications lab with a television studio, radio station, weather station, and a satellite earth station. The school has a biotech laboratory for genetic engineering experiments in cloning and cell fission as well as labs for research on energy and computers.

Corporate contributions to education, about $2 billion annually, have more than tripled over the past decade for a total of $13.4 billion. About 9 percent goes to elementary and secondary education and the rest to colleges, including grants to improve teacher preparation. *Fortune* magazine's third annual education poll of the *Fortune* Industrial 500 and Service 500 companies found that the percentage of businesses donating $1 million or more to education annually rose from 18 percent in 1990 to 24 percent in 1991.

If America's schools are to succeed in meeting the challenges of the twenty-first century, they will need to be funded at a level that provides quality educational experiences to students from a diverse array of backgrounds. Though innovative approaches to school funding have been developed, much remains to be done before both excellence and equity characterize all schools in the United States.

How Do Political Events Influence Education?

■ Parents, students, teachers, administrators, taxpayers, state and federal authorities, minorities and women, educational theorists and researchers, and businesses and corporations are among the groups that exert political influence on education.

■ Schools reflect the society they serve and thus are influenced by out-of-school factors such as the mass media, demographic shifts, international events, and social issues.

What Is the Role of the Local Community in School Governance?

■ Local school districts, which vary greatly in size, locale, organizational structure, demographics, and wealth, are responsible for the management and operation of schools.

■ Local schools boards, whose members are usually elected, set educational policies for a district; however, many people believe that boards should be reformed to be more well-informed and responsive.

■ The superintendent, the chief administrator of a local district, has a complex array of responsibilities and must work cooperatively with the school board and others in an environment that is often politically turbulent.

■ Through groups like the PTA or PTO, some parents are involved in local school activities and reform efforts; others are involved with private schools; and some actively promote alternative approaches to education such as school choice, voucher systems, and home schooling.

■ As part of the restructuring movement, schools are changing their policies for governance, curricula, and community collaboration; the Chicago School Reform Act is one example of restructuring based on school-based management which empowers teachers, principals, parents, community members, and students at local schools.

What Powers and Influence Do States Have in Governing Schools?

■ The state legislature, state courts, and the governor significantly influence education by setting policies related to the management and operation of schools within a state.

■ The state board of education, the highest educational agency in a state, regulates education and advises the governor and others on important educational policies.

■ The state department of education implements policies related to teacher certification, allocation of state and federal funds, enforcement of state and federal guidelines, school accreditation, and research and evaluation projects to improve education.

■ The chief state school officer oversees education within a state and, in collaboration with the governor, legislature, state board of education, and the public, provides leadership to improve education.

■ Professional standards boards set criteria for the certification and professional development of education personnel in some states; in others, state standards boards are limited to advising educational policymakers.

What Assistance Do Regional Education Agencies Provide?

■ The Regional Educational Service Agency (RESA), an intermediate unit of educational administration in about half of the states, provides assistance to two or more school districts for staff development, curriculum development, instructional media, and program evaluation.

How Does the Federal Government Influence Education?

■ The federal government influences education at the state level through funding general and categorical programs, establishing and enforcing standards and regulations, conducting and disseminating educational research, providing technical assistance to improve education, and encouraging equity and excellence for the nation's schools.

■ The national legislature, federal and Supreme courts, and the president significantly influence educational funding, regulations, research and dissemination, and policy development.

■ The U.S. Department of Education, a cabinet-level department, supports and disseminates educational research through ERIC, administers federal grants in education, and assists the president in developing and promoting a national agenda for education.

How Are Schools Financed in the United States?

■ Schools are supported with revenues from the local, state, and federal levels, with most funding now coming from the state level.

■ Local funding is provided through property taxes, which in many instances results in inequitable funding for schools located in areas with an insufficient tax base.

■ One challenge to financing schools has been the development of an equitable means of taxation for the support of education.

What Are Some Trends in Funding for Equity and Excellence?

■ Many state legislatures have enacted tax reforms including full-funding programs which set the same per-pupil expenditures for all schools and districts. Some states have achieved greater equity through redistricting—redrawing district boundaries to reduce funding inequities.

■ Some states achieve vertical equity by providing additional funding, or categorical aid, to educate students with special needs. Also, many local districts and schools receive additional funding through partnerships with the private sector.

■ School choice and voucher programs are two controversial approaches to providing parents the freedom to select the schools their children attend.

KEY TERMS AND CONCEPTS

Teacher's Journal

1. Reflect on this chapter's epigraph by Joel Spring: "Politicians compete among themselves for political positions, and workers and business people compete for higher wages and profits. Schools supply the arena for such competition" (Spring 1993, 47–48). Describe some examples of how politicians, workers, and business people are currently using schools to promote their interests within your state. Which actions do you support? Which do you oppose?

2. From this chapter's list of factors that exert a press on schools ("How Do Political Events Influence Education?"), select one factor and describe how it is currently influencing education at the national level. How is this factor influencing schools at the local level in your area?

3. Imagine that you are given vouchers to send your child to any school in your state. What factors would you consider in making your choice? Compare your list with the following list, most important coming first, from a recent survey of parents: quality of teaching staff, maintenance of school discipline, courses offered, size of classes, and test scores of students. What are the similarities and differences between the lists? What do the differences reveal about your view of education and schools?

4. Think of businesses and agencies in your community that might be good partners for a school. Select one of them and develop a proposal outlining the nature, activities, and benefits (to both) of the partnership you envision.

Teacher's Database

1. Use the Internet and the World Wide Web to gather information about the structure of education and school funding in your state. How many districts are in your state? Which is the largest? What are enrollment figures, trends, and projections for your state? What are the figures for household income and poverty rate? What proportion of school funding in your state is from the local, state, and federal levels? What are the total expenditures and per-pupil expenditures?

Begin your data search in the U.S. Department of Education's National Center for Education Statistics (NCES) via the Institutional Communications Network (INET). The INET provides access to education research, statistics, and information about the U.S. Department of Education. The Office of Educational Research and Improvement (OERI) Gopher Server is an electronic pathway to NCES data.

Office of Educational Research and Improvement (OERI):
    Gopher: gopher.ed.gov

Over the OERI Server, the INET makes available NCES data from the *Digest of Education Statistics,* the *Condition of Education, Youth Indicators, Projections of Education Statistics,* the *Directory of Department of Education Publications,* the *Directory of Current OERI-Funded Projects,* and the *Directory of Computer Data Files.*

2. Find information on sources of funding for education, education budgets, and issues of education finance. Access the U.S. Department of Education Office of Educational Research and Improvement (OERI) Gopher Server, or contact:

NCESINFO@INET.ED.GOV.

1. Visit a private (secular, parochial, for-profit, or charter) school. Find out how teachers and other staff members are hired and how the school is organized and governed. How does the management and operation of this school differ from public schools?

2. Interview a school superintendent and ask him or her to comment on how federal, state, and local forces affect education in the district. To what extent do influences at these three levels help (and/or hinder) the district in accomplishing its goals?

3. Interview a teacher and ask how legislation at the federal and state levels affects the teacher's work. Would the teacher like to see the federal government more or less involved in education? Report your findings to the rest of the class.

4. Attend a meeting of a local school board and observe the communication and decision-making process at that meeting. To help you make this observation, ask your instructor for handout master M6.1, "Observing Community-Based Decision Making on Education."

5. To understand how school-based decision making works, observe a meeting of a site-based council (SBC) or local school council (LSC). For guidance in making this observation, ask your instructor for handout master M6.2, "Observing School-Based Decision Making."

Professional Portfolio

Prepare a profile of a school district. The district may be in your home town, your college or university community, or a community in which you would like to teach. Information on the district may be obtained from your university library, public library, school district offices, state board of education, or professional teacher associations.

Keeping in mind that school district statistics are more readily available in some cases than in others, your profile might include the following types of information:

- Organizational chart showing (if possible) personnel currently assigned to each position
- Tables showing numbers of school buildings, students, teachers, administrators, support personnel, etc.
- Graduation/dropout rate
- Scores on standardized achievement tests
- Total annual budget
- Expenditures per pupil
- Entitlement programs
- Demographic characteristics of population living in the area served by the district—age, race/ethnicity, socioeconomic status, unemployment rate, etc.
- Volunteer groups serving schools in the district
- Pupil-teacher ratio
- Percent of ethnic minority students, students with disabilities, etc.
- Percent of students going on to college

Teachers [must] balance public obligations with their personal beliefs and purposes in teaching.

—David T. Hansen
The Call to Teach

Legal Concerns
in American Education

*A*fter a year of open meetings for teachers, administrators, parents, and students, the school district in which you work narrowly approved a proposal requiring students at the district's three high schools to complete forty hours of community service during high school and to participate in reflective classroom discussions on those experiences. The new program has no opt-out feature; however, students may select from a wide array of pre-approved service projects, or they may develop their own.

It is now early September, and students in your third-period high school class have just returned to the classroom after attending an assembly at which the principal introduced the mandatory community service project. Before turning to a brief review of yesterday's lesson, you ask if any students have decided upon a service-learning project for the year.

"I'm gonna work on the stream," Dave says excitedly, referring to a clean-up project for the stream that runs behind the school.

"Me too," Carol says, smiling at Dave. A few students giggle, amused at Carol's willingness to acknowledge publicly the close friendship that has begun to develop recently between her and Dave.

"Hank, what are you going to do?" you ask, turning to acknowledge the waving hand to your left.

"I want to work at the after-school day care center," Hank says. "I think that'd be a trip. Like, help'n those little kids and everything."

"Well, I ain't gonna do nothin'," Richard suddenly blurts out from the back of the room. He scowls and emits a long groan before continuing. "I ain't gonna be nobody's servant."

"Hey, chill out," Frank says, turning in his seat to address his classmate. "Nobody wants you to be a servant. The whole idea is just to help somebody out . . . you know, improve things."

"Yeah, it's not a big deal," says Carol.

"Now, let's give him a chance to speak," you say, responding to the murmurs of several students who obviously disagree with Richard.

"That's a violation of my rights," Richard continues. "It's like slavery or something . . . makin' him (Dave) pick up garbage down at the stream."

"Well, that's not the district's intention," you say. At this point, you decide to refocus the discussion on students' choices for their service-learning projects. "Okay, let's hear what some other people are going to do." You look toward Jane seated next to the window and, with a slight sweep of your hand, invite her to speak.

After allowing the discussion to continue for a few minutes, you turn the class' attention to the review. As you proceed with the lesson, you wonder if Richard does have a right not to participate in the service-learning project.

■

The preceding scenario, based on actual events that culminated in the filing of a lawsuit against a school district, highlights the role that legal issues can play in the lives of teachers and students. In this instance, a student filed a lawsuit claiming that the mandatory service-learning project violated his rights under the Thirteenth and Fourteenth Amendments. The student's parents joined the lawsuit, claiming that they had a constitutional right to direct their son's education. A U.S. District Court ruled in favor of the school district, whereupon the family appealed to the U.S. Court of Appeals. The court agreed with the district court that the service-learning program did not resemble involuntary servitude addressed by the Thirteenth Amendment. Also, while the parents' "liberty interest" in raising their son was recognized by the Fourteenth Amendment, the parents did not object to the program on religious grounds; thus the court did not extend constitutional protection to their secular claim. Lastly, the court maintained that the program was reasonably related to the state's function of educating students (*Immediato v. Rye Neck School Dist.*, 1996).

In this chapter we examine significant legal decisions that affect the rights and responsibilities of teachers, administrators, students, and parents. Teachers must act in accordance with a wide range of federal and state legislation and court decisions. As a teacher, you may need to deal with such legal issues as the teacher's responsibility for accidents, discriminatory employment practices, freedom of speech, desegregation, student rights, and circumstances related to job termination or dismissal. Without knowledge of the legal dimensions of such issues, you will be ill-equipped to protect your rights and the rights of your students.

WHY DO YOU NEED A PROFESSIONAL CODE OF ETHICS [?]

The actions of professional teachers are determined not only by what is legally required of them, but also by what they know they *ought* to do. They do what is legally right, and they *do the right thing*. A specific set of values guides them. A deep and lasting commitment to professional practice characterizes their work. They have adopted a high standard of professional ethics and they model behaviors that are in accord with that code of ethics.

At present, the teaching profession does not have a uniform **code of ethics** similar to the Hippocratic oath, which all doctors are legally required to take when they begin practice. However, the largest professional organization for teachers, the National Education Association (NEA) has a code of ethics for its members (see the Teacher's Resource Guide at the back of this book for the complete text).

NEA Code of Ethics

The educator, believing in the worth and dignity of each human being, recognizes the supreme importance of the pursuit of truth, devotion to excellence, and the nurture of democratic principles. Essential to these goals is the protection of freedom to learn and to teach and the guarantee of equal opportunity for all. The educator accepts the responsibility to adhere to the highest ethical standards.

ETHICAL TEACHING ATTITUDES AND PRACTICES

Teaching is an ethical enterprise—that is, a teacher has an obligation to act ethically, to follow what he or she knows to be the most appropriate professional action to take. The best interests of students, not the teacher, provide the rule of thumb for determining what is ethical and what is not. Behaving ethically is more than a matter of following the rules or not breaking the law—it means acting in a way that promotes the learning and growth of students and helps them realize their potential.

Unethical acts break the trust and respect on which good student-teacher relationships are based. An example of unethical conduct would be public ridicule of Richard (described in this chapter's opening vignette) for his opposition to his school's service learning project. Other examples would be using grades as a form of punishment, expressing rage in the classroom, or intentionally tricking students on tests. You could no doubt think of other examples from your own experience as a student.

ETHICAL DILEMMAS IN CLASSROOM AND SCHOOL

Teachers routinely encounter **ethical dilemmas** in the classroom and in the school. They often have to take action in situations in which all the facts are not known or for which no single course of action can be called right or wrong. At these times it can be quite difficult to decide what an ethical response might be. Dealing satisfactorily with ethical dilemmas in teaching often requires the ability to see beyond short-range consequences to consider long-range consequences.

Consider, for example, the following three questions based on actual case studies. On the basis of the information given, how would you respond to each situation?

1. Should the sponsor of the high school literary magazine refuse to print a well-written story by a budding writer if the piece appears to satirize a teacher and a student?

What ethical dilemmas might this experiment pose for a teacher? How might you respond? On what moral or ethical grounds would you base your response? What legal concerns might be involved?

2. Is a reading teacher justified in trying to increase achievement for an entire class by separating two disruptive students and placing one in a reading group beneath his reading level?
3. Should a chemistry teacher punish a student (on the basis of circumstantial, inconclusive evidence) for a laboratory explosion if the example of decisive, swift punishment will likely prevent the recurrence of a similar event and thereby ensure the safety of all students?

WHAT ARE YOUR LEGAL RIGHTS AS A TEACHER ?

It is frequently observed that with each freedom comes a corresponding responsibility to others and to the community in which we live. As long as there is more than one individual inhabiting this planet, there is a need for laws to clarify individual rights and responsibilities. This necessary balance between rights and responsibilities is perhaps more critical to teaching than to any other profession. As Michael Imber and Tyll Van Geel (1993, 514) put it,

> The treatment of teachers is an extremely delicate area of education law. The school has both a right and an obligation to ensure that all its employees perform the legitimate duties of their jobs. However, the school's power over teachers is limited because they retain the same constitutional rights as any citizen. Many cases require balancing a teacher's constitutional rights against a school's need to promote its goal.

While schools do have limited "power over" teachers, teachers' rights to **due process** cannot be violated. Teachers, like all citizens, are protected from being treated arbitrarily by those in authority. A principal who disagrees with a teacher's methods cannot suddenly fire that teacher. A school board cannot ask a teacher to resign merely by claiming that the teacher's political activities outside of school are "disruptive" of the educational process. A teacher cannot be dismissed for "poor" performance without ample documentation that the performance was, in fact, poor and without sufficient time to meet clearly stated performance evaluation criteria.

CERTIFICATION

Karla Brown is a junior high school English teacher and lives in a state with a law specifying that a teacher must show proof of five years of successful teaching experience for a teaching certificate to be renewed. Last year was Karla's fifth year of teaching, and her principal gave her an unsatisfactory performance rating. Karla's principal told her that her teaching certificate cannot be renewed. Is the principal correct?

Karla's principal is mistaken about the grounds for nonrenewal of a teaching certificate. According to the state's law, *unsuccessful* performance, or a failure to complete the school year, is grounds for nonrenewal of a certificate—not performance that is judged to be *unsatisfactory.* Because state laws vary and *unsuccessful performance* is defined differently in different states, however, Karla's principal might have been correct if she taught in another state.

No teacher who meets all of a state's requirements for initial certification can arbitrarily be denied a certificate. And once obtained, a certificate may not be revoked without due process of law. For a certificate to be revoked, the reason must be job-related and demonstrably impair the teacher's ability to perform satisfactorily. In this regard, the case of a California teacher whose certificate was revoked because someone admitted to having a homosexual relationship with the teacher is often cited. The court determined that the teacher's homosexual conduct was not an impairment to the teacher's performance and ordered the certificate restored (*Morrison v. State Board of Education,* 1969). However, in another case the courts ruled in favor of the California State Board of Education that had revoked the certificate of a teacher who had committed a homosexual act on a public beach. The courts upheld the termination on the basis of the teacher's "unmoral conduct" and the teacher's "publicly held stance" in support of such conduct (*Sarac v. State Board of Education,* 1969).

TEACHERS' RIGHTS TO NONDISCRIMINATION

Harold Jones has met all the qualifications for teaching but is denied certification because he has a prison record. Several years ago he was convicted of a felony. Harold claims he is being discriminated against because of his past. Is he right?

States may impose certain limitations on initial certification as long as those limitations are not discriminatory in regard to race, religion, ethnic origin, sex, or age. Nearly all the states, for example, require that applicants for a teaching certificate pass a test that covers basic skills, professional knowledge, or academic subject areas. Qualifications for initial certification may also legally include certain personal qualities. The case of Harold Jones at the beginning of this section, for example, is based on an Oregon case involving a man who had successfully completed a teacher training program but was denied a certificate because he had once been found guilty of a felony and served a term in prison. The Oregon State Board of Education raised some legitimate questions regarding the moral character of the applicant. The court held that a criminal conviction is proof of bad moral character, and his character flaw is irremediable regardless of the passage of time and subsequent legal behavior. As a result, he was unable to obtain the teaching certificate he needed to be hired as a teacher (*Application of Bay v. State Board of Education,* 1963).

The right to **nondiscrimination** in regard to employment is protected by Title VII of the Civil Rights Act of 1964, which states:

It shall be an unlawful employment practice for an employer (1) to fail or refuse to hire or to discharge any individual, or otherwise to discriminate against any individual with respect to his compensation, terms, conditions, or privileges of employment, because of such individual's race, color, religion, sex, or national origin; or (2) to limit, segregate, or classify his employees or applicants for employment in any way which would deprive or tend to deprive any individual of employment opportunities or otherwise adversely affect his status as an employee, because of such individual's race, color, religion, sex, or national origin.

TEACHING CONTRACTS

A **teaching contract** represents an agreement between the teacher and a board of education. For a contract to be valid, it must meet these five criteria:

1. *Manifestation of mutual assent*—There must be a formal offer and acceptance of the terms of the contract by the employee.
2. *Consideration*—The teacher must receive valid and adequate consideration (i.e., promise of remuneration) for his or her services.
3. *Competence of the parties*—The parties entering into the contract with the school board must be competent. The board cannot enter into contracts beyond the authority given to it by the state, and the teacher must meet the criteria for employment.
4. *Legality of subject*—The subject of the contract must not be illegal or against public policy.
5. *Satisfaction of statutory requirements for formation of a contract*—The contract must satisfy state contract laws (Imber and Van Geel 1993).

Before you sign your teaching contract, it is important that you read it carefully and be certain that it is signed by the appropriate member(s) of the board of education or board of trustees. Ask for clarification of any sections you don't understand. It is preferable that any additional nonteaching duties be spelled out in writing rather than left to an oral agreement. Because all board of education policies and regulations will be part of your contract, you should also read any available teacher handbook or school policy handbook.

The importance of carefully reading a contract and asking for clarification is illustrated in the following case study:

> Victor Sanchez had just begun his first year as an English teacher at a high school in a city of about 300,000. Victor became quite upset when he learned that he had been assigned by his principal to sponsor the poetry club. The club was to meet once a week after school. Victor refused to sponsor the club, saying that the contract he had signed referred only to his teaching duties during regular school hours. Could Victor be compelled to sponsor the club?

Certain assignments, though not specified in a contract, may be required of teachers in addition to their regular teaching load, as long as there is a reasonable relationship between the teacher's classroom duties and the additional assignment. Furthermore, such assignments can include supervision of school events on weekends as well. Though Victor's contract did not make specific reference to club sponsorship, such a duty would be a reasonable addition to his regular teaching assignment.

When school authorities have assigned teachers to additional duties not reasonably related to their teaching, the courts have tended to rule in favor of teachers who file suit. For example, a school's directive to a tenured teacher of American history to assume the additional role of basketball coach was not upheld by a court of appeals (*Unified School Dist. No. 241 v. Swanson,* 1986).

DUE PROCESS IN TENURE AND DISMISSAL

Tenure is a policy that provides the individual teacher with job security by (1) preventing his or her dismissal on insufficient grounds and (2) providing him or her with due process in the event of dismissal. Tenure is granted to teachers by the local school district after a period of satisfactory teaching, usually two to five years. In most cases, tenure may not be transferred from one school district to another.

The following case study highlights the importance of tenure to a teacher's professional career:

> A teacher was dismissed from his teaching position by the school board after it learned that the teacher was a homosexual. The teacher filed suit in court, claiming that his firing was arbitrary and violated the provisions of tenure that he had been granted. The school board, on the other hand, maintained that his conduct was inappropriate for a teacher. Was the school board justified in dismissing the teacher?

The events in this case were actually heard by a court, which ruled that the teacher was unfairly dismissed (*Burton v. Cascade School Dist. Union High School,* 1975). The court said that the board violated the teacher's rights as a tenured employee by failing to show "good and just cause" for dismissal. The teacher was awarded the balance due under his contract and an additional one-half year's salary. In a similar case, however, a court upheld the dismissal of a teacher whose sexual orientation was the target of parents' complaints and students' comments. The court ruled that the teacher could no longer effectively carry out his teaching duties (*Gaylord v. Tacoma School District No. 10,* 1977).

The practice of providing teachers with tenure is not without controversy. Some critics point out that tenure policies make it too difficult to dismiss incompetent teachers and that performance standards are high in many other fields that do not provide employees with job security. Generally, however, the courts have held that "tenure is for the improvement of education and not for the special benefit of any one class [of teachers]" (Peterson, Rossmiller, and Volz 1978, 470).

Just about every state today has a tenure law that specifies that a teacher may be dismissed with good cause; what counts as a good cause varies from state to state. The courts have ruled on a variety of reasons for **dismissal**: (1) insubordination, (2) incompetence or inefficiency, (3) neglect of duty, (4) conduct unbecoming a teacher, (5) subversive activities, (6) retrenchment or decreased need for services, (7) physical and/or mental health, (8) age, (9) causing or encouraging disruption, (10) engaging in illegal activities, (11) using offensive language, (12) personal appearance, (13) sex-related activities, (14) political activities, and (15) use of drugs or intoxicants.

For a tenured teacher to be dismissed, a systematic series of steps must be followed so that the teacher receives due process and his or her constitutionally guaranteed rights are not violated. Due process involves a careful, step-by-step examination of the charges brought against a teacher. Most states have outlined procedures that adhere to the following nine steps:

1. The teacher must be notified of the list of charges.
2. Adequate time must be provided for the teacher to prepare a rebuttal to the charges.
3. The teacher must be given the names of witnesses and access to evidence.
4. The hearing must be conducted before an impartial tribunal.
5. The teacher has the right to representation by legal counsel.
6. The teacher (or legal counsel) can introduce evidence and cross-examine adverse witnesses.
7. The school board's decision must be based on the evidence and findings of the hearing.
8. A transcript or record must be maintained of the hearing.
9. The teacher has the right to appeal an adverse decision.

These steps notwithstanding, it should be noted that "the definition [of due process] in each instance depends largely on a combination of the specific facts in a situation, the law governing the situation, the particular time in history in which judgment is being rendered, and the predilections of the individual judge(s) rendering the decision" (LaMorte 1996, 6), as the following case study illustrates:

> Near the start of his fifth year of teaching at an elementary school in a small city, and two years after earning tenure, Mr. Mitchell went through a sudden and painful divorce. A few months later a woman whom he had met around the time of his divorce moved into the house he was renting.
>
> For the remainder of the school year he and the woman lived together. During this time, he received no indication that his life-style was professionally unacceptable, and his teaching performance remained satisfactory.
>
> At the end of the year, however, Mr. Mitchell was notified that he was being dismissed because of immoral conduct; that is, he was living with a woman he was not married to. The school board called for a hearing and Mr. Mitchell presented his side of the case. The board, nevertheless, decided to follow through with its decision to dismiss him. Was the school board justified in dismissing Mr. Mitchell?

Though at one time teachers could readily be dismissed for living, unmarried, with a member of the opposite sex, a life-style such as Mr. Mitchell's is not that unusual today. Because the board had not shown that Mr. Mitchell's alleged immoral conduct had a negative effect on his teaching, his dismissal would probably not hold up in court, unless the community as a whole was upset by his behavior. Moreover, Mr. Mitchell could charge that his right to privacy as guaranteed by the Ninth Amendment to the Constitution had been violated. Overall, it appears that the decision to dismiss Mr. Mitchell was arbitrary and based on the collective bias of the board. Nevertheless, teachers should be aware that courts frequently hold that teachers are role models, and the local community determines "acceptable" behavior both in school and out of school.

Teachers also have the right to organize and to join teacher organizations without fear of dismissal. In addition, most states have passed **collective bargaining** laws that require school boards to negotiate contracts with teacher organizations. Usually, the teacher organization with the most members in a district is given the right to represent teachers in the collective bargaining process.

An important part of most collective bargaining agreements is the right of a teacher to file a **grievance**, a formal complaint against his or her employer. A teacher may not be dismissed for filing a grievance, and he or she is entitled to have the grievance heard by a neutral third party. Often, the teachers' union or professional association that negotiated the collective bargaining agreement will provide a teacher who has filed a grievance with free legal counsel.

One right that teachers are not granted by collective bargaining agreements is the right to strike. Like other public employees, teachers do not have the legal right to strike. Teachers who do strike run the risk of dismissal (*Hortonville Joint School District No. 1 v. Hortonville Education Association,* 1976), though when teacher strikes occur a school board cannot possibly replace all the striking teachers.

ACADEMIC FREEDOM

A male high school English teacher assigned his students an article in the *Atlantic Monthly* that employed and explored the uses of a well-known vulgar term for an incestuous son. Several parents who learned of the assignment protested, and the school

Dear Mentor

NOVICE AND EXPERT TEACHERS ON OBLIGATIONS REGARDING CURRICULUM

Dear Danae,

To answer your initial question, I must state that I have never held a strong personal conviction that prohibited me from teaching the required curriculum. However, I have had to make some difficult decisions as to how best to serve my students. I am a special education teacher. I work at the intermediate level and am often forced to make decisions concerning my student's educational future based upon the laws, regulations, and legal guidelines for the special education program. As we all know, in teaching there are very few absolutes because each student, teacher, and school is different, requiring curriculum interventions appropriate to the needs of the specific student population. To make critical decisions, I would suggest, a new teacher first must know the curriculum requirements of the district and become really knowledgeable regarding the scope and sequence of the curriculum content.

Second, it is essential that you know the curriculum sequence assigned to you. This is an absolute must for all teachers. Remember, for every topic, be it "slavery" or the "first Thanksgiving," there are always multiple issues and concepts to explore. I have found in preparing units or lesson plans that there is always more than one approach that can be taken while presenting content to children. Before you decide you cannot teach a lesson because of your personal beliefs, ask yourself if there is any way that your opinion can be incorporated into the lesson in a fair and objective manner. You must keep in mind that your beliefs are simply your opinions, and you cannot teach your opinions as absolutes or present your values as facts.

> **Dear Mentor,**
>
> I would like to know if you have ever felt constricted by the law in instances of required or censored topics in the curriculum. What happens when required curricula and teachers' personal beliefs conflict?
>
> Danae Martinez

Finally, you must decide what moral obligation you have to your students, the school community, and to yourself. If you decide that the content of the assigned curriculum completely violates your personal beliefs, you must seek relief immediately. One strategy may be simply to find a colleague who would be willing to teach the problematic subject to your students, while you teach his or her students in a different subject area. However, before taking any step, always ask yourself, "Who am I helping or hurting by teaching or not teaching this material?"

In conclusion I would like to remind you that once you sign a contract, you are legally and morally obligated to do just what the contract states. Being a teacher is a wonderful experience, so do not allow yourself to become discouraged by legal mandates and curriculum frameworks. The most important thing to remember is that whatever you teach, however you teach it, will reflect the total of who you are and what you believe. So let the curriculum reflect off the image of YOU, and be the best that you can be. I wish you the best of luck with your career.

Stacey M. DeKnikker
Special Education Teacher

board ordered the teacher not to use the term in class again. The teacher refused and was suspended. Was the teacher acting within his rights?

The above case is based on actual events involving a teacher in Massachusetts. The teacher brought suit against the board to prevent it from carrying out its threat to fire him. In his suit the teacher cited the principle of **academic freedom** and said that the assignment called for a legitimate analysis of a serious piece of writing to illustrate inappropriate language and that the article was published in a respectable magazine. The First Circuit Court of Appeal, pointing out that the term was widely used and could be found in some books in the library, ruled in favor of the teacher. The board was prevented from firing the teacher (*Keefe v. Geanakos,* 1969).

FAMOUS CASES A landmark case involving academic freedom focused on John Scopes, a biology teacher who challenged a Tennessee law in 1925 that made it illegal to teach in a public school "any theory which denies the story of the Divine Creation of man as taught in the Bible, and to teach instead that man is descended from a lower order of animals." Scopes maintained that Darwin's theory about human origins had scientific merit and that the state's requirement that he teach the Biblical account of creation violated his academic freedom.

Scopes's trial, which came to be known as the Monkey Trial, attracted national attention. Prosecuting Scopes was the "silver-tongued" William Jennings Bryan, a famous lawyer, politician, and presidential candidate. The defending attorney was Clarence Darrow.

Scopes believed strongly in academic freedom and his students' right to know about scientific theories. He expressed his views in his memoirs, *Center of the Storm:*

> Especially repulsive are laws restricting the constitutional freedom of teachers, The mere presence of such a law is a club held over the heads of the timid. Legislation that tampers with academic freedom is not protecting society, as its authors piously proclaim. By limiting freedom they are helping to make robot factories out of schools; ultimately, this produces nonthinking robots rather than the individualistic citizens we desperately need—now more than ever before (1966, 277).

The Monkey Trial ended after eleven days of heated, eloquent testimony. Scopes was found guilty of violating the Butler Act and was fined $100. The decision was later reversed by the Tennessee Supreme Court on a technicality.

Since the Scopes trail, controversy has continued to surround the teaching of evolution. In many states during the 1980s, for example, religious fundamentalists won rulings that required science teachers to give equal time to both Creationism and Evolutionism in the classroom. The Supreme Court, however, in *Edwards v. Aguillard* (1987) ruled that such "balanced treatment" laws were unconstitutional. In the words of the Court: "Because the primary purpose of the [Louisiana] Creationism Act is to advance a particular religious belief, the Act endorses religion in violation of the First Amendment." In 1996, controversy over evolution again emerged in Tennessee when lawmakers defeated, by a 20–13 vote, legislation that would allow districts to dismiss teachers for "insubordination" if they taught evolution as fact.

Another case suggesting that a teacher's right to academic freedom is narrow and limited is *Krizek v. Cicero-Stickney Township High School District No. 201* (1989). In this instance, a District Court ruled against a teacher whose contract was not renewed because she showed her students an R-rated film (*About Last Night*) as an example of a modern-day parallel to Thornton Wilder's play *Our Town.* Although the teacher told her students that they would be excused from viewing the film if they or their parents objected, she did not communicate directly with their parents. The teacher's at-

Are there any legal constraints on what this teacher can teach to his students? On what grounds have cases on academic freedom been decided? How are cases involving teachers' rights to academic freedom similar to cases involving students' rights to self-expression? Should this teacher have any concerns about tort liability in this lesson?

tempt to consider the objections of students and parents notwithstanding, the Court concluded that

> . . . the length of the film indicates that its showing was more than an inadvertent mistake or a mere slip of the tongue, but rather was a planned event, and thus indicated that the teacher's approach to teaching was problematic. . . .

Though concerned more with the right of a school to establish a curriculum than with the academic freedom of teachers per se, other cases have focused on the teacher's use of instructional materials. In *Mozert v. Hawkins County Board of Education* (1987, 1988), for example, a group of Tennessee parents objected to "secular humanist" reading materials used by their children's teachers. In *Smith v. Board of School Commissioners of Mobile County* (1987), 624 parents and teachers initiated a court suit alleging that forty-four history, social studies, and home economics texts used in the Mobile County, Alabama, public schools encouraged immorality, undermined parental authority, and were imbued with the "humanist" faith. In both cases, the courts supported the right of schools to establish a curriculum even in the face of parental disapproval. In *Smith v. Board of School Commissioners of Mobile County*, the Eleventh Circuit Court stated that "[i]ndeed, given the diversity of religious views in this country, if the standard were merely inconsistency with the beliefs of a particular religion there would be very little that could be taught in the public schools. . . ."

STATES' RIGHTS   The preceding cases notwithstanding, the courts have not set down specific guidelines to reconcile the teacher's freedom with the state's right to require teachers to follow certain curricular guidelines. The same federal court, for example, heard a similar case regarding a high school teacher who wrote a vulgar word for sexual intercourse on the blackboard during a discussion of socially taboo words. The court actually sidestepped the issue of academic freedom and ruled instead that the regulations authorizing teacher discipline were unconstitutionally vague and, therefore, the teacher could not be dismissed. The court did, however, observe that a public school teacher's right to traditional academic freedom is "qualified," at best, and the "teacher's right must yield to compelling public interests of greater constitutional significance." In reviewing its decision, the court also said, "Nothing herein suggests that school authorities are not free after they have learned that the teacher is using a teaching method of which they disapprove, and which is not appropriate to the proper teaching of the subject, to suspend him [or her] until he [or she] agrees to cease using the method" (*Mailloux v. Kiley,* 1971).

Although some teachers have been successful in citing academic freedom as the basis for teaching controversial subjects, others have been unsuccessful. Teachers have been dismissed for ignoring directives regarding the teaching of controversial topics related to sex, polygamy, race, and religion. Though the courts have not been able to clarify just where academic freedom begins and ends, they have made it clear that the state does have a legitimate interest in what is taught to impressionable children.

Evaluating Statements about Academic Freedom

Edward B. Jenkinson (1990, 60) suggests that the following statements about restrictions on teachers' academic freedom are myths:

- Attempts to censor school materials occur mainly in the Bible Belt.
- Irate citizens in small towns are more likely to attempt to rid the schools of so-called offensive books than people in cities.
- Rural communities are more likely to experience censorship than cities and suburbs.
- Appointed school boards censor more books than elected ones.
- All parents want their children to be well-read and to think critically.
- Parents do not want public schools to advance particular religious beliefs.
- Textbooks adopted on a statewide basis are not likely to be attacked by anyone.
- Literary classics are beyond reproach.
- Rational argument will save any book, course, film, or teaching method.

Do you agree with Jenkinson? What examples can you provide to support his observations? How should a teacher respond to a perceived attempt to restrict his or her academic freedom? Are censorship attempts always a threat to academic freedom?

DO STUDENT TEACHERS HAVE THE SAME RIGHTS

Do student teachers have the same legal status as certified teachers? Read the following case study:

Meg Grant had really looked forward to the eight weeks she would spend as a student teacher in Mrs. Walker's high school English classes. Meg knew that Mrs. Walker was one of the best supervising teachers she might have been paired with, and she was anxious to do her best.

In Mrs. Walker's senior class, Meg planned to teach *Brave New World.* Mrs. Walker pointed out to Meg that this book was controversial and some parents might object. She asked Meg to think about selecting an additional title that students could read if their parents objected to *Brave New World.* Meg, however, felt that Mrs. Walker was bowing to pressure from conservative parents, so she decided to go ahead and teach the book.

Two weeks later Meg was called down to the principal's office where she was confronted by an angry father who said, "You have no right to be teaching my daughter this Communist trash; you're just a student teacher." What should Meg do? Does she have the same rights as a fully certified teacher?

In some states, a student teacher such as Meg might have the same rights and responsibilities as a fully certified teacher; in others, her legal status might be that of an unlicensed visitor. The most prudent action for Meg to take would be to apologize to the father and assure him that if any controversial books are assigned in the future, alternative titles would be provided. In addition, Meg should learn how important it is for a student teacher to take the advice of his or her supervising teacher.

The exact status of student teachers has been the subject of controversy in many states. In fact, one study found that the authority of student teachers to teach was established by law in only forty states, and no state had a statutory provision regulating the dismissal of a student teacher, the assignment of a student teacher, or the denial of the right to student teach (Morris and Curtis 1983). Nevertheless, student teachers should be aware that a potential for liability exists with them just as it does with certified teachers.

One area of debate regarding student teachers is whether they can act as substitutes for their cooperating teachers or even other teachers in a school building. Unfortunately, many school districts have no policy regarding this practice. Depending on statutes in a particular state, however, a student teacher may substitute under the following conditions:

- A substitute teacher is not immediately available.
- The student teacher has been in that student teaching assignment for a minimum number of school days.
- The supervising teacher, the principal of the school, and the university supervisor agree that the student teacher is capable of successfully handling the teaching responsibilities.
- A certificated classroom teacher in an adjacent room or a member of the same teaching team as the student teacher is aware of the absence and agrees to assist the student teacher if needed.
- The principal of the school or the principal's representative is readily available in the building.
- The student teacher is not paid for any substitute service (Shoop and Dunklee 1992, 98).

Given the ambiguous status of student teachers, it is important that you begin your student teaching assignment with a knowledge of the legal aspects of teaching and a clear idea of your rights and responsibilities. To accomplish this, read "A Bill of Rights for Student Teachers" in the Teacher's Resource Guide and follow the recommendations in Figure 7.1 made by school law experts Julie Mead and Julie Underwood.

FIGURE 7.1 Legal advice for student teachers (Source: Julie Mead and Julie Underwood, "A Legal Primer for Student Teachers." In Gloria Slick (Ed.), *Emerging Trends in Teacher Preparation: The Future of Field Experiences.* Thousand Oaks, CA: Corwin Press, Inc., 1995, pp. 49–50.)

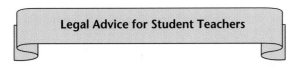

Legal Advice for Student Teachers

1. **Read the teacher's handbook, if one is available, and discuss its contents with the cooperating teacher. Be sure you understand its requirements and prohibitions.**

2. **Thoroughly discuss school safety rules and regulations. Be certain you know what to do in case of emergency, before assuming complete control of the classroom.**

3. **Be aware of the potential hazards associated with any activity and act accordingly to protect children from those dangers.**

4. **Be certain you know what controls the district has placed on the curriculum you will be teaching. Are there specific texts and/or methodologies that district policy requires or prohibits?**

5. **Be certain that student records are used to enhance and inform your teaching. Make certain that strict confidentiality is respected.**

6. **Document any problems you have with students, or as a teacher, in case you are called upon to relate details at a later time.**

WHAT ARE YOUR LEGAL RESPONSIBILITIES AS A TEACHER ?

Teachers are, of course, responsible for meeting the terms of their teaching contracts. As noted previously, teachers are responsible for duties not covered in the contract if they are reasonably related to teaching. Among these duties may be club sponsorship; lunchroom, study hall, or playground duty; academic counseling of students; and record keeping.

Teachers are also legally responsible for the safety and well-being of students assigned to them. Although it is not expected that a teacher be able to control completely the behavior of young, energetic students, a teacher can be held liable for any injury to a student if it is shown that the teacher's negligence contributed to the injury.

AVOIDING TORT LIABILITY

An eighth-grade science teacher in Louisiana left her class for a few moments to go to the school office to pick up some forms. While she was gone, her students continued to do some laboratory work that involved the use of alcohol-burning devices. Unfortunately, one girl was injured when she tried to relight a defective burner. Could the teacher be held liable for the girl's injuries?

The events described above actually occurred in 1974 (*Station v. Travelers Insurance Co.*). The court that heard the case determined that the teacher failed to provide adequate supervision while the students were exposed to dangerous conditions. Considerable care is required, the court observed, when students handle inherently dangerous objects, and the need for this care is magnified when students are exposed to dangers they don't appreciate.

At times, teachers may have concerns about their liability for damages as a result of their actions. The branch of law concerned with compensating an individual who suffers losses resulting from another's negligence is known as tort law. "A tort is a civil wrong in which one suffers loss as a result of the improper conduct of another" (LaMorte 1996, 373). The harm inflicted on the injured party may be the result of "intentional wrongdoing, recklessness, or simple carelessness" (Imber and Van Geel 1993, 575). According to **tort liability** law, an individual who is negligent and at fault in the exercise of his or her legal duty may be required to pay monetary damages to an injured party. Generally, the standard of behavior applied by the courts is "that of a reasonable person acting prudently in light of the circumstances" (Imber and Van Geel 1993, 594) to avoid a reasonably forseeable injury. However, teachers are held to a higher standard than ordinary citizens, and certain teachers (e.g., physical education and chemistry teachers) are held to an even higher standard because of the increased risk of injury involved in the classes they teach. Table 7.1 presents several examples of cases where students were injured and educators were found to have breached their duty of care.

NEGLIGENCE In contrast to the decision reached by the Louisiana court mentioned above, the courts have made it clear that there are many accidents that teachers cannot reasonably foresee that do result in student injuries. For example, a teacher on playground duty was found to be not negligent when a student threw a rock that struck another student in the eye. After the teacher walked past a group of boys, one boy threw a small rock that hit a larger rock on the ground and then bounced up to

TABLE 7.1

Selected court decisions in which educator's "breach of duty" was found to contribute to students' injuries

- A regular classroom teacher left a lighted candle on her desk, and a child whose costume came in contact with the flame was badly burned.

  Smith by Smith v. Archbishop of St. Louis, 632 S.W.2d 516 (Mo. Ct. App. 1982).

- A teacher left a classroom of mentally retarded teenagers unattended for a half hour, and one student threw a wooden pointer, injuring the eye of another.

  Gonzalez v. Mackler, 241 N.Y.S.2d 254 (N.Y. App. Div. 1963).

- A student was abducted from school by an intruder and raped. The doors of the school were not locked, and there was a history of sexual assaults and other violent crimes in the neighborhood.

  District of Columbia v. Doe, 524 A.2d 30 (D.C. 1987).

- A student was pushed out of a bathroom window by other students in a school with racial tensions.

  Lauricella v. Board of Education of Buffalo, 381 N.Y.S.2d 566 (N.Y. App. Div. 1976).

- On the school playground, students engaged in slap boxing for five to ten minutes until one student fell, mortally fracturing his skull.

  Dailey v. Los Angeles Unified School District, 470 P.2d 360 (Cal. 1970) *(en banc).*

- A student was injured when permitted to wear mittens while playing on the jungle gym.

  Ward v. Newfield Central School District No. 1. 412 N.Y.S.2d 57 (N.Y. App. Div. 1978).

- Students were required to play a game of line soccer in gym with little experience or technical instruction in soccer skills. A melee occurred as the students kicked for possession of the ball, and one student was hurt.

  Keesene v. Board of Education of New York, 235 N.Y.S.2d 300 (N.Y. Sup. Ct. 1962).

- In shop, a student was injured using a drill press while the instructor, who had not properly instructed students in use of the press or provided safety warnings, was absent from the shop.

  Roberts v. Robertson County Board of Education, 692 S.W.2d 863 (Tenn. Ct. App. 1985).

- A fifteen-year-old student employee stole chemicals from an unlocked chemistry lab and left them in bushes outside the school. The chemicals were found by an eight-year-old boy who was burned when he put a match to them.

  Kush by Marszalek v. Buffalo, 449 N.E. 2d 725 (N.Y. 1983).

- On a school-sponsored field trip, a child unsupervised while swimming in the ocean was hurt by a rolling log.

  Morris v. Douglas County School District No. 9, 403 P.2d 775 (Or. 1965) *(en banc).*

(Source: Based on material presented in Michael Imber and Tyll Van Geel, *Education Law* [New York: McGraw-Hill, 1993], pp. 596–597.)

---

hit the other boy in the eye. The court ruled that "[w]here the time between an act of a student and injury to a fellow student is so short that the teacher had no opportunity to prevent injury, it cannot be said that negligence of the teacher is a proximate cause of the injury" (*Fagen v. Summers,* 1972). In another case, the court ruled that a New York teacher could not have anticipated that the paper bag she asked a student to pick up contained a broken bottle upon which the student cut herself (*West v. Board of Education of City of New York,* 1959). In two almost identical cases, the courts ruled that a teacher of a class with a good behavior record could not reasonably be expected to anticipate that a student would be injured by a pencil thrown by a classmate while the teacher was momentarily out of the room attending to her usual duties (*Ohman v. Board of Education,* 1950; *Simonetti v. School District of Philadelphia,* 1983).

When a court considers a case involving tort liability, evidence is examined to determine whether the responsible party (the school district, the administrator, or the teacher) acted negligently. For a school official to be considered liable, the following must be shown to be present:

1. A legal duty to conform to a standard of conduct for the protection of others,
2. A failure to exercise an appropriate standard of care,
3. A causal connection, often referred to as *proximate cause,* between the conduct and the resultant injury, and
4. Actual loss or damage as a result of the injury (LaMorte 1996, 389–390).

As a teacher, you should be especially alert when conditions exist that might lead to accidental injury of one or more students. You will have a duty in regard to your pupils, and you could be held liable for injuries that students incur as a result of your **negligence**. This does not mean, however, that your liability extends to any and all injuries your students might suffer; only if you fail to provide the same degree of care for pupils that a reasonable and prudent person would have shown in similar circumstances can you be held liable. Our review of court cases involving the tort liability of teachers suggests that most cases involve at least one of the following:

- Inadequate supervision
- Inadequate instruction
- Lack of or improper medical treatment of pupils
- Improper disclosure of defamatory information concerning pupils—for example, release of school records that contain negative statements about a student

Teachers' concern about their potential monetary liability for failing to act reasonably and prudently in preventing injury to their students has been lessened by the availability of liability insurance. Many professional organizations for teachers offer liability coverage as part of their membership benefits, and teachers may also purchase individual liability insurance policies. In addition, some states that provide school districts with full or partial immunity from tort liability are considering extending the same protection to school employees. Georgia, for example, has extended immunity to teachers and principals (LaMorte 1996).

EDUCATIONAL MALPRACTICE   Since the mid-1970s the possibility of school districts and school personnel being held liable for an unusual kind of injury has increased. Several plaintiffs have charged in their **educational malpractice** suits that schools should be responsible for a pupil whose failure to achieve is significant. In the first of such cases, the parents of Peter W. Doe charged that the San Francisco Unified School District was negligent because it allowed him to graduate from high school with a fifth-grade reading level and this handicap would not enable him to function in adult society. In particular, they charged that the "defendant school district, its agents and employees, negligently and carelessly failed to provide plaintiff with adequate instruction, guidance, counseling and/or supervision in basic academic skills such as reading and writing, although said school district had the authority, responsibility, and ability [to do so]." They sought $500,000 for the negligent work of the teachers who taught Peter.

In evaluating the claim of Peter W. Doe and his parents, the court pointed out that the alleged injury was not within the realm of tort law and that many factors beyond a school's responsibility or control can account for lack of achievement. The court did not hold the school responsible for Peter's lack of achievement and made it clear that to do so would be to set a precedent with potentially drastic consequences: "To hold [schools] to an actionable duty of care, in the discharge of their academic functions, would expose them to the tort claims—real or imagined—of disaffected students and parents in countless numbers. . . . The ultimate consequences, in terms of public time and money, would burden them—and society—beyond calculation" (*Peter Doe v. San Francisco Unified School District,* 1976).

REPORTING CHILD ABUSE

Teachers, who are now *required* by law to report any suspected child abuse, are in positions to monitor and work against the physical, emotional, and sexual abuse and the neglect and exploitation of children. Teachers' professional journals and information from local, state, and federal child welfare agencies encourage teachers to be more observant of children's appearance and behavior in order to detect symptoms of child abuse. Such sources often provide lists of physical and behavioral indicators of potential child abuse, similar to that shown in Table 7.2 on page 216. Many communities, through their police departments or other public and private agencies, provide programs adapted for children to educate them about their rights in child-abuse situations and to show them how to obtain help.

Schools usually have a specific process for dealing with suspected abuse cases, involving the school principal and nurse as well as the reporting teacher. Because a child's physical welfare may be further endangered when abuse is reported, caution and sensitivity are required. Teachers are in a unique position to help students who are victims of child abuse, both because they have daily contact with them and because children learn to trust them.

OBSERVING COPYRIGHT LAWS

The continuing rapid development of technology has resulted in a new set of responsibilities for teachers in regard to observing **copyright laws** pertaining to the use of photocopies, videotapes, and computer software programs. In 1976 Congress revised the Copyright Act by adding the doctrine of **fair use**. Although the fair use doctrine cannot be precisely defined, it is generally interpreted as it was in *Marcus v. Rowley* (1983). In this case, Eloise Marcus successfully sued Shirley Rowley for using almost half of her copyrighted cake-decorating booklet in a high school food-service class. An appellate court concluded that Rowley's use of Marcus' material went beyond the fair use doctrine—i.e., one may "use the copyrighted material in a reasonable manner without [the copyright holder's] consent" as long as that use does not reduce the demand for the work or the author's income.

PHOTOCOPIES   To clarify the fair use doctrine as it pertained to teachers photocopying instructional materials from books and magazines, Congress endorsed a set of guidelines developed by educators, authors, and publishers. These guidelines allow teachers to make single copies of copyrighted material for teaching or research but are more restrictive regarding the use of multiple copies. The use of multiple copies of a work must meet the tests of brevity, spontaneity, and cumulative effect.

- *Brevity* means that short works can be copied. Poems or excerpts cannot be longer than 250 words, and copies of longer works cannot exceed 1,000 words or 10 percent of the work (whichever is less). Only one chart or drawing can be reproduced from a book or an article.

TABLE 7.2

Physical and behavioral indicators of child abuse and neglect

Type of Child Abuse/Neglect	Physical Indicators	Behavioral Indicators
Physical Abuse	Unexplained bruises and welts: ■ on face, lips, mouth ■ on torso, back, buttocks, thighs ■ in various stages of healing ■ clustered, forming regular patterns ■ reflecting shape of article used to inflict (electric cord, belt buckle) ■ on several different surface areas ■ regularly appear after absence, weekend, or vacation ■ human bite marks ■ bald spots Unexplained burns: ■ cigar, cigarette burns, especially on soles, palms, back, or buttocks ■ immersion burns (sock-like, glove-like, doughnut-shaped on buttocks or genitalia) ■ patterned like electric burner, iron, etc. ■ rope burns on arms, legs, neck, or torso Unexplained fractures: ■ to skull, nose, facial structure ■ in various stages of healing ■ multiple or spiral fractures Unexplained lacerations or abrasions: ■ to mouth, lips, gums, eyes ■ to external genitalia	Wary of adult contacts Apprehensive when other children cry Behavioral extremes: ■ aggressiveness ■ withdrawal ■ overly compliant Afraid to go home Reports injury by parents Exhibits anxiety about normal activities, e.g., napping Complains of soreness and moves awkwardly Destructive to self and others Early to school or stays late as if afraid to go home Accident prone Wears clothing that covers body when not appropriate Chronic runaway (especially adolescents) Cannot tolerate physical contact or touch
Physical Neglect	Consistent hunger, poor hygiene, inappropriate dress Consistent lack of supervision, especially in dangerous activities or long periods Unattended physical problems or medical needs Abandonment Lice Distended stomach, emaciated	Begging, stealing food Constant fatigue, listlessness, or falling asleep States there is no caretaker at home Frequent school absence or tardiness Destructive, pugnacious School dropout (adolescents) Early emancipation from family (adolescents)

■ The criterion of *spontaneity* means that the teacher doing the copying would not have time to request permission from the copyright holder.

■ The criterion of *cumulative effect* limits the use of copies to one course and limits the material copied from the same author, book, or magazine during the semester. Also, no more than nine instances of multiple copying per class are allowed during a semester.

VIDEOTAPES   Guidelines for the use of videotapes made by teachers of television broadcasts were issued by Congress in 1981 (a copy of these guidelines is presented

Type of Child Abuse/Neglect	Physical Indicators	Behavioral Indicators
Sexual Abuse	Difficulty in walking or sitting ■ torn, stained, or bloody underclothing Pain or itching in genital area Bruises or bleeding in external genitalia, vaginal, or anal areas Venereal disease Frequent urinary or yeast infections Frequent unexplained sore throats	Unwilling to participate in certain physical activities Sudden drop in school performance Withdrawal, fantasy, or unusually infantile behavior Crying with no provocation Bizarre, sophisticated, or unusual sexual behavior or knowledge Anorexia (especially adolescents) Sexually provocative Poor peer relationships Reports sexual assault by caretaker Fear of or seductiveness toward males Suicide attempts (especially adolescents) Chronic runaway Early pregnancies
Emotional Maltreatment	Speech disorders Lags in physical development Failure to thrive (especially in infants) Asthma, severe allergies, or ulcers Substance abuse	Habit disorders (sucking, biting, rocking, etc.) Conduct disorders (antisocial, destructive, etc.) Neurotic traits (sleep disorders, inhibition of play) Behavioral extremes: ■ compliant, passive ■ aggressive, demanding Overly adaptive behavior: ■ inappropriately adult ■ inappropriately infantile Developmental lags (mental, emotional) Delinquent behavior (especially adolescents)

(Source: C. C. Tower, *How Schools Can Help Combat Child Abuse and Neglect*, 2d ed. [Washington, D.C.: National Education Association, 1987], 162–163. Adapted from *Early Childhood Programs and the Prevention and Treatment of Child Abuse and Neglect*, by D. D. Broadhurst et al., The User Manual Series, 1979, Washington, D. C.: U.S. Department of Health, Education and Welfare.)

on page 549 in the Teacher's Resource Guide). Videotaped material may be used in the classroom only once by the teacher within the first ten days of taping. Additional use is limited to reinforcing instruction or evaluation of student learning, and the tape must be erased within forty-five days.

COMPUTER SOFTWARE Computer software publishers have become concerned about the abuse of their copyrighted material. Limited school budgets and the high cost of computer software have led to the unauthorized reproduction of software. To address the problem, the Copyright Act was amended in 1980 to apply the fair use doctrine to software. Accordingly, a teacher may now make one backup copy of a program. If a teacher were to make multiple copies of software, the fair use doctrine would be violated because the software is readily accessible for purchase and making multiple copies would substantially reduce the market for the software.

The increased practice of networking computer programs—that is, storing a copy of a computer program on a network file server and serving the program to a computer on the network—is also of concern to software publishers. As yet, the practice has not yet been tested in the courts. As more public schools develop computer networks, however, the issue of networked software will most likely be debated in the courts.

ELECTRONIC MAIL AND THE INTERNET With the huge increase in the transmission of documents via electronic mail (E-mail) and the Internet, copyright laws have been extended to cyberspace. Material transmitted online is copyright protected by the originator unless accompanied by a statement such as the following: "Permission is granted to distribute this document freely through electronic or by other means, provided it remains completely intact and unaltered, the source is acknowledged, and no fee is charged for it."

WHAT ARE THE LEGAL RIGHTS OF STUDENTS AND PARENTS?

As a prospective teacher, you have an obligation to become familiar with the rights of students. Since the 1960s students have increasingly confronted teachers and school districts with what they perceived to be illegal restrictions on their behavior. In this section we discuss briefly some of the major court decisions that have clarified students' rights related to freedom of expression, suspension and expulsion, search and seizure, privacy, and nondiscrimination.

FREEDOM OF EXPRESSION

The case of *Tinker v. Des Moines Independent Community School District* (1969) is perhaps the most frequently cited case concerning students' **freedom of expression**. The Supreme Court ruled in *Tinker* that three students, ages thirteen, fifteen, and sixteen, had been denied their First Amendment freedom of expression when they were suspended from school for wearing black arm bands in protest of the Vietnam War. The court ruled that neither teachers nor students "shed their rights to freedom of speech or expression at the schoolhouse gate." In addition, the court found no evidence that the exercise of such a right interfered with the school's operation.

CENSORSHIP One area of student expression that has generated frequent controversy is that of student publications. Prior to 1988, the courts generally made it clear that student literature enjoyed constitutional protection, and it could only be regulated if it posed a substantial threat of school disruption, if it was libelous, or if it was judged vulgar or obscene *after publication*. However, school officials could use "prior **censorship**" and require students to submit literature before publication if such controls were necessary to maintain order in the school. Some courts issued the following guidelines for controlling student literature prior to publication:

1. Schools must issue clear and narrowly drawn regulations in advance to notify students of what is required.
2. School procedures must ensure a prompt decision by school authorities on submitted materials.
3. Timely and fair (informal) hearings and a prompt appeal to higher authority on decisions to censor must be ensured (Valente 1987, 317).

Within these guidelines, students frequently successfully defended their right to freedom of expression. For example, the right of high school students to place in the school newspaper an advertisement against the war in Vietnam was upheld (*Zucker v. Panitz,* 1969). Students were also upheld in their right to distribute information on birth control and on laws regarding marijuana (*Shanley v. Northeast Independent School District,* 1972). And other cases upheld the right of students to publish literature that was critical of teachers, administrators, and other school personnel (*Scoville v. Board of Education of Joliet Township High School District 204* 1971; *Sullivan v. Houston Independent School District,* 1969).

In January of 1988, however, the Supreme Court, in a five-to-three ruling in *Hazelwood School District v. Kuhlmeier,* departed from the earlier *Tinker* decision and gave public school officials considerable authority to censor school-sponsored student publications. The case involved a Missouri high school principal's censorship of articles in the school newspaper, the *Spectrum,* on teenage pregnancy and the impact of divorce on students. The principal believed the articles were inappropriate because they might identify pregnant students and because references to sexual activity and birth control were inappropriate for younger students. Several students on the newspaper staff distributed copies of the articles on their own and later sued the school district, claiming that their First Amendment rights had been violated.

Writing for the majority in *Hazelwood School District v. Kuhlmeier,* Justice Byron White (who had voted with the majority in *Tinker*) said school officials could bar "speech that is ungrammatical, poorly written, inadequately researched, biased or prejudiced, vulgar or profane, or unsuitable for immature audiences." White also pointed out that *Tinker* focused on a student's right of "personal expression," and the Missouri case dealt with school-sponsored publications that were part of the curriculum and bore the "imprimatur of the school." According to White, "Educators do not offend the First Amendment by exercising editorial control over the style and content of student speech in school-sponsored expressive activities so long as their actions are reasonably related to legitimate pedagogical concerns."

A case involving an attempt to regulate an "underground" student newspaper entitled *Bad Astra,* however, had a different outcome. Five high school students in Renton, Washington, produced a four-page newspaper at their expense, off school property, and without the knowledge of school authorities. *Bad Astra* contained articles that criticized school policies, a mock poll evaluating teachers, and several poetry selections. The students distributed 350 copies of the paper at a senior class barbecue held on school grounds.

After the paper was distributed, the principal placed letters of reprimand in the five students' files, and the district established a new policy whereby student-written, non-school-sponsored materials with an intended distribution of more than ten were subject to predistribution review. The students filed suit in federal district court, claiming a violation of their First Amendment rights. The court, however, ruled that the new policy was "substantially constitutional." Maintaining that the policy was unconstitutional, the students filed an appeal in 1988 in the Ninth Circuit Court and won. The court ruled that *Bad Astra* was not "within the purview of the school's exercise of reasonable editorial control" (*Burch v. Barker,* 1987, 1988).

DRESS CODES   Few issues related to the rights of students have generated as many court cases as have dress codes and hairstyles. The demand on the courts to hear such cases prompted Supreme Court Justice Hugo L. Black to observe that he did not believe "the federal Constitution imposed on the United States Courts the burden of supervising the length of hair that public school students should wear" (*Karr v. Schmidt,* 1972). In line with Justice Black's observation, the Supreme Court has repeatedly refused to review the decisions reached by the lower courts.

In general, the courts have suggested that schools may have dress codes as long as such codes are clear, reasonable, and students are notified. However, when the legality of such codes has been challenged, the rulings have largely indicated that schools may not control what students wear unless it is immodest or is disruptive of the educational process.

Students in private schools, however, do not have First Amendment protections provided by *Tinker v. Des Moines Independent Community School District* because private schools are not state affiliated. As a result, students at private schools can be required to wear uniforms, and "[d]isagreements over 'student rights' . . . are generally

Issues in Education

- Why can students in private schools be required to wear uniforms?
- How might the public school students react if told they had to wear uniforms too?
- Why is student dress a continuing issue today?
- What factors are considered in evaluating student dress?
- Under what circumstances can public school students' freedom of expression through dress be censored?
- What social commentary about the issue of dress codes does this cartoonist make?
- Do you agree or disagree with the cartoonist's point of view? Why?

"HA! At our school we don't have to wear uniforms."

resolved by applying contract law to the agreement governing the student's attendance" (LaMorte 1996, 94).

At one time, educators' concerns about student appearance may have been limited to hairstyles and immodest dress; however, today's educators, as Michael LaMorte (1996, 93) points out, may be concerned about "T-shirts depicting violence, drugs such as marijuana leafs, racial epithets, or characters such as Bart Simpson; ripped or baggy jeans; sneakers with lights; colored bandannas, baseball or other hats; words shaved into scalps, brightly colored hair, distinctive hair cuts, styles, or ponytails for males; exposed underwear; Malcolm X symbols; Walkmen, cellular phones, or beepers; backpacks; tattoos, pierced noses, or earrings; and decorative dental caps."

Since gangs, hate groups, and violence in and around public schools have become more prevalent during the last decade, rulings that favor schools are becoming more common when the courts "balance the First Amendment rights of students to express themselves against the legitimate right of school authorities to maintain a safe and disruption-free environment" (LaMorte 1996, 93). This balance is clearly illustrated in *Jeglin v. San Jacinto Unified School District,* 1993). In this instance, a school's dress code prohibiting the wearing of clothing with writing, pictures, or insignia of professional or college athletic teams was challenged on the grounds that it violated students' freedom of expression. The court acknowledged that the code violated the rights of elementary and middle school students, but not those of high school students. Gangs, known to be present at the high school, had intimidated students and faculty in connection with the sports-oriented clothing. The court ruled that the curtailment of students' rights did not "demand a certainty that disruption will occur, but only the existence of facts which might reasonably lead school officials to forecast substantial disruption."

To reduce disruption and violence in schools, some school districts and policy makers have considered requiring students to wear uniforms. For example, in his 1996 State of the Union Address, President Clinton said, "if it means that teenagers will stop killing each other over designer jackets, then our public schools should be able to require the students to wear school uniforms" (*Education Week,* January 31, 1996, 21). The U.S. Department of Education later distributed guidelines to schools for formulating and implementing a uniform policy.

DUE PROCESS IN SUSPENSION AND EXPULSION

In February and March of 1971, a total of nine students received ten-day suspensions from the Columbus, Ohio, public school system during a period of citywide unrest. One student, in the presence of his principal, physically attacked a police officer who was trying to remove a disruptive student from a high school auditorium. Four others were suspended for similar conduct. Another student was suspended for his involvement in a lunchroom disturbance that resulted in damage to school property. All nine students were suspended in accordance with Ohio law. Some of the students and their parents were offered the opportunity to attend conferences prior to the start of the suspensions, but none of the nine was given a hearing. Asserting that their constitutional rights had been denied, all nine students brought suit against the school system.

In a sharply divided five-to-four decision, the Supreme Court ruled that the students had a legal right to an education, and that this "property right" could be removed only through the application of procedural due process. The court maintained that suspension is a "serious event" in the life of a suspended child and may not be imposed by the school in an arbitrary manner (*Goss v. Lopez,* 1975).

Exclusion from School for 10 Days or Less

- Notice of charges must be presented.
- The notice should specify a time and place for the hearing that allow the defense to prepare.
- The hearing should be before an impartial tribunal, often the board of education.
- The accused student should have an opportunity to present evidence and refute adverse evidence.
- A finding of guilt must be based on substantial evidence —i.e., the burden of proof is on the school district.

Long-term Suspensions and Expulsions

- The provision of a list of witnesses prior to the hearing. The majority of the courts have held that this is not required.
- The right to confront and question adverse witnesses. A number of courts permit testimony in the form of anonymous affidavits, but others do not.
- The admissibility of hearsay, with most courts permitting it.
- Whether impartiality is compromised when the school board's own attorney presents the case against the student. The courts are about evenly split on this question.
- The right to be represented by an attorney. Once again, the courts are split.
- The right to a recording or transcript of the hearing. Most courts do not recognize this right.
- The right to a written statement of reasons explaining the decision to suspend, also not required by most courts.

FIGURE 7.2 Due process in suspension and expulsion (Source: Adapted from Michael Imber and Tyll Van Geel, *Education Law*, New York: McGraw-Hill, Inc., 1993.)

As a result of cases such as *Goss v. Lopez*, every state has outlined procedures for school officials to follow in the suspension and expulsion of students. In cases of short-term suspension (defined by the courts as exclusion from school for ten days or less), the due process steps are somewhat flexible and determined by the nature of the infraction and the length of the suspension. As Figure 7.2 shows, however, long-term suspension (more than ten days) and expulsion require a more extensive due process procedure. The disciplinary transfer of a disruptive student to an alternative school, designed to meet his or her needs, is not considered an expulsion (LaMorte 1996).

In response to an increase of unruly students who disrupt the learning of others, a few districts and states have granted teachers the authority to suspend students for up to ten days. Teachers in Cincinnati and Dade County, Florida, for example, have negotiated contracts that give them authority to remove disruptive students from their classrooms; however, district administrators decide how the students will be disciplined. In 1995, Indiana became the first state to grant teachers the power to suspend students, and the following year New York's governor proposed legislation to allow teachers to remove students from their classrooms for up to ten days for "committing an act of violence against a student, teacher, or school district employee; possessing or threatening to use a gun, knife, or other dangerous weapon; damaging or destroying school district property; damaging the personal property of teachers or other employees; or defying an order from a teacher or administrator to stop disruptive behavior" (Lindsay 1996, 24).

REASONABLE SEARCH AND SEIZURE

As a teacher you have reason to believe that a student has drugs, and possibly a dangerous weapon, in his locker. Do you have the right to search the student's locker

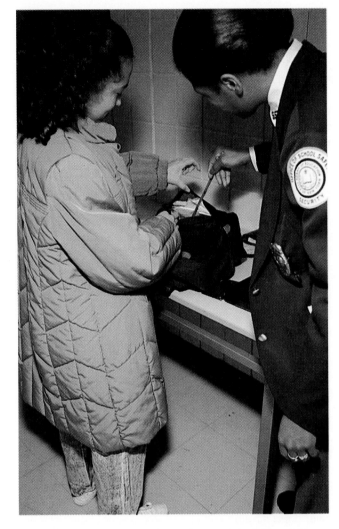

What are these students' rights with regard to their persons, lockers, personal property, and records in school and on school grounds? How are school districts' rights of search and seizure decided? In what ways have students' rights to privacy been upheld?

and seize any illegal or dangerous items? According to the Fourth Amendment, citizens are protected from **search and seizure** conducted without a search warrant. With the escalation of drug use in schools and school-related violence, however, cases involving the legality of search and seizure in schools have increased. These cases suggest guidelines that you can follow if confronted with a situation such as that described here.

The case of *New Jersey v. T.L.O.* (1985) involved a fourteen-year-old student (T.L.O.) whom a teacher found smoking a cigarette in a rest room. The teacher took the student to the principal's office, whereupon the principal asked to see the contents of her purse. On opening the purse, the principal found a pack of cigarettes and what appeared to be drug paraphernalia and a list titled "People who owe me money." T.L.O. was arrested and later found guilty of delinquency charges.

After being sentenced to one year's probation, T.L.O. appealed, claiming that the evidence found in her purse was obtained in violation of the Fourth Amendment and that her confession to selling marijuana was tainted by an illegal search. The United States Supreme Court found that the search had been reasonable. The Court also developed a two-pronged test of "reasonableness" for searches: (1) A school official must have a reasonable suspicion that a student has violated a law or school policy and (2) the search must be conducted using methods that are reasonable in scope.

Another case focused on the use of trained dogs to conduct searches of 2,780 junior and senior high school students in Highland, Indiana. During a two-and-a-half- to three-hour period, six teams with trained German shepherds sniffed the students. The dogs alerted their handlers a total of 50 times. Seventeen of the searches initiated by the dogs turned up beer, drug paraphernalia, or marijuana. Another eleven students singled out by the dogs, including thirteen-year-old Diane Doe, were strip searched in the nurse's office. It turned out that Diane had played with her dog, who was in heat, that morning and that the police dog had responded to the smell of the other dog on Diane's clothing.

Diane's parents later filed suit, charging that their daughter was searched illegally. The court ruled that the use of dogs did not constitute an unreasonable search, nor did holding students in their homerooms constitute a mass detention in violation of the Fourth Amendment. The court did, however, hold that the strip searches of the students were unreasonable. The court pointed out that the school personnel did not have any evidence to suggest that Diane possessed contraband because, prior to the strip search, she had emptied her pockets as requested. Diane was awarded $7,500 in damages (*Doe v. Renfrow,* 1980, 1981).

Court cases involving search and seizure in school settings have maintained that school lockers are the property of the schools, not students, and may be searched by school authorities if reasonable cause exists. In addition, students may be sniffed by police dogs if school authorities have a reasonable suspicion that illegal or dangerous items may be found. Lastly, courts have tended not to allow strip searches; however, as *Cornfield v. Consolidated High School District No. 230* (1993) illustrates, strip searches may be constitutional depending upon the circumstances giving rise to the search, the age of the student, and the severity of the suspected infraction. In *Cornfield,* the court allowed a strip search of a 16-year-old student suspected of "crotching" drugs. The court's decision was influenced by "allegations of several recent prior incidents such as dealing in drugs, testing positive for marijuana, possession of drugs, having 'crotched' drugs during a police raid at his mother's house, failing a urine analysis for cocaine, unsuccessful completion of a drug rehabilitation program, and a report by a bus driver that there was a smell of marijuana where the student sat on the bus" (LaMorte 1996, 140).

In general, the courts have tried to balance the school's need to obtain information and the student's right to privacy. In balancing these two rights, courts consider the following factors: "(1) the purpose of the search, (2) the person doing the searching, (3) the place being searched, (4) the background of the person being searched, (5) the severity of the penalties resulting from the search, and (6) the degree to which the person's privacy was invaded by the search" (Shoop and Dunklee 1992, 144–145).

Some schools use drug testing as a requirement for either attendance or interscholastic participation, including sports competition, or as a means of discipline. A 1988 court case upheld a urinalysis drug test for randomly selected student athletes because those who tested positively were suspended only from participating in sports for a period of time and no disciplinary or academic penalties were imposed (*Schaill v. Tippecanoe School Corporation,* 1988). Similarly, the U.S. Supreme Court reversed a lower court's ruling and stated that a school district's desire to reduce drug use justified the degree of intrusion required by random tests of student athletes' urine (*Acton v. Vernonia School District,* 1995). A few school districts have attempted to implement mandatory drug testing of teachers. So far the courts have upheld the decision rendered in *Patchogue-Medford Congress of Teachers v. Board of Education of Patchogue-Medford Union Free School District* (1987) that drug testing of teachers violates the Fourth Amendment's prohibition of unreasonable searches.

PRIVACY

Prior to 1974 students and parents were not allowed to examine school records. On November 19, 1974, Congress passed the Family Educational Rights and Privacy Act (FERPA), which gave parents of students under eighteen and students eighteen and older the right to examine their school records. Every public or private educational institution must adhere to the law, known as the **Buckley Amendment**, or lose federal money.

Under the Buckley Amendment, schools must do the following:

1. Inform parents or eligible students of their rights

Keepers of the Dream

Marian Wright Edelman

Founder of Children's Defense Fund

Marian Wright Edelman knew discrimination even as a child. When she was five she was scolded by a friend for drinking from a water fountain reserved for whites only in a downtown department store in her hometown of Bennettsville, South Carolina. When she went to the movies there, she was not permitted to sit in seats on the first floor—they, too, were reserved for whites only. But the incident that angered her the most was seeing discrimination in the rescue workers at the scene of an accident on the highway near her home. The ambulance picked up the slightly injured white truck driver and left behind the seriously hurt black migrant workers who had been in the car the truck had hit. "I remember watching children like me bleeding," she recalls, "I remember the ambulance driving off. You never, ever forget" (Terry 1993, 4).

When she was fourteen, her father suffered a heart attack and was rushed to a hospital. Riding in the ambulance with him, Edelman listened to his dying wish for her, "Don't let anything get in the way of your education." Ten

"You never, ever forget."

days after his death the Supreme Court outlawed school segregation in its *Brown v. Board of Education* decision.

Edelman followed her father's advice, graduating first from Spelman College and then from Yale Law School. When she obtained her law degree she returned to Mississippi, where she became the first African American woman to be admitted to the state's bar. After the Voting Rights Act of 1965 was passed, Edelman took up the cause of the poor.

Recognizing the need for a lobbying agency for children, she founded the Children's Defense Fund in Washington D.C. As its president she seeks "to educate the nation about the needs of children and encourage preventive investment in children before they get sick, drop out of school, suffer too-early pregnancy or family breakdown, or get into trouble."

Edelman's message for teachers is to see that all children, especially those who are poor, are taught how to read, write, and compute so that they can have positive and healthy options in their future. She believes strongly that

all Americans must commit personally and as voters to a national crusade of conscience and action that will ensure that no child is left behind. Only we—individually and collectively—can transform our nation's priorities and assure its future as we face a new century and begin a new millennium (Edelman 1993, 20).

2. Facilitate access to records by parents or eligible students by providing information on the types of educational records that exist and the procedures for gaining access to them
3. Permit parents or eligible students to review educational records, request changes, request a hearing if the changes are disallowed, and add their own statement by way of explanation, if necessary
4. Ensure that the institution does not give out personally identifiable information without the prior written, informed consent of a parent or an eligible student
5. Allow parents and eligible students to see the school's record of disclosures (Fischer and Sorenson 1996, 89)

The Buckley Amendment actually sets forth the minimum requirements that schools must adhere to, and many states and school districts have gone beyond these minimum guidelines in granting students access to their records. Most high schools, for example, now grant students under eighteen access to their educational records, and all students in Virginia, elementary through secondary, are guaranteed access to their records.

A number of exceptions are allowed by the Buckley Amendment. The teacher's gradebook, psychiatric or treatment records, notes or records written by the teacher for his or her exclusive use or to be shared with a substitute teacher, or the private notes of school law enforcement units, for example, are not normally subject to examination (Fischer and Sorenson 1996).

STUDENTS' RIGHTS TO NONDISCRIMINATION

Schools are legally bound to avoid discriminating against students on the basis of race, sex, religion, disability, marital status, or infection with a noncommunicable disease such as HIV/AIDS. One trend of the 1980s and 1990s that has confronted schools with the need to develop more thoughtful and fair policies has been the epidemic in teenage pregnancies.

In regard to students who are married, pregnant, or parents, the courts have been quite clear: Students in these categories may not be treated differently. A 1966 case in Texas involving a sixteen-year-old mother established that schools may provide separate classes or alternative schools on a *voluntary* basis for married and/or pregnant students. However, the district may not *require* such students to attend separate schools, nor may they be made to attend adult or evening schools (*Alvin Independent School District v. Cooper,* 1966).

The courts have made an about-face in their positions on whether students who are married, pregnant, or parents can participate in extracurricular activities. Prior to 1972 participation in these activities was considered a privilege rather than a right, and restrictions on those who could participate were upheld. In 1972, however, cases in Tennessee, Ohio, Montana, and Texas established the right of married students (and, in one case, a divorced student) to participate (*Holt v. Sheldon,* 1972; *Davis v. Meek,* 1972; *Moran v. School District No. 7,* 1972; and *Romans v. Crenshaw,* 1972). Since then, restrictions applicable to extracurricular activities have been universally struck down.

Since the mid-1980s, many school districts have become embroiled in controversy over the issue of how to provide for the schooling of young people with HIV/AIDS and whether school employees with HIV/AIDS should be allowed to continue working. As one observer put it:

> Public schools now face the difficulty of balancing two equal and opposing rights: the right of a student with AIDS to an education and the right of students who are not infected with HIV to be protected against infection. The latter right is fueled by fear that one can be infected with HIV through casual contact, even though no medical evidence has found or remotely suggested that HIV can be transmitted through casual contact. The practical result of attempts to balance those rights has been to open a floodgate to discrimination against students infected with this insidious virus (Alali 1995, 3).

In rulings on HIV/AIDS-related cases, the courts have sided with the overwhelming medical evidence that students with AIDS pose no "significant risk" of spreading the disease. "To date, courts have revealed a high degree of sensitivity to students with HIV or AIDS and to their being included in the public school mainstream" (LaMorte 1996, 167). In 1987, for example, a judge prevented a Florida school district from requiring that three hemophiliac brothers who were exposed to HIV/AIDS through transfusions be restricted to homebound instruction (*Ray v. School District of DeSoto County,* 1987).

To stem the spread of HIV/AIDS, school systems in many large cities—New York, Los Angeles, San Francisco, and Seattle, to name a few—have initiated programs to distribute condoms to high school students. According to a 1994 poll by Public Agenda, 55 percent of Americans believe it is appropriate to allow schools to distribute condoms to students, while 43 percent oppose it (Public Agenda 1994, 28).

New York's condom-distribution program, which initially did not require parental consent, was challenged in 1993 (*Alfonso v. Fernandez*). The court ruled that the program was a "health issue" and that the district could not dispense condoms without prior parental approval. The court maintained that the program violated parents' due process rights under the Fourteenth Amendment to raise their children as they see fit; however, the program did not violate parents' or students' freedom of religion.

WHAT ARE SOME ISSUES IN THE LEGAL RIGHTS OF SCHOOL DISTRICTS ?

Clearly, the law touches just about every aspect of education in America today. Daily, the media remind us that ours is an age of litigation; no longer are school districts as protected as they once were from legal problems. Corporal punishment, sexual harassment, religious expression, and home schooling are among the issues in the legal rights of school districts.

CORPORAL PUNISHMENT

The practice of **corporal punishment** has had a long and controversial history in American education. Recall, for example, our reference in Chapter 3 to seventeenth-century Latin grammar school teachers who routinely hit students for unsatisfactory recitations. Currently, policies regarding the use of corporal punishment vary widely from state to state, and even from district to district.

Critics believe that "corporal punishment is neither a necessary nor an effective response to misbehavior in school" (Slavin 1994, 413). In addition,

> corporal punishment inhibits learning, interferes with the accomplishment of each of the important developmental tasks of children, and has the potential for physical harm to the child. The practice has been labeled anachronistic, counterproductive, and most damaging to children who are already emotionally disturbed. Moreover, children who witness physically punitive adult behavior are more likely themselves to behave aggressively and antisocially (Parkay and Conoley 1982, 33–34).

In spite of such arguments against its effectiveness, corporal punishment continues to be widespread. Nevertheless, almost half of the states and many school districts currently ban corporal punishment, and many others restrict its use (LaMorte 1996).

The most influential Supreme Court case involving corporal punishment is *Ingraham v. Wright*, decided in 1977. In Dade County, Florida, in October 1970, junior high school students James Ingraham and Roosevelt Andrews were paddled with a wooden paddle. Both students received injuries as a result of the paddlings, with Ingraham's being the most severe. Ingraham, who was being punished for being slow to respond to a teacher's directions, refused to assume the "paddling position" and had to be held over a desk by two assistant principals while the principal administered twenty "licks." As a result, Ingram "suffered a hematoma requiring medical attention and keeping him out of school for several days."

The court had two significant questions to rule on in *Ingraham*: Does the Eighth Amendment's prohibition of cruel and unusual punishment apply to corporal punishment in the schools? And, if it does not, should the due process clause of the Fourteenth Amendment provide any protection to students before punishment is administered? In regard to the first question, the Court, in a sharply divided five-to-four decision, ruled that the Eighth Amendment was not applicable to students being disciplined in school, only to persons convicted of crimes. On the question of due process, the Court said, "We conclude that the Due Process clause does not require notice and a hearing prior to the imposition of corporal punishment in the public schools, as that practice is authorized and limited by the common law." The Court also commented on the severity of the paddlings in *Ingraham* and said that, in such cases, school personnel "may be held liable in damages to the child and, if malice is shown, they may be subject to criminal penalties."

Though the Supreme Court has upheld the constitutionality of corporal punishment, many districts around the country have instituted policies banning its use. Where corporal punishment is used, school personnel are careful to see that it meets criteria that have emerged from other court cases involving corporal punishment:

1. It is consistent with the existing statutes.
2. It is a corrective remedy for undesirable behavior.
3. It is neither cruel nor excessive.
4. There is no permanent or lasting injury.
5. Malice is not present.
6. The punishment is suitable for the age and sex of the child.
7. An appropriate instrument is used (O'Reilly and Green 1983, 144–145).

SEXUAL HARASSMENT

Though few victims report it, sexual harassment affects about four out of every five teenagers in schools across the nation, according to a survey of eighth- through eleventh-graders sponsored by the American Association of University Women (1993). Students' responses were based on the following definition: "Sexual harassment is *unwanted* and *unwelcome* sexual behavior which interferes with your life" (American Association of University Women 1993, 6). Although most teens report that they are harassed by their schoolmates, one-fourth of the girls and one-tenth of the boys said they had been harassed by school employees. Figure 7.3 shows the percentage of students reporting various types of **sexual harassment.** In addition, the survey indicated that only 7 percent of the victims told the school about the sexual harassment, and more than half didn't even know if their school had a policy on sexual harassment.

Data from the AAUW study were further analyzed by four University of Michigan researchers who came to the surprising conclusion that "the large majority of adolescents who experience harassment have also harassed someone else during their school life. Over half of all students, equivalent by gender, have experienced harassment both as victim and perpetrator" (Lee et al. 1996, 399–400). They also concluded that "we cannot say which came first, harassing others or being harassed" and that their findings "run counter to any explanation of sexual harassment based solely on differential social or power status" (399). To address the alarming problem of sexual harassment in schools, the University of Michigan team recommended the following:

■ The discussion of sexuality, both wanted and unwanted, should be included in the formal and informal curriculum.

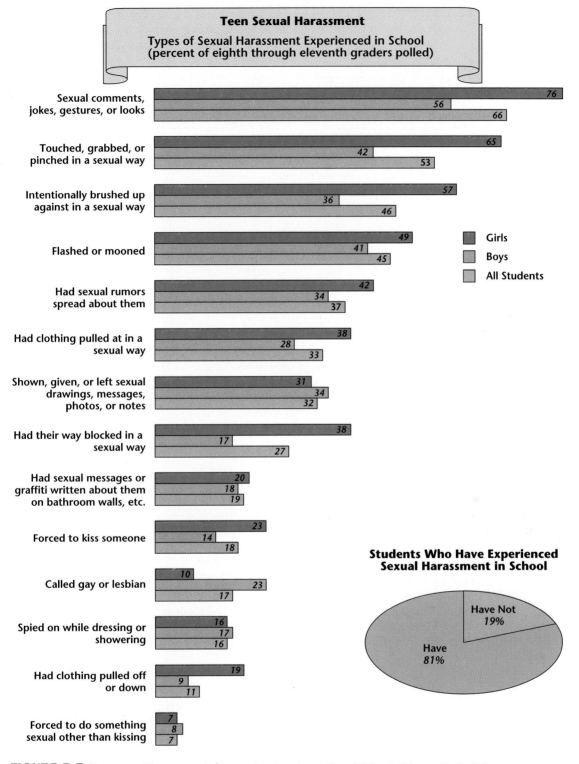

FIGURE 7.3 Teen sexual harassment (Source: American Association of University Women, *Hostile Hallways: The AAUW Survey on Sexual Harassment in America's Schools,* New York: Louis Harris and Associated, 1993, pp. 7, 9.)

- Helping students understand, recognize, and address their own ambivalence about sexual harassment (indeed, about sexuality generally) should be a meaningful component of every secondary school's curriculum.
- Adults in schools should serve as models for respectful cross-status relations (410).

In addition to harassment by the opposite sex, same-sex harassment, usually against gay and lesbian students, is a problem at some schools. At a hearing of Massachusetts' Commission on Gay and Lesbian Youth, for example, many "young people came forward to talk about how miserable their lives had been made. They reported that often adults were standing by and participating, permitting other students to mock them" (Yaffe 1995, K7). In 1996, three gay students in Minnesota and Illinois were among the first homosexual students to file lawsuits claiming that their school districts failed to maintain safe environments and to discipline students who regularly tormented them (Walsh 1996, 5). Currently, at least five states and several school districts have education policies that prohibit discrimination based on sexual orientation.

Increased reports of sexual harassment of students and a Supreme Court ruling in 1992 (*Franklin v. Gwinnett County Public Schools*) that students could sue and collect damages for harassment under Title IX of the Education Act of 1972 are causing some teachers to be apprehensive about working closely with students, and a small number of teachers even report that they fear being falsely accused by angry, disgruntled students. As a school superintendent put it, "There's no question but that the attitudes of personnel in schools are changing because of the many cases [of sexual harassment] that have come up across the country. I think all of us are being extremely cautious in how we handle students and in what we say and do with students and employees" (*Spokesman Review,* June 4, 1993, 1A). To address the problem, many school districts have suggested guidelines that teachers can follow to show concern for students, offer them encouragement, and congratulate them for their successes.

RELIGIOUS EXPRESSION

Conflicts over the proper role of religion in schools are among the most heated in the continuing debate about the character and purposes of American education. Numerous school districts have found themselves embroiled in legal issues related to school prayer, Bible reading, textbooks, creationism, singing of Christmas carols, distribution of religious literature, New Age beliefs, secular humanism, religious holidays, use of school buildings for religious meetings, and the role of religion in moral education, to name a few. On the one hand, conservative religious groups wish to restore prayer and Christian religious practices to the public schools; on the other, secular liberals see religion as irrelevant to school curricula and maintain that public schools should not promote religion. In addition, somewhere between these two positions are those who believe that, while schools should not be involved in the *teaching of* religion, they should *teach about* religion.

During the last 50 years, scores of court cases have addressed school activities related to the First Amendment principle of separation of church and state. As Michael Imber and Tyll Van Geel put it: "By far the most common constitutional objection raised against a school program in the latter half of the twentieth century is that it fails to respect the wall of separation between church and state" (1993, 88). In one of these landmark cases (*Engel v. Vitale,* 1962), the United States Supreme Court ruled that recitation of a prayer said in the presence of a teacher at the beginning of each school day was unconstitutional and violated the First Amendment which states: "Congress shall make no law respecting an establishment of religion, or prohibiting the free exercise thereof." Justice Hugo Black, who delivered the opinion of the Court, stated " . . . it is no part of the business of government to compose official prayers for any group of the American people to recite as a part of a religious program carried on by government."

The following year, the U.S. Supreme Court ruled that Bible reading and reciting the Lord's Prayer in school were unconstitutional (*School District of Abington Township v. Schempp*, 1963). In response to the district's claim that unless these religious activities were permitted a "religion of secularism" would be established, the Court stated that "We agree of course that the State may not establish a 'religion of secularism' in the sense of affirmatively opposing or showing hostility to religion, thus 'preferring those who believe in no religion over those who do believe.' We do not agree, however, that this decision in any sense has that effect."

To determine whether a state has violated the separation of church and state principle, the courts refer to the decision rendered in *Lemon v. Kurtzman* (1971). In this instance, the U.S. Supreme Court struck down an attempt by the Rhode Island legislature to provide a 15 percent salary supplement to teachers of secular subjects in nonpublic schools and Pennsylvania legislation to provide financial supplements to nonpublic schools through reimbursement for teachers' salaries, texts, and instructional materials in certain secular subjects. According to the three-part test enunciated in *Lemon v. Kurtzman,* governmental practices "must (1) reflect a clearly secular purpose; (2) have a primary effect that neither advances nor inhibits religion; and (3) avoid excessive entanglement with religion" (LaMorte 1996, 38). Though criticized vigorously by several Supreme Court justices since 1971, the so-called **Lemon test** has not been overruled.

During the mid 1990s, the courts heard several cases addressing the question of whether parents' right to direct their children's upbringing meant they could demand curricula and learning activities that were compatible with their religious beliefs. Without exception, the courts have rejected "parent-rights" cases against the schools; those rights, according to a U.S. Court of Appeals ruling in support of a school-wide assembly on HIV/AIDS, "do not encompass a broad-based right to restrict the flow of information in the public schools" (*Brown v. Hot, Sexy and Safer Productions, Inc.,* 1996). In a similar case, parents objected to a Massachusetts school district's policy of distributing condoms to junior and senior high school students who requested them. The state's Supreme Judicial Court rejected the parental rights argument and their argument that the program infringed on their First Amendment right to free exercise of religion: "Parents have no right to tailor public school programs to meet their individual religious or moral preferences" (*Curtis v. School Committee of Falmouth,* 1996).

HOME SCHOOLING

One spinoff of the heightened awareness during the 1980s of the problems that schools face has been the decision by some parents to educate their children in the home. While most home-schoolers view home schooling as an opportunity to provide their children with a curriculum based on religious values, "a new breed of home-schooler is emerging, motivated not by religious doctrine but by more practical concerns ranging from school violence to poor academic quality to overzealous peer pressure" (Schnaiberg 1996, 24). Estimates on the number of school-age children being taught at home vary—one puts it at between half a million and one million students (Schnaiberg 1996), another at between half a million and two million students (Weston 1996).

Home schooling is legal in all the states and the District of Columbia; however, how it is regulated, and whether resources are allocated, vary greatly. Thirty-four states regulate home schooling, and twenty-nine require periodic evaluations of students' learning; however, forty states do not require parents to have specific qualifications for teaching (Schnaiberg 1996). In most states, home-schoolers must demonstrate that their instruction is "equivalent" to that offered in the public schools, a standard set in *New Jersey v. Massa* (1967).

Legal support for home schools has been mixed. In 1994, home-schoolers in Maine defeated legislative attempts to require that home schools be visited monthly by public school officials. In 1993 and 1994, legislation to require home-school teachers to be state certified were defeated in South Dakota and Kansas, and similar laws were overturned in Iowa and North Dakota. However, a federal district court upheld a West Virginia statute making children ineligible for home schooling if their standardized test scores fell below the 40th percentile (*Null v. Board of Education*, 1993). In Iowa, mandatory home-schooling reports to the state were upheld in *State v. Rivera* (1993); home-schoolers in that state must submit course outlines, weekly lesson plans, and provide the amount of time spent on areas of the curriculum.

As the preceding cases related to home schooling show, school law is not static—instead, it is continually evolving and changing. In addition, laws pertaining to education vary from state to state. Therefore, it is important for the beginning teacher to become familiar with current publications on school law in his or her state.

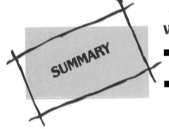

SUMMARY

Why Do You Need a Professional Code of Ethics?

- A professional code of ethics guides teachers' actions and enables them to build relationships with students based on trust and respect.
- A code of ethics helps teachers see beyond the short-range consequences of their actions to long-range consequences, and it helps them respond appropriately to ethical dilemmas in the classroom.

What Are Your Legal Rights as a Teacher?

- The right to due process protects teachers from arbitrary treatment by school districts and education officials regarding certification, nondiscrimination, contracts, tenure, dismissal, and academic freedom.
- Several court rulings have illustrated how the constitutional rights of teachers must be balanced against a school's need to promote its educational goals.

Do Student Teachers Have the Same Rights?

- Many states have not clarified the legal status of student teachers to teach. However, student teachers should be aware that a potential for liability exists for them just as it does with certified teachers, and they should clarify their rights and responsibilities prior to beginning student teaching.
- Depending upon state statutes, a student teacher may substitute under certain conditions for a cooperating teacher.

What Are Your Legal Responsibilities as a Teacher?

- Teachers are responsible for meeting the terms of their teaching contracts, including providing for their students' safety and well-being.

- Three legal responsibilities that concern teachers are: avoiding tort liability (specifically, negligence and educational malpractice), recognizing the physical and behavioral indicators of child abuse and then reporting suspected instances of such abuse, and observing copyright laws as they apply to photocopies, videotapes, and computer software.

What Are the Legal Rights of Students and Parents?

- Students' rights related to freedom of expression, suspension and expulsion, search and seizure, privacy, and nondiscrimination are based on several landmark legal decisions.
- Generally, students' freedom of expression can be limited if it is disruptive of the educational process or incongruent with the school's mission.
- Students can neither be suspended nor expelled without due process.
- Courts have developed a two-pronged test for search and seizure actions involving students: (1) School officials must have "reasonable" suspicion that a student has violated a law or school policy, and (2) the search must be done using methods that are reasonable and appropriate, given the nature of the infraction.
- Under the Buckley Amendment, students have the right to examine their school records, and schools may not give out information on students without their prior written consent.
- Schools may not discriminate against students on the basis of race, sex, religion, disability, marital status, or infection with a noncommunicable disease such as HIV/AIDS.

What Are Some Issues in the Legal Rights of School Districts?

- In spite of its proven ineffectiveness, corporal punishment has been upheld by the Supreme Court; however, almost half of the states and many school districts ban it, and many others restrict its use.
- About four out of five teenagers are affected by sexual harassment. According to a 1992 Supreme Court decision, schools can be held responsible for the sexual harassment of students.
- The First Amendment principle of separation of church and state has been applied to numerous court cases involving religious expression in the public schools. Court rulings banning school prayer, Bible reading, and other religious activities are often based on the three-part test developed in *Lemon v. Kurtzman* (1971). The courts have ruled consistently against parents who demand curricula and learning activities that are compatible with their religious beliefs.
- Home schooling is legal in all states, though most require home-schoolers to demonstrate that their instruction is "equivalent" to that in public schools.

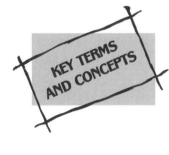
KEY TERMS AND CONCEPTS

academic freedom, 208
Buckley Amendment, 224
censorship, 218
code of ethics, 201
collective bargaining, 206
copyright laws, 215
corporal punishment, 227
dismissal, 205

due process, 202
educational malpractice, 214
ethical dilemmas, 201
fair use, 215
freedom of expression, 218
grievance, 206
Lemon test, 231

negligence, 214
nondiscrimination, 203
search and seizure, 223
sexual harassment, 228
teaching contract, 204
tenure, 204
tort liability, 212

Teacher's Journal

1. Read the NEA Code of Ethics in the Teacher's Resource Guide. Record in your journal examples of situations you observed or experienced in which you feel a teacher may have violated NEA principles. Include one example involving Principle I, a teacher's commitment to students, and one example involving Principle II, a teacher's commitment to the profession. Conclude your analysis of these cases with a personal statement about your goals for ethical conduct as a teacher.

2. What limits do you believe should be placed on *what* teachers teach? on *how* they teach? Which of the legal cases on academic freedom discussed in this chapter support your views?

3. What is your position regarding corporal punishment? Are there circumstances under which its use is justified?

4. Review the section on the legal rights of students (pp. 218–227). Can you recall a time when you believe your rights as a student (or the rights of a classmate) were denied? Describe those events. What court cases and parts of the U.S. Constitution would apply to the events you describe?

Teacher's Database

1. Conduct an Internet and Web search on one or more of the topics listed below or on another topic from Chapter 7. Narrow your search to issues and information relating to school law and the legal rights and responsibilities of school districts and schools, teachers and administrators, and students and parents. Include a search of news sources, such as *Education Week* online, for summaries of recent court rulings pertaining to education and school law. The texts of many policies, laws, and U.S. Supreme Court decisions are also available online. You may wish to select a particular court case from Chapter 7 to investigate.

Topics on legal issues to search from Chapter 7:

academic freedom	expulsion	school prayer
censorship	free speech	school uniforms
collective bargaining	gay and lesbian	search and seizure
copyright law	rights	sexual harassment
corporal punishment	home schooling	suspension
creation science	nondiscrimination	teacher dismissal
dress codes	privacy	teacher tenure
due process	professional ethics	

2. Using an index system or a keyword search engine, locate and visit the web sites of three or more of the following educational journals and publications. At each site, download or record information related to one or more of the education law issues discussed in Chapter 7.

American Educator	*Instructor*
American School Board Journal	*Kappa Delta Phi Record*
Childhood Education	*Phi Delta Kappan*
Educational Leadership	*PTA Today*
Elementary School Journal	*Teacher Magazine*
High School Journal	*Young Children*

1. Interview several students at a middle school or high school to get their views regarding the legal rights of students, discussed in this chapter. You may wish to develop a questionnaire that explores students' opinions in depth on a particular issue, such as freedom of expression or religion in the schools. Or you might get students' reactions to one of the legal cases summarized in this chapter. Present the results of your interview or survey to your classmates.

2. During an observation of a teacher's day, identify an ethical dilemma that the teacher confronts. Describe the dilemma and the teacher's response in a journal entry. To help you with this activity, ask your instructor for handouts M7.1, "Identifying Ethical Dilemmas in Teaching," and M7.2, "Analyzing Teachers' Responses to Ethical Dilemmas."

3. Interview a school superintendent or principal to find out about any instances of actual or threatened litigation that occurred in the district during the last year or so. Ask him or her to identify procedures the district has in place to ensure due process for teachers and students. Report your findings.

Professional Portfolio

Survey a group of students, teachers, and/or parents regarding a legal issue in education. Among the legal issues and questions you might address are the following:

- Should tenure for teachers be abolished? Does tenure improve the quality of education students receive?
- Under what circumstances should restrictions be placed on *what* teachers teach and *how* they teach?
- Should parents be allowed to provide home schooling for their children?
- Are parents justified in filing educational malpractice suits if their children fail to achieve in school?
- Under what circumstances should restrictions be placed on students' freedom of expression?
- Should schools have the right to implement dress codes? guidelines for students' hairstyles? school uniforms?
- Should corporal punishment be banned? If not, under what circumstances should it be used?
- How should schools combat the problem of sexual harassment?
- To combat drug abuse, should schools implement mandatory drug testing of students? of teachers?
- Should students have access to their educational records? should their parents or guardians?
- As part of an HIV/AIDS prevention program, should condoms be distributed to high school students? Should parental approval be required for participation?

The report summarizing the results of your survey should include demographic information such as the following for your sample of respondents: gender, age, whether they have children in school, level of education, and so on. When you analyze the results, look for differences related to these variables.

Prejudice is a burden which confuses the past, threatens the future, and renders the present inaccessible.

—Maya Angelou

chapter 8

Teaching Diverse Learners

Yvette is a twelve-year-old Puerto Rican girl who lives with her three older brothers and two younger sisters in an apartment in the city. Yvette and her brothers were born in Puerto Rico, and her sisters were born in New York. Yvette's mother and father brought the family to the mainland two years ago.

About three months earlier, Yvette transferred into your class. You suspect that she's having trouble adjusting to changes. You believe her work would improve if she got more involved; however, she gives the impression of being afraid to risk making mistakes, especially in the areas of reading and language arts.

Yvette seems to trust you, so you've decided to talk to her after school today—she usually waits in your classroom until her brother Juan arrives to walk her home. As she talks, timidly at first, then more openly and naturally, you realize that Yvette is struggling to adjust to the many new challenges of living on the mainland. She misses her grandmother who lived with the family in Puerto Rico. She also believes she does not speak English well enough and is worried that the other children will tease her if she speaks out in class. You also learn that Yvette has missed school frequently because she has been having bad headaches and stomach problems. When you ask Yvette if her parents are coming to the next PTA meeting, Yvette tells you they probably will not come because they do not speak English.

How can you get Yvette more involved in classroom activities? What strategies could you use to help her to increase her reading, speaking, and writing skills? How might you make Yvette's parents feel welcome and comfortable at the school?

This chapter looks at American cultural diversity and the challenges of equalizing educational opportunity for all students. Professional teachers see cultural diversity as an asset to be preserved and valued, not a liability. This country has always derived strength from the **diversity** of its people, and *all* students should receive a quality education so that they may make their unique contributions to society.

HOW IS DIVERSITY EMBEDDED IN THE AMERICAN WAY OF LIFE ?

The percentage of ethnic minorities in the United States has been growing steadily since the end of World War II. According to the U.S. Bureau of the Census, about 820,000 people immigrate to the United States annually. As a result, the number of students from diverse cultural backgrounds is increasing in most of America's schools (see Figure 8.1).

The increase in minority-group populations is having a profound effect on schools. The District of Columbia now has minority group enrollments of 96 percent; Hawaii, 76 percent; New Mexico, 57 percent; and Mississippi, 56 percent (National Center for Education Statistics 1996). It is estimated that by 2000 the majority of students in most urban school districts will be members of those groups traditionally thought of as minorities. Among the urban school districts where non-Hispanic white students already number less than 20 percent are Atlanta, Baltimore, Chicago, Detroit, Houston, Los Angeles, Miami, New Orleans, Oakland, Richmond, and San Antonio (National Center for Education Statistics 1996).

Clearly, the increasing diversity of American society has extensive implications for schools. There is, for example, an increased demand for bilingual programs and teachers. All but a few school districts are confronted with a critical shortage of minority teachers. And, there is a need to develop curricula and strategies that address the needs and backgrounds of all students—regardless of their social class, gender, sexual orientation, or ethnic, racial, or cultural identity.

THE MEANING OF CULTURE

As we pointed out in Chapter 4's discussion of the aims of education, one mission of the schools is to maintain the American culture. But what is the American cul-

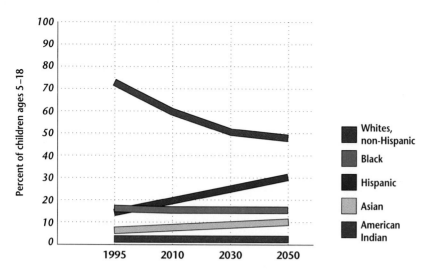

FIGURE 8.1 Changing school population (Note: Hispanic Americans can be of any race; figures for Anglo-European Americans are non-Hispanics; Asian Americans include Pacific Islanders; Native Americans include Eskimos and Aleuts. Percents do not add to 100 because the Hispanic population includes members of several races, including blacks and whites.) (Source: Census Bureau Projections.)

ture? Is there a single culture to which all Americans belong? Before we can answer that question we must define the term *culture*. Simply put, **culture** is *the way of life* common to a group of people. It consists of the values, attitudes, and beliefs that influence their traditions and behavior. It is also a way of interacting with and looking at the world. Though at one time it was believed that America was a "melting pot" in which ethnic cultures would melt into one, ethnic and cultural differences have remained very much a part of American life. A "salad-bowl" analogy captures more accurately the **cultural pluralism** of American society. That is, the distinguishing characteristics of cultures are to be preserved rather than blended into a single culture.

DIMENSIONS OF CULTURE Within our nation's boundaries, we find cultural groups that differ according to other distinguishing factors, such as religion, politics, economics, and geographic region. The regional culture of New England, for example, is quite different from that of the Southeast. Similarly, Californians are culturally different from Iowans.

However, Americans *do* share some common dimensions of culture. James Banks, an authority on multicultural education, has termed this shared culture the "national macroculture" (Banks 1994). In addition to being members of the national macroculture, Americans are members of ethnic groups. An **ethnic group** is made up of individuals within a larger culture who share a self-defined racial or cultural identity and a set of beliefs, attitudes, and values. Members of an ethnic group distinguish themselves from others in the society by physical and social attributes. In addition, you should be aware that the composition of ethnic groups can change over time, and that there is often as much variability within groups as between them.

CULTURAL IDENTITY In addition to membership in the national macroculture, each individual participates in an array of subcultures, each with its customs and beliefs. Collectively, these subcultures determine an individual's **cultural identity,** an overall sense of who one is. Other possible elements that might shape a person's cultural identity include age, racial identity, exceptionalities, language, gender, sexual orientation, income level, and beliefs and values. These elements have different significances for different people. For example, the cultural identity of some people is most strongly determined by their occupations; for others by their ethnicity; and for others by their religious beliefs.

Remember that your future students will have their own complex cultural identities, which are no less valid for being different. For some of them, these identities may make them feel "disconnected" from the attitudes, expectations, and values conveyed by the school. For example

> Students who come from homes where languages other than English are the medium of communication, who share customs and beliefs unique to their cultural community and/or home countries, or who face the range of challenges posed by economic insecurity will not often find much of their family, community, or national existence reflected in the school setting. Often these students feel that school is itself foreign, alienating, and unrelated to their beliefs and concerns (Rice and Walsh 1996, 9).

As a teacher, you will be challenged to understand the subtle differences in cultural identities among your students and to create a learning environment that enables all students to feel comfortable in school and "connected to" their school experiences.

LANGUAGE AND CULTURE   Culture is embedded in language, a fact that has resulted in conflict among different groups in our society. Some groups, although they support the preservation of ethnic cultures, believe that members of non-English-speaking groups must learn English if they are to function in American society. There is also conflict between those who wish to preserve linguistic diversity and those who wish to establish English as a national language.

Much of the debate has focused on **bilingual education,** that is, using two languages as the medium of instruction. Bilingual education is designed to help students maintain their ethnic identity and become proficient in both English and the language of the home, to encourage assimilation into the mainstream culture and integrate the home language and culture with a new one. Some people are staunchly opposed to any form of bilingual education, and others support it as a short-term way to teach English to students.

Language diversity is an important dimension of American cultural diversity regardless. Many students come from homes where English is not spoken. The National Clearinghouse for Bilingual Education estimates that the number of people from non-English-speaking backgrounds will reach almost 40 million by 2000. Currently, one in seven U.S. residents speaks a language other than English at home, most frequently Spanish, as Table 8.1 shows.

THE CONCEPT OF MULTICULTURALISM   **Multiculturalism** is a set of beliefs based on the importance of seeing the world from different cultural frames of reference and on recognizing and valuing the rich array of cultures within our nation and within our global community. For teachers, multiculturalism affirms the need to create schools where differences related to race, ethnicity, gender, disability, and social class are acknowledged and all students are viewed as valuable members and as human resources for enriching the teaching–learning process. Furthermore, a central purpose of teaching, according to the multiculturalist view, is to prepare students to live in a culturally pluralistic world. "In short, multiculturalism is a perspective that has far-reaching implications for all aspects of schooling, including instruction, curriculum, evaluation, home/school/community relationships, staffing, and extracurricular activities" (Grant and Gomez 1996, 264).

For teachers, multiculturalism also means actively seeking out experiences within other cultures that lead to increased understanding of and appreciation for those ways of life. To provide such cross-cultural experiences for their students, several teacher education programs have developed "cultural immersion" experiences that enable prospective teachers to live in their students' neighborhoods and com-

TABLE 8.1

The fifty most commonly spoken languages in the United States after English

Language	Number of Speakers	State with Highest % of Speakers	Language	Number of Speakers	State with Highest % of Speakers
1. Spanish	17,339,172	New Mexico	26. Gujarathi	102,418	New Jersey
2. French	1,702,176	Maine	27. Ukrainian	95,568	New Jersey
3. German	1,547,099	North Dakota	28. Czech	92,485	Nebraska
4. Italian	1,308,648	New York	29. Dutch (Pa.)	83,525	Pennsylvania
5. Chinese	1,249,213	Hawaii	30. Miao	81,877	Minnesota
6. Tagalog	843,251	Hawaii	31. Norwegian	80,723	North Dakota
7. Polish	723,483	Illinois	32. Slovak	80,388	Pennsylvania
8. Korean	626,478	Hawaii	33. Swedish	77,511	Minnesota
9. Vietnamese	507,069	California	34. Serbo-Croatian	70,964	New York
10. Portugese	429,860	Rhode Island	35. Kru	65,848	D.C.
11. Japanese	427,657	Hawaii	36. Romanian	65,265	New York
12. Greek	388,260	Massachusetts	37. Lithuanian	55,781	Illinois
13. Arabic	355,150	Michigan	38. Finnish	54,350	Minnesota
14. Hindi	331,484	New Jersey	39. Panjabi	50,005	California
15. Russian	241,798	New York	40. Formosan	46,044	California
16. Yiddish	213,064	New York	41. Croatian	45,206	Illinois
17. Thai/Lao	206,266	California	42. Turkish	41,876	New Jersey
18. Persian	201,865	California	43. Ilocano	41,131	Hawaii
19. French Creole	187,658	Florida	44. Bengali	38,101	New York
20. Armenian	149,694	California	45. Danish	35,639	South Dakota
21. Navajo	148,530	New Mexico	46. Syriac	35,146	Michigan
22. Hungarian	147,902	New Jersey	47. Samoan	34,914	Hawaii
23. Hebrew	144,292	New York	48. Malayalam	33,949	New York
24. Dutch	142,684	Utah	49. Cajun	33,670	Lousiana
25. Mon-Khmer	127,441	Rhode Island	50. Amharic	31,505	D.C.

(Source: *USA Today* analysis of Census Bureau data. *USA Today* [April 28, 1993]: 11A. Copyright 1993, *USA Today.* Used with permission.)

munities while student teaching. The University of Alaska-Fairbanks Teachers for Alaska Program, for example, enables students to live in remote Alaskan Native villages during their year-long student teaching experience. In the Urban Education Program of the Associated Colleges of the Midwest, prospective teachers live in a former convent in a multiracial, economically diverse neighborhood in Chicago. There the students teach and participate in structured activities that take them into the city's other ethnic neighborhoods. Students who participate in Indiana University's American Indian Project live in a dormitory on a reservation during their student teaching—an experience that one student says prepared her for student diversity in her future classroom:

> Learning about my students' home environment has done wonders. It's made me see things through other people's eyes. Now I know so much more about not only a specific

culture but likenesses and differences with just about anybody. I have had a lot of diverse experiences that have made me ready for anything (Wisconsin Center for Education Research 1994, 7).

ETHNICITY AND RACE

Your understanding of the distinction between ethnicity and race will enable you to provide students with educational experiences that reflect ethnic and racial diversity in meaningful ways. **Ethnicity** refers to "a shared feeling of common identity, a sense of peoplehood, and a shared sense of interdependence of fate. These feelings derive, in part, from a common ancestral origin, a common set of values, and a common set of experiences" (Banks 1994, 71).

On the other hand, the concept of **race** is used to distinguish among human beings on the basis of biological traits and characteristics. Numerous racial categories have been proposed, but because of the diversity among humans and the mixing of genes that has taken place over time, no single set of racial categories is universally accepted. People can be classified into as many as 300 "races," depending on the kind and number of genetic features chosen for measurement. In his classic book, *Man's Most Dangerous Myth: The Fallacy of Race,* anthropologist Ashley Montagu pointed out that

> It is impossible to make the sort of racial classifications which some anthropologists and others have attempted. The fact is that all human beings are so . . . mixed with regard to origin that between different groups of individuals . . . "overlapping" of physical traits is the rule (1974, 9).

Many Americans favor the addition of a "mixed race" category to the census to better reflect the realities of racial identity in the United States.

There are many ethnic groups in American society, and everyone belongs to at least one. However, as James Banks points out:

> an individual American is ethnic to the extent that he or she functions within ethnic subsocieties and shares their values, behavioral styles, and cultures. An individual, however, may have a low level of ethnicity or psychological identification with his or her ethnic group or groups (1997, 9).

It is also clear that racial and ethnic identities in America are becoming more complex. We now know that "racial and ethnic identities derive their meanings from social and historical circumstances, that they can vary over time, and that they can sometimes even be slipped on and off like a change of clothing" (Coughlin 1993, A7). For example, a third-generation descendent of a Japanese immigrant may choose to refer to him- or herself as a Japanese American, an American, or an Asian American. Furthermore, it is evident that "specific racial categories acquire and lose meaning over time" (Coughlin 1993, A7), and the use of ethnic and racial labels and expressions of group membership is largely self-selected and arbitrary.

THE CONCEPT OF MINORITIES

To understand the important concept of **minorities,** it may help to remember that even though the term *minority* technically refers to any *group* numbering less than half of the total population, in certain parts of the country "minorities" are actually the majority. However, more important than the numbers themselves is an appreciation of how many groups of people have continuously struggled to obtain full

Dear Mentor

NOVICE AND EXPERT TEACHERS ON TEACHING DIVERSE LEARNERS

Dear Moya,

American classrooms today are an exciting mixture of many diverse young people with many different cultural traditions. The salsa bowl analogy and your desire to address each student's uniqueness indicate a sensitivity and openness that will benefit your students and their families. Here is my advice to you:

As you get to know your students individually and share who you are, you will build the trust necessary to be an effective teacher. Use every opportunity to learn about your students and their families so your lesson planning will be personally directed. The more you know about them, their tradition, lifestyles, dreams, and problems, the better understanding you will have of what they need to learn and how they can best learn.

Continually evaluate and set new goals for yourself. Give yourself time to become the best you can be. Find ways to gain more knowledge about the subject matter you teach as well as the curriculum requirements so all of your students will have equal access to the content. Continue to add to and refine the variety of instructional, motivational, and organizational strategies you use. Take time to develop friendships among your colleagues as well as those outside of teaching, and have fun along the way. This journey will be demanding of your personal and professional growth, but it will also be rewarding.

I welcome you to teaching and send my best wishes. Your enthusiasm and caring is a wonderful gift to your students as both individuals and salsa bowl members. As

Dear Mentor,

A student in one of my education classes says that the United States is rapidly becoming a "salsa bowl." In a salsa bowl the different vegetables are distinctive but cannot be easily separated, and their combined taste is mostly the same in each bite. In a multicultural classroom, how can I teach the salsa bowl of American life and still address each student's individual ethnic style of learning?

Moya Lyttle

you begin your professional journey I'm confident that you will meet many other people who will support, encourage, and share the joy and humor of your odyssey.

Masako Kawase
Master Teacher

educational, economic, political, and social opportunities in our society. Along with minority racial and ethnic groups, others who have traditionally lacked power in American public life are immigrants, the poor, children and the elderly, non-English speakers, members of minority religions, and women. Groups that have been most frequently discriminated against in terms of the quality of education they have received include African Americans, Spanish-speaking Americans, Native Americans, Asian Americans, exceptional learners, people with disabilities, and females. There is mounting evidence that many students from these groups continue to receive a substandard education that does not meet their needs or help empower them to participate fully and equally in American life.

MINORITY ENROLLMENTS AND TEACHER RECRUITMENT   Data released in 1996 by the National Center for Education Statistics indicated the following percentages for enrollment in public elementary through secondary schools: 70.4 percent white, 16.1 percent African American, 9.9 percent Hispanic, 2.8 percent Asian or Pacific Islander, and 0.9 percent Native American/Native Alaskan. When contrasted with the diverse mosaic of student enrollments, especially in states and school districts with large minority populations and enrollments, the backgrounds of today's teachers reveal less diversity, a situation that has been labeled a "crisis" (King 1993). Recent U.S. Department of Education data indicate that the percentage of African-American teachers was 8.6 percent; Latino, 3.7 percent; Asian American/Pacific Islander, 1.0 percent; and Native American, 1.0 percent. Furthermore, the percentage of minority teachers may be declining; the Education Commission of the States estimates that by 2000 only 5 percent of teachers will be minorities while minorities will make up about one-third of the total school enrollment (Education Commission of the States 1992).

MINORITY GROUPS AND ACADEMIC ACHIEVEMENT   Minority-group students are disproportionately represented among students who have failed to master minimum competencies in reading, writing, and mathematics. In addition, many have limited abilities in the English language. It has been estimated that ethnic minority students are two to four times more likely than others to drop out of high school. Minority students are also expelled or suspended from school more often than nonminority students.

One of the most extensive studies comparing the academic achievement of students was done by James S. Coleman and his associates in 1966. The Coleman report, *Equality of Educational Opportunity*, looked at the test scores of 600,000 students at 4,000 schools in grades one, three, six, nine, and twelve. For each grade level, achievement for the average Mexican American, Puerto Rican, Native American, and African American was significantly lower than that for the average Asian American or Anglo-European American. Coleman also found that the achievement gap widened at higher grade levels. The reading scores of African Americans in the first grade, for example, were about six months behind; by the twelfth grade, this gap had widened to about three-and-a-half years (Coleman 1966).

A similar study in 1980, involving a national sample of high school sophomores, explored the relationships among minority group membership, social class, and academic achievement. Data from this study upheld the findings of the Coleman study. With the exception of the math scores of Asian-American students, the data reveal that as socioeconomic status increases, achievement also increases (National Center for Education Statistics 1980). Research clearly shows that socioeconomic status—not race, language, or culture—contributes most strongly to students' achievement in school.

One of the most comprehensive, ongoing studies of student achievement has been the **National Assessment of Educational Progress (NAEP)**. The NAEP assesses the achievement of students in several subject areas on a four- or five-year cycle. Several thousand youths, ages nine, thirteen, and seventeen, have been tested since 1969. Here, too, the data indicate that African-American and Hispanic students are consistently below the national average in their scores in reading, writing, history, mathematics, and science (see Table 8.2). Recent trends, however, show "modest growth in achievement among students from minority groups and from 'less advantaged' backgrounds" (Berliner and Biddle 1995, 27).

In considering the lower achievement levels of minority students, it is important to remember the strong connection between socioeconomic status (SES) and achievement and the much higher incidence of poverty among minority families. "Children from families with incomes below the poverty level are nearly twice as likely to be

TABLE 8.2

National assessment of educational progress, by subject and by race, 1992[*]

Reading	9-year-olds	13-year-olds	17-year-olds
National Average	210	260	290
White	218	266	297
African American	184	238	261
Hispanic	192	239	271
Writing	Grade 4	Grade 8	Grade 11
National Average	207	274	287
White	217	279	294
African American	175	258	263
Hispanic	189	265	274
Mathematics	9-year-olds	13-year-olds	17-year-olds
National Average	230	273	307
White	235	279	312
African American	208	250	286
Hispanic	212	259	292
Science	9-year-olds	13-year-olds	17-year-olds
National Average	231	258	294
White	239	267	304
African American	200	224	256
Hispanic	205	238	270

[*]National Assessment of Educational Progress scales in reading, writing, mathematics, and science range from 0 to 500.

(Source: National Center for Education Statistics, *The Condition of Education, 1996* [Washington, D.C.: National Center for Education Statistics], pp. 54,56,58,60.)

held back a grade as their more advantaged classmates, [and] the proficiency level of an average 17-year-old in a poor urban setting is equivalent to that of a typical 13-year-old in an affluent urban area" (National Commission on Children 1991, 182). Understandably, it is difficult for poor children to learn if they come to school hungry; endure the stress of living in unsafe, pollution-filled neighborhoods; or dwell in dilapidated homes.

LANGUAGE MINORITIES   The Census Bureau reported that in 1990 one in seven U.S. residents aged five years or older spoke a language other than English at home. Various bilingual education programs have been developed to meet the special needs of **language-minority students,** those whose language of the home is a language other than English, and students with **limited English proficiency (LEP),** a designation for students with limited ability to understand, read, or speak English and who have a first language other than English. Though most bilingual education programs serve Spanish-speaking students, there are bilingual education programs for the more than ninety other language groups in the United States. Figure 8.2 shows the distribution among the states of the nearly thirty-two million people who spoke a language other than English at home in 1990.

STEREOTYPING AND RACISM

While teachers should expand their knowledge of and appreciation for the diverse cultural backgrounds of their students, they should also guard against forming stereotypes or overgeneralizations about those cultures. **Stereotyping** is the process of attributing behavioral characteristics to all members of a group. In some cases, stereotypes are formed on the basis of limited experiences with and information about the group being stereotyped, and the validity of these stereotypes is not questioned.

Within any cultural group that shares a broad cultural heritage, however, considerable diversity exists. For example, two Puerto Rican children who live in the same community and attend the same school may appear alike to their teachers when, in reality, they are very different. One may come from a home where Spanish is spoken and Puerto Rican holidays are observed; the other child may know only a few words of Spanish and observe only the holidays of the majority culture.

In addition to being alert for stereotypes they and others may hold, teachers should learn to recognize **racism,** the prejudicial belief that one's ethnic or racial group is superior to others. In light of the arbitrariness of the concept of race, James A. Banks points out, "In most societies, *the social significance of race is much more important than the presumed physical differences among groups*" (1997, 74, italics in original). Unfortunately, many people attach great importance to the concept of race. If you believe "that human groups can be validly grouped on the basis of their biological traits and that these identifiable groups inherit certain mental, personality, and cultural characteristics that determine their behavior" (Banks 1997, 78) then you hold racist beliefs. When people use such beliefs as a rationale for oppressing other groups, they are practicing racism.

As a teacher, you will not be able to eliminate stereotypic thinking or racism in our society. However, you have an obligation to all your students to see that your curriculum and instruction are free of any forms of stereotyping or racism. The following Professional Reflection will help you examine, and possibly reassess, your cultural attitudes and values and determine if you have stereotypes about other cultural groups.

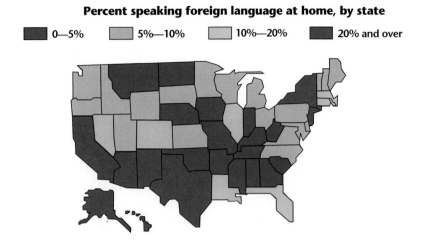

14% of the nation's population speaks a language other than English at home, compared to 11% in 1980. A look at this trend:

Percent speaking foreign language at home, by state

| ■ 0—5% | ■ 5%—10% | □ 10%—20% | ■ 20% and over |

Top Languages Spoken
(In Millions of Speakers)

Spanish	17.4
French	1.7
German	1.6
Italian	1.3
Chinese	1.3
Tagalog*	.84
Polish	.72
Korean	.63
Vietnamese	.51
Portugese	.43

Fastest Growing, Shrinking
(Percent Increase)

Mon-Khmer*	676%
Fr. Creole	654%
Gujarathi*	178%
Hindi*	155%
Vietnamese	150%

(Percent decrease)

-34%	Yiddish
-20%	Italian
-18%	Hungarian
-12%	Polish
-5%	Greek

*Tagalog is a language of the Philippines; Mon-Khmer is a language of Cambodia; Hindi and Gujarathi are languages of India.

FIGURE 8.2 Fewer speak English at home (Source: Taken from *Spokesman Review,* April 28, 1993: p. 2A.)

PROFESSIONAL REFLECTION

Reflecting on Your Cultural Identity

In a Teacher's Journal entry, describe *your* cultural identity. Who are you? What beliefs, customs, and attitudes are part of your culture? Which of these are most important to your cultural identity?

Next, think of the ethnic and cultural groups in America with which you are unfamiliar. When you become a teacher, some of your students may be from these groups. What are some stereotypes about these groups that you tend to believe? How might these stereotypes influence your teaching and teaching effectiveness? How will you test or change your beliefs as part of the process of becoming a teacher?

WHAT DOES EQUAL EDUCATIONAL OPPORTUNITY MEAN

To provide equal educational opportunity to all students means that teachers and schools promote the full development of students as individuals, without regard for race, ethnicity, gender, sexual orientation, socioeconomic status, abilities, or disabilities. More specifically, educators fulfill this important mission by continually evaluating the appropriateness of the curricular and instructional experiences they provide to each student.

In the following sections, we review the progress that has been made to provide students from diverse groups with equal educational opportunity, and we focus on strategies for teaching in diverse classrooms. We omit Anglo-European Americans from our review, not because students from this very diverse group always have had equal educational opportunities, but because this group represents the historically dominant culture. To a great extent, it has determined the curricular and instructional practices found in schools as well as the "formal institutions, official language, social values, and other aspects of life in [our] society" (Bennett 1995, 45).

Like the groups we discuss, however, "Anglo-European American" is not a single, monolithic culture. Americans whose ethnic heritage is English, Polish, German, Italian, Irish, Czechoslovakian, Russian, or Swedish, for example, often differ greatly in religious and political traditions, beliefs, and values. Their individual ethnic identity may or may not be strengthened by recent immigrants from their country of origin. European ethnics have, nevertheless, assimilated into the mainstream American society more completely than others.

EDUCATION AND AFRICAN AMERICANS

Of the more than 259 million persons living in America, approximately 13 percent are African Americans. According to Harold Hodgkinson's 1992 publication *A Demographic Look at Tomorrow,* the African-American population is expected to rise from 30 million in 1990 to 44 million by 2020. The incidence of social problems such as unemployment, crime, drug abuse, poverty, inadequate housing, and school dropouts is proportionally greater for African Americans than for whites. The struggle of African Americans to improve their quality of life after the end of slavery has been hampered for generations by persistent racism, discrimination, poverty, crime, unemployment, and underemployment.

The civil rights movement of the 1960s and 1970s made it clear that African Americans had been denied full access to many aspects of American life, including the right to a good education. A 1976 report by the United States Commission on Civil Rights, for example, revealed that a Southern school district in the 1930s spent nearly eighteen times as much for the education of white pupils as it did for the education of African Americans.

THE DESEGREGATION ERA

Perhaps the most blatant form of discrimination against African Americans has been school segregation and unequal educational opportunity. As you learned in Chapter 3, the attempt was made to justify segregation by the idea of separate-but-equal schools. It was not until the National Association for the Advancement of Colored People (NAACP) brought suit on behalf of a Kansas family (*Brown v. Board of Education of Topeka, Kansas*) in 1954 that the concept of separate-but-equal schools was decidedly struck down.

What is the legacy of school desegregation today? What are some outcomes of education research and curriculum reform related to the African-American experience?

The parents of Linda Brown felt that the education their fourth-grader was receiving in the segregated Topeka schools was inferior. When their request that she be transferred to a white school was turned down, they filed suit. In a landmark decision, the U.S. Supreme Court ruled that segregated schools are "inherently unequal" and violate the equal protection clause of the Fourteenth Amendment. American citizens, the justices asserted, have a right to receive an equal opportunity for education.

As a result of opportunities created during the civil rights movement, a substantial number of African Americans are now members of the middle class. Affirmative action programs have enabled many African Americans to attain high-ranking positions in the business, medical, legal, and educational professions. Such gains lead James Banks to point out that

> [A]ny accurate and sophisticated description of the status of African Americans on the threshold of the twenty-first century must describe not only the large percentage of Blacks who are members of the so-called underclass, but also the smaller and significant percentage of African Americans who have entered the middle and upper classes and who function in the mainstream society. Many of the children of the new middle class are not only unacquainted with poverty, but also have been socialized in mainstream middle- and upper-class communities. They have little first-hand experience with traditional African American culture (Banks and Banks 1997, 228–229).

RESEARCH ON LEARNING NEEDS OF AFRICAN-AMERICAN STUDENTS   Research on factors related to students' success in school suggest that our schools are monoethnic and do not take into account the diverse needs of ethnic minority-group students (Bennett 1995). In the case of African-American students, the failure of the school curriculum to address their learning needs may contribute to high dropout rates and below-average achievement. For example, research indicates that teaching strategies that emphasize cooperation—not competition—often result in higher achievement among African-American (and Mexican-American) students (Aronson and Gonzalez

1988). In addition, Christine Bennett, an expert on multicultural education, has found that because many African Americans have grown up in an oral tradition, they may learn better through oral/aural activities—for example, reading aloud and listening to audiotapes (Bennett 1995). However, she cautions against assuming that *all* African Americans learn better aurally.

AFROCENTRIC SCHOOLS   To address the educational inequities that African-American and other minority-group students may experience as a result of segregation, many communities have tried to create more ethnically and racially diverse classrooms through the controversial practice of busing students to attend schools in other neighborhoods. Also, some African Americans have recently begun to call for **Afrocentric schools**—that is, schools that focus on African-American history and cultures for African-American pupils. Proponents believe that the educational needs of African-American students can be met more effectively in schools that offer Afrocentric curricula.

Private Afrocentric schools, or "black academies," have sprung up across the country in recent years, many supported by the growing number of African Americans who practice Islam, a religion based on the teachings of the prophet Mohammed. Curricula in these schools emphasize the people and cultures of Africa and the history and achievements of African Americans. Teaching methods are often designed for culture-based learning styles, such as choral response, learning through movement, and sociality.

EDUCATION AND LATINO AND HISPANIC AMERICANS

Hispanic Americans are the fastest growing minority group in the Unites States. According to the 1990 census, 9 percent of Americans are of Hispanic heritage, and it has been estimated that an additional five million illegal aliens who speak Spanish may be in the country. By the year 2010, the Hispanic population is expected to be 14 percent, surpassing African Americans as the nation's largest minority group. And, by the year 2050, 23 percent of the population will have Hispanic roots.

Included in the category of Hispanic Americans are people who call themselves Latinos and Chicanos and who report their ancestry as Mexican, Puerto Rican, Cuban, Central American, or South American. Five states have populations that are more than 10 percent Hispanic: California, Texas, New Mexico, Arizona, and Colorado. In some states, efforts have been made to pass English-only laws and to restrict Hispanic immigrants' access to education. For example, U.S. English, a political action group, had been instrumental in getting English-only laws passed in 16 states by 1990, including Arizona, Colorado, and Florida (Banks 1997). In addition, California voters approved Proposition 187 in 1994, which prevents public schools from educating the children of illegal aliens.

HISTORICAL, CULTURAL, AND SOCIOECONOMIC FACTORS   Although some Spanish-speaking immigrants come to the United States hoping to escape a life of poverty in their home country, many others come because they have relatives in the United States or they wish to take advantage of business opportunities in this country. For those Spanish-speaking immigrants who lack job skills and have little education, however, adjusting to the complexities and demands of life in America may be difficult.

Cultural factors that affect the school experience of Hispanic and Latino students include values and attitudes that represent a fusion of Spanish colonial and Native-American cultures. A historian describes this fusion as a spiritual and romantic individualism that emphasized soul, honor, self-respect, integrity, and personal self-expression, combined with mutual trust, strong family and communities, and a Roman Catholic heritage (Olson 1979). It is noteworthy that this cultural heritage, shared by most Spanish-speaking Americans, cuts across all racial distinctions.

Socioeconomic factors affect the education of some Hispanics, such as the children of migrant farm workers. Among the estimated one million or so migrant farm workers in this country, more than 70 percent are Spanish-speaking. The dropout rate among all migrant workers is 90 percent, and 50 percent leave school before finishing the ninth grade (Bennett 1995). Migrant children are handicapped by the language barrier, deprivation resulting from poverty, and irregular school attendance. Some states have educational intervention programs in place for reaching this group.

RESEARCH ON NEEDS OF SPANISH-SPEAKING LEARNERS What can easily happen to Spanish-speaking learners if they are taught by teachers who are not sensitive to their learning needs is illustrated in Christine I. Bennett's portrait of Jesús, a student with limited English proficiency (LEP):

> Jesús Martinez was a bright, fine-looking six-year old when he migrated with his family from Puerto Rico to New York City. At a time when he was ready to learn to read and write his mother tongue, Jesús was instead suddenly thrust into an English-only classroom where the only tool he possessed for oral communication (the Spanish language) was completely useless to him. Jesús and his teacher could not communicate with each

Issues in Education

- What does the main character in this cartoon represent?
- With what education issue is the character concerned?
- What is the character's apparent solution to this issue?
- What, do you think, is the cartoonist's opinion of this solution? How could you infer the cartoonist's point of view from the cartoon?
- Do you agree or disagree? Why?
- What is your solution to the issue? to the larger problem of which the issue is a part?

other because each spoke a different language and neither spoke the language of the other. Jesús felt stupid, or retarded; his teacher perceived him to be culturally disadvantaged and beyond her help (Bennett 1995, 7).

Bennett also captures well the dilemma that many Spanish-speaking LEP students find themselves in: "LEP students are often caught up in conflicts between personal language needs—for example, the need to consolidate cognitive skills in the native language—and a sociopolitical climate that views standard English as most desirable and prestigious" (Bennett 1995, 247). The degree to which students from Spanish-speaking backgrounds are motivated to learn English varies from group to group. Mexican-American students who live in the southwest may retain the Spanish language to maintain ties with family and friends in Mexico. Recently arrived Cubans, on the other hand, may have a stronger motivation to learn the language of their new country. In regard to what they wish to learn, children take their cues from the adults around them. If their parents or guardians and friends and relatives have learned English and are bilingual, then they will be similarly motivated. Many Hispanic-Americans who value assimilation over their traditional culture favor English-only education.

However, the limited English proficiencies of many children raised in native Spanish-speaking families contribute significantly to the difficulties they have in school. To address the needs of these students, federally funded bilingual-bicultural programs encourage teachers to view bicultural knowledge as a bridge to the school's curriculum. Bilingual education is examined in detail later in this chapter.

EDUCATION AND ASIAN AMERICANS AND PACIFIC ISLANDERS

Asian Americans and Pacific Islanders represent about 3 percent of America's total population; by the year 2050, the percentage is expected to increase to almost 7 percent, or about 10 million people. This group is tremendously diverse and includes, for example, people from South Asia, primarily Bangladesh, India, and Pakistan; Southeast Asia, including Indochina (Laos, Thailand, Indonesia, Malaysia, and Vietnam) and the Philippines; East Asia, including China, Hong Kong, Japan, Korea, and Taiwan; and the Pacific Islands, including Hawaii, Guam, and Samoa. About 54 percent of the total Asian-American and Pacific-Islander population lives in the western United States, compared to 21 percent of the total population (U.S. Bureau of the Census 1993a).

HISTORICAL, CULTURAL, AND SOCIOECONOMIC FACTORS   The three largest Asian American groups are Chinese (23.8 percent of Asian Americans), Filipinos (20.4 percent), and Japanese (12.3 percent) (U.S. Bureau of the Census 1993a). While these groups differ significantly, each "came to the United States seeking the American dream, satisfied important labor needs, and became victims of an anti-Asian movement designed to prevent their further immigration to the United States. [They] also experienced tremendous economic, educational, and social mobility and success in U.S. society" (Banks 1997, 438).

The California gold rush of 1849 brought the first immigrants from Asia, Chinese men who worked in the mines, on railroads, and on farms, and who planned to return to their families and homeland. Early Chinese immigrants encountered widespread discrimination in their new country, with anti-Chinese riots occurring in San Francisco, Los Angeles, and Denver between 1869 and 1880. In 1882, Congress passed the Immigration Act, which ended Chinese immigration until 1902. The Chinese were oriented toward maintaining traditional language and religion and established tight-knit urban communities, or "Chinatowns." Recently, many upwardly mobile, professional Chinese Americans have been assimilated into suburban communities, while newly arrived, working-class immigrants from China and Hong Kong are settling in redeveloped Chinatowns.

Japanese immigrants began to arrive in Hawaii and the U.S. mainland in the late 1800s; most worked in agriculture, fisheries, the railroads, or industry and assimilated rapidly despite racial discrimination. The San Francisco Board of Education, for example, began to segregate all Japanese students in 1906, and the Immigration Act of 1924 ended Japanese immigration until 1952. During World War II, the United States was at war with Japan. In response to war hysteria over the "yellow peril," the United States government interned 110,000 Japanese-Americans, most of them American-born, in ten detention camps from 1942 to 1946. Since World War II, Japan has developed into one of the world's leading economic and technological powers—an accomplishment that has contributed, no doubt, to a recent decline in Japanese immigration to the United States.

Filipinos began to immigrate to Hawaii and the mainland as field laborers during the 1920s. They, too, encountered American racism; in 1934 Congress passed the Tydings-McDuffie Act, which limited Filipino immigration to the United States to 50 persons annually. The following year, President Roosevelt signed the Repatriation Act, which provided free transportation to Filipinos willing to return to the Philippines. While most early Filipino immigrants had little education and low income, recent immigrants have tended to be professional, technical workers who hope to obtain employment in the U.S. more suitable for their education and training than they could in the Philippines (Banks 1997).

In what ways are Asian Americans among the most diverse groups in the U.S.? How can stereotypes of Asian Americans interfere with students' success in school?

TEACHER'S CONCERNS ABOUT ASIAN-AMERICAN STUDENTS Asian Americans are frequently stereotyped as hard-working, conscientious, and respectful of authority, what Sue and Sue (1990) term a "model minority." The unreliability of such stereotypes notwithstanding, Asian-American parents do tend to require their children to respect authority and value education. In fact, one-third of the Asian-American adults immigrating to this country have a college degree (Hodgkinson 1986). Families often pressure children to be successful academically through sacrifice and hard work. At the same time, there has been an increase in the number of Asian-American youth who are in conflict with their parents' way of life. Leaders in Asian-American communities have expressed concern about increases in dropout rates, school violence, and declining achievement. Teachers need to be sensitive to cultural conflicts that may contribute to problems in school adjustment and achievement. Some Indochinese Americans, for example, face deep cultural conflict in our schools. Values and practices that are accepted in American culture, such as dating and glorification of the individual, are sources of conflict between many Indochinese students and their parents.

An authority on the education of Asian Americans, B. H. Suzuki, suggests that the tendency of Asian-American students to try to conform to the expectations of schools and teachers may result in their failure to grow in other ways:

> [Many] teachers stereotype Asian and Pacific American students as quiet, hard-working, and docile, which tends to reinforce conformity and stifle creativity. Asian and Pacific American students, therefore, frequently do not develop the ability to assert and express themselves verbally and are channeled in disproportionate numbers into the technical/scientific fields. As a consequence, many Asian and Pacific American students undergo traumatic family/school discontinuities, suffer from low self-esteem, are overly conforming, and have their academic and social development narrowly circumscribed (Suzuki 1983, 9).

To help Asian-American students adjust to the U.S. culture, Qiu Liang offers teachers the following advice based on his school experiences as a Chinese immigrant:

> They [teachers] should be more patient [with an immigrant child] because it is very difficult for a person to be in a new country and learn a new language. Have patience.

> If the teacher feels there is no hope in an immigrant child, then the child will think, "Well, if the teacher who's helping me thinks that I can't go anywhere, then I might as well give up myself" (Igoa 1995, 99–100).

Similarly, Dung Yoong offers these recommendations based on her educational experiences as a Vietnamese immigrant:

> Try to get them to talk to you. Not just everyday conversation, but what they feel inside. Try to get them to get that out, because it's hard for kids. They don't trust—I had a hard time trusting and I was really insecure because of that.

> [P]utting an immigrant child who doesn't speak English into a classroom, a regular classroom with American students, is not very good. It scares [them] because it is so different. [Teachers] should start [them] slowly and have special classes where the child could adapt and learn a little bit about American society and customs (Igoa 1995, 103).

EDUCATION AND AMERICAN INDIANS AND ALASKAN NATIVES

American Indians and Alaskan Natives peopled the Western hemisphere more than 12,000 years ago. Today, they represent less than 1 percent of the total U.S. population, or about 2 million people (U.S. Bureau of the Census 1993a). This group consists of 517 federally recognized and 365 state-recognized tribes, each with its own language, religious beliefs, and way of life. The four largest groups are the Cherokee Nation of Oklahoma, over 308,000 members; the Navajo Nation, 219,000; the Chippewa Nation, 104,000; and the Sioux Nation of the Dakotas, 103,000 (U.S. Bureau of the Census 1993b). Approximately 760,000 American Indians live on 275 reservations located primarily in the West. More than half of the American Indian and Alaskan Native population lives in six states: Alaska, Arizona, California, New Mexico, Oklahoma, and Washington (Manning and Baruth 1996). Though most Indians live in cities, many are establishing connections with reservation Indians as a means of strengthening their cultural identities.

American Indians are an example of the increasing ambiguity of racial and ethnic identities in the United States. For example, controversy exists over who is an American Indian. "Some full-blooded native people do not regard a person with one-quarter native heritage to qualify, while others accept 1/128" (Bennett 1995, 128). While most American Indians consider a person with one-quarter or more tribal heritage to be a member, the U.S. Census Bureau considers anyone who claims native identity to be a member. An expert on American Indians and Alaskan Natives, Arlene Hirschfelder, points out that fifty-two legal definitions of Native Americans have been identified (Hirschfelder 1986). American Indians were declared U.S. citizens in 1924, and native nations have been recognized as independent, self-governing territories since the 1930s (Bennett 1995).

HISTORICAL, CULTURAL, AND SOCIOECONOMIC FACTORS   Perhaps more than any other minority group, Native Americans have endured systematic long-term attempts to eradicate their languages and cultures. Disease, genocide, confinement on reservations, and decades of forced assimilation have devastated Native-American cultures. Today, the rates of unemployment, poverty, and lack of educational attainment among Native Americans are among the nation's highest. Since the 1970s, however, there has been a resurgence of interest in preserving or restoring traditional languages, skills, and land claims.

There are hundreds of Indian languages, which anthropologists have attempted to categorize into six major language families (Banks 1994). Older tribal members fluent in the original tribal language and younger members often speak a form of so-called "reservation English." The challenge of educating Native Americans from diverse language backgrounds is further complicated by the difference in size of various Native American populations. These range from the more than 300,000 Cherokee to the 200 or so Supai of Arizona. As a result of the extreme diversity among Native Americans, it has even been suggested that "There is no such thing as an 'Indian' heritage, culture, or value system. [N]avajo, Cherokee, Sioux, and Aleut children are as different from each other in geographic and cultural backgrounds as they are from children growing up in New York City or Los Angeles" (Gipp 1979, 19).

Education for Native-American children living on reservations is currently administered by the federal government's Bureau of Indian Affairs (BIA). The **Indian Education Act of 1972** and its **1974 amendments** supplement the BIA's educational programs and provide direct educational assistance to tribes. The act seeks to improve Native-American education by providing funds to school districts to meet the special needs of Native-American youth, to Indian tribes and state and local education agencies to improve education for youth and adults, to colleges and universities for the purpose of training teachers for Indian schools, and to Native-American students to attend college.

RESEARCH ON NATIVE-AMERICAN WAYS OF KNOWING   Considerable debate has occurred over the best approaches for educating Native Americans. For example, Banks points out that "since the 1920s, educational policy for Native Americans has vacillated between strong assimilationism to self-determination and cultural pluralism" (Banks 1994, 22). In any case, the culture-based learning styles of many American Indians and Alaskan Natives differ from that of other students. The traditional upbringing of Native-American children generally encourages them to develop a view of the world that is holistic, intimate, and shared. "They approach tasks visually, seem to prefer to learn by careful observation which precedes performance, and seem to learn in their natural settings experientially" (Deyhle and Deyhle 1987, 350). Bennett suggests the following guideline to ensure that the school experiences of Native-American students are in harmony with their cultural backgrounds: "An effective learning environment for Native Americans is one that does not single out

What factors contribute to below-average achievement levels of Native-American children? How do forces toward assimilation and cultural preservation coexist in the Native-American experience?

the individual but provides frequent opportunities for the teacher to interact privately with individual children and with small groups, as well as opportunities for quiet, persistent exploration" (Bennett 1995, 189).

Increasingly, Native Americans are designing multicultural programs to preserve their traditional cultures and ways of knowing. While these programs are sometimes characterized as emphasizing separatism over assimilation, for many Native Americans they are a matter of survival. The Heart of the Earth Survival School in Minneapolis, for example, was created to preserve the languages and cultures of the northern Plains Indians. Native-American teachers at the school provide bilingual instruction in Ojibwe and Dakota. Students are encouraged to wear traditional dress and practice traditional arts, such as drumming and dancing.

Cultural preservation is also the primary concern at Eskimo schools in remote parts of western Alaska and schools in the Marietta Independent School District of Stillwell, Oklahoma. In Alaska, elders come into the classroom to teach children how to skin a seal, an education that few Eskimo children receive today at home. In Oklahoma, schools try to keep alive the diverse languages of peoples forced to relocate to reservations there from the Southwestern United States in the last century. Students of mixed Cherokee, Creek, and Seminole descent become fluent and literate in the Cherokee language.

WHAT IS MEANT BY BILINGUAL EDUCATION ⁇

Bilingual education programs are designed to meet the learning needs of students whose first language is not English by providing instruction in two languages. Regardless of the instructional approach used, one outcome for all bilingual programs is for students to become proficient in English. Additionally, students are encouraged to become **bicultural,** that is, able to function effectively in two or more linguistic and cultural groups.

In 1968, Congress passed the Bilingual Education Act, which required that language-minority students be taught in both their native language and English. In response to the Act, school districts implemented an array of bilingual programs that varied greatly in quality and effectiveness. As a result, many parents filed law suits, claiming that bilingual programs were not meeting their children's needs. In 1974, the Supreme Court heard a class action suit (*Lau v. Nichols*) filed by 1,800 Chinese students in San Francisco who charged that they were failing to learn because they could

Immersion programs: **Students learn English and other subjects in classrooms where only Eng is spoken. Aides who speak the first language of students are sometimes available, or students may also listen to equivalent audiotaped lessons in their first language.**

Transition programs: **Students receive reading lessons in their first language and lessons in English as a Second Language (ESL). Once they sufficiently master English, students are placed in classrooms where English is spoken and their first language is discontinued.**

Pull-out programs: **On a regular basis, students are separated from English-speaking students that they may receive lessons in English or reading lessons in their first language. These are sometimes called sheltered English programs.**

Maintenance programs: **To maintain the student's native language and culture, instruction in English and instruction in the native language are provided from kindergarten through twelfth grade. Students become literate.**

FIGURE 8.3 Four types of bilingual education programs

not understand English. The students were enrolled in all-English classes and received no special assistance in learning English. In a unanimous ruling, the Court asserted that federally funded schools must "rectify the language deficiency" of students who "are certain to find their classroom experiences wholly incomprehensible." That same year, Congress adopted the Equal Educational Opportunity Act (EEOA), which stated in part that a school district must "take appropriate action to overcome language barriers that impede equal participation by its students in its instructional programs."

Bilingual programs, most of which serve Latino and Hispanic-American students, are tremendously varied and reflect "extreme differences in student composition, program organization, teaching methodologies and approaches, and teacher backgrounds and skills" (Griego-Jones 1996, 115). Generally, however, four types of bilingual education programs are currently available to provide special assistance to the 3.6 million language-minority students in the United States (see Figure 8.3). Only about 315,000 students actually participate in some kind of bilingual program.

RESEARCH AND DEBATE ON BILINGUAL PROGRAMS

Research on the effectiveness of bilingual programs is mixed. Some who have examined the research conclude that bilingual programs have little effect on achievement (Rossell 1990; Baker 1991). Others have found that well-designed bilingual programs do increase students' achievement and are superior to monolingual programs (Willig 1987; Schmidt 1991; Cziko 1992; Nieto 1992; Trueba, Cheng, and Kenji 1993).

Considerable debate surrounds bilingual programs in the United States. Those in favor of bilingual education make the following points:

- Students are better able to learn English if they are taught to read and write in their native language.
- Bilingual programs allow students to learn content in their native language rather than delaying that learning until they master English.

- Further developing competencies in students' native languages provides important cognitive foundations for learning English and academic content.
- Second-language learning is a positive value and should be as valid for a Spanish-speaker learning English as for an English-speaker learning Spanish.
- Bilingual programs support students' cultural identity, social context, and self-esteem.

On the other hand, those opposed to bilingual programs make the following points:

- Public schools should not be expected to provide instruction in all the first languages spoken by their students, nor can schools afford to pay a teacher who might teach only a few students.
- The cost of bilingual education is high. Bilingual programs divert staff and resources away from English-speaking students.
- If students spend more time exposed to English, they will learn English more quickly.
- Bilingual programs emphasize differences among and barriers between groups; they encourage separateness rather than assimilation and unity.
- Bilingual education is a threat to English as the nation's first language.

ADVICE FOR MONOLINGUAL TEACHERS

While the future of bilingual education in the United States is uncertain, teachers must continue to meet the needs of language-minority students. These needs are best met by teachers who speak their native language as well as English. However, this is often not possible, and monolingual teachers will find increasing numbers of LEP students in their classrooms. Table 8.3 presents several general strategies teachers can follow to create classroom environments that facilitate the learning of LEP students, and Table 8.4 on page 260 presents instructional strategies for improving their literacy skills. Developed by bilingual/ESL education expert Gisela Ernst and her colleagues, these strategies can be used whether or not a teacher is bilingual.

WHAT IS MULTICULTURAL EDUCATION?

Multicultural education is committed to the goal of providing all students—regardless of socioeconomic status, gender, sexual orientation or ethnic, racial, or cultural backgrounds—with equal opportunities to learn in school. Multicultural education is also based on the fact that students do not learn in a vacuum—their culture predisposes them to learn in certain ways. And finally, multicultural education recognizes that current school practices have provided, and continue to provide, some students with greater opportunities for learning than students who belong to other groups. The suggestions in Tables 8.3 and 8.4 are examples of multicultural education in practice.

As multiculturalism has become more pervasive in America's schools, controversy over the need for multicultural education and its purposes has emerged. Carl Grant has identified as "myths" the following six arguments against multicultural education: "(1) It is both divisive and so conceptually weak that it does little to eliminate structural inequalities; (2) it is unnecessary because the United States is a melting pot; (3) multiculturalism—and by extension multicultural education—and political correctness are the same thing; (4) multicultural education rejects the notion of a common culture; (5) multicultural education is a 'minority thing'; and (6) multicultural

TABLE 8.3

Teaching in multilingual/multicultural settings: Creating classroom environments that support second-language learners

Classroom Environment and Attitude	Cross-cultural Communication and Understanding
1. Relax and enjoy. Language is more caught than taught. Your relaxed, receptive, interested concern will be the magical ingredient for enhancing the teaching and learning process.	1. Become informed about the different cultures and languages represented in your classroom. This can be done by designing activities wherein your students become the "experts" by sharing part of their culture with the class.
2. Provide a warm, encouraging environment in which help is readily available to LEP students.	2. If you find a student's behavior to be unusual or disconcerting, you might ask students or parents to clarify its meaning (e.g., Native-American and Asian-American students avoid eye contact with authority figures out of respect). This could prevent misunderstandings further down the road.
3. Books that are sensitive to the adjustments of the new student can be shared with the class (e.g., *Crow Boy* by Yashima; *I Hate English* by Levine; *What Does the Rooster Say, Yoshio?* by Battles).	3. Try to talk individually with your students as much as possible. This lets them know you are interested in them as individuals, not just as students.
4. Fill the room with meaningful, relevant print. These are springboards for discussion and rudiments of second-language literacy.	4. Avoid forcing students to speak and allow a wait time for students to answer.
5. Label as many objects in the classroom as possible and invite your students to provide labels in their own language.	5. LEP students need instruction to be clear and interesting. By using exaggerated facial expressions, a slower speech rate, abundance of gestures, and enunciating clearly you can reach more students. Many times our expressions and gestures can help students understand what we are saying when our words do not.
6. Increase possibilities for success by using a satisfactory/unsatisfactory option for grading until students are able to successfully complete classroom assignments.	6. Try to incorporate tutors who speak students' native languages.
7. Try to avoid anglicizing your students' names. Sometimes their names are the only connection they have with their native language, culture, and country.	7. Start by asking questions (backed by visual aids) that can be answered with yes or no. Then move, little by little, to questions requiring slightly longer answers.

(Source: Gisela Ernst, Margaret Castle, and Lauren C. Frostad, "Teaching in Multilingual/Multicultural Settings: Strategies for Supporting Second-Language Learners," *Curriculum in Context* [Fall/Winter 1992]: 14–15. Used by permission of the authors and the publisher.)

TABLE 8.4

Teaching in multilingual/multicultural settings: Strategies for enhancing the learning and literacy of second-language learners

Instructional Techniques and Strategies	Literacy and Oral Language Development
1. Whenever possible, try to use a variety of formats that go beyond the traditional lecture format. This will enable you to target different learning styles in your classroom.	1. Keep in mind specialized vocabulary that is content specific. Each content area has specific terminology that can confuse most second-language learners. Math, for example, has several terms for the function of addition (e.g., add, plus, combine, sum, increased by).
2. Organize, when possible, cooperative-learning activities. Small groups give second-language learners a chance to use their second-language skills in a non-threatening environment.	2. Whenever possible define key terms in several ways.
3. The use of videos, films, drama/role plays, manipulatives (great for math), pictures, artifacts, posters, music, nursery rhymes, games, filmstrips, maps, charts, and fieldtrips can enhance teaching and learning.	3. Make use of pictionaries.
4. Your school ESL specialist is a wonderful source of knowledge and information about what to do and what materials to use with your LEP students.	4. Encourage the use of bilingual dictionaries, materials, and content-area books in students' first language. They can help students understand new concepts both in their native language and in English.
Encourage students to indicate when they are confused or do not understand. Students may feel more comfortable indicating understanding rather than acknowledging confusion.	5. Consult your media specialist for books appropriate for students' reading/comprehension level.
When testing we need to be sensitive to students' cultural background. Culturally biased tests are a major hurdle for second-language learners. Standardized tests can be a common culprit. Misinterpreting terms, directions, or situational cues can cause your students' test performance to drop drastically.	
When planning lessons or assignments, think about the following questions: What background knowledge do students have? Will the assignment use academic language or critical thinking skills unfamiliar to your students?	
Restate, rephrase, summarize, and review frequently.	

(Source: Gisela Ernst, Margaret Castle, and Lauren C. Frostad, "Teaching in Multilingual/Multicultural Settings: Strategies for Supporting Second-Language Learners," *Curriculum in Context* [Fall/Winter 1992]: 14–15. Used by permission of the authors and the publisher.)

education will impede learning the basic skills" (Grant 1994, 5). Though multicultural education is being challenged by those who promote these beliefs, we believe that public dialogue and debate about how schools can more effectively address diversity is healthy—an indicator that our society is making real progress toward creating "a mosaic culture incorporating the values of the diverse groups that make up America's population" (Robeson 1993, 1).

DIMENSIONS OF MULTICULTURAL EDUCATION

According to James A. Banks, "Multicultural education is at least three things: an idea or concept, an educational reform movement, and a process" (Banks 1993, 3). More specifically, Banks suggests that multicultural education may be conceptualized as consisting of five dimensions: (1) content integration, (2) knowledge construction, (3) prejudice reduction, (4) an equity pedagogy, and (5) an empowering school culture (see Figure 8.4 on page 262). As you progress through your teacher-education program and eventually begin to prepare curriculum materials and instructional strategies for your multicultural classroom, remember that integrating content from a variety of cultural groups is just one dimension of multicultural education. Multicultural education is not "something that is done at a certain time slot in the school day where children eat with chopsticks or listen to Peruvian music . . . [it is] something that is infused throughout the school culture and practiced daily" (Henry 1996, 108).

Multicultural education promotes students' positive self-identity and pride in their heritage, acceptance of people from diverse backgrounds, and critical self-assessment. In addition, multicultural education can prompt students, perhaps with guidance from their teachers, to take action against prejudice and discrimination within their school. Indeed, as Joel Spring says, "multicultural education should create a spirit of tolerance and activism in students. An understanding of other cultures and of differing cultural frames of reference will . . . spark students to actively work for social justice" (Spring 1996, 164). For example, students might reduce the marginalization of minority-group students in their school by inviting them to participate in extracurricular and after-school activities.

MULTICULTURAL CURRICULA

As a teacher you will teach students who historically have not received full educational opportunity—students from the many racial and ethnic minority groups in America, students from low-income families or communities, students with exceptional abilities or disabilities, students who are gay or lesbian, and students who are male or female. You will face the challenge of reaching out to all students and teaching them that they are persons of worth and can learn.

In your diverse classroom your aim is not to develop a different curriculum for each group of students—that would be impossible and would place undue emphasis on differences among students. Rather, your curriculum should help increase students' awareness and appreciation of the rich diversity in American culture. A **multicultural curriculum** addresses the needs and backgrounds of all students regardless of their cultural identity. As Banks suggests, the multicultural curriculum "enable[s] students to derive valid generalizations and theories about the characteristics of ethnic groups and to learn how they are alike and different, in both their past and present experiences. . . . [It] focus[es] on a range of groups that *differ* in their racial characteristics, cultural experiences, languages, histories, values, and current problems" (Banks 1997, 15). Teachers who provide multicultural education recognize the

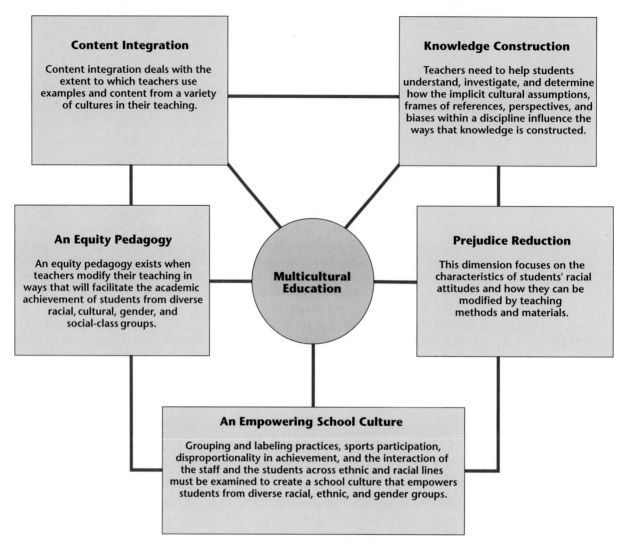

FIGURE 8.4 Banks' dimensions of multicultural education (Source: From Banks, James A. and Cherry A. McGee Banks. *Multicultural Education: Issues and Perspectives,* 3d ed., Copyright © 1997 by Allyn and Bacon. Reprinted by permission, p. 24.)

importance of asking questions such as those posed by Valerie Ooka Pang: "Why is a child's home language important to keep? What strengths does culture give children? What impact does culture have on learning? What does racism, sexism, or classism look like in schools?" (Pang 1994, 292).

In developing a multicultural curriculum, you should be sensitive to how your instructional materials and strategies can be made more inclusive so that they reflect cultural perspectives, or "voices," that previously have been silent or marginalized in discussions about what should be taught in schools and how it should be taught. "Non-dominant groups representing diversity in the school whose voices traditionally have not been heard include those defined by race, language, gender, sexual orientation, alternative family structures, social class, disability, bilingualism, and those with alien or refugee status" (Henry 1996, 108). Effective teachers attend to these previously unheard voices not as an act of tokenism but with a genuine desire to make the curriculum more inclusive and to "create space for alternative voices, not just on the periphery but in the center" (Singer 1994, 286).

MULTICULTURAL INSTRUCTIONAL MATERIALS AND STRATEGIES

To create classrooms that are truly multicultural, teachers must select instructional materials that are sensitive, accurately portray the contributions of ethnic groups, and reflect diverse points of view. Teachers must also recognize that "[s]ome of the books and other materials on ethnic groups published each year are insensitive, inaccurate, and written from mainstream and insensitive perspectives and points of view" (Banks 1997, 124). (See the Teacher's Resource Guide, "Selected Resources for Multicultural Education.") Some guidelines for selecting multicultural instructional materials follow:

- Books and other materials should accurately portray the perspectives, attitudes, and feelings of ethnic groups.
- Fictional works should have strong ethnic characters.
- Books should describe settings and experiences with which all students can identify and yet should accurately reflect ethnic cultures and life-styles.
- The protagonists in books with ethnic themes should have ethnic characteristics but should face conflicts and problems universal to all cultures and groups.
- The illustrations in books should be accurate, ethnically sensitive, and technically well done.
- Ethnic materials should not contain racist concepts, clichés, phrases, or words.
- Factual materials should be historically accurate.
- Multiethnic resources and basal textbooks should discuss major events and documents related to ethnic history (Banks 1997, 125–126).

Yvonne Wilson, a first-grade teacher in Talmoon, Minnesota, and an Ojibwe Indian, points out that a teacher's willingness to learn about other cultures is very important to students and their parents:

> People in the community know if you are trying to understand their culture. Students also see it. Becoming involved—going to a pow-wow or participating in other cultural events—shows people that here is a teacher who is trying to learn about our culture.

Participating wholeheartedly in cross-cultural experiences will help you to grow in the eight areas outlined in Figure 8.5 as essential for successful teaching in a diverse society.

FIGURE 8.5 Eight essentials for successful teaching in a diverse society (Source: From Banks, James A. and Banks, Cherry M. McGee. *Multicultural Education: A Cultural Perspective*, 3d ed. Copyright © 1997 by Allyn and Bacon: Reprinted by permission.)

Eight Essentials for Successful Teaching in a Diverse Society

1. The ability to communicate with students who are different from you

2. Skills in diagnosing the knowledge and abilities of culturally diverse students

3. Knowledge about the psychology, dynamics, and impact of prejudice

4. The ability to discover differences among value systems relating to cultural and class differences

5. Knowledge of one's own and other cultures leading to the realization that people are more alike than they are different

6. An increased capacity for humane, sensitive, and critical inquiry into multicultural issues as they relate to curriculum and instruction

7. An increased willingness and openness to examine and to reassess one's own cultural attitudes, beliefs, and values

8. An increased ability to respond positively and sensitively to the diversity of behavior present in multicultural settings

Keepers of the Dream

James A. Banks

Distinguished Scholar/Researcher on Minority Education

"You must first transform yourself."

James A. Banks is a widely recognized authority in the fields of social studies and multicultural education and the author of eighteen books on those subjects. He was named "Distinguished Scholar/Researcher on Minority Education" by the American Educational Research Association and is a Professor of Education and Director of the Center for Multicultural Education at the University of Washington.

Born in Arkansas and educated in segregated communities in the South in the 1950s and 60s, Banks developed an early interest in becoming a teacher. His grandmother, a country school teacher, influenced him, but he also deeply admired his own teachers in the schools he attended. "My teachers were part of my community," he says, "and the respect we had for teachers was great." Banks also had a desire to serve others: "We have a tradition of helping in the African-American community." He made firm his decision to become a teacher when he attended a desegregated college in Chicago. "As a child of the Civil Rights Movement," Banks explains, "it was natural to move from civil rights to teaching." He graduated first in his class and launched his teaching career in a third- and fourth-grade combination class in nearby Joliet, Illinois, and later returned to Chicago to teach fifth grade.

Banks' decision to leave elementary school teaching to pursue graduate study was a difficult one: "One of the saddest days in my life—there were tears in my eyes and tears in students' eyes." But his larger goal was to create equal educational opportunities for all students in a wider arena. During his career as an educator, Banks' audiences have grown from the children in his first Illinois classroom to the students in his university classes, from students nationwide who read his textbooks to teachers and scholars in international academic communities. He is regarded as one of the founders of the field of multicultural education.

Banks emphasizes that "multicultural education is primarily a way of thinking, . . . a way of asking questions, a way of conceptualizing," (1994, 88). For example:

> When we speak about the Westward Movement, we should ask, "Westward to whom?" To the Native American tribes, the Westward Movement was the Invasion from the East. . . . Teachers should help students become participants in constructing knowledge, not just consumers of knowledge.

Students need to learn to ask questions like "Westward to whom?" and to deconstruct concepts like "pioneers" and "settlers."

They should be given opportunities to investigate and determine how cultural assumptions, frames of references, perspectives, and the biases within a discipline influence the ways that knowledge is constructed. Students should also be given opportunities to create knowledge themselves and identify ways in which the knowledge they construct is influenced and limited by their personal assumptions, positions, and experiences (1996, 21).

Banks advises teachers who wish to teach more multiculturally to begin by examining their own beliefs: "Before you transform the world you must first transform yourself. Start with yourself, your own attitudes, and ask yourself, 'What is my attitude toward differences?' " Banks proposes that teachers help students understand five distinct but interacting types of knowledge: "personal/cultural knowledge, popular knowledge, mainstream academic knowledge, transformative academic knowledge, and school knowledge" (1996, 5). School knowledge tends to reflect and emphasize popular knowledge and mainstream academic knowledge but may conflict with the personal/cultural knowledge that students bring with them from their ethnic backgrounds. According to Banks, "Although the school should recognize, validate, and make effective instructional use of the personal and cultural knowledge in instruction, an important goal of education is to free students from their cultural and ethnic boundaries and enable them to cross cultural borders freely" (Banks 1996, 12).

Banks' dream for teachers is "that they be given the respect and regard in the nation that they deeply deserve." His dream for children is "to help create a world where we can all get along. Our work is incomplete as we pass the torch to the younger generation. They will need to help create that world."

HOW IS GENDER A DIMENSION OF MULTICULTURAL EDUCATION ?

Though it may be evident that gender affects students' learning in many ways, it may not be evident that gender is an important dimension of multicultural education. However, as Tozer, Violas, and Senese point out:

> Traditional definitions of culture have centered around the formal expression of a people's common existence—language, art, music, and so forth. If culture is more broadly defined to include such things as ways of knowing, ways of relating to others, ways of negotiating rights and privileges, and modes of conduct, thought, and expression, then the term "culture" applies not only to ethnic groups but to people grouped on the basis of gender. [G]ender entails cultural as well as physiological dimensions (Tozer, Violas, and Senese 1993, 310).

GENDER DIFFERENCES

Evidence abounds that schools have made significant contributions to the divisions between the sexes. From kindergarten on, girls traditionally have been and may still be reinforced for certain behaviors, boys for others. Girls were supposed to play with dolls, boys with trucks. Girls were supposed to be passive, boys active. On the one hand, part of the hidden curriculum girls encountered at school might make them feel that they should prepare to become homemakers by learning about home economics and family living, or secretaries by taking typing, shorthand, and bookkeeping. Boys, on the other hand, came to believe that girls might become nurses, while boys might become doctors. Girls might become teachers, but boys might become superintendents. Girls might become legal secretaries, but boys might become lawyers. Girls might become executive secretaries, but boys might become executives.

It is a well-established fact that women in our society are employed at lower levels than men, and, when they are employed at the same level, they earn less. Some commentators have suggested that there is a "glass ceiling" in the workplace that prevents women from achieving their full potential. For example, although most public elementary and high school teachers are women, 95 percent of superintendents and 72 percent of principals are men. Since the 1960s, women's groups such as the National Organization for Women (NOW) and an array of feminist publications have alerted all of us to the dynamics of **sexism**—discrimination that is based on the belief that one's sex is superior to the other. Most recently, the National Organization for Men (NOM) has similarly increased our awareness of the forms of sexism that men encounter in American society.

The cultural differences between males and females are shaped by society's traditional expectations of them. Families, the media, the schools, and other powerful social forces condition boys and girls to act differently. As we mentioned in Chapter 4, one of the aims of schools is to socialize students to participate in our society. One dimension of the **sex role socialization** process conveys to students certain expectations about the way boys and girls are "supposed" to act. Evidence suggests that "the school environment, confounded by society's sex-role socialization of children, stretches and stresses boys while it encourages girls to let their abilities atrophy" (Stanford 1992, 87). How have you been influenced by sex-role socialization during your school experiences?

Reflecting on Your School Experiences in Relation to Gender

Reflect on your K–12 school experiences with the following questions in mind.

- Were you encouraged by your teachers to behave in certain ways because of your gender? How did those behaviors influence your self-perceptions? What were the teachers' implicit messages about how boys and girls "should" behave?
- Do you recall instances when teachers encouraged other students to behave in certain ways because of their gender? For example, were girls complimented on their neatness, pretty handwriting, grooming and clothing, and boys on their competitiveness, accomplishments, and athletic prowess?
- Do you think that your treatment in school as a male or female influenced your achievement or your educational choices? In what ways?
- In what ways did the curriculum and instructional materials to which you were exposed portray your own and the opposite sex?

Students may be socialized into particular gender-specific roles as a result of the curriculum materials they use at school. By portraying males in more dominant, assertive ways and portraying females in ways that suggest that they are passive and helpless, textbooks can subtly reinforce expectations about the way girls and boys "should" behave. Within the last few decades, though, publishers of curriculum materials have become more vigilant about avoiding these stereotypes.

The feminist movement and sociological research of the past few decades have drawn attention to the problem of **sex role stereotyping** and sex discrimination in our society. Evidence abounds that schools significantly contributed to these problems.

Teachers may not be aware of how their behavior and attitudes promote sex-role stereotyping. For example, "teachers [may] say nice things about boys concerning their academic work and bad things about their behavior—throwing chalk and making noise. Girls tend to have more compliments given them about their nonacademic work—how neat and clean they are, how pretty they look" (Jacklyn 1981, 114–115). Research has confirmed that teachers tend to have lowered expectations for girls.

GENDER AND ACHIEVEMENT

As noted in chapter 3, it was not until Title IX of the Education Amendments Act was passed in 1972 that women were guaranteed (on paper, at least) equality of educational opportunity in educational programs receiving federal assistance. Title IX has had the greatest impact on athletic programs in schools; in fact, the strong showing of women athletes at the 1996 Summer Olympics was attributed in part to Title IX. The law requires that both sexes have equal opportunities to participate in and benefit from the availability of coaches, sports equipment, resources, and facilities. For contact sports such as football, wrestling, and boxing, sports that were not open to women, separate teams are allowed.

The right of females to equal educational opportunity was further enhanced with the passage of the **Women's Educational Equity Act (WEEA)** of 1974. This act provides the following opportunities:

What impact has civil rights legislation had on the education of females? Why and in what ways does gender bias persist in many American classrooms and schools?

- Expanded math, science, and technology programs for females
- Programs to reduce sex-role stereotyping in curriculum materials
- Programs to increase the number of female educational administrators
- Special programs to extend educational and career opportunities to minority, disabled, and rural women
- Programs to help school personnel increase the educational opportunities and career aspirations for females
- Encouragement for more females to participate in athletics

Despite reforms stemming from WEEA, several reports in the early 1990s criticized schools for subtly discriminating against girls in tests, textbooks, and teaching methods. Research on teacher interactions in the classroom pointed to widespread unintentional gender bias against girls. Two of these studies, *Shortchanging Girls, Shortchanging America* (1991) and *How Schools Shortchange Girls* (1992), both commissioned by the American Association of University Women (AAUW), found that textbooks contained few female role models, that girls were not encouraged in math and science, that teachers favored boys' intellectual growth over that of girls, and that girls received lower SAT scores despite earning higher grades than boys.

Myra Sadker, David Sadker, and Susan Klein, pioneers in research on gender equity, analyzed over 400 studies and concluded that at all educational levels "males are both given, and through their behaviors attract, a higher number of teacher interactions" (Sadker, Sadker, and Klein 1991, 298). In their earlier study of 100 fourth-, sixth-, and eighth-grade classrooms in four states and the District of Columbia, the Sadkers also observed that the quality as well as the frequency of teacher attention given to boys was greater. Teachers provided boys with more specific and instructive feedback (Sadker and Sadker 1984).

In *How Schools Shortchange Girls,* the AAUW commissioned the Wellesley College Center for Research on Women to "gain a comprehensive understanding of the educational experiences of America's girls and boys" (AAUW 1992, ix). Reviewing over 1,300 articles and research studies, the team concluded that "girls do not receive equitable amounts of teacher attention, that they are less apt than boys to see themselves reflected in the materials they study, and that they often are not expected or encouraged to pursue higher-level mathematics and science courses" (AAUW 1992, 147). The report was regarded as "one impetus for the inclusion of a package of gender equity provisions in the 1994 Elementary and Secondary Education Act" (Tovey 1995, 4), which included the following provisions:

- teacher training to eliminate inequitable practices
- developing programs to increase girls' participation in math and science
- training to combat sexual harassment
- assisting pregnant teens and teenage parents to prevent dropping out
- promoting research and dissemination of models of gender equity programs

The Sadkers and AAUW's effectiveness in communicating the findings of two decades of research on gender equity have contributed to the reduction of sexism in schools. Lessons widely shared are that gender inequalities are costly for both genders. In *Failing at Fairness: How Our Schools Cheat Girls* (1994), for example, David and Myra Sadker address the costs of bias against boys in a chapter entitled "The Miseducation of Boys":

> While boys rise to the top of the class, they also land at the bottom. Labeled as problems in need of special control or assistance, boys are more likely to fail a course, miss promotion, or drop out of school. Prone to take risks, they jeopardize not only their academic future but their lives as they dominate accident, suicide, and homicide statistics (1994, 197).

Boys also tend to be stressed by the school environment, especially in elementary classrooms where their learning and activity styles could be at odds with those of their female teachers. Boys may be placed at risk for inaccurate diagnosis of learning problems, academic failure, and dropping out. Girls, in contrast, could be underchallenged and placed at risk for declines in skill level and self-confidence.

In the mid-1990s, some gender equity studies had more mixed findings. In their analysis of data on achievement and engagement of 9,000 eighth-grade boys and girls, University of Michigan researchers Valerie Lee, Xianglei Chen, and Becky A. Smerdon concluded that "the pattern of gender differences is inconsistent. In some cases, females are favored; in others males are favored" (Lee, Chen, and Smerdon 1996). Similarly, University of Chicago researchers Larry Hedges and Amy Nowell found in their study of 32 years of mental tests given to boys and girls that, while boys do better than girls in science and mathematics, they were "at a rather profound disadvantage" in writing and scored below girls in reading comprehension (Hedges 1996, 3). Other commentary discounts gender bias as a fabrication of radical feminism, a view put forth in the controversial book, *Who Stole Feminism? How Women Have Betrayed Women* (1994) by Clark University professor Christina Hoff Sommers. In the gender debate this author defends the view that boys more than girls are disadvantaged in the educational system (Sommers 1996).

In Scholastic Aptitude Tests (SAT) of 1996 college-bound seniors, boys surpassed girls by 35 points on the math section and by 4 points on the verbal section. In the 36-point scale of the American College Test (ACT) scores for the 1996 graduating class, boys outscored girls in science by 1.2 points and in math by 1.2 points and girls outscored boys in English and Reading by less than a point.

GENDER-FAIR CLASSROOMS AND CURRICULA

While research and debate about the bias boys and girls encounter in school will no doubt continue, it is clear that teachers must encourage girls and boys to develop to the full extent of their capabilities and provide them an education that is free from **gender bias**—subtle favoritism or discrimination on the basis of gender. Unfortunately, evidence such as that presented in Table 8.5 suggests that boys and girls continue to experience inequities in school.

Following is a list of basic guidelines for creating a **gender-fair classroom.** Adherence to these guidelines will help teachers "address the inequities institutional-

TABLE 8.5

Gender bias in the classroom

Girls

- In the early grades, girls score ahead of boys in verbal skills; their academic performance is equal to that of boys in math and almost equal to boys in science. However, as they progress through school, their achievement test scores show significant decline. The scores of boys, on the other hand, continue to rise and eventually reach and surpass those of their female counterparts, particularly in areas of math and science. Girls comprise the only group in our society that begins school ahead and ends up behind.

- In spite of performance decline on standardized achievement tests, girls frequently receive better grades in school. This may be one of the rewards they get for being more quiet and docile in the classroom. However, their silence may be at the cost of achievement, independence, and self-reliance.

- Girls are more likely to be invisible members of classrooms. They receive fewer academic contacts, less praise and constructive feedback, fewer complex and abstract questions, and less instruction on how to do things for themselves.

- Girls who are gifted, especially in math and science, are less likely to participate in special or accelerated programs to develop their talent. Girls who suffer from learning disabilities are also less likely to be identified or to participate in special-education programs than are learning-disabled boys.

Boys

- Boys are more likely to be scolded and reprimanded in classrooms. Also, boys are more likely to be referred to school authorities for disciplinary action than are girls.

- Boys are far more likely to be identified as exhibiting learning disabilities, reading problems, and mental retardation.

- Not only are boys more likely to be identified as having greater learning and reading disabilities, but they also receive lower grades, and are more likely to be grade repeaters.

- The National Assessment of Educational Progress indicates that males perform significantly below females in writing achievement.

(Source: Myra Sadker, David Sadker, and Lynette Long, "Gender and Educational Equity," in James A. Banks and Cherry A. McGee Banks (Eds.). *Multicultural Education: Issues and Perspectives,* 3rd ed. Boston: Allyn and Bacon, 1997, pp. 139–140.)

---

ized in the organizational structure of schools, the curriculum selected to be taught, the learning strategies employed, and their ongoing instructional and informal interactions with students" (Stanford 1992, 88).

- Become aware of differences in interactions with girls and boys.
- Promote boys' achievement in reading and writing and girls' achievement in mathematics and science.
- Reduce young children's self-imposed sexism.
- Teach about sexism and sex role stereotyping.
- Foster an atmosphere of collaboration between girls and boys.

In addition to gender bias, some students experience discrimination on the basis of their sexual orientation. To help all students realize their full potential, teachers should acknowledge the special needs of students who are or believe they are gay, lesbian, or bisexual, for "there is an invisible gay and lesbian minority in every school, and the needs of these students are often unknown and unmet" (Besner and Spungin 1995, xi). One study of 120 gay and lesbian students ages fourteen to twenty-one found that only one-fourth said they were able to discuss their sexual orientation with school counselors, and less than one in five said they could identify someone who had been supportive of them (Tellijohann and Price 1993). Moreover, a similar study of lesbian and gay youth reported that 80 percent of participants believed their teachers had negative attitudes about homosexuality (Sears 1991).

Based on estimates that the percentage of homosexuals in our society may be as high as 10 percent, a high school with an enrollment of 1,500 might have as many as 150 gay, lesbian, and bisexual students (Besner and Spungin 1995; Stover 1992). The National Education Association, the American Federation of Teachers, and several professional organizations have passed resolutions urging members and school districts to acknowledge the special needs of these students.

The nation's first dropout prevention program targeting gay, lesbian, and bisexual students was implemented in the Los Angeles school system. Known as Project 10, the program focuses on education, suicide prevention, dropout prevention, creating a safe environment for homosexual students, and HIV/AIDS education (Uribe and Harbeck 1991). In 1993, Massachusetts became the first state to adopt an educational policy prohibiting discrimination against gay and lesbian students and teachers.

Homosexual students can experience school-related problems and safety risks. Teachers and other school personnel can provide much-needed support. For example, a Milwaukee school commission found that "the hostility gay youths [can] encounter leaves them frightened and uncertain about their own worth. Their self-esteem plummets, and they quickly realize the necessity of hiding their sexual orientation. Terrified of being marked as 'different,' afraid they'll be rejected by friends and family, they grow up unable to reach out to others for help" (Stover 1992, 29).

Informed, sensitive, and caring teachers can play an important role in helping all students develop to their full potential. Such teachers realize the importance of recognizing diverse perspectives, and they create inclusive classroom environments that encourage students to respect differences among themselves and others and to see the contributions that persons from all groups have made to our society.

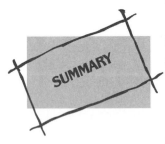

SUMMARY

How Is Diversity Embedded in the American Way of Life?

- The percentage of ethnic minorities in America has been growing steadily since World War II, and between 2030 and 2040 more than half of the school-age population will be students of color. Currently, the majority of students in several states and many urban districts are from groups traditionally thought of as minority.

- Culture is defined as the way of life common to a group of people, including beliefs, attitudes, habits, values, and practices.

- Dimensions of cultural identity include beliefs, attitudes, and values; racial identity; exceptionalities; language; gender; ethnicity; income level; and occupation.

- Ethnicity refers to a commonly shared racial or cultural identity and a set of beliefs, values, and attitudes. The concept of *race* is used to distinguish among people on the basis of biological traits and characteristics. A minority group is a group of people who share certain characteristics and are fewer in number than the majority of a population.

- The lower achievement levels of African-American, Latino and Hispanic-American, and American Indian students compared to that of their Anglo-European

American and Asian-American counterparts reflect the strong connection between socioeconomic status (SES) and achievement, since the incidence of poverty is highest among minority families.

■ Stereotyping is the process of attributing certain behavioral characteristics to all members of a group, often on the basis of limited experiences with and information about the group being stereotyped. Racism is the prejudicial belief that one's ethnic or racial group is superior to others.

What Does Equal Educational Opportunity Mean?

■ Equal educational opportunity means that teachers promote the full development of students without regard for race, ethnicity, gender, sexual orientation, socioeconomic status, abilities, or disabilities.

■ Past evidence indicates that four minority groups in America have been denied equality of educational opportunity through various forms of racism, discrimination, and neglect: African Americans, Latino and Hispanic Americans, Asian Americans and Pacific Islanders, and American Indians and Alaskan Natives. Teachers can meet the needs of students from these groups by becoming familiar with their cultural and linguistic backgrounds and learning styles.

What Is Meant by Bilingual Education?

■ Bilingual education programs provide instruction in a student's first language and English. The goal of bilingual programs is for students to learn English and become bicultural, able to function effectively in two or more linguistic/cultural groups. Four approaches to bilingual education are immersion, maintenance, pull-out, and transition programs.

■ Some research has found that bilingual programs have a positive effect on achievement, while others have found little effect. In light of inconclusive outcomes and mixed support, there has been a continuing debate over bilingual education in the United States.

What Is Multicultural Education?

■ Five dimensions of multicultural education have been suggested: content integration, knowledge construction, prejudice reduction, an equity pedagogy, and an empowering school culture.

■ A multicultural curriculum addresses the needs and backgrounds of all students—regardless of their cultural identity—and expands students' appreciation for diversity. Effective multicultural materials and instructional strategies include the contributions of ethnic groups and reflect diverse points of view or "voices" that previously may have been silenced or marginalized in our society.

How Is Gender a Dimension of Multicultural Education?

■ Gender includes ways of knowing and "modes of conduct, thought, and expression"; these are dimensions of culture.

■ The behavior of boys and girls in our society is influenced by *sexism, sex role socialization,* and *sex role stereotyping.*

- Both boys and girls experience inequities in the classroom; teachers, however, can provide both sexes with an education free of *gender bias* by creating gender-fair classrooms and curricula.
- Teachers should acknowledge the special needs of students who are gay, lesbian, or bisexual, and provide them with safe, supportive learning environments.

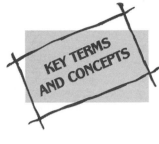

KEY TERMS AND CONCEPTS

Afrocentric schools, 250

bicultural, 256

bilingual education, 240

cultural identity, 239

cultural pluralism, 239

culture, 239

diversity, 238

ethnic group, 239

ethnicity, 242

gender bias, 268

gender-fair classroom, 268

Indian Education Act of 1972 and 1974 Amendments, 255

language-minority students, 246

limited English proficiency (LEP), 246

minorities, 242

multicultural curriculum, 261

multicultural education, 258

multiculturalism, 240

National Assessment of Educational Progress (NAEP), 245

race, 242

racism, 246

sexism, 265

sex role socialization, 265

sex role stereotyping, 266

stereotyping, 246

Women's Educational Equity Act (WEEA), 266

APPLICATIONS AND ACTIVITIES

Teacher's Journal

1. With which of the student groups discussed in this chapter do you feel most comfortable? Least comfortable? What reasons do you have for feeling as you do?

2. Reflecting on your experiences in schools and the five dimensions of multicultural education (see Figure 8.4 on page 264), describe the steps your teachers took to create an empowering school culture and social climate.

3. In your school years, did you ever experience discrimination as a member of a "different" group? Write about one outstanding incident that you feel affected your performance as a student.

4. As a teacher, what activities and materials might you use in a specific learning context to reduce the prejudices of students toward groups different from theirs?

5. Describe an example of sex-role stereotyping or gender bias that you experienced or observed in a school setting and how you felt about it.

Teacher's Database

1. Conduct an online keyword search for sources of information on one or more of the following diversity topics from Chapter 8. Share your findings with classmates before narrowing your search:

gender equity

cultural diversity

multicultural education

English as a Second Language (ESL)

bilingual education

English for Students of Other Languages (ESOL)

2. Experiment with using mailing lists by subscribing and unsubscribing to one of the following discussion mailing lists relating to diversity. Then conduct an online search for other mailing lists on diversity topics as a resource for beginning to teach.

MULTC-ED   Multicultural Education Discussion List
To subscribe: LISTSERV@umdd.umd.edu
      Type: SUBSCRIBE MULTC-ED your real name
To obtain a list of file archives: LISTSERV@umdd.umd.edu
      Type: INDEX MULTC-ED
To send articles: MULTC-ED@umdd.umd.edu

BILINGUE-L   Developmental Bilingual Elementary Education Discussion List
To subscribe: LISTSERV@reynolds.k12.or.us
      Type: SUBSCRIBE BILINGUE-L your real name
To participate: BILINGUE-L@reynolds.k12.or.us

Observations and Interviews

1. If possible visit a school that has an enrollment of students whose cultural or socioeconomic backgrounds differ from your own. What feelings and questions about these students emerge as a result of your observations? How might your feelings affect your teaching and teaching effectiveness? How might you go about finding answers to your questions?

2. Interview a teacher at the school identified in field assignment 1. What special satisfactions does he or she experience from teaching at the school? What significant problems relating to diversity does he or she encounter, and how are they dealt with?

Professional Portfolio

Prepare an annotated directory of local resources for teaching students about diversity, implementing multicultural curricula, and promoting harmony or equity among diverse groups. For each entry, include an annotation—that is, a brief description of the resource materials and their availability.

Resources for your personalized directory should be available through local sources such as your university library, public library, community agencies, and so on. Among the types of resources you might include are the following:

- Films, videos, audiocasettes, books, and journal articles
- Simulation games designed to improve participants' attitudes toward diversity
- Motivational guest speakers from the community
- Ethnic museums and cultural centers
- Community groups and agencies dedicated to promoting understanding among diverse groups
- Training and workshops in the area of diversity

Teaching, after all, is about knowing children well.

—Vito Perrone
A Letter to Teachers

Addressing Learners' Individual Needs

F O C U S
Q U E S T I O N S

1. How do students' needs change as they develop?

2. How do students vary in intelligence?

3. How do students vary in ability and disability?

4. What are special education, mainstreaming, and inclusion?

5. How can you teach all learners in your inclusive classroom?

It's late Friday afternoon, the end of the fourth week of school, and you've just finished arranging your classroom for the co-operative learning groups you're starting on Monday. Leaning back in the chair at your desk, you survey the room and imagine how things will go on Monday. Your mental image is positive, with one possible exception—11-year-old Rick. Since the first day of school, he's been very disruptive. His teacher last year described him as "loud, aggressive, and obnoxious."

Since school began, Rick has been belligerent and noncompliant. For the most part, he does what he wants, when he wants. As far as you know, he has no close friends; he teases the other kids constantly and occasionally gets into fights.

Rick's parents divorced when he was in the second grade. His father was given custody of Rick and his younger sister. Two years later, Rick's father married a woman with three children of her own. You've heard that Rick's two new half-brothers, thirteen and fifteen years old, are "out of control," and the family has been receiving counseling services from the local mental health clinic.

Rick's school records indicate that other teachers have had trouble with him in the past. Academically, he's below his classmates in all subjects except physical education and art. Comments from two of his previous teachers suggest Rick has a flair for artwork. Last year, Rick was diagnosed with mild learning and behavior disorders.

Mr. Chavez, the school psychologist, and Ms. Tamashiro, the school's inclusion facilitator, have been working with you on developing an individualized education program (IEP) for Rick. In fact, before school on Monday, you're meeting with Ms. Tamashiro to discuss how to involve Rick in the cooperative learning groups. You're anxious to get her suggestions, and you're confident that with her help and Mr. Chavez's, you can meet Rick's learning needs.

A s the preceding scenario about Rick suggests, teachers must understand and appreciate students' unique learning and developmental needs. They must be willing to learn about students' abilities and disabilities and to explore the special issues and concerns of students at three broad developmental levels—childhood, early adolescence, and late adolescence. The need to learn about the intellectual and psychological growth of students at the age level you plan to teach is obvious. In addition, understanding how their interests, questions, and problems will change throughout their school years will better equip you to serve them in the present. In this chapter, we look at how students' needs change as they develop and how their needs reflect various intelligences, abilities, and disabilities.

HOW DO STUDENTS' NEEDS CHANGE AS THEY DEVELOP

Development refers to the predictable changes that all human beings undergo as they progress through the life span—from conception to death. Although developmental changes "appear in orderly ways and remain for a reasonably long period of time" (Woolfolk 1995, 26), it is important to remember that students develop at different rates. Within a given classroom, for example, some students will be larger and physically more mature than others; some will be socially more sophisticated; and some will be able to think at a higher level of abstraction.

As humans progress through different **stages of development,** they mature and learn to perform the tasks that are a necessary part of daily living. There are several different types of human development. For example, as children develop physically, their bodies undergo numerous changes. As they develop cognitively, their mental capabilities expand so that they can use language and other symbol systems to solve problems. As they develop socially, they learn to interact more effectively with other people—as individuals and in groups. And, as they develop morally, their actions come to reflect a greater appreciation of principles such as equity, justice, fairness, and altruism.

Because no two students progress through the stages of cognitive, social, and moral development in quite the same way, teachers need perspectives on these three types of development that are flexible, dynamic, and, above all, useful. By becoming familiar with models of cognitive, social, and moral development, teachers at all levels, from preschool through college, can better serve their students. Three such models are Piaget's theory of **cognitive development,** Erikson's stages of **psychosocial development,** and Kohlberg's stages of **moral reasoning.**

PIAGET'S MODEL OF COGNITIVE DEVELOPMENT

Jean Piaget, the noted Swiss biologist and epistemologist, made extensive observational studies of children. He concluded that children reason differently from adults and even have different perceptions of the world. Piaget surmised that children learn through actively interacting with their environments, much as scientists do, and proposed that a child's thinking progresses through a sequence of four cognitive stages (see Figure 9.1). According to Piaget's theory of cognitive development, the rate of progress through the four stages varies from individual to individual.

During the school years, students move through the **preoperational stage,** the **concrete operations stage,** and the **formal operations stage;** yet, because of individual interaction with the total environment, each student's perceptions and learning will be unique. According to Piaget,

> A student who achieves a certain knowledge through free investigations and spontaneous effort will later be able to regain it; he will have acquired a methodology that can serve him for the rest of his life. . . . At the very least, instead of . . . subjugating his mind to exercise imposed from outside, he will make his reason function by himself and will build his own ideas freely (Piaget 1980, 93).

ERIKSON'S MODEL OF PSYCHOSOCIAL DEVELOPMENT

Erik Erikson's model of psychosocial development delineates eight stages, from infancy to old age (see Table 9.1 on page 278). For each stage a **psychosocial crisis** is central in the individual's emotional and social growth. Erikson expresses these

FIGURE 9.1 Piaget's stages of cognitive growth

1. **Sensorimotor Intelligence (birth to 2 years):** Behavior is primarily sensory and motor. The child does not yet "think" conceptually; however, "cognitive" development can be observed.

2. **Preoperational Thought (2 – 7 years):** Development of language and rapid conceptual development are evident. Children begin to use symbols to think of objects and people outside of their immediate environment. Fantasy and imaginative play are natural modes of thinking.

3. **Concrete Operations (7 – 11 years):** Children develop ability to use logical thought to solve concrete problems. Basic concepts of objects, number, time, space, and causality are explored and mastered. Through use of concrete objects to manipulate, children are able to draw conclusions.

4. **Formal Operations (11 – 15 years):** Cognitive abilities reach their highest level of development. Children can make predictions, think about hypothetical situations, think about thinking, and appreciate the structure of language as well as use it to communicate. Sarcasm, puns, argumentation, and slang are aspects of adolescents' speech that reflect their ability to think abstractly about language.

TABLE 9.1

Erikson's eight stages of development

Stage	Psychosocial Crisis	Virtue
Infancy	Trust vs. Mistrust	Hope
Early Childhood	Autonomy vs. Shame and Doubt	Will
Play Age	Initiative vs. Guilt	Purpose
School Age	Industry vs. Inferiority	Competence
Adolescence	Identity vs. Role Confusion	Fidelity
Young Adult	Intimacy vs. Isolation	Love
Adulthood	Generativity vs. Rejectivity	Care
Mature Love	Integrity vs. Despair	Wisdom

(Source: Adapted from *Childhood and Society,* 2d ed. by Erik H. Erikson, by permission of W. W. Norton & Co., Inc. Copyright 1950, © 1963 by W. W. Norton & Company, Inc. Copyright renewed 1978 by Erik H. Erikson.)

crises in polar terms; for instance, in the first stage, that of infancy, the psychosocial crisis is trust versus mistrust. Erikson explains that the major psychosocial task for the infant is to develop a sense of trust in the world but not to give up totally a sense of distrust. In the tension between the poles of trust and mistrust, a greater pull toward the more positive pole is considered healthy and is accompanied by a virtue. In this case, if trust prevails, the virtue is hope.

When we examine the issues and concerns of students in childhood and early and late adolescence later in this chapter, we will return to Erikson's model of psychosocial development. For further information on this significant and useful theory of development, we recommend that you read Erikson's first book, *Childhood and Society* (1963).

KOHLBERG'S MODEL OF MORAL DEVELOPMENT

According to Lawrence Kohlberg, the reasoning process people use to decide what is right and wrong evolves through three levels of development. Within each level, Kohlberg has identified two stages. Table 9.2 shows that at Level I, the preconventional level, the individual decides what is right on the basis of personal needs and rules developed by others. At Level II, the conventional level, moral decisions reflect a desire for the approval of others and a willingness to conform to the expectations of family, community, and country. At Level III, the postconventional level, the individual has developed values and principles that are based on rational, personal choices that can be separated from conventional values.

Kohlberg suggests that "over 50 percent of late adolescents and adults are capable of full formal reasoning [i.e., they can use their intelligence to reason abstractly, form hypotheses, and test these hypotheses against reality], but only 10 percent of these adults display principled (Stages 5 and 6) moral reasoning" (1993, 155). In addition, Kohlberg found that maturity of moral judgment is not highly related to IQ or verbal intelligence.

Some individuals have criticized Kohlberg's model as being too systematic and sequential, limited because it focuses on moral reasoning rather than actual behav-

TABLE 9.2

Kohlberg's theory of moral development

I. **Preconventional Level of Moral Reasoning**

Child is responsive to cultural rules and labels of good and bad, right or wrong, but interprets these in terms of consequences of action (punishment, reward, exchanges of favors).

Stage 1: Punishment-and-obedience orientation
Physical consequences of action determine its goodness or badness. Avoidance of punishment and deference to power are valued.

Stage 2: The instrumental-relativist orientation
Right action consists of that which satisfies one's own needs and occasionally the needs of others. Reciprocity is a matter of "You scratch my back and I'll scratch yours."

II. **Conventional Level of Moral Reasoning**

Maintaining the expectations of the individual's family, group, or nation is perceived as valuable, regardless of consequences.

Stage 3: The interpersonal concordance or "good boy-nice girl" orientation
Good behavior is that which pleases or helps others and is approved by them.

Stage 4: The "law and order" orientation
Orientation toward fixed rules and the maintenance of the social order. Right behavior consists of doing one's duty and showing respect for authority.

III. **Postconventional, Autonomous, or Principled Level of Moral Reasoning**

Effort to define moral principles that have validity and application apart from the authority of groups.

Stage 5: The social-contract, legalistic orientation
Right action defined in terms of rights and standards that have been agreed on by the whole society. This is the "official" morality of the American government and Constitution.

Stage 6: The universal-ethical-principle orientation
Right is defined by conscience in accord with self-chosen *ethical principles* appealing to logic and universality.

(Source: Adapted from Lawrence Kohlberg, "The Cognitive-Developmental Approach to Moral Education," in *Curriculum Planning: A New Approach*, 6th ed., eds. Glen Hass and Forrest W. Parkay [Boston: Allyn and Bacon, 1993], p. 154. The original version appeared in *Journal of Philosophy, 70,* 18 [October 25, 1973]: 631–632.)

ior, or biased because it tends to look at moral development from a male perspective (Bracey 1993). Carol Gilligan, for example, suggests that male moral reasoning tends to address the rights of the individual while female moral reasoning addresses the individual's responsibility to other people. In her book, *In a Different Voice* (1982), Gilligan refers to women's principal moral voice as the "ethics of care," which emphasizes care of others over the more male-oriented "ethics of justice." Thus, when confronted with a moral dilemma, females tend to suggest solutions based more on altruism and self-sacrifice than on rights and rules (Gilligan 1993).

The question remains, can moral reasoning be taught? Can teachers help students develop so that they live according to principles of equity, justice, caring, and empathy? Kohlberg suggests the following three conditions that can help children internalize moral principles:

1. Exposure to the next higher stage of reasoning
2. Exposure to situations posing problems and contradictions for the child's current moral structure, leading to dissatisfaction with his [her] current level
3. An atmosphere of interchange and dialogue combining the first two conditions, in which conflicting moral views are compared in an open manner (Kohlberg 1993, 161).

One approach to teaching values and moral reasoning is known as **character education,** a movement that stresses the development of students' "good character." As the following appraisal of our society indicates, the need for character education to make a "comeback" in today's schools is clear.

> Increasing numbers of people across the ideological spectrum believe that our society is in deep trouble. The disheartening signs are everywhere: the breakdown of the family; the deterioration of civility in everyday life; rampant greed at a time when one in five children is poor; an omnipresent sexual culture that fills our television and movie screens with sleaze, beckoning the young toward sexual activity at ever earlier ages; the enormous betrayal of children through sexual abuse; and the 1992 report of the National Research Council that says the United States is now *the* most violent of all industrialized nations (Lickona 1993, 6).

There is no single way for teachers to develop students' character, but Figure 9.2 illustrates twelve strategies Thomas Lickona suggests teachers can use to create moral classroom communities.

Some teachers, such as those at Dry Creek Elementary School in Clovis, California, Alexander Dumas School (K–8) in Chicago, and Allen Elementary School in inner-city Dayton, Ohio, emphasize specific moral values in their curricula. In 1989, for example, test scores at Allen rose to 28th out of the city's 33 elementary schools when teachers developed a character education program based on a "word of the week," such as self-control, patience, courage, cheerfulness, self-reliance, and helpfulness. Student behavior improved dramatically; by 1995 Allen's test scores were the highest in the city, suspensions plummeted, and teacher absenteeism was no longer a problem (McManus 1996, B3).

MASLOW'S MODEL OF A HIERARCHY OF NEEDS

Students' developmental levels also vary according to how well their biological and psychological needs have been satisfied. Psychologist Abraham Maslow (1970) formulated a model of a **hierarchy of needs** (see Figure 9.3 on page 282) which suggests that people are motivated by basic needs for survival and safety first. When these basic needs have been met sufficiently, people naturally seek to satisfy higher needs, the highest of which is self-actualization—the desire to use one's talents, abilities, and potentialities to the fullest. Students whose needs for safety have been fairly well satisfied will discover strong needs for friendship, affection, and love, for example. If efforts to satisfy the various needs are thwarted, the result can be maladjustment and interruption or delay in the individual's full and healthy development.

The hierarchy of needs model has particular relevance for teachers because students differ markedly in terms of where they are on Maslow's hierarchy of needs. Many families lack the resources to provide adequately for children's basic needs. Children from families that are concerned with day-to-day survival may not receive the support that could help them succeed in school. They come to school tired and hungry and may have trouble paying attention in class. Others may be well fed and clothed but feel unsafe, alien, or unloved; they may seek to protect themselves by withdrawing emotionally from activities around them.

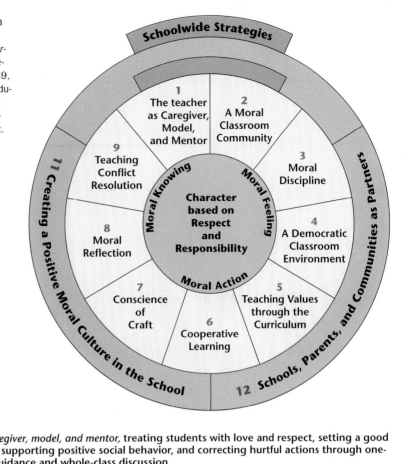

FIGURE 9.2 A comprehensive approach to values and character education (Source: Adapted from Thomas Lickona, *Educating for Character: How Our Schools Can Teach Respect and Responsiblity.* New York: Bantam Books, 1991, p. 69, and Thomas Lickona, "The Return of Character Education," *Educational Leadership,* November 1993: 10–11. Reprinted with permission of the Association for Supervision and Curriculum Development. © 1993. All rights reserved.)

1. *Act as caregiver, model, and mentor,* treating students with love and respect, setting a good example, supporting positive social behavior, and correcting hurtful actions through one-on-one guidance and whole-class discussion.

2. *Create a moral community,* helping students know one another as persons, respect and care about one another, and feel valued membership in, and responsibility to, the group.

3. *Practice moral discipline,* using the creation and enforcement of rules as opportunities to foster moral reasoning, voluntary compliance with rules, and a respect for others.

4. *Create a democratic classroom environment,* involving students in decision making and the responsibility for making the classroom a good place to be and learn.

5. *Teach values through the curriculum,* using the ethically rich content of academic subjects (such as literature, history, and science) as vehicles for teaching values and examining moral questions.

6. *Use cooperative learning* to develop students' appreciation of others, perspective taking, and the ability to work with others toward common goals.

7. *Develop the "conscience of craft"* by fostering students' appreciation of learning, capacity for hard work, commitment to excellence, and sense of work as affecting the lives of others.

8. *Encourage moral reflection* through reading, research, essay writing, journal keeping, discussion, and debate.

9. *Teach conflict resolution,* so that students acquire the essential moral skills of solving conflicts fairly and without force.

10. *Foster caring beyond the classroom,* using positive role models to inspire altruistic behavior and providing opportunities at every grade level to perform school and community service.

11. *Create a positive moral culture in the school,* developing a schoolwide ethos that supports and amplifies the values taught in classrooms.

12. *Recruit parents and the community as partners in character education,* letting parents know that the school considers them their child's first and most important moral teacher.

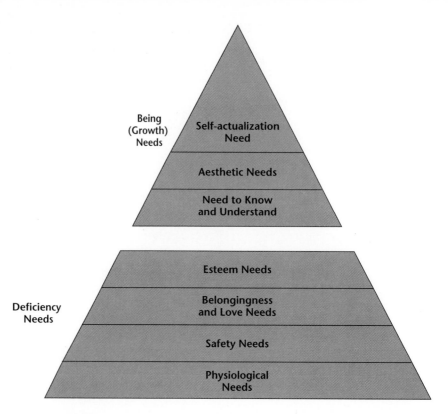

FIGURE 9.3 Maslow's hierarchy of needs. Note: The four lower-level needs are called deficiency needs because the motivation to satisfy them decreases when they are met. On the other hand, when being (growth) needs are met, motivation to fulfill them increases. (Source: Based on Abraham Maslow, *Motivation and Personality*, 2d. ed. New York: Harper & Row, 1970.)

DEVELOPMENTAL STRESSES AND TASKS OF CHILDHOOD

During Erikson's school-age stage, children strive for a sense of industry and struggle against feelings of inferiority. If successful, they gain the virtue of competence, believing in their abilities to do things. If children find evidence that they are inferior to others, if they experience failure when they try new tasks, and if they struggle without ever gaining a sense of mastery, then they feel incompetent.

Children gain the sense of industry needed at this age by playing seriously, mastering new skills, producing products, and being workers. When they first go to school they are oriented toward accomplishing new things (some kindergartners expect to learn to read on their first day of school and are disappointed when they don't). For young schoolchildren, the idea of work is attractive; it means that they are doing something grown-up.

Is childhood a time of carefree play or a period of stress? Certainly the answer depends upon the life circumstances and personality of the individual child. In a study of stressful events in the lives of more than 1,700 children in the second through the ninth grades in six countries, Karou Yamamoto and his associates found that the most stressful events "threaten[ed] one's sense of security and occasion[ed] personal denigration and embarrassment" (Yamamoto, et al. 1996, 139). Other studies have shown that serious stress is experienced by latchkey children, for example, who are left on their own or in each others' care for part or all of the day.

DEVELOPMENTAL STRESSES AND TASKS OF ADOLESCENCE

Many psychologists believe that adolescence contains two distinct stages: an early period covering the ages of ten to twelve through the ages of fourteen to sixteen, and a late period from approximately fifteen to sixteen through nineteen. Although a continuity exists in each individual's life, the psychosocial issues of adolescence—coping with change and seeking identity—vary in form and importance as individuals progress through the transition from childhood to adulthood.

In Erik Erikson's model of the eight stages of humans, identity versus role diffusion is the psychosocial crisis for the adolescent years. Although the quest for identity is a key psychosocial issue for both early and late adolescence, many believe that Erikson's identity-versus-role diffusion stage fits best for early adolescence. During this time, young adolescents, using their new thinking abilities, begin integrating a clearer sense of personal identity. Erikson's role diffusion refers to the variety of roles that adolescents have available to them.

According to Erikson's theory, when adolescents identify themselves with a peer group, with a school, or with a cause, their sense of fidelity—the "virtue" of this stage—is clear and strong. At this stage adolescents are loyal and committed, sometimes to people or ideas that may dismay or alarm their parents, sometimes to high ideals and dreams.

In late adolescence, the quest for identity shifts from relying on others to self-reliance. Young people continue to work on strengthening their sense of identity in late adolescence, but as they do so they draw less on the reactions of their peers and more

What needs must this child satisfy for healthy development? What childhood stresses does he face? What developmental tasks must he accomplish in his psychosocial development? What needs, stresses, and developmental tasks will affect this child as an adolescent? Why is information about development important to teachers?

Matty Rodriguez-Walling

Clarissa Hug Teacher of the Year

"The greatest feeling a teacher can have is to know you made a difference," Matty Rodriguez-Walling tells future teachers. Over the past twenty-four years, this versatile and enthusiastic educator has demonstrated that message in her work with students from kindergarteners to high school seniors and adults, in private and public schools, and in general-education, special-education, and adult-education classrooms.

Along the way Rodriguez-Walling has been recognized as *Outstanding High School Teacher, Dade County Public Schools Teacher of the Year, CEC (Council for Exceptional Children) Special Education Florida Teacher of the Year,* and in 1994 received the CEC's highest award, the *International CEC Clarissa Hug Teacher of the Year.* Throughout her

"Know that all children are special."

career, Rodriguez-Walling has encountered areas of student needs, has sought the necessary training and education to provide assistance, and has come to the aid of students, bettering their lives and learning.

The first way she made a difference was to help students with language needs. She recalls her own frustration when she came to the United States from Cuba at age eleven, not knowing a word of English. "For a whole year it was very frustrating. No one could understand me and I couldn't understand them." She decided then that she wanted to learn languages to help her future students avoid a similar struggle. Matty had "always wanted to be a teacher," in good measure because she had assisted her mother, who was a model classroom teacher in Cuba, but her uncomfortable initiation into the English language world helped her decide to become a foreign language teacher. In her first eight years of teaching she taught French, Spanish, and Italian to students in a private secondary school. Rodriguez-Walling next ventured into teaching in a public elementary school. When a major "boat lift" from Cuba took place, she was able to fulfill her dream of

on their own regard for what matters. Although late adolescents possess an array of interests, talents, and goals in life, they share a desire to achieve independence. More like adults than children, late adolescents are anxious to use newly acquired strengths, skills, and knowledge to achieve their own purposes, whether through marriage, parenthood, full-time employment, education beyond high school, a career, or military service.

The vulnerability of today's adolescents is portrayed graphically in *Great Transitions: Preparing Adolescents for a New Century,* a 1995 report by the Carnegie Council on Adolescent Development: "Altogether, nearly half of American adolescents are at high or moderate risk of seriously damaging their life chances. The damage may be near-term and vivid, or it may be delayed, like a time bomb set in youth" (Carnegie Council on Adolescent Development 1995). The list of alarming concerns in adolescence includes academic failure and retention, accidents, anorexia, assaultive behavior, criminal activity, cultism, depression, discipline problems, dropouts, drug abuse, homicides, incest, prostitution, runaways, school absenteeism, suicide, teenage pregnancy, vandalism, and the contraction of sexually transmitted diseases.

What can teachers do to help children and adolescents develop to their full potential? To help prevent the problems that place them at risk, an energetic, creative,

making life and learning easier for students with limited English knowledge.

Rodriguez-Walling became involved in special education for both professional and personal reasons. She had students with learning disabilities and emotional disturbances in her elementary school classes, and she had given birth to a son who was diagnosed with Down syndrome. In those pre-Public-Law 94-142 days, the doctors offered the distressed parents little hope that their son would ever go to school or be able to live outside of an institution. Rodriguez-Walling responded by earning a master's degree in special education. (Today, twenty-two years later, her son is "totally bilingual—he does everything in the house when I'm away—prepares dinner for my husband, does the laundry," and has a much fuller life than his doctors predicted.) When she discovered how motivating and learning-enhancing computers can be for students with special needs, she continued her studies, earning an Education Specialist degree in Computer Education.

The special education strategies and programs Rodriguez-Walling has designed and/or implemented are exciting: extensive use of computers and educational technology; a behavior management program to assist students in succeeding; a peer mediation conflict resolution program that integrates students from special education and general classrooms as peer mediators; and *The Winning Team Lab,* a computer laboratory in which exceptional students are paired with students in the general program as peer buddies. Because of their experience with technology, the students in Rodriguez-Walling's classes tutor the children in the regular program. "It is so good for their self-esteem," she observes.

Rodriguez-Walling now acts as a consulting teacher for Dade County Public Schools, helping classroom teachers better serve the needs of the exceptional children included in their classrooms. "Some teachers are frightened by students with special needs," she explains. She encourages them to "focus on students' strengths and talents and what they can do. Many times we focus on what they can't do." If one technique or approach does not work, she suggests that teachers try another. She is pleased when teachers realize that the special education techniques she demonstrates are good for all students, but is also aware that inclusion takes time to implement. "Full inclusion happens one school at a time, one student at a time, one attitude at a time. That's how it's happening and how it's going to work." Her advice for all teachers is: "Have high expectations for all children. See every child as a gifted child, and know that all children are special."

and multifaceted approach is necessary. Figure 9.4 on page 286 presents several strategies for helping students develop competence, positive self-concepts, and high esteem and for intervening to prevent or address problems that place them at risk.

HOW DO STUDENTS VARY IN INTELLIGENCE

In addition to developmental differences, students differ in terms of their intellectual capacity. Unfortunately, test scores, and sometimes intelligence quotient (IQ) scores, are treated as accurate measurements of students' intellectual ability because of their convenience and long-time use. What is intelligence and how has it been redefined to account for the many ways in which it is expressed? Though many definitions of intelligence have been proposed, the term has yet to be completely defined. One view is that **intelligence** is the ability to learn. As David Wechsler, the developer of the most widely used intelligence scales for children and adults, said: "Intelligence, operationally defined, is the aggregate or global capacity to act purposefully, to think rationally, and to deal effectively with the environment" (Wechsler 1958, 7). Other definitions of intelligence that have been proposed are the following:

1. **Provide opportunities and encouragement for students to develop competence.**

    • Provide a learning environment in which students can risk making mistakes.
    • Assign work that students can perform successfully and still be challenged.
    • Have realistic but high expectations for students.
    • Express belief in students' ability to succeed.
    • Encourage industry by letting students work on goals or projects of their choosing.
    • Provide opportunities for students to take special responsibility.
    • Assign older students to work with younger ones.
    • Reward industry and competence.

2. **Promote the development of positive self-concept and high self-esteem.**

    • Give praise more than criticism.
    • Take students and their work seriously.
    • Respect students' dignity.
    • Plan individual and group activities that boost morale.
    • Provide opportunities for students to interact and work cooperatively.
    • Teach and model acceptance of human diversity and individuality.
    • Develop systems for the recognition and reward of individual and group achievement.
    • Support students' efforts to achieve and appropriately express independence.

3. **Intervene to prevent or address problems that place students at risk.**

    • Provide a safe and structured learning environment where students feel secure.
    • Practice effective leadership and classroom management.
    • Provide opportunities to discuss preferences, values, morals, goals, and consequences.
    • Teach and model critical thinking, decision making, and problem solving.
    • Teach and model prosocial attitudes and behaviors and conflict resolution strategies.
    • Provide information on subjects of special concern to students and parents.
    • Cultivate family involvement.
    • Collaborate, consult, network, and refer on behalf of students.

FIGURE 9.4 What teachers can do to help children and adolescents develop

■ Goal-directed adaptive behavior
■ Ability to solve novel problems
■ Ability to acquire and think with new conceptual systems
■ Problem-solving ability
■ Planning and other metacognitive skills
■ Memory access speed
■ What people think intelligence is
■ What IQ tests measure
■ The ability to learn from bad teaching (Woolfolk 1995, 111)

INTELLIGENCE TESTING

The intelligence tests that we now use can be traced to the 1905 Metrical Scale of Intelligence designed by French psychologists Alfred Binet and Theodore Simon, who were part of a Paris-based commission that wanted a way to identify children who would need special help with their learning. Binet revised the scale in 1908, which was adapted for American children in 1916 by Lewis Terman, a psychologist at Stanford University. Terman's test was, in turn, further adapted, especially by the U.S. Army, which transformed it into a paper-and-pencil test that could be administered to large groups. The use of such intelligence tests has continued throughout the years. Approximately 67 percent of the population have an IQ between 85 and 115—the range of normal intelligence.

Individual intelligence tests are presently valued by psychologists and those in the field of special education because they can be helpful in diagnosing a student's strengths and weaknesses. However, group intelligence tests given for the purpose of classifying students into like-score groups have received an increasing amount of criticism.

The most significant and dramatic criticism of group IQ tests has been that test items and tasks are culturally biased, drawn mostly from white middle-class experience. Thus, the tests are more assessments of how informed students are about features in a specific class or culture than of how intelligent they are in general. This complaint became a formal, legal challenge when, on the basis of their IQ test scores, a group of African-American children were put into special classes for mentally retarded children. Their parents brought the complaint to the courts in 1971 and persisted with it all the way to the federal appellate court, where a decision was eventually made in their favor in 1984. In that well-known case, *Larry P. v. Riles* (1984), the court decided that IQ tests were discriminatory and culturally biased. However, in another case, *PASE v. Hannon* (1980), an Illinois district court ruled that when IQ tests were used in conjunction with other forms of assessment, such as teacher observation, they were not discriminatory for placement purposes. Although the criticism continues, a number of psychometricians are seeking other solutions by attempting to design culture-free intelligence tests.

MULTIPLE INTELLIGENCES

Many theorists believe that intelligence is a basic ability that enables one to perform mental operations in the following areas: logical reasoning, spatial reasoning, number ability, and verbal meaning. However, "the weight of the evidence at the present time is that intelligence is multidimensional, and that the full range of these dimensions is not completely captured by any single general ability" (Sternberg 1996, 11). Howard Gardner, for example, believes there are several "intelligences," which he defines as "biological and psychological potential[s]" (Gardner 1995, 202). Drawing on the theories of others and research findings on *idiots savants,* stroke cases, child prodigies, and so-called normal children and adults, Gardner suggests in *Frames of Mind* (1983) that there are at least seven human intelligences: logical-mathematical, linguistic, musical, spatial, bodily-kinesthetic, interpersonal, and intrapersonal (see Table 9.3 on page 288).

Gardner's theory of **multiple intelligences** is valuable for teachers. As Robert Slavin suggests, "Teachers must avoid thinking about children as 'smart' or 'not smart' because there are many ways to be 'smart' " (Slavin 1994, 135). Some students are talented in terms of their interpersonal relations and exhibit natural leadership abilities. Others seem to have a high degree of what Peter Salovey at Yale University and John Mayer at the University of New Hampshire term *emotional intelligence*—awareness of and ability to manage their feelings. Differences in musical, athletic, and mechanical abilities can be recognized by even the minimally informed observer. Because these intelligences are not tested or highlighted, they may go unnoticed and possibly wasted.

However, keep in mind Gardner's "reflections" twelve years after the publication of *Frames of Mind* (Gardner 1995, 206):

> MI [multiple intelligence] theory is in no way an educational prescription. [E]ducators are in the best position to determine the uses to which MI theory should be put. . . .

LEARNING MODES

Students vary greatly in regard to **learning modes,** the approaches to learning that work best for them. These differences have also been called *learning styles, learning*

TABLE 9.3

The seven intelligences

Intelligence	End-States	Core Components
Logical-mathematicial	Scientist Mathematician	Sensitivity to, and capacity to discern, logical or numerical patterns; ability to handle long chains of reasoning
Linguistic	Poet Journalist	Sensitivity to the sounds, rhythms, and meanings of words; sensitivity to the different functions of language
Musical	Composer Violinist	Abilities to produce and appreciate rhythm, pitch, and timbre; appreciation of the forms of musical expressiveness
Spatial	Navigator Sculptor	Capacities to perceive the visual-spatial world accurately and to perform transformations on one's initial perceptions
Bodily-kinesthetic	Dancer Athlete	Abilities to control one's body movements and to handle objects skillfully
Interpersonal	Therapist Salesperson	Capacities to discern and respond appropriately to the moods, temperaments, motivations, and desires of other people
Intrapersonal	Person with detailed, accurate self-knowledge	Access to one's own feelings and the ability to discriminate among them and draw on them to guide behavior; knowledge of one's own strengths, weaknesses, desires, and intelligences

(Source: H. Gardner and T. Hatch, "Multiple Intelligences Go to School: Educational Implications of the Theory of Multiple Intelligences," *Educational Researcher, 18*(8) (1989): 6. Copyright © 1989 by the American Educational Research Association. Reprinted by permission of the publisher.)

style preferences, or *cognitive styles* (Woolfolk 1995). The National Task Force on Learning Style and Brain Behavior suggests that there is a "consistent pattern of behavior and performance by which an individual approaches educational experiences. It is the composite of characteristic cognitive, affective, and physiological behaviors that serve as relatively stable indicators of how a learner perceives, interacts with, and responds to the learning environment."

Students' learning modes are determined by a combination of hereditary and environmental influences. Some more quickly learn things they hear; others learn faster when they see material in writing. Some need a lot of structure; others learn best when they can be independent and follow their desires. Some learn best in formal settings; others learn best in informal, relaxed environments. Some need almost total silence to concentrate; others learn well in noisy, active environments. Some are intuitive learners; some prefer to learn by following logical, sequential steps.

There is no one "correct" view of learning modes to guide teachers in their daily decision making. Culture-based differences in learning modes are subtle, variable, and difficult to describe; and learning modes change as the individual matures. Moreover, critics maintain that there is little evidence to support the validity of dozens of conceptual models for learning modes and accompanying assessment instruments. Nevertheless, you should be aware of the concept of learning modes and realize that any given classroom activity may be more effective for some students than for others. Knowledge of your own and your students' learning modes will help you to individualize instruction and motivate your students.

Identifying Your Learning Mode Preferences

Describe your preferred learning environment. Where, when, and how do you learn best? Does certain lighting, food, or music seem to enhance your learning? Think about how you acquire new information—do you prefer being analytical and abstract or commonsensical and concrete? Do you prefer thinking about things or doing things? Do you prefer to learn alone, in a small group, or in a large group? When given an assignment, do you prefer a lot of structure and details, or do you prefer more unstructured or open-ended assignments?

HOW DO STUDENTS VARY IN ABILITY AND DISABILITY

Students also differ according to their special needs and talents. Some enter the world with exceptional abilities or disabilities; others encounter life experiences that change their capabilities significantly, and still others struggle with conditions that medical scientists have yet to understand. Where possible, all of these exceptional children and youth are given a public education in America.

EXCEPTIONAL LEARNERS

Children "who require special education and related services if they are to realize their full human potential" (Hallahan and Kauffman 1994, 6) are referred to as **exceptional learners.** They are taught by special education teachers and by regular teachers into whose classrooms they have been integrated or *included.* Among the many exceptional children that teachers may encounter in the classroom are students who have physical, mental, or emotional disabilities and students who are gifted or talented.

Special-needs students are often referred to synonymously as *handicapped* or *disabled.* However, it is important for teachers to understand the following distinction between a disability and a handicap:

> A disability is an inability to do something, a diminished capacity to perform in a specific way. A handicap, on the other hand, is a disadvantage imposed on an individual. A disability may or may not be a handicap, depending on the circumstances. Likewise, a handicap may or may not be caused by a disability. For example, blindness is a disability that can be anything but a handicap in the dark. In fact, in the dark the person who has sight is the one who is handicapped. . . . (Hallahan and Kauffman 1994, 6).

In addition, teachers should know that current language use emphasizes the concept of "people first." In other words, a disabling condition should not be used as an adjective to describe a person. Thus, one should say "a child with a visual impairment," not a "blind child" or even a "visually impaired child."

Teachers should also realize that the definitions for disabilities are generalized, open to change, and significantly influenced by the current cultural perception of normality. For example, the American Association on Mental Retardation (AAMR) has changed its definition of mental retardation seven times since 1950 to reflect shifting views of people with cognitive disabilities.

Cautions about labeling should also apply to gifted and talented students. Unfortunately, people commonly have a negative view of gifted and talented youngsters. Like many ethnic groups, gifted students are "different" and thus have been the target of many myths and stereotypes. However, a landmark study of 1,528 gifted males and females begun by Lewis Terman (1925, 1947, 1959) in 1926 and to continue until 2010 has "exploded the myth that high-IQ individuals [are] brainy but physically and socially inept. In fact, Terman found that children with outstanding IQs were larger, stronger, and better coordinated than other children and became better adjusted and more emotionally stable adults" (Slavin 1994, 461).

STUDENTS WITH DISABILITIES

Table 9.4 shows that the percentage of all students participating in federally supported education programs for **students with disabilities** increased from 8.33 percent in 1976–77 to 11.97 percent in 1992–93. More than 5.3 million students participated in these programs in 1994 (Office of Special Education Programs 1995).

Various tests and other forms of assessment are used to identify persons in the categories of disability listed in Table 9.4. The following brief definitional characteristics of these categories are based on the Individuals with Disabilities Education Act

TABLE 9.4

Percent of children 0 to 21 years old in federal programs for students with disabilities, 1976–77 to 1992–93 *

Type of Disability	1976–77	1980–81	1984–85	1988–89	1992–93
Specific learning disabilities	1.80	3.58	4.67	4.94	5.50
Speech or language impairments	2.94	2.86	2.87	2.41	2.33
Mental retardation	2.16	2.03	1.77	1.40	1.21
Serious emotional disturbance	0.64	0.85	0.95	0.94	0.94
Hearing impairments	0.20	0.19	0.18	0.14	0.14
Orthopedic impairments	0.20	0.14	0.14	0.12	0.12
Other health impairments	0.32	0.24	0.17	0.11	0.15
Visual impairments	0.09	0.08	0.07	0.06	0.05
Multiple disabilities	—	0.17	0.17	0.21	0.24
Deaf-blindness	—	0.01	****	****	****
Autism and other	—	—	—	—	0.04
Preschool disabled**	***	***	***	0.98	1.24
All disabilities	**8.33**	**10.13**	**11.00**	**11.30**	**11.97**

*Includes students served under Chapter I and Individuals with Disabilities Education Act. Based on enrollment in public schools, PreK–12.

**Includes preschool children 0–5 years served under Chapter I and IDEA.

***Prior to 1987–88, these students were included in the counts by disabling condition.

****Less than .005.

—Data not available.

NOTE—Counts are based on reports from the 50 states and District of Columbia only. Increases since 1987–88 are due in part to new legislation enacted in 1986, which mandates public school special education services for all children with disabilities ages 3 through 5.

(Source: U.S. Department of Education, Office of Special Education and Rehabilitative Services, *Annual Report to Congress on the Implementation of The Individuals with Disabilities Education Act,* various years, and unpublished tabulations; and National Center for Education Statistics, Common Core of Data survey. This table was prepared June 1995. Taken from National Center for Education Statistics, *Digest of Education Statistics 1995* [Washington, DC: National Center for Education Statistics], p. 65.)

(IDEA) and definitions used by professional organizations dedicated to meeting the needs of persons in each category.

1. *Specific learning disabilities (LD)*—Learning is significantly hindered by difficulty in listening, speaking, reading, writing, reasoning, or computing
2. *Speech or language impairments*—Significant difficulty in communicating with others as a result of speech or language disorders
3. *Mental retardation*—Significant limitations in cognitive ability
4. *Serious emotional disturbance (SED)*—Social and/or emotional maladjustment that significantly reduces the ability to learn
5. *Hearing impairments*—Permanent or fluctuating mild to profound hearing loss in one or both ears
6. *Orthopedic impairments*—Physically disabling conditions that affect locomotion or motor functions
7. *Other health impairments*—Limited strength, vitality, or alertness caused by chronic or acute health problems
8. *Visual impairments*—Vision loss that significantly inhibits learning
9. *Multiple disabilities*—Two or more interrelated disabilities
10. *Deaf-blindness*—Vision and hearing disability that severely limits communication
11. *Autism and other*—Significantly impaired communication, learning, and reciprocal social interactions

Students with learning disabilities account for more than half of all students ages six through twenty-one with disabilities. From 1976 to 1994, the proportion of special-education students with learning disabilities more than doubled, from 23.8 percent to 51.1 percent (Schnaiberg 1995, 25). Since the term **learning disability (LD)** was first introduced in the early 1960s, there has been no universally accepted definition. In 1989 the National Joint Committee on Learning Disabilities issued the following definition:

> Learning disabilities is a generic term that refers to a heterogenous group of disorders manifested by significant difficulties in the acquisition and use of listening, speaking, reading, writing, reasoning or mathematics abilities. These disorders are intrinsic to the individual and presumed to be due to central nervous system dysfunction, and may occur across the life span.

> Problems in self-regulatory behaviors, social perception and social interaction may exist with learning disabilities but do not by themselves constitute a learning disability (National Joint Commission on Learning Disabilities 1989, 1).

Imagine that you are concerned about two of your new students—Mary and Bill. Mary has an adequate vocabulary and doesn't hesitate to express herself, but her achievement in reading and mathematics doesn't add up to what you believe she can do. Often, when you give the class instructions, Mary seems to get confused about what to do. In working with her one-on-one, you've noticed that she often reverses letters and numbers the way much younger children do—she sees a *b* for a *d* or a *6* for a *9*. Mary may have a learning disability, causing problems in taking in, organizing, remembering, and expressing information. Like Mary, students with learning disabilities often show a significant difference between their estimated intelligence and their actual achievement in the classroom.

Bill presents you with a different set of challenges. He is obviously bright, but he frequently seems to be "out of sync" with classroom activities. He gets frustrated when he has to wait for his turn. He sometimes blurts out answers before you've even asked a question. He can't seem to stop wiggling his toes and tapping his pencil, and he often comes to school without his backpack and homework. Bill may have **attention deficit hyperactivity disorder (ADHD),** one of the most commonly diagnosed disabilities among children. Students with ADHD have difficulty remaining still so they can concentrate. Students with an **attention deficit disorder (ADD)** have difficulty focusing their attention long enough to learn well. Children with ADD/ADHD do not qualify for special education unless they also have another disability in a federally defined category.

Treatment for students with ADD/ADHD includes behavior modification and medication. Since the early 1980s, Ritalin has become the most commonly prescribed drug for ADD/ADHD, and more than one million American children are currently estimated to take Ritalin to increase their impulse control and attention span.

By being alert for students who exhibit several of the following characteristics, teachers can help in the early identification of students with learning disabilities so they can receive the instructional adaptations or special education services they need.

- normal intelligence or even giftedness
- discrepancy between intelligence and performance
- delays in achievement
- attention deficit or high distractibility
- hyperactivity or impulsiveness
- poor motor coordination and spatial relation ability

Issues in Education

- To what extent might each choice affect this student's school experience and academic success?
- What other labels can you think of that might be added to the selection?
- In what contexts might labels be necessary or useful? Why is labeling nevertheless undesirable?
- To what extent, do you think, does the student in this cartoon have a choice of labels? That is, what point is the cartoonist making about assigning responsibility for student outcomes?

- difficulty solving problems
- perceptual anomalies, such as reversing letters, words, or numbers
- difficulty with self-motivated, self-regulated activities
- overreliance on teachers and peers for assignments
- specific disorders of memory, thinking, or language
- immature social skills
- disorganized approach to learning (Smith and Luckasson 1995)

STUDENTS WHO ARE GIFTED AND TALENTED

You are concerned about the poor performance of Paul, a student in your eighth-period high school class. Paul is undeniably bright. When he was ten, he had an IQ of 145 on the Stanford-Binet. Last year, when he was sixteen, he scored 142. Paul's father is a physician, and his mother is a professor. Both parents clearly value learning and are willing to give Paul any needed encouragement and help.

Throughout elementary school, Paul had an outstanding record. His teachers reported that he was brilliant and very meticulous in completing his assignments. He entered high school amid expectations by his parents and teachers that he would continue his outstanding performance. Throughout his first two years of high school, Paul never seemed to live up to his promise. Now, halfway through his junior year, Paul is failing English and geometry. Paul seems to be well adjusted to the social side of school. He has a lot of friends and says he likes school. Paul explains his steadily declining grades by saying that he doesn't like to study.

Paul may be gifted. **Gifted and talented** students, those who have demonstrated a high level of attainment in intellectual ability, academic achievement, creativity, or visual and performing arts, are evenly distributed across all ethnic and cultural groups and socioeconomic classes. Although you might think it is easy to meet the needs of gifted and talented students, you will find that this is not always the case. "Gifted and talented students often challenge the 'system' of the school, and they can be verbally caustic. Their superior abilities and unusual or advanced interests demand teachers who themselves are highly intelligent, creative, and motivated" (Hallahan and Kauffman 1994, 432). The ability of such students to challenge the system is reflected in a recent U.S. Department of Education study that found that gifted and talented elementary schoolchildren have mastered 35 percent to 50 percent of the grade curriculum in five basic subject areas *before* starting the school year.

There are many forms that giftedness may take; Joseph S. Renzulli (1982), Director of the National Research Center on the Gifted and Talented at the University of Connecticut, for example, suggests a distinction between academic giftedness and creative/productive giftedness. The trend during the last few decades has been to broaden our view of what characterizes giftedness.

Drawing from the work of Renzulli and his colleagues, Woolfolk (1995) defines *giftedness* "as a combination of three basic characteristics: above-average general ability, a high level of creativity, and a high level of task commitment or motivation to achieve in certain areas. Truly gifted children are not the students who simply learn quickly with little effort. The work of gifted students is original, extremely advanced for their age, and potentially of lasting importance" (Woolfolk 1995, 123).

Variations in criteria used to identify gifted and talented students are especially evident in the reported incidence of giftedness from state to state; for example, North Dakota identifies only 1.0 percent of its students as gifted and talented, while Michigan identifies 11.6 percent (National Center for Education Statistics 1995, 67). Depending on the criteria used, estimates of the number of gifted and talented students range from 3 to 5 percent of the total population.

Strategies for teaching students who are gifted and talented begin with effective teachers. Gallagher and Gallagher (1994) suggest that effective teachers of the gifted challenge their students through *enrichment, acceleration, sophistication,* and *novelty.* Educational psychologist Anita Woolfolk suggests that "Teaching methods for gifted students should encourage abstract thinking (formal-operational thought), creativity, and independence, not just the learning of greater quantities of facts. In working with gifted and talented students, a teacher must be imaginative, flexible, and unthreatened by the capabilities of these students. The teacher must ask, What does this child need most? What is she or he ready to learn? Who can help me to help?" (Woolfolk 1995, 126).

A study of the differences between outstanding and average teachers of gifted and talented students showed that the outstanding teachers were characterized by the following:

■ Enthusiasm for own work with gifted students
■ Confidence in their ability to be effective
■ Ability to facilitate other people as resources and learners
■ Ability to apply knowledge of theory to practice
■ A strong achievement orientation
■ Commitment to the role of educator of gifted students
■ Supporter of gifted education programs (Daurio 1979)

Several innovative approaches exist for meeting the educational needs of gifted students.

Acceleration: Accelerated programs for intellectually precocious students have proven successful. For example, one survey that spanned a fifty-year period and examined 200 studies of accelerated programs found that two-thirds were beneficial (Daurio 1979). One example of acceleration is a suburban Chicago alternative school where high-potential at-risk students work at their own pace in high-tech classrooms. They engage in "integrative accelerative learning," which offers advanced curricula and encourages individual creativity, positive reinforcement, and relaxation. At the National Research Center on Gifted and Talented Education, teachers in experimental classrooms practice thematic "curriculum compacting," which encourages brighter students to forge ahead in the regular curriculum while all students work to their strengths and less able students still get the time and attention they need. Also, many colleges and universities now participate in accelerated programs whereby gifted youth who have outgrown the high school curriculum may enroll in college courses.

Self-directed or independent study: For some time, self-directed or independent study has been recognized as an appropriate way for teachers to maintain the interest of gifted students in their classes. Gifted students usually have the academic backgrounds and motivation to do well without constant supervision and the threat or reward of grades.

Individual education programs: Since the passage of PL 94-142 and the mandating of Individual Education Programs (IEPs) for special education students, IEPs have been promoted as an appropriate means for educating gifted students. Most IEPs for gifted students involve various enrichment experiences, self-directed study, and special, concentrated instruction given to individuals or small groups in pull-out programs. For example, at Columbia Teachers College in New York, economically disadvantaged students identified as gifted participate in Project Synergy, which pairs students with mentors who nurture their talents and guide them through advanced academic content.

Alternative or magnet schools: Several large-city school systems have developed magnet schools organized around specific disciplines, such as science, mathematics, fine arts, basic skills, and so on. The excellent programs at these schools are designed to attract superior students from all parts of the district. Many of these schools offer outstanding programs for gifted and talented youth. E. Paul Torrence, a noted researcher in gifted education and children's creative thinking skills, says of such schools: "Students in these schools [stay] for hours after school and [return] on weekends. They [are] enthusiastic, intense, and satisfied" (Torrance 1986, 634).

WHAT ARE SPECIAL EDUCATION, MAINSTREAMING, AND INCLUSION❓

Prior to the twentieth century, children with disabilities were usually segregated from regular classrooms and taught by teachers in state-run and private schools. Today, an array of programs and services in general and special education classrooms is aimed at developing the potential of exceptional students. Three critical concepts to promote the growth, talents, and productivity of exceptional students are special education, mainstreaming, and inclusion.

Special education refers to "specially designed instruction that meets the unusual needs of an exceptional student" (Hallahan and Kauffman 1994, 14). Teachers who are trained in special education become familiar with special materials, techniques, and equipment and facilities for students with disabilities. For example, children with visual impairment may require reading materials in large print or Braille; students with hearing impairment may require hearing aids and/or instruction in sign language; those with physical disabilities may need special equipment; those with emotional disturbances may need smaller and more highly structured classes; and children with special gifts or talents may require access to working professionals. Related services—special transportation, psychological assessment, physical and occupational therapy, medical treatment, and counseling—may be necessary if special education is to be effective (Hallahan and Kauffman 1994, 14).

SPECIAL EDUCATION LAWS

Until 1975, the needs of students with disabilities were primarily met through self-contained special education classes within regular schools. That year, however, Congress passed the **Education for all Handicapped Children Act (Public Law 94-142).** This act guaranteed to all children with disabilities a free and appropriate public education. The law, which applied to every teacher and every school in the country, outlined extensive procedures to ensure that exceptional students between the ages of three and eighteen were granted due process in regard to identification, placement, and educational services received. As a result of PL 94-142, the participation of students with disabilities in all classrooms and school programs became routine.

In 1990, PL 94-142 was replaced by the **Individuals with Disabilities Education Act (IDEA).** IDEA included the major provisions of PL 94-142 and extended the availability of a free, appropriate education to youth with disabilities between the ages of three and twenty-one years of age. IDEA, which is one of the most important and far-reaching pieces of educational legislation ever passed in this country, has several provisions with which all teachers should be familiar.

Least restrictive environment: IDEA requires that all children with disabilities be educated in the **least restrictive environment.** In other words, a student must be mainstreamed into a general education classroom whenever such integration is feasible and appropriate and the child would receive educational benefit from such placement.

Individualized education program: Every child with a disability is to have a written **individualized education program (IEP)** that meets the child's needs and specifies educational goals, methods for achieving those goals, and the number and quality of special educational services to be provided. The IEP must be reviewed annually by five parties: (1) a parent or guardian, (2) the child, (3) a teacher, (4) a professional who has recently evaluated the child, and (5) others, usually the principal or a special-education resource person from the school district.

Confidentiality of records: IDEA also ensures that records on a child are kept confidential. Parental permission is required before any official may look at a child's records. Moreover, parents can amend a child's records if they feel information in it is misleading, inaccurate, or violates the child's rights.

Due process: IDEA gives parents the right to disagree with an IEP or an evaluation of their child's abilities. If a disagreement arises, it is settled through an impartial due process hearing presided over by an officer appointed by the state. At the hearing, parents may be represented by a lawyer, give evidence, and cross-examine, and are entitled to receive a transcript of the hearing and a written decision on the case. If either the parents or the school district disagree with the outcome, the case may then be taken to the civil courts.

MEETING THE MAINSTREAMING CHALLENGE

To help teachers satisfy the provisions of IDEA, school districts across the nation have developed inservice programs designed to acquaint classroom teachers with the unique needs of students with disabilities. In addition, colleges and universities with preservice programs for educators have added courses on teaching students with special educational needs.

The guidelines for IDEA suggest that schools must make a significant effort to include, or mainstream, *all* children in the classroom. However, it is not clear how far schools must go to meet this **mainstreaming** requirement. For example, should children with severe disabilities be included in general education classrooms if they are unable to do the academic work? Recent court cases have ruled that students with severe disabilities must be included if there is a potential benefit for the child, if the class would stimulate the child's language development, or if other students could act as appropriate role models for the child. In one case, the court ordered a school district to place a child with an IQ of 44 in a regular second-grade classroom and rejected as exaggerated the district's claim that the placement would be prohibitively expensive (*Board of Education, Sacramento City Unified School District v. Holland,* 1992). In another case, the court rejected a school district's argument that inclusion of a child with a severe disability would be so disruptive as to significantly impair the learning of the other children (*Oberti v. Board of Education of the Borough of Clementon School District,* 1992).

To meet the mainstreaming challenge, teachers must have knowledge of various disabilities and the teaching methods and materials appropriate for each. The effective teacher is also characterized by his or her positive attitudes toward special education students. In this regard, a study of 212 K–12 student teachers found that "developing acceptance and pupil self-confidence" was judged to be the most important competency for teaching mainstreamed students (Leyser 1985).

In addition, Hallahan and Kauffman suggest that *all* teachers should be prepared to participate in the education of exceptional learners. Teachers should be willing to do the following:

1. Make maximum effort to accommodate individual students' needs
2. Evaluate academic abilities and disabilities

3. Refer [students] for evaluation [as appropriate]
4. Participate in eligibility conferences [for special education]
5. Participate in writing individualized education programs
6. Communicate with parents or guardians
7. Participate in due process hearings and negotiations
8. Collaborate with other professionals in identifying and making maximum use of exceptional students' abilities (Hallahan and Kauffman 1994, 22–23)

THE DEBATE OVER INCLUSION

While mainstreaming refers to the application of the least restrictive environment clause of PL 94-142, **inclusion** goes beyond mainstreaming to integrate all students with disabilities into general education classes and school life with the active support of special educators and other specialists and service providers, as well as assistive technology and adaptive software. Advocates of inclusion believe that "if students cannot meet traditional academic expectations, then those expectations should be changed. They reject the mainstreaming assumption that settings dictate the type and intensity of services and propose instead the concept of inclusion" (Friend and Bursuck 1996, 4).

Full inclusion goes even further and calls for "the integration of students with disabilities in the general education classrooms at all times regardless of the nature or severity of the disability" (Friend and Bursuck 1996, 4). According to the full-inclusion approach, if a child needs support services, these are brought *to the child*; the child does not have to participate in a pull-out program to receive support services. Advocates of full inclusion maintain that pull-out programs stigmatize participating students because they are separated from their general-education classmates, and pull-out programs discourage collaboration between general and special education teachers. Those who oppose full inclusion maintain that classroom teachers, who may be burdened with large class sizes and be assigned to schools with inadequate support services, often lack the training and instructional materials to meet the needs of all exceptional students.

In addition, some parents of children with disabilities believe that full inclusion could mean the elimination of special education as we know it along with the range of services currently guaranteed by federal special education laws. Full inclusion, they reason, would make them depend upon individual states, not the federal government, to meet their children's needs. Moreover, some parents believe that special education classes provide their children with important benefits. For example, in 1994, parents of exceptional children attending Vaughn Occupational High School in Chicago protested a decision by the Chicago Board of Education to include the children in neighborhood schools. The Chicago Board was responding to the Illinois State Board of Education's threat to withhold state and federal funds from the school if students were not included in regular classrooms. In response, the parents picketed a Chicago Board of Education meeting with signs reading "The board's inclusion is exclusion." One parent expressed concern that inclusion would deny her son essential vocational training: "I know [my son] won't go to college so I don't expect that, just for him to learn everyday living and work skills" (Spring 1996, 143).

The general public also has reservations about full inclusion. According to the 1995 Gallup/Phi Delta Kappa Poll of the Public's Attitudes Toward the Public Schools, 66 percent believed exceptional students should be educated in special classes of their own; 26 percent believed they should be put in the same classes with regular students; and 8 percent said they "don't know" (Elam and Rose 1995, 49). Nevertheless, the trend toward full inclusion continues. The number of school-age students with disabilities increased by nearly 10 percent between 1990 and 1995; almost half of exceptional students aged six to eleven spent most of their school day in regular classrooms in 1995, as did 30 percent of students aged twelve to seventeen (Office of Special Education Programs 1995).

How do classroom teachers feel about inclusion? The following comments by four teachers express both the successes and the struggles teachers can experience in inclusive schools:

Successes

"Inclusion is good for kids. It helps students really understand diversity. And students learn how to help each other. It teaches students that they can learn from each other; that the teacher is not the only source in the classroom."

"Inclusion brings the staff together. We had to talk through a lot of issues to get ready for inclusion. Now we all talk about what we're teaching and how we're teaching it. If we have a problem with a student, we talk about it. We support each other more than we ever did before."

How might this student's exceptionality or disability be defined? What laws enable the student to receive special education services in this general education classroom? What must the teacher do to provide equal educational opportunity for *all* the students in the class? What are the key issues in the debate about inclusion?

Struggles

"I had a student with an emotional disability placed in my class. He would bite other students and blow in their faces. He wouldn't stay in one place for a minute. I spent the entire year worrying that he would seriously injure another student. I don't think he should have been in my classroom. I think I should have had more help."

"Sometimes I felt like I wasn't a teacher, more like a traffic cop. The special-education teacher came in sometimes. The aide came in every day. The speech therapist was here twice a week. I didn't have time to do my own planning, much less planning for everyone else. It almost would have been better to be left alone" (Friend and Cook 1993, 54–55).

EQUAL OPPORTUNITY FOR EXCEPTIONAL LEARNERS

Like many groups in our society, exceptional learners have often not received the kind of education that most effectively meets their needs. Approximately 10 percent of the population aged three to twenty-one is classified as exceptional; that is, "they require special education because they are markedly different from most children in one or more of the following ways: They may have mental retardation, learning disabilities, emotional or behavioral disorders, physical disabilities, disorders of communication, autism, traumatic brain injury, impaired hearing, impaired sight, or special gifts or talents" (Hallahan and Kauffman 1994, 7).

Just as there are no easy answers for how teachers should meet the needs of students from diverse cultural backgrounds, there is no single strategy for teachers to follow to ensure that all exceptional students receive an appropriate education. The key, however, lies in not losing sight of the fact that *"the most important charac- teristics of exceptional children are their abilities"* (Hallahan and Kauffman 1994, 6).

To build on students' strengths, classroom teachers must work cooperatively and collaboratively with special education teachers, and students in special educa- tion programs must not become isolated from their peers. In addition, teachers must understand how some people can be perceived as "different" and presumed to be "handicapped" because of their appearance or physical condition. Evidence sug- gests, for example, that people who are short, obese, or unattractive are often vic- tims of discrimination, as are people with conditions such as AIDS, cancer, multiple sclerosis, or epilepsy. Significantly, many individuals with clinically diagnosable and classifiable impairments or disabilities do not perceive themselves as *handicapped.* The term itself means permanently unable to be treated equally.

Officially labeling students has become a necessity with the passage of the laws that provide education and related services for exceptional students. The classifica- tion labels help determine which students qualify for the special services, educational programs, and individualized instruction provided by the laws, and they bring to ed- ucators' attention many exceptional children and youth whose educational needs could be overlooked, neglected, or inadequately served otherwise. Detrimental as- pects include the fact that classification systems are imperfect and have arbitrary cut- off points that sometimes lead to injustices. Also, labels tend to evoke negative expectations, which can cause teachers to avoid and underteach these students, and their peers to isolate or reject them, thereby stigmatizing individuals, sometimes per- manently. The most serious detriment, however, is that students so labeled are taught to feel inadequate, inferior, and limited in terms of their options for growth.

HOW CAN YOU TEACH ALL LEARNERS IN YOUR INCLUSIVE CLASSROOM ?

Teachers have a responsibility to address all students' developmental, individual, and exceptional learning needs. Although addressing the range of student differ- ences in the inclusive classroom is challenging, it can also be very rewarding. Con- sider the comments of three first-year teachers who reflect on their successes with diverse learners:

> I taught a boy with ADD. His first-grade teacher segregated him from other students, but I had him stay with his peer group. Soon, I heard from other teachers that he was not being a troublemaker anymore. By year's end, he had published his own booklet for a writing project.

> I had a troubled student who dropped out of school mid-year after I had spent a con- siderable amount of time working with him. He went to court over a trespassing charge, so I went to court with him. His mother wrote me a letter saying I had been such a pos- itive influence on him and she was very grateful. It was the relationships I was able to establish with these kids that meant so much to me. The opportunity to take kids with disciplinary problems and make them your kids—to get them to trust you and do what they need to do—is the most rewarding part of teaching.

> One little girl in my kindergarten class had neurological problems, but all the children joined together in helping her. By the end of the year, she was kicking and screaming,

not because she had to come to school, but because she had to leave! (Sallie Mae Corporation 1994, 5, 11).

Though it is beyond the scope of this book to present in-depth instructional strategies to address students' diverse learning needs, the general guidelines presented in Figure 9.5 are appropriate for teaching all learners. In addition, attention to three key areas will enable you to create a truly inclusive classroom: collabora-

FIGURE 9.5 Examples of instructional strategies for teaching all learners (Source: Pamela Maniet-Bellerman, *Mainstreaming Children with Learning Disabilities: A Guide to Accompany "L.D." Does NOT Mean Learning Dumb!* Pittsburgh: Upward Bound Press; as presented in R. R. McCown and Peter Roop, *Educational Psychology and Classroom Practice: A Partnership*, Boston: Allyn and Bacon, 1992, pp. 424–425.)

1. Present material on tape for students who cannot read successfully. School volunteers, older students, or parents can be asked to make recordings of assigned material.

2. Allow students to tape-record answers if writing is difficult or their handwriting is illegible.

3. Provide lots of visual reminders (pictures, maps, charts, graphs) for students who have trouble listening or attending.

4. Present handouts that are clear, legible, and uncrowded. Blurred copies [can be] very hard for [students with disabilities] to read.

5. Break directions and assignments into small steps. Completion of each step is an accomplishment—reward it.

6. Give tests orally if the child has trouble with reading, spelling, or writing. Testing that demonstrates what the student knows rather than language skills gives you a clearer picture of the student's abilities. The student demonstrates abilities, not disabilities.

7. Emphasize quality rather than quantity of writing.

8. Be consistent with directions, rules, discipline, and organization.

9. Arrange the class schedule so that the exceptional student does not miss important activities when he or she goes to the resource room.

10. Dispense encouragement freely but fairly. If students make errors, help them find the correct answers, and then reward them.

11. Discover the exceptional student's strengths and special interests. Capitalize on them in the regular classroom.

12. Carefully establish routines so that the student does not become further handicapped by the confusion of unclear expectations.

13. Arrange desks, tables, and chairs so every person can be easily seen and every word easily heard. Remember, students with hearing impairments need to see your face as you speak.

14. If possible, schedule difficult subjects when there are no outside noises, such as a class at recess.

15. Provide carrels or screens—an "office"—for students who are easily distracted.

16. When checking students' work, check correct answers rather than incorrect answers. The student is still informed of mistakes, but sees his or her successes emphasized.

17. Allow the exceptional student to tape lectures or arrange for a classmate who writes neatly to use carbon paper. Either the carbon copy or a copy of the teacher's notes can be given to the exceptional student.

18. Correct deficient lighting, glare from windows, and light-blocking partitions. Small light problems can be distractions for some exceptional students.

19. Fit the furniture to the child. Discomfort leads to distraction and restlessness.

20. Generally, become sensitive to the obstacles which prevent the exceptional student from exercising his or her abilities.

tive consultation, partnerships with parents, and assistive technology for special learners.

COLLABORATIVE CONSULTATION

One approach to meeting the needs of all students is known as **collaborative consultation,** an approach in which a classroom teacher meets with one or more other professionals (a special educator, school psychologist, or resource teacher, for example) to focus on the learning needs of one or more students. The following first-year teacher describes how collaborative consultation enabled her to meet the needs of a special student.

> I taught a Down's syndrome child who was very frustrated. I convened a meeting that included district experts, his parent, and a resource teacher, suggesting a change in educational strategy. All agreed to pilot the plan, and things have worked more smoothly ever since. It was a very rewarding experience (Sallie Mae Corporation 1994, 11).

Collaborative consultation is based on mutuality and reciprocity (Hallahan and Kauffman 1994), and participants assume equal responsibility for meeting students' needs. Friend and Bursuck (1996) make the following suggestions for working with a consultant:

1. Do your homework. Working with a consultant should be an intervention you seek only after you have attempted to identify and resolve the problem by analyzing the situation yourself, talking about it with parents, presenting it at a grade-level meeting, and so on.
2. Demonstrate your concern with documentation. At your initial meeting with a consultant, bring samples of student work, notes recounting specific incidents in the classroom, records of correspondence with parents, and other concrete information.
3. Participate actively. If you clearly describe the problem, contribute specific information about your expectations for how the situation should change, offer your ideas on how best to intervene to resolve the problem, implement the selected strategy carefully, and provide your perception of the effectiveness of the strategy, you will find consultation very helpful.
4. Carry out the consultant's suggestions carefully and systematically.
5. Contact the consultant if problems occur (Friend and Bursuck 1996, 96).

WORKING WITH PARENTS

In addition to working with education professionals to meet the learning needs of all students, effective teachers develop good working relationships with parents. Parents of exceptional children can be a source of valuable information about the characteristics, abilities, and needs of their children; they can be helpful in securing necessary services for their children; and they can assist you by reviewing skills at home and praising their children for their learning. The power of partnerships with parents is evident, for instance, at Central Park East Secondary School (CPESS) in Harlem where the only special admissions requirement is that parents must take an active role in their child's education. Parents apply in writing to the school, along with their children, and at least one parent must promise to work closely with teachers. As a result, school attendance is 100 percent, 90 percent of students graduate, and 95 percent of those go on to four-year colleges and universities (Smith 1995).

Communicating Effectively with Parents of Exceptional Students

The following case illustrates the importance of communicating effectively with parents of exceptional students. Read the case and then respond to the questions at the end in a Teacher's Journal entry.

> Chris' parents, Mr. and Mrs. Werner, arrived promptly for their after-school meeting with Ms. MacDougal, the middle school inclusion facilitator, and Mr. Saunders, the seventh-grade team leader. Mrs. Werner began by declaring that the school was discriminating against Chris because of her learning disability. Mr. Werner asserted that Chris was not to be singled out in any way because of her special needs and that he had learned that she was receiving tutoring during a lunch-period study hall. He strongly expressed that the family provides tutoring for Chris so that this type of discrimination does not occur at school. Further, Mr. and Mrs. Werner showed the teachers examples of modified assignment sheets, another example of discrimination. When Mr. Saunders started to explain that he was modifying Chris' work so she could learn more in his class, Mr. Werner cut him off, stating that a teacher's poor instructional practices was no excuse to destroy a child's self-concept through public humiliation (Friend and Bursuck 1996, 74).

Imagine that you are Mr. Saunders—how would you want Ms. MacDougal to react to the parents' concerns? What are the keys to effective communication between teachers and parents of exceptional students?

ASSISTIVE TECHNOLOGY FOR SPECIAL LEARNERS

The ability of teachers to create inclusive classrooms has increased dramatically as a result of many technological advances that now make it easier for exceptional students to learn and communicate. For example, computer-based word processing and math tutorials can greatly assist students with learning disabilities in acquiring literacy and computational skills. Students with hearing impairments can communicate with other students by using telecommunications equipment, and students with physical disabilities can operate computers through voice commands or with a single switch or key. Among the recent developments in **assistive technology** are the following:

1. talking word processor
2. speech synthesizer
3. touch-sensitive computer screens
4. computer screen image enlarger
5. teletypewriter (TTY) (connects to telephone and types a spoken message to another TTY)
6. customized computer keyboards
7. ultrasonic head controls for computers
8. voice-recognition computers
9. television closed-captioning
10. Kurzweil reading machine (scans print and reads it aloud)

On the Internet, technology-related special education resources and curriculum materials are available. One of these sites, The National Center to Improve Practice in Special Education Through Technology, Media and Materials

(http://hkein.school.net.hk/ Overseas/WWWEDGOV/pubs/TeachersGuide/NCIP.html)

also maintains discussion forums for teachers of students with disabilities. Clearly, the dazzling revolution in microelectronics will continue to yield new devices to enhance the learning of all students.

Dear Mentor

NOVICE AND EXPERT TEACHERS ON PARENTAL INVOLVEMENT

Dear Lori,

I believe your concerns are justified in regard to parental involvement. Parents often share your same concerns. Creating communication is essential. Let me suggest a few strategies that have worked for me in this area.

A class newsletter for parents can provide information about their children's class as well as invite participation. I distribute a newsletter the first day of school. In it, I introduce myself, my family, and desires to further the educational development of their child. The newsletter conveys my commitment and passion for teaching. I also invite parents to observe a school day in which they can experience the educational process and become familiar with me as a teacher and person.

Another strategy I have found to be quite successful is the use of video. I often videotape classroom learning and activities. Students then share the tapes with their families at home. Parents are able to experience the classroom environment and how exciting learning can be. The tapes can become a subject of conversation between student and parent, often leading to greater motivation to achieve, and between teacher and parent, often leading to parent-generated ideas and greater family involvement.

Dear Mentor,

When I think about my first time teaching, I have concerns about dealing with parents. I know that parental involvement and support have a significant impact on student achievement. What strategies have you used to gain this type of involvement, and what are some alternatives when parental support is just not possible?

Lori Iwamoto

When parental support is just not possible, you may have to pursue others, such as grandparents or older siblings, or other family members who sometimes are the significant adults in the student's education. Once again videos can be a tool to involve these people when there are time constraints or other barriers to communication.

Parents often are unsure of how to react to teachers and of the nature and importance of parents' roles in children's education. Again, communication is the key. Using the newsletter and video strategies described above, I have been successful in getting parents not only to be involved in their child's learning process but also to contribute to the entire class.

Paul A. Flores
Elementary School Teacher

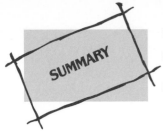

SUMMARY

How Do Students' Needs Change as They Develop?

- People move through different stages of cognitive, psychosocial, and moral development throughout their life spans.
- Piaget maintains that children, who reason differently than adults, pass through four stages of cognitive development as they mature. Effective teachers are aware of the characteristics of school-age children's thinking during three of these stages: the preoperational stage, the concrete operations stage, and the formal operations stage.
- According to Erikson's model of psychosocial development, people pass through eight stages of emotional and social development throughout their lives. Each stage is characterized by a "crisis" with a positive and negative pole. Healthy development depends upon a satisfactory, positive resolution of each crisis.
- Kohlberg believes that moral development, the reasoning people use to decide between right and wrong, evolves through three levels. Evidence suggests that males may base their moral reasoning on rights and rules, and females on altruism and self-sacrifice. Many teachers and schools emphasize character education to "teach" moral reasoning and values.
- Maslow suggests that human growth and development depends upon how well the individual's biological and psychological needs have been met. According to his hierarchy of needs model, people must satisfy their survival and safety needs before addressing "higher" needs such as self-actualization.
- Teachers must be aware of the developmental stresses and tasks students encounter during childhood and early and late adolescence.

How Do Students Vary in Intelligence?

- There are conflicting definitions of *intelligence;* they range from "what IQ tests measure" to "goal-directed adaptive behavior." Some theorists believe intelligence is a single, basic ability, though recent research suggests that there are many forms of intelligence.
- According to Howard Gardner's theory of multiple intelligences, there are at least seven human intelligences.
- Students differ in their learning modes—the patterns of behavior they prefer to use while learning. While there is conflict about the concept of learning modes, effective teachers are aware of differences among students regarding their preferences for learning activities.

How Do Students Vary in Ability and Disability?

- Some students are "exceptional" because they have abilities or disabilities that distinguish them from other students. Students with physical, cognitive, or emotional disabilities and students who are gifted and talented have unique learning needs.
- There is a lack of agreement regarding the definition of *learning disability (LD).* Teachers can identify students with learning disabilities by noting difficulties they have acquiring and processing new information. Learning disabilities are the most common disability among students, with attention deficit hyperactiv-

ity disorder (ADHD) and attention deficit disorder (ADD) the most common learning disabilities.

■ There are many forms of giftedness. Among the approaches used to meet the learning needs of gifted students are acceleration, self-directed or independent study, individual education programs, special or magnet schools, and weekend and summer programs.

What Are Special Education, Mainstreaming, and Inclusion?

■ Special education includes a variety of educational services to meet the needs of exceptional students. Key provisions of the Individuals with Disabilities Education Act (IDEA) include least restrictive environment, individualized education program (IEP), confidentiality of records, and due process.

■ *Mainstreaming* is the process of integrating students with disabilities into regular classrooms.

■ *Inclusion* integrates all students with disabilities into regular classrooms, with the support of special education services as necessary. *Full inclusion* is the integration of students with disabilities in general education classrooms at all times regardless of the severity of the disability.

How Can You Teach All Learners in Your Classroom?

■ Though challenging, teachers have a responsibility to create inclusive classrooms that address the developmental, individual, and exceptional learning needs of all students.

■ Through collaborative consultation, an arrangement whereby the regular classroom teacher collaborates with other education professionals, teachers can meet the needs of exceptional students. Collaborative consultation is based on mutuality and reciprocity, and all participants assume responsibility for meeting students' needs.

■ By developing effective relationships with parents of exceptional students, teachers acquire valuable information and support.

■ An array of assistive technologies and resources is available to help exceptional students learn and communicate in inclusive classrooms.

KEY TERMS AND CONCEPTS

Teacher's Journal

1. Through a series of vignettes, relate Erikson's stages of psychosocial development to your own experiences as a child and as an adolescent. How did sources of stress, psychosocial crises, and your resolutions of them affect your learning in school?

2. Do you know your IQ or recall participating in an IQ test? How do you regard yourself in terms of intelligence and how did you come by your beliefs about your intelligence? Do you think these beliefs influenced your motivation, choices, and achievement as a student? Do you think they influenced your school or class placements? Do you think they influenced the way your teachers and peers responded to you? What criteria would you use now to evaluate the fairness of IQ testing and the appropriateness of use of IQ scores?

3. Recount an experience you had as an exceptional student or one that involved a person with disabilities. What did you learn from this experience or from your reflection upon it that could help you as a teacher?

Teacher's Database

1. Investigate sources of information on students with disabilities or exceptional learners in the ERIC Clearinghouse on Disabilities and Gifted Education. The databases in this clearinghouse are maintained by the Council for Exceptional Children (CEC) in Reston, Virginia.

ericed@inet.ed.gov

Then visit the National Information Center for Children and Youth with Disabilities (NICHCY) on the SpecialNet. This government clearinghouse answers questions about disability issues, refers you to disability organizations, provides fact sheets, and identifies relevant educational resources in your state.

nichcy@capcon.net

2. Observe children online. Locate newsgroups by and for children and youth. As an adult you may not be allowed to participate, but in many cases you will be invited to visit (called "lurking" in Internet jargon). Try the following sites first. What educational interests, needs, and concerns do students share with one another? How might visiting students' sites online be viewed as an extension of your field experiences as an education major or a student teacher? What teacher observation techniques and protocols could you use in this situation? What are some ethical concerns about this practice? How might any new knowledge of students gained in this way help to make you a more effective teacher?

Student Newsgroups:

   k12.chat.elementary—elementary students' forum for grades K–5
   k12.chat.junior—elementary students' focus groups for grades 6–8
   k12.chat.senior—high school students' forum
   alt.kids-talk—open discussion among children

Observations and Interviews

1. Observe in a classroom that has exceptional students. What steps does the teacher take to meet the needs of these students? Interview the teacher to determine what he or she sees as the challenges and rewards of teaching exceptional students.

2. Observe and interview a student in the age group you wish to teach to conduct a brief case study that focuses on common developmental tasks for that age group and the areas of individual differences highlighted in this chapter. Then prepare a written portrait of the student. To help you with this activity, ask your instructor for handouts M9.1, "Who Are the Students in the Classroom?," and M9.2, "Conversations with Students in the School."

3. Visit a school at the level you plan to teach. Interview the counselor, asking questions about the problems that bring students to the counselor most often. If possible, shadow the school counselor for a day.

4. Attend an extracurricular event such as a high school basketball game or Little League soccer game. Observe the students on the field as well as any students watching the players. Notice the differences among the students in terms of their physical appearance, clothing and hairstyles, athletic abilities, social skills, and evidence of personal interests and confidence. Share your observations in class.

Professional Portfolio

For a grade level and content area you are preparing to teach, identify learning activities that address each of the seven multiple intelligences identified by Gardner. For example, you might plan activities such as the following. For one activity in each category, list the preparations you would need to make and/or the materials you would need to gather, and add this information to your portfolio.

Logical-Mathematical
- Design an experiment on . . .
- Describe the rules for a new board game called . . .

Linguistic
- Write a short story about . . .
- Write a biographical sketch of . . .

Musical
- Write song lyrics for . . .
- Locate music that sounds like . . .

Spatial
- Draw, paint, or sculpt a . . .
- Create an advertisement for . . .

Bodily-Kinesthetic
- Role play a person who is . . .
- Do a dance that shows . . .

Intrapersonal
- Assess your ability to . . .
- Describe how you feel about . . .

Interpersonal
- Show one or more of your classmates how to . . .
- In a small group, construct a . . .

Simply stated, a school becomes a community
for learning when it is:

- a purposeful place,
- a communicative place,
- a just place,
- a disciplined place,
- a caring place, and
- a celebrative place.

—Ernest L. Boyer
The Basic School: A Community for Learning

chapter 10

Creating a Community of Learners

FOCUS QUESTIONS

1. What determines the culture of the classroom?
2. How can you create a positive learning environment?
3. What are the keys to successful classroom management?
4. What teaching methods do effective teachers use?
5. What are some characteristics of effective teaching?

Terry-Sue slid lower in her seat, propped her feet on the chair in front, her head on the desk behind, closed her eyes, and slipped away. Philip sat alert, hands folded on a pile of books and binders, pencils sharpened, ready for whatever I had to dish out. Steven sat muttering self-deprecating remarks to anyone who would listen; no one would, we had heard them all before.

After writing about Shakespeare's England and reading Charles and Mary Lamb's version of *Romeo and Juliet*, we were ready to begin reading the play. I had no idea how the language would be handled by students of such low ability, so I began reading aloud to them. Previously, I had told them that there were two things that they must always do when reading: have a pencil in-hand for underlining key words and putting question marks in the margins beside points that they wanted to return to for clarification and use a finger or pencil for tracking while reading.

We read line-by-line, scene-by-scene, discussing as we went along, until we had finished Act I. They wrote about what they had read and heard, interpreting and summarizing on their own. They shared their writing and talked some more. It was late December, time to wish each other happy holidays and go home.

Throughout the holidays I found myself trying to puzzle out ways to make the reading easier. The vocabulary seemed to be just too difficult. At one point I considered abandoning the play, but I knew that this would have been a big disappointment for all of us and we could not afford such a setback. Nothing was resolved when I returned to work in January. As it turned out, David had the answer.

David scoots by me and into the classroom, tapping my shoulder (the far one) as he goes by. Reflexively, I look the wrong way to see who has touched me. He laughs, his big, crossed, brown eyes twinkling with delight, "Gotcha!" he cries. I laugh, too. We do this every day.

David loves to be the center of things. To this end, he has entertained classes year after year with clever, clown-ish antics, until this year he was suspended from school and the bus for continuing to "moon" the neighborhood after repeated discussions and warnings. His seemingly harmless pranks have evolved into a pattern of disruptive behavior. David is now trying hard to break out.

"How come you never let us read aloud?" he asks. Perched on my stool at the front of the class, I feel choked as I scrounge for an answer. I think all the wrong things and I know that they are the wrong things . . . "your skills are too weak, you're not capable, it's too hard . . ." I choose to lie. "I was just about to ask for volunteers," I answer. David's hand shoots up. The others, all but Terry-Sue, follow his lead. "Act II, scene i, *Romeo and Juliet*," he falters and then continues reading laboriously, monotone through to the end of the first speech. The group, including Terry-Sue this time, responds by clapping, pounding their desks, and shouting out the names of the parts that they want to read. David beams at me and I beam back. We are on the road to Verona.

■

The opening scenario for this chapter, written by Judith McBride, a special education teacher at a suburban high school, illustrates how teachers make decisions based on the unfolding dynamics of classroom life. Sensitivity to the ebb and flow of classroom events is the hallmark of a professional, reflective teacher. For teacher education students such as yourself, making the transition between the study of teaching and actual teaching can be a challenge. The more you understand how "the classroom learning environment develops gradually, in response to the teacher's communication of expectations, modeling of behavior, and approach to classroom management" (Good and Brophy 1994, 131), the better prepared you will be to make the transition smoothly.

WHAT DETERMINES THE CULTURE OF THE CLASSROOM ?

As you learned in Chapter 8, one definition of *culture* is the way of life common to a group of people. In much the same way, each classroom develops its own culture. The culture of a classroom is determined by the manner in which teachers and students participate in common activities.

The activities that teachers and students engage in are influenced by several factors. "There are characteristics of the physical milieu (building, materials, resources, etc.) and social milieu (norms, rules, expectations, grouping, climate, distribution of power, accountability structure) that affect life in . . . classroom[s]"

(Woolfolk and Galloway 1985, 80). Anita Woolfolk and Charles Galloway have identified the following six "interdependent and interacting sources of influence" on classroom culture:

1. The activity format, procedure, or delivery system for instruction
2. The academic content itself
3. The physical, spatial, and temporal constraints of the particular classroom
4. The accountability structure: how, when, where, against what standards, and by whom student responses (oral and written) will be evaluated
5. The players in the classroom drama
6. The dynamic interaction among participants, activities, content, materials, etc. (Woolfolk and Galloway 1985, 80–81).

CLASSROOM CLIMATE

Part of the environment of the classroom is **classroom climate**—the atmosphere or quality of life in a classroom. The climate of your classroom will be determined by how you interact with your students and "by the manner and degree to which you exercise authority, show warmth and support, encourage competitiveness or cooperation, and allow for independent judgment and choice" (Borich 1996, 470).

In addition to promoting learning, the classroom climate should make students feel safe and respected. In light of the finding in *The Metropolitan Life Survey of the American Teacher 1996, Students Voice their Opinions on: Their Education, Teachers and Schools* that 42 percent of students would give their teachers a grade of "C" or worse on "treating students with respect," it is important that your classroom fosters respect for others and be a place where students feel supported while learning.

Classroom climates are complex and multidimensional; their character is determined by a wide array of variables, many of which are beyond the teacher's control. Nevertheless, our observations of high-performing teachers have confirmed that they take specific steps to create classroom climates with the following eight characteristics:

- a productive, task-oriented focus
- group cohesiveness
- open, warm relationships between teacher and students
- cooperative, respectful interactions among students
- low levels of tension, anxiety, and conflict
- humor
- high expectations
- frequent opportunities for student input regarding classroom activities

These dimensions of classroom climates are within teachers' spheres of influence and are promoted, consciously or unconsciously, by their styles of communicating and treating students. Consider the following description of a classroom in terms of the preceding climate dimensions:

The front room is alive with activity. David and Maurice are building a runway with wooden blocks. Darlene, their teacher, sits in the middle of the block pile offering support and assistance. "Beautiful, David. It's going really well. Here, Maurice, use this big one, get some more of the long ones from over there."

David and Maurice are intent on building the longest runway they can make. Carl comes and joins them, but they hardly notice. Their attention is on the task at hand. Shaquan and Ebony occupy a small block building in one corner where they seem to be putting dolls to bed and then waking them up. "This is my hotel," says Ebony. "And it's only for me and my friends."

Maurice pushes a perilously high stack of long blocks slowly across the room toward the runway. Just as it arrives at its destination, it crashes loudly to the floor, and David laughs and rushes up to untangle the wreckage and keep the runway going.

"Teacher," Pete wails. "Someone took my glue."

"Doesn't everyone have a cup?" Marilyn asks.

"Yea, but she dipped in mine."

"Okay, Natika. This is yours. And Pete, there's more if you run out." Changing directions, she asks, "Doesn't glue feel funny on your fingers?"

Pete frowns and says, "It's yukky." Afrinique dips her whole hand in the glue and, watching the thick white drops fall back into the cup, smiles contentedly (Ayers 1989, 98).

How would you describe this classroom climate using the eight dimensions above? What changes in the teacher's behavior could transform the overall climate?

Although teachers influence the classroom climate by the way they regard and treat students, they also shape it by their instructional decisions. David Johnson and Roger Johnson, two researchers in the area of classroom communication and dynamics, delineate three types of interactions promoted by instructional decisions: cooperative or positive interdependence, competitive or negative interdependence, and individualistic or no interdependence (Johnson and Johnson 1994). To illustrate the three types, Johnson and Johnson suggest that a group project to measure classroom furniture would promote cooperative interdependence; a race to be the first student to measure the furniture would call for competitive interdependence; and having a student measure the furniture independently would be an example of no interdependence. Johnson and Johnson believe that teachers should use strategies that foster all three forms of interactions, depending on their instructional goals, but that, ideally, the emphasis should be on furthering cooperative interdependence.

What words would you use to describe the apparent climate of this classroom? In what ways does this classroom appear to be an effective learning environment? What would you look for to determine if this is a caring classroom?

CLASSROOM DYNAMICS

Interactions between teachers and students are the very core of teaching. The quality of these interactions reveals to students how the teacher feels about them. Teachers who empathize with students, genuinely respect them, and expect them to learn are more likely to develop a classroom climate free of management problems. In classrooms with positive group dynamics, teachers and students work toward a common goal—learning. In classrooms with negative interactions, the energy of teachers and students may be channeled into conflict rather than into learning.

There is no precise formula to guarantee success in the classroom; however, Robert Rosenthal, one of the first researchers to point out how teacher expectations influence student achievement, has suggested four rules of thumb that teachers can follow to increase student achievement through positive interactions:

1. Establish warm social-emotional relationships with children
2. Give students more feedback about their performance
3. Teach students more (and more difficult) material
4. Give students more opportunities to respond and to ask questions (Rosenthal 1974).

TEACHER COMMUNICATION   Successful teachers possess effective communication skills. They express themselves verbally and nonverbally (and in writing) in a manner that is clear, concise, and interesting. They "are able to communicate clearly and directly to their students without wandering, speaking above students' levels of comprehension, or using speech patterns that impair the clarity of what is being presented" (Borich 1996, 11). In addition, they are good listeners. Their students feel that not only are they heard, they are understood.

Effective teachers relish the live, thinking-on-your-feet dimensions of classroom communication. Their communication skills enable them to respond appropriately to events that could sabotage the plans of less effective teachers: a student's clowning, announcements on the public address system, interruptions by other teachers or parents, students' private arguments or romances, or simply the mood of the class at that particular time.

One of the findings in the studies of teachers' thinking is that teachers who ignore student reactions and continue to focus on the lesson plan objectives are not as effective as those who attend to and adjust to students' responses. Closely related to this is the finding that experienced teachers were better able to read their students and thus could adjust the content of the lessons according to their students' abilities and interest levels. *The Harvard Education Letter*'s (July 1986, 7) summary of this finding applies to elementary teachers, but it could be extended to secondary teachers as well:

> Experienced teachers, compared to beginners, know a great deal about children in general—what they do outside of school, how many are likely to need special help, and so on—and analyze classroom events in a more sophisticated way. . . .

> While all teachers reprimanded the unruly and aided the confused, experienced teachers were five times as likely as novices to respond to "positive cues"—a giggle of excitement, an item of news, a nod of comprehension, or an unexpected insight. . . .

> At all points in the processes of planning and teaching, experienced teachers keep the responses of their particular students near the center of their minds.

STUDENT INTERACTION   In addition to engaging in positive, success-oriented interactions with their students, effective teachers foster positive, cooperative interactions among students. As a result, students feel supported by their peers and free to devote their attention to learning. Richard Schmuck and Patricia Schmuck (1971) describe the climate of such classrooms as "mature" and "self-renewing." Their research on classroom group processes has led them to identify the four sequential stages of group development portrayed in Figure 10.1 on page 314.

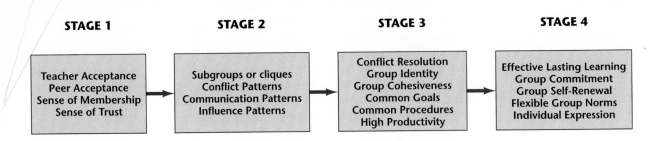

STAGE 1	STAGE 2	STAGE 3	STAGE 4
Teacher Acceptance Peer Acceptance Sense of Membership Sense of Trust	Subgroups or cliques Conflict Patterns Communication Patterns Influence Patterns	Conflict Resolution Group Identity Group Cohesiveness Common Goals Common Procedures High Productivity	Effective Lasting Learning Group Commitment Group Self-Renewal Flexible Group Norms Individual Expression

FIGURE 10.1 Characteristics of groups at four stages of development

During Stage 1 of a class's group development, students are on their best behavior. Teachers who are aware of this "honeymoon period" use it to their advantage; they discuss and teach classroom rules and procedures, outline their goals, and deliberately set the classroom tone and standards they want. During Stage 2, teachers seeking to promote group development are advised to encourage student participation and communication and to discourage the formation of cliques.

Groups that have met the requirements of the preceding stages move into Stage 3, which lasts for the majority of the expected life of the group (i.e., the semester or the school year). This stage is characterized by the group's willingness to set clear goals, share tasks, and agree on deadlines. At Stage 4, the final stage, group members fully accept responsibility for the group's quality of life, and they continuously strive to improve it.

In addition, teachers who effectively orchestrate group processes in their classrooms recognize that, for good or ill, students as well as teachers exert leadership in classrooms. Wise teachers quickly identify student leaders and develop ways to focus their leadership abilities on the attainment of goals that benefit the entire class. Teachers should also encourage their students to develop leadership skills.

HOW CAN YOU CREATE A POSITIVE LEARNING ENVIRONMENT

A positive classroom climate and positive classroom dynamics are prerequisites for a good learning environment. Creating and then maintaining a positive learning environment is a multidimensional challenge. While no single set of strategies will ensure success in all situations, educational researchers have identified teacher behaviors that tend to be associated with high levels of student learning. Effective teachers also know *how* to use these behaviors and *for what purposes* they are best suited. The following sections address three important dimensions of positive learning environments: the caring classroom, the physical classroom environment, and classroom organization, including procedures for grouping students for instruction and managing time.

THE CARING CLASSROOM

At this point in your preparation to become a teacher, you may feel uncertain of your ability to create a positive classroom climate and to orchestrate the complex dynamics of the classroom so that you and your students become a cohesive, productive, and mutually supportive group. In your quest to achieve these aims, it will help to remember that an authentic spirit of caring is at the heart of an effective learning environment. "[C]aring interactions between teachers, students, and parents often make the difference between positive school experiences and frustration or alienation" (Chaskin and Rauner 1995, 667–668).

How do teachers establish a **caring classroom?** First, teachers demonstrate caring through their efforts to help all students learn to their fullest potential. "Teachers display genuine caring for students when they find out about students' abilities and motivations. They continue this pervasive caring by providing all their students with the appropriate amount of support, structure, and expectations they need in order to be self-directed, responsible learners" (Zehm and Kottler 1993, 54). In addition, teachers realize that *how* they speak and listen to students determines the extent to which students believe their teachers care about them. Knowledge about the speaking and listening that occur in classes taught by effective, caring teachers was increased greatly by the Beginning Teacher Evaluation Study (BTES), a pioneering long-term study that in one phase focused on twenty second-grade and twenty fifth-grade classrooms. On the basis of student achievement during two-week units of instruction in reading and mathematics, the researchers found that the behaviors of the more effective teachers created a climate of care.

> [They] enjoyed teaching and were generally polite and pleasant in their daily interactions. They were more likely to call their students by name, attend carefully to what they said, accept their statements of feeling, praise their successes, and involve them in decision making.
>
> The more effective teachers were less likely to ignore, belittle, harass, shame, put down, or exclude their students. Their students were less likely to defy or manipulate the teachers. Thus, the more effective classes were characterized by mutual respect, whereas the less effective classes sometimes showed evidence of conflict (Brophy and Good 1986, 350–351).

In a comprehensive review of 8,000 studies of how elementary- and secondary-level students learn best, Herbert Walberg confirmed the findings of the earlier BTES study—caring interaction between teachers and students is vital to student achievement: "Students who perceive their classroom morale as friendly, satisfying, goal-directed, and challenging tend to learn more. Those who perceive student cliques, disorganization, apathy, favoritism, and friction learn less" (Walberg 1991, 52).

While students learn best in caring classrooms, Nel Noddings has suggested that students also must learn to care for others. Toward this end, she recommends reorganizing the school curriculum around "themes of care" and points out that "educators must recognize that caring for students is fundamental in teaching and that developing people with a strong capacity for care is a major objective of responsible education" (Noddings 1995, 678).

THE CLASSROOM AS A PHYSICAL ENVIRONMENT

When you become a teacher, the physical environment you work in will probably be similar to that of schools you attended. However, we encourage you, with the help of your students, to make your surroundings as safe, pleasant, and convenient as possible. Fresh air; plants; clean, painted walls; displays of students' work; a comfortable reading or resource area; and a few prints or posters can enhance the quality of teacher-student relationships. Seating arrangements and the placement of other classroom furniture also do much to shape the classroom environment. Although seating by rows may be very appropriate for whole-group instruction or examinations, other arrangements may be more beneficial for other activities. For example, you can enhance small-group activities by moving desks into small clusters in different parts of the room. Figure 10.2 shows the arrangement of a classroom at an exemplary elementary school. The room is designed to encourage students to learn through discovery at learning centers located around the room.

However you design your classroom, take care to ensure that seating arrangements do not reduce the opportunity of some students to learn. For example, students in some classrooms receive more attention if they are seated in the "action zone," the middle front-row seats and seats on the middle aisle. Teachers often stand near this area and unknowingly give students seated there more opportunities to speak.

FIGURE 10.2 Learning centers in an elementary classroom

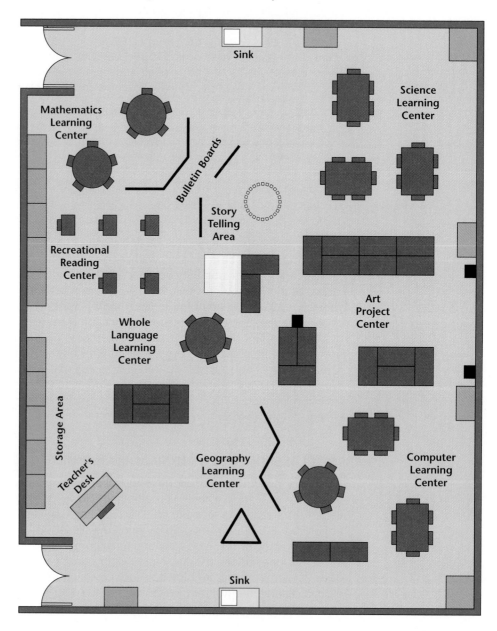

CLASSROOM ORGANIZATION

A factor in positive learning environments is **classroom organization**—the way teachers and students are grouped for instruction, the way learning tasks are structured, and other resources used. The following sections focus on these aspects of classroom organization.

GROUPING STUDENTS BY ABILITY   Two common approaches for grouping students on the basis of shared characteristics are between-class ability grouping, often called tracking, and within-class ability grouping. Students who attend schools where **between-class ability grouping** is practiced are assigned to classes on the basis of ability or achievement (usually determined by scores on standardized tests). Another form of between-class ability grouping, especially at the high school level, is based on students' goals after graduation. Many high schools, for example, have a college preparatory track, a vocational track, and a business education track.

Research suggests that, for the most part, between-class ability grouping does not contribute to greater achievement (Good and Brophy 1994). Supporters nevertheless claim that teachers are better able to meet the needs of students in homogeneous groupings. Among the alternatives to between-class ability grouping are heterogeneous (or mixed-ability) grouping, regrouping by subject area, the Joplin Plan (regrouping students for reading instruction by ability across grade levels), and cooperative learning (Manning and Lucking 1993).

Within-class ability grouping often is used for instruction in reading and mathematics within a class, where a teacher instructs students in homogeneous, small groups. Within-class grouping is used widely in elementary classrooms. Perhaps you can recall learning to read in a small group with a name such as the Eagles, the Redbirds, or the Mustangs. Like tracking, within-class ability grouping can heighten preexisting differences in achievement between groups of students, especially if teachers give high-achieving groups more attention. Also, once students are grouped, they tend not to be regrouped, even when differences in achievement are reduced.

At best, evidence to support student groupings is mixed. Whether students are grouped on the basis of ability, curricular interests, or disabling condition, there is a danger that some group labels can evoke negative expectations, causing teachers to "underteach" certain students, and their peers to isolate or reject them. The most serious consequence, of course, is that students so labeled are taught to feel inadequate, inferior, and limited in their options for growth.

GROUPING STUDENTS FOR COOPERATIVE LEARNING   **Cooperative learning** is an approach to teaching in which students work in small groups, or teams, sharing the work and helping one another complete assignments. Student-Team-Learning, for example, is a cooperative approach teachers use to increase the basic skills achievement of at-risk students. In cooperative learning arrangements, students are motivated to learn in small groups through rewards that are made available to the group as a whole and to individual members of the group. Cooperative learning includes the following key elements:

- Small groups (four to six students) work together on learning activities.
- Assignments require that students help one another while working on a group project.
- In competitive arrangements, groups may compete against one another.
- Group members contribute to group goals according to their talents, interests, and abilities.

Keepers of the Dream

Nel Noddings

Leader in the Challenge to Care

Nel Noddings, author of over 100 articles and chapters, a philosophy textbook, and a number of books, including the popular and influential works, *Caring* (1984) and *The Challenge to Care in Schools* (1992), is also the mother of ten children. She and her husband, a high school classmate, planned to have a large family. After they had five children very close together, they decided to adopt rather than contribute to the population explosion. Among their five additional children are three Amerasians whom they adopted through the Pearl Buck Welcome House. When Noddings suggests that teachers view education as "parents who are engaged in the task of

"Keep reflecting on everything you do. . . ."

raising a huge heterogeneous family" (1992, 177), she brings her heart and personal experience to the metaphor.

Noddings, a Stanford University professor and leader of a current movement to emphasize care in schools, describes herself as "incurably domestic—I really do like family and homemaking, and I'm incurably intellectual—read all the time." She taught mathematics at the secondary level in New Jersey for many years and then sought a doctorate in philosophy at Stanford University. There she remained, teaching courses in philosophy and education, serving as dean, and writing articles on theories of knowledge.

It was through an effort to combine the twin treasures in her life, her family and her superb analytical training, that Noddings developed the concept of caring. When she introduced the idea, the feedback she received was enthusiastic; the timing of her work was well matched with Americans' growing sense of alarm over the increase

In addition, cooperative learning is an instructional method that can strengthen students' interpersonal skills. When students from different racial, ethnic, and cultural backgrounds and mainstreamed special-needs students all contribute to a common group goal, friendships increase and group members tend to view one another as more equal in status and worth. The contribution that cooperative learning can make to the culture of the classroom is expressed by a teacher as follows: "The best rewards for the teacher are those signs that cooperation is becoming second nature with the children. I'm always impressed when a group finishes its work and then, without being told or even asked, goes to help other groups" (Pearson 1979, 36). Similarly, a fifth-grade science teacher who uses cooperative learning describes how her students learn a variety of roles and responsibilities in addition to learning subject matter content:

> I have the class divided into groups of five students and each group works as a team. The job duties are as follows: principle investigator (PI), materials manager (MM), reader, recorder, and reporter. The PI is the leader of the group and helps mediate when problems occur. The PI is the only student who can come to me with questions during the actual procedure. This rule enables me to monitor the groups and also teaches the group to work independently.
>
> Students change job duties within their group [for] each activity and every six weeks students change groups. This plan gives each student the experience of working with different classmates as well as learning the responsibility of group participation through performing the different job duties.

of violence and the erosion of character and moral behavior. Schools unwittingly or unwillingly have contributed to the problem. As Noddings observes, "Secondary schools—where violence, apathy, and alienation are most evident—do little to develop the capacity to care. Today, even elementary teachers complain that the pressure to produce high test scores inhibits the work they regard as central to their mission: the development of caring and competent people" (1995, 679).

Noddings contends that our educational efforts should promote more than adequate academic achievement. "We will not achieve even that meager success unless our children believe that they themselves are cared for and learn to care for others" (1995, 675–76). Noddings' perception of caring is not that of soft sentimentality, but rather the quality of care that involves deep commitment. "When we care, we want to do our very best for the objects of our care" (1995, 676). She suggests organizing the curriculum around themes of care: caring for self, for intimate others, for strangers and global others, for the natural world and its nonhuman creatures, for the human-made world, and for ideas (1992). She encour-

ages teachers to collaborate in developing curricula according to these broad themes or to emphasize these common themes in their separate curricula. She also recommends that teachers introduce themes of care in response to events that occur in the school or neighborhood. When faced with a tragedy, schools too often rely on outside experts, "when what children really need is the continuing compassion and presence of adults who represent constancy and care in their lives" (1995, 678).

Noddings' advice to teachers is "to keep reflecting on everything you do to see whether, in fact, what you do does promote the growth of loving, lovable, competent, and caring people. When you examine everything you do—how you grade, the rules you make—from this perspective, you will change the way you operate." She agrees with John Dewey's warning: "What the best and wisest parent wants for his own child, that must the community want for all its children. Any other ideal for our schools is narrow and unlovely; acted upon, it destroys our democracy" (Dewey 1902, 3).

STRUCTURING ACTIVITY FORMATS   The activity format, procedure, or delivery system for instruction is a key element in creating positive learning environments. What the teacher does and what students do have powerful influences on learning and on the quality of classroom life. A common activity format in elementary schools consists of students doing seatwork on their own or listening to their teachers and participating in whole-class recitations. In addition, students participate in reading groups, games, and discussions; take tests; check work; view films; give reports; help clean up the classroom; and go on field trips.

A teacher must answer the question "What activity will enable me to accomplish my instructional goals?" Teachers also must realize that learning activities should meet *students'* goals; that is, the activities must be meaningful and authentic for students. **Authentic learning tasks** enable students to see the connections between classroom learning and the world beyond the classroom—both now and in the future. To understand how authentic learning tasks can motivate students to learn, reflect upon your own school experiences. Do you recall memorizing facts only because they would appear on a test? Did you ever wonder why a teacher asked you to complete a learning task? Did you ever feel that a teacher asked you to do "busywork"? What kinds of learning tasks motivated you the most?

Herbert A. Thelen (1981, 86) contends that authenticity is "the first criterion all educational activity must meet." According to Thelen, an activity is authentic for a person if he or she "feels emotionally 'involved' and mentally stimulated . . . is aware of choices and enjoys the challenge of making decisions," and feels he or she "has something to bring to the activity and that its outcome will be important" (Thelen 1981, 86). A recent nationwide study of more than 800 successfully restructured schools reported that "authentic pedagogy" helps students to (1) "construct knowledge" through the use of higher-order thinking, (2) acquire "deep knowledge" (relatively complex understandings of subject matter), (3) engage in "substantive conversations" with teachers and peers, and (4) make connections between substantive knowledge and the world beyond the classroom (Newmann and Wehlage 1995). In addition, the study found that authentic pedagogy boosts achievement for all students.

STRUCTURING THE USE OF TIME   How teachers use time affects student learning. **Allocated time** is the time teachers allocate for instruction in various areas of the curriculum. Teachers vary widely in their instructional use of time. Educational researchers Tom Good and Jere Brophy report, for example, that "some students [may receive] as much as four times more instructional time in a given subject than other students in the same grade" (Good and Brophy 1994, 32).

Researchers have shown that **time on task**—the amount of time students are actively engaged in learning activities—is directly related to learning. As anyone

FIGURE 10.3 Percent instructional time for two physical science teachers (Source: Andrew Porter, "Opportunity to Learn," *Brief No. 7* (Madison, Wisc.: Center on Organization and Restructuring of Schools, Fall 1993), p. 3.)

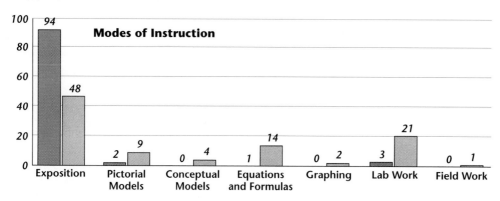

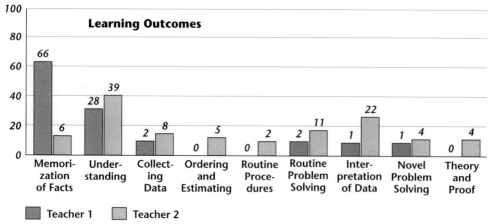

who has ever daydreamed while appearing to pay attention can confirm, time on task is difficult to measure. In response to this difficulty, Charles Fisher and his colleagues introduced the concept of **academic learning time**—the amount of time a student spends working on academic tasks with a high level of success (80 percent or higher) (Fisher et al. 1978). Not surprisingly, learning time, like allocated time, varies greatly from classroom to classroom. For example, Fisher found that some second-grade students spend between three and forty-two minutes a day successfully engaged in reading (Fisher et al. 1978).

An additional concept that is proving useful in understanding teachers' use of time in the classroom is known as **opportunity to learn (OTL)**. OTL is based on the premise that teachers should use time to provide all students with challenging content through appropriate instruction. Many states are developing OTL standards for how teachers should use time in the classroom. Figure 10.3 on the previous page, based on the results of a study of OTL in high school science and mathematics classes, shows how two physical science teachers in different states used time differently (Porter 1993).

To increase the time available for active learning, many high schools have implemented block scheduling arrangements. **Block scheduling** uses longer blocks of time each class period, with fewer periods each day. Longer blocks of time allow more in-depth coverage of subject matter and lead to deeper understanding and higher-level applications. Block scheduling also gives teachers more time to present complex concepts and students more time to practice applying those concepts to authentic problems.

PROFESSIONAL REFLECTION

Creating a Positive Learning Environment

The following excerpt is from an interview with a teaching candidate participating in a pilot study for the Praxis Series: Professional Assessments for Beginning Teachers. What steps did this teacher take to create a positive classroom culture? How did she group students for instruction? What instructional methods did she use?

> We started out reading "Tracker" by Gary Paulsen. I chose it because it's short and I believed it would challenge them and hold their attention. But there were neither lesson plans nor a teacher's guide, so I had to invent these and hope that what I was doing would work.
>
> What I did was have the students work in pairs and read to each other. This seemed to work well; the more advanced readers helped the less able ones. I also gave them a choice when it came to activities based on their reading. One set of activities I designed for the students who were struggling, and the other for the more advanced students. I never labeled them slow or fast, just gave them a choice. Given this particular group of students I feel I really should have four reading groups, but because I can't manage that many at one time, I work with two levels.
>
> I also used my background in graphic arts to make the classroom interesting. I wanted the students to feel excited coming into the room, so I decorated it with posters and diagrams and bright colors that would be visually stimulating. I even had more experienced teachers asking me for help with their classrooms (Dwyer and Villegas 1992, 3).

WHAT ARE THE KEYS TO SUCCESSFUL CLASSROOM MANAGEMENT?

For most new teachers, classroom management is a primary concern. How can you prevent discipline problems from arising and keep students productively engaged in learning activities? While effective classroom management cannot be reduced to a cookbook recipe, there are definite steps you can take to create an effective learning environment in your classroom. First, it is important to understand that **classroom management** refers to how teachers structure their learning environments to prevent, or minimize, behavior problems; *discipline* refers to the methods teachers use *after* students misbehave. *Classroom management* is prevention-oriented, while *discipline* is control-oriented. Second, it is important to recognize that "the key to good management is use of techniques that elicit student cooperation and involvement in activities and thus *prevent* problems from emerging in the first place" (Good and Brophy 1994, 131). In addition, sound classroom management techniques are based on the guidelines for creating an effective learning environment presented previously in this chapter—in other words, (1) creating a caring classroom, (2) organizing the physical classroom environment, (3) grouping students for instruction, (4) providing authentic learning tasks, and (5) structuring the use of time to maximize students' learning. Positive leadership and preventive planning thus are central to effective classroom management.

THE DEMOCRATIC CLASSROOM

Research findings suggest that teachers who allow students to participate in making decisions about the physical classroom environment, classroom rules and procedures, modifications to the curriculum, and options for learning activities also have fewer discipline problems. Students in **democratic classrooms** have both more power and more responsibility than students in conventional classrooms. On the premise that if students are to live in a democracy, they must learn to manage freedom responsibly, teachers model democracy by giving their students some choices and some control over classroom activities. For instance, Michael Manczarek, a sixth-grade teacher at a middle school in Torrance, California, establishes a "quality environment" democratically, based on the principles William Glasser outlines in *The Quality School: Managing Students Without Coercion* (1990) and *The Quality School Teacher* (1993). Manczarek begins the school year by having the class discuss questions such as What is a quality learning environment? What do students expect for themselves? for others? What do they think quality is? and What would a quality assignment be? For Manczarek, a quality environment must include trust and care: "Students need to feel that they can trust you and care for each other in order for school to be effective and enjoyable" (Abrams 1993, E2).

PREVENTIVE PLANNING

In what other ways can teachers prevent discipline problems from occurring? The key to prevention is excellent planning and an understanding of life in the classroom. In addition, teachers who have mastered the essential teaching skills have fewer discipline problems because students recognize that such teachers are prepared, well organized, and have a sense of purpose. They are confident of their ability to teach all students, and their task-oriented manner tends to discourage misbehavior.

In a seminal study of how teachers prevent discipline problems, Jacob Kounin looked at two sets of teachers: those who managed their classrooms smoothly and productively with few disruptions and those who seemed to be plagued with discipline problems and chaotic working conditions. He found that the teachers who managed their classrooms successfully had certain teaching behaviors in common: (1) they displayed the proverbial eyes-in-the-back-of-the-head, a quality of alertness Kounin referred to as *withitness*, (2) they used individual students and incidences as models to communicate to the rest of the class their expectations for student conduct—Kounin's *ripple effect*, (3) they supervised several situations at once effectively, and (4) they were adept at handling transitions smoothly (Kounin 1970). In addition to the principles of effective classroom management that emerge from Kounin's study, two key elements of preventive planning are establishing rules and procedures and organizing and planning for instruction.

ESTABLISHING RULES AND PROCEDURES Educational researchers have found that effective classroom managers have carefully planned rules and procedures, which they teach early in the year using clear explanations, examples, and practice (Evertson et al. 1994; Good and Brophy 1994). Your classroom rules should be clear, concise, reasonable, and few in number. For example, five general rules for elementary-age students might include: (1) Be polite and helpful; (2) Respect other people's property; (3) Listen quietly while others are speaking; (4) Do not hit, shove, or hurt others; and (5) Obey all school rules. Rules for the secondary level might stipulate the following: (1) Bring all needed materials to class; (2) Be in your seat and ready to work when the bell rings; (3) Respect and be polite to everyone; (4) Respect other people's property; (5) Listen and stay seated while someone else is speaking; and (6) Obey all school rules (Evertson et al. 1994).

It is important to enforce classroom rules consistently and fairly. "Consistency is a key reason why some rules are effective while others are not. Rules that are not enforced or that are not applied evenly and consistently over time result in a loss of prestige and respect for the person who has created the rules and has the responsibility for carrying them out" (Borich 1996, 364).

Procedures—the routines your students will follow as they participate in learning activities—also are essential for smooth classroom functioning and minimizing opportunities for misbehavior. How will homework be collected? How will supplies be distributed? How will housekeeping chores be completed? How will attendance be taken? How do students obtain permission to leave the classroom? Part of developing classroom rules and procedures is to decide what to do when students do not follow them. Students must be made aware of the consequences for failing to follow rules or procedures. For example, consequences for rule infractions can range from an expression of teacher disapproval to penalties such as loss of privileges, detention after school, disciplinary conference with a parent or guardian, or temporary separation from the group.

ORGANIZING AND PLANNING FOR INSTRUCTION The ability to organize instructional time, materials, and activities so that classes run smoothly are skills that will enable you to keep your students engaged in learning, thereby reducing the need for discipline. Time spent planning authentic learning activities that are appropriate to students' needs, interests, and abilities will enable you to enjoy the professional satisfaction that comes from having a well-managed classroom.

In the following words, a first-year junior high school teacher tells how organization and planning helped her to have a successful first day of teaching.

All I could think about all the way home [after the first day of school] was just that it was as smooth as it could be. I was prepared. . . . I guess I just planned well enough. I knew what I was going to say (Bullough 1989, 23).

Six months later, the same teacher comments on how she came to realize that planning for routine classroom management is also an essential teaching skill.

I thought that if you planned the *curriculum* really well, the management just falls into place. I really thought that when I was student teaching. If you are not well planned you are *going* to have problems. . . . Now [after six months], I plan a lot more things, like transition time and walking into the other room [to check on the students] (Bullough 1989, 25).

EFFECTIVE RESPONSES TO STUDENT BEHAVIOR

When student misbehavior does occur, effective teachers draw from a repertoire of problem-solving strategies. These strategies are based on their experience and common sense, their knowledge of students and the teaching-learning process, and their knowledge of human psychology. There are many structured approaches to classroom management; some are based on psychological theories of human motivation and behavior, while others reflect various philosophical views regarding the purposes of education. None of these approaches, however, is appropriate for all situations or for all teachers or for all students, and the usefulness of a given method depends, in part, on the teacher's individual personality and leadership style and ability to analyze the complex dynamics of classroom life. In addition, what works should not be the only criteria for evaluating structured or "packaged" approaches to discipline; what they teach students about their self-worth, acting responsibly, and solving problems is also important (Curwin and Mendler 1988).

SEVERITY OF MISBEHAVIOR   Your response to student misbehavior will depend, in part, on whether an infraction is mild, moderate, or severe and whether it is occurring for the first time or is part of a pattern of chronic misbehaviors. For example, a student who throws a wad of paper at another student might receive a warning for the first infraction, while another student who repeatedly throws objects at other students might receive an after-school detention. Definitions of the severity of misbehavior vary from school to school and from state to state. Table 10.1 presents one classification of examples of mild, moderate, and severe misbehaviors and several alternative responses.

CONSTRUCTIVE ASSERTIVENESS   The effectiveness of your responses to students' misbehavior will depend, in part, on your ability to use "constructive assertiveness" (Evertson et al. 1994). Constructive assertiveness "lies on a continuum between aggressive, overbearing pushiness and timid, submissive, or weak responses that allow students to trample on the teacher's and other students' rights. By using assertiveness skills you communicate to students that you are serious about teaching and about maintaining a classroom in which everyone's rights are respected" (Evertson et al. 1994, 132). Communication based on constructive assertiveness is neither hostile, sarcastic, defensive, nor vindictive; it is clear, firm, and concise.

Evertson and colleagues (1994) suggest that constructive assertiveness has three basic elements:

- A clear statement of the problem or concern.
- Body language that is unambiguous (e.g., eye contact with student, erect posture, facial expressions that match the content and tone of corrective statements).
- Firm, unwavering insistence on appropriate behavior.

TABLE 10.1 ▨▨▨▨▨▨▨▨▨▨▨▨▨▨▨▨▨▨▨▨▨▨▨▨▨▨▨▨▨▨▨▨

Mild, moderate, and severe misbehaviors and some alternative responses

Misbehaviors	Alternative Responses
Mild misbehaviors	**Mild responses**
Minor defacing of school property or property of others	Warning
	Feedback to student
Acting out (horseplaying or scuffling)	Time out
Talking back	Change of seat assignment
Talking without raising hand	Withdrawal of privileges
Getting out of seat	After-school detention
Disrupting others	Telephone/note to parents
Sleeping in class	
Tardiness	
Throwing objects	
Exhibiting inappropriate familiarity (kissing, hugging)	
Gambling	
Eating in class	
Moderate misbehaviors	**Moderate responses**
Unauthorized leaving of class	Detention
Abusive conduct towards others	Behavior contract
Noncompliant	Withdrawal of privileges
Smoking or using tobacco in class	Telephone/note to parents
Cutting class	Parent conference
Cheating, plagiarizing, or lying	In-school suspension
Using profanity, vulgar language, or obscene gestures	Restitution of damages
Fighting	Alternative school service (e.g., clean up, tutoring)
Severe misbehaviors	**Severe responses**
Defacing or damaging school property or property of others	Detention
Theft, possession, or sale of another's property	Telephone/note to parents
Truancy	Parent conference
Being under the influence of alcohol or narcotics	In-school suspension
Selling, giving, or delivering to another person alcohol, narcotics, or weapons	Removal from school or alternative school placement
Teacher assault or verbal abuse	
Incorrigible conduct, noncompliance	

(Source: Gary Bovich, *Effective Methods,* 3d ed. Englewood Cliffs, NJ: Merrill, 1996, p. 527.)

- What observation about student misbehavior, do you think, is the cartoonist making?
- In your opinion, what should happen before a teacher sends a student to the principal's office for misbehavior?
- As a teacher, how, specifically, might the severity of misbehavior affect your response to students?
- As a teacher, at what point in classroom management would you involve parents? Why?
- As Arnold's teacher, how might you work with Mrs. Jennings to prevent misbehavior in school? What would you say to her to enlist her support?
- As Arnold's teacher, how could you directly teach Arnold and his classmates how to behave? To what extent do you think this teaching would help prevent discipline problems?
- Which approach would you try first in your classroom management: Lee Cantor's assertive discipline or William Glasser's reality therapy? Why?
- For maximum effectiveness, what role would you take in a problem-solving conference with Arnold, Arnold's mother, and the principal?

"Mrs. Jennings, I asked you here so we could discuss Arnold's aggressive behavior."

Lee Cantor developed an approach to discipline based on teacher assertiveness. The approach calls on teachers to establish firm, clear guidelines for student behavior and to follow through with consequences for misbehavior. Cantor (1989, 58) comments on how he arrived at the ideas behind assertive discipline: "I found that, above all, the master teachers were assertive; that is, they *taught* students how to behave. They established clear rules for the classroom, they communicated those rules to the students, and they taught students how to follow them." **Assertive discipline** requires teachers to do the following:

1. Make clear that they will not tolerate anyone preventing them from teaching, stopping learning, or doing anything else that is not in the best interest of the class, the individual, or the teacher.
2. Instruct students clearly and in specific terms about what behaviors are desired and what behaviors are not tolerated.
3. Plan positive and negative consequences for predetermined acceptable or unacceptable behaviors.
4. Plan positive reinforcement for compliance. Reinforcement includes verbal acknowledgment, notes, free time for talking, and, of course, tokens that can be exchanged for appropriate rewards.
5. Plan a sequence of steps to punish noncompliance. These range from writing a youngster's name on the board to sending the student to the principal's office (MacNaughton and Johns 1991, 53).

TEACHER PROBLEM SOLVING   When a teacher's efforts to get a student to stop misbehaving are unsuccessful, a problem-solving conference with the student is warranted. A problem-solving conference may give the teacher additional understanding of the situation, thus paving the way for a solution. A conference also helps teacher and student understand the other's perceptions better and begin to build a more positive relationship.

The goal of a problem-solving conference is for the student to accept responsibility for his or her behavior and make a commitment to change it. While there is no "right way" to conduct a problem-solving conference, the **reality-therapy** approach to classroom management includes a conferencing procedure that is flexible and appropriate for most situations. According to William Glasser, a psychiatrist who developed the reality-therapy approach, good discipline begins with teachers who create positive, caring relationships with students and encourage them to take responsibility for their behavior. Through such relationships, teachers help misbehaving students see that the choices they make may not lead to the results they want. Glasser believes that students will usually make good choices (i.e., behave in an acceptable manner) if they experience success and know that teachers care about them.

Glasser (1969, 1975, 1986, 1990, and 1993) suggests the following steps for a problem-solving conference based on the reality-therapy approach to classroom discipline:

1. Establish warm, positive relationships with each student.
2. Have the misbehaving student evaluate and take responsibility for his or her behavior. Often, a good first step is for the teacher to ask "What are you doing?"
3. Have the student make a plan for a more acceptable way of behaving. If necessary, the student and the teacher brainstorm solutions. Agreement is reached on how the student will behave in the future and the consequences for failure to follow through.

4. Require the student to make a commitment to follow the plan.

5. Don't accept excuses for failure to follow the plan.

6. Don't use punishment or react to a misbehaving student in a punitive manner. Instead, point out to the student that there are logical consequences for failure to follow the plan.

7. Don't give up on the student. If necessary, remind the student of his or her commitment to desirable behavior. Periodically ask "How are things going?"

WHAT TEACHING METHODS DO EFFECTIVE TEACHERS USE ?

As we pointed out in our discussion of educational philosophy in Chapter 5, beliefs about teaching and learning, students, knowledge, and what is worth knowing influence the instructional methods a teacher uses. In addition, instruction is influenced by variables such as the teacher's style, learners' characteristics, the culture of the school and surrounding community, and the resources available. All of these components contribute to the "model" of teaching the teacher uses in the classroom. A model of teaching provides the teacher with rules of thumb to follow to create a particular kind of learning environment, or, as Bruce Joyce and Marsha Weil point out in *Models of Teaching* (1996, 11), a model of teaching is "a description of a learning environment."

Effective teachers use a repertoire of teaching models and assessment strategies, depending upon their situations and the goals and objectives they wish to attain. Your teaching strategies in the classroom will most likely be eclectic, that is, a combination of several models and assessment techniques. Also, as you gain classroom experience and acquire new skills and understanding, your personal model of teaching will evolve, enabling you to respond appropriately to a wider range of teaching situations.

METHODS BASED ON LEARNING NEW BEHAVIORS

Many teachers use instructional methods that have emerged from our greater understanding of how people acquire or change their behaviors. **Direct instruction,** for example, is a systematic instructional method that focuses on the transmission of knowledge and skills from the teacher (and the curriculum) to the student. Direct instruction is organized on the basis of observable learning behaviors and the actual products of learning. Generally, direct instruction is most appropriate for step-by-step knowledge acquisition and basic skill development but not appropriate for teaching less structured, higher-order skills such as writing, the analysis of social issues, and problem solving.

To help teachers be successful with direct instruction, Rosenshine and Stevens provide the following summary of the research findings from seven major studies conducted with students ranging in age from elementary to senior high school:

- Begin a lesson with a short review of previous, prerequisite learning
- Begin a lesson with a short statement of goals
- Present new material in small steps, with student practice after each step
- Give clear and detailed instructions and explanations
- Provide a high level of active practice for all students

Dear Mentor

NOVICE AND EXPERT TEACHERS ON CLASSROOM DISCIPLINE

Dear Connie,

Your question is a relevant one for all educators today. Classrooms are a microcosm of our society at large. They represent the richness that makes this country distinctive. My advice to you is to look within yourself and decide how you are going to approach this challenge. Your beliefs about diversity will determine the message your students receive regarding their value in your eyes.

If you believe diversity to be an exhilarating challenge that provides you and your students an opportunity to acquire new ways of resolving problems, your students will be likely to accept others' views and ways of interpreting the world. As a safe environment is created in your classroom and the students' defensive posture diminishes, students will be able to share their strengths with their classmates.

There are many worthwhile inservice training programs that teach conflict resolution, cooperative learning, and learner characteristics of particular ethnic groups. There are also preservice classes, graduate courses, and professional development programs on multicultural education, student-centered curriculum, and developmentally appropriate practices. If you believe that diversity in the classroom is a problem that must be addressed through a strict discipline policy, I suspect that these programs and classes would not provide you with successful results. But, if you believe that the diversity of your classroom is a vital asset, the extra inservice training will give you tools to help your students get the most from their classroom experience.

I believe the key is to set high standards of behavior for all members of your learning community, based on respect, and to provide varied and multiple opportunities for learning and sharing. All students can learn if that is what you expect of them.

> Moyra Contreras
> Teacher Mentor and
> Elementary School Principal

> ### Dear Mentor,
>
> I have many questions about my education as a teacher. I am especially concerned about dealing with student diversity and classroom discipline. What is the best way for me to prepare myself for these challenges? I have heard that some school districts require attendance at inservice professional development workshops. Are there seminars or workshops I should plan to attend as a preservice teacher?
>
> Connie Dougherty

- Ask a large number of questions, check for student understanding, and obtain responses from all students
- Guide students during initial practice
- Provide systematic feedback and corrections
- Provide explicit instruction and practice for seatwork exercises and, where necessary, monitor students during seatwork (Rosenshine and Stevens 1986, 377).

A direct instruction method called **mastery learning** is based on two assumptions about learning: (1) virtually all students can learn material if given enough time and taught appropriately and (2) students learn best when they participate in a structured, systematic program of learning that enables them to progress in small, sequenced steps (Carroll 1963; Bloom 1981):

1. Set objectives and standards for mastery.
2. Teach content directly to students.
3. Provide corrective feedback to students on their learning.
4. Provide additional time and help in correcting errors.
5. Follow a cycle of teaching, testing, reteaching, and retesting.

In mastery learning, students take diagnostic tests and then are guided to do corrective exercises or activities to improve their learning. These may take the form of programmed instruction, workbooks, computer drill and practice, or educational games. After the corrective lessons, students are given another test and are more likely to achieve mastery.

Computer-assisted instruction (CAI) is a vehicle for mastery learning, especially software programs that follow the five steps in the mastery learning process. Figure 10.4 presents several student-centered and technology-centered advantages of the instructional use of computers.

Instructional uses of computers also include (1) record keeping through data banks and spread sheets, (2) electronic workbooks for drill and practice, (3) interactive multimedia simulations for self-directed study or problem solving, (4) word processing, involving all stages of the writing process, (5) programming, involving the development of logic and other higher cognitive functions, (6) networking, in which teachers and students communicate with others worldwide through electronic mail, and (7) accessing information online through the Internet.

Since the early 1980s, computers have revolutionized the teaching–learning process. Virtually all schools now have computers, and many classrooms have several. In 1996–97, U.S. school districts spent about $4.1 billion on computers, software, training, and online services (Quality Education Data 1996). Though slightly more than half of schools had computer links to the Internet in 1996, cable television companies pledged to provide nearly all public schools with free online services (Trotter 1996).

METHODS BASED ON CHILD DEVELOPMENT

As you learned in Chapter 9, children move through stages of cognitive, psychosocial, and moral development. Effective instruction includes methods that are developmentally appropriate, meet students' diverse learning needs, and recognize the importance of learning that occurs in social contexts. For example, one way that students reach higher levels of development is to observe and then imitate their parents, teachers, and peers, who act as models. As Woolfolk (1995, 223) points out:

> Modeling has long been used, of course, to teach dance, sports, and crafts, as well as skills in subjects such as home economics, chemistry, and shop. Modeling can also be

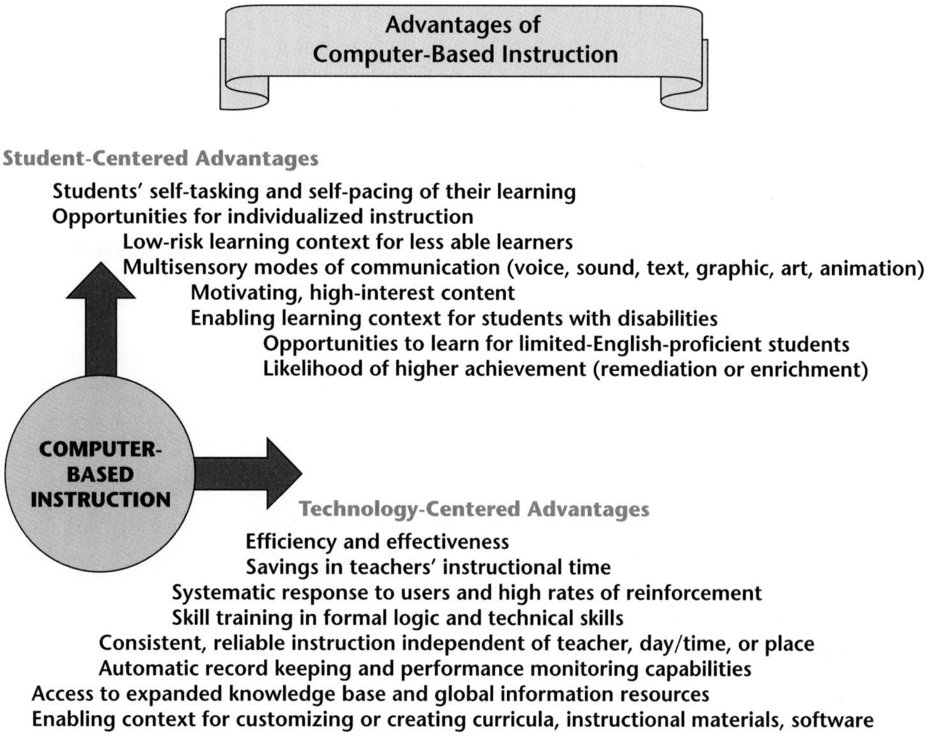

Student-Centered Advantages

Students' self-tasking and self-pacing of their learning
Opportunities for individualized instruction
Low-risk learning context for less able learners
Multisensory modes of communication (voice, sound, text, graphic, art, animation)
Motivating, high-interest content
Enabling learning context for students with disabilities
Opportunities to learn for limited-English-proficient students
Likelihood of higher achievement (remediation or enrichment)

COMPUTER-BASED INSTRUCTION

Technology-Centered Advantages

Efficiency and effectiveness
Savings in teachers' instructional time
Systematic response to users and high rates of reinforcement
Skill training in formal logic and technical skills
Consistent, reliable instruction independent of teacher, day/time, or place
Automatic record keeping and performance monitoring capabilities
Access to expanded knowledge base and global information resources
Enabling context for customizing or creating curricula, instructional materials, software

FIGURE 10.4 Advantages of computer-based instruction

applied deliberately in the classroom to teach mental skills and to broaden horizons—to teach new ways of thinking. Teachers serve as models for a vast range of behaviors, from pronouncing vocabulary words, to reacting to the seizure of an epileptic student, to being enthusiastic about learning.

Effective teachers also use **modeling** by "thinking out loud" and following three basic steps of "mental modeling" (Duffy and Roehler 1989):

1. Showing students the reasoning involved
2. Making students conscious of the reasoning involved
3. Focusing students on applying the reasoning

In this way, teachers can help students become aware of their learning processes and enhance their ability to learn.

At the same time, students "do not merely passively receive or copy input from teachers or textbooks. Instead, they actively mediate it by trying to make sense of it and relate it to what they already know (or think they know) about the topic" (Good and Brophy 1994, 414). That is, "*Students develop new knowledge through a process of active construction*" (414). Teachers with this constructivist view of learning focus on students' thinking about the material being learned and, through carefully orchestrated cues, prompts, and questions, help students arrive at a deeper understanding of the material. The common elements of **constructivist teaching** include the following:

■ The teacher's role is not just to present information but also to [r]espond to students' learning efforts.

- The students' role is not just to absorb or copy input but also to actively make sense and construct meaning.
- Students' prior knowledge about the topic is elicited and used as a starting place for instruction. . . .
- The teacher creates a social environment in the classroom . . . a learning community featuring discourse or dialogue designed to promote understanding (Good and Brophy 1994, 425–426).

Like constructivist teaching, contingent teaching is based on principles of cognitive development. In **contingent teaching,** teachers vary the amount of help they give children

> on the basis of their moment-to-moment understanding. If they do not understand an instruction given at one level, then more help is forthcoming. When they do understand, the teacher steps back and gives the child more room for initiative. In this way, the child is never left alone when he [or she] is in difficulty nor is he [or she] "held back" by teaching that is too directive and intrusive (Wood 1988, 81).

The concept of contingent teaching, sometimes called *scaffolding,* is based on the work of L. S. Vygotsky, a well-known Soviet psychologist. Vygotsky coined the term *zone of proximal development* to refer to the point at which students need assistance in order to continue learning. The effective teacher is sensitive to the student's zone of development and ensures that instruction neither exceeds the student's current level of understanding nor underestimates the student's ability.

METHODS BASED ON THE THINKING PROCESS

Some instructional methods are derived from the mental processes involved in learning, thinking, remembering, problem solving, and creativity. **Information processing,** for example, is a branch of cognitive science concerned with how people use their long- and short-term memory to access information and solve problems. The computer is often used as an analogy for information-processing views of learning: "Like the computer, the human mind takes in information, performs operations on it to change its form and content, stores the information, retrieves it when needed, and generates responses to it. Thus, processing involves gathering and representing information, or *encoding;* holding information, or *storage;* and getting at the information when needed, or *retrieval.* The whole system is guided by *control processes* that determine how and when information will flow through the system" (Woolfolk 1995, 243).

While several systematic approaches to instruction are based on information processing—teaching students how to memorize, think inductively or deductively, acquire concepts, or use the scientific method, for example—they all focus on how people acquire and use information. Table 10.2 presents general teaching guidelines based on ideas from information processing.

In **inquiry learning** and **discovery learning** students are given opportunities to inquire into subjects so that they "discover" knowledge for themselves. When teachers ask students to go beyond information in a text to make inferences, draw conclusions, or form generalizations; and when teachers do not answer students' questions, preferring instead to have students develop their own answers, they are using methods based on inquiry and discovery learning. These methods are best suited for teaching concepts, relationships, and theoretical abstractions, and for having students formulate and test hypotheses. The following example shows how inquiry and discovery learning in a first-grade classroom fostered a high level of student involvement and thinking.

TABLE 10.2

Using information processing ideas in the classroom

- Make sure you have the students' attention. For example, begin a lesson by asking a question that stimulates interest in the topic.
- Help students separate essential from nonessential details and focus on the most important information as it relates to instructional objectives.
- Help students make connections between new information and what they already know.
- Provide for repetition and review of information and the practice of skills.
- Present material in a clear, organized, concrete way. For example, give students a brief outline to follow and summarize lessons.
- Focus on meaning, not memorization.

(Source: Adapted from Anita E. Woolfolk, *Educational Psychology,* 6th ed. Boston: Allyn and Bacon, 1995, p. 257.)

The children are gathered around a table on which a candle and jar have been placed. The teacher, Jackie Wiseman, lights the candle and, after it has burned brightly for a minute or two, covers it carefully with the jar. The candle grows dim, flickers, and goes out. Then she produces another candle and a larger jar, and the exercise is repeated. The candle goes out, but more slowly. Jackie produces two more candles and jars of different sizes, and the children light the candles, place the jars over them, and the flames slowly go out. "Now we're going to develop some ideas about what has just happened," she says. "I want you to ask me questions about those candles and jars and what you just observed" (Joyce and Weil 1996, 3).

METHODS BASED ON PEER-MEDIATED INSTRUCTION

Student peer groups can be a deterrent to academic performance (Steinberg et al. 1996), but they can also motivate students to excel. Because "learning takes place in a social situation" (Woolfolk 1995, 277), **peer-mediated instruction** provides teachers with options for increasing students' learning. Cooperative learning, described earlier in this chapter, is an example of peer-mediated instruction. Another example is **group investigation** in which the teacher's role is to create an environment that allows students to determine what they will study and how. Students are presented with a situation to which they "react and discover basic conflicts among their attitudes, ideas, and modes of perception. On the basis of this information, they identify the problem to be investigated, analyze the roles required to solve it, organize themselves to take these roles, act, report, and evaluate these results" (Thelen 1960, 82).

The teacher's role in group investigation is multifaceted; he or she is an organizer, guide, resource person, counselor, and evaluator. The method is very effective in increasing student achievement (Sharan and Sharan 1990, 17–21), positive attitudes toward learning, and the cohesiveness of the classroom group. The model also allows students to inquire into problems that interest them and enables each student to make a meaningful, authentic contribution to the group's effort based on his or her experiences, interests, knowledge, and skills.

Other common forms of peer-mediated instruction include peer tutoring and cross-age tutoring. In **peer-tutoring** arrangements, students are tutored by other pupils in the same class or the same grade. **Cross-age tutoring** involves, for example, sixth-grade students tutoring second-grade students in reading. Research clearly shows that with proper orientation and training, cross-age tutoring can greatly benefit both "teacher" and learner (Sharpley et al. 1993). Pilot programs pairing students at risk of dropping out of school with younger children and with special-needs students have proved especially successful.

WHAT ARE SOME CHARACTERISTICS OF EFFECTIVE TEACHING [?]

The *outcomes* of effective teaching are relatively easy to enumerate: (1) students acquire an understanding of the subject at hand; (2) they can apply what they have learned to new situations; and (3) they have a desire to continue learning. However, if we wish to identify the *characteristics* of effective teaching, we find ourselves confronted with a more difficult task.

What do effective teachers do when they are teaching? How do they communicate with students? How do they manage classroom activities? What models of teaching do they use? As the previous discussions of classroom cultures, learning environments, classroom management, and teaching methods suggest, answers to questions such as these are not easy to formulate. However, one broad helpful view of the characteristics that underlie all effective teaching is the "Framework for Defining Teaching," developed as part of the Praxis Series: Professional Assessments for Beginning Teachers. According to the Praxis framework, teachers must be able to perform four teaching tasks: (1) organize content knowledge for student learning, (2) teach for student learning, (3) create an environment for student learning, and (4) develop as professionals. Teachers must be able to perform these tasks while taking into account individual, developmental, and cultural differences among students and differences among subjects. Figure 10.5 shows what teachers should be able to perform within each teaching task.

Describe this learning environment in terms of apparent student grouping, the activity format, and the kind of teaching method in use. What are three other types of teaching models that effective teachers use? How do effective teachers link teaching methods with goals and assessment?

ESTABLISHING GOALS

One characteristic of successful teachers is that they focus on the outcomes—the results or consequences of their teaching. Regardless of the instructional method used, teaching "is most effective when used as part of a coherent instructional program that is *goals driven*—designed to accomplish clear goals that

Organize Content for Student Learning

- Articulate clear learning goals that are appropriate to the students.
- Demonstrate an understanding for the connections between past, present, and future content.
- Become familiar with relevant aspects of students' prior knowledge, skills, and cultural experiences.
- Create or select instructional materials or other resources and learning activities that are appropriate to the students and are clearly linked to the goals of the lesson.
- Create or select evaluation strategies that are appropriate for the students and clearly related to the goals of the lesson.

Teach for Student Learning

- Communicate high expectations for each student.
- Make specific learning expectations clear to students.
- Make content comprehensible to students.
- Encourage students to extend their thinking.
- Monitor students' understanding of content through a variety of means, providing feedback to students to assist learning and adjust lessons as needed.
- Use instructional time effectively.

Create an Environment for Student Learning

- Create a climate that promotes equity.
- Establish and maintain rapport with students in ways that are appropriate to the students' developmental needs.
- Establish and consistently maintain clear standards of mutually respectful classroom interaction and behavior.
- Make the physical environment as safe and conducive to learning as possible.

Develop as a Professional

- Reflect on the extent to which the instructional goals were met and explain how insights gained from teaching can be used in the future.
- Demonstrate a sense of efficacy and acceptance of responsibility for student learning.
- Build professional relationships with colleagues to share teaching insights and coordinate learning activities for students.
- Communicate with parents or guardians regarding student learning.

FIGURE 10.5 The Praxis framework for four teaching tasks (Source: Carol Anne Dwyer and Ana Maria Villegas, *Foundations for Tomorrow's Teachers—No. 3, Defining Teaching* (Princeton, NJ: Educational Testing Service, 1992, pp. 4–5.) Reprinted by permission of Educational Testing Service.)

are phrased in terms of student outcomes or capabilities to be developed" (Good and Brophy 1994, 374).

Goals are general statements of purpose that guide schools and teachers as they develop instructional programs. Instructional goals can be derived from the curriculum or content being taught; or, as you saw in Chapter 5, they can be derived from various educational philosophies. Goals range from very broad statements of purpose that apply to a large number of students to those that apply to students in a particular classroom. In addition, teachers evaluate their teaching by how well students master certain objectives. **Learning objectives** are specific, measurable outcomes of learning that students are to demonstrate. For example, "Students will identify the structural elements of cells and explain their functions" might be a specific objective toward a larger goal of "understanding biological concepts and principles."

Successful teachers also realize that the quality of their teaching depends upon what students can *do,* not only on what they *know.* To evaluate their effectiveness in this area, teachers assess students' mastery of performance tasks in which they apply their learning to a new problem. Figure 10.6 on page 336 illustrates two different approaches to lesson planning that take into account targeted goals, objectives, and performance tasks.

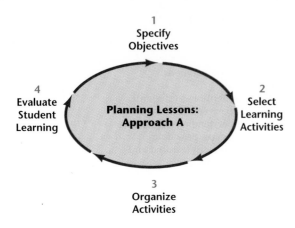

1
Specify Objectives

2
Select Learning Activities

3
Organize Activities

4
Evaluate Student Learning

Planning Lessons: Approach A

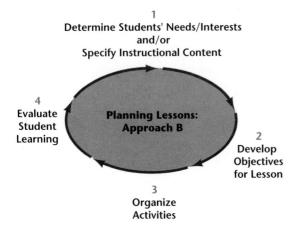

1
Determine Students' Needs/Interests and/or Specify Instructional Content

2
Develop Objectives for Lesson

3
Organize Activities

4
Evaluate Student Learning

Planning Lessons: Approach B

FIGURE 10.6 Two approaches to planning lessons

LINKING ASSESSMENT WITH INSTRUCTION

In assessing students' learning, teachers make judgments about the performance of students *and* about their own performance as teachers. Successful teachers continually evaluate the effectiveness of their teaching because they recognize that how well students learn depends upon how well they teach. **Assessment** has been defined as "the process of obtaining information that is used to make educational decisions about students, to give feedback to the student about his or her progress, strengths, and weaknesses, to judge instructional effectiveness and curricular adequacy, and to inform policy" (American Federation of Teachers et al. 1990, 2).

To assess students' learning, teachers use measurement and evaluation techniques. **Measurement** is the gathering of quantitative data related to the knowledge and skills students have acquired. Measurement yields scores, rankings, or ratings that teachers can use to compare students. **Evaluation** involves making judgments about or assigning a value to those measurements. **Formative evaluation** occurs when the teacher measures students' learning for instruction. **Summative evaluation** is used by teachers to determine grades at the end of a unit, semester, or year and to decide whether students are ready to proceed to the next phase of their education.

Authentic assessments (sometimes called *alternative assessments*) require students to use higher-level thinking skills to perform, create, or solve real-life problems—not just choose one of several designated responses as on a multiple-choice test. The authentic assessments a teacher might use include evaluating the quality of individual and small-group projects, videotaped demonstrations of skills, or participation in community-based activities. In science, for example, students might design and conduct an experiment; in mathematics, they might explain in writing how they solved a problem. Authentic assessments require students to solve problems or to work on tasks that approximate as much as possible those they will encounter beyond the classroom. **Portfolio assessment** is based on "a purposeful collection of student work that exhibits the student's efforts, progress, and achievements in one or more areas. The collection must include student participation in selecting contents, the criteria for judging merit, and evidence of student self-reflection" (Paulson et al. 1991, 60). **Performance assessment** is used to determine what students can *do* as well as what they know. In some cases, the teacher observes and then evaluates an actual performance or application of a skill; in others, the teacher evaluates a product created by the student.

The following sections present brief portraits of three effective teachers in action. As you read each portrait, look for evidence that shows how these teachers create effective learning environments.

AN EFFECTIVE ELEMENTARY SCHOOL TEACHER

Maya Dawson teaches kindergarten at a private school in New York City. As you read the following portrait, notice how effectively Maya communicates with her students.

Maya articulates with precision. Her voice is warm and soft, with a reminder of the rural South only in the slowness and sweetness of her speech. She is trim and energetic, a medium Afro forming a black halo around her open, friendly face. Her hands are in motion as she talks, softly hammering home a point, underlining a word, sweeping away an argument.

"Listen to the plans now," she says. "Yesterday you painted some wonderful penguins. And the day before we painted a beautiful Antarctic background. Today I want some of you to cut out penguins and paste them on the background in the hall."

"Me!"

"Me!"

"Me!"

Maya holds up her hand. "Wait a minute. Quiet now. We'll talk first and then we'll decide who will do what. So some of you will make a mural of millions and millions of penguins. Now, who didn't make a card for Spring [a student who is moving to Italy]?"

"I did! I made a red one."

"No," Maya smiles. "No, my question is who did not make a card?"

Not a hand goes up. "Good. Everyone made one."

"I did."

"Yes!"

"Yes."

"Okay, good. Now, I wrote a message on the chalkboard, and I'd like someone to read it." About a half dozen hands shoot up, and these children go to the board one at a time to read out loud: "Dear Spring. We Will Miss You."

Maya selects five volunteers to cut out penguins.

"There's a lot of work to do there so you better get right to it. And don't forget to get scissors and paste." Off they go.

"We haven't done little books in a long time. Who wants to do little books at the table?" Ben, Vanessa, and Angola raise their hands and troop off to get supplies. "I'll be over in a minute," Maya calls after them (Ayers, 1989, 122–123).

AN EFFECTIVE MIDDLE SCHOOL TEACHER

Mr. Gebhart is a seventh- and eighth-grade art teacher at a middle school on the West Coast. Notice how he is able to create what he calls a "delicate balance between control and freedom" in a ceramics class.

At first no teacher is visible. Then he can be discerned in his open-necked shirt and clay-streaked pants, bending over one student's project discussing the aesthetic quality of the glaze, then over another's to suggest how to solve the problem of reattaching pieces that fell off in the first firing. Two minutes after the bell has summoned the faithful, Mr. Gebhart stands up. He has already had individual consultation with five students.

"Bo, turn off the radio please, till everyone is working."

A boy from the non-working table silences the music. Most of the students look up for a moment, then resume work. Some approach him with questions concerning evaluation of their work, further directions, or technical or aesthetic problems demanding solution. Mr. Gebhart attends briefly to them, but directs his attention to the back table where a girl is wrapping her scarf around Bo's head, talking.

"Penny, what are you working on?" She shrugs. "Don't just sit there and chat. You've had enough time to get started." Mr. Gebhart turns to somebody else. Penny pulls out a lacy clay shoe and starts smoothing out its high heel.

The radio is turned on. "Leave that off till everyone is working. I'll say when everyone is working." The radio is turned off. Students admonish one another to get to work. Fifteen minutes into the period Mr. Gebhart turns the music on. Another work-day is in progress.

Every two weeks or so Mr. Gebhart introduces a new lesson. He asks the students to gather round, which they do, some perched on the front tables, one on crutches, balanced dangerously between two tables. This lesson involves sculpting a figure, "doing something, not looking like it just died," from a small block of clay. Mr. Gebhart demonstrates the basic cuts and twists which produce a human form, telling students to attend to proportion, not detail. He shows them how to use their bodies to determine arm length. The students seem captivated by the emerging figure. Working quickly, Mr. Gebhart notes that the figure should be posed after its basic form is established, and then brings forth a seated figure, torso twisted, knee raised.

Having given basic directions, Mr. Gebhart shows the students illustrations in *Sports and Games in Art*—Bellows' boxers, Moore's abstractions, Greek wrestlers. He brings the pictures to life: "This one was probably made in clay first like you're doing." "We call this 'abstracted.' Just put in what you think is essential." "Notice how this conveys a feeling of movement." He throws his body forward to walk. "In art we create the same process by throwing the whole body off center."

Pointing to a Giacometti with slender legs, "What's the problem with this one if you were making it out of clay?" ("It wouldn't stand.") "How could you solve that problem?" With no hesitations solutions are offered, "put wire inside and clay around it"; "a platform"; "support."

Mr. Gebhart expands on the students' answers, showing further illustrations and reminding them to think about how they will present their figure. Then he recaps several tips adapting ideas from existing art pieces, planning before starting, using one's body as a guide, adding details last.

During the fourteen-minute lecture, Mr. Gebhart has the students' attention. Barb, chin on hands, has her eyes riveted to him and the book, nodding to herself. Valerie is unobtrusively observing from behind some more assertive students. Even Bo and Penny watch. "Continue with your work," concludes Mr. Gebhart. The students disperse, and the day continues in the usual manner of individual instruction. Seven or eight different types of projects are under way (Catford 1994, 310–314).

AN EFFECTIVE HIGH SCHOOL TEACHER

Finally, let us visit Mrs. LeFluir's high school Spanish class. Notice how Mrs. LeFluir gradually changes the demands placed on her students. She first focuses on the memorization of rules and vocabulary; then she turns to completion and fill-in exercises; and last, she has students practice their oral delivery.

MRS. LeFLUIR: Today we will study the gender of nouns. In Spanish all nouns are either masculine or feminine. Nouns ending in *o* are generally masculine, and those ending in *a* are generally feminine. Tisha, can you identify the following nouns as either masculine or feminine? (writes on board)

libro

	pluma
	cuaderno
	gramática
TISHA:	(correctly identifies each)
MRS. LEFLUIR:	Now, let's see how you identified each of the words and what each word means.
TISHA:	Well, I followed the rule that if it ends in an *o* it will be masculine but if it ends in an *a* it will be feminine. I think the words are *book, pen, notebook,* and *grammar.*
MRS. LEFLUIR:	Good. Now for the next step, you've all used indefinite articles *a* or *an* many times in your speaking and writing. In Spanish the word *un* is used for *a* or *an* before a masculine noun, and *una* is used for *a* or *an* before a feminine noun. In Spanish the article is repeated before each noun. Now, using the vocabulary words on the board, let's place the correct form of the indefinite article in front of each word (shifting the task demand). Why don't you take the first one, Ted?
TED:	It would be *un libro.*
MRS. LEFLUIR:	Mary.
MARY:	*Una pluma.*
MRS. LEFLUIR:	Bob and Mike, take the next two.
BOB:	*Un cuaderno.*
MIKE:	*Una gramática.*
MRS. LEFLUIR:	OK. Now, we are ready to put our knowledge to work. I will give you a sentence in English and you translate it into Spanish, being sure to include the correct form of the indefinite article (shifting the task demand again). For this you will need to remember your vocabulary from last week. If you need to, look up the words you forgot. Mark, let's start with you. Come up to the board and write: Do you want a book?
MARK:	(writes on board) *Desea usted un libro?*
MRS. LEFLUIR:	Good. And how did you decide to use *un* instead of *una?*
MARK:	The noun ended in *o.*
MRS. LEFLUIR:	(continues with three other examples)
	Do you need grammar?
	Do you want to study a language?
	Do you need a notebook?
	(After the students respond, she shifts the task demand again by moving to the following activity.) Now, read each sentence on the transparency and write down the correct form of the indefinite article that goes before the noun (shows transparency) (Borich 1996, 406–407).

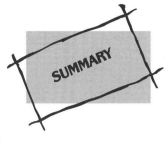

What Determines the Culture of the Classroom?

■ The culture of the classroom, which has a significant influence on students' learning, comprises six interdependent and interacting elements: (1) the activity format, procedure, or delivery system for instruction; (2) the academic content itself; (3) the physical, spatial, and temporal constraints; (4) the accountability structure; (5) the players in the classroom drama; and (6) the dynamic interaction among participants, activities, content, and materials.

■ Classroom climate refers to the atmosphere or quality of life in a classroom. The climates established by high-performing teachers are characterized by a productive, task-oriented focus; group cohesiveness; open, warm relationships between teacher and students; cooperative, respectful interactions among students; low levels of tension, anxiety, and conflict; humor; high expectations; and frequent opportunities for student input regarding classroom activities.

How Can You Create a Positive Learning Environment?

■ An important element of a positive learning environment is a caring classroom climate. Teachers show care for students by providing support, structure, and appropriate expectations.

■ The physical environment of a classroom—seating arrangements and the placement of other classroom furniture, for example—can make a positive contribution to students' learning.

■ Classroom organization, how students are grouped for instruction and how time is used, is an important element of the effective learning environment. Among the patterns for organizing classrooms are grouping students by ability, grouping students for cooperative learning, using activity formats based on authentic learning tasks, and using time to maximize students' learning.

What Are the Keys to Successful Classroom Management?

■ The key to successful classroom management is preventing problems before they occur. Teachers who prevent problems foster effective, harmonious interpersonal interactions; understand how their leadership style influences students; and facilitate the development of the classroom group so that it becomes more cohesive and supportive.

■ Teachers who establish a democratic classroom climate that allows students to participate in making decisions about the classroom environment, rules and procedures, curriculum materials, and learning activities have fewer discipline problems.

■ When management problems occur, effective teachers use a repertoire of problem-solving skills based on experience, common sense, and understanding of the teaching–learning process. Regardless of the management strategy used, effective teachers base their response to problems on three elements of "constructive assertiveness": a clear statement of the problem or concern; unambiguous body language; and a firm, unwavering insistence on appropriate behavior.

What Teaching Methods Do Effective Teachers Use?

■ While it is difficult to identify *all* the skills teachers need, research indicates that effective teachers use a repertoire of models of teaching based on students' learning behaviors, child development, the thinking process, and peer mediation.

■ Direct instruction, mastery learning, and computer-assisted instruction are based on the view that learning is the acquisition of new behaviors.

■ Modeling, constructivism, and contingent teaching are based primarily on an understanding of how students construct meaning as they learn new material.

- Information processing, inquiry learning, and discovery learning are based on our understanding of the cognitive processes involved in learning.
- Peer-mediated instruction, which views learning as taking place in social situations, includes cooperative learning, group investigation, and peer- and cross-age tutoring.

What Are Some Characteristics of Effective Teaching?

- Effective teaching focuses on outcomes—the results or consequences of teaching. Outcomes include clear goals, objectives, and performance tasks that students are to master.
- Successful teachers modify their instruction based on assessments of students' understanding.
- Measurement refers to gathering data related to students' knowledge and skills, while evaluation involves making judgments about or assigning value to those judgments. In addition to traditional tests, teachers can use authentic assessments, portfolio assessments, and performance assessments to measure and evaluate students' learning.

KEY TERMS AND CONCEPTS

academic learning time, 320
allocated time, 320
assertive discipline, 326
assessment, 335
authentic assessments, 336
authentic learning tasks, 319
between-class ability grouping, 317
block scheduling, 320
caring classroom, 315
classroom climate, 311
classroom management, 322
classroom organization, 317

computer-assisted instruction (CAI), 330
constructivist teaching, 331
contingent teaching, 331
cooperative learning, 317
cross-age tutoring, 333
democratic classroom, 322
direct instruction, 328
discovery learning, 332
evaluation, 336
formative evaluation, 336
group investigation, 333
information processing, 332
inquiry learning, 332
learning objectives, 335

mastery learning, 328
measurement, 336
modeling, 331
opportunity to learn (OTL), 320
peer-mediated instruction, 333
peer-tutoring, 333
performance assessment, 336
portfolio assessment, 336
reality therapy, 327
summative evaluation, 336
time on task, 320
within-class ability grouping, 317

APPLICATIONS AND ACTIVITIES

Teacher's Journal

1. Recall the teachers and classmates you had during your school career. Select one class and analyze its group processes in terms of the stages of group development discussed in this chapter. At what stage of development was the group near the end of the school year? What conditions facilitated or impeded the development of this group?

2. Describe the "ideal" physical classroom environment for you. How would the seating arrangement facilitate the attainment of your instructional goals and objectives? How would you involve students in arranging the classroom?

3. Describe your leadership style as it relates to classroom management. In which aspects of leadership and classroom management do you feel most and

least confident? What might you do, or what skills might you acquire, to strengthen your effectiveness in areas you feel you lack confidence? Develop your ideas into a statement of professional goals.

Teacher's Database

1. Visit the home pages of three or more of the following research publications on the Web. These journals focus on educational research, learning theories, student and teacher attitudes and behaviors, and the effectiveness of teaching methods. Some journals especially emphasize the implications of educational psychology theory and research for educational policy and applications to teaching practice. Note the kinds of studies and research topics each selected journal reports. How might articles in these journals help you as an education major? as a classroom teacher? as a teaching professional?

American Educational Research Journal	*Cognition and Instruction*
Contemporary Educational Psychology	*Educational Psychologist*
Educational Psychology Review	*Educational Researcher*
Journal of Educational Psychology	*Review of Research in Education*
Journal of Teaching and Teacher Education	*Social Psychology of Education*
Review of Educational Research	

2. What resources are available on the Internet for developments in educational assessment? Begin in the ERIC Clearinghouse on Assessment and Evaluation. This clearinghouse contains the Test Locator service, searchable testing databases, tips on how to best evaluate a test, and information on fair testing practices.

Gopher: gopher.cua.edu
Select: Special Resources/ERIC Clearinghouse of Assessment and Evaluation

Then visit CRESST (The National Center for Research on Evaluation, Standards, and Student Testing), which houses a database of alternative approaches to assessment, including portfolio and performance assessments.

Gopher: spinoza.cse.ucla.edu

Observations and Interviews

1. Observe several teachers at the level for which you are preparing to teach and try to identify the teaching methods they are using as part of their instructional repertoires.

2. Form a team with several other classmates and analyze three to five classrooms in terms of the eight dimensions of effective classroom climates presented on page 311. Rate each class on each dimension in terms of a five-point scale representing a continuum between the negative and positive qualities. Let 5 stand for *a most productive, task-oriented focus* and 1 stand for *a least productive, task-oriented focus*. Compare ratings and discuss your observations with the rest of the class.

3. Interview a classroom teacher about the assessment of students' learning. How do the assessment methods used by this teacher relate to his or her goals and objectives? To what extent does the teacher use authentic assessments?

Professional Portfolio

Prepare a poster depicting a classroom arrangement appropriate for the subject area and grade level for which you are preparing to teach. The poster should indicate the seating arrangement and location of other classroom furniture. In addition, make a list of classroom rules that will be posted in the room. You may wish to organize the rules according to the following categories.

- Rules related to academic work
- Rules related to classroom conduct
- Rules that must be communicated on your first teaching day
- Rules that can be communicated later

Lastly, prepare a flow chart depicting routine activities for a typical day. This chart could include procedures for the following:

- Handling attendance, tardy slips, and excuses
- Distributing materials
- Turning in homework
- Doing seatwork or various in-class assignments
- Forming small groups for cooperative learning activities
- Returning materials and supplies at the end of class

An educator is entrusted with the most serious work that confronts humankind: the development of curricula that enable new generations to contribute to the growth of human beings and society.

—William H. Schubert
Curriculum: Perspective, Paradigm, and Possibility

chapter 11

Developing and Implementing the Curriculum

William Cordasco, a first-year teacher, is at a meeting of the school-wide curriculum development committee recently formed at his school. The committee is exploring ways to integrate the school curriculum so that it treats various subject areas as a unified whole rather than as separate, disconnected parts.

The committee is discussing the pros and cons of a theme-based curriculum. The thematic approach would organize the curriculum around several themes, each of which would address a key concept (how the animal world has influenced the lives of human beings on earth, for example). As students explored such themes they would learn relevant material from areas such as language, reading, mathematics, science, social studies, art, movement and drama, and music.

At this point, Dolores, an experienced teacher who volunteered to serve as a mentor to William, is speaking in favor of curriculum integration: "It's really artificial to say that children learn best by focusing first on science, then on math, then on reading," she says. "These divisions have been created by adults and imposed on kids because . . . "

"I think that's overstating things," another teacher says, interrupting Dolores. "How are we going to be sure that our kids master the basics if we organize the curriculum around these themes? That's not what the parents of our children want. And . . . what would students actually *do* in a curriculum that focused on how animals and humans live on earth?"

"Oh, they could do a lot of things," Dolores says, smiling. "They could study the biological characteristics of animals in science, sing about animals in music, move like different animals in physical education, and read stories about animals in reading. In math they could calculate how much animals must eat to stay alive."

William decides to get involved in the discussion. "I support the integrated approach," he says. "One of the main goals of our curriculum should be for students to go beyond the basics. We want them to know how to use the material they learn, how to solve problems. An integrated approach is the best way to accomplish that."

"I'm not sure I agree," a teacher seated across the table from William says. "The purpose of our curriculum should be to learn the basics. We want our kids to do well on the state's test of basic skills. If they don't do well on that, they're less likely to continue their education. What we're talking about here has been tried before, and it didn't work."

What should be the purpose of the school curriculum in today's schools? How should the curriculum be organized? What learning activities should students experience? How should teachers assess students' learning?

■

Think back to your experiences as a student at the elementary, middle, junior, and secondary schools you attended. What things did you learn? Certainly, the curriculum you experienced included reading, computation, penmanship, spelling, geography, and history. In addition to these topics, though, did you learn something about cooperation, competition, stress, football, video games, popularity, and the opposite sex? Or, perhaps, did you learn to love chemistry and to hate English grammar?

WHAT IS TAUGHT IN THE SCHOOLS ⟨?⟩

The countless things you learned in school make up the curriculum that you experienced. Curriculum theorists and researchers have suggested several different definitions for **curriculum,** with no one definition universally accepted. Here are some definitions in current use.

1. A course of study, derived from the Latin *currere,* meaning "to run a course"
2. Course content, the information or knowledge that students are to learn
3. Planned learning experiences
4. Intended learning outcomes, the *results* of instruction as distinguished from the *means* (activities, materials, etc.) of instruction
5. All the experiences that students have while at school

No one of these five is in any sense the "right" definition. The way we define curriculum depends on our purposes and the situation we find ourselves in. If, for example, we were advising a high school student on the courses he or she needed to take in order to prepare for college, our operational definition of curriculum would most likely be "a course of study." However, if we were interviewing sixth-grade students for their views on the K–6 elementary school they had just graduated from, we would probably want to view curriculum as "all the experiences that students have while at school." Let us posit an additional definition of curriculum: *Curriculum refers to the experiences, both planned and unplanned, that enhance (and sometimes impede) the education and growth of students.*

KINDS OF CURRICULUM

Elliot Eisner, a noted educational researcher, has said that "schools teach much more—and much less—than they intend to teach. Although much of what is taught is explicit and public, a great deal is not" (1994, 87). For this reason, we need to look at the four curricula that all students experience. The more we understand these curricula and how they influence students, the better we will be able to develop educational programs that do, in fact, educate.

EXPLICIT CURRICULUM   The explicit, or overt, curriculum refers to what a school intends to teach students. This curriculum is made up of several components: (1) the goals, aims, and learning objectives the school has for all students, (2) the actual courses that make up each student's course of study, and (3) the specific knowledge, skills, and attitudes that teachers want students to acquire. If we asked a principal to describe the educational program at his or her school, our inquiry would be in reference to the explicit curriculum. Similarly, if we asked a teacher to describe what he or she wished to accomplish with a particular class, we would be given a description of the explicit curriculum.

In short, the **explicit curriculum** represents the publicly announced expectations the school has for its students. These expectations range from learning how to read, write, and compute to learning to appreciate music, art, and cultures other than one's own. In most instances, the explicit curriculum takes the form of written plans or guides for the education of students. Examples of such written documents are course descriptions, curriculum guides that set forth the goals and learning objectives for a school or district, texts and other commercially prepared learning materials, and teachers' lesson plans. Through the instructional program of a school, then, these curricular materials are brought to life.

HIDDEN CURRICULUM   The hidden, or implicit, curriculum refers to the behaviors, attitudes, and knowledge the culture of the school unintentionally teaches students. In addition, the **hidden curriculum** addresses "aspects of schooling that are recognized only occasionally and remain largely unexamined, particularly the schools' pedagogical, organizational, and social environments, and their interrelations" (Cornbleth 1990, 48). For example, one study of an "effective" inner-city elementary school revealed that students had "learned" that grades depended as much or more on their attitudes and behavior as on their academic ability. When asked "How do you earn grades for your report card?" the responses of fifth- and sixth-grade students included the following (Felsenthal 1982, 10):

> If you want to earn good grades you got to hand in your work on time. You got to sit up straight and don't talk to no one.

> You have to be quiet, be a nice student and know how to write and read and stuff.

As a result of the hidden curriculum of schools, students learn more than their teachers imagine. Although teachers cannot directly control what students learn through the hidden curriculum, they can increase the likelihood that what it teaches will be positive. By allowing students to help determine the content of the explicit curriculum, by inviting them to help establish classroom rules, and by providing them with challenges appropriate for their stage of development, teachers can ensure that the outcomes of the hidden curriculum are more positive than negative.

NULL CURRICULUM   Discussing a curriculum that cannot be observed directly is like talking about dark matter or black holes, unseen phenomena in the universe whose existence must be inferred because their incredible denseness and gravitational fields do not allow light to escape. In much the same way, we can consider the curriculum that we *do not* find in the schools; it may be as important as what we *do* find. Elliot Eisner has labeled the intellectual processes and content that schools do not teach "the **null curriculum**—the options students are not afforded, the perspectives they may never know about, much less be able to use, the concepts and skills that are not a part of their intellectual repertoire" (1994, 106–107).

For example, the kind of thinking that schools foster among students is largely based on manipulations of words and numbers. Thinking that is imaginative, subjective, and poetic is stressed only incidentally. Also, students are seldom taught anthropology, sociology, psychology, law, economics, filmmaking, or architecture.

Eisner points out that "certain subject matters have been traditionally taught in schools not because of a careful analysis of the range of other alternatives that could be offered but rather because they have traditionally been taught. We teach what we teach largely out of habit, and in the process neglect areas of study that could prove to be exceedingly useful to students" (1994, 103).

PROFESSIONAL REFLECTION

Identifying Kinds of Curriculum

Reflect on your experiences with the curriculum as an elementary, middle, or high school student. Then, focusing on one part of the explicit curriculum that you experienced—a particular subject or a particular class—identify possible aspects of the hidden curriculum and possible areas of null curriculum. What conclusions might you draw about beliefs and values concerning the curriculum held by educators? local communities? the wider society? How did those beliefs and values affect you and your education?

EXTRACURRICULAR/COCURRICULAR PROGRAMS   The curriculum includes school-sponsored activities—music, drama, special interest clubs, sports, student government, and honor societies, to name a few—that students may pursue in addition to their studies in academic subject areas. When such activities are perceived as additions to the academic curriculum, they are termed *extracurricular*. When these activities are seen as having important educational goals—and not merely as extras added to the academic curriculum—they are termed *cocurricular*. To reflect the fact that these two labels are commonly used for the same activities, we use the term *extracurricular/cocurricular activities*.

Though **extracurricular/cocurricular programs** are most extensive on the secondary level, many schools at the elementary, middle, and junior high levels also provide their students with a broad assortment of extracurricular/cocurricular activities. For those students who choose to participate, such activities provide an opportunity to use social and academic skills in many different contexts.

Research shows that the larger a school is, the less likely it is that a student will take part in extracurricular/cocurricular activities. At the same time, those who do participate tend to have higher self-concepts than those who do not (Goodlad 1984, 225). The actual effects that extracurricular/cocurricular activities have on students' development, however, are not entirely clear. While it is known that students who participate in extracurricular/cocurricular activities receive higher grades than nonparticipants, it is not known if participation influences achievement, or if achievement influences participation. However, research has shown that participation has a positive influence on the level of education and the occupation one aspires to and eventually attains (Holland and Andre 1987, 437-466; Brown et al. 1991). Furthermore, students themselves tend to identify extracurricular/cocurricular activities as a high point in their school careers.

It is also clear that students who might benefit the most from participating in extracurricular/cocurricular activities—those below the norm in academic achievement and students at risk—tend not to participate. In addition, students from low socioeconomic backgrounds participate less often. Table 11.1, for example, indicates that low-socioeconomic-status tenth-grade students had a lower rate of participation in eight out of nine areas of extracurricular/cocurricular activities.

TABLE 11.1

Percentage of public school seniors participating in selected extracurricular activities by socioeconomic status (SES) of student and affluence of school, 1992

Selected Activity	All Students*	Low SES Students		High SES Students	
		Less Affluent Schools	More Affluent Schools	Less Affluent Schools	More Affluent Schools
Any extracurricular activity	79.9	74.7	73.0	86.8	87.6
Sports (individual and team)	42.4	34.3	33.2	48.6	53.1
Performing arts	27.5	25.0	20.7	32.0	29.2
Academic clubs	26.2	20.2	20.5	36.2	32.3
Vocational/professional clubs	20.8	29.2	25.6	16.0	11.8
Honor societies	18.1	10.3	10.0	30.8	29.9
Publications	17.0	17.6	9.5	22.4	20.0
Student government	15.5	12.6	9.9	17.5	20.9
Service clubs	15.2	10.0	9.4	25.0	21.1
Hobby clubs	8.5	8.2	6.9	9.4	9.6

*Includes students in middle two quartiles.

(Source: *Educational Policy Issues: Statistical Perspectives: Extracurricular Participation and Student Involvement.* Washington, DC: National Center for Education Statistics, 1995.)

TABLE 11.2

Degree of emphasis for high school students

	More Emphasis %	Less Emphasis %	Some Emphasis %	Don't Know %
Mathematics	82	1	17	*
English	79	2	19	*
Science	75	3	22	*
History/U.S. government	62	6	31	1
Geography	61	7	31	1
Foreign language	52	16	32	*
Music	31	22	46	1
Art	29	24	46	1

*Less than one-half of 1%.

(Source: Stanley M. Elam, Lowell C. Rose, and Alec M. Gallup, "The 26th Annual Phi Delta Kappa/Gallup Poll of the Public's Attitudes Toward the Public Schools," *Phi Delta Kappan,* September 1994, p. 51.)

CURRICULUM CONTENT

Our nation's schools teach what the larger society believes young people should learn. For example, Table 11.2 shows that respondents to the 1994 Gallup Poll of the Public's Attitudes Toward the Public Schools believed that, at the high school level, more emphasis should be placed on the "basics," which most people interpret as "reading, writing, and arithmetic." Similarly, the 1994 Public Agenda report, *First Things First: What Americans Expect from the Public Schools* revealed that 60 percent of respondents believed that "not enough emphasis on the basics such as reading, writing, and math" was a "serious problem" in their local schools (Johnson and Immerwahr 1994, 13). The comments of two parents who participated in the Public Agenda survey illustrate this concern:

> Education is becoming more about social issues as opposed to reading, writing, and arithmetic. Some of it's fine, but I think schools need to stay with the basics. . . . You can't get by in the business world on social issues if you can't add and subtract.

> They all talk all the time about this "whole child educational process". . . . It's not your business to make a "whole child." Your business is to teach these students how to read, how to write, and give them the basic skills to balance their checkbook. It's not to make new Emersons out of them (Johnson and Immerwahr 1994, 13)

In addition to the basics, the public also places a high priority on computer literacy and students' ability to access information through cyberspace; for example, 80 percent of respondents to the 1996 Gallup Poll believed it was "very important" or "somewhat important" for students to have "access to global electronic communications systems."

Curriculum content also reflects social and regional differences; however, the educational programs of most schools in this country are more alike than different. Goodlad found that what schools teach is characterized more by uniformity than by diversity (1983, 14–15).

Our data, whatever the source, reveal not only the curricular dominance of English/language arts and mathematics but also the consistent and repetitive attention to basic facts and skills. Developing "the ability to read, write, and handle basic arithmetical operations" pervades instruction from the first through the ninth grades and the lower tracks of courses beyond.

HOW IS THE SCHOOL CURRICULUM DEVELOPED ⁇

Although there is no easy-to-follow set of procedures for developing curriculum, Ralph Tyler has provided four fundamental questions that must be answered in developing any curriculum or plan of instruction. These four questions, known as the **Tyler rationale,** are as follows (Tyler 1949, 1):

1. What educational purposes should the school seek to attain?
2. What educational experiences can be provided that are likely to attain these purposes?
3. How can these educational experiences be effectively organized?
4. How can we determine whether these purposes are being attained?

Tyler's classic work has been used by a great number of school systems to bring some degree of order and focus to the curriculum development process.

THE FOCUS OF CURRICULUM PLANNING   In discussing curriculum development, it is helpful to clarify the focus of curriculum planning. Figure 11.1 on page 352 illustrates two dimensions of this planning process: the target and the time orientation. The target of curriculum planning may be at the macro- or the micro-level. At the macro-level, decisions about the content of the curriculum apply to large groups of students. The national goals for education and state-level curriculum guidelines are examples of macro-level curricular decisions. At the micro-level, curriculum decisions are made that apply to groups of students in a particular school or classroom. To some extent, all teachers are micro-level curriculum developers—that is, they make numerous decisions about the curricular experiences they provide students in their classrooms.

Another dimension of curriculum planning is the time orientation—does the planning focus on the present or the future? In addition to the national goals and state-level curriculum

How do curricula vary regionally? Why is what schools teach characterized more by uniformity than by diversity?

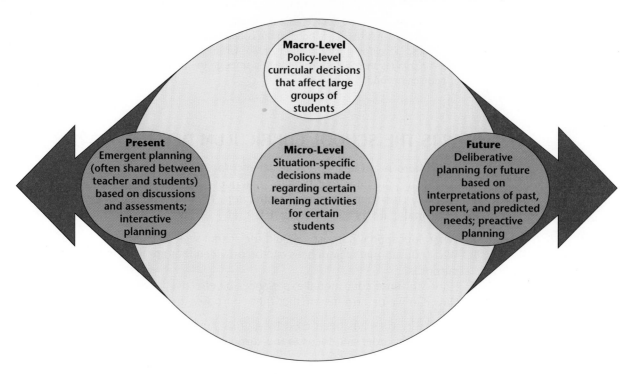

FIGURE 11.1 Two dimensions of curriculum planning

guidelines, the semester-long or monthly plans or unit plans that teachers make are examples of future-oriented curriculum planning. Present-oriented curriculum planning usually occurs at the classroom level and is influenced by the unique needs of specific groups of students. The daily or weekly curriculum decisions and lesson-plans that teachers make are examples of present-oriented curriculum planning.

STUDENT-CENTERED VERSUS SUBJECT-CENTERED CURRICULA   A key concern in curriculum development is whether greater emphasis should be given to the requirements of the subject area or to the needs of the students. It is helpful to imagine where a school curriculum might be placed on the following continuum.

Although no course is entirely subject- or student-centered, curricula vary considerably in the degree to which they emphasize one or the other. The **subject-centered curriculum** places primary emphasis on the logical order of the discipline students are to study. The teacher of such a curriculum is a subject-matter expert and is primarily concerned with helping students understand the facts, laws, and principles of the discipline. Subject-centered curricula are more typical of high school education.

Some teachers develop curricula that reflect greater concern for students and their needs. Though teachers of the **student-centered curriculum** also teach content, they emphasize the growth and development of students. This emphasis is generally more typical of elementary school curricula.

THE INTEGRATED CURRICULUM   The opening scenario for this chapter is based on the integrated approach to developing the school curriculum. Used most frequently with

Dear Mentor

NOVICE AND EXPERT TEACHERS
ON STUDENT-CENTERED CURRICULUM AND INSTRUCTION

Dear John,

You asked me how to motivate students with different abilities and backgrounds. I know of no better advice than my own motto: "A teacher must be motivated first in order to motivate others." When teachers make a commitment to their job, they want to accomplish two things: get youngsters to respond to them, and set high expectations for each youngster. Remember that your students have different goals regarding education than you do. As the facilitator, you need to internalize their primary goals and have the students "buy in" to them. I have no doubt that if you make your class student-centered, instead of teacher-centered, your students will respond.

I would like to suggest several strategies:

1. Differentiate your assignments to suit the variety of learning styles and learning abilities, or allow the students to select which problems they would like to tackle.
2. As well as using mixed-ability groupings, include projects that give each student an opportunity to work with peers who are at his or her own level.
3. Use different students' actual names in class practices or problems. Students who make some personal connection to a problem feel more involved in solving it.
4. Most important, give constant feedback, including lots of positive reinforcement through spontaneous praise and written and oral comments.

The flip side of your commitment to students is having strong parental contact and involvement. Distribute to your students' families copies not just of your curriculum goals but of goals for the entire school. Work with a language teacher to translate the goals to accommodate different ethnic backgrounds and languages of your students and their families. Make frequent phone calls informing parents of even a slight observation of growth, such as a child's grade, participation, or behavior improving. Too often teachers call home just for disciplinary actions. Urge your students' parents to come into class to observe their child, to work alongside their child, or to make a presentation to the class. When you reach out to the children's families and structure your teaching and the classroom for encouragement, you will have begun to pique your students' interest.

Overall, John, I urge you to stick to your high expectations and provide incentives for all students' achievement. Between what each student already knows and can do and what he or she has yet to learn, all students can accept a challenge and can succeed. I know that you will do a splendid job in your career as an educator.

Elizabeth A. Haden
High School Mathematics Teacher
Sallie Mae First Class Teacher Award

Dear Mentor,

I have a small group of students who excel; some have been classified as gifted. At the same time I have another small group of students who cannot read at even a first-grade level. I also have some who are fluent in English and others very limited; some who are very boisterous and others shy and withdrawn. Everybody's background and family life is different, too. How can I motivate students who have such different abilities and come from such different backgrounds?

John Gage

elementary-age students, the **integrated curriculum** draws from several different subject areas and focuses on a theme or concept rather than on a single subject. In *The Integrated Early Childhood Curriculum,* Suzanne Krogh suggests that an integrated approach is more "natural" for children: "When children learn in a way that is most natural to themselves, they unconsciously integrate subject areas into a complex whole based on their current interests. Teachers who consciously adapt this method of learning to the classroom see the curriculum as a fully spun web that incorporates a number of components at one time" (Krogh 1990, 77).

According to a national survey of elementary teachers' views on the integrated curriculum, 89 percent believed that integration was the "most effective" way to present the curriculum. As one teacher who was surveyed said, "I'm not interested in presenting isolated facts which children seem to memorize and forget. I want to help students put each lesson in perspective" (Boyer 1995, 83). In *The Basic School: A Community for Learning,* the late Ernest Boyer suggested that the elementary school curriculum should be integrated according to eight themes or "core commonalities": The Life Cycle, The Use of Symbols, Membership in Groups, A Sense of Time and Space, Response to the Aesthetic, Connections to Nature, Producing and Consuming, and Living with Purpose (Boyer 1995).

WHO PLANS THE CURRICULUM?

Only 35 percent of teachers in the country believe they have "considerable influence" over school policies for selecting course content and topics in the curriculum in their classrooms (Anderson 1994). However, Figure 11.2, based on Boyer's survey of elementary teachers, shows that most teachers believe "groups of teachers working together" should control the curriculum.

The model presented in Figure 11.3 shows how various agencies and persons external to the school are involved in curriculum planning. Textbook publishers, for example, influence what is taught because many teachers use textbooks as curriculum guides. The federal government contributes to curriculum planning by setting national education goals, and state departments of education develop both broad aims for school curricula and specific minimum competencies for students.

Within a given school, the curriculum-planning team and the classroom teacher plan the curriculum that students actually experience. As a teacher you will draw from a reservoir of curriculum plans prepared by others, thus playing a vital role in the curriculum-planning process. Whenever you make decisions about what material to include in your teaching, how to sequence content, and how much time to spend teaching certain material, you are planning the curriculum.

FIGURE 11.2 Who do you think best controls the content of the school curriculum? (Source: The Carnegie Foundation for the Advancement of Teaching and the George H. Gallup International Institute, The International Schooling Project, 1994 (United States). In Ernest L. Boyer, *The Basic School: A Community for Learning.* Princeton, NJ: The Carnegie Foundation for the Advancement of Teaching, 1995, p. 36.)

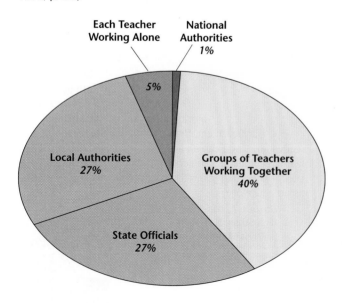

Each Teacher Working Alone
National Authorities 1%
5%
Local Authorities 27%
Groups of Teachers Working Together 40%
State Officials 27%

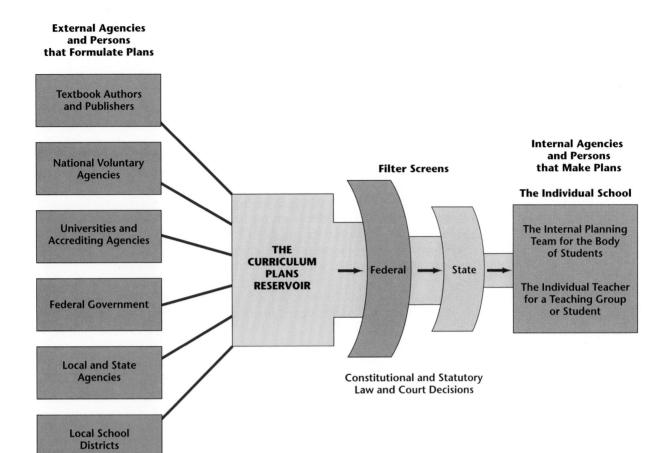

External Agencies and Persons that Formulate Plans

Textbook Authors and Publishers

National Voluntary Agencies

Universities and Accrediting Agencies

Federal Government

Local and State Agencies

Local School Districts

THE CURRICULUM PLANS RESERVOIR

Filter Screens

Federal → State

Constitutional and Statutory Law and Court Decisions

Internal Agencies and Persons that Make Plans

The Individual School

The Internal Planning Team for the Body of Students

The Individual Teacher for a Teaching Group or Student

FIGURE 11.3 The curriculum plans reservoir (Source: J. Gaylen Saylor, *Who Planned the Curriculum? A Curriculum Plans Reservoir Model with Historical Examples* (West Lafayette, IN: Kappa Delta Pi, 1982), p. 3. Used with permission.)

WHAT INFLUENCES CURRICULAR DECISIONS? ?

From the earliest colonial schools to schools of the 1990s, curricula have been broadly influenced by a variety of religious, political, and utilitarian agendas. Among the factors that influence curricula are community pressures, court decisions, students' life situations, testing results, national reports, teachers' professional organizations, and research results. Some factors have a more direct influence on curriculum development at the school level—students' needs and school district policies, for example. Other factors, more removed from the school setting, may have less obvious or direct effects on the school curriculum—the results of educational research, national educational legislation, or federal court decisions, for example. In addition, the culture of a school itself affects how the school responds to curricular influences. Let us examine some of these influences in greater detail.

SOCIAL ISSUES AND CHANGING VALUES   Values that affect curriculum planning include prevailing educational theories and teachers' educational philosophies. In addition, curriculum planners respond to social issues and changing values in the wider society. As a result, current social concerns find their way into textbooks, teaching aids, and lesson plans. Often curriculum changes are made in the hope that changing what students learn will help solve social problems or achieve local, statewide, or national goals.

Because the United States is so culturally diverse, proposed curriculum changes also reflect divergent interests and values. This divergence then leads to controversies over curriculum content and conflicting calls for reform. Some groups may demand that Christian teachings and observances be included in the public school curricula, for example, or that materials regarded as objectionable on religious grounds be censored or banned. Other groups may call for the elimination of all activities or symbols that have their origins in organized religion, including even secularized or commercialized ones such as Halloween and the Easter bunny. Curriculum changes to promote greater social integration or equity among racial or ethnic groups may draw complaints of irrelevancy or reverse discrimination. Traditionalists may object to curriculum changes that reflect feminist views.

As you can imagine, consensus on many curriculum reform issues is never achieved. However, because of their public accountability, schools must consider how to respond to those issues. A 1992 survey revealed that during a one-year period, half the school districts in Florida received complaints about curriculum content. Included were complaints claiming that the schools were undermining family values, overemphasizing globalism, underemphasizing patriotism, permitting profanity and obscenity, and teaching taboo subjects such as satanism and sex (Sheuerer and Parkay 1992, 112–118).

TEXTBOOK PUBLISHING   Textbooks greatly influence the curriculum. According to one study, "with nearly 95 percent of classroom instruction in grades K–8 and 90 percent of homework time derived from printed materials, textbooks predominate the school day" (Venezky 1992, 444). In addition, textbook publishers influence school curricula by providing teaching objectives, learning activities, tests, audiovisual aids, and other supplements to assist their customers.

Like curriculum planners, textbook authors and publishers are influenced by trends in education and by social issues. In response to criticism, for example, publishers now tend to avoid bias in terms of gender, religion, class, race, and culture. However, because the goal of business is profit, publishers are most responsive to market trends and customer preferences. They are often reluctant to risk losing sales by including subjects that are controversial or that may be offensive to their bigger customers. They may also modify textbooks to appeal to decision makers in populous states that make statewide adoptions of textbooks, such as California and Texas. Currently, 22 states have statewide adoption policies that school districts must follow in selecting textbooks (Sowell 1996).

Educators have criticized textbooks for inoffensiveness to the point of blandness, for artificially lowered reading levels (called "dumbing down"), and for pedagogically questionable gimmicks to hold students' attention. "The quality problem [with textbooks also] encompasses [f]actors such as poor writing, poor content 'coverage,' and failure to engage students in the skills needed to created the knowledge contained in a particular area of study" (Sowell, 1996, 158). Although the publishing industry continually responds to such criticisms, you would be wise to follow systematic guidelines in evaluating and selecting textbooks and other curriculum materials.

WHAT REFORM EFFORTS HAVE AFFECTED THE CURRICULUM ?

The content of the curricula in America's schools has changed frequently since the colonial period. These modifications came about as the goals of the schools were debated, additional needs of society became evident, and the characteristics of student populations shifted. The following list is a sampling of goals the schools have set for themselves at different times in our history:

- Prepare students to carry out religious and family responsibilities
- Provide employers with a source of literate workers
- Desegregate society
- Reduce crime, poverty, and injustice
- Help our country maintain its competitive edge in the world economy
- Provide the scientists needed to keep our country strong
- Educate students for intelligent participation in a democracy

Glenn Hass and Forrest W. Parkay (1993, 49) suggest that three interrelated "social forces" or "demands" influence the school curriculum. In any society, the curriculum must equip the individual learner to "provide for his or her *vocational demands and requirements,* the *demands of citizenship,* and the *demands of self-fulfillment.*" The timeline presented in Figure 11.4 on page 358 shows how school curricula have shifted in their degree of emphasis on these three demands since 1620.

CHURCH, NATION, AND SCHOOL

From 1620 to 1760, the primary aim of the curriculum was to train students in religious beliefs and practices. It was only later that a distinction was made between civil and religious life. Basic skills were taught for the purpose of learning religious catechisms and reading prayers. In addition to taking courses with religious content, students also studied such practical subjects as surveying, navigation, bookkeeping, architecture, and agriculture.

From 1770 to 1860 the development of citizenship provided the curriculum's major focus. The U.S. had just won its independence from England, and many policymakers believed that literacy was essential to the preservation of freedom. Accordingly, students were taught history, geography, health, and physical training, as well as the basic skills of reading, writing, and computation. In 1821, the nation's first public high school was opened in Boston, and two years later the first private normal school for teachers opened in Concord, Vermont. The first English-speaking kindergarten, taught by Elizabeth Peabody, opened in Boston in 1860.

By the beginning of the Civil War, the basic skills of reading, writing, and mathematics were well established in the curriculum. Various types of schools had been incorporated into state systems, and in 1852 the first compulsory school attendance law was passed in Massachusetts. Parents in every section of the country wanted more and better opportunities for their children. Through a curriculum that stressed individual virtue, literacy, hard work, and moral development, reformers wished to improve social conditions and to provide more opportunities for the poor.

The development of citizenship continues to influence school life and school curricula. All students, for example, are required to study United States history and the United States Constitution at some time during their school career. Presidents' birthdays and national holidays are built into the school year calendar. Issues concerning

1620	1620	Emphasis on basic skills needed to learn religious catechisms and read prayers. Curriculum also includes surveying, navigation, and bookkeeping. Education primarily for the elite.
1640	1636	Latin grammar (college-prep) schools established and, like Harvard and Yale Colleges emphasize Latin, Greek, theology, and philosophy for those preparing to enter law or religion.
1660	1647	Massachusetts Law of 1647 mandates a reading and writing teacher for towns of 50 or more families; a Latin teacher for towns of 100 or more. Females taught basics to enable them to carry out religious and family responsibilities.

Religious Emphasis — 1620–1740

- **1680**
- **1700** — 1700: Public schools teach reading, writing, and basic mathematics (counting, adding, and subtracting) to prepare students for jobs and apprenticeships.
- **1720**
- **1740**

Political Emphasis on Citizenship — 1740–1820

- Early 1750s: Academies teach secondary students a practical curriculum (drawing, surveying, navigation, merchant's accounting, etc.) to become tradespeople and workers.
- **1760**
- **1780**
- **1800**

Vocational Emphasis — 1820–1880

- **1820**
- 1821: First public high school teaches basic skills and history, geography, health, and physical training.
- **1840**
- **1860** — 1860: First English-speaking kindergarten emphasizes growth, activity, play, songs, and physical training.
- **1880** — 1874: Free public schooling now includes high schools that place emphasis on vocational education and reading, writing, and mathematics.

FIGURE 11.4 A chronology of major emphases in the school curriculum

civil liberties and the expression of patriotism often become educational issues, as in controversies during the last decades over treatment of the American flag and the recitation of the Pledge of Allegiance in schools.

CHILDREN AND SCHOOL

Vocational goals for the curriculum were most prominent from 1860 to 1920. The turn of the century brought with it many changes that profoundly influenced the curriculum. The dawning of the machine age altered the nature of industry, transportation, and communication. The growth of cities and the influx of millions of immigrants re-

Education for Masses		
	1900	1893 — Committee of Ten asserts that high schools are for college-bound and curriculum should emphasize mental disciplines in humanities, language, and science.
		1918 — Commission on Reorganization of Secondary Education focuses on individual differences. Curriculum to stress Seven Cardinal Principles.
	1920	
The Excellence Movement	**1940**	1930s | 1940s — Progressive education movement stresses curriculum based on student's needs and interests. Home economics, health, family living, citizenship, and wood shop added to the curriculum.
	1960	1957 — Russia's Sputnick sparks emphasis on science, mathematics, and languages.
		1960s — Calls for relevancy result in expanded course offerings and electives.
		Mid-1970s — Back-to-basics movement emphasizes reading, writing, mathematics, and oral communication.
	1980	1983 — *Nation at Risk* report calls for "five new basics"— English, mathematics, science, social studies, and computer science.
		1985 — Rigorous core curricula advocated at all levels in an effort to increase standards and to ensure quality.
		1989 — The Carnegie Council on Adolescent Development report, *Turning Points*, recommends the creation of learning communities and a core academic program for middle-level students.
	1990	1990 — President Bush unveils national educational goals in six areas: readiness for school; high school completion; student achievement and citizenship; science and mathematics; adult literacy and lifelong learning; and safe, disciplined, and drug-free schools.
		1992 — President Clinton proposes a program of national service for America's youth.
	2000	Mid-1990s — National standards committees meet in the subject areas. Renewed emphasis on developing curricula for schooling in an increasingly diverse society.

sulted in new functions for all social institutions, and home life was forever changed. As a result, curricula came to be based on vocationally oriented social and individual need rather than on subject matter divisions. Subjects were judged by the criterion of social utility rather than by their ability to develop the intellect.

During this period, several national committees met for the purpose of deciding what should be taught in elementary and secondary schools. Initially, these committees espoused goals formed by educators at the college and private secondary school levels—that is, uniform curricula with standardized methods of instruction. Gradually, though, these appointed groups began to recommend curricula that were more flexible and based on the needs of children. This shift is seen clearly in the recommendations made by three of the more influential committees during this period: the Committee of Ten, the Committee of Fifteen, and the Commission on Reorganization of Secondary Education.

THE COMMITTEE OF TEN   During 1892–93, the directors of the National Education Association appropriated $2,500 for a **Committee of Ten** to hold nine conferences that focused on the following subjects in the high school curriculum: (1) Latin; (2) Greek; (3) English; (4) other modern languages; (5) mathematics; (6) physics, astronomy, and chemistry; (7) natural history (biology, botany, and zoology); (8) history, civil government, and political science; and (9) geography (physical geography, geology, and meteorology). The group's members decided that the primary function of high schools was to take intellectually elite students and prepare them for life. Their recommendations stressed mental discipline in the humanities, languages, and science.

THE COMMITTEE OF FIFTEEN   The report of the Committee of Ten sparked such discussion that in 1893 the National Education Association appointed the **Committee of Fifteen** to examine the elementary curriculum. In keeping with the view that high schools were college preparatory institutions, the committee's report, published in 1895, called for the introduction of Latin, the modern languages, and algebra into the elementary curriculum. In addition, the curriculum was to be organized around five basic subjects: grammar, literature, arithmetic, geography, and history.

THE REORGANIZATION OF SECONDARY EDUCATION   In 1913 the National Education Association appointed the Commission on the **Reorganization of Secondary Education.** The commission's report, *Cardinal Principles of Secondary Education,* was released in 1918 and called for a high school curriculum designed to accommodate individual differences in scholastic ability. Seven educational goals were to provide the focus for schooling at all levels: health, command of fundamental processes (reading, writing, and computation), worthy home membership, vocation, citizenship, worthy use of leisure time, and ethical character.

STANDARDS AND THE SCHOOLS

From 1920 to the present, schools have become increasingly accountable for providing all students with curricular experiences based on high standards. The following comments made by U.S. Education Secretary Richard Riley at a Washington, D.C., junior high school in 1993, for example, reflect the nation's concern about current standards in schools (1993/1994, 3):

> We are not doing any children any favors by praising them for their skill on the basketball court but continuing the conspiracy of low expectations. Excellence and equality are not incompatible. We've just never tried hard enough to achieve them for all of our children.

> Ultimately, if we want our children to get smart and come into their own as full citizens of this great democracy, we need to raise the bar and help our children jump a little higher academically.

To meet these demands for higher standards, schools have undertaken numerous curricular reforms over the years and used more sophisticated methods for measuring the educational outcomes of these reforms.

THE PUSH FOR MASS EDUCATION   Since 1920, schools have been expected to provide educational opportunities for all Americans. During this period, curricula have been developed to meet the needs and differences of many diverse student groups: disabled, bilingual, gifted, delinquent, and learning-disabled students, for example. Moreover, these curricula have been used not only in public and private schools but also in alternative schools: night schools, schools without walls, summer schools, vocational schools, continuation schools, schools-within-schools, magnet schools, and so on. In 1973 there were more than 600 alternative public schools. A survey done in 1981 found that the number of public alternative schools had mushroomed to over 10,000, with an estimated three million children enrolled (Raywid 1981, 551–554)!

THE PROGRESSIVE CURRICULUM   The concern in this country for educating all our youth has drawn much of its initial energy from the progressive education movement. During the 1920s, the Progressive Education Association reacted against the earlier emphasis on the mental disciplines and called for elementary schools to develop curricula based on the needs and interests of all students. Throughout the 1930s, progressive ideas were promoted on the secondary level as well.

Though there was no single set of beliefs that united all Progressives, there was general agreement that students should be involved in activities that parallel those found in society. Furthermore, those activities should engage students' natural interests and contribute to their self-fulfillment. With these guidelines in mind, the progressive education movement expanded the curriculum to include such topics as home economics, health, family living, citizenship, and wood shop. The spirit of the progressive education movement is expressed well in a statement made in 1926 by the Director of the School of Organic Education in Fairhope, Alabama (Johnson 1926, 350–351):

> We believe that education is life, growth; that the ends are immediate; that the end and the process are one. We believe that all children should have the fullest opportunity for self-expression, for joy, for delight, for intellectual stimulus through subject matter, but we do not believe that children should be made self-conscious or externalized by making subject matter an end. Our constant thought is not what do the children learn or do, but what are the "learning" and the "doing" doing to them. . . .

> We believe that society owes all children guidance, control, instruction, association, and inspiration—right conditions of growth—throughout the growing years until physical growth is completed. No child may know failure—all must succeed. Not "what do you know" but "what do you need," should be asked, and the nature of childhood indicates the answer.

THE EIGHT-YEAR STUDY   One of the most ambitious projects of the progressive education movement was the **Eight-Year Study,** which ran from 1932 to 1940. During this period, thirty public and private high schools were given the opportunity to restructure their educational programs according to progressive tenets and without regard for college and university entrance requirements. Over 300 colleges and universities then agreed to accept the graduates of these schools. The aim of the study, according to its director, was "to develop students who regard education as an enduring quest for meanings rather than credit accumulation" (Aiken 1942, 23). The curricula developed by these schools emphasized problem solving, creativity, self-directed study, and more extensive counseling and guidance for students.

Ralph Tyler evaluated the Eight-Year Study by matching nearly 1,500 graduates of the experimental schools who went on to college with an equal number of college freshmen who graduated from other high schools. He found that students in the experimental group received higher grades in every subject area except foreign languages and had slightly higher overall grade point averages. Even more significant, perhaps, was the finding that the experimental group had higher performance in such areas as problem solving, inventiveness, curiosity, and motivation to achieve. Unfortunately, the Eight-Year Study failed to have any lasting impact on American education—possibly because World War II overshadowed the study's results.

THE PUSH FOR EXCELLENCE Concern with excellence in our schools ran high during the decade that spanned the late 1950s to the late 1960s. The Soviet Union's launching of the satellite Sputnik in 1957 marked the beginning of a great concern in this country over the content of the schools' curricula. Admiral Hyman G. Rickover was a leading proponent of an academically rigorous curriculum and urged the public to see that our strength as a nation was virtually linked to the quality of our educational system. He wrote in his 1959 book *Education and Freedom* (188):

> The past months have been a period of rude awakening for us. Our eyes and ears have been assaulted by the most distressing sort of news about Russia's giant strides in technology, based on the extraordinary success she has had in transforming her educational system. All but in ruins twenty-five years ago, it is today an efficient machine for producing highly competent scientists and engineers—many more than we can hope to train through our own educational system which we have so long regarded with pride and affection.

> We are slowly thinking our way through a thicket of bitter disappointment and humiliating truth to the realization that America's predominant educational philosophy is as hopelessly outdated today as the horse and buggy. Nothing short of a complete reorganization of American education, preceded by a revolutionary reversal of educational aims, can equip us for winning the educational race with the Russians.

Fueled by arguments like Rickover's, many curriculum reform movements were begun in the 1950s and 1960s. The federal government became involved and poured great sums of money into developing curricula in mathematics, the sciences, modern languages, and, to a lesser extent, English and history. Once again, the focus of the curriculum was on the mental disciplines and the social and psychological needs of children were secondary. Testing and ability grouping procedures were expanded in an effort to identify and to motivate academically able students.

THE INQUIRY-BASED CURRICULUM The prevailing view of what should be taught in the schools during this period was influenced significantly by Jerome Bruner's short book, *The Process of Education*. A report on a conference of scientists, scholars, and educators at Woods Hole, Massachusetts, in 1959, Bruner's book synthesized current ideas about intelligence and about how to motivate students to learn. Bruner believed that students should learn the "methods of inquiry" common to the academic disciplines. For example, in an **inquiry-based curriculum,** instead of learning isolated facts about chemistry, students would learn the principles of inquiry common to the discipline of chemistry. In short, students would learn to think like chemists; they would be able to use principles from chemistry to solve problems independently.

Bruner's ideas were used as a rationale for making the curriculum more rigorous at all levels. As he pointed out in an often-quoted statement in *The Process of Education,* "Any subject can be taught effectively in some intellectually honest form to any child at any stage of development" (1960, 33). Bruner advocated a spiral curriculum wherein children would encounter the disciplines at ever-increasing levels of complexity as they progressed through school. Thus, elementary students could be taught physics in a manner that would pave the way for their learning more complex principles of physics in high school.

THE RELEVANCY-BASED CURRICULUM   The push for a rigorous academic core curriculum was offset in the mid-1960s by a call for a **relevancy-based curriculum.** Many educators, student groups, and political activists charged that school curricula were unresponsive to social issues and significant changes in our culture. At some schools, largely high schools, students actually demonstrated against educational programs they felt were not relevant to their needs and concerns. In response to this pressure, educators began to add more courses to the curriculum, increase the number of elective and remedial courses offered, and experiment with new ways of teaching. This concern with relevancy continued until the back-to-basics movement began in the mid-1970s.

THE CORE CURRICULUM   In the early 1980s, the public was reminded anew that our country's well-being depended on its system of education, and once again our schools were found lacking in excellence. Several national reports claimed that curriculum standards had eroded. The 1983 report by the National Commission on Excellence in Education asserted, for example, that secondary school curricula had become "homogenized, diluted, and diffused." And even Admiral Rickover, in his characteristically terse, hard-hitting manner, pointed out in 1983 that school curricula had become less rigorous (Rickover 1983):

> Student performance is lower than in 1957 at the time of Sputnik, when many so-called reforms were initiated. Some curricula involve expensive gimmicks, trivial courses and quick fixes of dubious value. Teachers are often poorly trained and misused on nonacademic tasks. Many students have settled for easy, so-called relevant and entertaining courses. They and their parents are deceived by grade inflation. And the lack of national standards of performance blinds everyone to how poor our education system is.

The push for excellence in the high school curriculum received a boost at the end of 1987 when U.S. Secretary of Education William J. Bennett proposed an academically rigorous **core curriculum** for all high school students. In a U.S. Department of Education booklet entitled *James Madison High School: A Curriculum for American Students,* Bennett described what such a curriculum might look like for an imaginary high school. His course of study called for four years of English consisting of four year-long literature courses; three years each of science, mathematics, and social studies; two years of foreign language; two years of physical education; and one semester each of art and music history. Twenty-five percent of his program would be available for students to use for electives.

OUTCOME-BASED EDUCATION   A recent approach to reforming the curriculum to ensure that all students learn and perform at higher levels is known as **performance-based** or **outcome-based education.** The performance-based approach focuses on assessing students' mastery of a set of rigorous learning goals or outcomes. By the early 1990s, Kentucky, Oregon, Connecticut, and Washington were among the states that had begun to develop statewide performance-based curriculum goals. Washington, for example, passed the Performance-Based Education Act of 1993 calling for the implementation of a performance-based education system by 2000–2001. The system, which will include mandatory assessments of students' performance at the elementary, middle, and high school levels, is based on the following four goals, each of which includes several outcomes and essential learning requirements:

Goal 1: Communicate effectively and responsibly in a variety of ways and settings

Goal 2: Know and apply the core concepts and principles of mathematics; social, physical, and life sciences; arts; humanities; and healthful living

Goal 3: Think critically and creatively, and integrate experience and knowledge to form reasoned judgments and solve problems

Goal 4: Function as caring and responsible individuals and contributing members of families, work groups, and communities

WHAT ARE SOME CURRENT SUBJECT-AREA TRENDS ⁉️

The final section of this chapter examines briefly some of the current trends and issues regarding what is taught in elementary, middle, junior high, and high schools. (For information on obtaining "Free Curriculum Materials," consult the Teachers' Resource Guide at the end of this book.)

READING AND WRITING

The importance of attaining a minimum level of literacy in our society cannot be underestimated; the language arts are the tools through which students learn in nearly all other areas of the curriculum. Most students who are deficient in reading and writing skills are at a significant disadvantage when it comes to seeking employment or additional education.

The teaching of reading at all levels should focus on acquiring basic comprehension skills and learning to appreciate literature in its various forms: novels, essays, poetry, short stories, and so on. Reading teachers, however, are currently far from united as to how these aims should be realized. Does instruction in phonics enhance reading comprehension? Is a whole-language approach to the teaching of reading superior to teaching isolated decoding and comprehension skills? Should children be taught the alphabet before learning to read? While media coverage frequently dichotomizes the teaching of reading between the phonics approach and the whole-language approach, Cheeks, Flippo, and Lindsey (1997, 130) contend that "this polarization is more political than representative of the real issues. Those who advocate for whole language do not believe that phonics is not important. Instead they argue about how it should be presented to students."

Advocates of the **whole-language approach** believe that reading is part of general language development, not an isolated skill students learn apart from listening, speaking, and writing. Teachers in whole-language classrooms seldom use textbooks; instead, young students write stories and learn to read from their writing, and older students read literature that is closely related to their everyday experiences.

Literature-based reading instruction is important. The 1994 National Assessment of Educational Progress (NAEP) in reading, given to fourth-, eighth-, and twelfth-grade students, provided insight into the methods the fourth-grade teachers used to teach reading. Only 20 percent primarily used trade books vs. textbooks for reading instruction; 69 percent had students read books of their own choosing almost every day; 49 percent used a variety of books almost every day; and 30 percent asked students to write about what they have read almost every day.

Keepers of the Dream

Sylvia Ashton-Warner

Whole Language Pioneer

Sylvia Ashton-Warner mixed her abilities as a writer with her insights as an educator to create the book *Teacher*, an autobiographical account of the lessons she learned teaching the Maori children in New Zealand. The book, now a classic in the field of education, made its author and her teaching methods famous around the world, particularly in America.

Though developed in the 1950s, Ashton-Warner's methods are being rediscovered in the 1990s because of their relevance and effectiveness. Her teaching approach, the "Creative Teaching Scheme," can be thought of as a precursor to today's whole-language movement.

Recognizing that the traditional British readers and teaching strategies were ineffective with her Maori students, Ashton-Warner developed a method for teaching her students to read which she called *organic reading*. Using this approach, Ashton-Warner helped each student develop a key vocabulary of words of personal significance. Each day the children would tell her the words they wanted to learn to read, and she would write them on cards. The next day she would spill the box of cards on a rug and the children would select their own, team up with a partner, and practice reading the words to each other. The process was a crucial element of her program, because, as she observed, "All this . . . takes time and involves noise and movement and personal relations and actual reading, and above all communication, one with an-

"All this . . . takes time."

other: the vital thing so often cut off in a schoolroom." Ashton-Warner discarded the words that were forgotten, reasoning that they were not truly important to the children. The key vocabulary that remained was used for writing as well as for reading, and the children created their own stories with them.

Creativity was a key force in Ashton-Warner's theory. She passionately supported the belief that creativity releases energies that would otherwise be destructive. In *Teacher* she wrote, "I see the mind of a five-year-old as a volcano with two vents; destructiveness and creativeness. And I see that to the extent that we widen the creative channel, we atrophy the destructive one." Further, she saw her efforts to release destructive tendencies in positive ways in the infant room as extending to a more peaceful future society: "And the design of my work is that creativity in this time of life when character can be influenced forever is the solution to the problem of war" (Ashton-Warner 1965, 88).

Ashton-Warner's passion could be regarded as her hallmark. It gave edge and energy to her writing, expressed itself in her creative teaching strategies, and invigorated her pursuit of worthy causes. Fortunately for educators, with it she has provided a model of teaching commitment in her work with the Maori children and in her words: "Not just part of us becomes a teacher. It engages the whole self—the woman or man, wife or husband, mother or father, the lover, scholar or artist in us" (Levy 1984, 192). Ashton-Warner has left a legacy that guides teachers to use their own creativity and tap that of their students so that classrooms will be lively, even joyful centers for learning.

During the last two decades, several new approaches have been incorporated into the language arts curriculum. Many English teachers have reduced the amount of time spent on grammar, electing instead to teach grammar as needed within the context of a writing program. Since the 1960s, English teachers have generally broadened their view of literature to include more contemporary forms of writing and the literary contributions of minority or ethnic writers. Teaching in the English classroom now frequently includes such techniques as creative writing, drama, journal writing, guided fantasy exercises, and group discussions. In addition, many teachers are using the word-processing capabilities of computers to explore new ways to teach students reading and writing.

After three years of collaborative development, the International Reading Association and the National Council of Teachers of English released voluntary national standards for English-language arts in 1996. Debate over these standards continues to stimulate discussion and debate about the goals of language arts instruction (*Education Week* 1996, March 20, 13).

Based on their review of literacy research, Cheeks, Flippo, and Lindsey (1997, 83–84) recommend that teachers do the following to develop students' language abilities.

1. Allow many opportunities for social imaginative play and other verbal peer interaction, which enhance language and cognitive development.
2. Develop learning activities that integrate listening, speaking, reading, and writing (oral and written language).
3. Use art, music, and drama activities to further develop language opportunities.
4. Read many books and stories to children every day.
5. Choose books and stories that you believe will be of high interest to children and will further stimulate their interest in reading books.
6. Give children opportunities to respond to the books and stories you read.
7. Reread favorite stories as often as children request them.
8. Give children opportunities to retell and/or act out stories in their own words after listening to you read them.
9. Give children many opportunities to make their own books. Children can dictate stories as the teacher writes the stories down in the children's own words. Children also can write their own books using scribble writing, pictures, and invented spellings to tell their stories in their own words.
10. Give children many opportunities to share with others the stories they write.
11. Accept "less than perfect" readings, retellings, writing, and other literacy attempts for all children.
12. Provide classroom activities and an environment that enhances the idea that literacy is part of communication and that meaning is essential for communication to take place.

MATHEMATICS

With the publication of *Curriculum and Evaluation Standards for School Mathematics* in 1989, the National Council of Teachers of Mathematics (NCTM) made it clear that "basic mathematical skills for the 21st century" should consist of more than computation skills. According to the NCTM, the mathematics curriculum should emphasize twelve critical skills: problem solving, communicating mathematical ideas, mathematical reasoning, applying mathematics to everyday situations, alertness to reasonableness of results, estimation, appropriate computational skills, algebraic thinking, measurement, geometry, statistics, and probability (NCTM 1989).

Since their introduction, the NCTM *Standards* have been widely supported. For example, the 1996 National Assessment of Educational Progress (NAEP) in Mathematics was revised to reflect what NAEP (1996a) termed "the national goals for mathematics education." With input from the NCTM, the 1996 NAEP assessments were revised to measure students' performance in five major areas, or "content strands," of mathematics (see Figure 11.5). In addition to mastery of the content strands, students were to demonstrate mastery of the following:

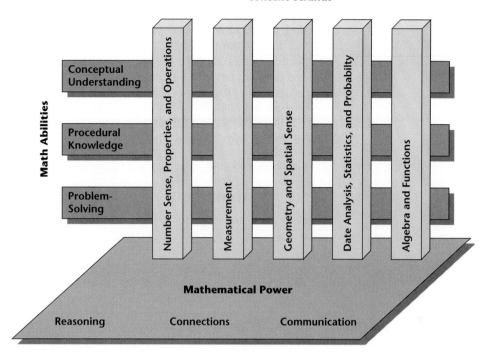

Content Strands

Math Abilities: Conceptual Understanding, Procedural Knowledge, Problem-Solving

Number Sense, Properties, and Operations · Measurement · Geometry and Spatial Sense · Date Analysis, Statistics, and Probability · Algebra and Functions

Mathematical Power

Reasoning Connections Communication

FIGURE 11.5 A framework for mathematics assessment (Source: *Assessing Mathematics— Achieving Goals: The 1996 National Assessment of Educational Progress in Mathematics.* Washington, DC: National Assessment Governing Board, U.S. Department of Education, 1996.)

- Productive use of mathematical concepts, procedural skills, and problem-solving strategies.
- Grasp of process skills in reasoning, communicating, and making connections with mathematics and between mathematics and other disciplines.
- Knowledge of when and how to employ technology, most notably calculators, in solving mathematics problems (NEAP 1996a).

In the 1990s, mathematics programs, from the elementary through secondary levels, still tended to focus on the mechanical acquisition of skills. A 1992 study by Boston College's Center for the Study of Testing, Evaluation, and Educational Policy pointed out that efforts to increase the mathematics and science competencies of students were not succeeding because textbooks were measuring low-level skills such as memorization—not the higher-order reasoning and problem-solving skills students need. Similarly, *A Splintered Vision: An Investigation of U.S. Science and Mathematics Education* (1996), a report by the U.S. Department of Education and the International Institute of Education, asserted that publishers included shallow analyses of many different topics to appeal to as many school districts as possible. Compared to the mathematics curricula of other nations, the report asserted, the U.S. curriculum in mathematics is "a mile wide and an inch deep."

What is needed is **problem-centered learning,** in which students work in small groups on problems that have many or open-ended solutions. Rather than memorizing facts, working on sets of problems in textbooks, and competing against their classmates, students discover concepts, solve problems similar to those they will encounter in life, and learn to cooperate in small groups. For example, one mathe-matics-reform group developed a curriculum unit on testing blood for diseases that asks students to use quadratic and cubic equations to decide when to pool samples of blood rather than test each sample individually (Viadero 1996, 33). The use of manipulative materials such as Cuisinnaire rods, balance beams, counting sticks, and measuring scales also has positive effects on students' achievement in mathe-matics (Walberg 1991). Use of manipulatives supports active learning. As researcher Herbert Walberg says, "Students can handle the material, see the relation of ab-stract ideas and concrete embodiments, and check hypothesized answers by doing quick empirical tests—without having to wait for quiz results or teacher feedback" (1991, 57).

SCIENCE AND TECHNOLOGY

Perhaps more than any other area of the curriculum, the teaching of science in the United States has come under increasingly critical scrutiny. On the elementary level, the science curriculum consists of assorted science-related topics: animals, plants, seasons, light, sound, heat, weather, magnets, the stars and planets, basic electric-ity, nutrition, oceanography, and so on. These topics are often restudied in greater depth at the middle or junior high level in courses variously titled Earth Science, Gen-eral Science, Physical Science, or Life Science. At the high school level, students typ-ically may select from only a limited number of basic science courses: Biology, Chemistry, Physical Science, Anatomy and Physiology, and Physics. Many high schools do, however, distinguish between science courses that are applied (for the noncollege-bound) and those that are academic.

Several leading science educators and national committees have recommended changes in the science curriculum. Nearly all stress the need for students to learn more science and to acquire scientific knowledge, skills, and processes through an inquiry, discovery, or problem-centered method. The teacher's primary role is to guide students in their search for knowledge rather than to act solely as a source of information and/or right answers.

To assess students' achievement in science, for example, the 1996 National As-sessment of Educational Progress (NAEP) in Science included a "Knowing and Doing Science" dimension that focused on the following goals:

- Students should acquire a rich collection of scientific information that will en-able them to move from simply being able to provide reasonable interpreta-tions of observations to providing explanations and predictions.
- Appropriate to their age and grade level, students will be assessed on their ability to acquire new information, plan appropriate investigations, use a vari-ety of scientific tools, and communicate the results of their investigations.
- By grade 12, students should be able to discuss larger science- and technol-ogy-linked problems not directly related to their immediate experience. Exam-ples include waste disposal, energy uses, air quality, water pollution, noise abatement, and the trade-offs between the benefits and adverse conse-quences of various technologies (NAEP 1996b).

Similarly, the American Association for the Advancement of Science issued a set of recommendations based on Project 2061: Education for a Changing Future (2061 refers to the year Halley's comet returns). The Association recommended (1) integrat-ing science and mathematics with other disciplines, (2) preparing students to become inquirers and critical thinkers rather than sources of right answers, and (3) focusing on

In what ways might these students be meeting the curriculum goals of the National Assessment of Educational Progress in Science?

the contributions science can make to current social issues—population growth, environmental pollution, waste disposal, energy, and birth control (Rutherford and Ahlgren 1990).

Recently, the National Science Foundation (NSF) released *Indicators of Science and Mathematics Education* (1996), highlighting a positive trend for science education in America. Student performance on the NAEP science and mathematics tests had improved slightly for all age and ethnic groups since 1980. In addition, the NSF found that 94 percent of science teachers and 97 percent of mathematics teachers reported they enjoyed teaching.

SOCIAL STUDIES

Goals for the social studies lack the precision that we find in other subject areas. Consider, for example, Charles Beard's comment in 1938 that the social studies aim at the "creation of rich and many-sided personalities, equipped with practical knowledge and inspired by ideals so that they can make their way and fulfill their mission in a changing society which is part of a world complex" (1938, 179). Or the assertion in 1979 by the National Council for the Social Studies (NCSS) that "the basic goal of social studies education is to prepare young people to be humane, rational, participating citizens in a world that is becoming increasingly interdependent" (1979, 262).

Or finally, the following ten "strands" from the NCSS's (1994) *Expect Excellence: Curriculum Standards for Social Studies:*

1. Culture and cultural diversity
2. Human beings' views of themselves over time
3. People, places, and environments
4. Individual development and identity
5. Interactions among individuals, groups, and institutions
6. How structures of power, authority, and governance are changed
7. The production, distribution, and consumption of goods and services
8. Relationships among science, technology, and society
9. Global interdependence
10. Citizenship in a democratic society

The content of traditional social studies courses has remained comparatively unchanged during the last decade. Trends include fewer offerings in ancient history and civics and more offerings in psychology, economics, world cultures, and marriage and the family. Experimental courses or units in subjects such as African-American studies,

Latino and Hispanic culture, and women's history have been criticized variously as gratuitous, distorting, misrepresentative, ethnocentric, or defamatory. As you read in Chapter 8, the development of a truly multicultural curriculum is a subject of debate.

The National Center for History in the Schools at UCLA became embroiled in controversy in 1994 when it issued a set of voluntary U.S. and world history standards. The Council for Basic Education and other groups believed that the standards' authors were overly concerned about including the stories of minorities and women and the discrimination they experienced, with the result that they omitted significant historical figures and positive features of the U.S. and the West. Others complained that the new standards were "politically correct" to the extent that they contained an anti-Western bias. With input from two independent, bipartisan national review panels appointed by the Council for Basic Education; 33 national education organizations; and more than 1,000 educators, the National Center for History rewrote the standards and released the revised edition in 1996 with endorsements from several groups that had criticized the previous standards.

FOREIGN LANGUAGES

As we become increasingly aware of our interconnectedness with other nations, the small number of students who study foreign languages at the elementary through secondary levels is alarming. Support for foreign languages increased briefly immediately following Russia's launching of Sputnik in 1957, but foreign language enrollments declined dramatically during the 1960s and 1970s.

Currently, more than one-third of high school students enroll in a foreign language course (National Center for Education Statistics 1995), though the majority enroll in one of only three languages: Spanish, French, or German. Only a few schools in the country offer a course in the world's first and third most commonly spoken languages—Mandarin and Hindi. To enhance foreign language instruction in the United States in an era of expanding global interdependence, several states have developed guidelines for foreign language study, and government and private groups are working cooperatively with foreign language organizations to promote the need for foreign language study.

In *Standards for Foreign Language Learning: Preparing for the 21st Century,* the American Council on the Teaching of Foreign Languages (1996) asserted that:

> The United States must educate students who are linguistically and culturally equipped to communicate successfully in a pluralistic American society and abroad. This imperative envisions a future in which ALL students will develop and maintain proficiency in English and at least one other language, modern or classical. Children who come to school from non-English backgrounds should also have opportunities to develop further proficiencies in their first language.

To reach this goal, the Council recommended that foreign language instruction focus on the following "five C's of foreign language education":

> *Communication:* Communicate in languages other than English
> *Cultures:* Gain knowledge and understanding of other cultures
> *Connections:* Connect with other disciplines and acquire information
> *Comparisons:* Develop insight into the nature of language and culture
> *Communities:* Participate in multilingual communities at home and around the world (American Council on the Teaching of Foreign Languages 1996)

Rarely are students introduced to foreign language study at the optimal time for learning a second language—as early as second grade. The first year of a foreign language, usually Spanish or French, is sometimes offered at the middle school or junior high school level. Students typically study the first part of Spanish I, for example, in the sixth or seventh grade and complete the course next year. As high school freshmen, then, they are ready for Spanish II.

Some schools have broadened their foreign language offerings to include such languages as Russian, Japanese, and Chinese. At a few schools, foreign language study has even become a central part of the curriculum. La Salle Language Academy in Chicago, for example, provides its K–8 students daily instruction in French, Spanish, Italian, or German. In addition, parents are encouraged to take special morning or evening language classes, and seventh- and eighth-grade students may participate in a foreign-exchange program.

THE ARTS

More than any other area of the curriculum, the arts hold an insecure position. When schools are faced with budgetary cutbacks or pressure to raise scores on basic skills tests, a cost-conscious public often considers the elimination of music and art. The arts, however, have much to contribute to the education of students. As Ernest Boyer said, "The arts give rise to many voices, and make it possible for people who are socially, economically, and ethnically separated to understand one another at a deeper, more authentic level. The arts help build community" (1995, 76).

Typically, elementary art and music are limited to one period a week, and this instruction is given either by regular teachers or by special teachers who travel from school to school. In addition, most elementary students have occasional opportunities to use crayons, watercolors, clay, and other art materials as they learn in other subject areas. And, from time to time, many children even have the opportunity to experience dance, puppetry, role-playing, pantomime, and crafts.

At the middle and junior high level, instruction in art and music becomes more structured, as well as more voluntary. Students may choose from band, chorus, arts, and crafts. At the high school level, art and music are usually offered as electives. Depending on the school's resources, however, students frequently have a wide assortment of classes to choose from: jazz band, glee club, band, orchestra, drama, chorus, photography, sculpture, ceramics, and filmmaking, to name a few. In addition, middle school and high school students may receive instruction in practical arts, such as sewing, cooking, woodworking and metalworking, automotive shop, print shop, and courses teaching agricultural knowledge and skills. A noteworthy trend is for students of both sexes to take courses in all the practical arts rather than follow traditional sex-role stereotypes; that is, you increasingly find boys and girls both in the kitchen and in the garage.

In spite of the tenuous position of the arts in the curriculum, art educators are working to create a new awareness of the unique contribution that the arts can make to all areas of the curriculum. Several reform reports of the 1980s underscored the importance of the arts in the curriculum. In its study of the academic preparation that students need for college, the College Board included the visual and performing arts as one of the six essential areas of the basic academic curriculum. The observation team for the Carnegie Foundation's report on high schools in America found the arts "shamefully neglected" and recommended that "all students study the arts to discover how human beings use nonverbal symbols and communicate not only with words but through music, dance, and the visual arts (Boyer 1983, 98)."

Art education in American schools received considerable attention in the mid-1980s when the Getty Center for Education in the Arts, funded by the J. Paul Getty

What determines content-area coverage in the curriculum? What do curriculum reformers propose for keeping and even expanding art education programs in the public schools?

Trust, began to call for a "discipline-based" approach to art education. **Discipline-based art programs** emphasize art production, art criticism, art history, and aesthetics. Since the late 1980s, the Getty center has spearheaded five major efforts to influence the quality of art education in the schools (Duke 1988, 445):

- Public advocacy for the value of art in education
- Professional development programs for school administrators and teachers
- Development of the theoretical bases of discipline-based art education
- Development of model programs to demonstrate discipline-based art education in the classroom
- Development of discipline-based curricula

In 1996, the Getty Center and the College Board launched "The Role of the Arts in Unifying the High School Curriculum," a four-year research and development project to study how the arts can unify the school curriculum across all subject areas. Five high schools, including arts magnet and comprehensive high schools from rural and urban areas in Massachusettes, New Mexico, Texas, Maryland, and Washington, were selected to develop and test model curricula to integrate the arts with subjects such as history, literature, language, and science. Project teams at these schools will share their work with other schools over online school networks.

PHYSICAL EDUCATION

The ultimate aim of physical education is to promote physical activities that develop a desire in the individual to maintain physical fitness throughout life. In addition, students in physical education programs may receive instruction in health and nutrition, sex education, and driver education.

At one time, physical education programs consisted largely of highly competitive team sports. Many children, less aggressive and competitive than their peers, did not do well in such programs and experienced a lowered sense of self-esteem. Gradually, instructors began to offer activities designed to meet the needs and abilities of all students, not just the athletically talented. In addition to traditional team sports such as football, baseball, and basketball, and individual sports such as swimming and wrestling, many students in grades K–12 may now participate in a broad array of physical activities, including aerobics, archery, badminton, dodgeball, folk and square dancing, gymnastics, handball, hockey, table tennis, golf, racquetball, shuffleboard, skating, volleyball, soccer, and yoga.

In addition to becoming more sensitive to the needs and abilities of individual students, physical education programs were required by law to provide more opportunities for female students. In 1972, Congress enacted Title IX of the Education Amendments Act, which said, "No person in the United States shall, on the basis of sex, be excluded from participation in, be denied benefits of, or be subjected to discrimination under any education or activity receiving federal financial assistance." Following Title IX, girls became much more involved in school athletic programs. The National Federation of State High School Associations, for example, found that 1.85 million young women participated in high school athletics in 1980–81 compared to only 240,000 in 1970–71. In 1995, the National Center for Education Statistics reported that almost 29 percent of female high school seniors participated in school-sponsored athletic activities.

VOCATIONAL EDUCATION

In addition to their academic (or college preparatory) curricula, many comprehensive high schools offer programs in vocational education; and some high schools offer only a vocational education program. **Vocational education** programs vary from those that actually prepare students to take jobs in business and industry after graduation to those that merely introduce students to career possibilities.

Unfortunately, vocational education in American has had an image problem. As the MIT Commission on Industrial Productivity concluded in its 1989 report, *Made in America* (Dertouzon, Lester, and Solow, 1989, 85): "though high school vocational education in the U.S. has been supported by the federal government for over 70 years and enrolls about five million students annually, it has a very disappointing performance and is not generally viewed as a viable preemployment training system." Also, vocational students in comprehensive high schools often have lower achievement levels than students in nonvocational programs. Finally, as the following blunt comments suggest, the curriculum and instructional methods found in vocational education programs may not be of the same quality as those found in academic programs (Aring, 1993, 400):

> The curricula used to instruct [vocational] students generally do not reflect the needs of the future labor market, in which one worker will be required to do sophisticated tasks previously done by several workers. Academic courses for students in vocational tracks are usually out of date and watered down to the lowest possible level. . . . Finally, the method of instruction is almost always teacher-centered, and students gain little or no experience in teamwork, communication, and how to go about solving complex problems.

In the mid-1990s, many high schools formed partnerships with the private sector and began to develop **school-to-work programs** to address current and future needs in industry. Curricula were revised to emphasize the transfer of knowledge and skills learned at school to the job setting. For example, from 1994 to 1996, Forrest Parkay and a colleague helped teachers at Rogers High School in Spokane, Washington, redesign the curriculum according to five "career pathways": Business and Marketing, Communications and Arts, Science and Nature, Health and Human Services, and Industry and Technology. As part of this new "real-world" curriculum, all students would select a career pathway and take courses that prepare them to pursue the pathway at the "entry," "skilled/technical," or "professional" levels after graduation. Within the Business and Marketing pathway, for example, a student at the entry level would take courses to prepare to become a cashier or salesperson; a student at the professional level would take courses appropriate for an eventual career as an accountant or business executive. In addition, students could select from pathway-appropriate opportunities for internships, summer work, and job shadowing.

As America continues to be concerned about its productivity compared with other nations, and as employers continue to expect schools to graduate students

Issues in Education

- What does this cartoon suggest about the need for career education as a part of the standard school curriculum?
- Do you agree? Why or why not?
- How might career education be integrated across the curriculum? differentiated from vocational education?
- What is your opinion of the current emphasis on preparing students for the world of work as the chief aim of education? What influences have created this emphasis?
- What curriculum goals might be sacrificed through a focus on turning out good employees?

"RIGHT NOW I'M KINDA LEANING TOWARD A CAREER IN VIDEO GAMES."

who have mastered the basic skills and learned how to learn, it seems likely that vocational education will continue to be an important part of the school curriculum. Through school–business partnerships such as the one at Rogers High, a new definition of vocational education will be forged—one based on new, rigorous standards cooperatively developed by educators and employers from various industrial sectors.

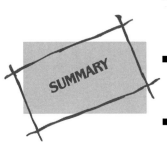

What Is Taught in the Schools?

- There are many different definitions for the term *curriculum*. A general definition is that curriculum refers to the experiences, both planned and unplanned, that either enhance or impede the education and growth of students.
- There are four curricula that all students experience. In addition to learning what teachers intend to teach (the explicit curriculum), students learn from the hidden curriculum, the null curriculum, and extracurricular/cocurricular programs.
- From school policies to national politics, many factors influence what is taught (and not taught) in the schools.

How Is the School Curriculum Developed?

- Curricula are based on the needs and interests of students and also reflect a variety of professional, commercial, local, state, national, and international pressures.
- Teachers must be prepared to assume important roles in the curriculum development process, especially in developing student-centered and integrated curricula.

What Reform Efforts Have Affected the Curriculum?

- Historical forces affecting the aims of education have influenced curriculum reform. Religion and the need to educate for citizenship in a democracy have played important roles in the development of American school curricula. In any historical period, curriculum content reflects society's beliefs and values about education.
- Recent systematic efforts to establish curriculum reforms have focused on curriculum standards, core curricula, and education for equity and excellence.

What Are Some Current Subject-Area Trends?

- Alternative curricula for literacy, multicultural curricula, character education, art as curriculum, problem-centered learning, thinking skills, computer literacy, and career education are examples of curriculum trends today.
- Curriculum trends also involve, for example, redefining foreign language study and sex/health education, developing school-to-work programs, providing for active and authentic learning, determining what students will need to know and be able to do in the 21st century, and establishing national standards in the content areas.

APPLICATIONS AND ACTIVITIES

Teacher's Journal

1. List in order of importance the five factors that you believe have the greatest impact on the curriculum. Then list the five factors that you believe *ideally* should have the greatest influence. What differences do you notice between your actual and ideal lists? What might be done to reduce the differences between the two lists?

2. Reflect on the 12,000 or so hours that you have spent as a student in K–12 classrooms. What did the nonexplicit curricula in the classes teach you about yourself?

3. What religious and political emphases affected your learning as a student in elementary school or high school? Which experiences do you view as having been positive? Which do you view as having been negative for you?

4. In your opinion, how should teachers and schools respond to censorship issues in the curricula and complaints about the content of instructional materials?

Teacher's Database

1. Visit the ERIC Clearinghouse for a curricular area you plan to teach, and record information for your portfolio on the resources available to you as a teacher in that content area. E-mail askeric@ericir.syr.edu and request information about contacting, for example, one of the following clearinghouses for educators:

Languages and Linguistics (Center for Applied Linguistics, Washington, DC)
Reading, English and Communication (Indiana University)
Science, Mathematics and Environmental Education (Ohio State University)
Social Studies (Indiana University)

2. Survey the Internet to begin locating and bookmarking web sites, schools, networks, and teacher discussion groups that you could use to help develop a subject-area curriculum for your students. For example, visit (gopher) informns.k12.mn.us for curriculum resources developed at Minnesota Schools, the Discovery Channel School (http://school.discovery.com), the Eisenhower National Clearinghouse for Mathematics and Science Education (ENC) (galileo.enc.org), the Teachers Network (www.teachnet.org), and Steve Linduska's K-12 Resources (http:// www.public.iastate.edu).

3. Find the professional curriculum standards for your subject area(s) online and compare them to the curriculum standards for that subject area in a state where you plan to teach. For example, you might download the National Council for Teachers of Mathematics (NCTM) standards and then compare them with the mathematics curriculum in Georgia's Quality Core Curriculum on Georgia College EduNet (gcedunet.peachnet.edu).

Observations and Interviews

1. Spend a half-day at school at the level you plan to teach and record your impressions regarding the types of curricula. If possible, chat briefly with administrators, teachers, and students about your impressions. Include observations of students outside the classroom during the school day.

2. As a collaborative project, conduct an informal survey on what people think are the four most important subjects to be taught at the elementary, middle, junior, and senior high levels. Compare your data with the information in this chapter.

3. With classmates, as an experiment, practice the process of curriculum development described in this chapter. Assign some members of the group to observe and report on their observations in relation to concepts presented in in this chapter.

Professional Portfolio

Compare and contrast two or more textbooks or curriculum guides that are currently used by teachers to teach a unit in a subject area and at a grade level you are preparing to teach. Assess the strengths and weaknesses of the unit in each textbook or curriculum guide. Would you use the materials in your classroom? How would you improve them? What other curriculum materials would you incorporate? How would you integrate educational technology? How would you adapt the curriculum for the unit for individual students according to their needs and characteristics?

. . . images of leadership have come to prominence where teachers are involved in and exercise substantial leadership at [the] school level.

—Andy Hargreaves
Changing Teachers, Changing Times

Teachers as Educational Leaders

F O C U S
Q U E S T I O N S

1. To what extent is teaching a full profession?

2. What is professionalism in teaching?

3. How do teachers help shape education as a profession?

4. What new leadership roles for teachers are emerging?

5. How do teachers contribute to educational research?

6. How are teachers involved in school restructuring and curriculum reform?

7. How are teachers innovators in the use of educational technology?

It is near the end of your third year of teaching at a school in a working-class neighborhood in a city of about 300,000. Approximately 35 percent of the students are ethnic minorities, and the school has the largest American Indian enrollment in the state. Fifty percent of the students are on free and reduced lunch. According to a needs assessment conducted by a teacher, approximately 30 percent of students are "at risk" (i.e., they possess two or more at-risk characteristics such as "erratic attendance," "signs of abuse/neglect," "assignments not turned in or incomplete," or "chronic behavior problems").

The school serves the diverse needs of its students well and is generally acknowledged as one of the most innovative in the district. Three years ago, for example, the local newspaper did a two-page feature on the role that teachers were playing in restructuring the school. The article also highlighted the school's partnership with a university and described how two professors were facilitating the change effort and how their students were helping teachers with curriculum development.

You and five other teachers (one of whom is the school's representative on the teachers' union) sit on the Site-Based Council (SBC) that also includes the principal, two assistant principals, and two parents. It is two weeks before the end of school, and the SBC is meeting to discuss the composition of next year's SBC and how it will function.

You enter the conference room and take a seat just as the principal says, "So, today, we've got to decide who's responsible, and ultimately accountable, for what."

The teachers' union representative nods her head in agreement and says, "We need to remember that other teachers, most of whom belong to the union, want the membership of the new SBC to represent their interests

vigorously. As professionals, we play a key role in providing leadership for change."

"I agree," adds another teacher. "We've worked extremely hard at restructuring for three years—developing an entirely new curriculum, a mentoring program for new teachers, a peer coaching program, and so on."

The teacher next to you adds, "What we're saying is that next year's SBC has got to continue to place teachers at the center of this change effort. Regardless of how the SBC functions, teacher leadership is essential."

As several members of the group, including you, nod in agreement, you reflect on what you've just heard. What does it really mean to be a professional? What are the characteristics of a profession, and to what extent does teaching reflect those characteristics? What new leadership roles for teachers are emerging? What leadership roles will you play in educational reform?

■

Andy Hargreaves' *Changing Teachers, Changing Times: Teachers' Work and Culture in the Postmodern Age* (1994) provides the title for Part Four of this book because it captures so well the condition of education at the start of the 21st century. School reform efforts, as the preceding scenario illustrates, are continuing to change dramatically what it means to be a teacher. Teacher empowerment, the professionalization of teaching, shared decision making, and mentor teacher programs are just a few of the educational changes that are providing unprecedented, exciting opportunities for teachers to assume leadership roles beyond the classroom.

We have referred to teaching as a **profession** throughout this book; however, if we compare teaching with other professions—law and medicine, for example—we find some significant differences. As a result of these differences, current opinion is divided as to whether teaching actually is a full profession. Some have labeled teaching a *semi*-profession (Etzioni 1969), an *emerging* profession (Howsam et al. 1976), an *uncertain* profession (Powell 1980), an *imperiled* profession (Duke 1984; Sykes 1983; Freedman et al. 1983; Boyer 1990), an *endangered* profession (Goodlad 1983), and a *not-quite* profession (Goodlad 1990)!

TO WHAT EXTENT IS TEACHING A FULL PROFESSION ?

We use the terms *professional* and *profession* quite frequently, usually without thinking about their meanings. Professionals "possess a high degree of *specialized theoretical knowledge*, along with methods and techniques for applying this knowledge in their day-to-day work. . . . [and they] are united by a high degree of in-group solidarity, stemming from their common training and common adherence to certain doctrines and methods" (Abrahamsson 1971, 11–12).

From several sociologists and educators who have studied teaching come additional characteristics of occupations that are highly professionalized, summarized in Figure 12.1. As you read each characteristic in Figure 12.1, think about the degree to which it applies to teaching.

Now let us examine the extent to which teaching satisfies each of these commonly agreed-on characteristics of full professions.

INSTITUTIONAL MONOPOLY OF SERVICES   On one hand, teachers do have a monopoly of services. As a rule, only those who are certified members of the profession may teach in public schools. On the other hand, the varied requirements we find for certification and for teaching in private schools weaken this monopoly. In addition, any claim teachers might have as exclusive providers of a service is further eroded by the practice of many state systems to approve temporary, or emergency, certification measures to deal with teacher shortages—a move that establishes teaching as the only profession that allows noncertified individuals to practice the profession. The National Commission on Teaching and America's Future (1996), for example, recently reported that more than 25 percent of the nation's teachers were not fully licensed, and about one-fourth of the high school teachers surveyed lacked a minor degree in their primary field of instruction. Furthermore, a decline of inadequately licensed teachers seemed unlikely, given the Commission's projection that the nation would need more than 2 million new teachers in the next ten years.

FIGURE 12.1   Characteristics of a profession

1. Professionals are allowed to institutionalize a monopoly of essential knowledge and services. For example, only lawyers may practice law; only physicians may practice medicine.

2. Professionals are able to practice their occupation with a high degree of autonomy. They are not closely supervised, and they have frequent opportunities to make their own decisions about important aspects of their work. Professional autonomy also implies an obligation to perform responsibly, to self-supervise, and to be dedicated to providing a service rather than meeting minimum requirements of the job.

3. Professionals must typically undergo a lengthy period of education and/or training before they may enter professional practice. Furthermore, professionals usually must undergo a lengthy induction period following their formal education or training.

4. Professionals perform an essential service for their clients and are devoted to continuous development of their ability to deliver this service. This service emphasizes intellectual rather than physical techniques.

5. Professionals have control over their governance, their socialization into the occupation, and research connected with their occupation.

6. Members of a profession form their own vocational associations, which have control over admissions to the profession, educational standards, examinations and licensing, career development, ethical and performance standards, and professional discipline.

7. The knowledge and skills held by professionals are not usually available to nonprofessionals.

8. Professionals enjoy a high level of public trust and are able to deliver services that are clearly superior to those available elsewhere.

9. Professionals are granted a high level of prestige and higher-than-average financial rewards.

Perhaps the most significant argument against teachers claiming to be the exclusive providers of a service, however, is the fact that a great deal of teaching occurs in informal, nonschool settings and is done by people who are not teachers. Every day, thousands of people teach various kinds of how-to-do-it skills: how to water-ski, how to make dogs more obedient, how to make pasta from scratch, how to tune a car's engine, and how to meditate.

TEACHER AUTONOMY In one sense teachers have considerable autonomy. They usually work behind a closed classroom door, and only seldom is their work observed by another adult. In fact, one of the norms among teachers is that the classroom is a castle of sorts, and teacher privacy a closely guarded right. Although the performance of new teachers may be observed and evaluated on a regular basis by supervisors, veteran teachers are observed much less frequently, and they usually enjoy a high degree of autonomy.

Teachers also have extensive freedom regarding how they structure the classroom environment. They may emphasize discussions as opposed to lectures. They may set certain requirements for some students and not for others. They may delegate responsibilities to one class and not another. And, within the guidelines set by local and state authorities, teachers may determine much of the content they teach.

There are, however, constraints placed on teachers and their work. Teachers, unlike doctors and lawyers, must accept all the "clients" who are sent to them. Only infrequently does a teacher actually "reject" a student assigned to him or her.

Teachers must also agree to teach what state and local officials say they must. Moreover, the work of teachers is subject to a higher level of public scrutiny than that found in other professions. Because the public provides "clients" (students) and pays for schools, it has a significant say regarding the work of teachers.

YEARS OF EDUCATION AND TRAINING As sociologist Amitai Etzioni (1969) points out in his classic discussion of the "semi-professions," the training of teachers is less lengthy than that required for other professionals—lawyers and physicians, for example. The professional component of teacher education programs is the shortest of all the professions—only 15 percent of the average bachelor's degree program for a high school teacher is devoted to professional courses. However, as we learned in Chapter 2, several colleges and universities have begun five-year teacher education programs. Similarly, in its comprehensive report, *What Matters Most: Teaching for America's Future,* the National Commission on Teaching and America's Future (1996) recommended that teacher education be moved to the graduate level. If the trend toward five-year and graduate-level teacher education programs continues, the professional status of teaching will definitely be enhanced.

In most professions, new members must undergo a prescribed induction period. Physicians, for example, must serve an internship or residency before beginning practice, and most lawyers begin as clerks in law firms. In contrast, teachers usually do not go through a formal induction period before assuming full responsibility for their work. Practice teaching comes closest to serving as an induction period, but it is often relatively short, informal, and lacking in uniformity. As the National Commission on Teaching and America's Future (1996) noted, "Our society can no longer accept the [s]ink-or-swim induction [of teachers]."

PROVISION OF ESSENTIAL SERVICE Although it is generally acknowledged that teachers provide a service that is vital to the well-being of individuals and groups, the pub-

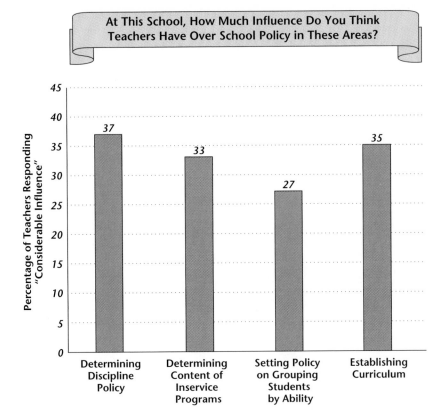

At This School, How Much Influence Do You Think Teachers Have Over School Policy in These Areas?

FIGURE 12.2 At this school, how much influence do you think teachers have over school policy in these areas? (Source: Based on Judith Anderson, "Who's In Charge? Teachers' Views on Control Over School Policy and Classroom Practices," *Research Report,* U.S. Department of Education, Office of Educational Research and Improvement, August 1994. In Ernest L. Boyer, *The Basic School: A Community for Learning.* The Carnegie Foundation for the Advancement of Teaching, 1995.)

lic does need to be reminded of this fact from time to time. This importance was driven home on a large scale during the early 1980s when several reports calling for school reform linked the strength of our country to the quality of its schools.

In a sense, it is no exaggeration to say that teaching is a matter of life and death:

> every moment in the lives of teachers and pupils brings critical decisions of motivation, reinforcement, reward, ego enhancement and goal direction. Proper professional decisions enhance learning and life; improper decisions send the learner towards incremental death in openness to experience and in ability to learn and contribute. Doctors and lawyers probably have neither more nor less to do with life, death, and freedom than do teachers (Howsam et al. 1976, 15).

DEGREE OF SELF-GOVERNANCE The limited freedom of teachers to govern themselves has detracted from the overall status of the profession. In many states, licensing guidelines are set by government officials who may or may not be educators; and at the local level, decision-making power usually resides with local boards of education, largely made up of persons who have never taught. As a result, teachers have had little or no say over what they teach, when they teach, whom they teach, and, in extreme instances, *how* they teach.

However, recent efforts to empower teachers and to professionalize teaching are creating new roles for teachers and expanded opportunities to govern important aspects of their work. At schools such as the one portrayed in this chapter's opening scenario, teachers are having a greater voice in decisions related to curriculum development, staffing, budger, and the day- to-day operation of schools. Figure 12.2, for example, compares the percentage of teachers in public and private schools who report that they have a "great deal of influence" over schoolwide discipline policies, faculty training programs, grouping students by ability, and establishing the curriculum.

PROFESSIONAL ASSOCIATIONS Teachers, like other professionals, have formed a number of vocational associations that are vitally concerned with issues such as admission

To What Extent is Teaching a Full Profession? **383**

to the profession, educational standards, examinations and licensing, career development, ethical and performance standards, and professional discipline. It is clear, though, that the more than 500 national teacher organizations have not progressed as far as other professions have in gaining control of these areas.

PROFESSIONAL KNOWLEDGE AND SKILLS   Professionals are granted a certain status because they possess knowledge and skills not normally held by the general public. Within the profession of teaching, however, the requirements for membership are less precise. In spite of the ongoing efforts of educational researchers, there is less than unanimous agreement on the knowledge and skills considered necessary to teach. This lack of agreement is reflected in the varied programs at the 1,300 or so colleges and universities that train teachers.

During the last ten years, the National Board for Professional Teaching Standards (NBPTS) has made significant progress toward clarifying the knowledge base for teaching. As we learned in Chapter 2, the NBPTS (the majority of whose members are teachers) offers board certification to teachers who possess a high level of NBPTS-identified knowledge and skills. By 1996, the NBPTS had granted national certification to 376 teachers (*Education Week,* September 4, 1996, 4), and that same year the National Commission on Teaching and America's Future (1996) called for the NBPTS to certify 105,000 teachers during the coming decade, enough to put a board-certified teacher in every school.

LEVEL OF PUBLIC TRUST   The level of trust the public extends to teachers as professionals varies greatly. On the one hand, the public appears to have great confidence in the work that teachers do. Because of its faith in the teaching profession, the public invests teachers with considerable power over its children. For the most part, parents willingly allow their children to be molded and influenced by teachers, and this willingness must be based on a high degree of trust. In addition, most parents expect their children to obey and respect teachers.

Though all professions have some members who might be described as unprofessional, teaching is especially vulnerable to such charges. The sheer size of the teaching force makes it difficult to maintain consistently high professional standards. Moreover, teaching is subject to a level of public scrutiny and control that other, more established, professions traditionally have not tolerated. However, the era of widespread public trust may be running out for these other professions as well. Mushrooming malpractice suits against doctors, for example, may be a sign that here, too, public confidence has significantly eroded.

PRESTIGE, BENEFITS, AND PAY   Though one of the few studies of occupational prestige to include teachers ranked them well above average in status (Siegel 1971), teachers have not received salaries in keeping with other professions. Although considerable salary gains have been made for teachers in most states since the start of the 1980s, teachers still earn less than members of other professional groups. And if comparisons are made with professions requiring approximately the same amount of schooling, the discrepancies are still significant. Nevertheless, there is support for reducing the salary gap—on the 1996 Phi Delta Kappa/Gallup Poll, the public ranked "raise teachers salaries" fifth out of 20 items when asked what they would do if "additional money became available to spend on your public schools" (Elam, Rose, and Gallup 1996, 56).

WHAT IS PROFESSIONALISM IN TEACHING ⁉️

We believe that the current thrust among teachers, teacher educators, policymakers, and the general public is in the direction of making teaching a full profession. Be aware, too, that countless career teachers find teaching immensely satisfying. In spite of problems that confront the profession today, morale among most teachers is high. As one lifelong teacher put it:

> I hope that awareness of the problems . . . will not discourage talented young men and women from entering our profession. Some problems will be solved; the others can be lived with. All professions have their problems. If I were making a career choice in the twenty-first century, I would have no hesitation about becoming a teacher because I firmly believe that teaching, done well, is still the most personally satisfying of all the professions as well as the one offering the greatest long-range service to the human race (Woodring 1983, 121).

The following sections look at three dimensions of professionalism in teaching.

PROFESSIONAL BEHAVIOR

The professional teacher is guided by a specific set of values. He or she has made a deep and lasting commitment to professional practice. He or she has adopted a high standard of professional ethics and models behaviors that are in accord with that code of ethics. The professional teacher also engages in serious, reflective thought about how to teach more effectively. Moreover, he or she does this *while* teaching, continually examining experiences to improve practice.

REFLECTION-IN-ACTION   Donald Shön (1983, 1987, and 1991) has described this professional behavior as **reflection-in-action**, and he describes how a teacher might use it to solve a problem in the classroom:

An artful teacher sees a child's difficulty in learning to read not as a defect in the child but as a defect "of his own instruction." And because the child's difficulties may be unique, the teacher cannot assume that his repertoire of explanations will suffice, even though they are "at the tongue's end." He must be ready to invent new methods and must "endeavor to develop in himself the ability of discovering them" (1983, 66).

The professional teacher Schön describes makes careful, sensitive observations of classroom events, reflects on

What characteristics distinguish teaching as a profession? What characteristics might distinguish this teacher as a professional?

the meaning of those observations, and then decides to act in a certain way. Steven Lacy, selected by the Walt Disney Company as the Outstanding General Elementary Teacher for 1994–95, describes the reflective decision-making process this way:

> Our effectiveness as teachers is not reflected in the materials and structures of our pedagogy as much as it is in the countless decisions we make every day, decisions that are made in an instant. [D]o I help him with that problem or let him struggle? Do I pursue her question or stick with the lesson? Does this behavior need to be punished or ignored? Does this composition need to be criticized or praised (Levey 1996, 2–3)?

BECOMING A MENTOR Because of their positions and their encounters with young people, teachers may find opportunities to become mentors to some of their students. Accepting this responsibility is another example of professionalism. The role of **mentor** is unique in several ways. First, mentorship develops naturally and is not an automatic part of teaching, nor can it be assigned to anyone. True mentorships grow from teaching relationships and cannot be artificially promoted. Second, the role of mentor is a *comprehensive* one: Mentors express broad interest in those whom they mentor. Third, the role of mentor is *mutually* recognized by student and teacher; both realize that their relationship has a special "depth." Fourth, the role of mentor is significant and has the potential to change the quality and direction of students' lives. And fifth, the opportunity to work with a mentor is free, what Gehrke (1988) terms the mentor's "gift of care."

The longer you teach, the more you will encounter opportunities for mentorships to develop, discovering that you can mentor less experienced teachers and student teachers as well as students. The rewards that come from the unique role of mentor are among the most satisfying.

LIFELONG LEARNING

The professional teacher is dedicated to continuous learning—both about the teaching-learning process and about the subject taught. No longer is it sufficient for career teachers to obtain only a bachelor's degree and a teaching certificate. Rather, teachers are lifelong members of learning communities.

Several states have mandated continuing education for teachers. The content of the curriculum as well as methods and materials for teaching that content are changing so rapidly that teachers must be involved in continuous learning to maintain their professional effectiveness. In addition, we feel that teachers must practice what they preach. A teacher who is not continuously learning raises serious questions for students: If it's not important for our teachers to learn, why should we? The attitude toward learning that teachers model for students may be as important as the content they teach.

Many opportunities are available for teachers to learn new knowledge and skills. Nearly every school district makes provisions for inservice training or staff development. Topics can range from classroom-focused issues such as authentic assessment, using the Internet, classroom management, integrated curricula, or learning styles to schoolwide management issues such as restructuring, shared governance, or school-community partnerships. Beyond these inservice opportunities, professional teachers actively seek additional avenues for growth, as this teacher observes during her fourth year of teaching: "After realizing what it could mean to work with colleagues and support colleagues in their work, I began arranging my own 'inservice' opportunities in my building and in the professional community. Even though I am a young teacher,

I learned that I too am responsible for continuing my own learning in my profession" (Visconti 1996, 154).

INVOLVEMENT IN THE PROFESSION

Today's teachers realize that they have the most important role in the educational enterprise and that, previously, they have not had the power they needed to improve the profession. Therefore, they are taking an increasingly broader view of the decisions that, as professionals, they have the right to make, as this elementary teacher points out:

> One of the problems is legislative people deciding what the education reforms should be and how they should be handled. I think it entails a lack of trust in the teachers by these authorities, and I think it's passed on to the public by the authorities. . . . Every time they start reforming education, they start reforming the teachers. For example, there's all the talk about competency testing and we're going to get rid of all the bad teachers. Teachers have the feeling that they're talking about all of us. We sometimes are used as public relations by authorities. And then often they take credit for what we do (Godar 1990, 264).

Across the country, professional teachers are deeply involved with their colleagues, professional organizations, teacher educators, legislators, policy makers, and others in a push to make teaching more fully a profession. Through their behaviors and accomplishments, they are demonstrating that they are professionals, that the professional identity of teachers is becoming stronger. During the last decade, for example, teachers have become more involved in teacher education reform, teacher certification, and professional governance. And, through the efforts of scores of teacher organizations, teachers have also made gains in working conditions, salaries, and benefits.

TO WHAT PROFESSIONAL ORGANIZATIONS DO TEACHERS BELONG

The expanding leadership role of teachers has been supported through the activities of more than 500 national teacher organizations (*National Trade and Professional Associations of the United States* 1996). These organizations and the scores of hardworking teachers who run them support a variety of activities to improve teaching and schools. Through lobbying in Washington and at state capitols, for example, teacher associations acquaint legislators, policymakers, and politicians with critical issues and problems in the teaching profession. Many associations have staffs of teachers, researchers, and consultants who produce professional publications, hold conferences, prepare grant proposals, engage in school improvement activities, and promote a positive image of teaching to the public. In the quest to improve the professional lives of all teachers, two national organizations have led the way: the National Education Association (NEA) and the American Federation of Teachers (AFT). These two groups have had a long history of competition for the allegiance of teachers.

THE NATIONAL EDUCATION ASSOCIATION

Membership in the **National Education Association (NEA),** the oldest and largest of the two organizations, includes both teachers and administrators. Originally called the

National Teachers Association when it was founded in 1857, the group was started by forty-three educators from a dozen states and the District of Columbia (West 1980, 1).

The NEA has affiliates in every state plus Puerto Rico and the District of Columbia, and its local affiliates number more than 13,000. About two-thirds of the teachers in this country belong to the NEA. More than 78 percent of NEA's 2.2 million members are teachers; about 12 percent are guidance counselors, librarians, and administrators; almost 3 percent are university professors; about 2 percent are college and university students; about 3 percent are support staff (teacher aides, secretaries, cafeteria workers, bus drivers, and custodians); and about 2 percent are retired members (personal communication, NEA, October 8, 1996).

To improve education in this country, the NEA has standing committees in the following areas: affiliate relationships, higher education, human relations, political action, teacher benefits, and teacher rights. These committees engage in a wide range of activities, among them preparing reports on important educational issues, disseminating the results of educational research, conducting conferences, working with federal agencies on behalf of children, pressing for more rigorous standards for the teaching profession, helping school districts resolve salary disputes, developing ways to improve personnel practices, and enhancing the relationship between the profession and the public.

Currently, more than two-thirds of states have passed some type of collective bargaining laws that apply to teachers. There is little uniformity among these laws, with most of the thirty-one states permitting strikes only if certain conditions have been met. The NEA has gone on record as supporting a federal statute that would set up uniform procedures for teachers to bargain with their employers.

The NEA continues today to focus on issues of concern to teachers, primarily in the area of professional governance. Efforts are being made to broaden teachers' decision-making powers related to curriculum, extracurricular responsibilities, staff development, and supervision. To promote the status of the profession, the NEA conducts annual research studies and opinion surveys in various areas and publishes *NEA Today*, the *NEA Research Bulletin,* and its major publication, *Today's Education.*

THE AMERICAN FEDERATION OF TEACHERS

The **American Federation of Teachers (AFT)** was founded in 1916. Three teachers' unions in Chicago issued a call for teachers to form a national organization affiliated with organized labor. Teacher unions in Gary, Indiana; New York City; Oklahoma; Scranton, Pennsylvania; and Washington, D.C., joined the three Chicago unions to form the AFT.

The AFT differs from the NEA in that it is open only to teachers and nonsupervisory school personnel. The AFT is active today in organizing teachers, collective bargaining, public relations, and developing policies related to various educational issues. In addition, the organization conducts research in areas such as educational reform, bilingual education, teacher certification, and evaluation, and also represents members' concerns through legislative action and technical assistance.

The AFT has 907,000 members who are organized through 2,265 local affiliates (personal communication, AFT, October 8, 1996).

The AFT is affiliated with the American Federation of Labor–Congress of Industrial Organizations (AFL-CIO), which has over fourteen million members. To promote the idea that teachers should have the right to speak for themselves on important issues, the AFT does not allow superintendents, principals, and other administrators to join. As an informational brochure on the AFT states, "Because the AFT believes in action—in 'getting things done' rather than issuing reports, letting someone else do the 'doing'—a powerful, cohesive structure is necessary."

Unlike the NEA, the AFT has been steadfastly involved throughout its history in securing economic gains and improving working conditions for teachers. Though the AFT has been criticized for being unprofessional and too concerned with bread-and-butter issues, none other than the great educator and philosopher John Dewey took out the first AFT membership card in 1916. After twelve years as a union member, Dewey made his stance on economic issues clear:

> It is said that the Teachers Union, as distinct from the more academic organizations, overemphasizes the economic aspect of teaching. Well, I never had that contempt for the economic aspect of teaching, especially not on the first of the month when I get my salary check. I find that teachers have to pay their grocery and meat bills and house rent just the same as everybody else (Dewey 1955, 60–61).

Traditionally, the AFT has been strongest in urban areas. Today, the AFT represents teachers not only in Chicago and New York but in Philadelphia, Washington, D.C., Kansas City, Detroit, Boston, Cleveland, and Pittsburgh. NEA membership has tended to be suburban and rural. The NEA has always been the larger of the two organizations, and it is presently more than twice the size of its rival.

OTHER PROFESSIONAL ORGANIZATIONS

In addition to the NEA and AFT, teachers' professional interests are represented by more than 500 other national organizations. Several of these are concerned with improving the quality of education at all levels and in all subject areas. **Phi Delta Kappa (PDK),** for example, is a professional and honorary fraternity of educators concerned with enhancing quality education through research and leadership activities. Founded in 1906, Phi Delta Kappa now has a membership of 166,000 (personal communication, PDK, October 8, 1996). Members, who are graduate students, teachers, and administrators, belong to one of 666 chapters. To be initiated into Phi Delta Kappa, one must have demonstrated high academic achievement, have completed at least fifteen semester hours of graduate work in education, and have made a commitment to a career of educational service. Phi Delta Kappa members receive *Phi Delta Kappan,* a journal of education published ten times a year.

Another example is the **Association for Supervision and Curriculum Development (ASCD),** a professional organization of teachers, supervisors, curriculum coordinators, education professors, administrators, and others. The ASCD is interested in school improvement at all levels of education. Founded in 1921, the association has a membership of 177,000 (personal communication, ASCD, October 8, 1996). ASCD provides professional development experiences in curriculum and supervision, disseminates information on educational issues, and encourages research, evaluation, and theory development. ASCD also conducts several National Curriculum Study Institutes around the country each year and provides a free research information service to members. Members receive *Educational Leadership*, a well-respected journal printed eight times a year. ASCD also publishes a yearbook, each one devoted to a particular educational issue, and occasional books in the area of curriculum and supervision.

In addition, as you will see in the Teacher's Resource Guide at the back of this book, many professional associations exist for teachers of specific subject-areas, such as mathematics, English, social studies, music, physical education, and so on, as well as for teachers of specific student populations, such as exceptional learners, young children, and students with limited English proficiency.

Keepers of the Dream

Sandra MacQuinn

**High School Teacher,
Fulbright Scholar**

Traveling through Rumania and Bulgaria for six weeks on a bus, high school English teacher Sandra MacQuinn met with other teachers and students to talk about educational restructuring. "They do more with nothing than we do with so much money. All they were asking for was an economics book with a copyright past the 1970s. They were hungry for learning and saw us as angels there to help them," MacQuinn exclaimed when she returned from her 1996 Summer Fulbright experience. By fall she had already gained a senator's assistance, secured an agreement with UPS to transport books in their spare space, and involved her students in collecting books. She and the teachers she met in Rumania and Bulgaria also began the process for creating a literary magazine to be made available internationally on the Internet.

*"Many Voices—
One Vision."*

We will focus on four or five topics in history and English, such as oppression, families, and work. We'll send writings back and forth on e-mail, getting student feedback and editing them for desktop publishing of the journal (personal communication September 1, 1996).

Given MacQuinn's track record, these efforts will succeed. The recipient of four teaching awards, she has founded or coordinated her school's "All School Renaissance Faire," "The Teaching Academy," a Cultural Diversity/Equity Committee, a peer meditation program for conflict resolution, a drop-out prevention program, and numerous projects involving community–school partnerships. With the Renaissance fair, she explained, "I did what most people who are excited about life do—followed my own interests." In this case her love of costumes, music, and plays launched the now-annual schoolwide event.

MacQuinn also recognizes the value of including the local community in school endeavors:

Any time we have successes in schools they involve people outside of school. We teachers don't have enough expertise. Our gift is being generalists, but it also limits us. We need to draw on the interests of the people in our communities.

WHAT NEW LEADERSHIP ROLES FOR TEACHERS ARE EMERGING?

Teachers' roles are changing in fundamental and positive ways as we enter the twenty-first century. Greater autonomy and an expanded role in educational policy-making has led to "unprecedented opportunities for today's teachers to extend their leadership roles beyond the classroom" (Gmelch and Parkay 1995, 48). To prepare for this future, today's teachers will need to develop leadership skills to a degree not needed in the past.

TEACHER INVOLVEMENT IN TEACHER EDUCATION AND CERTIFICATION

Teacher input into key decisions about teacher preparation and certification is on the rise. Through their involvement with professional development schools and the National Board for Professional Teaching Standards (see Chapter 2), state profes-

Restructuring concerns rank high in MacQuinn's priorities. She was elected to be the liaison and on-site coordinator of a school-university partnership between Rogers High School and Washington State University's College of Education. Restructuring was one of the partnership's goals. MacQuinn recognizes that any real change in education is a challenge, observing that "consensus is unwieldy and difficult" and admitting that she is nervous—in an excited way—about restructuring, but she maintains that schools have no choice but to accept the challenge to change significantly for the sake of students:

> We're watching students who can't do anything. We love them and want to see them accomplish things in their lives, but students are graduating with second and third grade reading levels.

Though MacQuinn regards the task as "monumental," she is convinced that teachers working and talking together can do it, because of the worthiness of their common goal. A poster she placed on the wall by her office door proclaims her perspective:

> Many Voices—One Vision. All Restructuring Efforts Are for KIDS.

One of MacQuinn's collaborative projects aimed at motivating students to better their lives is "The Teaching Academy," a service learning program. In the Academy, the high school students learn about themselves, classroom management, learning styles, and group dynamics and are then placed in an elementary school where they observe, work with small groups, and eventually teach the whole class one hour a day. Their service frees elementary teachers to assist students who need individual attention and provides children with role models who open the world of teaching to them. In return, the high school students, who are treated as adults by the staff and eat lunch in the faculty room, get a taste of being a professional and sample the pleasure of teaching and serving children.

MacQuinn's advice for new teachers is "to draw others into what you love most and find some peers on the staff that like to do what you like to do." She reassures that "change naturally falls from that, and administrators support enthusiastic, creative people." She counsels teachers to be adventurous and not reluctant to "grow where planted." MacQuinn never thought she would be "walking through the same parking lot for the past twenty-six years," always thinking she would move to the excitement of the city. Now she realizes and demonstrates in her teaching and leadership that "exciting things are happening wherever you are."

sional standards boards (see Chapter 6), and scores of local, state, and national education committees, teachers are changing the character of teacher education. For example, in 1992, the National Board for Professional Teaching Standards (NBPTS) established a network designed to allow nearly 7 percent of the nation's 2.5 million teachers to participate in field-testing various components of the NBPTS certification system. The NBPTS allocated $1 million to teachers, in the form of honoraria, for helping to field-test the NBPTS assessment materials. In commenting on the teachers' role in the field-test network, the NBPTS vice-president for assessment and research said, "Teachers are indispensable for the development of these assessments. We need their real-world perspective" (National Board for Professional Teaching Standards Press Release, June 22, 1992, 3).

For the most part, teachers recommend that greater emphasis be placed on field experiences for preservice teachers. For example, when asked how universities could prepare preservice teachers better, one group of more than 2,700 teachers recommended "more emphasis on pedagogical skills, particularly for generating

TABLE 12.1

What specific actions would improve teacher preparation for the middle grades?

Action	Percent Listing
Improve field experiences and student teaching	58
Greater variety of teaching and assessment techniques	40
More on social relationships and self-awareness	33
More on classroom management	29
More on early adolescent development	29
Deeper academic subject control	29

(N = 439)

(Source: *Windows of Opportunity: Improving Middle Grades Teacher Preparation* [Chapel Hill: University of North Carolina, September 1992], p. 8.)

student motivation, and more time in clinical settings to develop these skills" (Cohn and Kottkamp 1993, 227). Similarly, in 1992 the Center for Early Adolescence at the University of North Carolina at Chapel Hill found that 58 percent of 439 randomly selected middle-level teachers in eight states believed that field experience and student teaching should be improved (see Table 12.1).

TEACHER-LEADERS

As the titles of several recent books suggest, the term **teacher-leader** has become part of our vocabulary: *Educating Teachers for Leadership and Change* (O'Hair and Odell 1995), *Teachers as Leaders: Perspectives on the Professional Development of Teachers* (Walling 1994), *Becoming a Teacher Leader: From Isolation to Collaboration* (Boleman and Deal 1994), *When Teachers Lead* (Astuto 1993), and *Teachers as Leaders: Evolving Roles* (Livingston 1992).

"In their new leadership roles, teachers are being called upon to form new partnerships with business and industry; institutions of higher education; social service agencies; professional associations; and local, state, and federal governmental agencies. In this new role, teachers will be the key to promoting widespread improvement of our educational system" (Gmelch and Parkay 1995, 50–51). A brief look at Sandra MacQuinn's professional activities illustrates the wide-ranging roles of a teacher-leader (see the "Keepers of the Dream"). Here are just a few of MacQuinn's work-related activities (in addition to teaching): writing grants for teacher-developed projects; helping other teachers write grants; facilitating the development of an integrated school-to-work curriculum; preparing newsletters to keep faculty up-to-date on restructuring; organizing and facilitating staff development training; developing connections with area businesses and arranging "job shadowing" sites for students; working with a community college to create an alternative school for Rogers High students at the college; scheduling substitute teachers to provide Rogers teachers with release-time to work on restructuring; making presentations on the Rogers High restructuring at state and regional conferences; arranging for Rogers students to visit Washington State University (WSU); meeting with the principal, assistant principals, WSU professors, and others to develop short- and long-range plans for implementing site-based management; chairing meetings of the site-based council, the restructuring steering committee, and other restructuring-related committees.

At West Forest Intermediate School in Opelika, Alabama, which has several schools within a school, teachers have the following roles: coordinator of special education services and lead teacher, coordinator of the media center responsible for school-wide implementation of technology, and director of the school's whole-language program (Gerstner et al. 1994). At a Florida elementary school with a shared decision making (SDM) form of governance, teachers work on committees that make hiring, budget, and school policy decisions. In the words of one teacher at that school: "I'm not just a teacher in a classroom, I am a member of an organization, a company that helps to run the school. I'm not just alone in my room" (Ross and Webb 1995, 76).

DIMENSIONS OF TEACHER LEADERSHIP BEYOND THE CLASSROOM

Figure 12.3 illustrates ten dimensions of teacher leadership beyond the classroom. The many teachers whom we have assisted on school restructuring projects during the last few years have used these skills to reach an array of educational goals. Clearly, these teachers have modeled what Rallis (1990, 193) terms "an elevated conception of teaching."

At schools around the country, teachers and principals are using a "collaborative, emergent" approach to leadership; that is, the person who provides leadership for a particular schoolwide project or activity may or may not be the principal or a member of the administrative team (Parkay et al. 1997). Such schools are characterized by a "higher level of professional community" (Newmann and Wehlage 1995). They are similar to the schools Wohlstetter (1995, 24) identified as having successfully implemented school-based management (SBM): "[They] had principals who played a key role in dispersing power. [T]he principals were often described as facilitators and managers of change."

FIGURE 12.3 Ten dimensions of teacher leadership beyond the classroom

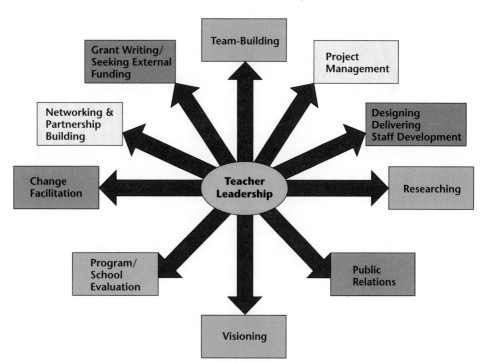

Working with Principals

The new calls to leadership for teachers suggest that teachers' essential knowledge and skills may not differ much from those traditionally required for educational administrators. The National Commission for the Principalship has identified the following "performance domains" for the Principalship. Which of these domains also apply to teacher-leaders? To what extent are the knowledge and skills required of teacher-leaders and of principals becoming similar?

I. **Functional Domains**
   1. *Leadership*
   2. *Information Collection*
   3. *Problem Analysis*
   4. *Judgment*
   5. *Organizational Oversight*
   6. *Implementation*
   7. *Delegation*

II. **Programmatic Domains**
   8. *Instructional Program*
   9. *Curriculum Design*
   10. *Student Guidance and Development*
   11. *Staff Development*
   12. *Measurement and Evaluation*
   13. *Resource Allocation*

III. **Interpersonal Domains**
   14. *Motivating Others*
   15. *Sensitivity*
   16. *Oral Expression*
   17. *Written Expression*

IV. **Contextual Domains**
   18. *Philosophical and Cultural Values*
   19. *Legal and Regulatory Applications*
   20. *Policy and Political Influences*
   21. *Public and Media Relationships* (National Commission for the Principalship)

HOW DO TEACHERS CONTRIBUTE TO EDUCATIONAL RESEARCH ?

Today's teachers play an increasingly important role in educational research. By applying research to solve practical, classroom-based problems, teachers validate the accuracy and usefulness of educational research and help researchers identify additional areas to investigate. As consumers of educational research, teachers improve their teaching, contribute to educational reform, and enhance the professional status of teaching.

In addition, increasing numbers of teachers are becoming competent researchers in their own right and making important contributions to our understanding of teaching and learning. Prior to the mid 1980s, teachers were the missing "voice" in educational research. However, as teachers and staff developers Holly and McLoughlin (1989, 309) noted almost a decade ago, "We've moved from research *on* teachers to research *with* teachers and lately to research *by* teachers." Since their observation, we have seen the emergence of the **teacher-researcher,** the professional teacher who conducts classroom research to improve his or her teaching.

Part of being a professional is the ability to decide *how* and *when* to use research to guide one's actions. For example, Emmerich Koller, a teacher of German at a suburban high school, describes in an article he wrote for the book *Teachers Doing Research: Practical Possibilities* (Burnaford et al. 1996) how he experimented with new

This teacher is conducting classroom research on the ways students come to understand a problem and to apply appropriate problem-solving skills. What are several ways the teacher might use this research as a professional?

teaching methods based on the latest findings from brain research and "accelerated learning," a strategy for optimizing learning by integrating conscious and unconscious mental processes. After determining how and when to put that research into practice, he commented, "At age 50, after 27 years of teaching, I have found something that has made teaching very exciting again" (Koller 1996, 180).

SOURCES OF EDUCATIONAL RESEARCH

Research findings are reported in scores of educational research journals (see "Professional Resources for Teachers: Periodicals and Publications" in the Teacher's Resource Guide). In addition, there are several excellent reviews of research with which you should become familiar during your professional preparation, such as the fourth edition of the *Handbook of Research on Teaching* (Simon & Schuster, 1998), a project sponsored by the American Educational Research Association. Its more than one thousand pages synthesize research in several areas, including research on teaching at various grade levels and in various subject areas. Other comprehensive, authoritative reviews of research you might wish to consult include the following:

- *Handbook of Research on Multicultural Education* (Macmillian, 1995)
- *Handbook of Research on Science Teaching and Learning* (Macmillan, 1994), sponsored by the National Science Teachers Association
- *Handbook of Research on the Education of Young Children* (Macmillan, 1993)
- *Handbook of Research on Mathematics Teaching and Learning* (Macmillan, 1992), sponsored by the National Council of Teachers of Mathematics
- *Research Ideas for the Classroom: Early Childhood Mathematics, Middle School Mathematics, and High School Mathematics* (Macmillan, 1993), three volumes sponsored by the National Council of Teachers of Mathematics
- *Encyclopedia of Educational Research,* Sixth Edition, four volumes (Macmillan, 1992)
- *Handbook of Research on Music Teaching and Learning* (Macmillan, 1992), sponsored by the Music Educators National Conference
- *Handbook of Research on Teaching the English Language Arts* (Macmillan, 1991), sponsored by the International Reading Association and the National Council of Teachers of English
- *Handbook of Research on Social Studies Teaching and Learning* (Macmillan, 1991), sponsored by the National Council for the Social Studies

GOVERNMENT RESOURCES FOR RESEARCH APPLICATION

The federal government supports several efforts designed to help teachers improve their practice through the application of research findings. In 1966, three agencies were created to support and disseminate research: **Educational Resources Information Center (ERIC), Research and Development Centers,** and **Regional Educational Laboratories.**

ERIC is a national information system made up of sixteen **ERIC Clearinghouses** and four adjunct clearinghouses—all coordinated by the central ERIC agency in Washington, D.C. (see "Educational Resources Information Clearinghouses [ERIC]" in the Teacher's Resource Guide). The ERIC system, available in most college and university libraries, contains descriptions of exemplary programs, the results of research and development efforts, and related information that can be used by teachers, administrators, and the public to improve education. Each Clearinghouse specializes in one area of education and searches out relevant documents or journal articles that are screened according to ERIC selection criteria, abstracted, and indexed.

Within the **Office of Educational Research and Improvement (OERI)** in Washington, D.C., the Office of Research (formerly the National Institute of Education) maintains fourteen research centers at universities around the country (see the "Selected National Educational Research and Improvement [OERI] Centers" in the Teacher's Resource Guide). The centers are devoted to high-quality, fundamental research at every level of education, with most of the research done by scholars at the host university. Among the areas these centers focus on are the processes of teaching and learning, school organization and improvement, the content of education, and factors that contribute to (or detract from) excellence in education.

OERI also houses Programs for the Improvement of Practice (PIP), which support exemplary projects at the state and local levels. PIP also maintains nine regional educational laboratories and sponsors a number of Assistance Centers (see the Teacher's Resource Guide). Each laboratory serves a geographic region and is a nonprofit corporation not affiliated with a university. Laboratory staff work directly with school systems, state educational agencies, and other organizations to improve education through the application of research findings.

CONDUCTING CLASSROOM ACTION RESEARCH

More than three decades ago, Robert Schaefer (1967, 5) posed the following questions in *The School as the Center of Inquiry:*

> Why should our schools not be staffed, gradually if you will, by scholar-teachers in command of the conceptual tools and methods of inquiry requisite to investigating the learning process as it operates in their own classroom? Why should our schools not nurture the continuing wisdom and power of such scholar-teachers?

Schaefer's vision for teaching has become a reality. Today, thousands of teachers are involved in action research to improve their teaching. Using their classrooms as "laboratories," these teacher-researchers are systematically studying the outcomes of their teaching through the application of various research methods. In addition, they are disseminating the results of their research at professional conferences and through publications, including *Teacher as Researcher,* a journal edited, written, and published by teachers.

Simply put, **action research** is the classroom-based study by teachers, individually or collaboratively, of how to improve instruction. As in the *reflection-in-action* approach described earlier in this chapter, action research begins with a teacher-identified question, issue, or problem. How can I more effectively motivate a group of students? How do students experience the climate in my classroom? What factors limit parental participation in our school? How can our department (or teacher team) become more collegial? How does computer use in the foreign language classroom affect students' oral communication?

Action research is also "a natural part of teaching. [T]o be a teacher means to observe students and study classroom interactions, to explore a variety of effective ways of teaching and learning, and to build conceptual frameworks that can guide one's work. This is a personal as well as a professional quest, a journey toward making sense out of and finding satisfaction in one's teaching. It is the work of teacher-researchers" (Fischer 1996, 33).

Action research can be used to study almost any dimension of teaching and learning. Calhoun (1992) identified five basic steps in the action research cycle:

1. *Problem-Identification:* What question will be answered?
2. *Planning:* What data will be collected? How will it be collected and analyzed?
3. *Organization:* How should data be organized and presented to provide a clear picture of the findings?
4. *Evaluation:* Analysis and interpretation of data.
5. *Action:* Revise activities based on research results.

Not surprisingly, becoming a teacher-researcher is hard work, given the daily demands of teaching itself. However, more school districts are redefining the teacher's role to include doing action research (Bennett 1993). These districts realize that action research can provide data on the effectiveness of educational programs, enhance student learning, and energize teachers for professional growth.

HOW ARE TEACHERS INVOLVED IN SCHOOL RESTRUCTURING AND CURRICULUM REFORM

Today's teachers welcome opportunities to become involved in school restructuring and curriculum reform. Although teachers may have played a limited role in school governance in the past, there are currently many opportunities for teachers to become involved in these areas. Table 12.2 on page 398 presents five streams of educational reform, each of which will offer teachers opportunities to shape policies during the next decade.

EMPOWERMENT AND COLLABORATION FOR SCHOOL REFORM

The key to successful school restructuring and curriculum reform is teacher empowerment and collaboration. A Metropolitan Life Survey showed that 83 percent of teachers believe that "principals and teachers should share time together after the school day to formally plan staff development, curriculum, and mangagment" (see Figure 12.4 on page 399). Lillian Brinkley, principal of the Willard Model School in Norfolk, Virginia, is typical of the new breed of principals who welcome such collaboration: "I don't ask teachers to do anything I wouldn't do. Every teacher is a leader at this school. When teachers have ownership, they give their best and see to it that their project succeeds" (Boyer 1995, 32).

TABLE 12.2

Five streams of educational reform

1. *Reforms in subject-matter teaching (standards, curriculum, and pedagogy).* Many of the current reforms aspire to more ambitious student outcomes. Among them are the whole-language and literature-based approach to language arts, the new National Council of Teachers of Mathematics (NCTM) standards, and the like. These reforms are incompatible with textbook-style teaching; they demand that teachers be well able to integrate various content areas into coherent lessons and to efficiently organize students' time. And these demands may represent a substantial departure from teachers' prior experience, established beliefs, and present practice.

2. *Reforms centered on problems of equity and the increasing diversity of the student population.* These reforms address the persistent achievement disparities among students from differing family backgrounds and seek to improve both the demonstrated achievement and school completion rates of the lowest achieving groups. Over past decades, such reforms have focused on remedying individual student deficiencies. Recent analyses have drawn attention to the ways in which school practices define and contribute to student failure. To address the institutional failure related to low achievement, teachers must learn to identify and alter classroom practices that contribute to student failure and undermine equal opportunity to learn.

3. *Reforms in the nature, extent, and uses of student assessment.* Some reform proposals seek more widespread and rigorous use of assessment that truly measures what students are learning. Yet, the technical advances in assessment are lagging behind the advances in curriculum design. State and local policymakers continue to judge the success of reform efforts on the basis of standardized test scores.

4. *Reforms in the social organization of schooling.* In recent years there has been a remarkable convergence of interest, activities, and funds around the broad image of school restructuring. State-supported initiatives in school restructuring, foundation-supported special projects, and projects sponsored by teachers' associations in concert with local schools and districts have appeared in nearly every state. The most ambitious of these are based on principles, rather than specific practices. They pose a deep dilemma for school leadership and for professional development programs because there are rarely any well-developed models of how these principles translate into specific instructional strategies and activities.

5. *Reforms in the professionalization of teaching.* The professionalization reforms at the state level focus on teachers' demonstrated knowledge base (as reflected in standards for accreditation of teacher education programs and candidate assessment), on teacher licensure requirements, and on the structure of career opportunities in teaching. Reforms to professionalize teaching mean that teachers will increasingly serve as mentors to new teachers, take on new responsibilities over time, and exert more leadership through site-based decision making.

(Source: Excerpted from Judith Warren Little, "Teacher Professional Development in a Climate of Educational Reform," *Educational Evaluation and Policy Analysis* [Summer 1993]: 129–151. Copyright 1993, by the American Educational Research Association; used by permission of the publisher. Excerpt taken from Consortium for Policy Research in Education, *CPRE Policy Briefs* [November 10, 1993]: 2.)

Teachers who have participated in the trend toward **teacher empowerment** often report a renewed zest for teaching. For example, several middle school teachers in Florida, participants in a faculty-driven school restructuring project, had this to say about becoming empowered and working collaboratively:

> For the first time inservice is meeting my needs. It's not something decreed from central administration that I don't care about.

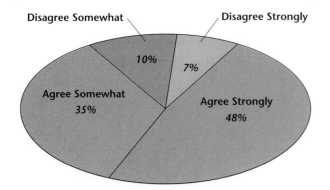

FIGURE 12.4 Principals and teachers should plan together
Note: Survey of 2,000 teachers—1,048 elementary, 430 junior high/middle school, and 443 high school teachers (79 taught both junior high and high school). (Source: Louis Harris and Associates. *The Metropolitan Life Survey of the American Teacher 1989: Preparing Schools for the 1990s* (New York: Louis Harris and Associates, 1990), p. 80. Used with permission.)

Before I didn't feel I had any power to get things done. Having an opportunity to initiate change was something I had never thought possible.

The [improvement] committees have been the most important part of this project. They give us [teachers] an opportunity to sit down and discuss issues and decide what we should do about problems (Parkay and Damico 1989, 12–13).

COLLABORATIVE SCHOOL REFORM NETWORKS

Many teachers are involved in restructuring and curriculum change through their schools' participation in collaborative networks for reform. Networks provide teachers with training and resources for restructuring, and they create opportunities for teachers at network schools to help teachers at non-network schools with their restructuring efforts. Among the many collaborative reform networks are the Coalition of Essential Schools, the National Network for Educational Renewal, Accelerated Schools, and state-based networks, such as the Washington State League of Schools.

COALITION OF ESSENTIAL SCHOOLS The **Coalition of Essential Schools,** started in 1984 by Theodore R. Sizer at Brown University, is a network of more than 150 public and private high schools in 30 states committed to redesigning America's high schools. No two Coalition schools are alike; each develops an approach to restructuring suited to its students, faculty, and community. However, the efforts of Coalition schools to restructure are guided by nine Common Principles extrapolated from Sizer's (1984, 1992) books on redesigning America's high schools and the beliefs that top-down, standardized solutions to school problems don't work and that teachers must play a key role in the operation of their schools. Recently, the Coalition organized resource centers so teachers at Coalition schools can provide non-Coalition schools with restructuring assistance.

NATIONAL NETWORK FOR EDUCATIONAL RENEWAL The Center for Educational Renewal at the University of Washington created the **National Network for Educational Renewal (NNER)** to encourage new opportunities for teachers to become involved in school restructuring, curriculum reform, and the preparation of teachers. Members of the NNER include 25 colleges and universities that collaborate with 93 school districts and 266 partner schools. The NNER is based on 19 postulates for reforming teacher education that John Goodlad presented in *Teachers for Our Nation's Schools* (1990). For a school to become a member of the NNER, its teachers must demonstrate that they "understand their appropriate role in site-based management and school renewal" (Goodlad 1994, 89).

Dear Mentor

NOVICE AND EXPERT TEACHERS
ON SHARING DECISION MAKING

Dear Kevin,

As you prepare to be a teacher, your concerns related to teacher leadership roles and co-teaching are two issues familiar to me. Classroom environment is a critical component to any teacher, so I will address co-teaching first and share what has worked for me. I have found that students can use their democratic vote to express their preferences. A student-centered curriculum and environment can start with students deciding their classroom rules. Later, the democratic process can handle more important issues such as choices for curriculum topics, student-developed tests, or decisions about which community service project to choose. Benefits occur when students are actively involved in their own education. Student input heightens the learning experience and teaches responsibility. Remember, the teacher can carefully plan parameters that allow maximum student input while maintaining needed control.

Leadership roles for first-year teachers can be demanding, but carefully chosen responsibilities can reap personal and professional benefits. "How the school is run" is the responsibility of teachers and administrators. A classroom teacher can offer guidance and leadership through self-initiated, planned activities. Try starting a weekly after-school activity. I started an embroidery class for fourth-grade girls. This encouraged another teacher to start a "jump rope for health"

class. Use your own personal interests and talents to stretch your leadership skills.

The more traditional form of teacher leadership is related to administrative endeavors. You may want to have input when a new teacher or administrator is hired, decide on how budget items will be funded, and/or decide how money will be spent. I suggest that you develop a good time-management program for yourself and take the plunge. Try to make yourself available for every school committee your time permits. Attend the next PTA meeting and closely pay attention to their agenda. You will become aware of the issues important to parents and the community. If you have any time left, attend monthly school board meetings. This kind of involvement can open the door to any desired leadership role you may wish to assume. After a while you will become a treasure of information for others. Good luck.

Elizabeth A. Lyles
Elementary School Teacher

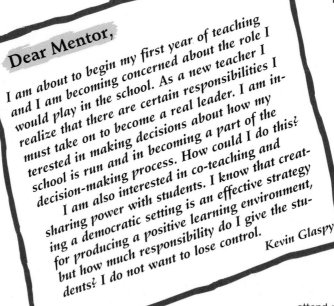

Dear Mentor,

I am about to begin my first year of teaching and I am becoming concerned about the role I would play in the school. As a new teacher I realize that there are certain responsibilities I must take on to become a real leader. I am interested in making decisions about how my school is run and in becoming a part of the decision-making process. How could I do this?

I am also interested in co-teaching and sharing power with students. I know that creating a democratic setting is an effective strategy for producing a positive learning environment, but how much responsibility do I give the students? I do not want to lose control.

Kevin Glaspy

ACCELERATED SCHOOLS   Stanford economist Henry M. Levin has developed a nationwide network of **accelerated schools** that provide enriched, rigorous curricula to "speed up" the learning of students at risk. Instead of placing at-risk students into remedial classes, Accelerated Schools provide students with challenging learning activities traditionally reserved for gifted and talented students. Accelerated Schools are based on the belief that teachers—in collaboration with administrators, parents, and community members—must be able to make important educational decisions, take responsibility for implementing those decisions, and take responsibility for the outcomes of those decisions. The National Center for the Accelerated Schools Project at Stanford operates eight regional Accelerated Schools Satellite Centers across the country. The Satellite Centers provide assistance to teachers and administrators who wish to restructure their schools according to the Accelerated Schools model.

STATE-BASED EDUCATIONAL PARTNERSHIPS   Many states have established state-based partnerships between a state university or college and a coalition of public schools. The Washington State League of Schools, for example, patterned after the League of Professional Schools started by Carl Glickman at the University of Georgia, is a network of 50 Washington public schools, Washington State University's (WSU) Center for Educational Partnerships, and other educational and community agencies. League schools exchange resources and ideas and support one another in their restructuring efforts. The League has established LeagueNet for member schools to share their restructuring experiences via the Internet. Teacher education students at WSU also use LeagueNet to discuss curriculum reform, action research, and teaching strategies with teachers at League schools.

HOW ARE TEACHERS INNOVATORS IN THE USE OF EDUCATIONAL TECHNOLOGY ⟨?⟩

In 1994 eighth-graders in three Massachusettes schools participated in a live, two-way, ninety-minute teleconference with ninth-graders in Karlsruhe, Germany. During previous teleconferences, students had exchanged information and opinions on issues such as nuclear power, antinuclear protests, the merits of nonfossil fuels, rap music, clothes, and fast foods. They also used various computer networks (such as international electronic mail [e-mail] and C.S. Net—a worldwide network funded by the National Science Foundation—for international data communication and project management). The students were part of KITES (Kids Interactive Telecommunications Experience by Satellite), a multiorganization partnership designed to advance students' crosscultural sensitivities and infuse the curriculum with the vitality of international perspectives.

In a classroom hundreds of miles away, nine-year-old Nancy is seated in front of a computer and color monitor, about to begin a lesson on insects. On the screen is a two-story house. Nancy reaches out to the screen and touches the burnished knob on the front door and it magically opens. The next screen shows the hallway and living room. At various points on the screen are purple bugs. Nancy touches a bug near the bottom of a bookcase. The bookcase fades away and reveals dozens of ants scurrying about. A pleasant-sounding voice comes on and begins to explain how insects and humans coexist. After giving Nancy information about the ants she has discovered, the voice invites her to explore the rest of the house to see what other insects she can find.

To enhance their classroom instruction, today's teachers can draw from a dazzling array of technological devices like the ones these students were using. Little more than a decade ago, the technology available to teachers who wished to use more than the chalkboard was limited to an overhead projector, a 16-mm movie projector, a tape recorder, and, in a few forward-looking school districts, television sets. Today, teachers and students use desktop and laptop computers with built-in modems, faxes, and CD-ROM players; videodisc players; camcorders; optical scanners; speech and music synthesizers; laser printers; digital cameras; and LCD projection panels. In addition, they use sophisticated software for e-mail, word processing, desktop publishing, presentation graphics, spreadsheets, databases, and multimedia applications.

THE IMPACT OF THE TELEVISION REVOLUTION

Since the 1950s, television has become an omnipresent feature of life in America. Compared to the computer, therefore, television has had a longer and possibly a more predictable impact of education. In fact, the effects of the television revolution—both positive and negative—on all facets of American life are still being studies, and for good cause. Children spend an estimated equivalent of two months of the year watching television. The typical child between six and eleven years of age watches about twenty-seven hours a week.

Critics of television point out that it encourages passivity in the young, may be linked to increases in violence and crime, often reinforces sexual and ethnic stereotypes, and retards growth and development. Some say that television robs children of the time they need to do homework, to read and reflect, and to build bonds with family members and others through interaction.

However, television can enhance students' learning. Excellent educational programs are aired by the Public Broadcasting Service and by some cable and other commercial networks. Television has also had a positive impact on how students are taught in schools. With the increased availability of video equipment, many schools have begun to have students produce their own television documentaries, news programs, oral histories, and dramas. Many schools have closed-circuit television systems that teachers use to prepare instructional materials for students in the district, and many districts have distance learning networks that use two-way, interactive telecommunications to provide enrichment instruction to students in remote areas or staff development to teachers.

THE COMPUTER REVOLUTION

The Franklin Park Magnet School, a science-technology-environment-math magnet school in Lee County, Florida, has created a computer-based, multimedia "experience" for students in a classroom setting. Each morning students broadcast "FPM News" live from the school's television studio, which is controlled by a computer that allows students to produce professional-quality video shows with video fades, wipes, or special effects. Teachers have computer workstations with overhead projectors and LCD (liquid crystal display) projection panels, and their students work at individual computer workstations. According to teacher Sandi Agle, FPM students are learning essential computer skills for the twenty-first century: "In the future, these students will be using similar computer tools, not paper, to disseminate information" (Poole 1995, 354).

Computer simulations and networking are particularly fascinating forms for computer-supported instruction. Simulations range from the lemonade stand that elementary school students can plan and run vicariously, practicing basic arithmetic and problem-solving skills, to a mock trial, which Harvard Law students can participate in via videodisc and computer. Recently available are computer-based simulations that give students direct learning experiences, such as visiting the great museums of the world or the bottom of the Pacific Ocean.

Through networking, your students can create community electronic bulletin boards of their own and conduct computer conferences within the classroom or between different classes. Your students can even talk to students in other schools or different countries. Data bases and on-line experts in many fields also change the way your students conduct research, as more computerized reference works—such as directories, dictionaries, and encyclopedias—become available.

CLASSROOM MEDIA MAGIC

Personal computers have so revolutionized the instructional media available to teachers that today it is no exaggeration to refer to the "magic" of media. Some of the most exciting forms of media magic involve CD-ROMS, videodiscs, and interactive multimedia.

Recent advances in computer technology have made it possible for students to become much more active in shaping their learning experiences. On a four-inch CD-ROM, they can access the equivalent of about 270,000 pages of text, about 900 300-page books; or on a twelve-inch videodisc they can access the equivalent of about 54,000 photographic slides. Computer-supported interactive multimedia allow students to integrate huge libraries of text, audio, and video information. Hypermedia systems consisting of computer, CD-ROM drive, videodisc player, video monitor, and speakers now allow students to control and present sound, video images, text, and graphics with an almost limitless array of possibilities. Students who use such systems can follow their curiosity, browse through enormous amounts of information, and develop creative solutions for multidimensional, real-life problem situations.

The term *hypermedia* refers to " 'nonsequential documents' composed of text, audio, and visual information stored in a computer, with the computer being used to link and annotate related chunks of information into larger networks or webs" (Heinich et al. 1993, 269). Hypermedia is an effective learning tool because it allows students to actively construct their own learning experiences based on their interests, preferences, and learning styles.

EFFECTS OF TECHNOLOGY ON LEARNING

The use of computers and other technologies in schools has grown enormously since the early 1980s. However, "no one knows for certain [h]ow it is used" or "how much it is used" (Mehlinger 1996, 403). Since educational technology is a tool to help teachers teach more effectively, how it is used is critical. For example, one science teacher might use computers primarily for student drills on science terminology, while another science teacher might have students use computer simulations to determine the impact of urbanization on animal populations.

The lack of information about how technology is being used in the schools aside, research results are just now beginning to appear on the long-term effects of technology on learning. One of the most informative research studies is based on the Apple Classrooms of Tomorrow (ACOT) project launched in seven K–12 classrooms in 1986. Participating students and teachers each received two computers—one for school and one for home. Eight years later, study results indicated that all ACOT students performed as well as they were expected without computers, and some performed better. More importantly, perhaps, "the ACOT students routinely and without prompting employed inquiry, collaboration, and technological and problem-solving skills" (Mehlinger 1996, 405). Also, 90 percent of ACOT students went on to college after graduating from high school, while only 15 percent of non-ACOT students did. Furthermore, the behavior of ACOT teachers also changed—they worked "more as mentors and less as presenters of information" (Mehlinger 1996, 404).

Another significant study reviewed the results of 133 research studies on educational technology from 1990 through 1994. The results of that study follow:

- Educational technology has a significant positive impact on achievement in all subject areas, across all levels of school, and in regular classrooms as well as those for special-needs students.
- Educational technology has positive effects on student attitudes.
- The degree of effectiveness is influenced by the student population, the instructional design, the teacher's role, how students are grouped, and the levels of student access to technology.

Issues in Education

- Is this cartoon likely to be for or against the use of computers for classroom instruction?
- In what sense might computer instruction be said to provide "artificial knowledge"?
- How might applications of computer technology in education change what students know? the nature of learning as a process? the nature of teaching as a profession?

" But won't artificial intelligence just give me artificial knowledge? "

- Technology makes instruction more student-centered, encourages cooperative learning, and stimulates increased teacher-student interaction.
- Positive changes in the learning environment evolve over time and do not occur quickly (Mehlinger 1996, 405).

Clearly, educational technology *does* have positive effects on learning and teaching, and indications are that technology will influence all aspects of education even more in the twenty-first century. As more funds are made available to purchase hardware and software, train teachers, and provide technical support, the benefits of classroom media magic will become even more widespread.

SUMMARY

To What Extent Is Teaching a Full Profession?

- For an occupation to be considered a profession, it must satisfy several criteria. Of the following nine criteria for a profession, teaching meets some more fully than others: (1) institutional monopoly of services, (2) teacher autonomy, (3) years of education and training, (4) provision of essential service, (5) degree of self-governance, (6) professional associations, (7) professional knowledge and skills, (8) level of public trust, and (9) prestige, benefits, and pay.
- While teaching does not currently satisfy all criteria for a profession, the collaborative efforts of individuals and groups such as the National Commission on Teaching and America's Future and the National Board for Professional Teaching Standards are rapidly professionalizing teaching.

What Is Professionalism in Teaching?

- The most potent force for enhancing the professional status of teaching is for teachers to see that their actions are professional and to commit themselves to lifelong learning and active involvement in the profession.
- Professional behavior as a teacher is characterized by reflection-in-action (the ability to observe sensitively in classrooms, reflect on those observations, and then act accordingly) and a willingness to serve as a mentor to those entering the profession.
- As lifelong learners, professional teachers actively seek opportunities for growth—from participating in training provided by a school district to arranging one's own "inservice" activities.

To What Professional Organizations Do Teachers Belong?

- Teachers help shape education as a profession through their leadership roles in more than 500 national teacher organizations.
- As the oldest and largest professional organization for educators, the National Education Association has played a key role in addressing issues of concern to the 78 percent of its members who are teachers.
- Affiliated with organized labor and open only to teachers and nonsupervisory personnel, the American Federation of Teachers has done much to secure greater financial rewards and improved working conditions for teachers.
- Teachers are members of professional associations for specific subject areas and student populations.

What New Leadership Roles for Teachers Are Emerging?

- Through their involvement with professional development schools, the National Board for Professional Teaching Standards, and local, state, and national education committees, teachers participate in making key decisions about teacher preparation and certification.
- In their new role as teacher-leaders, many teachers are playing a key role beyond the classroom as they form partnerships that focus on the transformation of America's schools.
- Teachers who work collaboratively with principals on school improvement use ten dimensions of teacher leadership beyond the classroom: team-building, project management, designing and delivering staff development, researching, public relations, visioning, program/school evaluation, change facilitation, networking and partnership building, and grant writing/seeking external funding.

How Do Teachers Contribute to Educational Research?

- Teachers validate the accuracy and usefulness of educational research and identify additional areas to research when they put "research into practice."
- In the role of teacher-researcher, many teachers conduct action research and systematically study the outcomes of their teaching. Teachers use a five-step action research cycle to study their classrooms and improve their teaching: problem identification, planning, organization, evaluation, and action.

How Are Teachers Involved in School Restructuring and Curriculum Reform?

- Five "streams" of educational reform provide teachers with many opportunities to become empowered and involved in school restructuring and curriculum reform.
- Through collaborative school reform networks such as the Coalition of Essential Schools, the National Network for Educational Renewal, Accelerated Schools, and the Washington State League of Schools, teachers provide leadership for restructuring their schools and help other teachers promote school reform at non-network schools.

How Are Teachers Innovators in the Use of Educational Technology?

- Through technologies such as two-way interactive telecommunications, CD-ROM players, interactive multimedia, and hypermedia, teachers are creating environments that allow students to become more active in shaping their learning experiences.
- Although how and to what extent computers and other technologies are being used in schools is not known, research indicates that technology has a positive impact on students' achievement and attitudes.

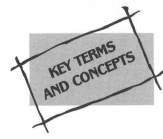

KEY TERMS AND CONCEPTS

accelerated schools, 401

action research, 396

American Federation of Teachers (AFT), 388

Association for Supervision and Curriculum Development (ASCD), 389

CD-ROM, 403

Coalition of Essential Schools, 399

computer simulations, 403

Educational Resources Information Center (ERIC), 396

ERIC Clearinghouses, 396

hypermedia, 403

interactive multimedia, 403

mentor, 386

National Education Association (NEA), 387

National Network for Educational Renewal, 399

networking, 403

Office of Educational Research and Improvement (OERI), 396

Phi Delta Kappa (PDK), 389

profession, 380

reflection-in-action, 385

Regional Educational Laboratories, 396

Research and Development Centers, 396

teacher empowerment, 398

teacher-leader, 392

teacher-researcher, 394

videodisc, 403

APPLICATIONS AND ACTIVITIES

Teacher's Journal

1. In your opinion, what accounts for public trust and lack of trust in the teaching profession? What might be the best way to increase that trust?

2. Review several recent issues of the NEA publication, *Today's Education,* and the AFT publication, *The American Teacher.* Compare and contrast concerns or issues that each publication addresses. What overall differences do you find between the NEA and AFT publications?

3. Do you plan to join a teacher's association such as the NEA or AFT? What are your reasons? What advantages and disadvantages are most important to you?

4. In your opinion, what are the most important benefits of technology for education, and what are its most important potential drawbacks?

Teacher's Database

1. With classmates, join or start an online discussion on one or more of the following topics or another topic in Chapter 12 of this text.

action research	mentoring
computer simulations	National Board for Professional Teaching Standards (NBPTS)
computer-assisted instruction	
educational reform	school restructuring
educational software	teacher empowerment
educational technology	teacher leadership
grant writing	teacher strikes
hypermedia	teacher unions
interactive multimedia	teacher-principal collaboration

2. Find out more about school networking and distance learning projects. How might you use distance networking in your preparation as a teacher? As a teacher, how might you and your students use distance networking in connection with your curriculum? What knowledge and skills do you need to start to participate in a school-based collaborative networking project? Develop a list of personal resources as you sample the following information sources:

ACADEMY ONE of the National Public Telecomputing Network (NPTN)

aa005@nptn.org

I*LEARN—The International Education and Research Network

edl@copenfund.igc.apc.org

COSNDISC—Consortium for School Networking mailing list.

cosndisc@yukon.cren.org

EDTECH—Mailing list on topics in educational technology.

edtech@ohstvma.bitnet

KIDSPHERE—Development of computer networks for students and teachers.

kidsphere@vms.cis.pitt.edu

CONSORTIUM FOR SCHOOL NETWORKING—To develop use of computer network technology in K–12 education and for teachers to contribute ideas, lesson plans, and projects to others over the Internet.

ferdi@digital.cosn.org

THE EMPIRE INTERNET SCHOOLHOUSE—Provides a wide variety of K–12 resources, including discussion groups and invitations to join Internet projects.

Gopher: nysernet.org 3000

ISTE (International Society for Technology in Education)—Articles on the improvement of education through computer-based technology.

Gopher: iste-gopher.uoregon.edu

ISTE also has a mailing list (SIGTEL-L) for the Special Interest Group for Telecommunications:

sigtel-l@unmvma.unm.edu

TECH-ED—Forum for technology educators.

tech-ed-request@fre.fsu.umd.edu

Observations and Interviews

1. Survey adults who are not involved in education to get their views on teaching as a profession. What images of teachers and teaching emerge? How do you account for these views?

2. Interview teachers about their involvement in professional associations and the teachers' union. What benefits do teachers obtain from their professional involvement?

3. Find out if teacher strikes are legal in your state. What risks do striking teachers face? How are disputes between teachers and school districts settled?

4. Collaborate with classmates to study a school that is involved in restructuring and participants' roles in the change process. Compare teachers' activities with the new leadership roles for teachers discussed in this chapter. Are any of the teachers involved in action research in the classroom? How does teacher research contribute to restructuring efforts?

5. Visit a school that has developed a partnership with one or more community agencies, schools of higher education, businesses, parent groups, or neighborhood associations. Arrange to observe a planning meeting between the school and the community representatives. Write a narrative account of the meeting followed by an evaluation of the effectiveness of this partnership. To help you with this activity, ask your instructor for handouts M12.1, "Observing a School-Community Partnership," and M12.2, "Evaluating the Effectiveness of a School-University Partnership."

6. Survey a local school district to determine the educational technologies used by teachers. How and how often are these technologies used for instruction? What is the availability of computers and software for student use?

Professional Portfolio

Prepare a catalog of interactive multimedia resources and materials that you will use as a teacher. For each entry, include an annotation that briefly describes the resource materials, how you will use them, and where they may be obtained. As with the selection of any curriculum materials, try to find evidence of effectiveness, such as results of field tests, published reviews of educational software, awards, or testimonials from educators. View and report on at least one program you have included in your personal catalog. Explain in your report how you will integrate this multimedia resource into your curriculum. For some ideas to get you started, ask your instructor for handout M12.6.

Before I began teaching, I was unsure about whether I could do everything that teachers have to do. But now that the first year's about over, I know I can do it. I feel really great.

—A First-Year Teacher

chapter

13

Your First Teaching Position

Your spring student teaching seminar ended minutes ago; now you and three other students are seated in the faculty–student lounge enjoying sodas and talking about finding a job.

"What was the interview like?" you ask one of your classmates, upon learning that he interviewed yesterday for a position at an urban school.

"Yeah, tell us," another student adds. "I'm really anxious about interviewing. I don't know what to expect. There're so many things they could ask."

"Well, I was interviewed by the principal and two people from the district office—I think they were in personnel. At first, they asked questions like the ones we used in our seminar role plays: 'Why do you want to teach? What are your weaknesses? Use five adjectives to describe yourself.' "

"What else?" you ask, anxious to complete a mental image of the interview process so you'll be ready for your first interview next week.

"They asked me to describe a student teaching lesson that went well," he continues. "After I did that, one of them asked 'How could the lesson have been better—either for the entire class or for a certain student?' That one took some thinking."

As he goes on to reconstruct his response, you imagine how you would answer the same question.

Moments later, he says, "Then, one that really surprised me came when I was asked 'What would you do if your principal told you to discontinue a classroom activity because it was too noisy and left a mess for the custodians to clean up? But, the activity really involved the kids and they learned a lot.'"

He pauses for a sip of soda and then continues, "Another one was, 'Give us an example of a principle that guides your teaching.'"

Impressed with the district's ability to pose challenging questions, you again imagine how you would respond.

A few minutes later, another student asks, "What about portfolios? Did they spend much time looking at yours?"

"Did they ever!" your classmate exclaims. "They looked at everything. Plus, they really wanted to see things that were related to how much my students learned while I was student teaching."

With the mention of portfolios, you're reminded that you want to double-check the contents of yours before next week's interview. You also wonder what else you should do to prepare and what steps you can follow to increase your chances of finding the best possible teaching position.

■

Upon completion of your teacher education program, you will still have several important steps to take before securing your first teaching position. Preparing well for these steps will go a long way toward helping you begin teaching with confidence.

It is natural that you feel both excited and a bit fearful when thinking about your first job. While taking the courses required in your teacher education program, you probably feel secure in your role as a student; you know what is expected of you. As a teacher, however, you will assume an entirely new role—a role that requires some time before it becomes comfortable. The aim of this chapter, then, is to help make the transition from student to professional teacher a positive, pleasant one. We first look at the steps you can take to become certified or licensed to teach and to identify current trends related to teacher supply and demand.

HOW WILL YOU BECOME CERTIFIED OR LICENSED TO TEACH ?

State certification is required for teaching in the public schools, and in many private schools as well. In some cases, large cities (e.g., Chicago, New York, Buffalo) have their own certification requirements that must be met. And certain local school districts have additional requirements, such as a written examination, before one can teach in those districts.

A **teaching certificate** is actually a license to teach. The department of education for each of the fifty states and the District of Columbia sets the requirements for certification. A certificate usually indicates at what level and in what content areas one may teach. One might, for example, be certified for all-level (K–12) physical education or art, secondary English, elementary education, or middle-level education.

In 1996, thirty-two states offered certification for teaching at the middle school or junior high level—an increase from 1987, when twenty-six states offered such certification. In addition, a certificate may list other areas of specialization, such as driver's training, coaching, or journalism. If you plan to go into nonteaching areas such as counseling, librarianship, or administration, special certificates are usually required.

STATE CERTIFICATION REQUIREMENTS

In order for a person to receive a teaching certificate, all states require successful completion of an approved teacher education program that culminates with at least a bachelor's degree. To be approved, programs must pass a review by the state department of education approximately every five years. In addition to approval at the state level, almost all of the 1,289 programs in the nation have regional accreditation, and 524 voluntarily seek accreditation by the **National Council for Accreditation of Teacher Education (NCATE)** (Andrews 1994, I-4). In 1996, all states required an average of six to eight semester credits of supervised student teaching. Alabama, Colorado, Idaho, Indiana, Nevada, New York, and Virginia require a master's degree for advanced certification; and Arizona, Maryland, Montana, Oregon, and Washington require either a master's degree or a specified number of semester credits after certification (Andrews 1994, D-2). Additional requirements may also include U.S. citizenship, an oath of loyalty, fingerprinting, or a health examination.

A few states, including Iowa, North Carolina, New Mexico, and Oklahoma, waive state licensing requirements for teachers certified by the National Board for Professional Teaching Standards (NBPTS). Other states, including Massachusetts and Ohio, accept NBPTS certification as an alternative to their own requirements. For a current listing of state and local action supporting NBPTS certification, call the NBPTS at (800)-22TEACH.

Nearly all states now require testing of teachers for initial certification. States use either a standardized test (usually the National Teacher Examination [NTE] or Praxis) or a test developed by outside consultants. Areas covered by the states' tests usually include basic skills, professional knowledge, and general knowledge. Many states also require an on-the-job performance evaluation for certification (see Table 13.1 on page 414).

There is a trend away from granting teaching certificates for life. Some states, for example, issue three- to five-year certificates, which may be renewed only with proof of coursework completed beyond the bachelor's degree. And, amid considerable controversy, Arkansas, Georgia, and Texas have enacted testing for **recertification** of experienced teachers.

Certification requirements differ from state to state, and they are frequently modified. To remain up-to-date on the requirements for the state in which you plan to teach, it is important that you keep in touch with your teacher placement office or certification officer at your college or university. You may also wish to refer to *Requirements for Certification for Elementary and Secondary Schools* (The University of Chicago Press), an annual publication that lists state-by-state certification requirements for teachers, counselors, librarians, and administrators. Or, you may contact the teacher certification office in the state where you plan to teach (see the Teacher's Resource Guide for a "Directory of State Teacher Certification Offices in the United States").

In 1996, thirty states were members of the **Interstate Certification Agreement Contract,** a reciprocity agreement whereby a certificate obtained in one state will be honored in another (see the Teacher's Resource Guide). If you plan to teach in a state other than the one in which you are currently studying, you should find out if both states share a reciprocity agreement.

TABLE 13.1

Assessment requirements for the initial teaching certificate

State	Basic Skills Exam					Subject Matter Exam	General Knowledge Exam	Knowledge of Teaching Exam	Assessment of Teaching Performance	Footnotes
	Reading	Math	Writing	Spelling	Other					
	1	2	3	4	5	6	7	8	9	
Alabama	(1)	(1)	(1)	(1)		(2)		(2)	X	(1) For admission to program (2) Institution's exit exam
Alaska										
Arizona	X	X	X		(1)					(1) Grammar
Arkansas	X	X	X			X		X		
California	X	X	X			(1)			X	(1) Or completion of an approved subject matter program
Colorado		X	X	X	(1)					(1) Language, oral and written
Connecticut	X	X	X			X				
Delaware	X	X	X							
D.C.	X	X	X			X		X	X	
Florida	X	X	X			X	X	X	X	
Georgia						X				
Hawaii	X	X	X		(1)	X	X	X	X	(1) Listening/oral communication
Idaho	X	X	X		(1)	X				(1) Listening
Illinois	X	X	X		(1)	X				(1) Grammar
Indiana	X		X		(1)	X	X	X		(1) Listening
Iowa										
Kansas	X	X	X			X		X		
Kentucky	(1)	(1)	(1)	X		X	X	X	X	(1) Required for admission to teacher education
Louisiana	X	X	X		(1)	X	X	X	X	(1) Communication skills
Maine							X	X		
Maryland	X		X	X	(1)	X	X	X		(1) Listening
Massachusetts										
Michigan	X	X	X			X	X			
Minnesota	X	X	X							
Mississippi	X	X	X	(1)	(1)	X	X	X		(1) Listening
Missouri	(1)	(1)	(1)	(1)		X		X		(1) For entry into teacher education
Montana	X	X	X		(1)		X	X		(1) Listening

(Source: Theodore E. Andrews, ed. *NASDTEC Manual on Certification and Preparation of Educational Personnel in the United States, Second Edition, 1994–95.* National Association of State Directors of Teacher Education & Certification, Dubuque, Iowa: Kendall/Hunt Publishing Company, p. B-4.)

The rightmost notes column of the table reads (top to bottom, aligned to the indicated rows):

- (1) Demonstrate competence by: a) college recommendation, b) possession of MA or higher, c) certification from state requiring basic skills test, d) statement from college
- (1) For elementary education
- (1) Listening
- (1) Prior to entry into teacher education (2) Listening
- (1) Prior to entry into teacher education
- (1) Communication Skills & General Knowledge Exams required for elementary (2) For Oregon graduates
- (1) Listening (2) Includes Math
- (1) Required for some prior to entering teacher education

State	1	2	3	4	5	6	7
Nebraska	X	X					
Nevada	X	X					X
New Hampshire	(1)	(1)					
New Jersey		X			X	(1)	X
New Mexico	X	X		(1)	X	X	
New York	X	X				X	
North Carolina	(1)	(1)		(2)	X	X	
North Dakota	(1)				X	X	
Ohio	X	X			X	X	
Oklahoma	X	X			X		X
Oregon	X	X		(1)	(1)	X	(2)
Pennsylvania	X	X		(1)	X	(2)	
Rhode Island	X	X	X		X	X	
South Carolina	X	X			X		
South Dakota					X		X
Tennessee	X	X			X	X	X
Texas	X	X			X	X	
Utah					X	X	X
Vermont							
Virginia	X	X			X	X	
Washington	(1)	(1)		(1)	(1)		
West Virginia	X				X		X
Wisconsin	X	X					
Wyoming							

What are some alternatives for becoming certified or licensed to teach? What are some current trends in certification and what conditions might account for those trends?

About 400,000 teachers, many of whom are noncertified, teach in America's growing system of private, parochial, for-profit, and charter schools (National Center for Education Statistics 1996, 72). Private and parochial schools supported largely by tuition and gifts, and for-profit schools operated by private educational corporations, usually have no certification requirements for teachers. Also, teacher-created and teacher-operated charter schools, though they are public, are often free of state certification requirements. A school's **charter** (an agreement between the school's founders and its sponsor—usually a local school board) may waive certification requirements if the school guarantees that students will attain a specified level of achievement.

ALTERNATIVE CERTIFICATION

Despite the national movement to make certification requirements more stringent, concern about a possible teacher shortage during the 1990s has resulted in increasing use of alternative teacher certification programs. In 1983, only eight states offered alternatives; by 1992, forty states had alternative routes to certification (Feistritzer and Chester 1993).

Alternative certification programs are designed for persons who already have at least a bachelor's degree in a field other than education and want to become licensed to teach. About 20,000 persons were licensed through alternative certification programs between 1985 and 1990; by 1992, the total number had increased to about 40,000 (Feistritzer and Chester 1993).

All but two states may grant certification to those who do not meet current requirements. Half of the states may even give a substandard credential to those who hold less than a bachelor's degree. In response to occasional shortages of teachers in particular subject and grade-level areas, many state systems approve temporary measures such as **emergency certification.** During the teaching shortage of the mid-1980s, for example, the National Education Association reported that one in thirteen teachers was not fully certified and one in six spent at least some time teaching a grade or subject in which he or she had received no training. Though strongly resisted by professional teacher organizations, alternative certification is likely to become even more widespread in the event of a teacher shortage.

THE NATIONAL TEACHER EXAMINATION AND PRAXIS

The **National Teacher Examination (NTE)** is required in most states for initial certification. The NTE consists of tests of communication skills, general knowledge, and professional knowledge (see the Teacher's Resource Guide). Each test is a separate two-hour examination, and specialty tests in twenty-eight subject areas are also available.

In 1992, Educational Testing Service (ETS), the developers of the NTE, announced to states the availability of a more sophisticated battery of tests for initial teacher certification. These tests will eventually replace the NTE. The new testing system, known as the **Praxis Series: Professional Assessments for Beginning Teachers**, was developed through consultation with teachers, educational researchers, the National Education Association, and the American Federation of Teachers. The Praxis Series (*praxis* means putting theory into practice) enables states to create a system of tests that meet their specific licensing requirements. Three types of assessments, beginning with entry into a teacher education program and culminating in actual classroom performance, are available through the Praxis Series. In 1995, ETS expanded the Praxis Series by introducing Principles of Learning and Teaching (PLT), a test of teachers' professional knowledge. The Teachers' Resource Guide includes descriptions of Praxis I, II, and III, and the PLT test.

WHERE WILL YOU TEACH 🔲

When you think ahead to a career in teaching, two questions you are likely to ask yourself are, How hard will it be to find a job? And, Where will I teach? From time to time, **teacher supply and demand** figures have painted a rather bleak picture for those entering the teaching profession. At other times, finding a position in a preferred location has been relatively easy.

During the early 1990s, a debate ensued about teacher supply and demand. Citing statistics related to the rising number of school-age children of baby boomers, increased teacher retirements, fewer college students going into teaching, and increased employment opportunities for women in other fields, some observers predicted a shortage of teachers by the turn of the century. Others, however, predicted that a teacher shortage would not develop. Their forecasts suggested that increases in teachers' salaries, the economic recession of the early 1990s, and alternative certification (discussed earlier in this chapter) would prevent a teacher shortage from occurring.

Despite the difficulty of predicting trends in teacher supply and demand, it is clear that, even during times of teacher surplus, talented, qualified teachers are able to find jobs. Teaching is one of the largest professions in the United States; out of a national population of about 261 million, about 51.7 million attended public and private elementary and secondary schools in fall 1996 (National Center for Education Statistics 1995). During 1994–95, the total instructional staff in our nation's public and private K–12 schools was about 2.9 million (National Center for Education Statistics 1995), and this number is expected to range between 3.25 and 3.44 million by the year 2003 (National Center for Education Statistics 1992). Within such a large profession, annual openings resulting from retirements and career changes alone are sizable.

A FAVORABLE JOB MARKET

Although the need for new teachers is difficult to determine, most analysts predict a favorable job market for teachers in all regions of the country during the early twenty-first century. Enrollments in elementary and secondary schools are expected to continue to increase into the next century and surpass the previous high set in 1971. Elementary school enrollment is expected to reach 39.4 million by the year 2005, while secondary school enrollment is expected to reach 16.4 million (see Figure 13.1 on page 418). Figure 13.2 on page 418 shows that the projected need for elementary and secondary classroom teachers will show a steady increase between now and the year 2006. These projections mean that qualified teachers—those with a real commitment to children—should have little difficulty securing desirable positions.

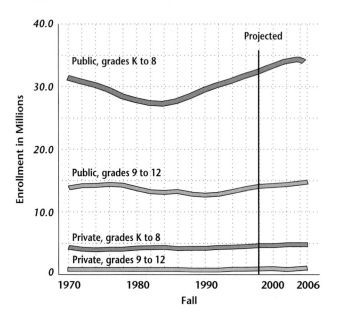

FIGURE 13.1 Enrollment in elementary and secondary schools, by level and control: Fall 1970 to fall 2006 (Source: National Center for Education Statistics, *Mini-Digest of Education Statistics 1995.* Washington, D.C.: U.S. Department of Education, Office of Educational Research and Improvement, p. 10.)

DEMAND BY SPECIALITY AREA AND GEOGRAPHIC REGION

The ease with which you will find your first teaching position is also related to your area of specialization and to the part of the country where you wish to locate. In 1997, for example, job seekers able to teach bilingual education or special education were in an especially favorable position. Also, Hawaii had the greatest overall demand for teachers, followed by the West, the South Central region, the Great Plains/Midwest, and the Southeast. For current employment opportunities according to speciality area and geographic region and for other job-search resources, check the following publications by the American Association for Employment in Education (820 Davis Street, Suite 222, Evanston, IL 60201-4445, (847) 864-1999). Be aware, however, that the Association does not provide placement services nor does it maintain lists of vacancies.

FIGURE 13.2 Elementary and secondary classroom teachers by organizational level and control of institution (Source: National Center for Education Statistics, *Projections of Education Statistics to 2006, Twenty-Fifth Edition.* Washington, D.C.: U.S. Department of Education, Office of Educational Research and Improvement, pp. 69–70.)

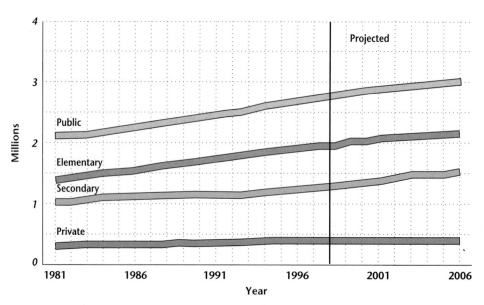

- *AAEE Annual: The Job Search Handbook for Educators* (Supply-demand data, interview techniques, résumé advice, and other job-search suggestions, $8.00).
- *Guide to Services and Activities for Teacher Employment* (Employment assistance services, career fair dates, contacts, teacher certification reciprocity among states, vacancy listing information, candidates' computer data banks, and other resources, $12.00).
- *AAEE Directory of Public School Systems in the United States* (Names, addresses, and phone numbers of contact persons, district size, school grade levels, and other information, $65.00 for complete directory; from no charge to $12.00 for individual state directories).

When considering supply and demand estimates, remember that jobs *are* to be had in oversupplied areas. Job hunting will be more competitive, though, and you may have to relocate to another region of the country.

OTHER CAREER OPPORTUNITIES FOR TEACHERS

There are also a great many nonteaching jobs in education and education-related fields, such as principal, assistant principal, librarian, and counselor. In addition, there are many jobs that, although removed from the world of the classroom, would nevertheless enable you to use your teaching skills.

The following outline lists several places other than schools where individuals with teaching backgrounds are often employed. The number of education-related careers is likely to increase in the coming decades.

Industry
- Publishers
- Educational materials and equipment suppliers
- Specialized educational service firms
- Communications industries
- Research and development firms
- Management consulting firms
- Education and training consultants
- Educational divisions of large corporations—Xerox, IBM, CBS, General Electric, Westinghouse, etc.

Government
- Federal agencies—U.S. Office of Education, Bureau of Prisons, Department of Labor, Office of Economic Opportunity, Department of Justice, Department of Health, Education and Welfare, etc.
- Federal programs—Bureau of Indian Affairs Schools, Bureau of Prisons Schools, Job Corps, Overseas Dependent Schools, Peace Corps, Teacher Corps, Upward Bound, VISTA, etc.
- Regional educational networks—Research and development centers, regional educational laboratories, sixteen clearinghouses of the Educational Resources Information Center (ERIC), etc.
- Jobs in state departments of education

Education-Related Associations
- Research centers and foundations
- Professional associations—National Council of Teachers of English, National Association of Mathematics Teachers, National Education Association, American Federation of Teachers, Phi Delta Kappa, Kappa Delta Pi, Educational Testing Service, etc.

Community Organizations

- Community action programs—Upward Bound, neighborhood health centers, legal services, aid to migrant workers, etc.
- Social service agencies—United Fund agencies, Boy Scouts, Girl Scouts, YMCAs and YWCAs, settlement houses, boys' and girls' clubs, etc.
- Adult education centers
- Museums
- Hospitals

HOW WILL YOU FIND YOUR FIRST TEACHING JOB ?

During the last year of your teacher education program, you will probably become increasingly concerned about finding a teaching position. The "Job Search Timetable Checklist" presented in the Teacher's Resource Guide may help you plan your job search. In the remainder of this section we discuss five critical steps in that sequence: finding out about teaching vacancies, preparing a résumé, writing letters of inquiry and letters of application, being interviewed, and selecting a position.

FINDING OUT ABOUT TEACHING VACANCIES

Your college or university probably has a **placement service** designed to help graduates find jobs. On a regular basis, placement offices usually publish lists of vacancies, which are posted and, in many cases, mailed to students who have registered with the office and set up a credentials file.

A **credentials file** (known as placement papers at some institutions) usually includes the following: background information on the applicant, the type of position sought, a list of courses taken, performance evaluations by the applicant's cooperative teacher, and three or more letters of recommendation. With each job application, the candidate requests that his or her credentials be sent to the appropriate person at the school district, or the school district itself may request the applicant's papers. Placement offices usually charge a small fee for each time a candidate's papers are sent out.

A job announcement describes the position and its requirements and provides the name and address of the individual to contact at the school district. For each position you are interested in, send a letter of application to the appropriate person along with your résumé. In addition, you may have your placement office send your credentials file. Placement offices also frequently set up on-campus interviews between candidates and representatives of school district personnel departments.

State department of education employment offices help teachers locate positions. Like college and university placement offices, states publish lists of job openings, which are then distributed to registered candidates. Because most of these states will assist out-of-state candidates, you can register in more than one state.

Personal networking will play an important role in landing the right job. Let people know you are looking for a job—friends, teachers at schools you've attended, faculty at the school where you student teach, and people you meet at workshops and conferences. Also, with access to the Internet, you can conduct a global job search and even make your résumé available to millions of people. An easy-to-use, free job-search service on the Internet is the National Teacher/Educational Job Listings (http://www.ldol.state.la.us/ajb/ajbtmain.HTML) maintained by the Louisiana

Department of Labor. This service allows the user to search specific states for teacher and education-related job openings that are listed with America's Job Bank (http://www.ajb.dni.us:80/ajb/job.search/), a comprehensive, free job-search service linked to 2,000 state employment offices. Many individuals who know the computer coding language HTML (HyperText Markup Language) can create their own "home pages" on the Internet to make their résumés available to network users.

PREPARING YOUR RÉSUMÉ

A **résumé** presents a concise summary of an individual's professional experiences, education, and skills. Résumés must be typed and preferably no longer than one page, two pages at most. Though there is no right way to prepare a résumé, it should present—in a neat, systematic way—key information that will help an employer determine your suitability for a particular position. Because your résumé will most likely be your first contact with an employer, it must make a good impression.

Ordinarily, a résumé contains the following information:

- Personal data
- Education
- Certificates held
- Experience

- Activities and interests
- Honors and offices held
- Professional memberships
- References

Figure 13.3 on page 422 is a résumé prepared by Linda M. Rodriguez that you can use as a model. To prepare an effective résumé, read "Résumé Advice for Educators" in the Teacher's Resource Guide.

WRITING LETTERS OF INQUIRY AND APPLICATIONS

As a job seeker, you will most likely have occasion to write two kinds of letters: letters of inquiry and letters of application. A **letter of inquiry** is used to determine if a school district has, or anticipates, any teaching vacancies. This type of letter states your general qualifications and requests procedures to be followed in making a formal application (see Figure 13.4 on page 423). A letter of inquiry should also include your résumé as well as a self-addressed, stamped envelope for the school district's convenience. Be prepared not to receive a reply for each letter of inquiry you send out. Many school districts are unable to respond to all inquiries.

A **letter of application** (often called a cover letter) indicates your interest in a particular position and outlines your qualifications for that job. As most districts have several vacancies at any given time, it is important that the first sentence of your letter refer to the specific position for which you are applying. The body of the letter should then highlight why you would be an excellent choice to fill that position. Also, inform the reader that your credentials file will be sent on request or is being sent by your placement office. Close the letter by expressing your availability for an interview (see Figure 13.5 on page 424).

PARTICIPATING IN A JOB INTERVIEW

The interview is one of the most important steps in your search for an appropriate position. As the dialogue in the scenario at the beginning of this chapter suggests, school district representatives may ask a wide range of questions, both structured and open-ended.

Linda M. Rodriguez

Personal Data

Born: October 16, 1977

Address and Phone: 948 W. Third
                        Spokane, WA 99206
                        (509) 924-1234
                        lmrodrig@abc.com

Education

B.A., Elementary Education, Washington State University, June 1998.

Certificates Held

Major Area: Elementary Education, K–8

Minor Area: Bilingual Education

Experience

Student Teaching, Garden Springs Elementary, W. 5116 Garden Springs Road, Spokane, WA 99204, Spring 1998. Cooperating teacher: Mrs. Becky Jones. Observed, assisted, and taught regular and accelerated 3rd grade classes in a multilingual setting. Organized after-school tutoring program and developed a unit on using the World Wide Web in the classroom. Attended site-based council meetings with Mrs. Jones and assisted in the development of community-based partnerships.

Camp Counselor and Recreation Director, YWCA Summer Camp, Spokane, WA.
Directed summer recreation program comprised of 10 counselors and 140 elementary aged girls.

Volunteer Telephone Counselor, Spokane County Crisis Hotline, June 1996–June 1997.

Activities and Interests

Spokane County Historical Society, Secretary, 1997.

Member, Washington State University Community Service Learning Center.

Hobbies: Jogging, Aerobics, Piano, Water Skiing.

Honors

B.A. with Honors, Washington State University, June 1998.

Washington State Scholarship, 1996–1998.

Professional Memberships

Washington Association for Supervision and Curriculum Development.

Kappa Delta Pi.

Instructional Technology Skills

Word processing, Internet and World Wide Web, optical scanner, interactive electronic whiteboard, LCD computer projection panel, NovaNET (computer-based learning system).

Career Objective

Seeking K-8 position in multicultural/multilingual setting.

References

References and credentials file available upon request.

FIGURE 13.3 Résumé

Linda M. Rodriguez
948 W. Third
Spokane, Washington 99206

April 5, 1998

Dr. Lawrence Walker
Office of Personnel Services
City School District
100 Post Oak Boulevard
Houston, Texas 77056

Dear Dr. Walker:

This letter is to express my interest in a teaching position in the Houston City School District. Specifically, I would like to know if you anticipate any vacancies at the elementary level for fall of 1998. This June I will receive my B.A. (with honors) in elementary education from Washington State University. My supporting endorsement will be in bilingual education.

As a student teacher this spring semester, I taught regular and accelerated 3rd grade classes at Garden Springs Elementary School in Spokane, Washington. One class had 25 students, 3 of whom were diagnosed as having learning disabilities. At Garden Springs, I introduced students to science resources on the World Wide Web, and each student learned how to send e-mail messages to students in other countries.

My education at Washington State University, I believe, has prepared me well to teach in today's classrooms. I have had a course that focuses on meeting the needs of at-risk learners, and my supporting endorsement in bilingual education has prepared me to meet the challenges of working with students from diverse linguistic backgrounds. If possible, I would like a position that would allow me to develop programs for students with non–English backgrounds.

Enclosed you will find my résumé, which provides additional information about my experiences and activities. If there are any positions for which you think I might be suited, please send application materials in the enclosed stamped, self-addressed envelope. I appreciate your consideration, and I look forward to hearing from you.

Sincerely,

Linda M. Rodriguez

Linda M. Rodriguez

FIGURE 13.4 Letter of inquiry

Linda M. Rodriguez
948 W. Third
Spokane, Washington 99206

May 5, 1998

Dr. Mary Lamb
Associate Superintendent for Personnel
Metropolitan School District
Wacker Office Building
773 Ranier Avenue
Seattle, Washington 98504

Dear Dr. Lamb:

This letter is in support of my application for the position of 4th grade teacher at City Elementary School. This June I will receive my B.A. (with honors) in elementary education from Washington State University. My supporting endorsement will be in bilingual education.

As my enclosed résumé indicates, I just completed my student teaching at Garden Springs Elementary School in Spokane. During that 16-week period, I taught regular and accelerated 3rd grade classes. One class had 25 students, 3 of whom were diagnosed as having learning disabilities. I also organized an after-school tutoring program and assisted my cooperating teacher in developing community-based partnerships.

A major interest of mine is using technology in the classroom. I am familiar with various hypermedia programs and NovaNET, a computer-based learning system. At Garden Springs, I introduced students to science resources on the World Wide Web, and each student learned how to send e-mail messages to students in other countries.

As a result of my rewarding experiences at Garden Springs Elementary and in light of my preparation in bilingual education, I believe I could make a significant contribution to the educational program at City Elementary.

I have arranged for my credentials to be forwarded from Washington State University's placement office. If you require additional information of any sort, please feel free to contact me. At your convenience, I am available for an interview in Seattle. I thank you in advance for your consideration.

Sincerely,

Linda M. Rodriguez

Linda M. Rodriguez

FIGURE 13.5 Letter of application

What questions might you be asked in an interview for a teaching position? What questions should you have about the teaching position? about the school?

In some districts, you might be interviewed by the principal only; in others, the superintendent, the principal, and the department chairperson might interview you; and in still others, classroom teachers might interview you. Regardless of format, the interview enables the district to obtain more specific information regarding your probable success as an employee, and it gives you an opportunity to ask questions about what it is like to teach in the district. By asking questions yourself, you demonstrate your interest in working in the district. The Teacher's Resource Guide presents seventeen questions you can ask (see "Sample Interview Questions for Candidates to Ask").

PROFESSIONAL REFLECTION

Anticipating Interview Questions

The following questions were gathered from school hiring officials and are representative of those that you are likely to encounter in your job interviews. Circle the *one* question in each section that you feel *least* prepared to answer and develop answers on a separate sheet or in your teacher's journal.

Motivation/Experience/Training

1. Tell us about yourself.
2. Why did you enter the field of teaching?
3. What experiences have you had related to teaching?
4. What qualities do you have that make you an effective teacher?
5. Do you have experience with special education students?
6. Why do you want to teach in our school district?
7. Do you have (multicultural, urban, learning problems) teaching experience?
8. What do you remember most about your own education?

Teaching Effectiveness

9. How do you meet the range of skills and needs commonly present in a classroom?

10. When do you use an individual, group, and/or whole-class teaching approach? Why?
11. Let's imagine we are going to observe a teacher teaching a lesson. I tell you in advance to expect a superb lesson. What would you expect to see in that lesson?
12. How do you diagnose your students' needs?
13. How do you stimulate active participation in the classroom?
14. How would you use parents in the classroom?

Teacher Planning/Preparation

15. What kinds of planning do you see a teacher doing?
16. How do you plan for a year? A week? A day?
17. How do you know what you will cover?
18. What types of resource materials do you like to use?

Classroom Management/Discipline

19. What are some characteristics of a well-managed classroom?
20. What discipline methods work for you?
21. What is your primary goal with student discipline?
22. What are some examples of rules you would have in your classroom?
23. How would you be sure your rules are carried out?
24. How much responsibility for their learning do you feel students should have to take?
25. What types of rewards and consequences would you use?
26. Describe your most difficult student discipline situation and how you handled it.

Staff Development/Professional Growth

27. What do you see yourself doing over the course of the next several years to improve your abilities as a professional?
28. What professional development topics most interest you?

Staff Rapport/Relationships

29. As a teacher new to a school, what would you see yourself doing to contribute to healthy staff relationships and to become part of the staff?
30. What should a principal expect from teachers?
31. What should teachers expect from the principal?

Grading Systems

32. What grading system works for you?
33. Under what conditions, if any, would most of your pupils receive D's and F's? How and why could this happen?

Closing Comments/Questions

34. What additional talents and skills do you have?
35. What extracurricular activities can you supervise?
36. Do you have questions or additional comments for us (Johnston, Morehead, and Burns 1992, 23–24)?

ACCEPTING AN OFFER

One day you are notified that a school district would like to hire you. Your job search efforts have paid off! In the competition for positions, you have been successful. However, accepting your first teaching position is a major personal and professional step. Before signing a contract with a district, you should carefully consider job-related questions such as the following:

- In regard to my abilities and education, am I suited to this position?
- Would I like to work with this school's students, administrative staff, and teachers?
- Is the salary I am being offered sufficient?
- Will this position likely be permanent?
- Would I like to live in or near this community?
- Would the cost of living in this community enable me to live comfortably?
- Are opportunities for continuing education readily available?

If you accept the offer, you will need to return a signed contract to the district along with a short letter confirming your acceptance. As a professional courtesy, you should notify other districts to which you have applied that you have accepted a position elsewhere.

WHAT CAN YOU EXPECT AS A BEGINNING TEACHER ?

Once you accept the professional challenge of teaching, it is important to prepare well in advance of the first day of school. In addition to reviewing the material you will teach, you should use this time to find out all you can about the school's students, the surrounding community, and the way the school operates. Also reflect on your expectations.

THE FIRST DAY

The first day of school can be both exciting and frightening, as the experiences of the following beginning teachers suggest:

> I teach first grade. There's a stigma attached to being a first-year first-grade teacher. [On the first day] a parent said (in a skeptical tone), "So, you're a first-year teacher?" Later, that same parent called me on Back-to-School Night and conceded, "You know your stuff, don't you?" That parent was a partner with me in the child's education the remainder of the year and wrote a recommendation to my principal supporting my nomination for the Sallie Mae Award (Sallie Mae 1995, 5).

> —First-grade teacher

> . . . my first day on the job. It was very weird because I felt very young. Everyone here is pretty much settled in. I felt like I was a rookie—a greenhorn. The other teachers made jokes about it, too. I'm sure they didn't mean anything by it. My first day actually in the classroom, facing my kids—that was really interesting. I was real nervous about what my kids were going to be like and what kind of students I was going to have. I ended up with some really nice classes so it was kind of a treat (Dollase 1992, 23).

> —Middle school teacher

> I was nervous, of course. I had done substitute work before, but this was like the real show. I think my anxiety was evident, although students couldn't detect it because they

Vito Perrone

Wise Adviser of Teachers

As the Director of Programs in Teacher Education at the Harvard Graduate School of Education and former public school teacher, Vito Perrone has spent his professional life focusing on the concerns of teachers. In his book, *A Letter to Teachers* (1991), he points out that teachers need to keep in mind the "large purposes" of education. New teachers can easily become overwhelmed by the required textbooks to be read and the state and district curricula to be digested. He encourages them instead to trust and draw on their basic beliefs about the large purposes of education. To Perrone, "education at its best is first and foremost a moral and intellectual endeavor, always beginning with children and young people and their intentions and needs. . . . If we kept such a view about children and young people constantly before us," he says, "we wouldn't be so quick to assume clinical approaches to education, approaches so full of labels. We would put our energy into seeking out students' strengths and not their deficits" (pp. 1–3).

"[Teachers] need to be seen as real people. . . ."

In response to the concerns new teachers express regarding discipline and classroom management, he observes that teachers should reduce the limitations they place on students:

> I believe the limits we need are few, revolving almost exclusively on how individuals treat others in the environment and how they treat each other's work. Most of the negative exchanges in schools between teachers and students stem from too many rules that are rooted mostly in control and not in concern for student learning (p. 32).

He disagrees with the "Don't smile until Christmas" advice so many people give first-year teachers. Instead he tells teachers to be real people to their students and to not keep their distance or try to keep their students off guard:

> Teachers needn't reveal themselves completely; few people do this, even among good friends. But they need to be seen as real people who care, have strong beliefs, live fully in the world (p. 31).

Perrone suggests that new teachers remain students, students of teaching. By reflecting on their teaching, analyzing it, and growing from it, teachers can become empowered teachers. Teachers also need to reflect on their practice together, collaborating on solutions to the daily challenges they face. From someone whose teaching has never stopped, these words are wise advice.

---

were as nervous as I was. Actually, it went very well, very well. I had planned out some games which the kids were really into. It was such a well-planned day for me. I had planned everything for the first few days so it went well (Dollase 1992, 35).

—High school social studies teacher

Creating a pleasant, learning-oriented climate on the first day, as this teacher went on to do, will contribute greatly to your success during the first year. On the first day, students are eager to learn and are hopeful that the year will be a productive one. In addition, nearly all students will be naturally receptive to what you have to say. To them, you are a new, unknown quantity, and one of their initial concerns is to find out what kind of a teacher you will be. It is therefore critical that you be well organized and ready to take charge.

ADVICE FROM EXPERIENCED TEACHERS

In our work with schools and teachers, we have gathered recommendations on preparing for the first day from experienced K–12 teachers in urban, suburban, and rural schools. Teachers' recommendations focus on planning, establishing effective management practices, and following through on decisions.

> There are little things you can do, such as having a personal note attached to a pencil welcoming each child. You may want to do a few little tricks in science class or read them your favorite children's story. But, don't put all your energy into the first day and have that day be the highlight of the year. Be well prepared and have plenty of things to do. Don't worry if you don't get everything done. Remember, you have all year.
>
> —Middle school science teacher

> It really helps on the first day to have plenty of material to cover and things to do. I'd recommend taking the material you plan to cover that day and doubling it. It's better to have too much than to run out. What you don't use the first day, you use the next. It takes a while to get a feeling for how fast the kids are going to go.
>
> —Third-grade teacher

> The first day is a good time to go over rules and procedures for the year. But don't overdo it. Be very clear and specific about your expectations for classroom behavior.
>
> —Sixth-grade teacher

> From the beginning, it's important to do what you're there to do—that's teach. Teach the class something, maybe review material they learned last year. That lets them know that you're in charge, you expect them to learn. They'll look to you for direction—as long as you give it to them, you're fine.
>
> —Junior high language arts teacher

> What I've found very helpful is to get in touch with all my kids' parents right after the first day. I tell them a bit about how I run my class, what we're going to do that year, and how pleased I am to have their child in my room. I keep it upbeat, very positive. We're going to have a great year! It takes time to do that—everyone's so busy at the start of the year—but it's worth it. It pays off during the rest of the year.
>
> —First-grade teacher

HOW CAN YOU BECOME A PART OF YOUR LEARNING COMMUNITY ?

Your success in your first year of teaching will be determined by the relationships you develop with the pupils, their families, your colleagues, school administrators, and other members of the school community. All of these groups contribute to your effectiveness as a teacher, but the relationships you establish with students will be the most important (and complex) you will have as a teacher.

RELATIONSHIPS WITH STUDENTS

The quality of your relationships with students will depend in large measure on your knowledge of students and commitment to improving your interactions with them. As one beginning teacher put it:

> More than anything, you need to understand the students and what kinds of different things they're bringing into the classroom. . . . Every student is different, every student

needs to be treated differently. . . . I still feel I need to improve in learning to understand students. I can think of specific cases where I was a little bit hard on them, and I forgot to give them the opportunity to tell me why they were acting that way. . . . Another thing I need to work on, too, is my attitude with students who are always causing me to have to speak to them. My patience is shorter with them. It's easy to jump on those persons, you're always jumping on them for doing something (Dollase 1992, 29, 31).

Your relationships with students will have many dimensions. Principally, you must see that each student learns as much as possible; this is your primary responsibility as a professional teacher. You will need to establish relationships with a great diversity of students based on mutual respect, caring, and concern. Without attention to this personal realm, your effectiveness as a teacher will be limited. In addition, teachers are significant models for students' attitudes and behaviors.

RELATIONSHIPS WITH COLLEAGUES AND STAFF

Each working day, you will be in close contact with other teachers and staff members. As the experience of the following teacher suggests, it will definitely be to your advantage to establish friendly, professional relationships with them:

> I was on a staff with a group of teachers who really supported me. They made it a part of their day to come into my room and see how I was doing and to share things. They made it easy to ask questions and work with them. They started me on the track of co-operating with other teachers and sharing my successes and failures with them.

> They did such a good job of taking care of each other that my needs were always met. I had plenty of supplies, counseling help, administrative help. The school was a community. Anything I needed to be successful was provided.

During your first few months at the school, it would be wise to communicate to colleagues that you are willing to learn all you can about your new job and to be a team player. In most schools it is common practice to give junior faculty members less desirable assignments, reserving the more desirable ones for senior faculty. By demonstrating your willingness to take on these responsibilities with good humor and to give them your best effort, you will do much to establish yourself as a valuable faculty member.

Your colleagues may also appreciate learning from you about new approaches and materials—if you share in a manner that doesn't make others feel inferior. The following comments by a high school department chair, for example, illustrate a first-year Spanish teacher's positive influence on others:

> She won the respect of all her colleagues in the school who have dealt with her almost immediately, not because she's so competent in Spanish and not because she's so competent as a teacher, but because she handles everything with such sensitivity and sensibleness.

> Because of the way she operates—which is quietly but effectively—she has raised the whole tenor of expectations in the department. We have some very fine faculty in Spanish, but I would speculate they don't see their group self-image as intellectuals but rather as "people people." Because of what Elizabeth has brought to the school: the knowledge about how to use computers, her knowledge of foreign language oral proficiency, her knowledge of Spanish film and Spanish authors, she has kind of lifted everybody up and helped her colleagues see themselves in a little bit different light and to improve professionally (Dollase 1992, 49).

It is important that you get along with your colleagues and contribute to a spirit of professional cooperation or **collegiality** in the school. Some you will enjoy being around; others you may wish to avoid. Some will express obvious enthusiasm for

Dear Mentor

NOVICE AND EXPERT TEACHERS ON SOLVING CLASSROOM DISCIPLINE PROBLEMS

Dear Eddie,

Classroom management is a top concern among teachers, principals, and parents within the education community. Problem solving is a valid concern for teachers of any grade level. Teachers must have a clear, organized plan for handling classroom problems. This plan should be well-defined with clear rules and consistent consequences.

Discipline in the classroom is an issue all teachers deal with daily in their classroom. The first step in dealing with your students is getting to know each student's personality. Each child has a different background and family history. This process should begin soon after school starts by reviewing the students' academic and confidential files. Teachers must search for patterns of behavior in the comment section of past report cards. Major events in the child's family history such as divorce and abuse can lead to changes in students' behavior. Teachers must be cautious not to stereotype students before they have an opportunity to develop their own opinions during the school year.

I believe a teacher must be involved in the everyday problems among students. The teacher sets the tone for the environment of the classroom. The students will often "test" the teacher by seeing how much they can get away with. Teachers should be firm and fair when dealing with student behavior. Teachers should not ignore the petty situations, otherwise those situations often develop into larger, more serious problems.

Dear Mentor,

An area of concern for me has been problem solving within the classroom. How much involvement should I have with everyday problems among students? Should I ignore petty situations, such as making fun or taking pencils, and only intercede in more serious misbehavior, such as hitting, name calling, or throwing objects? I have tried to deal with all issues, but I also think that students should learn to solve their own problems.

Eddie Franco

Teachers must also use a wide range of resources when dealing with student discipline. Involve the parents as much as possible when problems arise. Daily notes, home visits, and conferences all provide a base of communication between the school and home. Your school's guidance counselor is a valuable resource. With more time to talk with the students, the counselor can often search deeper for solutions. The last resource is documentation of student problems and parent conferences. Detailed student records are crucial to the success of the teacher in the area of classroom management.

When dealing with difficult students, teacher documentation often becomes the center of meetings between the principal and parents.

School discipline is a hot topic in communities all across the United States. A teacher with genuine concern for students will find a system of rules and consequences that will enable the students to learn and the teachers to teach.

Paul Liner
Teacher at Hidenwood Elementary
School in Newport News, Virginia.
Virgina's 1995 Sallie Mae First-
Year Teacher Award winner.

teaching; others may be bitter and pessimistic about their work. Be pleasant and friendly with both types. Accept their advice with a smile, and then act on what you believe is worthwhile.

RELATIONSHIPS WITH ADMINISTRATORS

Pay particular attention to the relationships you develop with administrators, department heads, and supervisors. Though your contacts with them will not be as frequent as with other teachers, they can do much to ensure your initial success. They are well aware of the difficulties you might encounter as a first-year teacher, and they are there to help you succeed.

The principal of your new school will, most likely, be the one to introduce you to other teachers, members of the administrative team, and staff. He or she should inform you if there are assistant principals or department heads who can help you enforce school rules, keep accurate records, and obtain supplies, for example. The principal may also assign an experienced teacher to serve as a mentor during your first year. In addition, your principal will indicate his or her availability to discuss issues of concern, and you should not hesitate to do so if the need arises.

RELATIONSHIPS WITH PARENTS

Developing positive connections with your students' parents can contribute significantly to students' success and to your success as a teacher. In reality, teachers and parents are partners—both concerned with the learning and growth of the children in their care. As U.S. Secretary of Education Richard Riley stated in his 1996 State of American Education Address, parents can have a significant impact on schools: "If all parents in America made it their patriotic duty to find an extra thirty minutes every day to help their children learn more, it would revolutionize American education" (U.S. Department of Education 1996, 1). Unfortunately, research indicates that mothers typically spend less than Riley's recommended 30 minutes per day talking with or reading to their children, and fathers spend less than 15 minutes. The time parents spend interacting with their children differs as much as five times from family to family (Sadker and Sadker 1994).

It is important that you become acquainted with parents at school functions, at meetings of the Parent–Teacher Association or Organization (PTA or PTO), at various community events, and in other social situations. To develop good communication with parents, you will need to be sensitive to their needs, such as their work schedules and the language spoken at home.

By maintaining contact with parents and encouraging them to become involved in their children's education, you can significantly enhance the achievement of your students. Research has shown, for example, that parental involvement is a key factor in children's reading achievement and reading group placement (Goldberg 1989, 329–352) and in overall academic achievement (Epstein 1991, 344–349). Parental involvement also increases the achievement levels of students in urban schools (Flaxman and Inger 1991, 2–6; Comer 1988, 42–48, 1986, 442–446; Brandt 1986, 13–17). It is important that you be willing to take the extra time and energy to pursue strategies such as the following for involving parents:

- Ask parents to read aloud to the child, to listen to the child read, and to sign homework papers.
- Encourage parents to drill students on math and spelling and to help with homework lessons.

- Encourage parents to discuss school activities with their children and suggest ways parents can help teach their children at home. For example, a simple home activity might be alphabetizing books; a more complex one would be using kitchen supplies in an elementary science experiment.
- Send home suggestions for games or group activities related to the child's schoolwork that parent and child can play together.
- Encourage parents to participate in school activities such as a sports booster club, career day, and music and drama events.
- Involve parents in their children's learning by having them co-sign learning contracts and serve as guest speakers.

In 1996 the Goals 2000: Educate America Act funded parent resource centers in twenty-eight states (see "Parent Resource Centers" in the Teacher's Resource Guide). To help families get involved in their children's learning, these centers offer training for parents, hotlines, mobile training teams, resource and lending libraries, support groups, and referral networks. That same year, the U.S. Department of Education also launched the national Family Involvement Partnership for Learning, designed to help students act as a link between their teachers and schools and their families and communities. (For information, call 1-800-USA-LEARN.)

Family involvement resources are also available on the Internet through the National Parent Information Network (NPIN), a project sponsored by the ERIC system (http://ericps.ed.uiuc.edu/npin/npinhome.html or (800) 583-4135). NPIN resources include information for parents on child development, testing, working with teachers,

Issues in Education

- What realities of home life tend to reduce the amount and quality of family interaction, reading, and homework preparation?
- What other forces operate against parents' involvement in their children's education at home and in school?
- In what ways and to what extent does parental involvement really affect student achievement?
- How can teachers promote family-based learning and parental involvement in the schools?

"ISN'T IT WONDERFUL THAT WE SPEND SO MUCH TIME TOGETHER AS A FAMILY?... HONEY?...KIDS?..."

and home learning activities. AskERIC Question & Answer Service (http://ericir. syr.edu/Qa/) provides forums for parents and teachers to address mutual concerns, listings of useful and inexpensive learning materials, and descriptions of model parent involvement programs. Other online resources for parental involvement in schools can be obtained from the Consortium for School Networking (http://cosn.org:80/).

COMMUNITY RELATIONS

Communities provide significant support for the education of their young people and determine the character of their schools. In addition, communities often help their schools by recruiting volunteers, providing financial support for special projects, and operating homework hotline programs. For example, school–community partnerships have been formed through "The Employer's Promise," a national effort to involve communities in supporting the family's central role in children's learning:

- John Hancock sponsors educational activities for children during school vacations and holidays.
- Hewlett-Packard staggers start times for employees who volunteer at the corporation's on-site elementary school and accommodates the schedules of employees with school-age children.
- American College Testing's "Realize the Dream" program provides workshops and resources to involve parents in their children's education.

HOW CAN YOU PARTICIPATE IN TEACHER COLLABORATION ？

The relationships that build a learning community involve **collaboration**—working together, sharing decision making, and solving problems. As a member of a dynamic, changing profession, your efforts to collaborate will result in an increased understanding of the teaching–learning process and improved learning for all students. By working with others on school governance, curriculum development, school-community partnerships, and educational reform, you will play an important role in enhancing the professional status of teachers.

The heart of collaboration is meaningful, authentic relationships among professionals. Such relationships, of course, do not occur naturally; they require commitment and hard work. Friend and Bursuck (1996, 76–77) have identified seven characteristics of collaboration which are summarized in the following:

- Collaboration is voluntary; teachers make a personal choice to collaborate.
- Collaboration is based on parity; all individuals' contributions are valued equally.
- Collaboration requires a shared goal.
- Collaboration includes shared responsibility for key decisions.
- Collaboration includes shared accountability for outcomes.
- Collaboration is based on shared resources; each teacher contributes something—time, expertise, space, equipment, or other resource.
- Collaboration is emergent; as teachers work together, the degree of shared decision making, trust, and respect increases.

Schools that support the essential elements of collaboration are *collegial schools* "characterized by purposeful adult interactions about improving schoolwide teaching and learning" (Glickman 1995, 5). In the following, we examine four expressions of teacher collaboration: peer coaching, staff development, team teaching, and co-teaching.

PEER COACHING

Experienced teachers traditionally help novice teachers, but more formal peer coaching programs extend the benefits of collaboration to more teachers. **Peer coaching** is an arrangement whereby teachers grow professionally by observing one another's teaching and providing constructive feedback. The practice encourages teachers to learn together in an emotionally safe environment. According to Bruce Joyce and Marsha Weil (1996, 382), peer coaching is an effective way to create communities of professional educators, and all teachers should be members of coaching teams:

> If we had our way, *all* school faculties would be divided into coaching teams—that is, teams who regularly observe one another's teaching and learn from watching one another and the students. In short, we recommend the development of a "coaching environment" in which all personnel see themselves as one another's coaches.

Through teacher-to-teacher support and collaboration, peer coaching programs improve teacher morale and teaching effectiveness.

STAFF DEVELOPMENT

Increasingly, teachers are contributing to the design of staff development programs that encourage collaboration, risk-taking, and experimentation. Some programs, for example, give teachers the opportunity to meet with other teachers at similar grade levels or in similar content areas for the purpose of sharing ideas, strategies, and solutions to problems. A day or part of a day may be devoted to this kind of workshop or idea exchange. Teachers are frequently given released time from regular duties to visit other schools and observe exemplary programs in action.

One example of a collaborative staff development program is Project MASTER (Mathematics and Science Teachers Education Renewal), developed by the Chicago public schools. Groups of eight teachers (four in mathematics and four in science) from 10 high schools form collegial support groups or professional cadres at their schools. A department chair or lead teacher heads the mathematics and science cadres at each school. Participants read and discuss educational research, attend workshops, and form peer coaching groups. The groups also receive training in conferencing skills, classroom observation and data collection, and analysis of instruction. Participants visit other Project MASTER schools to exchange ideas and to practice coaching and instructional analysis skills. As the following comments by participants indicate, collaboration is a powerful catalyst for professional growth and change:

> The project strengthened my understanding of instructional leadership and my own instructional leadership skills. The focus was on improving instruction, and I became more aware of certain aspects of teaching through observation (Ponticell, Olson, and Charlier 1995, 104).

> We have a chance to share, to get together with each other as a staff; this helped us become a team and help each other (103).

TEAM TEACHING

In **team teaching** arrangements, teachers share the responsibility for two or more classes, dividing up the subject areas between them, with one preparing lessons in mathematics, science, and health, for instance, while the other plans instruction in reading and language arts. The division of responsibility may also be made in terms of the performance levels of the children, so that, for example, one teacher may teach the lowest- and highest-ability reading groups and the middle math group,

What are some forms of professional collaboration in which you will participate as a teacher? In what types of co-teaching arrangements might these teachers cooperate?

while the other teaches the middle-ability reading groups and the lowest and highest mathematics group. In many schools, team teaching arrangements are so extensive that children move from classroom to classroom for forty- to fifty-minute periods just as students do at the high school level.

The practice of team teaching is often limited by student enrollments and budget constraints. As integrated curricula and the need for special knowledge and skills increase, however, the use of faculty teams will become more common. **Faculty teams** can be created according to subject areas, grade levels, or teacher interests and expertise. The members of a team make wide-ranging decisions about the instruction of students assigned to the team, such as when to use large-group instruction or small-group instruction, how teaching tasks will be divided, and how time, materials, and other resources will be allocated.

CO-TEACHING

In **co-teaching** arrangements, two or more teachers, such as a classroom teacher and a special education teacher or other specialist, teach together in the same classroom. Co-teaching builds on the strengths of two teachers and provides increased learning opportunities for all students (Friend and Bursuck 1996). Typically, co-teaching arrangements occur during a set period of time each day or on certain days of the week. Among the several possible co-teaching variations, Friend and Bursuck (1996) have identified the following:

■ *One teach, one support:* one teacher leads the lesson; the other assists.
■ *Station teaching:* the lesson is divided into two parts; one teacher teaches one part to half of the students while the other teaches the other part to the rest. The groups then switch and the teachers repeat their part of the lesson. If stu-

dents can work independently, a third group may be formed, or a volunteer may teach at a third station.

- *Parallel teaching:* a class is divided in half, and each teacher instructs half the class individually.
- *Alternative teaching:* a class is divided into one large group and one small group. For example, one teacher may provide remediation or enrichment to the small group, while the other teacher instructs the large group.

HOW WILL YOUR PERFORMANCE AS A TEACHER BE EVALUATED ?

Most teachers are evaluated on a regular basis to determine if their performance measures up to acceptable standards, if they are able to create and sustain effective learning environments for students. Performance criteria used to evaluate teachers vary and are usually determined by the school principal, district office, the school board, or a state education agency. In most schools, the principal or a member of the leadership team evaluates teachers.

Teacher evaluations serve many purposes: to determine if teachers should be retained, receive tenure, or be given merit pay. Evaluations also help teachers assess their effectiveness and develop strategies for self-improvement. National studies indicate that "teachers want to be observed *more,* they want *more* feedback, and they want to talk *more* with other professionals about improving learning for their students" (Glickman 1995, 303).

QUANTITATIVE AND QUALITATIVE EVALUATION

Typically, supervisors use quantitative or qualitative approaches (or a combination) to evaluate teachers' classroom performance. **Quantitative evaluation** includes pencil-and-paper rating forms the supervisor uses to record classroom events and behaviors objectively in terms of their number or frequency. For example, a supervisor might focus on the teacher's verbal behaviors—questioning, answering, praising, giving directions, and critiquing.

Qualitative evaluation, in contrast, includes written, open-ended narrative descriptions of classroom events in terms of their qualities. These more subjective measures are equally valuable in identifying teachers' weaknesses and strengths. In addition, qualitative evaluation can capture the complexities and subtleties of classroom life that might not be reflected in a quantitative approach to evaluation.

CLINICAL SUPERVISION

Many supervisors follow the four-step **clinical supervision** model in which the supervisor first holds a preconference with the teacher, then observes in the classroom, analyzes and interprets observation data, and finally holds a postconference with the teacher (Goldhammer, Anderson, and Krajewski 1993; Acheson and Gall 1992; Pajak 1993). During the preconference, the teacher and supervisor schedule a classroom observation and determine its purpose and focus and the method of observation to be used. At the postconference, the teacher and supervisor discuss the analysis of observation data and jointly develop a plan for instructional improvement.

Fulfilling the clinical supervision model is difficult and time-consuming, and time-pressed administrators must often modify the approach. For example, Kim Marshall, principal at a Boston elementary school with 39 teachers, makes four random, unannounced five-minute visits to classrooms each day. This schedule allows him to observe every teacher during a two-week period, and each teacher about 19 times during a year. To make the most of his five-minute classroom visits, he follows these guidelines:

- Be a perceptive observer in order to capture something interesting and helpful to say during the feedback session.
- Give teachers a mixture of praise, affirmation, suggestions, and criticism.
- When sharing critical observations with teachers, be tactful and nonthreatening but totally honest.
- Use good judgment about when to deliver criticism and when to hold off (Marshall 1996, 344).

Regardless of the approach a school district will use to evaluate your performance as a beginning teacher, remember that evaluation will assist your professional growth and development. Experienced teachers report that periodic feedback and assistance from knowledgeable, sensitive supervisors is very beneficial; such evaluation results in "improved teacher reflection and higher-order thought, more collegiality, openness, and communication, greater teacher retention, less anxiety and burnout, greater teacher autonomy and efficacy, improved attitudes, improved teaching behaviors, and better student achievement and attitudes" (Glickman 1995, 306).

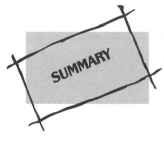

How Will You Become Certified or Licensed to Teach?

- State certification is required for teaching in public schools and in many private schools. Some large cities and local school districts have additional criteria for certification. Certification requirements for teachers vary from state to state and are frequently modified. Some states waive licensing requirements for teachers certified by the National Board for Professional Teaching Standards (NBPTS).
- Most states require testing of teachers for initial certification, and some require recertification after a three- to five-year period.
- States that are members of the Interstate Certification Agreement Contract honor teaching certificates granted by certain other states.
- Private, parochial, for-profit, and charter schools employ about 400,000 non-certified teachers. Many states offer alternative and emergency certification programs.
- The National Teacher Examination (NTE) is required in most states for initial certification. The Praxis Series: Professional Assessments for Beginning Teachers, which will eventually replace the NTE, includes assessments of academic (basic) skills, subject matter knowledge, and classroom performance.

Where Will You Teach?

- Teacher supply and demand in content areas and geographic regions influences finding a teaching position.
- Teaching is a large profession, involving more than 50 million students in public and private K–12 schools and almost 3 million teachers.
- Job vacancies result from retirements, relocation, and career changes. Elementary and secondary enrollments and the demand for new teachers will increase through 2006.
- Education-related career opportunities for teachers include principal, assistant principal, librarian, counselor, and teaching roles in government and the private sector.

How Will You Find Your First Teaching Job?

- Information about teaching vacancies may be obtained through placement services, state departments of education, and personal networking on the Internet.
- A résumé is a concise summary of an individual's experiences, education, and skills. A letter of inquiry is used to find out if a school district has any teaching vacancies, and a letter of application (or cover letter) indicates an individual's interest in and qualifications for a teaching position.

What Can You Expect as a Beginning Teacher?

- Beginning teachers should prepare instructional strategies and materials and learn about their students and the community well in advance of the first day of school.
- Experienced teachers' recommendations for beginning teachers focus on planning, organizing, and following through.

How Can You Become a Part of Your Learning Community?

- The learning community includes students, their families, colleagues, and members of the community.
- Research indicates that parental involvement is a key factor in children's academic achievement.
- Training programs, hotlines, referral networks, and partnership programs are among the resources teachers can use to involve parents and members of the community.

How Can You Participate in Teacher Collaboration?

- Teachers collaborate through participation in school governance, curriculum development, school-community partnerships, and educational reform.
- Four approaches to teacher collaboration are peer coaching, staff development, team teaching, and co-teaching.

How Will Your Performance as a Teacher Be Evaluated?

- Performance criteria for evaluating teachers are developed by school principals, districts, school boards, or states.
- Quantitative approaches to teacher evaluation focus on the incidence, frequency, or amount of teacher or student behavior in various categories.
- Qualitative approaches to teacher evaluation are usually written narratives focusing on the qualities of classrooms and events, such as classroom climate and teaching style.

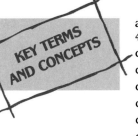

Teacher's Journal

1. What is your view of an ideal teaching position for you? In your description include characteristics of the school, students, and community; resources available for effective teaching; and ideal on-the-job relationships.

2. Record in your journal your plan for becoming certified or licensed to teach.

3. Develop answers to possible interview questions and brainstorm questions to ask.

4. Envision your first day as a teacher and describe what you see.

5. When you become a teacher, in what collaborations and partnerships will you participate? How might these activities contribute to your effectiveness as a teacher? How might your involvement enhance students' learning and your relationships with them?

Teacher's Database

1. Explore and compare teacher proficiencies and teaching standards according to state boards of education, national standards organizations, and teacher and subject area organizations. Begin by locating the following organizations online and information about your school's education program in relation to state and national standards.

National Council for Accreditation of Teacher Education (NCATE)
National Board for Professional Teaching Standards (NBPTS)
National Association of State Directors for Teacher Education and Certification (NASDTEC)
National Association for State Boards of Education (NASBE)

Continue your search by accessing the government or education department of a locality, region, or state where you plan to teach and gathering information about becoming a teacher there.

2. Formulate a research question concerning demographic aspects of teachers and schools in the United States. Then go online to gather current national and state statistics on your question. For example, your question might relate to one or more of the following topics.

teacher recruitment	information about school districts
teacher shortages	public schools compared to private schools
teaching salaries and benefits	independent and private schools
characteristics of the teaching force	characteristics of parochial schools
attitudes of teachers	

Begin your data search in the U.S. Department of Education's National Center for Education Statistics (NCES) via ERIC or the Institutional Communications Network (INET). The INET is an Internet Gopher Server providing the public with access to education research, statistics, and information about the U.S. Department of Education and its programs (Gopher: gopher.ed.gov). The National Data Resource Center (NDRC) is a INET government resource for information about teachers and schools (NDRC@INET.ED.GOV).

Observations and Interviews

1. If you can arrange it, observe the first day of classes at a local school. What strategies did the teachers use to begin the year on a positive, task-oriented note? What evidence did you see that the teachers followed the advice given by the experienced teachers in this chapter? Record your qualitative observations on hand-out master M13.3 (Qualitative Observation Log) and share them with your classmates. What common themes do you detect in the data?

2. Survey teachers at a local school to get information about how they prepare for the first day of school. To help you develop questions for your survey, ask your instructor for the handout master that supports this activity (M13.1, Developing and Conducting a Survey 1).

3. Prepare a questionnaire and then survey a group of experienced teachers for their recollections about the triumphs and defeats they experienced as beginning teachers. What lessons are evident in their responses to your questionnaire? Are there common themes that characterize the triumphs they recall? The defeats? For help in developing the items for your questionnaire, ask your instructor for hand-out master M13.2, Developing and Conducting a Survey 2.

4. Interview teachers and administrators about their experiences with professional collaboration and parental involvement. What examples do they provide, and how do these reflect the seven characteristics of collaboration presented in this chapter? How do students benefit from collaboration and parental involvement? What suggestions do the teachers and administrators have for improving collaboration and parental involvement?

Professional Portfolio

1. Draft a preliminary professional résumé. Review the section in this chapter titled "Preparing Your Résumé" and "Résumé Advice for Educators" in the Teacher's Resource Guide. In addition, examine the résumé prepared by Linda M. Rodriguez (Figure 13.3).

In your résumé, under "Personal Data," provide a current address and a permanent address. Also, under "Education," specify an anticipated graduation date. Under "Experience," include work experience that indicates your ability to work with people. Begin with your most recent experiences and present information in reverse chronological order.

When you have finished your preliminary résumé, critique it against "Résumé Advice for Educators."

2. Draft an essay describing what you will bring to your first year of teaching. It may help to review the essay you wrote for the Chapter 1 portfolio entry on what has drawn you to teaching.

As we enter the new information age, we cannot deny children the rich resources for learning that can so powerfully expand their knowledge, spark their creativity, and intellectually transport them to classrooms in their neighborhoods, around the world, and even to the galaxies beyond.

—Ernest L. Boyer
The Basic School: A Community for Learning

chapter 14

Education Issues
for the 21st Century

**F O C U S
Q U E S T I O N S**

1. What will students need to know and be able to do?

2. How can teachers and schools reach all learners?

3. How can community-based partnerships address social problems that hinder students' learning?

4. How will the privatization movement affect equity and excellence in education?

5. What can teachers and schools learn from international education?

6. How will cyberspace change teaching and learning?

7. What is our vision for the future of education?

What does the 21st century hold for education? How will teaching change? What learning activities will characterize schools of the future? Will the following descriptions of how students learn at an elementary school and at four high schools linked electronically become widespread?

The science curriculum for the 500 students at this K–5 school focuses on restoring a nearby creek that students found devoid of life and polluted. First-graders maintain a tank stocked with salmon fingerlings which will eventually be released into the creek. Students monitor the fish as they progress through the life cycle. Second- and third-grade students study water pollution and other environmental issues that impact fish and other animals. Fourth-grade students regularly check the creek's water quality. Each year, the school holds a "Salmon Celebration" when the fingerlings are released into the creek.

Building on the students' work, the community has developed a project to install a new storm drainage system to improve water quality. The project's board of directors includes members of the PTA and the city government.

Students at four high schools participate in "Connections: The Cross-District Classroom," a network of databases and telecommunication systems tied together by a coordinated curriculum.

Students collaborate on projects in which they study global issues through a five-phase program of community study, simulation, issue analysis, action planning, and plan presentation.

Students work together in teams to investigate and share information on their social, political, and cultural environments. In cross-district teams they identify such focus topics as human rights, world health, education, the environment, and global distribution of wealth.

The teams then research and analyze these issues, explore possible solutions, and work across district lines to develop a comprehensive action plan. They communicate by means of on-line telecommunications, telephones, fax, and mail. The teams take part in a high-tech conference where they meet with experts and leaders in business and industry to perfect their plans. Aided by multimedia technologies, student teams then present and defend their action plans in an interdistrict forum attended by invited experts from business, industry, universities, and social organizations.

Each "Connections" classroom is equipped with student research, production, and communications centers, providing the means for students to develop joint products. Teleconferencing and facsimile are used to connect students and are used by teachers for planning, curriculum development, and coordination. The project has created a model of the teacher's role as curriculum designer, co-learner, and facilitator, while fostering the role of the student as worker, researcher, communicator, peer-teacher, and creative problem-solver (National Foundation for the Improvement of Education, n.d., 14).

Though no one has an educational crystal ball that will give us a totally accurate glimpse of how students will be taught in the twenty-first century, we believe there is a high probability that students will learn in the manner just described. In fact, these descriptions are based on actual schools. Jackson Elementary School in Everett, Washington, has restored nearby Pigeon Creek, and high school students in Wayne County, Michigan, participate in "Connections."

WHAT WILL STUDENTS NEED TO KNOW AND BE ABLE TO DO

What knowledge and skills will students need to succeed in the world of the future? Teachers in every generation have asked that question. As we enter the twenty-first century, the answer is confounded by conflicting theories, expectations, and values. One thing everyone agrees on, however, is that increasing cultural diversity in the United States and other countries and increasing global economic interdependence will call for communication and cooperation skills. People will need to be able to live together well and use environmental resources wisely. To equip students to do this, teachers of the future will need to dedicate themselves to ensuring that all students develop knowledge, skills, attitudes, and values in nine key areas (see Figure 14.1). Though these nine areas of learning will not be all that students will need, learning in these areas will best enable them to meet the challenges of the future.

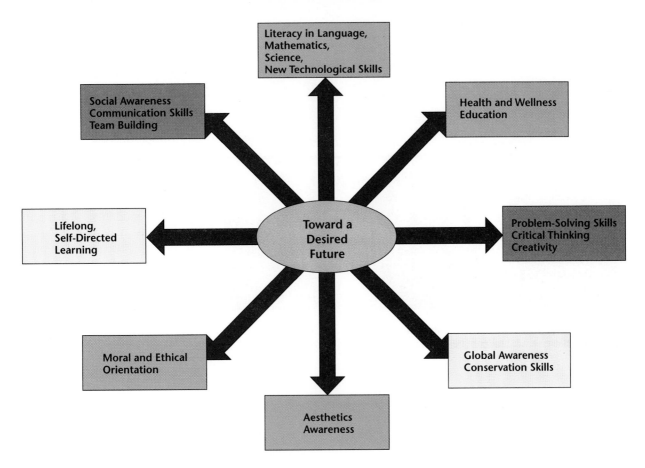

FIGURE 14.1 Educational priorities for the future

LITERACY IN LANGUAGE, MATHEMATICS, AND SCIENCE To solve the problems of the future, students will need to be able to write and speak clearly and succinctly. To access critical information from enormous data banks, they will need to be able to read complex material with a high degree of comprehension. Moreover, the continued development of "user-friendly" technologies such as voice-activated computers and reading machines will not reduce the need for high-level language arts literacy. Students will also need to be able to apply mathematical and scientific concepts to solve new problems. For example, they will need to be able to analyze unfamiliar situations, pose appropriate questions, use trial-and-error methods to gather and evaluate relevant data, and summarize results.

NEW TECHNOLOGICAL SKILLS Students of the future will also need to attain high levels of skill in computer-based technologies. To teach students skills in accessing the vast stores of information that computers routinely handle today, our nation's schools will become more technologically rich and teachers more technologically sophisticated. No longer able to resist the "irresistible force" of Information Age technology (Mehlinger 1996), schools will join the larger society where "the computer is a symbol of the future and all that is good about it" (Morton 1996, 417). In such an environment, students will not only learn to use computers as "tools" to

What knowledge and skills for the twenty-first century does this learning activity support? What else will students need to know and be able to do in the future?

access information—they will use computers to communicate worldwide and to generate creative solutions to real-world problems.

PROBLEM SOLVING, CRITICAL THINKING, AND CREATIVITY

Students of the future will need to be able to think rather than to remember. Although the information that students learn in schools may become outdated or useless, the thinking processes they acquire will not. These processes focus on the ability to find, obtain, and use information resources for solving problems or taking advantage of opportunities. Students will need to learn how to cope with change, how to anticipate alternative future developments, how to think critically, and how to analyze and synthesize large amounts of complex data.

Forecasts about the future share one thing in common—they place a priority on creative thinking to solve future problems. The acquisition of structured bodies of knowledge, while important, is not sufficient preparation for the future. Students must learn to think creatively to solve unforeseen problems. Students who are stretched to develop their creativity today will become the adults who invent ways to solve tomorrow's problems.

Can creative thinking be taught? William J. J. Gordon (1968, 1971a, 1971b, 1975), who has devoted his career to the study of creativity, believes it can. Gordon developed synectics, a teaching method based on the thinking process that is designed to "teach" creativity through the use of metaphor and analogy. **Synectics** is based on the assumptions that (1) creativity is important; (2) creativity is not mysterious; (3) in all fields, creative invention draws from the same underlying intellectual processes; and (4) the creativity of individuals and groups is similar (Joyce and Weil 1996).

SOCIAL AWARENESS, COMMUNICATION SKILLS, AND TEAM BUILDING   Tomorrow's students must be able to communicate with people from diverse cultures. The ability to create a better world in the future, then, will surely depend on our willingness to celebrate our rich diversity through the kind of communication that leads to understanding, friendly social relations, and the building of cohesive teams. "[T]he classroom should be a laboratory for collaborative decision making and team building" (Uchida, Cetron, and McKenzie 1996, 8).

GLOBAL AWARENESS AND CONSERVATION SKILLS   Tomorrow's students will need to recognize the interconnectedness they share with all countries and with all people.

Our survival may depend on being able to participate intelligently in a global economy and respond intelligently to global threats to security, health, environmental quality, and other factors affecting the quality of human life. The curriculum of the future must emphasize cultural diversity, interdependence, respect for the views and values held by others, an orientation toward international cooperation for resolving global issues, and practical knowledge and skills on, for example, the conservation of natural energy resources.

HEALTH AND WELLNESS EDUCATION With ever-increasing health care costs, the spread of diseases such as AIDS, increased risks of cancer, and longer life spans, it is imperative that students of the future acquire appropriate knowledge, skills, and attitudes in the area of health education. To live healthy lives, then, students of tomorrow will need consumer education to select from among an increasingly complex array of health care services. In addition, they will need to be able to make informed choices among alternatives for the prevention or treatment of problems relating to substance abuse, nutrition, fitness, and mental health. Sex education, still a matter for debate in some communities, seems more critical today than at any time in the past.

MORAL AND ETHICAL ORIENTATION The school culture and the curriculum reflect both national and community values. The traditional practice of using values-clarification activities in the classroom, however, has been criticized by some for promoting relativism at the expense of family values or religious doctrines. Yet, as we witness the effects of gang warfare, racial violence, sexual exploitation of children, drunk driving, white-collar crime, false advertising, unethical business practices, excessive litigation, and so on, many Americans are calling for schools to pay more attention to issues of public morality and ethical behavior. "[T]o survive and prosper in the twenty-first century, students will need self-discipline, which entails an ethical code and the ability to set and assess progress toward their own goals" (Uchida, Cetron, and McKenzie 1996, 17).

AESTHETICS AWARENESS Another challenge for teachers and schools is to encourage creativity and greater appreciation for the arts. Many observers of American education point out that emotional, spiritual, aesthetic, and reflective, or meditative, dimensions of life receive less emphasis than analytical thinking and practical life skills. Although literature and drama are standard fare in curricula, most students know little, for example, about music, painting, and sculpture. Public school students are rarely taught art history or principles of design or other criteria for evaluating creative works. As a result, students may lack the concepts and experiences that lead to an appreciation of beauty and the development of aesthetic judgment.

LIFELONG, SELF-DIRECTED LEARNING The key educational priority that should guide teachers of the future is to create within each student the ability, and the desire, to continue self-directed learning throughout his or her life.

It has often been said that one of the primary purposes of schooling is for students to learn how to learn. In a world characterized by rapid social, technological, economic, and political changes, all persons must take responsibility for their own learning. Career changes will be the norm, and continuing education over a lifetime will be necessary.

HOW CAN TEACHERS AND
SCHOOLS REACH ALL LEARNERS ?

While we don't know exactly what teaching will be like in the twenty-first century, we do know that teachers will continue to have a professional and moral obligation to reach all learners, many of whom will be from environments that provide little support for education. Imagine, for example, that one of your students is Dolores, described in the following scenario.

Fifteen-year-old Dolores and her twin brother, Frank, live with their mother in a housing project in a poor section of the city. Their mother divorced her third husband two years ago, after she learned that he had been sexually abusing Dolores. Since then, Dolores' mother has been struggling to make ends meet with her job as a custodian at a hospital. Two evenings a week, she goes to a neighborhood center to learn English. She hopes to become proficient enough in English to get a job as a secretary.

Dolores wishes her mother and Frank didn't fight so much. The fights usually revolve around Frank missing school and his drinking. Just last night, for example, Frank came home drunk and he and his mother got into another big fight. When she accused him of being involved in a street gang, Frank stormed out and went to spend the night at his cousin's apartment two blocks away.

At 6:30 that morning, Dolores awoke just as her mother left for work. The hinges on the apartment door, painted over by a careless maintenance worker, creaked loudly as she closed the door behind her. Dolores felt reassured by the sound of her mother locking the dead bolt—the apartment beneath them had been burglarized last week. Like Frank, she wasn't getting along well with her mother lately, so it would be nice to have the apartment to herself while she got ready for school.

Dolores got up slowly, stretched, and looked around the cluttered livingroom of the one-bedroom apartment. Her mother slept in the bedroom, and Frank, when he wasn't out all night or at his cousin's, slept on the other couch in the living room.

She had trouble sleeping last night. Now that it was winter, the radiator next to the beige couch on which she slept clanked and hissed most of the night. Also, she was worried—two weeks ago a doctor at the neighborhood clinic confirmed that she was pregnant. Yesterday, she finally got up enough courage to tell her boyfriend. He got angry at her and said he "wasn't gonna be no father."

Dolores knew she ought to be seeing a doctor, but she dreaded going to the clinic alone. Her mother took a day off from work—without pay—when she went two weeks ago. Right after that, her mother complained about missing work and said, "Don't expect me to take off from work every time you go to the clinic. You should have thought about that before you got in trouble."

Later that morning, Dolores is in your class, sitting in her usual spot in the middle of the back row. While your students work on an in-class writing assignment, you glance at Dolores and wonder why she hasn't been paying attention during the last few weeks like she usually does. At that moment, Dolores, wearing the same clothes she wore yesterday, stifles a yawn.

As you continue to move about the room, checking on students' progress and answering an occasional question, you wonder if you should talk with Dolores after class. You don't want to pry into her life outside of school, but you're worried about what might be causing her to act differently.

Although the family will continue to remain a prominent part of our culture, evidence indicates that many children, like Dolores and Frank, live in families that are under acute stress. Soaring numbers of runaway children and cases of child abuse suggest that the family is in trouble. In addition, teachers will continue to find that more and more of their students are from families that are smaller, have working mothers, have a single parent present, or have unrelated adults living in the home.

EQUITY FOR ALL STUDENTS

A dominant political force as we enter the twenty-first century will be continued demands for equity in all sectors of American life, particularly education. For example, the constitutionality of school funding laws will be challenged where inequities are perceived, and tax reform measures will be adopted to promote equitable school funding. Classroom teachers will continue to be held accountable for treating all students equitably.

In Chapter 8, you learned about the importance of preparing multicultural instructional materials and strategies to meet the learning needs of students from diverse cultural, ethnic, and linguistic backgrounds. In Chapter 9, you learned how to create an inclusive classroom to meet the needs of all students, regardless of their developmental levels, intelligences, abilities, or disabilities. In addition, you should create a learning environment in which high-achieving and low-achieving students are treated the same. Thomas Good and Jere Brophy (1994) reviewed the research in this area and found that several teacher behaviors indicated unequal treatment of students. The behaviors identified include waiting less time for them to answer questions, interacting with them less frequently, giving less feedback, calling on them less often, seating them farther way, failing to accept and use their ideas, smiling at them less often, making less eye contact, praising them less, demanding less, grading their tests differently, and rewarding inappropriate behaviors.

Effective teachers establish respectful relationships with *all* students; they listen to them; they give frequent feedback and opportunities to ask questions; and they demand higher-level performance. In their assessment of student's learning, they give special attention to the questions they ask of students. Research indicates that most questions teachers ask are **lower-order questions,** those that assess students' abilities to recall specific information. Effective teachers, however, also ask **higher-order questions** that demand more critical thinking and answers to questions such as, Why? What if . . . ? In addition, to reach all learners and prepare them for the future, effective teachers provide students with active, authentic learning experiences.

ACTIVE, AUTHENTIC LEARNING

Since the 1970s, educational researchers have increased our understanding of the learning process. Though learning theorists and researchers disagree about a definition for *learning,* most agree that **learning** "occurs when experience causes a relatively permanent change in an individual's knowledge or behavior" (Woolfolk 1995, 196). Research into multiple intelligences and multicultural learning modes has broadened our understanding of this definition of learning. In addition, research in the fields of neurophysiology, neuropsychology, and cognitive science will continue to expand our understanding of how people think and learn.

Our growing understanding of learning indicates that all students learn best when they are actively involved in authentic activities that connect with the "real world." Small-group activities, cooperative learning arrangements, field trips, experiments, and integrated curricula are among the instructional methods you should incorporate into your professional repertoire.

HOW CAN COMMUNITY-BASED PARTNERSHIPS ADDRESS SOCIAL PROBLEMS THAT HINDER STUDENTS' LEARNING ?

Earlier in this book, we examined social problems that affect schools and place students at risk of dropping out: poverty, family stress, substance abuse, violence and crime, teen pregnancy, HIV/AIDS, and suicide (see Chapter 4). We also looked at intervention programs schools have developed to ensure the optimum behavioral, social, and academic adjustment of at-risk children and adolescents to their school experiences: peer counseling, full-service schools, school-based interprofessional case management, compensatory education, and alternative schools and curricula. Here, we describe innovative, community-based partnerships that some schools have developed recently to *prevent* social problems from hindering students' learning.

The range of school-community partnerships found in today's schools is extensive; Figure 14.2, for example, illustrates the partnerships Turner Middle School in West Philadelphia has developed with the surrounding community. With support from a grant the University of Pennsylvania (Penn) obtained from United Parcel Ser-

FIGURE 14.2 The West Philadelphia Improvement Corps (WEPIC) Program at Turner Middle School (Source: Karen Prager, "Community Partnerships Bring Community Revitalization," *Issues in Restructuring Schools, 5* (Madison: University of Wisconsin–Madison, Center on Organization and Restructuring of Schools, Fall 1993), p. 14. Used with permission of the publisher.)

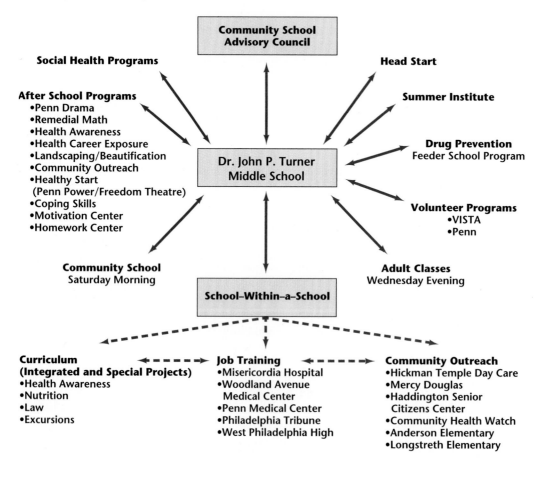

vice Foundation, the school has developed eighteen separate partnerships with various community organizations and agencies.

THE COMMUNITY AS A RESOURCE FOR SCHOOLS

To assist schools in addressing the social problems that impact students, many communities are acting in the spirit of a recommendation made by Ernest Boyer: "Perhaps the time has come to organize, in every community, not just a *school* board, but a *children's* board. The goal would be to integrate children's services and build, in every community, a friendly, supportive environment for children" (Boyer 1995, 169). In partnerships between communities and schools, individuals, civic organizations, or businesses select a school or are selected by a school to work together for the good of students. The ultimate goals of such projects are to provide students with better school experiences and to assist students at risk.

CIVIC ORGANIZATIONS   To develop additional sources of funding, many local school districts have established partnerships with community groups interested in improving educational opportunities in the schools. Some groups raise money for schools. The American Jewish Committee and the Urban League raised funds for schools in Pittsburgh, for example. Other partners adopt or sponsor schools and enrich their educational programs by providing funding, resources, or services.

VOLUNTEER MENTOR PROGRAMS   Mentorship is a trend in community-based partnerships today, especially with students at risk. Parents, business leaders, professionals, and peers volunteer to work with students in neighborhood schools. Goals might include dropout prevention, high achievement, improved self-esteem, and healthy decision making. Troubleshooting on life-style issues often plays a role, especially in communities plagued by drug dealing, gang rivalry, casual violence, and crime. Mentors also model success.

Some mentor programs target particular groups. A volunteer service group in Washington, DC, known as the Concerned Black Men, for example, targets inner-city African-American boys. About three dozen African-American men—lawyers, businessmen, government workers, and students from Howard University—participate as mentors in an area elementary school. Their goal is to serve as positive adult male role models for boys who are living only with their mothers or grandmothers and who lack male teachers in school.

CORPORATE-EDUCATION PARTNERSHIPS   Business involvement in schools has taken many forms, including, for example, contributions of funds or materials needed by a school, release time for employees to visit classrooms, adopt-a-school programs, cash grants for pilot projects and teacher development, educational use of corporate facilities and expertise, employee participation, student scholarship programs, and political lobbying for school reform. Extending beyond advocacy, private sector efforts include job initiatives for disadvantaged youths, inservice programs for teachers, management training for school administrators, minority education and faculty development, and even construction of school buildings.

Business-sponsored school-building experiments focus on creating model schools or laboratory schools or on addressing particular local needs. Minneapolis, for example, boasts two new schools dedicated to improving student performance through nongrouped classes, small class sizes, and high expectations of students. With the support of Minneapolis's superintendent, school board, and local teachers' union, corporate innovators have implemented programs in which teachers are chosen on the basis of talent and telephones are installed in the classrooms for greater communication between teachers and parents.

In addition to contributing more resources to education, chief executive officers and their employees are donating more time; 83 percent of the top managers surveyed by a recent *Fortune* poll said they "participate actively" in educational reform, versus 70 percent in 1990. At Eastman Kodak's Rochester, New York, plant, for example, hundreds of employees serve as tutors or mentors in local schools. In some dropout prevention programs, businessmen and businesswomen adopt individual students, visiting them at school, eating lunch with them once a week, meeting their families, and taking them on personal field trips.

SCHOOLS AS RESOURCES FOR COMMUNITIES

A shift from the more traditional perspective of schools needing support from the community to meet the needs of students whose lives are impacted by social problems is the view that schools should serve as multipurpose resources *for* the community. By focusing not only on the development of children and youth, but on their families as well, schools ultimately enhance the ability of students to learn. As Ernest Boyer (1995, 168) put it, "No arbitrary line can be drawn between the school and life outside. Every [school] should take the lead in organizing a *referral service*—a community safety net for children that links students and their families to support agencies in the region—to clinics, family support and counseling centers, and religious institutions."

BEYOND THE SCHOOL DAY   Many schools and school districts are serving their communities by providing educational and recreational programs before and after the traditional school day and during the summers. A recent report by the National Education Commission on Time and Learning (1994, 7) pointed out that "Time is learning's warden. Our time-bound mentality has fooled us all into believing that schools can educate all of the people all of the time in a school year of 180 six-hour days." Proposals for year-round schools and educationally oriented weekend and after-school programs address the educational and developmental needs of students impacted by social problems. According to the San Diego-based National Association for Year-Round Education, more than 2,000 public schools now extend their calendars into the summer, and more than one million elementary students go to school year-round. Futurist Marvin Cetron predicts that, soon, "schools will educate and train both children and adults around the clock: the academic day will stretch to seven hours for children; adults will work a 32-hour week and prepare for their next job in the remaining time" (Uchida, Cetron, and McKenzie 1996, 35).

Programs that extend beyond the traditional school day also address the needs of parents and the requirements of the work world. Nearly two million elementary-age, "latchkey" children come home to an empty home every afternoon, according to Census Bureau figures. As an elementary teacher in Missouri said, "Many of my students just hang around at the end of every day. They ask what they can do to help me. Often there's no one at home, and they're afraid to go home or spend time on the streets" (Boyer 1995, 165).

Proposals for providing services to children beyond the traditional school day include the **Educare system,** which would provide day-long, year-round public schooling for children six months through twelve years of age. The late Ernest Boyer argued that schools should adapt their schedules to those of the workplace so that parents could become more involved in their children's education, and that businesses, too, should give parents more flexible work schedules. Drawing on the model of Japan, Boyer suggested that the beginning of the school year could be a holiday to free parents to attend opening day ceremonies and celebrate the launching and continuation of education in the same way that we celebrate its ending.

For several years, the After-School Plus (A+) Program in Hawaii has operated afternoon enrichment programs from 2:00 to 5:00 for children in kindergarten through sixth grade. The children, who are free to do art, sports, drama, or homework, develop a sense of *ohana,* or feeling of belonging (Cohen 1990, 1). Since the mid-1970s, schools in Buena Vista, Virginia, have operated according to a Four Seasons Calendar that includes an optional summer enrichment program. Buena Vista's superintendent estimates that the district saves more than $100,000 a year on retention costs; though some students take more time, they are promoted to the next grade (Boyer 1995). Similarly, research indicates that extended school days and school calendars have a positive influence on achievement (Gandara and Fish 1994; Center for Research on Effective Schooling for Disadvantaged Students 1992).

HEALTH AND SOCIAL SERVICES In response to the increasing number of at-risk students, many schools are also providing an array of health and social services to their communities. In a gripping *New York Times* editorial, Bob Herbert (1993, A24) presents the acute need for support services for inner-city youth.

> The teen-ager called to ask if he could be excused from classes. Something bad had happened. He had attended a christening and a shootout had erupted. "I have to go with my mother to visit my brother in jail," the boy told school officials. "He's up for attempted murder. Then I'm going with her to bring my other brother's body home. He was killed in the shootout and I still have to go to the doctor because I got shot in the pelvis." Officials of the Bushwick Outreach Center, an alternative high school in Brooklyn, were understanding. They said yes, the boy could be excused.

> Another time a student asked if he could "delay" coming to school for a week. "We found my brother dead in the hallway this morning," he said. Yes, school officials replied. Of course. A week's absence would be O.K.

> Once there was a time when kids stayed home because of the flu, or a cold, or a stomachache. Serious illness was unusual and the death of a student was rare. This is no longer the case in inner-city schools. Like a poisonous wind, misfortune and tragedy are sweeping relentlessly across the children of the big cities.

In Chapter 4, we looked at how full-service schools provide educational, medical, social and/or human services, and how the school-based interprofessional case management model uses case managers to deliver services to at-risk students and their families. While many believe that schools should not provide such services, scenarios like Herbert's suggest that the trend is likely to continue, with more schools following the lead of schools in Charlotte-Mecklenburg, North Carolina; Seattle; and Palm Beach County, Florida. Charlotte-Mecklenburg schools organized a Children's Services Network, "which brings together all of the community agencies concerned with children, coordinates the services, increases support, and prepares a report card on progress" (Boyer 1995, 169). In Seattle, a recent referendum required that a percentage of taxes be set aside to provide services to elementary-age children. And Palm Beach County officials created the Children's Services Council to address sixteen areas, from reducing the dropout rate to better child care. From parent support groups, to infant nurseries, to programs for students with special needs, the council has initiated scores of projects to benefit the community and its children.

HOW WILL THE PRIVATIZATION MOVEMENT AFFECT EQUITY AND EXCELLENCE IN EDUCATION ?

One of the most dramatic reforms in American education during the last decade has been the development of charter schools and for-profit schools, both of which were developed to provide an alternative to the perceived inadequacies of the public schools. On many different levels—governance, staffing, curricula, funding, and accountability—the **privatization movement** is a radical departure from schools as most people have known them.

CHARTER SCHOOLS

In 1991, Minnesota passed the nation's first charter school legislation calling for up to eight teacher-created and -operated, outcome-based schools that would be free of most state and local rules and regulations. When the St. Paul City Academy opened its doors in September 1992, it became the nation's first charter school.

Charter schools are independent, innovative, outcome-based, public schools. "The charter school concept allows a group of teachers, parents, or others who share similar interests and views about education to organize and operate a school. Char-

Issues in Education

- What roles of public education and private education might need to be rethought?
- Why is now a time to rethink those roles?
- In this cartoon what does the implied contrast between "Chapter One" and "Channel One" mean?
- How might that contrast constitute a dilemma for tomorrow's teachers and schools?
- If you as a teacher were faced with such a dilemma, how might you respond? What are your reasons for your answer?

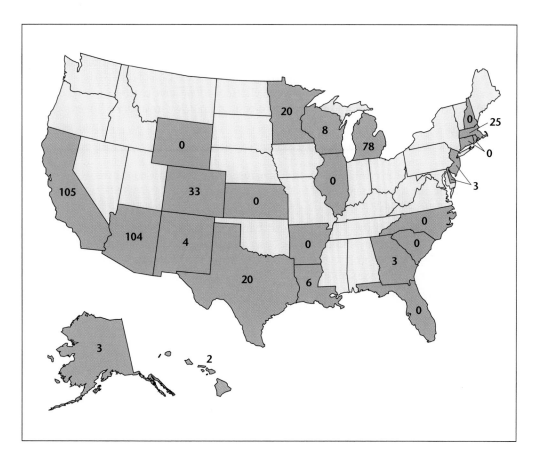

FIGURE 14.3 Total number of charters approved (Source: *Moscow-Pullman Daily News,* October 12–13, 1996, p. 3A.)

ters can be granted by a local school district, by the state, or by the national government. In effect, charter schools offer a model for restructuring that gives greater autonomy to individual schools and promotes school choice by increasing the range of options available to parents and students within the public schools system" (Wohlstetter and Anderson 1994, 486). As of late 1996, twenty-five states, in addition to Minnesota, had adopted charter school legislation (see Figure 14.3), and President Clinton called on every state to enact charter school provisions by 1997. Currently, more than 600 charter schools are operational, with California and Arizona accounting for more than 200. Charter schools in Arizona range from those focusing on the fine arts to charter schools in remote regions of the state that serve American Indian communities.

To open a charter school, an original charter (or agreement) is signed by the school's founders and a sponsor (usually the local school board). The charter specifies the learning outcomes that students will master before they continue their studies. Charter schools, which usually operate in the manner of autonomous school districts (a feature that distinguishes them from the alternative schools that many school districts operate), are public schools and must teach all students. If admission requests for a charter school exceed the number of available openings, students are selected by drawing.

Because charter schools are designed to promote the development of new teaching strategies that can be used at other public schools, they can prove to be an effective tool for promoting educational reform and the professionalization of teaching as we enter the twenty-first century. Moreover, as Milo Cutter, one of the two teachers who founded St. Paul City Academy points out, charter schools give teachers unprecedented leadership opportunities and the ability to respond quickly to students' needs:

> [We had] the chance to create a school that takes into account the approaches we know will work. We listen to what the students want and need, because we ask them. And each day we ask ourselves if we are doing things the best way we can. We also have the flexibility to respond. We can change the curriculum to meet these needs as soon as we see them. Anywhere else it would take a year to change. It is much better than anything we have known in the traditional setting (North Central Regional Education Laboratory 1993, 3).

Murnane and Levy (1996) suggest that charter schools are "too new to have a track record," and they should not be seen as a "magic bullet" that will dramatically, and with little effort, improve students' achievement. In addition, they suggest four questions that observers should pose to determine if individual charter schools promote both equity and excellence.

- Does the charter school commit itself to a goal, such as mastery of critical skills for all its students, or will it emphasize other goals?
- Does the charter school commit itself to serve a fair share of the most difficult-to-educate children, and does it have a strategy for attracting such children—or will it discourage applications from such children?
- Does the charter school's contract with the school district provide enough time and enough financial support for the school to persevere and learn from the mistakes that are inevitable in any ambitious new venture?
- Does the charter school commit itself to providing information about student achievement that will allow parents to make sound judgments about the quality of the education their children are receiving (Murnane and Levy 1996, 113)?

FOR-PROFIT SCHOOLS

Concerned about the slow pace of educational reform in the United States, Christopher Whittle launched the $3 billion Edison Project in 1992—an ambitious plan to develop a national network of private secondary schools. Whittle Communications Inc., based in Knoxville, Tennessee, plans to build more than 1,000 **for-profit schools** by 2010 at a cost comparable to public schools. Eventually, about two million children, each paying $6,000 (the average cost to taxpayers of educating a public school student in 1996) would attend Whittle schools, and the corporation would make a yearly profit of 12 to 15 percent.

Significant start-up funding for Channel One is becoming another controversial project that Whittle began in 1990. Watched daily by about seven million teenagers in more than 10,000 public and private schools in nearly every state, Channel One is a ten-minute news broadcast, with two minutes of commercials. Schools receive the program free, including the loan of thousands of dollars of electronic equipment. Professional associations such as the National Education Association and educational leaders have maintained that advertisements have no place in the classroom. California's education department challenged Channel One in court during 1992, saying that it violated the state's constitutional requirement that schools engage only in educational activities. The court refused to temporarily ban a public school from showing the program, but ordered a full trial on whether the program could continue to include advertisements.

In late 1996, testing results for students at the first four schools run by the Edison Project were released by Educational Testing Service. At two of the schools, kindergarten and first-grade students showed substantial reading gains compared to students at comparison schools (Walsh 1996, 3). Lack of appropriate comparison-group schools made it difficult to interpret scores at the other two schools.

Another approach to for-profit schools has been developed by Education Alternatives Inc. (EAI), a Minneapolis-based company that negotiates with school districts to operate their public schools. Participating school districts give the company the same per-pupil funding to operate the school that the district would have used. The company, using its own curricula and cost-saving techniques, agrees to improve student performance and attendance in return for the opportunity to operate schools at a profit. Education Alternatives Inc., which began operating its first for-profit school in Dade County, Florida, in 1991, became the first private company to run an entire school district when the Duluth, Minnesota, School Board awarded the company a three-month contract in 1992 to serve as interim superintendent for the district. In Baltimore, where EAI operated twelve public schools in 1995, critics challenged the achievement gains the company claimed. The school board later terminated its contract with EAI, citing budget constraints.

WHAT CAN TEACHERS AND SCHOOLS LEARN FROM INTERNATIONAL EDUCATION ?

The world has truly become smaller and more interconnected as telecommunications, cyberspace, and travel by jet bring diverse people and countries together. As we continue to move closer together, it is clear that education is crucial to the wellbeing of every country and to the world as a whole. The challenges and opportunities awaiting teachers in the twenty-first century are remarkably similar worldwide, and there is much we can learn from one another. For example, an observation in a *Bangkok Post* editorial on the need to prepare Thai youth for a changing world echoes calls for educational reform in the United States: "The country's policy planners [s]hould seriously review and revamp the national education system to effectively prepare our youths [for] the next century" (Sricharatchanya 1996, 15). Similarly, a community leader's comments about educating young substance abusers in Bangkok's Ban Don Muslim community could apply to youth in scores of American communities: "We are in an age of cultural instability. Children are exposed to both good and bad things. [I]t's hard to resist the influences and attitudes from the outside world that are pulling at the children's feelings" (Rithdee 1996, 11). Lastly, the curriculum goals at Shiose Junior High School in Nishinomiya, Japan, are based on Japan's fifteenth Council for Education and would "fit" American junior high schools as well; according to principal Akio Inoue (1996, 1), "Students will acquire the ability to survive in a changing society, that is, students will study, think and make judgments on their own initiative. It is also important that we provide a proper balance of knowledge, morality, and physical health, and that we nurture humanity and physical strength for that purpose." As a result of the universal challenges that confront educators, we are entering an era of increasing cross-national exchanges that focus on sharing resources, ideas, and expertise for the improvement of education worldwide.

COMPARATIVE EDUCATION

As the nations of the world continue to become more interdependent, policies for educational reform in the United States will be influenced increasingly by **comparative**

Keepers of the Dream

Kristi Rennebohm Franz

Multicultural Educator

"Reweaving the Global Tapestry . . ."

First graders in Kristi Rennebohm Franz's class in Sunnyside Elementary School, Pullman, Washington, think that using the Internet to exchange drawings with children around the world and taking daily Spanish lessons from a teacher in Argentina are just part of going to school. The students also took in stride talking to their teacher while she attended an international conference in Budapest and participating in an hour-long live video-conferencing session with twelve teachers from other countries. "Their communication skills are innate at that young age," Franz explains. "It's so natural for them to want to communicate with people, and technology becomes a natural way to do it."

What moved Franz most, as she watched from Budapest, was seeing her young students in Pullman form a huddle to figure out how to talk with one of the conference teachers who spoke only Spanish. After sharing their bits of knowledge, they said several sentences in Spanish to her. Franz was also pleased to have students discover that people in other countries were interested in learning about them, noting that "multicultural education tends to focus only on learning about *other* people and places."

As an educator and lifelong learner, Franz has developed a rich array of skills and talents, which serve her well as she designs motivating future-oriented curricula that tap students' varied learning modalities. In college she studied speech therapy and upon graduation became a speech therapist in the public schools in Champaign, Illinois. She later earned a degree in music therapy so she could "use speech and music therapy together to help students with special needs." When she moved to Washington State with her husband, a university professor, she taught cello lessons and chamber music and

education, the study of educational practices in other countries. Comparative education studies show how school systems in other countries work and how American students compare with students in other countries on certain measures of schooling and achievement. For instance, in Hungary 61 percent of thirteen-year-old students spend two hours or more on all homework every day, 16 percent watch television five hours or more every day, 71 percent use calculators in school, and 31 percent use computers for school work. In the United States, comparable statistics are, respectively, 31 percent (two or more hours of homework daily), 22 percent (five or more hours of television daily), 54 percent (calculators in school), and 37 percent (computers for schoolwork) (Educational Testing Service 1993, 108–109). In addition, research in comparative education enables professionals to share information about successful innovations internationally. Teachers can collaborate on global education projects and test change models that other countries have used to help match educational and societal needs and goals.

INTERNATIONAL COMPARISONS OF ACHIEVEMENT The first **International Assessment of Educational Progress (IAEP)** in 1991 revealed that the achievement levels of U.S. students are often below that of students from other countries. Figure 14.4 on page 460 is based on that first IAEP and compares the percentages of geography, math-

played in the Washington Symphony. Traveling with her husband for a sabbatical in Nairobi, Kenya, she taught kindergarten at an international school.

Her rich storehouse of experiences contributes to Franz's forward-looking perspective. The title of the project that Franz shared at the international conference in Budapest was "Reweaving the Global Tapestry of Education for Today's Students: Multicultural Education." Franz and her internet colleague, Jane McLane Kimball, collaborated with teachers in twelve schools around the world, "on every continent except Antartica," to exchange their young students' drawings of their families along with brief texts written by the children in their native languages explaining what they had drawn. Franz observes that including the brief texts, locally translated, helped the students "comprehend the multilingual aspect of our planet." The children then e-mailed their reactions to each others' drawings and discussed how families are different and alike in different countries. A full description of the project can be located on the internet at http://www.igc.apc.org/iearn/ which is the home page for I*EARN, the International Education and Resource Network.

To teachers who want to begin using educational technology in their classrooms, Franz advises: "Choose what you feel are important curricular concepts and start by looking for ways software and telecommunications can enhance your teaching and learning with the children." She suggests that teachers find two or three recommended Web sites to explore in depth, well enough to integrate them with their curriculum. "Partnering up with another school to develop a social context for learning" is the next step. Franz's first graders exchange e-mail daily with another class across their state, sometimes sending a letter with each line contributed by a different child.

Franz began using computers and telecommunication technology with her students when she realized that it was "a way to enhance their learning about the world." She learned along with the children, discovering a unique form of student–teacher collaborative learning—a process that "is making major changes in how we do our teaching and learning." Franz believes strongly in global awareness, multiculturalism, educational technology and telecommunications, environmental education, and teaching to all learning modalities. As a Visiting Scholar at Harvard University's Graduate School of Education, Franz will assist in the development of a summer institute on technology for teachers to help prepare students for the global future.

ematics, and science questions answered correctly by thirteen-year-old students in nine countries. Subsequent IAEP comparisons have shown some improvement in the rankings of American students in mathematics and science. Gains in literacy, however, have been more significant; for example, *A First Look—Findings from the National Assessment of Educational Progress* reported that U.S. fourth-graders ranked second in 1995 on a thirty-two-nation survey of reading skills.

Since the publication of *A Nation at Risk* in 1983, there has been an unbroken trend for the media and some observers of American education to decry the perceived poor performance of U.S. students on international comparisons of achievement. A statement from *Transforming America's Schools* typifies these observations: "The poor performance of American schools is now so well known that it makes the front page of the daily newspaper and is a source of public humiliation" (Murphy and Schiller 1992, 1).

A closer examination of international comparisons, however, reveals the seldom-reported fact that America's position in country-by-country rankings is based on *aggregate* achievement scores—in other words, achievement scores of all students are used to make the comparisons. Not taken into account is America's commitment to educating *all* students (not just the academically able or those from home environments that encourage education), the widely varying quality of U.S.

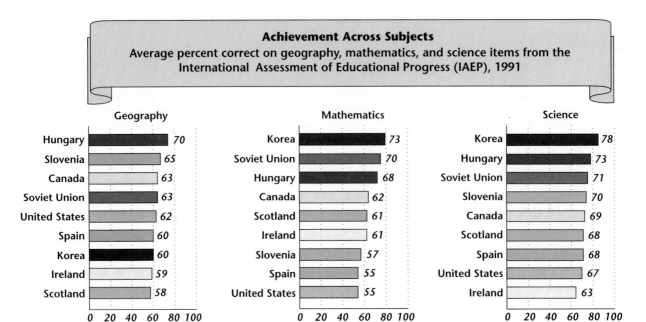

FIGURE 14.4 Achievement across subjects (Source: Educational Testing Service, 1992. From *The National Education Goals Report, 1992*. Washington, D.C.: U.S. Government Printing Office, 1992, p. 7.)

schools, and differences in students' *opportunity to learn* the content covered in achievement tests. That is, when only the top students of each country are compared, the rankings of U.S. students improve dramatically. As David Berliner and Bruce Biddle point out in *The Manufactured Crisis: Myths, Fraud, and the Attack on America's Public Schools* (1995, 52), "If one actually looks at and thinks about the comparative evidence, [o]ne discovers that it does *not* confirm the myth of American educational failure. Indeed, it suggests that in many ways American education stands head and shoulders above education in other countries."

To illustrate their point, Berliner and Biddle summarize Ian Westbury's (1992) analysis of data from the International Association for the Evaluation of Educational Achievements' (IEA) Second International Mathematics Study, which purported to show U.S. eighth-graders significantly behind their Japanese peers in mathematics achievement. Westbury noted that Japanese eighth-grade students were *required* to take courses that covered algebra, while American students typically take such courses a year or two later. When Westbury compared the achievement of U.S. and Japanese students who had taken prealgebra and algebra, the achievement of U.S. students matched or exceeded that of Japanese students (see Figure 14.5).

Berliner and Biddle (1995, 63) go on to offer these cautions about interpreting cross-national studies of educational achievement.

- Few of those studies have yet focused on the unique values and strengths of American education.
- Many of the studies' results have obviously been affected by sampling biases and inconsistent methods for gathering data.
- Many, perhaps most, of the studies' results were generated by differences in curricula—in opportunities to learn—in the countries studied.

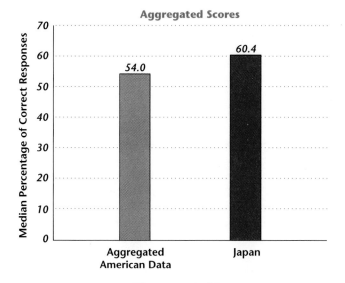

Aggregated Scores

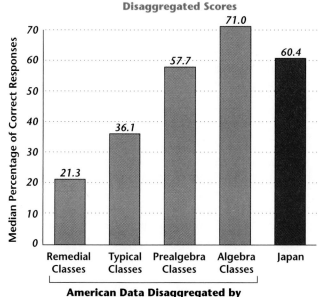

Disaggregated Scores

American Data Disaggregated by Type of Mathematics Courses Taken

FIGURE 14.5 Japanese and American achievement scores for students age 13—from The Second International Mathematics Study of the IEA (Source: Ian Westbury. (1992). "Comparing American and Japanese Achievement: Is the United States Really a Low-Achiever?" *Educational Researcher, 21*(5), 18–24. Taken from David C. Berliner and Bruce J. Biddle, *The Manufactured Crisis: Myths, Fraud, and the Attack on America's Public Schools.* Reading, MA: Addison-Wesley Publishing Company, 1995, p. 57.)

- Aggregate results for American schools are misleading because of the huge range of school quality in this country—ranging from marvelous to terrible.
- The press has managed to ignore most comparative studies in which the United States has done well.

A NATIONAL CURRICULUM? Decisions about the operation of schools in America are made largely at the district or individual school level. However, in some countries (Japan, Korea, and England, for example) education is centralized and teachers follow a standardized national curriculum. Since the first International Assessment of Educational Progress (IAEP) in 1991 revealed that the achievement levels of U.S. students are often below that of students from other countries (many of which have national curricula), some have proposed a **national curriculum** for the United States. Proposals for a national curriculum are also supported by the public. On the last Gallup Poll of the Public's Attitudes Toward the Public Schools that asked for opinions about a national curriculum and national examinations, 46 percent believed they were "very important" and 27 percent "quite important" (Elam, Rose, and Gallup 1995, 48).

Although there is widespread support for national examinations and a national curriculum, there is also widespread opposition to such a system. For example, educational researchers Thomas Kellagan and George Madaus have identified several disadvantages to a system of national examinations (1991, 91):

- The examinations narrow the curriculum in the sense that approaches to learning are limited and subjects and aspects of subjects not covered in the examinations are excluded or neglected.
- The cost of examining oral and practical skills is quite high, forcing most systems to rely on written tests.
- It is impossible to assess in a terminal examination such factors as student planning, perseverance, and adaptability in the execution of a project.

- External [i.e., national] examinations promote the tendency to emphasize lower-order skills in teaching, because these are more easily examined than higher-order ones.
- Examinations are unsuitable for assessing some students (particularly lower achieving ones).
- Examinations engender a diminished professional role for teachers, because important curriculum descisions are in effect decided by the examination.

LESSONS FROM OTHER COUNTRIES

American educators can learn a great deal from their colleagues around the world regarding what works and what doesn't work in other countries. When considering the possibility of adopting practices from other countries, however, it is important to remember that educational practices reflect the surrounding culture. When one country tries to adopt a method used elsewhere, a lack of support from the larger society may doom the new practice to failure. In addition, it is important to realize that the successes of another country's educational system may require sacrifices that are unacceptable to our way of life. Nevertheless, there are many practices in other countries that American educators and policy makers should consider.

SUPPORT FOR TEACHERS AND TEACHING   In many other countries, teachers and teaching receive a level of societal support that surpasses that found in the United States. For example, teachers in many countries, while perhaps not paid more, are accorded greater respect than their American counterparts. In addition, most U.S. teachers have about one hour or less per day for planning; "[T]his leaves them with almost no regular time to consult together or learn about new teaching strategies, unlike their peers in many European and Asian countries where teachers spend between fifteen and twenty hours per week working jointly on refining lessons, coaching one another, and learning about new methods" (National Commission on Teaching and America's Future 1996, 14). Similarly, *A Splintered Vision: An Investigation of U.S. Science and Mathematics Education,* a study by the U.S. Department of Education and the International Institute on Education (1996), reported that American high school teachers teach about thirty classes a week, compared with twenty by teachers in Germany and fewer than twenty by Japanese teachers. Lastly, Ernest Boyer and a Carnegie Foundation for the Advancement of Teaching research team found that, among teachers in twelve countries, U.S. teachers were third highest (behind teachers in Russia and Zimbabwe) in the percentage who reported they "seldom/never" met with one other teacher to "plan and prepare together" (Boyer 1995, 38).

The National Commission on Teaching and America's Future (1996) also found that other countries invest their resources in hiring more teachers, who comprise about 60 to 80 percent of total staff compared to only 43 percent in the United States (see Figure 14.6). In the United States, the Commission (1996, 15) noted that in U.S. schools "too many people and resources are allocated to activities outside of classrooms, sitting on the sidelines rather than the front lines of teaching and learning." Many other countries also invest more resources in staff development than U.S. schools, a fact reflected in the finding by Boyer and his colleagues that the United States leads other nations surveyed in the percentage of teachers who describe their ongoing training as "disappointing" (see Table 14.1).

PARENTAL INVOLVEMENT   The powerful influence of parental involvement on students' achievement is well documented (Booth and Dunn 1996; Buzzell 1996; Epstein 1992; ERIC Clearinghouse 1993). Japan probably leads the world when it comes

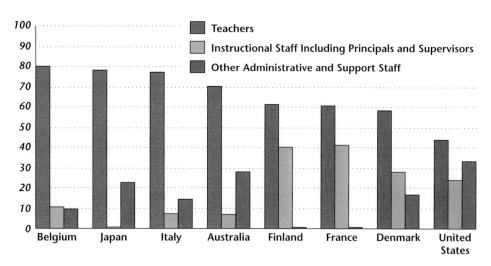

FIGURE 14.6 Comparisons of educational staff by function (Source: Organization for Economic Cooperation and Development (OECD), *Education at a Glance: OECD Indicators* (Paris, OECD 1995), table, p. 31, pp. 176–177. Taken from National Commission on Teaching and America's Future, *What Matters Most: Teaching for America's Future.* New York: National Commission on Teaching and America's Future, p. 15.)

TABLE 14.1

Most of the time I have spent in ongoing training has been disappointing

	Percentage of Teachers Responding "Yes"
United States	40%
Italy	35
Great Britain	32
Russia	29
Japan	24
Germany	24
Israel	23
Chile	19
China	19
Turkey	14
Mexico	12
Zimbabwe	12

(Source: the Carnegie Foundation for the Advancement of Teaching and the George H. Gallup International Institute, The International Schooling Project, 1994. Taken from Ernest L. Boyer, *The Basic School: A Community for Learning.* Princeton, NJ: The Carnegie Foundation for the Advancement of Teaching, p. 45.)

to parental involvement in education. Japanese mothers frequently go to great lengths to ensure that their children get the most out of the school's curriculum. The *kyoiku mama* (literally, education mother) will tutor her child, wait for hours in lines to register her child for periodic national exams, prepare healthy snacks for the child to eat while studying, forego television so her child can study in quiet, and ensure that her child arrives on time for calligraphy, piano, swimming, or martial arts lessons. Though few American parents might wish to assume the role of the *kyoiku parent,* it seems clear that American students would benefit from greater parental involvement. For example, Boyer and his colleagues report that the United States leads other nations surveyed in the percentage of parents who believe "families are not taking enough responsibility for the welfare of their children" (see Table 14.2 on page 464).

PRESSURE TO EXCEL   There have been many calls to make American schooling more rigorous—a longer school calendar, longer school days, more homework, and harder examinations, for example, have all been proposed. These changes, it is assumed, would increase student achievement and find favor with the majority of the public that wants greater academic rigor in the schools. More often than not, Japan, Korea, and other Asian countries are held up as models for the direction American education should take.

But should America's schools be patterned after schools in these countries? Several of those who have studied and experienced Asian schools are beginning to think not. For example, Paul George (1995), who studied the Japanese public school his son attended for two years, reports in *The*

TABLE 14.2

Families are not taking enough responsibility for the welfare of their children

	Percentage of Parents Agreeing
United States	89%
Great Britain	71
Chile	65
Mexico	54
Germany	54
China	53
Zimbabwe	51
Russia	47
Japan	46
Italy	41
Turkey	38
Israel	29

(Source: the Carnegie Foundation for the Advancement of Teaching and the George H. Gallup International Institute, The International Schooling Project, 1994. Taken from Ernest L. Boyer, *The Basic School: A Community for Learning,* Princeton, NJ: The Carnegie Foundation for the Advancement of Teaching, p. 50.)

Japanese Secondary School: A Closer Look that large numbers of students, deprived of sleep from having attended *jukus* (cram schools) to do well on college entrance exams, waste time in school, having been told by their *juku* instructors not to pay attention to their teachers. Additionally, a teacher of English in rural Japan reports that 70 percent of students at her school attend *jukus* and frequently are awake past midnight (Bracey 1996). According to Gerald Bracey (1996, 128), if American parents want their children to achieve at the level of Asian students, which is often only a few percentage points higher on standardized examinations, they must understand the sacrifices made by Asian students and their parents and be prepared to adhere to these guidelines:

1. [W]hen their children come home from public school, they should feed them and then ship them off to a private school or tutor until 10 p.m.; most youngsters, both elementary and secondary, will need to go to school all day on Sunday, too.
2. [They should] spend 20 to 30 percent of their income on [a]fter-school schools.
3. [W]hen their children turn four, they should take them on their knees and tell them, "You are big boys and girls now, so you need to start practicing for college entrance examinations" (Bracey 1996, 128).

In addition, American students would need to realize that "if they sleep four hours a night, they will get into college, but if they sleep five hours a night, they won't; they must study instead" (Bracey 1996, 128).

HOW WILL CYBERSPACE CHANGE TEACHING AND LEARNING

Carol Gilkinson's classroom looks like those of talented teachers everywhere—lively, filled with displays of students' work, photos of field trips, and information-filled posters. A closer look, however, reveals how **cyberspace** has transformed teaching and learning in her classroom. Several computers in the room allow students to communicate via the Internet with other students in Germany, Holland, Russia, and Australia. Gilkinson's students also use child-oriented "search engines" like *Yahooligans!* (http://www.yahooligans.com) and *KidsLink* (http://gnn.digital.com/gnn/wic/ed.35.html) to search for information about whales, the Brazilian rain forest, or the planet Mars on the World Wide Web. They go to "chat rooms" or "newsgroups" for children, such as *k12chat.elementary* for kindergarten through fifth-grade students, where they can "talk" to other children around the world, or participate in various global networking projects for children.

CYBERSPACE AND THE CHALLENGE TO SCHOOLS

Clearly, the Internet, the World Wide Web, and related telecommunications technologies have the potential to transform teaching and learning. However, one of the education issues for the twenty-first century is how committed are teachers, administrators,

Dear Mentor

NOVICE AND EXPERT TEACHERS ON EDUCATIONAL TECHNOLOGY

Dear Pam,

Computers have been a part of the educational scene for more than ten years and are just beginning to have an impact on teaching and learning. One of the chief strengths of using technology in the classroom is that it enables me to adapt my instruction to the individual needs and learning styles of the students. As computer activities can be tailored to student needs, the class becomes more student centered. CD-ROM, videodisc, and captioned instructional television present information visually and allow students to learn complex material more easily.

Individual teachers are using technology to improve instruction, but it has not yet changed the way most teachers teach. "To use these tools well, teachers need visions of the technologies' potential, opportunities to apply them, training and just-in-time support, and time to experiment" (OTA Report on Teachers and Technology). What technology's role will be in the classroom depends to a large extent on the training and support provided by the educational system.

Dear Mentor,

As a prospective teacher I will be entering the classroom soon for my student teaching. One of the many questions I have is how to incorporate computer use in instruction. Do you think fourth and fifth graders could learn computers effectively enough to do a science lab on them? What is the prospect of implementing the whole curriculum via computer? I have a lot of issues about the role of teachers in relation to computers and about where technology is going in education. I guess I'm also a little afraid.

Pam Schnelbach

As more classrooms become connected to the information superhighway, teachers and students will have access to more resources and increased communication. Teacher isolation is reduced as teachers connect with others working on similar projects. Community involvement will increase as public libraries provide more electronic resources for learners of all ages. Senator Kerry feels that classrooms and living rooms will be networked together so that study in the home and study in the school become indistinguishable from each other.

This reality may be a long way off, but it is certainly one vision of the future.

Carol Gilkinson
Christa McAuliffe Educator

policy makers, parents, and the general public to enabling students to realize the full impact that cyberspace can have on their learning? As Howard Mehlinger (1996, 403) says, the future of schools may depend on their response to this challenge.

> The genie is out of the bottle. It is no longer necessary to learn about the American War of Independence by sitting in Mrs. Smith's classroom and hearing her version of it. There are more powerful and efficient ways to learn about the Revolutionary War, and they are all potentially under the control of the learner. Either schools will come to terms with this fact, or schools will be ignored.

Additionally, educators must develop new assessment techniques to evaluate students' learning that occurs through the use of advanced telecommunications like the Internet and the World Wide Web. The number of correct responses on homework, quizzes, and examinations will no longer suffice to measure students' learning. As Chris Morton (1996, 419) points out:

> For the most part, computer environments will not drastically improve students' attainment in the traditional content that we adhere to in our current curricula and that we reinforce with our didactic methods. If teachers want students to be able to use ditto masters, then they shouldn't spend thousands of dollars on systems that support computer-assisted instruction. If teachers want to reinforce their didactic role and their role as information providers, then they should also leave computers alone.

> [Educators] must understand that the promise of computer environments is that they support changes in the educational structure, in instructional processes, and in the development of lifelong learning within the whole population.

THE NATIONAL INFORMATION INFRASTRUCTURE (NII)

In 1995, President Clinton created the **National Information Infrastructure (NII),** to encourage all schools, libraries, hospitals, and law enforcement agencies to become connected to the "Information Superhighway." As part of this effort, the National Center for Education Statistics (1995) conducted the *Survey of Advanced Telecommunications in U.S. Public Schools, K–12* to determine the degree to which public schools had access to advanced telecommunications. Table 14.3, based on the survey, shows that America's educational system was hardly ready to "go online" in 1994; only 35 percent of all public schools and 3 percent of all classrooms had access to the Internet. Furthermore, that same year schools reported a host of barriers to either the acquisition or the use of advanced telecommunications, the most significant of which were lack of funds and equipment (see Table 14.4 on page 468).

WHAT IS OUR VISION FOR THE FUTURE OF EDUCATION

When you think about your future as a teacher, that future may seem at once exciting and frightening, enticing and threatening. How, you may ask, can I meet the many educational challenges identified in this book? In a very real sense, it is in the hands of persons such as yourself to shape with vision and commitment the profession of tomorrow. Our vision for the future of education that follows is designed to help you begin the process of planning for that future.

THE SCHOOL OF TOMORROW

Imagine that it is the year 2020, and we are visiting Westside Elementary school, a school in a medium-sized city in a midwestern state. All of the teachers at Westside

TABLE 14.3

Percent of public schools having access to the Internet and the percent of all instructional rooms across the country with an Internet connection, by school characteristics: 1994

School Characteristic	Percent of Schools Having Access to the Internet	Percent of All Instructional Rooms Across the Country with Internet Access[1]
All public schools	35	3
Instructional[2]		
Elementary	30	3
Secondary	49	4
Size of enrollment		
Less than 300	30	3
300 to 999	35	3
1,000 or more	58	3
Metropolitan status		
City	40	4
Urban fringe	38	4
Town	29	3
Rural	35	3
Geographic region		
Northeast	34	3
Southeast	29	2
Central	34	3
West	42	5

[1]The percent of instructional rooms across the country is based upon the total number of instructional rooms (e.g., classrooms, computer labs, library/media centers) in all regular public elementary and secondary schools.

[2]Data for combined schools are not reported as a separate instructional level because there were very few in the sample. Data for combined schools are included in the totals and in analyses by other school characteristics.

(Source: U.S. Department of Education, National Center for Education Statistics, Fast Response Survey System, "Survey on Advanced Telecommunications in U.S. Public Schools, K–12," FRSS 51, 1994. Taken from *Advanced Telecommunications in U.S. Public Schools, K–12*. Washington, DC: U.S. Department of Education, Office of Educational Research and Improvement, 1995, p. 10.)

have been certified by the National Board for Professional Teaching Standards (NBPTS). The salaries of the board-certified teachers are on a par with those of other professionals with comparable education and training. About half of the fifty-five teachers at Westside have also earned the advanced professional certificate now offered by the NBPTS. These teachers are known as lead teachers and may earn as much as $125,000 per year. Westside has no principal; the school is run by an executive committee of five lead teachers elected by all teachers at the school. One of these lead teachers is elected to serve as committee chair for a two-year period. In addition, the school has several paid interns and residents who are assigned to lead teachers as part of their graduate-level teacher preparation program. Finally, teachers are assisted by a diagnostician; hypermedia specialist; computer specialist; video specialist; social worker; school psychologist; four counselors; special remediation teachers in reading, writing, mathematics, and oral communication; bilingual and ESL teachers; and special-needs teachers.

Westside Elementary operates many programs that illustrate the close ties the school has developed with parents, community agencies, and businesses. The school houses a daycare center that provides after-school employment for several students from the nearby high school. On weekends and on Monday, Wednesday, and Friday evenings the school is used for adult education and for various community group activities. Executives from three local businesses spend one day a month at the school visiting with classes and telling students about their work. Students from a nearby college participate in a tutoring program at Westside, and the college has several on-campus summer enrichment programs for Westside students.

TABLE 14.4

Percent of all public schools indicating the extent to which various factors are barriers to either the acquisition or the use of advanced telecommunications: 1994

Barrier	Minor or No Barrier	Moderate Barrier	Major Barrier
Lack of or poor equipment	30	20	50
Inadequate hardware upkeep and repair	50	22	28
Lack of instructional software	47	28	24
Software too complicated to use	79	14	7
Too few access points in building	35	19	47
Telecommunications equipment not easily accessible	36	20	44
Telecommunications links not easily accessible	42	18	39
Variability of telecommunications rates from service providers	64	17	19
Problems with telecommunications service provider	78	9	13
Lack of time in school schedule	45	27	28
Lack of technical support or advice	46	27	27
Use of advanced telecommunications does not fit with the educational policy of this school	90	6	4
Lack of or inadequately trained staff	33	31	36
Lack of teacher awareness regarding ways to integrate telecommunications into curriculum	32	34	34
Not enough help for supervising student computer use	49	26	25
Lack of administrative support or initiative	69	17	14
Lack of teacher interest	65	28	8
Lack of parent or community interest	77	16	7
Lack of student interest	92	6	2
Funds not specifically allocated for telecommunications	16	15	69

Note: Percents may not sum to 100 because of rounding.

(Source: U.S. Department of Education, National Center for Educations Statistics, Fast Response Survey System, "Survey on Advanced Telecommunications in U.S. Public Schools, K–12," FRSS 51, 1994. Taken from *Advanced Telecommunications in U.S. Public Schools, K–12.* Washington, DC: U.S. Department of Education, Office of Educational Research and Improvement, 1995, p. 19.)

Westside has a school-based health clinic that offers health care services and a counseling center that provides individual and family counseling. In addition, from time to time Westside teachers and students participate in service-learning activities in the community. At the present time, for example, the fifth-grade classes are helping the city develop a new recycling program.

All the facilities at Westside—classrooms, library, multimedia learning center, gymnasium, the cafeteria, and private offices for teachers—have been designed to create a teaching/learning environment free of all health and safety hazards. The cafeteria, for example, serves meals based on findings from nutrition research about the best foods and methods of cooking. The school is carpeted, and classrooms are soundproofed and well lit. Throughout, the walls are painted in soft pastels tastefully accented with potted plants, paintings, wall hangings, and large murals depicting life in different cultures.

The dress, language, and behaviors of teacher, students, and support personnel at Westside reflect a rich array of cultural backgrounds. In the cafeteria, for example, it is impossible not to hear several languages being spoken and to see at least a few students and teachers wearing non-Western clothing. From the displays of students' work on bulletin boards in hallways and in classrooms, to the international menu offered in the cafeteria, there is ample evidence that Westside is truly a multicultural school and that gender, race, and class biases have been eliminated.

Each teacher at Westside is a member of a teaching team and spends at least part of his or her teaching time working with other members of the team. Furthermore, teachers determine their schedules, and every effort is made to assign teachers according to their particular teaching expertise. Students attend Westside by choice for its excellent teachers; its curricular emphasis on problem solving, human relations, creative thinking, and critical thinking; and its programs for helping at-risk students achieve academic success.

Instruction at Westside is supplemented by the latest technologies. The school subscribes to several computer databases and cable television services, which teachers and students use regularly. The hypermedia learning center has an extensive collection of CD-ROMs and computer software, much of it written by Westside teachers. The center also has virtual-reality interactive videodisc systems, workstations equipped with the latest robotics, and an extensive lab with voice-activated computers. The computer-supported interactive multimedia in the center use the CD-ROM format and the more advanced Integrated Services Digital Network (ISDN) delivery system based on the optical fiber.

Every classroom has a video camera, fax machine, hypermedia system, and telephone that, in addition to everyday use, are used frequently during satellite video teleconferences with

What vision of the school of the future does this photograph suggest? What might you add to the image to achieve a broader perspective on tomorrow's teachers and learners?

business executives, artists, scientists, scholars, and students at schools in other states and countries. Westside Elementary's technological capabilities permit students to move their education beyond the classroom walls, as they determine much of how, when, where, and what they learn.

TOMORROW'S TEACHER

Teaching and the conditions under which teachers work may change in some fundamental and positive ways during the next two decades. Teaching will become increasingly professionalized, for example, through such changes as more lengthy and rigorous preprofessional training programs, salary increases that put teaching on a par with other professions requiring similar education, and greater teacher autonomy and an expanded role for teachers in educational policy making. There will be more male teachers who are African Americans, Hispanic and Latino, or members of other minority groups. There will be greater recognition for high-performing teachers and schools through such mechanisms as merit pay plans, master teacher programs, and career ladders. Tomorrow's teachers will achieve new and higher levels of specialization. The traditional teaching job will be divided into parts. Some of the new jobs may be the following:

- Learning diagnostician
- Researcher for software programs
- Courseware writer
- Curriculum designer
- Mental health diagnostician
- Evaluator of learning performances
- Evaluator of social skills
- Small-group learning facilitator
- Large-group learning facilitator
- Media-instruction producer
- Home-based instruction designer
- Home-based instruction monitor

Though we cannot claim to have handed you an educational crystal ball so that you can ready yourself for the future, we hope you have gained both knowledge and inspiration from our observations in this chapter. Certainly, visions of the future, such as the one of Westside Elementary, will not become a reality without a lot of dedication and hard work. The creation of schools like Westside will require commitment and vision on the part of professional teachers like you.

PROFESSIONAL REFLECTION

Anticipating the Impacts of Innovations and Trends in Education

Following is a list of educational innovations and trends that are shaping tomorrow's classrooms. For each item, indicate with an *X* whether you are "highly committed," "somewhat committed," "opposed," or "neutral" toward having that innovation or trend characterize your teaching. After responding to the items, reflect on those to which you are "highly committed." What steps will you take from this point on to ensure that those items will, in fact, characterize your future in teaching five, ten, and fifteen years from now? How will those items be reflected in your professional life as a teacher?

Innovation//Trend	Highly Committed	Somewhat Committed	Opposed	Neutral
1. Alternative/authentic assessment of students' learning	___	___	___	___
2. Cross-age tutoring/mentoring	___	___	___	___
3. Peer counseling/peer coaching	___	___	___	___
4. Faculty teams/team teaching	___	___	___	___
5. Business-school partnerships	___	___	___	___
6. Community-school teaming	___	___	___	___
7. School-based clinics/counseling centers	___	___	___	___
8. Year-round schools	___	___	___	___
9. School restructuring	___	___	___	___
10. Equity in school funding	___	___	___	___
11. Open enrollment/school choice	___	___	___	___
12. Telephones in the classroom	___	___	___	___
13. Student computer networking	___	___	___	___
14. Video teleconferencing	___	___	___	___
15. Interactive multimedia/hypermedia	___	___	___	___
16. Sex education	___	___	___	___
17. AIDS education	___	___	___	___
18. Moral orientation on curricula	___	___	___	___
19. Globalism/multiculturalism	___	___	___	___
20. Aesthetics orientation	___	___	___	___
21. Alcohol and drug intervention	___	___	___	___
22. Reduction of gender bias	___	___	___	___
23. Reduction of racial/ethnic prejudice	___	___	___	___
24. Teacher empowerment	___	___	___	___
25. Constructivist approaches to teaching	___	___	___	___
26. Charter schools	___	___	___	___
27. Corporate-education partnerships	___	___	___	___
28. For-profit schools	___	___	___	___

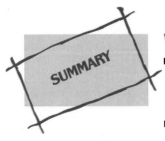

SUMMARY

What Will Students Need to Know and Be Able to Do?

■ Conflicting theories, expectations, and values make it difficult to answer what students need to know and be able to do in the future; however, increasing cultural diversity and global economic interdependence call for communication and cooperation skills and wise use of environmental resources.

■ To meet the challenges of the future, students will need knowledge, skills, attitudes, and values in nine key areas: literacy in language, mathematics, and science; new technological skills; problem solving, critical thinking, and creativity; social awareness, communication skills, and team building; global awareness and conservation skills; health and wellness education; moral and ethical orientation; aesthetics awareness; and lifelong, self-directed learning.

How Can Teachers and Schools Reach All Learners?

■ To reach all learners, teachers must understand how some families are under acute stress, how crime and violence impact students' lives, and how to develop multicultural curricula and instructional repertoires that develop the potentialities of students from varied backgrounds.

■ In addition to preparing multicultural instructional materials and strategies for students from diverse cultural, ethnic, and linguistic backgrounds, teachers treat students equitably when they treat high- and low-achieving students the same. Research has identified several teacher behaviors that reflect inequitable treatment of low-achieving students: waiting less time for them to answer questions, interacting with them less frequently, giving them less feedback, calling on them less often, seating them farther away, failing to accept and use their ideas, smiling at them less often, making less eye contact, praising them less, demanding less, grading their tests differently, and rewarding inappropriate behaviors.

■ Effective teachers establish positive relationships with *all* students by listening to them, giving frequent feedback and opportunities to ask questions, and demanding higher-level performance by asking higher-order questions that require more critical thinking.

■ To reach all learners, teachers should provide them with active, authentic learning experiences.

How Can Community-Based Partnerships Address Social Problems That Hinder Students' Learning?

■ Communities help schools address social problems that hinder students' learning by providing various kinds of support.

■ Civic organizations raise money for schools, sponsor teams, recognize student achievement, award scholarships, sponsor volunteer mentor programs, and provide other resources and services to enrich students' learning.

■ Corporate-education partnerships provide schools with resources, release time for employees to visit schools, scholarships, job initiatives for disadvantaged youth, inservice programs for teachers, and management training for school administrators.

■ Schools serve as resources for their communities by providing educational and recreational programs before and after the school day, and by providing health and social services.

How Will the Privatization Movement Affect Equity and Excellence in Education?

■ Charter schools and for-profit schools, both part of the privatization movement, were developed in response to perceived inadequacies of the public schools.

■ Charter schools are independent, innovative, outcome-based public schools started by a group of teachers, parents, or others who obtain a *charter* from a local school district, a state, or the federal government.

■ The Edison Project's national network of private secondary schools and schools operated by Education Alternatives Inc. are examples of for-profit schools operated by private corporations.

What Can Teachers and Schools Learn from International Education?

- The challenges and opportunities for teachers in the twenty-first century are remarkably similar worldwide, and teachers in different countries can learn much from one another. Comparative education, the study of educational practices in other countries, enables educators to collaborate internationally.
- The International Assessment of Educational Progress (IAEP) has revealed that the achievement levels of U.S. students are lower than those of students in other countries; however, these results reflect America's commitment to educating *all* students and differences in *opportunity to learn* among countries.
- Education in many other countries is centralized and teachers follow a national curriculum. While some people support a national curriculum and national examinations for America's educational system, there are several disadvantages to such a system.
- Many other countries tend to provide greater support for teachers and teaching and have greater parental involvement, two practices that would benefit American education. However, pressure for students in other countries to excel is often extreme.

How Will Cyberspace Change Teaching and Learning?

- In many schools and classrooms, cyberspace has already transformed teaching and learning; however, teachers, administrators, policy makers, and parents must realize that advanced telecommunications will require new approaches to teaching and assessing students' learning.
- The National Information Infrastructure (NII) was developed to encourage all schools to use advanced telecommunications.

What Is Our Vision for the Future of Education?

- It is not unrealistic to imagine that teachers in schools during the year 2020 will be well-paid, NBPTS-certified, self-governing professionals who have developed specialized areas of expertise. This vision becomes more possible with each teacher who makes a commitment to its realization.

KEY TERMS AND CONCEPTS

APPLICATIONS AND ACTIVITIES

Teacher's Journal

1. Write a scenario forecasting how the teaching profession will change during the next two decades.

2. Select one of the following areas and develop several forecasts for changes that will occur during the next two decades: energy, environment, food, the economy, governance, family structure, demographics, global relations, media, and technology. On what current data are your forecasts based? How might these changes affect teaching and learning?

3. In your opinion, what is the most important benefit of advanced telecommunications for education, and what is the most important potential drawback?

4. Think about two children you know and project them into the future, twenty years from now. What skills are they likely to need? Which talents should help them? How can schools better promote the development of these skills and talents?

Teacher's Database

1. Explore the field of international education or comparative education and talk to teaching professionals in other countries online. Begin by checking the following sites:

Project Archive: URL:httpl//curry.edschool.virginia.edu/-tedcasesl
   Project Cape Town: Education and integration in South Africa, 1995.

Newsgroup: Usenet: k12.euro.teachers—teachers in Europe

Journal on the Web: *Comparative Education Review*

2. Explore the fee for service and fee for product opportunities that are available to teachers on the Internet. You might order and receive a special document, newsletter, or mailing list that addresses your interests or needs. Your school might subscribe to the educational services of a private organization, such as the National Geographic Society. Begin your exploration by getting information on two or more of the following services.

InterNIC Information Services publishes a *Newsletter* that gives information on all the networks that are on the Internet:

   InterNIC Information Services
   P.O. Box 85608
   San Diego, CA 92186-9784
   (619) 455-3990   Fax: (619) 455-3990
   INFO@IS.INTERNIC.NET

Learning Link—information about using television in the classroom and partnerships between schools and local public television stations, including online mentoring for novice teachers.

   (212) 708-3054

FrEdMAIL—information about a net tool for sending student writing from one school to another.

   (619) 475-4852

Classroom Connect is a monthly newsletter with practical advice on using the Internet to find instructional materials, design an online project, and get grants for going online. $39/yr, 9 issues.

   (800) 638-1639
   success@wentworth.com

The Educator's Internet Newsletter describes Internet resources that are provided by local school systems, provides information about Archie, and catalogues resources for music teachers. $18/yr, 6 issues.

P.O. Box 7085
Golden, CO 80403-0100

NetTeach News, a newsletter for both novice and experienced teachers, describes new sites, and provides information on site licensing that is available for public elementary and secondary education networks, conferences in education and technology, government-sponsored telecommunications grants, and What's New in K–12 Mosaics.

info@netteach.chaos.com

The Internet Handbook for School Users is a handbook for teachers from the Educational Research Service (ERS).

2000 Clarendon Boulevard
Arlington, Virginia 22201
(703) 243-2100   Fax: (703) 243-8316
ers@access.digex.net

Observations and Interviews

1. Interview the principal at a local or nearby school and ask him or her to describe what the school will be like in ten years. Now interview several teachers at the school. Compare the forecasts of the principal with those of the teachers. What might account for any differences you find?

2. Search for examples of school-community partnership arrangements in the local school district. Find out how these partnerships are progressing and propose a specific new one based on your knowledge of the community.

Professional Portfolio

Prepare a portfolio entry of instructional resources—curriculum guides, teaching tips, assessment strategies, relevant professional associations, books and articles, software, and online resources—related to one of the nine areas of learning students will need to meet the challenges of the future (i.e., literacy in language, mathematics, and science; new technological skills; problem solving, critical thinking, and creativity; social awareness, communication skills, and team building; global awareness and conservation skills; health and wellness education; moral and ethical orientation; aesthetics awareness; and lifelong, self-directed learning). For each entry include a brief annotation describing the materials, how you will use them, and where they may be obtained. After you have prepared this portfolio entry, meet with your classmates and exchange information.

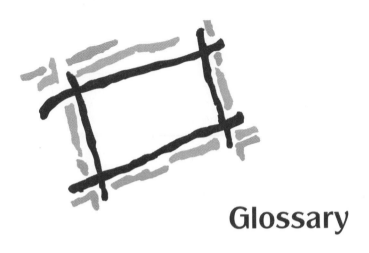

Glossary

A

Academic freedom (p. 208): the right of teachers to teach, free from external constraint, censorship, or interference.

Academic learning time (p. 320): the amount of time students spend working on academic tasks with a high level of success (80 percent or higher).

Academies (p. 75): early secondary schools with broader and more practical curricula than those found in grammar schools of the previous era.

Accelerated schools (p. 401): a national network of schools that provide enriched, rigorous curricula to "speed up" the learning of students at risk.

Accountability (p. 88): the practice of holding teachers responsible for adhering to high professional and moral standards and creating effective learning environments for all students.

Action research (p. 396): classroom-based study, by teachers, of how to improve their instruction.

Aesthetics (p. 138): the branch of axiology concerned with values related to beauty and art.

Afrocentric schools (p. 250): schools that focus on African-American history and cultures for African-American pupils.

Aims of education (p. 98): what a society believes the broad, general purposes of education should be—for example, socialization, achievement, personal growth, and social improvement.

Allocated time (p. 320): the amount of time teachers allocate for instruction in various areas of the curriculum.

Alternative certification (p. 416): a provision allowing people who have completed college but not a teacher education program to become certified teachers.

Alternative school (p. 125): a small, highly individualized school separate from a regular school; designed to meet the needs of students at risk.

American Federation of Teachers (AFT) (p. 388): a national professional association for teachers, affiliated with the AFL-CIO.

Assertive discipline (p. 326): an approach to classroom discipline requiring that teachers establish firm, clear guidelines for student behavior and follow through with consequences for misbehavior.

Assessment (p. 335): the process of gathering information related to how much students have learned.

Assistive technology (p. 302): technological advances (usually computer-based) that help exceptional students learn and communicate.

Association for Supervision and Curriculum Development (ASCD) (p. 389): a professional organization for educators interested in school improvement at all levels.

Attention deficit disorder (ADD) (p. 292): a learning disability characterized by difficulty in concentrating on learning.

Attention deficit hyperactivity disorder (ADHD) (p. 292): a learning disability characterized by difficulty in remaining still so that one can concentrate on learning.

Authentic assessments (p. 336): an approach to assessing students' learning that requires them to solve problems or work on tasks that approximate as much as possible those they will encounter beyond the classroom.

Authentic learning tasks (p. 319): learning activities that enable students to see the connections between classroom learning and the world beyond the classroom.

Axiology (p. 138): the study of values, including the identification of criteria for determining what is valuable.

B

Back-to-basics movement (p. 145): a movement begun in the mid-1970s to establish the "basic skills" of reading, writing, speaking, and computation as the core of the school curriculum.

Behaviorism (p. 151): based on behavioristic psychology, this philosophical orientation maintains that environmental factors shape people's behavior.

Between-class ability grouping (p. 317): the practice of grouping students at the middle and high school levels for instruction on the basis of ability or achievement, often called *tracking*.

Bicultural (p. 256): the ability to function effectively in two or more linguistic and cultural groups.

Bilingual education (pp. 240, 256): a curriculum for non-English-speaking and English-speaking students in which two languages are used for instruction and biculturalism is emphasized.

Block grants (p. 188): a form of federal aid given directly to the states, which a state or local education agency may spend as it wishes with few limitations.

Block scheduling (p. 320): a high school scheduling arrangement that provides longer blocks of time each class period, with fewer periods each day.

***Brown v. Board of Education of Topeka* (p. 87):** a 1954 landmark court case rejecting the "separate but equal" doctrine used to prevent African Americans from attending schools with whites.

Buckley Amendment (p. 224): a 1974 law, the Family Educational Rights and Privacy Act, granting parents of students under eighteen and students over eighteen the right to examine their school records.

Bureau of Indian Affairs (BIA) schools (p. 182): schools for Native American children operated by the U.S. Department of Interior.

Burnout (p. 16): an acute level of stress resulting in job dissatisfaction, emotional and physical exhaustion, and an inability to cope effectively.

C

Caring classroom (p. 315): a classroom in which the teacher communicates clearly an attitude of caring about students' learning and their overall well-being.

Categorical aid (p. 190): state-appropriated funds to cover the costs of educating students with special needs.

CD-ROM (p. 403): a small plastic disk (usually 4.72 or 5.25 inches in diameter) that holds 600 or more megabytes of information that can be read by a computer.

Censorship (p. 218): the act of removing from circulation printed material judged to be libelous, vulgar, or obscene.

Character education (p. 280): an approach to education that emphasizes the teaching of values, moral reasoning, and the development of "good" character.

Charter (p. 416): an agreement between a charter school's founders and its sponsors specifying how the school will operate and what learning outcomes students will master.

Charter schools (p. 454): independent schools, often founded by teachers, that are given a charter to operate by a school district, state, or national government, with the provision that students must demonstrate mastery of predetermined outcomes.

Chief state school officer (p. 180): the chief administrator of a state department of education and head of the state board of education, often called the commissioner of education or superintendent of public instruction.

Classroom climate (p. 311): the atmosphere or quality of life in a classroom, determined by how individuals interact with one another.

Classroom culture (p. 110): the "way of life" characteristic of a classroom group; determined by the social dimensions of the group and the physical characteristics of the setting.

Classroom management (p. 322): day-to-day teacher control of student behavior and learning, including discipline.

Classroom organization (p. 317): how teachers and students in a school are grouped for instruction and how time is allocated in classrooms.

Clinical supervision (p. 437): a four-step model supervisors follow in making teacher performance evaluations.

Coalition of Essential Schools (p. 399): a national network of public and private high schools that have restructured according to nine Common Principles.

Code of ethics (p. 201): a set of guidelines that defines appropriate behavior for professionals.

Cognitive development (p. 277): the process of acquiring the intellectual ability to learn from interaction with one's environment.

Cognitive science (p. 154): the study of the learning process that focuses on how individuals manipulate symbols and process information.

Collaboration (p. 434): the practice of working together, sharing decision making, and solving problems among professionals.

Collaborative consultation (p. 301): an approach in which a classroom teacher meets with one or more other professionals (such as a special educator, school psychologist, or resource teacher) to focus on the learning needs of one or more students.

Collective bargaining (p. 206): a process followed by employers and employees in negotiating salaries, hours, and working conditions; in most states, school boards must negotiate contracts with teacher organizations.

Collegiality (p. 430): a spirit of cooperation and mutual helpfulness among professionals.

Committee of Fifteen (p. 360): an NEA committee that recommended an academically oriented elementary curriculum (1895).

Committee of Ten (p. 360): an NEA committee that recommended an academically rigorous curriculum for high school students (1893).

Common schools (p. 77): free state-supported schools that provide education for all students.

Comparative education (p. 458): the comparative study of educational practices in different countries.

Compensatory education programs (p. 124): federally funded educational programs designed to meet the needs of low-ability students from low-income families.

Computer-assisted instruction (CAI) (p. 330): the use of microcomputers to provide individual instruction to students.

Computer simulations (p. 403): computer programs that present the user with multifaceted problem situations similar to those they will encounter in real life.

Concrete operations stage (p. 277): the stage of cognitive development (seven to eleven years of age) proposed by Jean Piaget in which the individual develops the ability to use logical thought to solve concrete problems.

Constructivism (p. 153): a psychological orientation that views learning as an active process in which learners *construct* understanding of the material they learn—in contrast to the view that teachers transmit academic content to students in small segments.

Constructivist teaching (p. 331): a method of teaching based on students' prior knowledge of the topic and the processes they use to *construct* meaning.

Contingent teaching (p. 331): an approach to teaching, sometimes called *scaffolding*, in which instruction is based on (or contingent on) the student's current level of understanding and ability; the teacher varies the amount of help given to students based on their moment-to-moment understanding of the material being learned.

Cooperative learning (p. 317): an approach to education in which students work in small groups, or teams, sharing the work and helping one another complete assignments.

Copyright laws (p. 215): laws limiting the use of photocopies, videotapes, and computer software programs.

Core curriculum (p. 363): a set of fundamental courses or learning experiences that are part of the curriculum for all students at a school.

Corporal punishment (p. 227): physical punishment applied to a student by a school employee as a disciplinary measure.

Cost of living (p. 10): the amount of money needed, on average, for housing, food, transportation, utilities, and other living expenses in a given locale.

Co-teaching (p. 436): an arrangement whereby two or more teachers teach together in the same classroom.

Credentials file (p. 420): a file set up for students registered in a teacher placement office at a college or university, which includes background information on the applicant, the type of position desired, transcripts, performance evaluations, and letters of recommendation.

Cross-age tutoring (p. 333): a tutoring arrangement in which older students tutor younger students; evidence indicates that cross-age tutoring has positive effects on the attitudes and achievement of tutee and tutor.

Cultural identity (p. 239): an overall sense of oneself, derived from the extent of one's participation in various subcultures within the national macroculture.

Cultural pluralism (p. 239): the preservation of cultural differences among groups of people within one society. This view is in contrast to the melting-pot theory that says that ethnic cultures should melt into one.

Culture (p. 239): the way of life common to a group of people; includes knowledge deemed important, shared meanings, norms, values, attitudes, ideals, and view of the world.

Curriculum (p. 346): the school experiences, both planned and unplanned, that enhance (and sometimes impede) the education and growth of students.

Cyberspace (p. 464): a vast global network of interconnected computers that make up the Internet and the World Wide Web.

D

Dame schools (p. 72): colonial schools, usually held in the homes of widows or housewives, for teaching children basic reading, writing, and mathematical skills.

Democratic classroom (p. 322): a classroom in which the teacher's leadership style encourages students to take more power and responsibility for their learning.

Department of Defense (DOD) overseas dependents schools (p. 182): schools operated by the U.S. Department of Defense for children of military personnel and federal employees on overseas assignments.

Departmentalization (p. 109): an organizational arrangement for schools in which students move from classroom to classroom for instruction in different subject areas.

Desegregation (p. 87): the process of eliminating schooling practices based on the separation of racial groups.

Direct instruction (p. 328): a systematic instructional method focusing on the transmission of knowledge and skills from the teacher to the students.

Discipline-based art programs (p. 372): art education in which students learn art production, art criticism, art history, and aesthetics.

Discovery learning (p. 332): an approach to teaching that gives students opportunities to inquire into subjects so that they "discover" knowledge for themselves.

Dismissal (p. 205): the involuntary termination of a teacher's employment; termination must be made for a legally defensible reason with the protection of due process.

Distance learning (p. 45): the use of technology such as video transmissions that enables students to receive instruction at multiple, often remote, sites.

Diversity (p. 238): differences among people in regard to gender, race, ethnicity, culture, and socioeconomic status.

Due process (p. 202): a set of specific guidelines that must be followed to protect individuals from arbitrary, capricious treatment by those in authority.

E

Educare system (p. 452): a proposal that would combine education and day care to provide day-long, year-round schooling for children six months through twelve years of age.

Education Consolidation and Improvement Act (ECIA) (p. 188): a 1981 federal law giving the states a broad range of choices for spending federal aid to education.

Education for All Handicapped Children Act (Public Law 94-142) (pp. 89, 295): a 1975 federal act that guarantees a free and appropriate education to all handicapped children (often referred to as the mainstreaming law or Public Law 94-142).

Educational malpractice (p. 214): liability for injury that results from the failure of a teacher, school, or school district to provide a student with adequate instruction, guidance, counseling, and/or supervision.

Educational philosophy (p. 132): a set of ideas and beliefs about education that guide the professional behavior of educators.

Educational reform movement (p. 43): a comprehensive effort made during the 1980s and into the 1990s to improve schools and the preparation of teachers.

Educational Resources Information Center (ERIC) (p. 396): a national information system made up of sixteen clearinghouses that disseminate descriptions of exemplary programs, results of research and development efforts, and related information.

Eight-Year Study (p. 361): an experiment in which thirty high schools were allowed to develop curricula that did not meet college entrance requirements (1932–1940).

Elementary and Secondary Education Act (p. 87): part of President Lyndon B. Johnson's Great Society Program, this act allocated federal funds on the basis of the number of poor children in school districts.

Emergency certification (p. 416): temporary, substandard certification requirements set by a state in response to a shortage of teachers.

Entitlements (p. 188): federal programs to meet the educational needs of special populations.

Epistemology (p. 137): a branch of philosophy concerned with the nature of knowledge and what it means to know something.

ERIC Clearinghouses (p. 396): sixteen Educational Resources Information Center Clearinghouses that disseminate descriptions of exemplary educational programs, the results of research and development efforts, and related information.

Essentialism (p. 144): formulated in part as a response to progressivism, this philosophical orientation holds that a core of common knowledge about the real world should be transmitted to students in a systematic, disciplined way.

Ethical dilemmas (p. 201): problem situations in which an ethical response is difficult to determine; that is, no single response can be called "right" or "wrong."

Ethics (p. 138): a branch of philosophy concerned with principles of conduct and determining what is good and evil, right and wrong, in human behavior.

Ethnic group (p. 239): individuals within a larger culture who share a racial or cultural identity and a set of beliefs, values, and attitudes and who consider themselves members of a distinct group or subculture.

Ethnicity (p. 242): a shared feeling of common identity that derives, in part, from a common ancestry, common values, and common experiences.

Evaluation (p. 336): making judgments about, or assigning a value to, measurements of students' learning.

Exceptional learners (p. 289): students whose growth and development deviate from the norm to the extent that their educational needs can be met more effectively through a modification of regular school programs.

Existentialism (p. 148): a philosophical orientation that emphasizes the individual's experiences and maintains that each individual must determine his or her own meaning of existence.

Expenditure per pupil (p. 184): the amount of money spent on each pupil in a school, school district, state, or nation; usually computed according to average daily attendance.

Explicit curriculum (p. 347): the behavior, attitudes, and knowledge that a school intends to teach students.

Extracurricular/cocurricular programs (p. 349): school-sponsored activities students may pursue outside of, or in addition to, academic study.

F

Faculty teams (p. 436): a small number of teachers, brought together on the basis of interests and expertise, who teach a group of students equal in number to what the teachers would have in their self-contained classrooms.

Fair use (p. 215): the right of an individual to use copyrighted material in a reasonable manner without the copyright holder's consent, provided that use meets certain criteria.

Female seminaries (p. 76): schools established in the early nineteenth century to train women for higher education and public service outside the home.

Field experiences (p. 45): opportunities for teachers-in-training to experience first-hand the world of the teacher, by observing, tutoring, and instructing small groups.

For-profit schools (p. 456): schools that are operated, for profit, by private educational corporations.

Formal operations stage (p. 277): the stage of cognitive development (eleven to fifteen years of age) proposed by Jean Piaget in which cognitive abilities reach their highest level of development.

Formative evaluation (p. 336): an assessment, or diagnosis, of students' learning for the purpose of planning instruction.

Freedmen's Bureau (p. 75): an organization that provided assistance, including education, to former slaves.

Freedom of expression (p. 218): freedom, granted by the First Amendment to the Constitution, to express one's beliefs.

Fringe benefits (p. 10): benefits (i.e., medical insurance, retirement, and tax-deferred investment opportunities) that are given to teachers in addition to base salary.

Full inclusion (p. 297): the policy and process of including exceptional learners in general education classrooms.

Full-funding programs (p. 189): state programs to ensure statewide financial equity by setting the same per-pupil expenditure level for all schools and districts.

Full-service schools (p. 123): schools that provide students and their families with medical, social, and human services, in addition to their regular educational programs.

G

Gender bias (p. 268): subtle bias or discrimination on the basis of gender; reduces the likelihood that the target of the bias will develop to the full extent of his or her capabilities.

Gender-fair classroom (p. 268): education that is free of bias or discrimination on the basis of gender.

G.I. Bill of Rights (p. 181): a 1944 federal law that provides veterans with payments for tuition and room and board at colleges and universities and special schools, formally known as the Servicemen's Readjustment Act.

Gifted and talented (p. 293): exceptional learners who demonstrate high intelligence, high creativity, high achievement, or special talent(s).

Goals 2000: Educate America Act (p. 99): a comprehensive funding program to help schools achieve a set of eight national goals emphasizing student achievement, effective learning environments, professional development for teachers, and parental involvement.

Grievance (p. 206): a formal complaint filed by an employee against his or her employer or supervisor.

Group investigation (p. 333): an approach to teaching in which the teacher facilitates learning by creating an environment that allows students to determine what they will study and how.

H

Hidden curriculum (p. 347): the behaviors, attitudes, and knowledge the school culture unintentionally teaches students.

Hierarchy of needs (p. 280): a set of seven needs, from the basic needs for survival and safety to the need for self-actualization, that motivate human behavior.

Higher-order questions (p. 449): questions that require the ability to engage in complex modes of thought (synthesis, analysis, and evaluation, for example).

Holmes Group (p. 43): a group of ninety-six colleges of education that prepared *Tomorrow's Teachers*, a 1986 report calling for all teachers to have a bachelor's degree in an academic field and a master's degree in education.

Horn book (p. 72): a copy of the alphabet covered by a thin transparent sheet made from a cow's horn.

Humanism (p. 150): a philosophy based on the belief that individuals control their own destinies through the application of their intelligence and learning.

Humanistic psychology (p. 150): an orientation to human behavior that emphasizes personal freedom, choice, awareness, and personal responsibility.

Hypermedia (p. 403): an interactive instructional system consisting of a computer, CD-ROM drive, videodisc player, video monitor, and speakers. Hypermedia systems allow students to control and present sound, video images, text, and graphics in an almost limitless array of possibilities.

I

Inclusion (p. 297): the practice of integrating all students with disabilities into general education classes.

Indian Education Act of 1972 and 1974 amendments (p. 255): a federal law and subsequent amendment designed to provide direct educational assistance to Native-American tribes and nations.

Individualized education program (IEP) (p. 296): a plan for meeting an exceptional learner's educational needs, specifying goals, objectives, services, and procedures for evaluating progress.

Individuals with Disabilities Education Act (IDEA) (p. 295): a 1990 federal act providing a free, appropriate education to disabled youth between three and twenty-one years of age. IDEA superseded the earlier Education for all Handicapped Children Act (Public Law 94-142).

Induction programs (p. 49): programs of support for beginning teachers, usually during their first year of teaching.

Information processing (p. 332): a branch of cognitive science concerned with how individuals use long- and short-term memory to acquire information and solve problems.

Inquiry-based curriculum (p. 362): a curriculum that teaches not only the content but also the thought processes of a discipline.

Inquiry learning (p. 332): an approach to teaching that gives students opportunities to explore, or *inquire* into, subjects so that they develop their own answers to problem situations.

Inservice workshops (p. 54): on-site professional development programs in which teachers meet to learn new techniques, develop curricular materials, share ideas, or solve problems.

Institution (p. 105): any organization a society establishes to maintain, and improve, its way of life.

Integrated curriculum (p. 354): a school curriculum that draws from two or more subject areas and focuses on a theme or concept rather than on a single subject.

Intelligence (p. 285): the ability to learn; the cognitive capacity for thinking.

Interactive multimedia (p. 403): computer-supported media that allow the user to interact with a vast, nonlinear, multimedia database to combine textual, audio, and video information.

Interactive teaching (p. 21): teaching characterized by face-to-face interactions between teachers and students in contrast to preactive teaching.

Internet (p. 56): a set of more than 10,000 interconnected computer networks created for the rapid dissemination of vast amounts of information around the world.

International Assessment of Educational Progress (IAEP) (p. 458): a program established in 1991 for comparing the achievement of students in the United States with that of students from other countries.

Internship programs (p. 49): programs of assistance and training for beginning teachers, usually for those who have not gone through a teacher education program.

Interstate Certification Agreement Contract (p. 413): a reciprocity agreement among approximately thirty states whereby a teaching certificate obtained in one state will be honored in another.

Interstate New Teacher Assessment and Support Consortium (INTASC) (p. 41): an organization of states established in 1987 to develop performance-based standards for what beginning teachers should know and be able to do.

J

Job analysis (p. 40): a procedure for determining the knowledge and skills needed for a job.

K

Kentucky Education Reform Act (KERA) (p. 178): comprehensive school-reform legislation requiring all Kentucky schools to form school-based management councils with authority to set policies in eight areas.

Kindergarten (p. 81): a school for children before they begin formal schooling at the elementary level; based on the ideas of German educator Friedrick Fröebel, *kindergarten* means "garden where children grow."

Knowledge base (p. 38): the body of knowledge that represents what teachers need to know and be able to do.

L

Language-minority students (p. 246): students whose language of the home is a language other than English.

Latchkey children (p. 117): children who, because of family circumstances, must spend part of each day unsupervised by a parent or guardian.

Latin grammar school (p. 72): colonial schools established to provide male students a precollege education; comparable to today's high schools.

Learning (p. 449): changes in behavior the individual makes in response to environmental stimuli; the acquisition and organization of knowledge and skills.

Learning disability (LD) (p. 291): a limitation in one's ability to take in, organize, remember, and express information.

Learning modes (p. 287): cognitive, affective, and physiological behaviors through which an individual learns most effectively; determined by a combination of hereditary and environmental influences.

Learning objectives (p. 335): specific, measurable outcomes of learning that students are to demonstrate.

Least restrictive environment (p. 295): an educational program that meets a disabled student's special needs in a manner that is identical, insofar as possible, to that provided to students in general education classrooms.

***Lemon* test (p. 231):** a three-part test, based on *Lemon v. Kurtzman,* to determine whether a state has violated the separation of church and state principle.

Letter of application (p. 421): a letter written in application for a specific teaching vacancy in a school district.

Letter of inquiry (p. 421): a letter written to a school district inquiring about teaching vacancies.

Limited English proficiency (LEP) (p. 246): a designation for students with limited ability to understand, read, or speak English and who have a first language other than English.

Local school council (p. 175): a group of community members that is empowered to develop policies for the operation of local schools.

Local school district (p. 167): an agency at the local level that has the authority to operate schools in the district.

Logic (p. 139): a branch of philosophy concerned with the processes of reasoning and the identification of rules that will enable thinkers to reach valid conclusions.

Lower-order questions (p. 449): questions that require students to recall specific information.

M

Magnet school (p. 104): a school offering a curriculum that focuses on a specific area such as the performing arts, mathematics, science, international studies, or technology. Magnet schools, which often draw students from a larger attendance area than regular schools, are frequently developed to promote voluntary desegration.

Mainstreaming (pp. 89, 296): the policy and process of integrating disabled or otherwise exceptional learners into regular classrooms with nonexceptional students.

Massachusetts Act of 1642 (p. 73): a law requiring each town to determine whether its young people could read and write.

Massachusetts Act of 1647 (p. 73): a law mandating the establishment and support of schools; often referred to as the Old Deluder Satan Act because education was seen as the best protection against the wiles of the devil.

Mastery learning (p. 328): an approach to instruction based on the assumptions that (1) virtually all students can learn material if given enough time and taught appropriately and (2) learning is enhanced if students can progress in small, sequenced steps.

McGuffey readers (p. 78): an immensely popular series of reading books for students in grades one through six, written in the 1830s by Reverend William Holmes McGuffey.

Measurement (p. 336): the gathering of data that indicate how much students have learned.

Mentor (pp. 53, 386): a wise, knowledgeable individual who provides guidance and encouragement to someone.

Mentoring (p. 53): an intensive form of teaching in which a wise and experienced teacher (the mentor) inducts a student (the protégé) into a professional way of life.

Metaphysics (p. 136): a branch of philosophy concerned with the nature of reality.

Microteaching (p. 46): a brief, single-concept lesson taught by a teacher education student to a small group of students; usually designed to give the education student an opportunity to practice a specific teaching skill.

Minorities (p. 242): groups of people who share certain characteristics and are smaller in number than the majority of a population.

Modeling (p. 331): the process of "thinking out loud" which teachers use to make students aware of the reasoning involved in learning new material.

Modes of teaching (p. 25): different aspects of the teaching function—for example, teaching as a way of being, as a creative endeavor, as a live performance, and so on.

Monitorial system (p. 70): a method of instruction through which a teacher, with the assistance of older students to monitor the learning of younger students, could teach hundreds of students at the same time.

Montesorri Method (p. 84): a method of teaching, developed by Maria Montessori, based on a prescribed set of materials and physical exercises to develop children's knowledge and skills.

Moonlight (p. 10): the practice of holding a second job to increase one's income.

Moral reasoning (p. 277): the reasoning process people follow to decide what is right or wrong.

Morrill Land-Grant Act (p. 79): an 1862 act that provided federal land that states could sell or rent to raise funds to establish colleges of agriculture and mechanical arts.

Multicultural curriculum (p. 261): a school curriculum that addresses the needs and backgrounds of all students regardless of their cultural identity and includes the cultural perspectives, or "voices," of people who have previously been silent or marginalized.

Multicultural education (p. 258): education that provides equal educational opportunities to all students—regardless of socioeconomic status; gender; or ethnic, racial, or cultural backgrounds—and is dedicated to reducing prejudice and celebrating the rich diversity of American life.

Multiculturalism (p. 240): a set of beliefs based on the importance of seeing the world from different cultural frames of reference and valuing the diversity of cultures in the global community.

Multiple intelligences (p. 287): a perspective on intellectual ability, proposed by Howard Gardner suggesting that there are at least seven types of human intelligence.

N

A Nation at Risk **(p. 23):** a 1983 national report critical of American education.

National Assessment of Educational Progress (NAEP) (p. 245): an ongoing, large-scale national testing program to assess the effectiveness of American education.

National Board for Professional Teaching Standards (NBPTS) (p. 40): a board established in 1987 that began issuing professional certificates in 1994–95 to teachers who possess extensive professional knowledge and the ability to perform at a high level.

National Council for Accreditation of Teacher Education (NCATE) (p. 413): an agency that accredits, on a voluntary basis, almost half of the nation's teacher education programs

National curriculum (p. 461): a standardized curriculum set at the national level and delivered to students at all schools throughout the country. Usually, countries with national curricula have nationwide testing to assess students' mastery of the curriculum.

National Defense Education Act (p. 85): a 1958 federally sponsored program to promote research and innovation in science, mathematics, modern foreign languages, and guidance.

National Education Association (NEA) (p. 387): the oldest and largest professional association for teachers and administrators.

National Governor's Association (p. 178): an association of state governors that influences policies in several areas, including teacher education and school reform.

National Information Infrastructure (NII) (p. 466): a federal plan to create a telecommunications infrastructure linking all schools, libraries, hospitals, and law enforcement agencies to the Internet and the World Wide Web.

National Network for Educational Renewal (p. 399): a national network of colleges and universities that collaborate with school districts and partner schools to reform education according to nineteen postulates in John Goodlad's *Teachers for Our Nation's Schools.*

National Teacher Examination (NTE) (p. 416): examination (prepared by Educational Testing Service) that covers communication skills, general knowledge, and professional knowledge; currently required for teacher certification in most states.

Negligence (p. 214): failure to exercise reasonable, prudent care in providing for the safety of others.

Networking (p. 403): the process of using computers to communicate—for example, exchanging information through electronic bulletin boards and electronic mail (e-mail).

Nondiscrimination (p. 203): conditions characterized by the absence of discrimination; for example, employees receive compensation, privileges, and opportunities for advancement without regard for race, color, religion, sex, or national origin.

Normal school (p. 78): schools that focus on the preparation of teachers.

Null curriculum (p. 348): the intellectual processes and subject content that schools do not teach.

O

Observations (p. 45): field experiences wherein a teacher education student observes a specific aspect of classroom life such as the students, the teacher, the interactions between the two, the structure of the lesson, or the setting.

Office of Educational Research and Improvement (OERI) (p. 396): a federal agency that promotes educational research and improving schools through the application of research results.

Open-space schools (p. 109): schools that have large instructional areas with movable walls and furniture that can be rearranged easily.

Opportunity to learn (OTL) (p. 320): the time during which a teacher provides students with challenging content and appropriate instructional strategies to learn that content.

Outcome-based assessment (p. 363): standards for assessing the degree to which teachers have mastered desired outcomes—that is, what they know and are able to do.

Outcome-based education (p. 363): an educational reform that focuses on developing students' ability to demonstrate mastery of certain desired outcomes or performances.

Outcome-based teacher education (p. 39): an approach to teacher education emphasizing outcomes (what teachers should be able to do, think, and feel) rather than the courses they should take.

P

Parochial schools (p. 71): schools founded on religious beliefs.

Peer coaching (p. 435): an arrangement whereby teachers grow professionally by observing one another's teaching and providing constructive feedback.

Peer counseling (p. 122): an arrangement whereby students, monitored by a school counselor or teacher, counsel one another in such areas as low achievement, interpersonal problems, substance abuse, and career planning.

Peer-mediated instruction (p. 333): approaches to teaching, such as cooperative learning and group investigation, that utilize the social relationships among students to promote their learning.

Peer tutoring (p. 333): an arrangement whereby students tutor other students in the same classroom or at the same grade level.

Perennialism (p. 142): a philosophical orientation that emphasizes the ideas contained in the Great Books and maintains that the true purpose of education is the discovery of the universal, or perennial, truths of life.

Performance assessment (p. 336): the process of determining what students can *do* as well as what they know.

Performance-based education (p. 363): an educational reform that focuses on developing students' ability to demonstrate mastery of certain desired performances or outcomes.

Performance-based teacher education (p. 39): an approach to teacher education emphasizing performances (what teachers should be able to do, think, and feel) rather than the courses they should take.

Personal-development view (p. 39): the belief that teachers become more effective by increasing their self-knowledge and developing themselves as persons.

Phi Delta Kappa (p. 389): a professional and honorary fraternity of educators with 650 chapters and 130,000 members.

Placement service (p. 420): a school, government, or commercial service that matches job applicants with job openings and arranges contacts between employers and prospective employees.

Portfolio assessment (p. 336): the process of determining how much students have learned by ex-

School culture (p. 108): the collective "way of life" characteristic of a school; a set of beliefs, values, traditions, and ways of thinking and behaving that distinguish it from other schools.

School restructuring (p. 112): approaches to school improvement that change the way students are grouped for instruction, uses of classroom time and space, instructional methods, and procedures for decision making and governance.

School-to-work programs (p. 373): educational programs, often developed collaboratively by schools and industry, that emphasize the transfer of knowledge and skills learned at school to the job setting.

School traditions (p. 109): those elements of a school's culture that are handed down from year to year.

School-within-a-school (p. 125): an alternative school (within a regular school) designed to meet the needs of students at risk.

Scientific management (p. 80): the application of management principles and techniques to the operation of big business and large school districts.

Search and seizure (p. 223): the process of searching an individual and/or his or her property if that person is suspected of an illegal act; reasonable or probable cause to suspect the individual must be present.

Self-assessment (p. 54): the process of measuring one's growth in regard to the knowledge, skills, and attitudes possessed by professional teachers.

Self-contained classroom (p. 109): an organizational structure for schools in which one teacher instructs a group of students (typically, twenty to thirty) in a single classroom.

Service learning (p. 102): an approach to teaching in which students participate in community-based service activities and then reflect on the meaning of those experiences.

Sexism (p. 265): the belief that one's sex is superior to the other; used to justify discrimination.

Sex-role socialization (p. 265): socially expected behavior patterns conveyed to individuals on the basis of gender.

Sex-role stereotyping (p. 266): beliefs that subtly encourage males and females to conform to certain behavioral norms regardless of abilities and interests.

Sexual harassment (p. 228): unwanted and unwelcome sexual behavior directed toward another person, whether of the same or opposite sex.

Social reconstructionism (p. 146): a philosophical orientation based on the belief that social problems can be solved by changing, or *reconstructing,* society.

Socratic questioning (p. 67): a method of questioning designed to lead students to see errors and inconsistencies in their thinking, based on questioning strategies used by Socrates.

Sophists (p. 67): traveling Greek educators criticized by Socrates for accepting large fees from their students.

Special education (p. 295): a teaching specialty for meeting the special educational needs of exceptional learners.

Stages of development (p. 276): predictable stages through which individuals pass as they progress through life.

State aid (p. 187): money given by a state to its cities and towns to provide essential services, including the operation of public schools.

State board of education (p. 178): the highest educational agency in a state, charged with regulating the state's system of education.

State department of education (p. 179): the branch of state government, headed by the chief state school officer, charged with implementing the state's educational policies.

Stereotyping (p. 246): the process of attributing behavioral characteristics to all members of a group; formulated on the basis of limited experiences with and information about the group, coupled with an unwillingness to examine prejudices.

Student-centered curriculum (p. 352): curricula that are organized around students' needs and interests.

Student diversity (p. 6): differences among students in regard to gender, race, ethnicity, culture, and socioeconomic status.

Student-mobility rates (p. 12): the proportion of students within a school or district who move during an academic year.

Student variability (p. 6): differences among students in regard to their developmental needs, interests, abilities, and disabilities.

Students at risk (p. 113): students whose living conditions and backgrounds place them at risk for dropping out of school.

Students with disabilities (p. 290): students who need special education services because they possess one or more of the following disabilities: learning disabilities, speech or language impairments, mental retardation, serious emotional disturbance, hearing impairments, orthopedic impairments, visual impairments, or other health impairments.

Subject-centered curriculum (p. 352): a curriculum that emphasizes learning an academic discipline.

Substitute teaching (p. 50): Temporary teachers who replace regular teachers absent due to illness, family responsibilities, personal reasons, or professional workshops and conferences.

Successful schools (p. 111): schools characterized by a high degree of student learning, results that surpass those expected from comparable schools, and steady improvement rather than decline.

Summative evaluation (p. 336): an assessment of student learning made for the purpose of assigning grades at the end of a unit, semester, or year and deciding whether students are ready to proceed to the next phase of their education.

Superintendent (p. 172): the chief administrator of a school district.

Synectics (p. 446): a method for "teaching" creativity through the use of metaphors and analogies.

T

Teach for America (p. 8): a program that enables recent college graduates without a teaching certificate to teach in districts with critical shortages of teachers and, after taking professional development courses and supervision by state and school authorities, earn a teaching certificate.

Teacher accountability (p. 25): society's expectations that teachers will adhere to high professional and moral standards and create effective learning environments for all students.

Teacher centers (p. 55): centers where teachers provide other teachers with instructional materials and new methods and where teachers can exchange ideas.

Teacher empowerment (p. 398): the trend to grant teachers greater power and more opportunities to make decisions that affect their professional lives.

Teacher-leader (p. 392): a teacher who assumes a key leadership role in the improvement and/or day-to-day operation of a school.

Teacher-researcher (p. 394): a teacher who regularly conducts classroom research to improve his or her teaching.

Teacher-student ratios (p. 12): a ratio that expresses the number of students taught by a teacher.

Teacher supply and demand (p. 417): the number of school-age students compared to the number of available teachers; may also be projected based on estimated numbers of students and teachers.

Teachers' thought processes (p. 22): the thoughts that guide teachers' actions in classrooms. These thoughts typically consist of thoughts related to planning, theories and beliefs, and interactive thoughts and decisions.

Teaching certificate (p. 412): a license to teach issued by a state or, in a few cases, a large city.

Teaching contract (p. 204): an agreement between a teacher and a board of education that the teacher will provide specific services in return for a certain salary, benefits, and privileges.

Teaching simulations (p. 46): an activity in which teacher education students participate in role-plays designed to create situations comparable to those actually encountered by teachers.

Team teaching (p. 435): an arrangement whereby a team of teachers teaches a group of students equal in number to what the teachers would have in their self-contained classrooms.

Tenure (pp. 10, 204): an employment policy in which teachers, after serving a probationary period, retain their positions indefinitely and can be dismissed only on legally defensible grounds.

Time on task (p. 320): the amount of time students are actively and directly engaged in learning tasks.

Title IX (p. 89): a provision of the 1972 Education Amendments Act prohibiting sex discrimination in educational programs.

Tort liability (p. 212): conditions that would permit the filing of legal charges against a professional for breach of duty and/or behaving in a negligent manner.

Tyler rationale (p. 351): a four-step model for curriculum development in which teachers identify purposes, select learning experiences, organize experiences, and evaluate.

V

Vertical equity (p. 190): an effort to provide equal educational opportunity within a state by providing different levels of funding based on economic needs within school districts.

Videodisc (p. 403): a twelve-inch plastic disc, each side of which holds about thirty minutes of motion video, or 54,000 frames of video; each frame can be frozen with a high degree of clarity.

Vocational education (p. 373): schooling that prepares students for particular jobs or provides them with the basic skills and career awareness needed to enter the world of work.

Voucher system (p. 192): funds allocated to parents that they may use to purchase education for their children from public or private schools in the area.

W

Whole-language approach (p. 364): the practice of teaching language skills (listening, reading, and writing) as part of students' everyday experiences rather than as isolated experiences.

Within-class ability grouping (p. 317): the practice of creating small, homogeneous groups of students within a single classroom for the purpose of instruction, usually in reading or mathematics, at the elementary level.

Women's Educational Equity Act (WEEA) (p. 266): a 1974 federal law that guarantees equal educational opportunity for females.

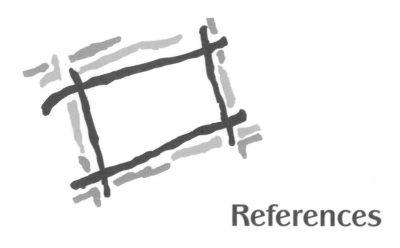

References

Abrahamsson, B. (1971). *Military professionalization and political power.* Stockholm: Allmanna Forlagret.

*Abrams, G. (1993, February 15). Teaching kids to think for themselves. *Los Angeles Times.*

*Acheson, A. A., and Gall, M. D. (1992). *Techniques in the clinical supervision of teachers, 3d ed.* New York: Longman.

Acton v. Vernonia School District, 66 F.3d 217 (9th Cir. 1995); 115 S. Ct. 2386 (1995).

*Adler, M. (1981). *Six great ideas.* New York: Macmillan.

Aiken, W. M. (1942). *The story of the Eight-Year Study.* New York: Harper and Row.

Alali, A. A. (Ed.). (1995). *HIV and AIDs in the public schools: A handbook for curriculum development, teacher education, and the placement of affected students, with a directory of resources.* Jefferson, NC: McFarland.

*Alan Guttmacher Institute. (1994). *Sex and America's teenagers.* New York: Alan Guttmacher Institute.

Alfonso v. Fernandez, 606 N. Y. S.2d 259 (N. Y. App. Div. 1993).

Alvin Independent School District v. Cooper, 404 S. W.2d 76 (Tex. Civ. App. 1966).

American Association of University Women (AAUW). (1992). *How schools shortchange girls: The AAUW report.* (Researched by The Wellesley College Center for Research on Women.). Washington, D.C.: The AAUW Educational Foundation.

American Association of University Women. (1993). *Hostile hallways: The AAUW survey on sexual harassment in America's schools.* New York: Louis Harris and Associates.

*American Council on the Teaching of Foreign Languages. (1996). *Standards for foreign language learning: Preparing for the 21st century.* Lawrence, KS: American Council on the Teaching of Foreign Languages.

American Federation of Teachers (1993). *Research report: Survey and analysis of salary trends, 1993.* Washington, DC: American Federation of Teachers.

American Federation of Teachers, National Council on Measurement in Education, and National Education Association. (1990). *Standards for teacher competence in educational assessment of students,* ERIC document No. ED323 186.

*Anderson, J. (1994, August). Who's in charge? Teachers' views on control over school policy and classroom practices. *Research Report*. Washington, DC: U.S. Department of Education, Office of Educational Research and Improvement.

Andrews, S., Sherman, R., and Webb, R. (Winter 1983). Teaching: The isolated profession. *Journal of Thought*.

*Andrews, T. (ed.) (1994). *NASDTEC Manual on Certification and Preparation of Educational Personnel in the United States, Second Edition, 1994–95,* National Association of State Directors of Teacher Education and Certification, Dubuque, IA: Kendall/Hunt Publishing Company

*Anyon, J. (1996). Social class and the hidden curriculum of work. In E. Hollins (Ed.). *Transforming curriculum for a culturally diverse society.* Mahwah, NJ: Lawrence Erlbaum, 179–203.

*Applegate, J. R., and Andrews, T. (1991). The preparation of educational personnel in the 1990s. *Action in Teacher Education, 12*(4).

Application of *Bay v. State Board of Education, 233* Ore. 609, 378 P.2d 558 (1963).

Aring, M. K. (1993, January). What the "V" word is costing America's economy. *Phi Delta Kappan.*

Aristotle. (1941). *Politics* (Book VIII). In Richard McKoen (Ed.). *The basic works of Aristotle.* New York: Random House.

Aronson, E., and Gonzalez, A. (1988). Desegregation, jigsaw, and the Mexican-American experience. In P. A. Katz, and D. A. Taylor (Eds.). *Eliminating racism: Profiles in controversy.* New York: Plenum Press.

*Ashton-Warner, S. (1965). *Teacher.* New York: Simon & Schuster.

*Astuto, T. (ed.). (1993). *When teachers lead.* University Park, PA: University Council for Educational Administration.

Ayers, W. (1989). *The good preschool teacher: Six teachers reflect on their lives.* New York: Teachers College Press.

*B. M. v. Montana, 649 P.2d 425 (Mont. 1982).

Bagley, W. C. (1934). *Education and emergent man.* New York: Ronald Press.

*Baker, K. A. (1991). *Bilingual Education.* Bloomington, IN: Phi Delta Kappa.

*Ballantine, J. H. (1993). *The sociology of education: A systematic analysis.* Englewood Cliffs, NJ: Prentice Hall.

Bandura, A. (1977). *Social learning theory.* Englewood Cliffs, NJ: Prentice Hall, 12.

Banks, J. A. (1994). *An introduction to multicultural education.* Boston: Allyn and Bacon.

Banks, J. A. (1994). *Multiethnic education: Theory and practice, 3d ed.* Boston: Allyn and Bacon.

*Banks, J. A. (1997). *Teaching strategies for ethnic studies,* 6th ed. Boston, Allyn and Bacon.

Banks, J. A. (Ed.) (1996). Multicultural education, transformative knowledge, and action: Historical and contemporary perspectives. New York: Teachers College Press.

*Banks, J. A., and Banks, C. A. (Eds.). (1997). *Multicultural education: Issues and perspectives,* 3rd ed. Boston: Allyn and Bacon.

*Barker, E. (1980). *The politics of Aristotle.* London: Oxford University Press.

*Barrow, R. (1976). *Plato and education.* London: Routledge & Kegan Paul.

Barth, J. (1987). "Teacher." In L. Rubin (Ed.), *An apple for my teacher.* Chapel Hill, NC: Algonquin Books.

Barth, R. (1990). *Improving schools from within: Teachers, parents, and principals can make the difference.* San Francisco: Jossey-Bass Publishers

Bassuk, E. L. (December 1991). Homeless families. *Scientific American.*

Beard, C. (1938). *The nature of the social sciences.* New York: Charles Scribner.

Bell, T. H. (1986, March). Education policy development in the Reagan administration. *Phi Delta Kappan.*

*Bennett, C. I. (1995). *Comprehensive multicultural education: Theory and practice,* 3d ed. Boston: Allyn and Bacon.

*Bennett, C. K. (1993, October). Teacher-researchers: All dressed up and no place to go. *Educational Leadership.*

*Berliner, D. C., and Biddle, B. J. (1995). *The manufactured crisis: Myths, fraud, and the attack on America's public schools.* Reading, MA: Addison-Wesley Publishing Company.

Bertocci, P. A. (1956). Unless educators be philosophers, and philosophers be educators. . . . *Harvard Educational Review, 26.*

*Besner, H. F., and Spungin, C. I. (1995). *Gay and lesbian students: Understanding their needs.* Washington, DC: Taylor & Francis.

*Bloom, B. S. (1981). *All our children learning: A primer for parents, teachers, and other educators.* New York: McGraw-Hill, Inc.

*Board of Education, Sacramento City Unified School District v. Holland, 786 F. Supp. 874 (ED Cal. 1992).

*Boleman, L. G., and Deal, T. E. (1994). *Becoming a teacher leader: From isolation to collaboration.* Thousand Oaks, CA: Corwin Press.

*Booth, A., and Dunn, J. F. (eds.). (1996). *Family-school links: How do they affect educational outcomes?* Mahwah, NJ: Lawrence Erlbaum Associates, Publishers.

*Borich, G. D. (1996). *Effective teaching methods,* 3d ed. Englewood Cliffs, NJ: Merrill.

Boyer, E. (1989). New fuel for school reform, in K. Sidey, (Ed.), *The blackboard fumble.* Wheaton, IL: Victor Books.

*Boyer, E. (1990). Teaching in America. In M. Kysilka (Ed.). *Honor in Teaching: Reflections.* West Lafayette, ID: Kappa Delta Pi.

Boyer, E. (1995a). *The basic school: A community for learning.* Princeton, NJ: The Carnegie Foundation for the Advancement of Teaching.

Boyer, E. (1995b, September). Common sense wins out in school reform. *Instructor.*

Boyer, E. L. (1983). *High school: A report on secondary education in America.* New York: Harper

*Bracey, G. W. (1996, October). The sixth Bracey report on the condition of public education. *Phi Delta Kappan.*

Bracy, G. W. (1993). Now then, Mr. Kohlberg, about moral development in women . . . " In Hass, G., and Parkay, F. W. (eds.). *Curriculum planning: A new approach,* 6th ed. Boston: Allyn and Bacon.

Brameld, T. (1956). *Toward a reconstructed philosophy of education.* New York: Holt, Rinehart and Winston.

Brameld, T. (1959). Imperatives for a reconstructed philosophy of education. *School and Society, 87.*

*Brandt, R. (1986, February). On improving achievement of minority children: A conversation with James Comer. *Educational Leadership.*

Brillingsley, K. L. (Ed.). (1994). Voices on choice: The education reform debate. San Francisco: Pacific Research Institute for Public Policy.

Brooks, V. W. (1956). *Helen Keller: Sketch for a portrait.* New York: E. P. Dutton.

Brophy, J., and Good, Thomas L. (1986). Teacher behavior and student achievement. In Wittrick, M. C. (ed.). *Handbook of research on teaching,* 3d ed. New York: Macmillan.

Broudy, H. S. (1979). Arts education: Necessary or just nice? *Phi Delta Kappan, 60.*

Brown v. Board of Education of Topeka, Kansas, 347, U.S. 483, 74 S. Ct. 686 (1954); *Brown v. Board of Education of Topeka, Kansas,* 349, U.S. 294, 75 S. Ct. 753 (1955).

Brown v. Hot, Sexy and Safer Productions, Inc., 68 F.3d 525 (1st Cir. 1995), cert. denied, 116 S. Ct. 1044 (1996).

*Brown, F. B., Kohrs, D., and Lanzarro, C. (1991). The academic costs and consequences of extracurricular participation in high school. Paper presented at the Annual Meeting of Educational Research Association.

*Brown, M. E. (1994). Computer simulation: Improving case study methods for preservice and inservice teacher education. ERIC Document Reproduction Services No. ED371 730.

Bruner, J. S. (1960). *The process of education.* New York: Random House.

*Bryk, A. S., Deabster, P. E., Easton, J. Q., Lupescu, S., and Thum, Y. M. (1994, May). Measuring achievement gains in the Chicago Public Schools. *Education and Urban Society.*

Bullough, R. V. (1989). *First-year teacher: A case study.* New York: Teachers College Press.

Burch v. Barker, 651 F. Supp. 1149 (W. D. Wash. 1987) & *Burch v. Barker,* 861 F. 2d 1149 (9th Cir. 1988).

*Bureau of Census. (1975). *Historical statistics of the U.S., colonial times to 1970, bicentennial edition.* Washington, DC: U.S. Department of Commerce.

Bureau of Census. (1982–83). *Statistical abstract of the United States.* Washington, DC: U.S. Department of Commerce.

*Burnaford, G., Fischer, J., and Hobson, D. (1996). *Teachers doing research: Practical possibilities.* Mahwah, NJ: Lawrence Erlbaum Associates, Publishers.

Burton v. Cascade School Dist. Union High School No. 5, 512 F.2d 850 (9th Cir. 1975).

Business Week, (1992 September 14). How Americans Grade the School System.

Button, H. W., and Provenzo, E. G. (1983). *History of education and culture in America.* Englewood Cliffs, NJ: Prentice Hall.

Butts, R. F., and Cremin, L. A. (1953). *A history of education in American culture.* New York: Holt, Rinehart and Winston.

*Buzzell, J. B. (1996). *School and family partnerships: Case studies for regular and special educators.* Albany, NY: Delmar Publishers.

*Calhoun, E. F. (1992, April). A status report on action research in the League of Professional Schools. Paper presented at the Annual Meeting

of the American Educational Research Association, San Francisco.

*Campbell, D. M., Cignetti, P. B., Molenyzer, B. J., Nettles, D. H., and Wyman, Jr., W. M. (1996). *How to develop a professional portfolio: A manual for teachers.* Boston: Allyn and Bacon.

Canfield, J. (1970). White teacher, black school. In K. Ryan (Ed.), *Don't simile until Christman: Accounts of the first year of teaching.* Chicago: University of Chicago Press.

Cantor, L. (1989). Assertive discipline—more than names on the board and marbles in a jar. *Phi Delta Kappan, 71,*(1).

Carmichael, L. B. (1981). *McDonogh 15: The making of a school.* New York: Avon Books.

Carnegie Council on Academic Development. (1995). *Great transitions: Preparing adolescents for a new century.* Carnegie Council on Academic Development.

*Carroll, J. (1963). A model of school learning. *Teachers College Record, 64.*

*Castle, E. B. (1967). *Ancient education and today.* Baltimore, MD: Penguin Books.

Catford, L. (1994). Portrait of a ceramics class: Control and freedom in a delicate balance. In Elliot W. Eisner, *The educational imagination: On the design and evaluation of school programs,* 3d ed. New York: Macmillan.

*Center for Research on Effective Schooling for Disadvantaged Students. (1992). Helping students who fall behind, report no 22. Baltimore, MD: The Johns Hopkins University.

Center on Organization and Restructuring of Schools. (Fall 1992). *Brief to Policymakers.* Madison: University of Wisconsin.

*Chaskin, R. J., and Rauner, D. M. (1995, May). Youth and caring: An introduction. *Phi Delta Kappan.*

*Cheeks, E. H., Flippo, R. F., and Lindsey, J. D. (1997). *Reading for success in elementary schools.* Madison, WI: Brown & Benchmark.

*Chubb, J. E., and Moe, T. (1990). *Politics, markets and America's schools.* Washington, DC: Brookings Institution.

Clinton, B. (1992, October). The Clinton plan for excellence in education. *Phi Delta Kappan.*

*Cohen, D. (1990, March 14). Hawaii program for after-school care irks private firms. *Education Week.*

Cohen, S. (ed.) (1974). *Massachusetts School Law of 1648. Education in the United States.* New York: Random House.

Cohn, M. M., and Kottkamp, R. B. (1993). *Teachers: The missing voice in education.* Albany: State University of New York Press.

Coleman, J. S., Campbell, E. Q., Hobson, C. J., McPartland, J., Mood, A. L., Weinfeld, F. D., and York, R. L. (1966). *Equality of educational opportunity.* Washington, DC: U.S. Government Printing Office.

Combs, A. (1979). *Myths in education: Beliefs that hinder progress and their alternatives.* Boston: Allyn and Bacon.

*Comer, J. (1986, February). Parent participation in the schools. *Phi Delta Kappan.*

*Comer, J. (1988, November). Educating poor minority children. *Scientific American.*

Comer, J. (1989). Children can! In R. B. Webb and F. W. Parkay (Eds.). *Children can: An address on school improvement.* Gainesville, FL: Research and Development Center on School Improvement, University of Florida.

Comfield v. Consolidated High School District No. 230, 991 F.2d 1316 (7th Cir. 1993).

Commager, H. S. (October 18, 1958). Noah Webster, 1758–1958. *Saturday Review, 41.*

Compayre, G. (1888). *History of pedagogy,* translated by W. H. Payne. Boston: Heath.

*Cornbleth, C. (1990). *Curriculum in context.* London: The Falmer Press.

Costa, A. L. (1984). A reaction to Hunter's knowing, teaching, and supervising. In P. L. Hosford (Ed.), *Using what we know about teaching.* Alexandria, VA: Association for Supervision and Curriculum Development.

Coughlin, E. K. (1993, March 24). Sociologists examine the complexities of racial and ethnic identity in America. *Chronical of Higher Education.*

*Council of Chief State School Officers. (1996). *Directory of Chief State School Officers 1996.* Washington, DC: Council of Chief State School Officers.

Counts, G. (1932). *Dare the school build a new social order?* New York: The John Day Co.

Cremin, L. A. (1961). *The transformation of the school: Progressivism in American education, 1876–1957.* New York: D. Appleton-Century.

*Csikszentmihalyi, M., and McCormack, J. (1986, February). The influence of teachers. *Phi Delta Kappan.*

Cuban, L. (1985, September). Conflict and leadership in the superintendency. *Phi Delta Kappan.*

Curtis v. School Committee of Falmouth, 116 S. Ct. 753 (1996).

*Curwin, R., and Mendler, A. (1988). Packaged discipline programs: Let the buyer beware. *Educational Leadership, 46*(2).

*Cziko, G. A. (1992, March). The evaluation of bilingual education: From necessity and probability to possibility. *Educational Researcher.*

Daniels, C. B. (1984). Quality of educational materials: A marketing perspective. In Parkay, F. W., Obrien, S., and Hennesey, M. (eds). *Quest for quality: Improving basic skills instruction in the 1980s.* Lanham, MD: University Press of America.

*Danzberger, J. P. (1994a, January). Governing the nation's schools: The case for restructuring local school boards. *Phi Delta Kappan.*

*Danzberger, J. P. (1994b, January). School board reform in West Virginia. *Phi Delta Kappan.*

Daurio, S. P. (1979). Educational enrichment versus acceleration: A review of the literature. In George, W. C., Cohn, S. J., and Stanley, J. C. (eds.). *Educating the gifted: Acceleration and enrichment.* Baltimore, MD: Johns Hopkins University Press.

David Hill. "Rising Star," *Teacher Magazine* (March 1993).

Davis v. Meek, 344 F. Supp. 298 N.D. Ohio (1972).

Dehyle, K. S., and Deyhle, D. (1978). Styles of learning and learning styles: Educational conflicts for American Indian/Alaskan Native youth. *Journal of Multilingual and Multicultural Development, 8.*

Dertouzon, M. L., Lester, R. K., and Solow, R. M. (1989). *Made in America: Regaining the productive edge.* Bambridge, MA: M.I.T. Press.

Dewey, J. (1902). *The school and society.* Chicago, IL: University of Chicago Press.

Dewey, J. (1916). *Democracy and education: An Introduction to the philosophy of education.* New York: Macmillan.

*Dewey, J. (1955). Quoted in *Organizing the teaching profession: The story of the American Federation of Teachers.* Glencoe, IL: The Commission on Educational Reconstruction.

Doe v. Renfrow, 635F.2d 582 (7th Cir. 1980), cert denied, 451 U.S. 1022, rehearing denied, 101 S. Ct. 3015 (1981).

*Dollase, R. H. (1992). *Voices of beginning teachers: Visions and realities.* New York: Teachers College Press.

Doyle, W. (1986). Classroom organization and management. In M. Wittrock (Ed.), *Handbook of research on teaching, 3d.* New York: Macmillan.

*Dryfoos, (1990). *Adolescents at risk: Prevalence and prevention.* New York: Oxford University Press.

*Dryfoos, (1994). *Full-service schools: A revolution in health and social services for children, youth, and families.* San Francisco: Jessy-Bass.

*Duffy, G., and Roehler, L. (1989). The tension between information-giving and mediation: Perspectives on instructional explanation and teacher change. In J. Brophy (ed.), *Advances in research on teaching,* Vol. 1. Greenwich, CT: JAI Press, Inc.

Duke, D. L. (1984). *Teaching—the imperiled profession.* Albany: State University of New York Press.

Duke, D. L. (1988, February), The Getty Center for Education in the Arts: A progress report. *Phi Delta Kappan.*

*Durlak, J. A. (1995). *School-based prevention programs for children and adolescents.* Thousand Oaks, CA: Sage Publications.

Dwyer, C. A., and Villegas, A. M. (1992). *Foundations for tomorrow's teachers—No. 3, Defining teaching.* Princeton, NJ: Educational Testing Service.

ERIC Clearinghouse. (1993). *Value search: Parent involvement in the educational process.* Eugene, OR: ERIC Clearinghouse on Educational Management.

Edelman, M. W. (1990). Children at risk. *Proceedings of the Academy of Political Science, 27*(2), 20–30.

Edelman, M. W. (1993). *The measure of our success: A letter to my children.* New York: Harper Perennial.

*Education Commission of the States. (1992). *New strategies for producing minority teachers.* Denver: Education Commission of the State.

*Education Week (1996, January 10). Studies seek to adjust for pay variables."

*Education Week. (1996, April 24). "Virginia. Governor Victorious in Rejecting Goals 2000."

*Education Week. (1996, September 4). Board certifies 108 teachers, 4.

*Educational Testing Service. (1993). *The national education goals report, vol. 1: The national report, 1993.* Washington, DC: U.S. Government Printing Office.

Educational Testing Service. (1995, spring). Bringing volunteers into teacher education programs. *ETS Policy Notes,* 8–9.

Edwards v. Aguillard, 482 U.S. 578(1987).

*Edwards, P., and Young L. (1992). Beyond parents: family, community, and school involvement. *Phi Delta Kappan, 74*(1).

*Eisner, E. (1994). *The educational imagination: On the design and evaluation of school programs,* 3d ed. New York: Macmillan.

Elam, S. M., Rose, L. C., and Gallup, A. M. (1992, September). The 24th annual Phi Delta Kappa Gallup Poll of the public's attitudes toward the public schools. *Phi Delta Kappan.*

Elam, S. M., Rose, L. C., and Gallup, A. (October 1993). The 25th annual Phi Delta Kappa Gallup Poll of the public's attitudes toward the public schools. *Phi Delta Kappan.*

*Elam, S. M., Rose, L. C., and Gallup, A. M. (September 1995). The 27th annual Gallup poll of the public's attitudes toward the public schools. *Phi Delta Kappan.*

*Elam, S. M., Rose, L. C., and Gallup, A. M. (September, 1996). The 28th annual Phi Delta Kappa/Gallup poll of the public's attitudes toward the public schools, 41–59.

Emmer, E. T., Evertson, C. M., Clements, R. S., and Worsham, M. E, (1997a). *Classroom management for secondary teachers,* 4th ed. Boston: Allyn and Bacon.

**Engel v. Vitale,* 370 U.S. 421 (1962).

*Epstein, J. (January 1991). Paths to partnership. *Phi Delta Kappan, 72*(5).

*Epstein, J. L. (1992). School and family partnerships. *Encyclopedia of educational research,* 6th ed. Alkin, M. C. (ed.). New York: Macmillan.

Erikson, E. (1963). *Childhood and society.* New York: W. W. Norton.

Etzioni, A. (1969). *The semi-professions and their organization: Teachers, nurses, social workers.* New York: Free Press.

Evertson, C. M., Emmer, E. T., Clements, R. S., and Worsham, M. E. (1997b). *Classroom management for elementary teachers,* 4th ed. Boston: Allyn and Bacon.

FASE Video, "Good Morning, Miss Toliver," September 1993.

**Fagen v. Summers,* 498 P.2d 1227 (Wyo. 1972).

Farrell, E. *Hanging in and dropping out: Voices of at-risk high school students.* New York: Teachers College Press.

*Feinberg, W. (1995). The discourse of philosophy of education. In Wendy Kohli (Ed.). *Critical Conversations in Philosophy of Education.* New York: Routledge.

Feistritzer, E., and Chester, D. (1993). *Alternative teacher certification: A state-by-state analysis, 1992–93.* Washington, DC: National Center for Education Information.

Felsenthal H. (1982, March). Factors influencing school effectiveness: An ecological analysis of an "effective" school. Paper presented at the Annual Meeting of the American Educational Research Association, New York.

*Fischer, J. C. (1996). Open to ideas: Developing a framework for your research. In Burnaford, G., Fischer, J., and Hobson, D. (1996). *Teachers doing research: Practical possibilities.* Mahwah, NJ: Lawrence Erlbaum Associates, Publishers.

Fischer, L., and Sorenson, G. P. (1996). *School law for counselors, psychologists, and social workers, 3rd ed.* White Plains, NY: Longman.

Fisher, C., Filby, N., Marliave, R., Cahan, L., Dishaw, M., Moore, J., and Berliner, D. (1978). *Teaching behaviors, academic learning time, and student achievement.* Final report of Phase III-B Beginning Teacher Evaluation Study. San Francisco: Far West Laboratory for Educational Research and Development.

*Flaxman, E., and Inger, M. (1991). Parents and schooling in the 1990s. *The Eric Review, 1*(3).

Franklin v. Gwinnett County Public Schools, 112 S. Ct. 1028 (1992).

Franklin, B. (1993). Proposals relating to the education of youth in Pennsylvania, in Thomas Woody (Ed.), *Educational views of Benjamin Franklin.* New York: McGraw-Hill.

Freedman, S., Jackson, J., and Botes, K. (1983). Teaching: An imperiled profession. In Shulman, L., and Sykes, G. (eds.). (1983). *Handbook of teaching and policy.* New York: Longman.

*Freire, P. (1970). Pedagogy of the oppressed. (M. B. Ramos, Trans.). New York: Herder & Herder.

Friedman, J. (with B. Shaw). (1988, May 30). The quiet victories of Ryan White. *People Magazine.*

*Friend, M., and Bursuck, W. D. (1996). *Including students with special needs: A practical guide for classroom teachers.* Boston: Allyn and Bacon.

*Friend, M., and Cook, L. (1993, November/December). Inclusion: What it takes to make it work, why it sometimes fails, and how teachers really feel about it. *Instructor.*

*Frymier, J. (December 1988). Understanding and preventing teen suicide: An interview with Barry Garfinkel. *Phi Delta Kappan.*

*Fuligni, A. J., and Stevenson, H. W. (1995). Home environment and school learning. In Lorin W. Anderson (Ed.), *International encyclopedia of teaching and teacher education,* 2E Oxford: Pergamon, 378–382.

Gage, N. L. (1978). *The scientific basis of the art of teaching.* New York: Teachers College Press.

*Gallagher, J. J., and Gallagher, S. S. (1994). *Teaching the gifted child,* 4th ed. Boston: Allyn and Bacon.

Gallup. G. H. (September 1975). The 11th annual Gallup poll of the public's attitudes toward the public schools. *Phi Delta Kappan.*

*Gandara, P., and Fish, J. (Spring 1994). Year-round schooling as an avenue to major structural reform. *Educational Evaluation and Policy Analysis, 16.*

Gardner, H. (1983). *Frames of mind.* New York: Basic Books.

*Gardner, H. (1995, November). Reflections on multiple intelligences: Myths and messages. *Phi Delta Kappan.*

Gaylord v. Tacoma School District No. 10, 88 Wa. 2d 286, 599 P.2d 1340 (1977).

Gehrke, N. (Summer 1988). Toward a definition of mentoring. *Theory Into Practice.*

*George, P. (1995). *The Japanese secondary school: A Closer look.* Columbus, OH: National Middle School Association; and Reston, VA: National Association of Secondary School Principals.

*Gerard, D. E., and Hussar, W. J. (1991). *Projections of education statistics to 2002.* Washington, DC: National Center for Education Statistics.

*Gerstner, L. V., Semerad, R. D., Doyle, D. P., and Johnston, W. B. (1994). *Reinventing education: Entrepreneurship in America's public schools.* New York: Dutton.

Gilligan, C. (1982). *In a different voice: Psychological theory and women's development.* Cambridge, MA: Harvard University Press.

Gipp, G. (1979, August-September). Help for Dana Fast Horse and friends. *American Education, 15.*

Glasser, W. R. (1969). *Schools without failure.* New York: Harper and Row.

Glasser, W. R. (1975). *Reality therapy: A new approach to psychiatry.* New York: Harper and Row.

*Glasser, W. R. (1986). *Control theory in the classroom.* New York: Harper and Row.

*Glasser, W. R. (1990). *The quality school: Managing students without coercion.* New York: Perennial Library.

*Glasser, W. R. (1993). *The quality school teacher.* New York: Harper Perennial.

*Glickman, C. (1995). *Supervision of instruction: A developmental approach.* Boston: Allyn and Bacon.

*Gmelch, W. H., and Parkay, F. W. (1995). Changing roles and occupational stress in the teaching profession. In O'Hair, M. J., and Odell, S. J. *Educating teachers for leadership and change: Teacher*

education yearbook III. Thousand Oaks, CA: Corwin Press, Inc.

Godar, J. (1990). *Teachers talk.* Macomb, IL: Glenbridge Publishing.

Goldberg, C. N. (Fall 1989). Parents' effects on academic grouping for reading: Three case studies. *American Education Research Journal.*

Goldberg, M. F. (1995, February). "A Portrait of Ernest Boyer," *Educational Leadership,* LII.

*Goldhammer, R., Anderson, R. H., and Krajewski, R. J. (1993). *Clinical supervision: Special methods for the supervision of teachers, 3d ed.* Fort Worth: Harcourt Brace Jovanovich.

*Good, T. E., and Brophy, J. E. (1994). Looking in classrooms, 6th ed. New York: Harper Collins.

Goodlad, J. (1990). *Teachers for our nation's schools.* San Francisco: Jossey-Bass Publishers.

*Goodlad, J. (1994). Educational renewal: Better teachers, better schools. San Francisco: Jossey-Bass.

Goodlad, J. (Spring 1983). Teaching: An endangered profession. *Teachers College Record,* 575–578.

Goodlad, J. I. (1983, April). What some schools and classrooms teach. *Educational Leadership.*

Goodlad, J. I. (1984). *A place called school.* New York: Macmillan.

Gordon, D. (September 1993). Materials for FASE video "Good Morning, Miss Toliver." Washington, DC: Foundation for Advancements in Science and Education (FASE) Outreach.

Gordon, W. J. J. (1968). *Making it strange.* (Books 1 & 2). Evanston, IL: Harper & Row.

*Gordon, W. J. J. (1971a). *What color is sleep?* Cambridge, MA: Porpoise Books.

*Gordon, W. J. J. (1971b). *Invent-o-rama.* Cambridge, MA: Porpoise Books.

*Gordon, W. J. J. (1975). *Strange and familiar.* (Book 1). Cambrdige, MA: Porpoise Books.

Goss v. Lopez, 419 U.S. 565 (1975).

*Grant, C. A. (Winter 1994). Challenging the myths about multicultural education. *Multicultural Education.*

Grant, C. A., and Gomez, M. L. (1996). Making schooling multicultural: Campus and classroom. Englewood Cliffs, NJ: Prentice Hall.

Grant, G. (1988). *The world we created at Hamilton High.* Cambridge, MA: Harvard University Press.

*Grant, P. G., Richard, K. J., and Parkay, F. W. (1006. April). *Using video cases to promote reflection among preservice teachers: A qualitative inquiry.* Paper presented at the Annual Meeting of the

American Educational Research Association, New York.

*Greene, M. (1995). What counts as philosophy of education? In Wendy Kohli (Ed.). *Critical conversations in philosophy of education.* New York: Routledge.

*Griego-Jones, T. (1996). Reconstructing bilingual education from a multicultural perspective. In C. A. Grant, and M. L. Gomez, *Making schooling multicultural: Campus and classroom.* Englewood Cliffs, NJ: Merrill.

*Gutek, G. L. (1986). *Education in the United States: An historical perspective.* Englewood Cliffs, NJ: Prentice Hall.

*Haberman, M. (1995, June). Selecting "star" teachers for children and youth in urban poverty. *Phi Delta Kappan.*

Hallahan, D. P., and Kauffman, J. M. (1994). *Exceptional children: Introduction to special education,* 6th ed. Boston: Allyn and Bacon.

*Hansen, D. T. (1995). *The call to teach.* New York: Teachers College Press.

*Hargreaves, A. (1994). *Changing teachers, changing times: Teachers' work and culture in the postmodern age.* New York: Teachers College Press.

Harvard Education Letter. (1986, July). Researchers look at teachers' thinking. Vol. II, No. 4.

Harvard Education Letter. (1987, March). Some third graders are passing because I work with them. Vol. III, No. 2.

*Hass, G., and Parkay, F. W. (eds.) (1993). *Curriculum planning: A new approach,* 6th ed. Boston: Allyn and Bacon.

Hazelwood School District v. Kuhlmeier, 56 U.S.L.W. 4079, 4082 (1988); 484 U.S. 260, 108 S. Ct. 562 (1988).

Hedges, L. V. (1996). Quoted in: Hedges finds boys and girls both disadvantaged in school. *Education News,* The Department of Education, The University of Chicago.

Heinich, R., Molenda, M., and Russell, J. D. (1993). *Instructional media and the new technologies of instruction,* 4th ed. New York: Macmillan.

*Henry, E, Huntley, J., McKamey, C., and Harper, L. (1995). *To be a teacher: Voices from the classroom.* Thousand Oaks, CA: Corwin Press, Inc.

*Henry, M. (1993). *School cultures: Universes of meaning in private schools.* Norwood, NJ: Ablex Publishing Corporation.

*Henry, M. E. (1996). *Parent-school collaboration: Feminist organizational structures and school

leadership.* Albany, NY: State University of New York Press.

*Hirschfelder, A. B. (1986). Happily may I walk: American Indians and Alaska Natives today. New York: Charles Scribner.

*Herbert, B. (1993, June 27). Listen to the children. *New York Times, OP-ED.*

Hess, G. A., Jr. (1995). Restructuring urban schools: A Chicago perspective. New York: Teachers College Press.

Hewlett, S. A. (1991). *When the bough breaks: The cost of neglecting our children.* New York: Basic Books.

Hill, D. (March 1993). Rising star. *Teacher Magazine.*

Hodgkinson, H. L. (1986, January). What's ahead for education? *Principal.*

Hodgkinson, H. L. (1992, June). *A demographic look at tomorrow.* Washington, DC: Institute for Educational Leadership/Center for Demographic Policy.

*Holland, A., and Andre, T. (Winter 1987). Participation in extracurricular activities in secondary schools. *Review of Educational Research.*

*Holly, M. L., and McLoughlin, C. (eds.). (1989). *Perspectives on teacher professional development.* New York: Falmer Press.

Holt v. Shelton, 341 F. Supp. 821 (M.D. Tenn. 1972).

Hortonville Joint School District No. 1 v. Hortonville Education Association, 426 U.S. 482, 96 S. Ct. 2308 (1976).

Howsam, R. B. Corrigan, D. C., Denemark, G. W., and Nash, R. J. (1976). *Educating a profession.* Washington, DC: American Association of Colleges for Teacher Education.

Huling-Austin, L. (1990). Teacher induction programs and internships, in W. R. Houston (Ed.), *Handbook of research on teaching.* New York: Macmillan.

*Hun-Choe. (November 15, 1996). Bringing the cane down on school bullies. *Bangkok Post,* 8.

Hutchins, R. M. (1963). *A conversation on education.* Santa Barbara, CA: The Fund for the Republic.

Igoa, C. (1995). *The inner world of the immigrant child.* New York: Lawrence Erlbaum Associates, Publishers.

Imber, M., and Van Geel, T. (1993). *Education law.* New York: McGraw-Hill, Inc.

Immediato v. Rye Neck School Dist., 73 F.3d 454 (2d Cir. 1996).

Ingraham v. Wright, 430 U.S. 651 (1977).

*Inoue, A. (1996, October 10). Creating schools with special characteristics. Paper presented at the eighth Washington State University College of Education/Nishinomiya Education Board Education Seminar. Washington State University, Pullman.

Interstate New Teacher Assessment and Support Consortium, A Project of the Council of Chief State School Officers. (1993). *Model standards for beginning teacher licensing and development: A resource for state dialogue (draft for comments)*. Washington, DC: Council of Chief State School Offices.

Isiah B. v. State 176 Wis. 2d 639, 500 N. W.2d 637 (Wis. 1993), *cert. denied,* 510 U.S. 883, 114 S. Ct. 231 (1993).

*Jacklyn, C. (1981). Quoted in L. C. Dowling, *The Cinderella complex*. New York: Summit Books.

*Jackson, P. (1986). *The practice of teaching.* New York: Teachers College Press.

*Jackson, P. (1990). *Life in classrooms.* New York: Teachers College Press.

Jeglin v. San Jacinto Unified School District, 827 F. Supp. 1459 (Cal. 1993).

*Jenkinson, E. B. (1990) Lessons learned from three schoolbook protests. In A. Ochoa (Ed.), *Academic freedom to teach and to learn: Every teacher's issue*. Washington, DC: National Education Association).

Jersild, A. (1955). *When teachers face themselves.* New York: Teachers College Press.

Johnson, D. W., and Johnson, R. T. (1994). *Learning together and alone: Cooperative, competitive, and individualistic learning,* 4th ed. Boston: Allyn and Bacon.

*Johnson, J., and Immerwahr, J. (1994). *First things first: What Americans expect from the public schools, a report from Public Agenda.* New York: Public Agenda.

Johnson, J., and Yates, J. (1982). A national survey of student teaching programs. DeKalb, IL: Northern Illinois University, Teaching Programs. Eric Document Reproduction Services No. ED 232 963.

Johnson, M. (1926). The educational principles of the School of Organic Education, Fairhope, Alabama. In Whipple, G. M. (ed.). *The twenty-sixth yearbook of the National Society for the Study of Education.* Bloomington, IL: Public School Publishing Company.

Johnston, C. B., Morehead, M. A., and Burns, C. (1992). *1992 ASCUS Annual: The Job Search Handbook for Educators.* Evanston, IL: Association for School, College and University Staffing.

*Joyce, B., and Weil, M. (1986). *Models of teaching, 5d.* Englewood Cliffs, NJ: Prentice Hall.

Kahn, A. P. (1988). Parent Teacher Association, National Congress of Parents and Teachers. In R. A. Gorton, G. T. Schneider, and J. C. Fisher (Eds.). *Encyclopedia of school administration & supervision.* Phoenix: Oryx Press.

*Kalafat, J. (May 1990). Adolescent suicide and the implications for school response programs. *School Counselor.*

Karr v. Schmidt, 401 U.S. 1201, 91 S. Ct. 592, 27 L. Ed.2d 797 (1972).

Keefe v. Geanakos, 418 F.2d 359 (1st Cir.) (1969).

Kellagan, T., and Madaus, G. F. (1991, November). National testing: Lessons for America from Europe. *Educational Leadership.*

Keller, H. (1954). *The Story of My Life.* Garden City, NY: Doubleday, 443.

*King, S. H. (Summer 1993). The limited presence of African-American teachers. *Review of Educational Research.*

*Knezevich, S. J. (1984). *Administration of public education: A source book for the leadership and management of educational institutions, 4th ed.* New York: Harper and Row.

Kohlberg, L. (1993). The cognitive-developmental approach to moral education. In Hass, G., and Parkay, F. W. (eds.). *Curriculum planning: A new approach,* 6th ed. Boston: Allyn and Bacon, 670–677.

*Koller, E. (1996). Overcoming paradigm paralysis: A high school teacher revists foreign language education. In Burnaford, G., Fischer, J., and Hobson, D. (1996). *Teachers doing research: Practical possibilities.* Mahwah, NJ: Lawrence Erlbaum Associates, Publishers.

Kounin, J. (1970). *Discipline and group management in classrooms.* New York: Holt, Rinehart and Winston.

Kozol, J. (1991). *Savage inequalities: Children in America's schools.* New York: Crown Publishers, Inc.

Krizek v. Cicero-Stickney Township High School District No. 201 713 F. Supp.1131(1989).

Krogh, S. L. (1990). *The integrated childhood curriculum.* New York: McGraw-Hill, Inc.

Lal, R. (1991). *A study of strategies employed by junior high school administrators to overcome disruptive gang-related activities.* Unpublished doctoral dissertation. Los Angeles: University of California, Los Angeles.

*Lamorte, M. W. (1996). *School law: Cases and concepts.* Boston: Allyn and Bacon.

Larry P. v. Riles, 793 F.2d 969 (9th Cir. 1984).

Lash, J. P. (1980). *Helen and Teacher: The Story of Helen Keller and Anne Sullivan Macy.* New York: Dell.

Lau v. Nichols, 414 U.S. 563 (1974).

*Lawton, M. (1991, April 10). More than a third of teens surveyed say they have contemplated suicide. *Education Week,* 5.

*Lee, V. E., Chen, X., and Smerdon, B. A. (1996). *The influence of school climate on gender differences in the achievement and engagement of young adolescents.* American Association of University Women.

*Lee, V. E., Croninger, R. G., Linn, E., and Chen, X. (Summer 1996). The culture of sexual harassment in secondary schools. *American Education Research Journal.*

Lemon v. Kurtzman, 403 U.S. 602, 91 S. Ct. 2105, 291 L. Ed.2d 745 (1971).

*Levey, S. (1996). *Starting from scratch: One classroom builds its own curriculum.* Portsmouth, NH: Heinemann.

*Levine, D. U., and Levine, R. F. (1996). Society and education, 9th ed. Boston: Allyn and Bacon.

*Levy, M., (ed). (1985). *The annual obituary, 1984.* Chicago: St. James Press.

Leyser, Y. (1985, December). Competencies needed for teaching individuals with special needs. *Clearing House.*

Lickona, T. (1993, November). The return of character education. *Educational Leadership.*

*Lieberman, A. (1990). Foreword. In Mei-ling Yee, S. *Careers in the classroom: When teaching is more than a job.* New York: Teachers College Press.

*Lieberman, A. (1995) Restructuring schools: The dynamics of changing practice, structure, and culture. In Ann Lieberman (Ed.), The work of restructuring schools: Building from the ground up. New York: Teachers College Press, 1–17.

Lightfoot, S. L. (1978). *Worlds apart: Relationships between families and schools.* New York: Basic Books.

*Lindsay, D. (1996, March 13). N. Y. bills give teachers power to oust pupils. *Education Week.*

Livingston, C. (ed.). (1992). *Teachers as leaders: Evolving roles.* Washington, DC: National Education Association.

Lortie, D. (1975). *Schoolteacher.* Chicago: University of Chicago Press.

Lortie, D. (1975). *Schoolteacher: A sociological study.* Chicago: The University of Chicago Press.

*Louis Harris and Associates, Inc. (1990). *The Metropolitan Life survey of the American teacher 1990:*

New teachers: Expectations and ideals. New York: Louis Harris and Associates, Inc.

Louis Harris and Associates, Inc. (1991). *The Metropolitan Life survey of the American teacher, 1991: Coming to terms—teachers' views on current issues in education.* New York: Louis Harris and Associates.

*Louis Harris and Associates, Inc. (1995). *The Metropolitan Life survey of the American teacher, 1984–1995: Old problems, new challenges.* New York: Author.

MacNaughton, R. H., and Johns, F. A. (1991, September). Developing a successful schoolwide discipline program. *NASSP Bulletin.*

Mailloux v. Kiley, 323 F., 448 F.2d 1242 Supp. 1387, 1393 (1st Cir. 1971).

Maloy, K. (1993). *Toward a new science of instruction.* Washington, DC: U.S. Department of Education, Office of Educational Research and Improvement.

Manen, M. van (1991). *The tact of teaching: The meaning of pedagogical thoughtfulness.* Albany: State University of New York Press.

Mann, H. (1868). *Annual reports on education,* in Mary Mann (Ed.). *The life and works of Horace Mann,* vol. 3. Boston: Horace B. Fuller.

Mann, H. (1957). *Twelfth annual report.* In Lawrence A. Cremin (Ed.). *The republic and the school: Horace Mann on the education of free men.* New York: Teachers College Press.

*Manning, M. L., and Baruth, L. G. (1996). *Multicultural education of children and adolescents.* Boston: Allyn and Bacon.

Manning, M. L., and Lucking, R. (1993). Ability grouping: Realities and alternatives. In Hass, G., and Parkay, F. W. (eds.). *Curriculum planning: A new approach,* 6th ed. Boston: Allyn and Bacon.

Marcus v. Rowley 695 F.2d 1171 (9th Cir. 1983).

Marian Wright Edelman, *The Measure of Our Success: A Letter to My Children and Yours* (New York: Harper Perennial, 1993).

*Marshall, K. (1996, January). How I confronted HSPS (hyperactive superficial principal syndrome) and began to deal with the heart of the matter. *Phi Delta Kappan.*

*Maslow, A. (1954). *Motivation and personality.* New York: Basic Books.

*Maslow, A. (1962). *Toward a psychology of being.* New York: Van Nostrand.

Matlen, L. (1993). *The effects of violent youth gang subcultures on the cultures of four secondary schools.* Unpublished doctoral dissertation. Pullman, WA: Washington State University.

*Mayer, F. (1973). *A history of educational thought.* Columbus, OH: Merrill.

*McCloud, B., and McKenzie, F. D. (1994, January). School boards and superintendents in urban districts. *Phi Delta Kappan.*

*McManus, M. (1996, July 1). Words to live by. *Spokesman Review.*

*Mead, J., and Underwood, J. 1995). A legal primer for student teachers. In G. A. Slick (Ed.), *Emerging trends in teacher preparation: The future of field experiences.* Thousand Oaks, CA: Corwin Press, Inc.

*Mehlinger, H. D. (1996, February). School reform in the Information Age. *Phi Delta Kappan.*

*Meyer, A. E. (1972). *An educational history of the Western world.* New York: McGraw Hill.

Miller, A. (May 1983). Those who teach also can sell, organize, compute, write, market, design, manage . . . *Instructor.*

*Monroe, P. (1939). *Source book of the history of education for the Greek and Roman period.* New York: Macmillan.

Montagu, A. (1974). *Man's most dangerous myth: The fallacy of race,* 5th ed. New York: Oxford University Press.

Moore, D. R. (1992). Voice and choice in Chicago. In W. H. Clune, and J. F. Witte (Eds.). *Choice and control in American education: Volume II. The practice of choice, decentralization and school restructuring.* Philadelphia: The Falmer Press.

*Moran v. School District No. 7, 350 F. Supp. 1180 (D.C. Mont. 1972).

*Morris, J. E. & Curtis, K. F. (1983, March/April). Legal issues relating to field-based experiences in teacher education. *Journal of Teacher Education,* 2–6.

Morris, V. C., and Pai, Y. (1976). *Philosophy and the American school: An introduction to the philosophy of education.* Boston: Houghton Mifflin.

Morrison v. State Board of Education, 82 Cal. Rptr. 175, 461 P.2d 375 (Cal. 1969).

*Morton, C. (1996, February). The modern land of Laputa: Where computers are used in education. *Phi Delta Kappan.*

Moyers, B. D. (1989). *A world of ideas: Conversations with thoughtful men and women.* New York: Doubleday.

*Mozert v. Hawkins County Board of Education, 827 F.2d 1058 (6th Cir. 1987), *cert. denied,* 484 U.S. 1066 (1988).

*Murnane, R. J., and Levy, F. (October 1996). What General Motors can teach U.S. schools about the proper role of markets in education reform. *Phi Delta Kappan.*

*Murphy, J., and Schiller, J. (1992). *Transforming America's schools.* LaSalle, IL: Open Court Publishing Co.

*Nathan, J., and Ysseldyke, J. (1994, May). What Minnesota has learned about school choice. *Phi Delta Kappan.*

National Assessment of Educational Progress (NAEP). (1994). *Results from the NAEP 1994 Reading Assessment—At a glance.* Washington, DC: Office of Educational Research and Improvement.

National Assessment of Educational Progress. (1996a). *Assessing mathematics—Achieving goals.* Washington, DC: National Assessment Governing Board, U.S. Department of Education.

National Assessment of Educational Progress. (1996b). *Measuring essential learning in science.* Washington, DC: National Assessment Governing Board, U.S. Department of Education.

National Board for Professional Teaching Standards. (1995). *An invitation to national board certification.* Detroit: National Board for Professional Teaching Standards.

National Board for Professional Teaching Standards. (1991). *Toward high and rigorous standards for the teaching profession: Initial policies and perspectives of the National Board for Professional Teaching Standards,* 3rd ed. Detroit: National Board for Professional Teaching Standards.

*National Center for Education Statistics (1995). *Public school teacher cost differences across the United States.* Washington, DC: National Center for Education Statistics.

National Center for Education Statistics. (1980). *High school and beyond study.* Washington, DC: National Center for Education Statistics.

National Center for Education Statistics. (1989). *Digest of Education Statistics 1989.* Washington, DC: U.S. Department of Education, U.S. Government Printing Office.

National Center for Education Statistics. (1992). *Projection of Education Statistics to 2003.* Washington, DC: U.S. Department of Education, Office of Educational Research and Improvement.

*National Center for Education Statistics. (1995). *Digest of education statistics 1995.* Washington, DC: U.S. Department of Education, Office of Educational Research and Improvement.

National Center for Education Statistics. (1995). *Mini-Digest of Education Statistics 1995.* Washington,

DC: U.S. Department of Education, Office of Educational Research and improvement.

*National Center for Education Statistics. (1995). *Survey of Advanced telecommunications in U.S. Public Schools, K-12.* Washington, DC: National Center for Education Statistics.

*National Center for Education Statistics. (1996). *Projection of Education Statistics to 2006, Twenty-Fifth Edition.* Washington, DC: U.S. Department of Education, Office of Educational Research and Improvement.

*National Commission for the Principalship. (n.d.). *Principals for our changing schools: preparation and certification.* Reston, VA: National Association of Elementary School Principals.

*National Commission on Children. (1991). *Beyond rhetoric: A new American agenda for children and families.* Washington, DC: U.S. Government Printing Office.

National Commission on Excellence in Education. (1983). *A Nation at risk: Imperative for educational reform.* Washington, DC: Government Printing Office.

*National Commission on Teaching and America's Future. (1996). *What matters most: Teaching for America's future.* New York: National Commission on Teaching and America's Future.

National Council for the Social Studies. (1979). *Initial draft, Curriculum standards for the social studies.* Washington, DC: National Council for the Social Studies.

*National Council for the Social Studies. (1994). *Expect excellence: Curriculum standards for the social studies.* Washington, DC: National Council for the Social Studies.

*National Council of Teachers of Mathematics. (1989). *Curriculum and evaluation standards for school mathematics.* Reston, VA: National Council of Teachers of Mathematics.

National Defense Fund (July 1993). "A Brief Biography of Marian Wright Edelman."

*National Education Commission on Time and Learning. (1994). *Prisoners of time.* Washington, DC: Government Printing Office.

*National Education Goals Panel. (1993). *The national education goals report, volume two: State reports.* Washington, DC.

National Foundation for the Improvement of Education. (n.d.). *Images in action: Learning tomorrow: Linking Technology and restructuring.*

National Joint Commission on Learning Disabilities. (1989, September 18). *Letter from NJCLD to member organizations.*

*National Science Foundation. (1996). *Indicators of science and mathematics education.* Washington, DC: National Science Foundation.

*National Trade and Professional Associations of the United States. (1996). New York: Columbia Books, Inc.

National defense Fund. (1993, July). A brief biography of Marian Wright Edelman. Author.

*Nelson, J. L., Carlson, K., and Palonsky, S. B. (1996). *Critical issues in education: A dilectical approach.* New York: McGraw-Hill, Inc.

*New Jersey v. Massa, 231 A.2d 252 (N.J. Sup. Ct. 1967).

New Jersey v. T.L.O. 221 Cal. Rptr. 118, 105 S. Ct. 733 (1985).

*Newmann, F. M., and Wehlage, G. G. (1995). *Successful school restructuring: A report to the public and educators by the Center on Organization and Restructuring of Schools.* Madison, WS: University of Wisconsin, Center on Organization and Restructuring of Schools.

*Newsweek (1996, February 26). The Hit Men.

*Nieto, S. (1992). *Affirming diversity: The sociopolitical context of multicultural education.* White Plains, NY: Longman.

*Noddings, N. (1984). *Caring: A feminine approach to ethics and moral education.* Berkeley, CA: University of California Press.

*Noddings, N. (1992). *The challenge to care in schools: An alternative approach to education.* New York: Teacher's College Press.

*Noddings, N. (1995, May). Teaching themes of care. *Phi Delta Kappan, 76*(9).

*North Central Regional Educational Laboratory. (1993). *Policy briefs, report 1, 1993.* Elmhurst, IL: Author.

*Null v. Board of Education, 815 F. Supp. 937 (W. Va. 1993).

O'Hair, M. J. and Odell, S. J. (eds.) (1995). *Educating Teachers for Leadership and Change: Teacher education yearbook III.* Thousand Oaks, CA: Corwin Press, Inc.

O'Reilly, R. C., and Green, E. T. (1983). *School law for the practitioner.* Westport, CN: Greenwood Press.

*Oaks, M. M, Worthy, J., and Remaley, A. (1993). Confronting our nation's at-risk and dropout dilemma. In G. Hass, and F. W. Parkay, *Curricu-*

lum planning: A new approach. Boston: Allyn and Bacon.

Oberti v. Board of Education of the Borough of Clementon School District, 789 E. Supp. 1322 (D. N.J. 1992)

Odden, A. (1988). Financing of schools. In R. A. G. T. Schneider, and J. C. Fisher (Eds.). *Encyclopedia of school administration & supervision.* Phoenix: Oryx Press.

*Office of Special Education Progams (1995). *17th annual report to Congress on the implementation of the Individuals with Disabilities Education Act.* Washington, DC: Division for Innovation and Development.

Ohman v. Board of Education, 301 N.Y. 662, 93 N. E. 2d 927 (1950).

Olson, J. S. (1979). *The ethnic dimension in American history,* vol. 2. New York: St. Martin's Press.

PASE v. Hannon, 506F. Supp. 831 (N. D. Ill. 1980).

*PBS Television. (April 10, 1991). "All Our Children," with Bill Moyers.

*Pajak, E. (1993). *Approaches to clinical supervision: Alternatives for improving instruction.* Norwood, MA: Christopher-Gordon.

*Palikokas, K. L., and Rist, R. C. (1996, April 2). School uniforms: Do they reduce violence—or just make us feel better? *Education Week.*

*Pang, V. O. (1994, December). Why do we need this class: Multicultural education for teachers. *Phi Delta Kappan.*

Parkay, F. W. (April 1983). *A general theory of aesthetics for the conduct of educational research.* Paper presented at the Annual Meeting of the American Educational Research Association, Montreal.

Parkay, F. W. (Summer 1988). Reflections of a protégé. *Theory Into Practice.*

*Parkay, F. W., Shindler, J., and Oaks, M. M. (1997, January). Creating a climate for collaborative, emergent leadership at an urban high school: Exploring the stressors, role changes, and paradoxes of restructuring. *International Journal of Educational Reform.*

Parkay, F. W., and Conoley, C. (1982, September). Characteristics of educators who advocate corporal punishment: A brief report. *Journal of Humanistic Education and Development.*

Parkay, F. W., and Damico, S. B. (Spring 1989). Empowering teachers for change through faculty-driven school improvement. *Journal of Staff Development.*

Parkay, F. W., and Fillmer, H. T. (1984, November). Improving teachers' attitudes toward minority-group students: An experiential approach to multicultural inservice. *New Horizons.*

Patchogue-Medford Congress of Teachers v. Board of Education of Patchogue-Medford Union Free School District, 70 N.Y. 2d 57, 510 N.E. 2d 325 (1987).

*Paulson, F. L., Paulson, P. R., and Meyer, C. A. (1991). What makes a portfolio a portfolio? *Educational Leadership, 48*(5).

Pearson, C. (1979, March). Cooperative learning: An alternative to cheating and failure. *Learning.*

Perrone, V. (1991). *A Letter to teachers: Reflections on Schooling the the Art of teaching.* San Francisco: Jossey-Bass Publishers.

Perrone, V. (1991). *A letter to teachers: Reflections on schooling and the art of teaching.* San Francisco: Jossey-Bass.

Peter Doe v. San Francisco Unified School District, 131 Cal. Rptr. 854 (1976).

Peterson, L. J., Rossmiller, R. A., and Volz, M. M. (1978). *The law and public school operation,* 2d ed. New York: Harper and Row.

Piaget, J. (1980). *To understand is to invent: The Future of Education.* New York: Penguin Books.

Pickering v. Board of Education 391 U.S. 563 (1968).

*Ponticell, J. A., Olson, G. E., and Charlier, P. S. (1995). Project MASTER: Peer coaching and collaboration as catalysts for professional growth in urban high schools. In O'Hair, M. J., and Odell, S. J. (eds.). *Educating teachers for leadership and change: Teacher education yearbook III.* Thousand Oaks, CA: Corwin Press, Inc.

*Poole, B. J. (1995). *Education for an information age: Teaching in the computerized classroom.* Madison, WI: Brown & Benchmark.

Porter, A. (Fall 1993). Opportunity to learn. *Brief No. 7.* Madison, WS: Center on Organization and Restructuring of Schools.

Posner, G. J. (1993). *Field experience: A guide to reflective teaching, 3rd ed.* New York: Longman.

Powell, A., Farrar, E., and Cohen, D. K. (1985). *The shopping mall high school: Winners and losers in the educational marketplace.* Boston: Houghton Mifflin.

Powell, A. G. (1980). *The uncertain profession: Harvard and the search for educational authority.* Cambridge, MA: Harvard University Press.

Power, E. J. (1982). *Philosophy of education: Studies in philosophies, schooling, and educational policies.* Englewood Cliffs, NJ: Prentice Hall.

Power, E. J. (1996). *Education philosophy: A history from the ancient world to modern America*. New York: Garland Publishing, Inc.

Pratt, C. (1948). *I learn from children*. New York: E. P. Dutton.

Psychology Today. (1993, July/August). Marian Wright Edelman: An interview with the most concerned parent in America.

*Public Agenda. (1994). *First things first: What Americans expect from the public schools*. New York: Public Agenda.

*Quality Education Data. (1996). *1996–97 technology purchasing forecast*. Denver: Quality Education Data.

*Rallis, S. F. (1990). Professional teachers and restructured schools: Leadership challenges. In Mitchell, B., and Cunningham, L. L. (eds.), *Educational leadership and changing contexts of families, communities, and schools* (89th NSSE yearbook). Chicago: University of Chicago Press.

Ravitch, D. (1983). *The troubled crusade: American education, 1945–1980*. New York: Basic Books.

Ray v. School District of DeSoto County, 666 F. Supp. 1524 (M. D. Fla. 1987).

Raywid, M. A. (1981, April). The first decade of public school alternatives. *Phi Delta Kappan*.

Remembering Ernest L. Boyer, Sr. 1928–1995 (1996). *The Messiah College Bridge, Special Edition*.

*Renzulli, J. S. (1982). Dear Mr. and Mrs. Copernicus: We regret to inform you . . . *Gifted Child Quarterly, 26*.

*Rice, R., and Walsh, C. E. (1996). Equity at risk: The problem with state and federal education reform efforts. In C. Walsh, (Ed.), *Education reform and social change: Multicultural voices, struggles, and visions*. Mahwah, NJ: Lawrence Erlbaum Associates, Publishers.

Robeson, P. Jr. (1993). Paul Robeson, Jr. speaks to America. New Brunswick, NJ: Rutgers University Press.

Rickover, H. G. (1959). *Education and freedom*. New York: E. P. Dutton.

Rickover, H. G. (1983, February 3). Educating for excellence. *Houston Chronicle*.

*Riley, R. (1993/1994). Quoted in *Goals 2000, educate America community update*. Washington, DC: U.S. Department of Education.

Rippa, A. (1984). *Education in a free society*. New York: Longman.

*Rithdee, K. (1996, November 3–9). Fighting drugs with faith. *The Bangkok Post Sunday Magazine*.

Roberts v. City of Boston, 59 Mass. (5 Cush.) 198 (1850).

*Robinson, G. E., and Protheroe, N. (1994, September). Local school budget profiles study. *School Business Affairs*.

*Rogers, C. (1961). On becoming a person. Boston: Houghton Mifflin.

*Rogers, C. (1974). *Freedom to learn*. Columbus, OH: Charles E. Merrill.

*Rogers, C. (1982). *Freedom to learn in the eighties*. Columbus, OH: Charles E. Merrill.

Romans v. Crenshaw, 354 F. Supp. 868 (S.D. Tex. 1972).

Rosenshine, B. (1988). Explicit teaching. In D. Berliner and B. Rosenshine (Eds.), *Talks to teachers*. New York: Random House.

Rosenshine, B. (1992, April). The use of scaffolds for teaching higher-level cognitive strategies. *Educational Leadership*.

Rosenshine, B., and Stevens, R. (1986). Teaching functions. In Merlin C. Wittrock (ed.). *Handbook of research on teaching*, 3d ed. New York: Macmillan.

Rosenthal, R. (1974). *On the social psychology of the self-fulfilling prophecy: Further evidence for Pygmalion effects and their mediating mechanisms*. New York: MSS Modular Publications.

*Ross, D. D., and Webb, R. B. (1995). Implementing shared decision making at Brooksville Elementary School. In Lieberman, A. (ed.). *The work of restructuring schools: Building from the ground up*. New York: Teachers College Press.

*Rossell, C. H. (Winter 1990). The research on bilingual education. *Equity and Excellence*.

Rutherford, F. J., and Ahlgren, A. (1990). *Science for all Americans*. New York: Oxford University Press.

*Sadker, M., Sadker, D., and Klein, S. (1991). The issue of gender in elementary and secondary education. *Review of Research in Education, 17*.

*Sadker, M., and Sadker, D. (1984). *Year 3: Final report, promoting effectiveness in classroom instruction*. Washington, DC: National Institute of Education.

*Sadker, M., and Sadker, D. (1994). *Failing at fairness: How our schools cheat girls*. New York: Touchstone.

*Sadker, M. P., and Sadker, D. M. (1994). *Teachers, schools, and society*. New York: McGraw-Hill, Inc.

*Sallie Mae Corporation. (1995). *A report from the 1994 Sallie Mae symposium on quality education*. Washington, DC: Author.

Sarac v. State Board of Education, 249 Cal. App. 2d 58, 57 Cal. Rptr. 69 (Ct. App. 1967).

Sartre, Jean-Paul. (1972). Existentialism. In John Martin Rich (Ed.). *Readings in the philosophy of education.* Belmont, CA: Wadsworth.

Schaefer, R. (1967). *The school as the center of inquiry.* New York: Harper and Row.

Schaill v. Tippecanoe School Corporation, 864 F.2d 1309 (7th Cir. 1988).

*Schmidt, P. (1991, February 20). Three types of bilingual education effective, E. D. study concludes. *Education Week.*

Schmuck, R. A., and Schmuck, P. A. (1971). *Group processes in the classroom.* Dubuqe, IA: William C. Brown.

*Schnaiberg, L. (1995, November 1). Record increase in special-education students reported. *Education Week.*

*Schnaiberg, L. (1996, June 12). Staying home from school. *Education Week.*

Schön, D. (1983). *The reflective practitioner: How professionals think in action.* New York: Basic Books.

Schön, D. (1987). *Educating the reflective practitioner: Toward a new design for teaching and learning in the professions.* San Francisco: Jossey-Bass.

Schön, D. (1991). *The reflective turn: Case studies in an on educational practice.* New York: Teachers College Press.

School District of Abington Township v. Schempp, 374 U.S. 203, 83 S. Ct. 1560, 10 L.Ed. 2d 844 (1963).

*Schubert, W. (1986). *Curriculum: Perspective, paradigm, and possibility.* New York: Macmillan.

Schwartz, A. and Stallings, J. (1987). *Youth gangs and high schools in eastern Los Angeles County.* Los Angeles: University of Southern California.

Schwebel, A. I.; Schwebel, B. L.; Schwebel, C. R.; & Schwebel, M. (1992). *The Student Teacher's Handbook, 2nd ed.* Hillsdale, NJ: Lawrence Erlbaum Associates, Publishers.

*Scopes, J. (1966). *Center of the storm.* New York: Holt, Rinehart, and Winston.

Scoville v. Board of Education of Joliet Township High School District 204, cert. denied, 400 U.S. 826, 91 S. Ct. 51 (1970); 425 F.2d 10 (7th Cir. 1971).

*Sears, J. T. (1991). Educators, homosexuality and homosexual students: Are personal feelings related to professional beliefs? *Journal of Homosexuality,* 22.

Seattle Post Intelligencer (1994, December 5). "Teach for America is Tested in Seattle."

Shanley v. Northeast Independent School District, 462 F.2d 960 (5th Cir. 1972).

*Sharan, Y., and Sharan, S. (1989/1990, December/January). Group investigation expands cooperative learning. *Educational Leadership.*

Sharpley, A. M., Irvine, J. W., and Sharpley, C. F. (Spring 1993). An examination of the effectiveness of a cross-age tutoring program in mathematics for elementary school children. *American Educational Research Journal.*

Sheuerer, D., and Parkay, F. W. (1992). The new Christian right and the public school curriculum: A Florida report. In Smith, J. B. and Coleman, J. G. Jr. (eds.). *School library media annual: 1992,* vol. 10. Englewood, CO: Libraries Unlimited.

Shoop, R. J., and Dunklee, D. R. (1992). *School law for the principal: A handbook for practitioners.* Boston: Allyn & Bacon.

Siegel, P. M. (1971). *Prestige in the American occupational structure.* Ph.D. dissertation, University of Chicago.

Simonetti v. School District of Philadelphia, 308 Pa Super. 555, 454 A. 2d 1038 (Pa. Super. 1982).

Simonson, J. R., and Menzer, J. A. (???) *Catching up: A review of the Women's Educational Equity Act program.* Washington, DC: Citizens Council on Women's Education.

*Singer, A. (1994, December). Reflections on multiculturalism. *Phi Delta Kappan.*

*Sizer, T. (1984). *Horace's compromise: The dilemma of the American high school.* Boston: Houghton Mifflin.

*Sizer, T. (1992). *Horace's school: Redesigning the American high school.* Boston: Houghton Mifflin.

Skinner, B. F. (1972). Utopia through the control of human behavior. In John Martin Rich (Ed.). *Readings in the philosophy of education.* Belmont, CA: Wadsworth.

*Slavin, R. E. (1994). *Educational psychology: Theory and practice,* 4th ed. Boston: Allyn and Bacon.

Smith v. Board of School Commissioners of Mobile County 655 F. Supp. 939 (S. D. Ala.), *rev'd,* 827 F.2d 684 (11th Cir. 1987).

*Smith, D. D., and Luckasson, R. (1995). *Introduction to special education: Teaching in an age of challenge,* 2d ed. Boston: Allyn and Bacon.

Smith, H. (1995). *Rethinking America.* New York: Random House, Inc.

*Smith, K. B., and Meier, K. K. (1995). *The case against school choice: Politics, markets, and fools.* Armonk, NY: M.E. Sharpe, Inc.

*Smith, L. G., and Smith, J. K. (1994). *Lives in education: a narrative of people and ideas.* 2d ed. New York: St. Martin's Press.

*Sommers, C. H. (1996, June 12). Where the boys are. *Education Week.*

*Sowell, E. J. (1996). *Curriculum: An integrative introduction.* Boston: Allyn and Bacon. 158

Splintered vision (A): An investigation of U.S. science and mathematics education. (1996). Washington, D.C.: U.S. Department of Education and International Institute on Education.

Spokesman Review. (1993, June 4). Harassment claims vex teachers.

*Spring, J. (1990). *The American school 1642–1990, 2d ed.* New York: Longman.

*Spring, J. (1993). *Conflict of interests: The politics of American education, 2d ed.* New York: Longman.

*Spring, J. (1996). *American education,* 7th ed. New York: McGraw-Hill, Inc.

*Sricharatchanya, P. (1996, November 5). Education reforms are also crucial. *Bangkok Post.*

*St. Michel, T. (1995). *Effective substitute teachers: Myth, mayhem, or magic?* Thousand Oaks, CA: Corwin Press, Inc.

*Stanford, B. H. (1992). Gender equity in the classroom. In D. A. Byrnes, and G. Kiger, (Eds.), *Common bonds: Anti-bias teaching in a diverse society.* Wheaton, MD: Association for Childhood Education International.

State v. Rivera, 497 N. W.2d 878 (Iowa 1993).

Station v. Travelers Insurance Co., 292 So.2d 289 (La. Ct. App. 1974).

*Steinberg, L, Dornbusch, S., and Brown, B. (1996). *Beyond the classroom: Why school reform has failed and what parents need to do.* New York: Simon and Schuster.

*Sternberg, R. J. (1996, March). Myths, countermyths, and truths about intelligence. *Educational Researcher.*

Stover, D. (1992, March). The at-risk kids schools ignore. *The Executive Educator.*

Strike, K. A., and Soltis, J. F. (1985). *The ethics of teaching.* New York: Teachers College Press.

*Sue, D. W., and Sue, D. (1990). *Counseling the culturally different: Theory and practice.* 2d. ed. New York: John Wiley.

Sullivan v. Houston Independent School District, 475 F.2d 1071 (5th Cir. 1973), cert. denied 414 U.S. 1032 (1973).

Suzuki, B. H. (1983). The education of Asian and Pacific Americans: An introductory overview. In D. T. Nakanishi, and M. Hirano-Nakanishi, (Eds.), *The education of Asian and Pacific Americans: Historical perspectives and prescriptions for the future.* Phoenix: Oryx Press.

Sykes, G. (1983, October). Contradictions, ironies, and promises unfulfilled: A contemporary account of the status of teaching. *Phi Delta Kappan.*

*Taylor, F. W. (1980). Quoted in Brody, D. The American worker in the progressive age, in *The worker in industrial America: Essays on the twentieth century struggle.* London: Oxford University Press.

*Tellijohann, S. K., and Price, J. H. (1993). A qualitative examination of adolescent homosexuals' life experiences: Ramifications for secondary school personnel. *Journal of Homosexuality, 26.*

*Tenbusch, J., and Michael, G. (1993, April). *Organizational change at the local school level under Minnesota's open enrollment program.* Paper presented at the Annual Meeting of the American Educational Research Association, Atlanta.

*Terman, L. M., Baldwin, B. T., and Bronson, E. (1925). Mental and physical traits of a thousand gifted children. In L. M. Terman (ed.). *Genetic studies of genius* (vol. 1). Stanford, CA: Stanford University Press.

*Terman, L. M., and Oden, M. H. (1947). The gifted child grows up. In L. M. Terman (ed.). *Genetic studies of genius* (vol. 4). Stanford, CA: Stanford University Press.

*Terman, L. M., and Oden, M. H. (1959). The gifted group in mid-life. In L. M. Terman (ed.). *Genetic studies of genius* (vol. 5). Stanford, CA: Stanford University Press.

Terry, W. (1993, February 14). Make things better for somebody, *Parade Magazine.*

The Holmes Group. (n.d.). *Tomorrow's schools: Principles for the design of professional development schools.* East Lansing, MI: The Holmes Group.

The University of Memphis. (Winter 1994/95). Technology provides field experiences. *Perspectives.* Memphis: The University of Memphis, College of Education.

*Thelen, H. A. (1960). *Education and the human quest.* New York: Harper and Row.

*Thelen, H. A. (1981). *The classroom society: The construction of educational experience.* London: Croom Helm.

Thompson, M. M. (1951). *The history of education.* New York: Barnes & Noble.

Tinker v. Des Moines Independent Community School District, 393 U.S. 503 (1969).

Tolliver, K. (1993). The Kay Tolliver mathematics program. *The Journal of Negro Education, 62 (1).*

Torrance, E. P. (1986). Teaching creative and gifted learners. In Wittrock, M. C. (ed.). *Handbook of research on teaching,* 3d ed. New York: Macmillan.

*Torres, C. A. (1994). Paulo Freire as Secretary of Education in the municipality of Sao Paula. *Comparative Education Review 38*(2), 181–214.

*Tovey, R. (1995). A narrowly gender-based model of learning may end up cheating all students. *Harvard Education Letter, 9*(4).

*Tozer, S. E., Violas, P. C., and Senese, G. (1993). *School and society: Educational practice as social expression.* New York: McGraw-Hill, Inc.

*Trotter, A. (1996, August 7). Cable companies say they'll bring internet to most U.S. schools. *Education Week.*

*Trueba, H. T., Cheng, L. R. L., and Kenji, I. (1993). *Myth or reality: Adaptive strategies of Asian Americans in California.* Washington, DC: The Falmer Press.

*Tyack, F. D., and Hansot, E. (1982). *Managers of virtue: Public school leadership in America, 1820–1980.* New York: Basic Books.

Tyler, R. (1949). *Basic principles of curriculum and instruction.* Chicago: University of Chicago

*U.S. Bureau of the Census. (September 1993a). *We the American . . . Asians.* Washington, DC: U.S. Bureau of the Census.

U.S. Bureau of the Census. (September 1993b). *We the American . . . Asians.* Washington, DC: U.S. Bureau of the Census.

*U.S. Department of Education. (1996). *Community Update,* No. 33, March 1996.

*U.S. Department of Justice. (1996). 1995 national youth gang survey. Washington, DC: Author.

*U.S. Government Printing Office. (1990). *Who's Minding the Kids?.* Washington, DC: U.S. Government Printing Office.

*Uchida, D., Cetron, M., and McKenzie, F. (1996). *Preparing students for the 21st century.* Arlington, VA: American Association of School Administrators.

*Ulich, R. (1950). *History of educational thought.* New York: American Book Company.

**Unified School Dist.No 241 v. Swanson,* 717 P.2d 526 (Kan.App.1986).

*Uribe, V., and Harbeck, K. M. (1991). Addressing the needs of lesbian, gay and bisexual youth. *Journal of Homosexuality, 22.*

Valente, W. D. (1987). *Law in the schools,* 2d ed. Columbus, OH: Merrill.

Van Manen, M. (1991) The tact of teaching: The meaning of pedagogical thoughtfulness. Albany: State University of New York Press.

*Van Lehn, K., (1994). Applications of simulated students: An exploration. *Journal of Artificial Intelligence in Education, 5*(2).

*Venezky, R. L. (1992). Textbooks in school and society. In Jackson, P. W. (ed.). *Handbook of research on curriculum.* New York: Macmillan.

*Viadero, D. (1996, May 8). Math texts are multiplying. *Education Week.*

*Visconti, K. (1996). Stay in or get out? A "twenty-something" teacher looks at the profession. In Burnaford, G., Fischer, J., and Hobson, D. *Teachers doing research: Practical possibilities.* Mahwah, NJ: Lawrence Erlbaum Associates, Publishers.

WCER Highlights. Madison, WI: University of Wisconsin.

*Walberg, H. J. (1991). Productive teaching and instruction: Assessing the knowledge base. In Waxman, H. C. and Walberg, H. J. (eds.). *Effective teaching: Current research.* Berkeley, CA: McCutchan.

*Walberg, H. J., and Niemiec, R. P. (1994, May). Is Chicago school reform working? *Phi Delta Kappan.*

*Walberg, H. J., and Niemiec, R. P. (1996). Can the Chicago reforms work? *Education Week,* May 22, 1996.

Wallace Terry, "Make Things Better for Somebody," *Parade Magazine* (February 14, 1993): 4–5.

Waller, W. (1932). *The sociology of teaching* New York: John Wiley.

*Walling, D. R. (ed.). (1994). *Teachers as leaders: Perspectives on the professional development of teachers.* Bloomington, IN: Phi Delta Kappa Educational Foundation.

*Walsh, M. (1996, April 24). Gay students press abused claims against districts. *Education Week.*

*Walsh, M. (1996, October 16). Cautious analysis of Edison test data urged. *Education Week.*

*Wasserman, S. (1994, April). Using cases to study teaching. *Phi Delta Kappan,* 602–611.

Watson, J. B. (1925). *Behaviorism,* 2d ed. New York: People's Institute.

*Webb, L. D., Metha, A., and Jordan, K. F. (1996). *Foundations of American education, 2d ed.* Englewood Cliffs, NJ: Prentice Hall.

Wechsler, D. (1958). *The Measurement and appraisal of adult intelligence,* 4th ed. Baltimore: Williams and Wilkins.

Welsh, P. (1987). *Tales out of school.* New York: Penguin Books.

West v. Board of Education of City of New York, 187 N. Y. S.2d 88 8 A.D. 2d 291 (N.Y. App. 1959).

West, A. M. (1980). *The National Education Association: The power base for education.* New York: Free Press.

*Westbury, I. (1992). Comparing American and Japanese achievement: Is the United States really a low-achiever? *Educational Researcher, 21*(5).

*Weston, M. (1996, April 3). Reformers should take a look at home schools: Their numbers are growing, their students excel, and they use some well-hyped teaching techniques. *Education Week.*

Wigginton, E. (1985). *Sometimes a shining moment.* Garden City, NY: Anchor Press.

*Willig, A. C. (Fall 1987). Examining bilingual education research. *Review of Educational Research.*

Wirt, F. M., and Kirst, M. W. (1989). *Schools in conflict: The politics of education, 2d ed.* Berkeley, CA: McCutchan.

*Wisconsin Center for Education Research. (Fall 1994). Teachers prepare for diversity.

*Wohlstetter, P. (September 1995). Getting school-based management right: What works and what doesn't. *Phi Delta Kappan.*

Wohlstetter, P., and Anderson, L. (1994, February). What can U.S. charter schools learn from England's grant-maintained schools? *Phi Delta Kappan.*

Wood, D. (1988). *How children think and learn.* New York: Basil Blackwell.

Woodring, P. (1983). *The persistent problems of education.* Bloomington, IN: Phi Delta Kappa.

*Woolfolk, (1995). *Educational psychology,* 6th ed. Boston: Allyn and Bacon.

Woolfolk, A. E., and Galloway, C. M. (1985). Nonverbal communication and the study of teaching. *Theory into Practice, 24*(1), 80.

*Yaffe, E. (1995, November). Expensive, illegal, and wrong: Sexual harassment in our schools. *Phi Delta Kappan.*

*Yamamoto, K., Davis, O. L. Jr., Dylak, S., Whittaker, J., Marsh, C., and van der Westhuizen, P C. (Spring 1996). Across six nations: Stressful events in the lives of children. *Child Psychiatry and Human Development.*

*Zehm, S. J., and Kottler, J. A. (1993). *On being a teacher: The human dimension.* Newbury Park, CA: Corwin Press, Inc.

Zucker v. Panitz, 299 F. Supp. 102 (D.C.S.D. N.Y. 1969).

Teacher's Resource Guide

TEACHING LICENSURE AND TEACHER CERTIFICATION

THE NATIONAL TEACHER EXAMINATION

The NTE consists of three tests organized as follows:

Area Tested	Section (30 min. each)	Number of Questions
Communication Skills	Listening	40
	Reading	30
	Writing (multiple choice)	45
	Writing (essay)	essay
General Knowledge	Literature and Fine Arts	35
	Mathematics	25
	Science	30
	Social Studies	30
Professional Knowledge	Part I	35
	Part II	35
	Part III	35
	Part IV	35

Typical Questions from the Test of Professional Knowledge

1. ____ Which of the following is *not* part of the mastery learning approach to instruction? (A) Clearly specified objectives (B) Preset mastery standards (C) Additional time and help for those who don't achieve mastery (D) Ability grouping

2. ____ Which of the following is the best example of an extrinsic motivation? (A) Material reward such as a prize or money (B) Opportunity to interact with friends (C) Chance to participate in favorite activity (D) Learning something that will help with a personal problem

3. ____ John Dewey believed that (A) the teacher should try to structure the classroom like a democracy, (B) children should be allowed to do whatever they please, (C) students cannot learn much outside of the classroom, (D) students should not learn basic skills, or (E) the school curriculum should be based on the entrance requirements of the best colleges and universities.

4. ____ You believe that one of your students is being physically abused at home. Legally, you should (A) do nothing, (B) tell your principal or a social worker what you believe is happening, (C) talk with the student and try to find out the truth, or (D) visit the student's home and talk to a parent or guardian.

Note: The questions presented above are not from the NTE but are samples of the kind of questions found on the examinations.

THE PRAXIS SERIES: PROFESSIONAL ASSESSMENTS FOR BEGINNING TEACHERS

The Praxis Series is designed to be used in conjunction with other criteria by state authorities for the purpose of licensing beginning teachers. Based on knowledge and skills commonly required by states of beginning teachers, the Praxis Series is administered nationwide. The Praxis Series includes

- Praxis I: Academic Skills Assessments
- Praxis II: Subject Assessments
- Praxis III: Classroom Performance Assessments
- Principles of Learning and Teaching (PLT)

PRAXIS I, ACADEMIC SKILLS ASSESSMENTS Praxis I covers the "enabling skills" in reading, writing, and mathematics that all teachers need, regardless of grade or subject taught. Two formats, computer-based and pencil-and-paper, are available for the Praxis I assessment, which is given early in a student's teacher education program. To help students pass Praxis I, ETS has developed computer-delivered instructional components that consist of practice tests, a diagnostic skills assessment, and twenty to thirty hours of instructional modules.

PRAXIS II, SUBJECT ASSESSMENTS Praxis II measures teacher education students' knowledge of the subjects they will teach. In most cases, Praxis II tests are taken on completion of an undergraduate program. The tests, available in more than seventy subject areas, have a core content module required by every state, with the remaining modules selected on an individual basis by the states. The format of Praxis II tests includes multiple-choice and constructed-response items.

PRAXIS III, CLASSROOM PERFORMANCE ASSESSMENTS
Praxis III is a performance-based assessment system, not a test. Developed after extensive job analyses, reviews of research, and input from educators, Praxis III involves the assessment of actual teaching skills of the beginning teacher. The assessments focus on planning for instruction, implementing instruction, classroom management, and evaluating student progress and instructional effectiveness. In addition, Praxis III assesses the teacher's sensitivity to developmental levels and cultural differences among students. In-class assessments and pre- and post-observation interviews conducted by trained state and local personnel are the main component of Praxis III. The observations are supplemented by work samples—for example, lesson plans. Following Praxis III assessments, which normally are completed by the end of the first year of teaching, the state makes a decision about whether to grant a license to teach.

PRINCIPLES OF LEARNING AND TEACHING (PLT) The two-hour PLT test assesses teachers' professional knowledge through multiple-choice and constructed response questions. PLT is built around case histories of particular teaching situations and requires candidates to demonstrate understanding of when and how to apply a principle of learning and teaching. The PLT is available in three versions: K–4, 5–9 (middle grades), and 7–12.

MODELS OF PROFESSIONAL STANDARDS: STANDARDS FOR COLORADO EDUCATORS

PREAMBLE

Great educators are the keys to great schools. The State Board of Education has set licensure standards which must be met so that only the best and most promising candidates receive and retain educator licenses and that the training and professional development they experience contribute meaningfully to this end.

In concert with the move to a standards-based system where students demonstrate their skills and knowledge, educator preparation and licensing requirements assure the public that educators have the skills and knowledge needed to support students toward attaining high standards.

The knowledge and performance standards for educators serve as a foundation for the licensure system, from admission to a preparation program through Master Certification. But mastery of knowledge and competent performance are not enough.

Great educators also display dispositions or attributes which contribute to their success. They demonstrate a thirst for knowledge and their own professional development; they hold strong beliefs about the potential for all children and adults to learn and contribute to the school and the community; they are reasoned, consistent, and fair in decision making. They recognize their roles in the education endeavor and are confident in their abilities to lead schools into the future.

The following shall serve as standards for the development of teacher and special services professional education programs and as standards for the ongoing professional development of these educators.

KNOWLEDGE OF CONTENT AND LEARNING School professionals are knowledgeable about their subjects or specialties, are knowledgeable about state-adopted content standards, and know how to facilitate learning.

School professionals thoroughly understand and can demonstrate skills and competencies in their subjects and specialties. They also know and are able to demonstrate effective strategies that empower students to understand fully these subjects. School professionals understand the discipline specific to their subject; they understand the methodologies that make interdisciplinary learning successful. School professionals recognize how factors such as student background, attitudes, and perceptions about the subject can affect learning.

ASSESSMENT School professionals use a variety of assessment approaches to improve learning.

School professionals view assessment as an opportunity to enhance achievement levels and measure performance, as an essential part of the learning process. Assessment provides a continuous opportunity to demonstrate and recognize students' abilities to apply their learning to the complex problems that they will encounter as citizens, family members, and workers.

DEMOCRATIC IDEAL A primary purpose of an educational system is to develop productive citizens. In our society, that means citizens who function in and contribute to a democratic society. School professionals have a special responsibility to help students thoroughly understand our democracy.

In a democracy with compulsory schooling, school professionals have an inherent challenge to provide all students with an excellent education that attends to their needs, backgrounds, and cultural differences and leads to responsible citizenship. To accomplish this, school professionals need to interact with others in the learning community and to ask vital questions regarding practice and policies.

DIVERSITY Our diverse society is composed of individuals with varied experiences, values, and perspectives. The school professional appreciates and works with this diversity and provides opportunities to help students learn.

COMMUNICATION School professionals are effective communicators who draw from a wealth of communication tools and practices to understand and be understood by diverse groups of individuals.

School professionals understand that effective communication is central to all learning and takes place in diverse settings. School professionals use various forms of communication to meet student needs, foster collegial relationships, and to interact with parents and the community.

(Source: Colorado Department of Education, Educator Licensing, 201 East Colfax, Denver, Colorado 80203.)

MODELS OF PROFESSIONAL STANDARDS: KENTUCKY'S NEW TEACHER STANDARDS

Office of Teacher Education and Certification, 1826 Capital Plaza Tower, 500 Mero Street, Frankfort, KY 40601, (502) 564-4606, (FAX) (502) 564-6470.

PREAMBLE TO THE NEW TEACHER STANDARDS The New Teacher Standards describe what first year teachers should know and be able to do in authentic teaching situations and the academic content, teaching behaviors, and instructional processes that are necessary to promote effective student learning. They imply more than the mere demonstration of teaching competencies. They imply a current and sufficient academic content understanding that promotes consistent quality performance on teaching tasks. Authentic teaching tasks provide opportunities and contexts for performances by beginning teachers.

In Kentucky, all teaching and learning tasks address Kentucky's academic expectations. These identify what students need to be successful in the world of the future. Thus, teachers design and implement instruction and assess learning that develops students' abilities to:

1. **Use basic communication and mathematics skills** in finding, organizing, expressing, and responding to information and ideas.
2. **Apply core concepts and principles** from science, arts and humanities, mathematics, practical living studies, social studies, and vocational studies.
3. **Become a self-sufficient individual** who demonstrates high self-esteem, a healthy lifestyle, flexibility, creativity, self-control, and independent learning.
4. **Become a responsible group member** who demonstrates consistent, responsive, and caring behavior; interpersonal skills; respect for the rights and responsibilities of others; world views; and an open mind to other perspectives.
5. **Think and solve problems** including the ability to think critically and creatively, develop ideas and concepts, and make rational decisions.
6. **Connect and integrate experiences and new knowledge** throughout the curriculum, question and interpret ideas from diverse perspectives, and apply concepts to real-life situations.

NEW TEACHER STANDARDS

I. Designs/Plans Instruction

The teacher *designs/plans instruction* and *learning climates* that develop students' abilities to use communication skills, apply core concepts, become self-sufficient individuals, become responsible team members, think and solve problems, and integrate knowledge.

II. Creates/Maintains Learning Climates

The teacher *creates learning climates* that support the development of students' abilities to use communication skills, apply core concepts, become self-sufficient individuals, become responsible team members, think and solve problems, and integrate knowledge.

III. Implements/Manages Instruction

The teacher *introduces/implements/manages instruction* that develops students' abilities to use communication skills, apply core concepts, become self-sufficient individuals, become responsible team members, think and solve problems, and integrate knowledge.

IV. Assesses/Communicates Learning Results

The teacher *assesses learning and communicates results* to students and other with respect to student abilities to use communication skills, apply core concepts, become self-sufficient individuals, become responsible team members, think and solve problems, and integrate knowledge.

V. Reflects/Evaluates Teaching/Learning

The teacher *reflects on and evaluates specific teaching/learning situations* and/or programs.

VI. Collaborates with Colleagues/Parents/Others

The teacher *collaborates with colleagues, parents, and other agencies* to design implement, and support learning programs that develop students' abilities to use communication skills, apply core concepts, become self-sufficient individuals, become responsible team members, think and solve problems, and integrate knowledge.

VII. Engages in Professional Development

The teacher *evaluates his/her overall performance* with respect to modeling and teaching Kentucky's Learning Goals and *implements a professional development program* that enhances his/her own performance.

VIII. Demonstrates Content Knowledge

The teacher demonstrates a *current* and *sufficient academic knowledge* of certified content areas to develop student knowledge and performance in those areas.

INTERSTATE NEW TEACHER ASSESSMENT AND SUPPORT CONSORTIUM STANDARDS

1. The teacher understands the central concepts, tools of inquiry, and structures of the discipline(s) he or she teaches and can create learning experiences that make these aspects of subject matter meaningful for students.
2. The teacher understands how children learn and develop, and can provide learning opportunities that support their intellectual, social, and personal development.
3. The teacher understands how students differ in their approaches to learning and creates instructional opportunities that are adapted to diverse learners.
4. The teacher understands and uses a variety of instructional strategies to encourage students' development of critical thinking, problem solving, and performance skills.
5. The teacher uses an understanding of individual and group motivation and behavior to create a learning environment that encourages positive social interaction, active engagement in learning, and self-motivation.
6. The teacher uses knowledge of effective verbal, nonverbal, and media communication techniques to foster active inquiry, collaboration, and supportive interaction in the classroom.
7. The teacher plans instruction based upon knowledge of subject matter, students, the community, and curriculum goals.
8. The teacher understands and uses formal and informal assessment strategies to evaluate and ensure the continuous intellectual, social, and physical development of the learner.
9. The teacher is a reflective practitioner who continually evaluates the effects of his/her choices and actions on others (students, parents, and other professionals in the learning community) and who actively seeks out opportunities to grow professionally.
10. The teacher fosters relationships with school colleagues, parents, and agencies in the larger community to support students' learning and well-being.

(Source: *Model Standards for Beginning Teacher Licensing and Development: A Resource for State Dialogue [Draft for Comments]* Washington, DC: Interstate New Teacher Assessment and Support Consortium. A Project of the Council of Chief State School Officers, 1993, pp. 1–29.)

SELECTION FROM THE NBPTS PORTFOLIO ACTIVITIES

EARLY ADOLESCENCE/GENERALIST

PROFESSIONAL DEVELOPMENT AND SERVICE Candidate provides an overview of his professional career, highlighting the impact of his professional development and service.

- Reflects on professional growth and contributions to the profession
- Selects an area of practice that has been affected by professional development and an area of service that has contributed to the profession.
- Develops a vita with brief clarifying descriptions.
- Writes an account of each of the two selected areas.
- Selects colleagues to submit letters of support.

TEACHING AND LEARNING Candidate prepares a narrative describing her work with a class during a selected period of teaching and learning. The experiences of three students are presented as examples. A collection of exhibits illustrates the teaching and learning.

- Selects class and featured period of instruction.
- Selects from this class three students who represent a variety of learning characteristics.
- Regularly videotapes teaching-and-learning activities and collects samples of students' work, instructional artifacts, and teaching notes and reflections.
- Prepares narrative and illustrates it with exhibits.
- Writes a description of teaching situation and selected class.

- Writes a description of each of the three selected students.
- Writes an account of the teaching and learning that occurred over the featured period of instruction and illustrates it with selected exhibits.

ANALYZING YOUR LESSON   Candidate gives an account of a single lesson that occurred during the period of instruction featured in Teaching and Learning, focusing on five to seven points of particular importance.

- Selects an unedited videotape of 30–45 minutes of instruction.
- Chooses five to seven points of particular importance to highlight.
- Provides background information that serves as context for the videotaped instruction.
- At the Assessment Center, discusses the videotaped lesson addressing selected points and responding to interviewer questions.

(Source: National Board for Professional Teaching Standards. Taken from *Education Week,* April 20, 1994, p. 24.)

NBPTS ASSESSMENT CENTER ACTIVITIES

EARLY ADOLESCENCE/ENGLISH LANGUAGE ARTS

Content Knowledge Examination

- Completes three two-hour essay assignments that explore knowledge of composition, literature, and language and language development. Literature and articles from professional journals are provided as a stimulus for each task.

Analysis of Student Writing

- Analyzes a set of student papers and prepares to discuss the writing and instruction the candidate would design for the students.
- In a videotaped interview, discusses with an interviewer the writing analysis and how to help the students become better writers.

Instructional Analysis

- Reads a written commentary and watches a short videotape of a discussion led by a first-year teacher in a 6th-grade English language-arts class.
- Writes an analysis of the teacher and makes recommendations for improving her instruction, demonstrating an understanding of young adolescents and how they learn, cultural awareness, and the dynamics of discussion.

Cooperative Group Discussion

Candidate is asked to become familiar with eight novels for young adolescents before coming to the assessment center.

- After a preparation period, participates in a videotaped discussion with other candidates that simulates putting together a 7th-grade curriculum unit on personal relationships. Is given background about the school district and asked to select four of the eight novels for the instructional unit, discussing reasons and recommending ways for teaching the unit.

EARLY ADOLESCENCE/GENERALIST

Instructional Resources

Candidate is sent SimCity, an interactive computer simulation, and asked to become familiar with its potential for teaching history and social studies, science, and mathematics.

- Is asked to draw on knowledge of content, young adolescent learners, understanding of resources as learning tools, and school-site experience with the simulation to prepare a written analysis. May use brief notes in writing the analysis.

Instructional Analysis

- Candidate is given materials about a teacher's instruction in mathematics, including a videotape of the teacher's classroom and samples of students' work.
- Observes and comments on teacher's practice, suggesting strategies that might be more effective and recommending ways to extend the study of mathematics into the arts.

Exploring Curriculum Issues

Candidate is asked to think about how middle-grades students might investigate systems of government, ecosystems, and influences of the media.

- In a group discussion, three or four candidates are given a theme that might be useful in helping students examine the questions. They are asked how the theme might be explored with young adolescents. The discussion is to stimulate candidates' thinking and is not assessed.

- Completes a two-hour written assessment that describes the ways the candidate would develop a specified theme and how the content from one of the subjects studied at the school site might contribute to students' understanding.
- Takes three one-hour written subject examinations.

(Source: National Board for Professional Teaching Standards. Taken from *Education Week,* April 20, 1994, p. 27.)

U.S. STATE TEACHER CERTIFICATION OFFICES

KEY TO STATE CODES FOR TESTING REQUIREMENTS

No Code No testing is required.
1 State requires successful completion of its own examination.
2 State requires successful completion of its own examination *plus* completion of one or more national tests.
3 State requires successful completion of one or more national tests. States set their own minimum scores.

Alabama
Department of Education
Division of Instructional Service
5108 Gordon Persons Bldg.
50 North Ripley Street
Montgomery 36104-3833,
205-242-9960

Alaska
Department of Education
Teacher Education and Certification
Goldbelt Building
801 W. 10th Street, Suite 200
Juneau 99801-1894, 907-465-2831

Arizona 1
Department of Education
Teacher Certification Unit
P.O. Box 6490
Phoenix 85005-6490, 602-542-4368

Arkansas 3
Department of Education
Teacher Education and Licensure
#4 Capitol Mall, Rooms 106B/107B
Little Rock 72201, 501-682-4342

California 2
Commission on Teacher Credentialing
1812 9th Street
Sacramento 95814-7000, 916-445-0184

Colorado 1
Department of Education
Educator Licensing, Room 105
201 East Colfax Avenue
Denver 80203-1704, 303-866-6628

Connecticut 2
State Department of Education
Bureau of Certification and Professional Development
P.O. Box 2219
Hartford 06145, 860-566-5201

Delaware 3
State Department of Public Instruction
Office of Certification
Townsend Building, P.O. Box 1402
Dover 19903-1402, 302-739-4686

District of Columbia 3
Teacher Education and Certification Branch
Logan Administration Building
215 G Street, N.E., Room 101A
Washington 20002, 202-724-4246

Florida 1
Department of Education
Bureau of Teacher Certification
Florida Education Center
325 W. Gaines Street, Room 203
Tallahassee 32399-0400, 904-488-5724

Georgia 1 & 3
Professional Standards Commission
1452 Twin Towers East
Atlanta 30334, 404-657-9000

Hawaii 3
State Department of Education
Office of Personnel Services
P.O. Box 2360
Honolulu 96804, 808-586-3269

Idaho

Department of Education
Teacher Education and Certification
P.O. Box 83720
Boise 83720-0027, 208-334-3475

Illinois 1

State Board of Education
Division of Professional Preparation
100 North First Street
Springfield 62777-0001, 217-782-2805

Indiana 3

Professional Standards Board
Teacher Licensure
251 East Ohio Street, Suite 201
Indianapolis 46204-2133, 317-232-9010

Iowa

Board of Educational Examiners
Practitional Preparation and Licensure
 Bureau
Grimes State Office Building,
East 14th and Grand
Des Moines 50319-0146, 515-281-3245

Kansas 3

State Department of Education
Certification & Teacher Education
120 East 10th Avenue
Topeka 66612-1182, 913-296-2288

Kentucky 3

State Board of Education
Office of Teacher Education and
 Certification
1024 Capital Center Drive
Frankfort 40601, 502-573-4606

Louisiana 3

State Department of Education
Bureau of Higher Education, Teacher
 Certification and Continuing Education
P.O. Box 94064
Baton Rouge 70804-9064,
504-342-3490

Maine 3

Department of Education
Teacher Certification and Placement
23 State House Station
Augusta 04333-0023, 207-287-5944

Maryland 3

State Department of Education
Division of Certification and
 Accreditation
200 West Baltimore Street
Baltimore 21201, 401-767-0412

Massachusetts

Department of Education
Office of Teacher Certification
P.O. Box 9140
350 Main Street
Malden 02148-5023, 617-388-3300

Michigan 1

Department of Education
Office of Professional Preparation
 and Certification Services
608 West Allegan, 3rd Floor
P.O. Box 30008
Lansing 48933, 517-335-0406

Minnesota 3

State Department of Children, Families
 & Learning
Personnel Licensing
Capitol Square Building
550 Cedar Street
St. Paul 55101-2273, 612-296-2046

Mississippi 3

State Department of Education
Division of Teacher Certification
Sillers Building, Suite 802
P.O. Box 771
Jackson 39205-0771, 601-359-3483

Missouri 3

Department of Elementary & Secondary
 Education
Teacher Certification Office
P.O. Box 480
Jefferson City 65102-0480,
573-751-0051

Montana 3

Office of Public Instruction
Teacher Education and Certification
Capitol Building, Room 106
P.O. Box 202501
Helena 59620-2501, 406-444-3150

Nebraska 3

Department of Education
Teacher Education and Certification
310 Centennial Mall South, Box 94987
Lincoln 68509-4987, 402-471-0739

Nevada 3

Department of Education
1850 E. Sahara, Suite 207
Las Vegas 89104, 702-486-6457

New Hampshire

State Department of Education
Bureau of Credentialing
101 Pleasant Street
Concord 03301-3860, 603-271-2407

New Jersey 3

Department of Education
Professional Development & Licensing
100 River View Plaza, CN 500
Trenton 08625-0500, 609-984-1216

New Mexico 3

State Department of Education
Professional Licensure Unit
Education Building
Santa Fe 87501-2786, 505-827-6587

New York 1

State Department of Education
Office of Teaching
Cultural Education Center, Room 5A11
Nelson A. Rockefeller Empire State Plaza
Albany 12230, 518-474-3901

North Carolina 3

Department of Public Instruction
Licensure Section
301 N. Wilmington Street
Raleigh 27601-2825, 919-733-4125

North Dakota

Educational Standards
and Practices Board
600 East Boulevard Avenue
Bismarck 58505-0440, 701-328-2264

Ohio 3

Department of Education
Division of Teacher Education
 & Certification
65 S. Front Street, Room 412
Columbus 43215-4183, 614-466-3593

Oklahoma 1

State Department of Education
Professional Standards Section
Hodge Education Building
2500 North Lincoln Boulevard,
 Room 211
Oklahoma City 73105-4599,
405-521-3337

Oregon 2

Teacher Standards and Practices
 Commission
Public Service Building, Suite 105
225 Capitol Street, N.E.
Salem 97310, 503-378-3586

Pennsylvania 3

State Department of Education
Bureau of Teacher Preparation and
 Certification
333 Market Street, 3rd Floor
Harrisburg 17126-0333, 717-787-2967

Puerto Rico 3
Department of Education
Certification Office
P.O. Box 190759
San Juan 00919-0759, 787-759-2000

Rhode Island 3
Department of Education
Office of Teacher Certification
& Preparation
Roger Williams Building
22 Hayes Street
Providence 02908, 401-277-2675

South Carolina 3
Office of Organizational Development
Teacher Licensure Section
1015 Rutledge Building
Columbia 29201, 803-734-8466

South Dakota
Division of Education & Cultural Affairs
Office of Certification
Kneip Building,
700 Governor's Drive
Pierre 57501-2291, 605-773-3553

Tennessee 3
State Department of Education
Teacher Education and Accreditation
Andrew Johnson Tower, 6th Floor
710 James Robertson Parkway
Nashville 37243-0375, 615-741-6055

Texas 1
State Board for Educator Certification
1001 Trinity Street
Austin 78701, 512-469-3000

Utah
State Office of Education
Certification and Personnel
Development
250 East 500 South
Salt Lake City 84111, 801-538-7741

Vermont
State Department of Education
Licensing & Professional Standards
120 State Street
Montpelier 05620, 802-828-2445

Virginia 3
Department of Education
Division of Compliance
P.O. Box 2120
Richmond 23216-2120, 804-371-2522

Washington
Superintendent of Public Instruction
Professional Education and
Certification Office
P.O. Box 47200
Olympia 98504-7200, 360-753-6773

West Virginia 3
Department of Education
Office of Professional Preparation
1900 Kanawha Boulevard East
Building #6, Room B-337
Charleston 25305-0330, 304-558-2703

Wisconsin 3
Department of Public Instruction
Teacher Education & Licensing Teams
125 S. Webster Street,
P.O. Box 7841
Madison 53707-7841, 608-266-1027

Wyoming
Professional Teaching Standards Board
Hathaway Building, 2nd Floor
2300 Capital Avenue
Cheyenne 82002, 307-777-6248

St. Croix District 3
Department of Education
Educational Personnel Services
2133 Hospital Street
St. Croix, Virgin Islands 00820,
809-773-5844

St. Thomas/St. John District 3
Department of Education
Personnel Services
44-46 Kongens Gade
St. Thomas, Virgin Islands 00802,
809-774-5240

**United States Department of Defense
Dependent Schools** 3
Certification Unit
4040 N. Fairfax Drive
Arlington, Virginia 22203-1634
703-696-3081, ext 133

(Source: *1997 Job Search Handbook for Educators,* American Association for Employment in Education, 820
Davis St., Suite 222, Evanston, IL 60201-4445.)

PARTIES TO THE INTERSTATE CERTIFICATION AGREEMENT CONTRACT

State	AL	CA	CT	DE	FL	GA	HI	ID	IN	KY	ME	MD	MA	MI	MT	NH	NJ	NY	NC	OH	PA	RI	SC	TN	TX	UT	VI	VA	WA	WV	DC	PR
AL	•	X	X	X	X	X	X	X	X	X	X	X	X	X			X	X	X	X		X	X	X		X	X	X	X	X	X	
CA	X	•	X	X	X	X	X	X	X	X	X	X	X	X	X	X	X	X	X	X	X	X	X	X	X	X	X	X	X	X	X	X
CT	X	X	•	X	X		X	X		X	X	X	X				X	X	X	X	X	X	X	X			X	X	X	X	X	
DE	X	X	X	•	X		X	X	X	X	X	X	X	X		X	X	X	X	X	X	X	X	X	X	X	X	X	X	X	X	X
FL	X	X	X	X	•		X	X	X	X		X	X	X		X	X	X	X	X	X	X	X	X	X	X	X	X	X	X	X	X
GA	X	X			X	•	X	X	X								X	X										X	X	X	X	
HI	X	X	X	X	X	X	•	X	X	X	X	X	X	X	X	X	X	X	X	X	X	X	X	X		X	X	X	X	X	X	
ID	X	X	X	X	X	X	X	•	X	X	X	X	X	X	X	X	X	X	X	X	X	X	X	X		X	X	X	X	X	X	
IN	X	X		X	X	X	X	X	•	X		X	X	X		X	X	X	X	X	X	X	X	X		X	X	X	X	X	X	
KY	X	X	X	X	X			X	X	•	X	X	X			X	X	X	X	X	X	X	X	X			X	X	X	X	X	
ME	X	X	X	X	X				X		•	X	X	X		X	X	X	X	X	X		X	X			X	X	X	X	X	
MD	X	X	X	X	X	X	X	X	X	X	X	X	•	X		X	X	X	X	X	X	X	X	X		X	X	X	X	X	X	
MA	X	X	X	X	X	X	X	X	X	X	X	X	X	•	X	X	X	X	X	X	X	X	X	X		X	X	X	X	X	X	
MI		X		X	X	X	X	X	X			X	X	•	X	X		X	X	X	X		X			X	X	X	X	X	X	
MT		X		X	X	X	X	X			X	X	X	X	•	X		X		X	X	X	X	X			X	X	X	X		
NH	X	X	X	X	X	X	X	X	X	X	X	X	X	X	X	•	X	X	X	X	X	X	X	X	X	X	X	X	X	X	X	
NJ	X	X	X	X	X			X	X		X	X	X	X			X	•	X	X	X	X	X	X			X	X	X	X	X	
NY	X	X	X	X	X	X	X	X	X	X	X	X	X	X	X	X	X	•	X	X	X	X	X	X	X	X	X	X	X	X	X	X
NC	X	X	X	X	X	X	X	X	X	X	X	X	X	X	X	X	X	X	•	X	X	X	X	X	X	X	X	X	X	X	X	X
OH	X	X	X	X	X	X	X	X	X	X	X	X	X	X	X	X	X	X	X	•	X	X	X	X	X	X	X	X	X	X	X	
PA	X	X	X	X	X	X	X	X	X	X		X	X	X	X	X	X	X	X	X	•	X	X	X	X	X	X	X	X	X	X	X
RI	X	X	X	X	X	X	X	X	X	X	X	X	X		X	X	X	X	X	X	X	•	X	X			X	X	X	X	X	
SC	X	X	X	X	X	X	X	X	X	X	X	X	X	X	X	X	X	X	X	X	X	X	•	X	X	X	X	X	X	X		X
TN	X	X	X	X	X	X	X	X	X		X	X		X	X		X	X	X	X		X	X	•	X	X	X	X	X	X		
TX		X		X	X	X	X	X	X		X	X	X	X	X		X	X		X	X		X		•			X	X	X		
UT	X	X	X	X	X	X	X	X	X	X	X	X	X	X	X	X	X	X	X	X	X	X	X	X		•	X	X	X		X	
VT	X	X	X	X	X	X	X	X			X	X	X			X	X	X	X	X		X	X			X	•	X	X	X	X	
VA	X	X	X	X	X	X	X	X	X	X	X	X	X	X	X	X	X	X	X	X	X	X	X	X	X	X	X	•	X	X	X	
WA	X	X	X	X	X	X	X	X	X	X	X	X	X	X	X	X	X	X	X	X	X	X	X	X	X	X		X	•	X	X	
WV	X	X	X	X	X	X	X	X	X	X	X	X	X	X	X	X	X	X	X	X		X	X	X		X	X	X	X	•	X	
DC	X	X	X	X	X	X	X	X	X	X	X	X	X	X			X	X	X	X	X	X	X	X		X	X	X	X	X	•	
PR*																	X			X												•

*Commonwealth of Puerto Rico

Note: Parties to the contract as of September 1996. A fully certified teacher in a contract state may be issued a certificate for a minimum of one year by another contract state.

JOB SEARCH PLANNING AND DATA

JOB SEARCH TIMETABLE CHECKLIST

This checklist is designed to help graduating students who are seeking teaching positions make the best use of their time as they conduct job searches. We encourage you to use this checklist in conjunction with the services and resources available from your college or university career planning and placement office.

August/September (12 months prior to employment)	_____	Attend any applicable orientations/workshops offered by your college placement office.
	_____	Register with your college placement office and inquire about career services.
	_____	Begin to define career goals by determining the types, sizes, and geographic locations of school systems in which you have an interest.
October (11 months prior to employment)	_____	Begin to identify references and ask them to prepare letters of recommendation for your credential or placement files.
	_____	See a counselor at your college placement office to discuss your job-search plan.
November (10 months prior to employment)	_____	Check to see that you are properly registered at your college placement office.
	_____	Begin developing a résumé and a basic cover letter.
	_____	Begin networking by contacting friends, faculty members, etc., to inform them of your career plans. If possible, give them a copy of your résumé.
December/January (8–9 months prior to employment)	_____	Finalize your résumé and make arrangements for it to be reproduced. You may want to get some tips on résumé reproduction from your college placement office.
	_____	Attend any career planning and placement workshops designed for education majors.
	_____	Use the directories available at your college placement office to develop a list of school systems in which you have an interest.
	_____	Contact school systems to request application materials.
	_____	If applying to out-of-state school systems, contact the appropriate State Departments of Education to determine testing requirements.
February (7 months prior to employment)	_____	Check the status of your credential or placement file at your college placement office.
	_____	Send completed applications to school systems, with a résumé and cover letter.
	_____	Inquire about school systems which will be recruiting at your college placement office, and about the procedures for interviewing with them.
March/April (5–6 months prior to employment)	_____	Research school systems with which you will be interviewing.
	_____	Interview on campus and follow up with thank you letters.
	_____	Continue to follow up by phone with school systems of interest.
	_____	Begin monitoring the job vacancy listings available at your college placement office.

May/August		
(1–4 months prior to employment)	_____	Just before graduation, check to be sure you are completely registered with your college placement office, and that your credential or placement file is in good order.
	_____	Maintain communication with your network of contacts.
	_____	Subscribe to your college placement office's job vacancy bulletin.
	_____	Revise your résumé and cover letter if necessary.
	_____	Interview off campus and follow up with thank you letters.
	_____	If relocating away from campus, contact a college placement office in the area to which you are moving and inquire about available services.
	_____	Continue to monitor job vacancy listings and apply when qualified and interested.
	_____	Begin considering offers. Ask for more time to consider offers, if necessary.
	_____	Accept the best job offer. Inform those associated with your search of your acceptance.

*Adapted from material originally prepared at Miami University of Ohio.

(Source: American Association for Employment in Education, *1997 ASCUS Annual: A Job Search Handbook for Educators,* Evanston, IL: Association for School, College and University Staffing, Inc., p. 10. The *Handbook* is available for a fee.)

RÉSUMÉ ADVICE FOR EDUCATORS

A modern-day résumé is a written advertisement focused toward a prospective employer. In a résumé, however, the 'product' being advertised is you, the candidate.

Many job applicants become confused about what to include on a résumé. This article covers the most common informational categories, but you should strive to include any information that you feel will enhance your chances of being selected for an interview.

SEEKING THE "PERFECT" RÉSUMÉ   Just as every individual is different, each résumé presents a distinct combination of skills, abilities, and qualifications about the author. This is why it is impossible to find a perfect sample résumé and simply copy it. Your background is unique, and cannot be found in a book. However, reviewing other résumés will certainly be helpful because they will provide a rich supply of ideas and perspectives for your document.

While the perfect résumé may be an elusive concept, excellent résumés have many characteristics in common. An excellent résumé is one to two pages in length. It is free of typographical errors, produced on high-quality bond paper, accentuates your most salient qualities and qualifications, is organized and easy to read, and conveys a sense of who you are to the reader. This is easier said than done!

You need to remember that in today's job market, school principals are inundated with résumés. One or two pages is about the maximum they are willing to read about each candidate. As a prospective teacher, a résumé with any typographical error is a signal that you are poorly prepared to instruct others, so be sure to have your final document read by others, until all errors are eliminated.

Résumés for teaching and résumés for business have both similarities and differences. Organization, style, appearance, neatness, and punctuation issues apply to both. (If you need help with these issues, you will find useful books on the topic in your institution's career planning and placement office or at local bookstores.) However, educators' résumés typically include additional categories: student teaching, clinical experience, and certification information.

As you work to write the 'perfect' résumé, you will undoubtedly receive a variety of well-intentioned advice, and some of it will be conflicting. Everyone will have an opinion to offer. One of your most difficult tasks will be to evaluate what you hear. Pursue different opinions, and then decide what makes sense for you.

STATEMENT OF TEACHING OBJECTIVE   It is appropriate to include a "Career Objective" or "Teaching Objective" statement on you résumé. While optional, this statement is highly recommended because it helps identify the specific areas in which you wish to teach. Consider the advantages and disadvantages of the following three sample objectives, then develop your own to fit your requirements.

1. Elementary Teaching Position, K–6.
2. Seeking a classroom position in the upper elementary grades that provides an opportunity to facilitate academic, social, and personal growth of students.
3. Secondary or middle school position in science/math, in a suburban location. Qualified and interested in coaching track, volleyball, or swimming.

Objective "A" is descriptive and to the point. However, additional elements are incorporated into examples "B" and "C." Objective "C" is well thought out and developed, although unless you intend to decline all offers other than those in suburban locations, you should avoid using a phrase which defines location too tightly. The reader will assume that you mean what you say.

STUDENT TEACHING INFORMATION   It is important that beginning teachers provide information about their student teaching experiences. Do not assume that all student teaching experiences are alike, and therefore need not be described. Some principals remain interested in your student teaching experience even after you have several years of professional experience.

Review the two examples below, and then develop a section that accurately portrays your own experience.

1. Northwestern High School
   Rolling Hills, Illinois
      Student Teacher
      January–April, 1994
      Taught 11th grade chemistry and math courses in an open classroom format. Coordinated field study trips, and a "Careers in Science" day.

2. MacKenzie Elementary School
   Chicago, Illinois
      Student Teacher
      September–December, 1993
      Observed, assisted, and taught regular and accelerated classes. Developed daily lesson and unit plans. Assisted in after-school tutoring program. Coordinated a revised parent conference format that increased teacher-parent interaction. Refined an existing computer database for classroom record keeping.

Note how the examples include pertinent details of student teaching experiences beyond the routine aspects. It is this information that demonstrates ways in which you made yourself valuable. In your narrative, try to focus on how your presence made something better to make your experience stand out from those who merely developed lesson plans and assisted teachers.

PAST EMPLOYMENT INFORMATION   Normally, an employer wants to know about your last ten years of professional experience. As a prospective teacher, you should include any experiences in which you worked with K–12-age individuals. Examples of pertinent positions would include camp counselor, teacher's aide, tutor, Scout troop leader, and so forth.

Many candidates dismiss nonteaching experiences as unrelated, and fail to include them on their résumés. However, principals and school administrators can draw valuable inferences regarding your work habits from this information. Dependability, responsibility, and leadership potential are just a few of the desirable traits you can document with information about jobs you have held.

RELATED ACTIVITIES AND INTERESTS   Information about activities and interests helps you present the image of a well-rounded and versatile teacher. The following categories represent just a few of the areas you may want to include.

- Volunteer activities
- Professional memberships
- Special interests
- Honors and awards
- Committee work
- Training
- Study abroad
- Community involvement
- Fluency in languages other than English
- Computer skills
- Leadership activities
- Professional development activities
- Class projects
- Scholarships

Remember, the more areas of knowledge and expertise that you demonstrate, the more likely you are to become a desirable candidate in the eyes of school administrators. School districts actively seek candidates who are flexible and willing to take on a variety of tasks in the school.

A FEW FINAL DO'S AND DON'T'S Make sure that your résumé is not a jig saw puzzle of unrelated odds and ends, expecting that the principal will be able to piece them together. If those who receive your résumé have to work hard to figure it out, it is likely that they will just move on to the next résumé!

When your résumé is complete, print your final copy on a laser-jet printer, and have copies made at a printing service on high-quality, bond paper. Conservative paper—white, off-white or ivory—is always suitable. Your printing service can help you select a paper which has matching envelopes to enhance your presentation. Be sure to purchase blank paper which matches your résumé, so your cover letters will also match your presentation package.

Writing your résumé should be an introspective, exhilarating, positive, pat-yourself-on-the-back experience. If you approach it with this spirit, your résumé will be one of which you are justifiably proud.

(Source: Lorn B. Coleman, *1997 ASCUS Annual: The Job Search Handbook for Educators* [Evanston, IL: Association for School, College and University Staffing, Inc.], pp. 14–15. Used with permission.)

SAMPLE INTERVIEW QUESTIONS FOR CANDIDATES TO ASK

If you are serious about teaching in the district where you are interviewing, there are many questions to which you need to know the answers before you accept an offer. Your interviewer will surely cover some of your questions, but by asking pertinent questions you will show your interviewer that you do understand fundamental issues relating to teaching. You should have several questions in mind before you arrive for your interview. The following 17 questions should give you a good start.

1. What is the teacher/student ratio in your district?
2. Do you encourage teachers to earn advanced degrees?
3. How many classes a day will I be expected to teach?
4. Do you have teachers serving in areas for which they do not have full certification?
5. Tell me about the students who attend this school.
6. What textbooks does the district use in this subject area?
7. Do teachers participate in curriculum review and change?
8. What support staff members are available to help students and teachers?
9. How does the teaching staff feel about new teachers?
10. What discipline procedures does the district use?
11. Do parents support the schools? Does the community?
12. Do your schools use teacher aides or parent volunteers?
13. What allowances are provided for supplies and materials?
14. Does the administration encourage field trips for students?
15. How are teachers assigned to extracurricular activities? Is compensation provided?
16. Does the district have a statement of educational philosophy or mission?
17. What are prospects for future growth in this community and its schools?

(Source: American Association for Employment in Education. *1997. Job Search Handbook for Educators* [Evanston, IL: Association for School, College and University Staffing, Inc.], p. 23. Used with permission.)

CRITICAL INFORMATION TO KNOW ABOUT SCHOOL DISTRICTS

In your interviews with K–12 school district administrators, it is very important that you know as much as possible about the school, district, and community in which you might be employed. You might want to visit the district while classes are in session to visit the department and building in which you might be working. If at all possible, try to meet the department head and/or building principal by whom you would be supervised. Also, you should be prepared to ask about concerns and issues related to your employment that are of interest to you.

The following are topics about which job applicants typically have questions:

DISTRICT
- Type of district (elementary, high school, or unit)
- History and development of the district
- Characteristics of the student population and community
- Size of the district (number of elementary, junior high/middle, and high schools)
- Central office administrators and their roles
- Grades included at each level of education

CURRICULUM
- Courses in the curriculum in your discipline and their content, sequence, prerequisites, and status as electives or required courses
- Typical schedule of courses in the curriculum (first and/or second semester courses)
- Textbook and supplementary materials, the recency of their adoption, and district adoption procedures
- Availability of AV materials and equipment for classroom use
- New and/or innovative curriculum developments in your discipline in recent years
- Curriculum developments currently being planned

STUDENTS
- Type and size of student body in which a position is available
- Typical class size
- Procedures for student placement

- Characteristics of entering and exiting students (i.e., number or percentage who are enrolled in vocational and college preparatory curricula and the number or percentage who enroll in college on graduation)

INSTRUCTIONAL ASSIGNMENT
- Reasons why the position is available (enrollment increase, retirement, resignation, etc.).
- Number and type of teaching preparations (i.e., self-contained classes or team-taught classes)
- Other instructional assignments
- Methods and frequency of teacher evaluation
- Availability of summer employment
- Assignments on department, school, or district committees
- Duties in the supervision/sponsorship of student activities
- Starting and ending dates of employment
- Contract length

FACULTY
- Number of administrators in the building and their responsibilities
- Size of the faculty within departments and the building
- Number of new teachers hired each year
- Special interests and/or expertise of faculty

STUDENT SERVICES
- Student clubs, organizations, and sports
- Counselling and guidance personnel and services
- Social worker, school nurse, librarian, and other support staff and their roles

COMMUNITY
- Community support for education
- Involvement of parents and other community members in the school program
- Recreational and other facilities in the community
- Demographic information about community residents
- Cost of living and housing in the community

SALARY AND FRINGE BENEFITS
- District salary schedule

- Pay for extracurricular responsibilities
- Reimbursement policies for graduate study
- District requirements for continuing professional education
- Vacation and sick leave, personal leave, and other leave policies
- Substitute teacher procedures
- Payroll schedule
- Medical insurance

SELECTION PROCEDURES
- Number and type of interviews that job candidates can expect

- Individuals involved in the preliminary screening of candidates, interviews, and the final selection
- District requirements for residency of staff

FINAL SUGGESTIONS
- Be certain to read your employment contract carefully before signing it.

(*Source:* Jan E. Kilby, *The ASCUS Annual 1988: A Job Search Handbook for Educators* [Addison, IL: Association for School, College and University Staffing], p. 16. Used with permission.)

RESOURCES FOR TEACHING OUTSIDE THE UNITED STATES

Fulbright Teacher Exchange
Bureau of Educational and Cultural Affairs
U.S. Information Agency
E/ASX, Room 353
301 4th Street, SW
Washington, DC 20547
202-619-4555
E-mail: fulbrigh@xgate_. or fulbrigh@grad.visda.gov.

International Schools Services (ISS)
P.O. Box 5910
15 Roszeo Road
Princeton, NJ 08543
609-452-0990
WWW: iss@iss.edu
E-mail: www.iss.edu

U.S. Department of Defense
Office of Dependents Schools
Recruitment/Assignment Division
4040 North Fairfax Drive, 6th Floor
Arlington, VA 22203
703-696-4413

U.S. Department of State
Office of Overseas Schools
Room 245;
SA29 Dept. of State A/OS
Washington, DC 20522-2902

U.S. Peace Corps Recruiting Office
1990 K Street, NW, Suite 9102
Washington, DC 20526
800-424-8580

University of Northern Iowa
Overseas Placement Service for Educators
Student Services Center #19
Cedar Falls, IA 50614-0390
319-273-2083

ADVICE FOR SUBSTITUTE TEACHERS

FINDING POSITIONS

- Contact schools or school districts in your area and inquire about their method of booking substitute teachers.
- Don't overapply or overbook to the extent that you must turn down assignments too often to make you reliable as a substitute.
- Find out what credentials you must present, and prepare them. You also may be asked to provide proof of CPR or first aid training and the results of a physical examination.
- Substitutes are not limited to their areas of certification, but notify school officials in advance of any areas in which you do not wish to be a substitute teacher.
- Use a telephone answering device to ensure that you don't miss calls, and be prepared for short notice to report to work.
- Keep a calendar of teaching assignments so you can book future assignments accurately in light of your previous commitments.
- Confirm all dates with the school or service.
- When you report to each assignment, complete any paperwork required, making sure information is accurate (and your name and social security number are correct). Keep copies for your records to prove that you did substitute on a particular day.
- Be prepared to wait for your paycheck, and keep pay stubs as proof of payment. Take initiative in making certain that you are paid correctly for each day you teach.

BEING A GOOD SUBSTITUTE

- Arrive early and become familiar with the school, the classroom, and the lesson plans.
- Follow lesson plans as closely as possible. Try to complete lesson plans, but be prepared to be spontaneous as well.
- With or without lesson plans, keep students engaged in learning activities to decrease behavior problems.
- Introduce yourself and establish a positive class atmosphere.
- Enforce classroom and school rules. State your expectations for student behavior at the outset, and use appropriate methods of classroom management.
- Carefully take care of tasks such as recording attendance, collecting homework, and performing supervisory duties.
- Tidy the classroom at the end of the day, and leave a signed written note for the teacher, reporting on how the day went and what students did.
- When you have time, network with teachers, principals, and other staff. Through networking you may learn about full-time positions or long-term substitute assignments.

(Source: Adapted from American Association for Employment in Education, *1997 Job Search Handbook for Educators,* Evanston, IL: Association for School, College, and University Staffing, Inc., pp. 31–32.)

TEACHING AIDS
FOR BEGINNING TEACHERS

NEA BILL OF RIGHTS FOR STUDENT TEACHERS

As a citizen, a student, and a future member of the teaching profession, the individual student teacher has the right:

1. To freedom from unfair discrimination in admission to student teaching and in all aspects of the field experience. Student teachers shall not be denied or removed from an assignment because of race, color, creed, sex, age, national origin, marital status, political or religious beliefs, social or cultural background, or sexual orientation. Nor shall their application be denied because of physical handicap unless it is clear that such handicap will prevent or seriously inhibit their carrying out the duties of the assignment.

2. To be informed in advance of the standards of eligibility for student teaching and of the criteria and procedures for evaluation of his or her classroom performance.

3. To be consulted in advance and have effective voice in decisions regarding assignment, with respect to subject, grade level, school, and cooperating teacher.

4. To be assigned to a cooperating teacher who volunteers to work with the student-teaching program, who is fully qualified to do so, and is appropriately remunerated for the work and given sufficient time to carry out its responsibilities.

5. To be reimbursed by the college or university for any financial hardship caused by the student-teaching assignment; for example, for the costs of traveling excessive distances to the cooperating school district, or for the expenses incurred when the student teacher is assigned to a location so remote from his or her college/university that it is necessary to establish residence there, in addition to the college or university residence.

6. To be informed, prior to the student-teaching period, of all relevant policies and practices of the cooperating school district, including those regarding personnel, curriculum, student requirements, and student-teaching program.

7. To confidentiality of records. Except with the express permission of the student teacher, the college or university shall transmit to the cooperating school district only those student records that are clearly necessary to protect the health and welfare of the student teacher, the cooperating teacher, the students, and others in the cooperating school. All persons having access to the records of student teachers shall respect the confidentiality of those records, as required by law.

8. To be admitted to student teaching and to remain in the student-teaching assignment in the absence of a showing of just cause for termination or transfer through fair and impartial proceedings.

9. To a student-teaching environment that encourages creativity and initiative. The student teacher should have the opportunity, under the perceptive supervision of the cooperating teacher, to develop his or her own techniques of teaching.

10. To a student-teaching environment that encourages the free exploration of ideas and issues as appropriate to the maturity of the students and the topics being studied.

11. To carry out the student-teaching assignment in an atmosphere conducive to learning and to have authority under supervision of the cooperating teacher, to use reasonable means to preserve the learning environment and protect the health and safety of students, the student teacher, and others.

12. To participate, with the cooperating teacher and college/university supervisor, in planning the student-teaching schedule to include, in addition to work with the assigned cooperating teacher, observation of other classes, attendance at professional meetings, and involvement, as appropriate, in extracurricular activities that will enrich and broaden the range of the field experience.

13. To be assigned to duties that are relevant to the student teacher's learning experience. Student teachers shall not be required to act as substitute teacher or teacher aide, nor to handle any nonteaching duties that are not part of the cooperating teacher's duties.

14. To request transfer in the event of prolonged illness of, or serious personality conflict with the cooperating teacher and to have that request

TEACHER'S RESOURCE GUIDE

given favorable consideration without damage to any party's personal or professional status.

15. To a cessation of student-teaching responsibilities in the event and for the duration of a teacher strike at the cooperating school or school district to which the student teacher is assigned. If the strike is a prolonged one, the college or university has the responsibility to reassign the student teacher to another school district.

16. To the same liability protections as are provided by the school district for regularly employed certified teachers.

17. To influence the development and continuing evaluation and improvement of the student-teacher program, including the formulation and systematic review of standards of student teacher eligibility, and criteria and procedures of student teacher evaluation. Such influence shall be maintained through representation of student teachers and recent graduates of the student-teacher program on committees established to accomplish these purposes.

18. To frequent planning and evaluative discussions with the cooperating teacher.

19. To systematic, effective supervision by the college/university supervisor. Such supervision shall include (1) regularly scheduled classroom observations of sufficient frequency and length to permit thorough insight into the strengths and weaknesses of the student teacher's performance; (2) conferences with college/university supervisor immediately fol-

lowing observation, or as soon thereafter as possible, to discuss results of observation; and (3) regularly scheduled three-way evaluation conferences among student teacher, college supervisor, and cooperating teacher, to ensure that the student teacher is fully apprised of his or her progress and is given substantive assistance in assessing and remedying the weaknesses and reinforcing the strengths of his or her performance.

20. To see, sign, and affix written responses to evaluations of his or her classroom performance.

21. To an equitable and orderly means of resolving grievances relating to the student-teaching assignment. The college/university grievance procedure shall incorporate due process guarantees, including the right to be informed in writing of the reasons for any adverse action regarding his or her assignment, and to appeal any such action, with the right to have both student and teacher representation on committees formulated to hear and adjudicate student teacher grievances.

22. To be free to join, or not to join, on or off-campus organizations, and to enjoy privacy and freedom of life-style and conscience in out-of-school activities, unless it is clearly evident that those activities have a harmful effect on the student teacher's classroom performance.

(Source: National Education Association, 1201 16th Street N.W., Washington, D.C., 1977.)

GENERIC TEACHING KNOWLEDGE AND SKILLS

Teacher candidates should be able to do the following:

1. Analyze and interpret student abilities, cultural backgrounds, achievements, and needs:
   - Use school records, including standardized test scores, and anecdotal data, to identify the learner's needs
   - Recognize and interpret various exceptional conditions of children (e.g., limited sight or hearing, cognitive ability or outstanding gifted abilities)
   - Identify cultural backgrounds of students and interpret impact on learning

2. Design instruction that will meet learner needs through appropriate instructional materials, content, activities, format, and goals:
   - Plan a course of action for instruction over a school year, a semester, a grading period, a day, and a lesson
   - Develop lesson plans with objectives or expected outcomes, instructional sequences and activities, and an evaluation design
   - Decide the subject matter to be taught, including sequencing, pacing, emphases, activities, and evaluation
   - Select appropriate print, audiovisual, and computer materials according to established criteria and the needs of students

530   Teacher's Resource Guide

3. Conduct instruction to best facilitate learning:
- Present subject matter and manage activities to maximize learning
- Use a variety of instructional strategies including individual and small or large group instruction, peer teaching, independent study, field projects, computer-assisted instruction, lecture, etc.
- Use instructional technology, including computers, as appropriate

4. Manage the classroom to promote productive learning:
- Regulate classroom time to focus on learning activities
- Manage student interaction with each other and the teacher
- Organize the classroom physical setting to be an effective environment for learning activities

5. Manage student conduct to create a positive climate for student learning:
- Develop, explain, and monitor rules for student conduct
- Deal with distractions and competing tasks to maintain a smooth flow of attractive and challenging tasks for students
- Maintain a focus on productive learning by correcting deviant behavior, varying teaching strategies, and praising desirable conduct

6. Promote classroom communication to evoke and express academic information as well as personal feelings and relationships:
- Use and elicit Standard English in writing and speaking
- Use correct mathematical symbols and processes

- Use body language and other forms of nonverbal communication to express emotions as well as approval, disapproval, permission, etc.

7. Evaluate learning to determine the extent to which instructional objectives are achieved by students:
- Relate evaluation to instructional objectives and be able to select and develop appropriate questions and types of tests
- Elicit students' best efforts in preparation for and in taking examinations
- Create an appropriate environment for test-taking that encourages conscientious and ethical behavior
- Help students develop an acceptance of tests as an opportunity to demonstrate the accomplishment of goals and to identify areas that need strengthening
- Summarize students' performance on units of instruction and report that performance honestly and accurately to both students and parents
- Analyze test results and interpret achievement information meaningfully to students

8. Arrange for conferral and referral opportunities:
- Refer parents/pupils to appropriate professional expertise as necessary following detection of apparent student problems
- Conduct conferences as necessary with parents and special school personnel, such as the school nurse, psychologist, social worker, librarian/media specialist, and guidance counselor

(Source: American Association of Colleges for Teacher Education, *Educating a Profession: Profile of a Beginning Teacher,* Washington, D.C.: American Association of Colleges for Teacher Education, 1983).

NEGOTIATING A SCHOOL'S CULTURE: A POLITICAL ROADMAP FOR THE FIRST-YEAR TEACHER

Congratulations! You've completed your teacher education training program, become certified, and been offered a teaching position! As you begin your assignment, it is essential to keep in mind that successful teachers possess skills in many areas: teaching ability, content knowledge, interpersonal relations and communications, and those nebulous areas—"etiquette, politics and culture."

ETIQUETTE, POLITICS AND CULTURE What do those words—*etiquette, politics, and culture*—mean, and what impact do they have on first year teachers? Some refer to these as the "informal structure" of schools, the "rites of passage" that new teachers must experience.

- Every school has formal and informal cultures and political structures. Learn about these structures as soon as possible. Become acquainted with the informal leaders. The sooner you understand the established culture at the school—whether it is participating in football pools, sitting at a particular table at lunch, or joining in after school activities—the sooner you will be considered effective and involved.

■ Watch, listen, learn to ask questions! Know who to ask! Frequently, colleagues are available for assistance during those first days of school, but once classes begin, you may be left on your own. Ask for help, watch what others do, and be an intuitive observer.

■ Seek a mentor. New teachers all need someone to turn to for guidance and support. Identify another teacher you respect and like, and ask that teacher to provide information, counselling, and encouragement.

■ Volunteer! Join the PTA, work at the school carnival, chaperone a school dance. Become involved with curriculum committees. You'll get to meet many people this way, and your fellow teachers will respect your involvement.

■ Volunteer, but don't be "pushy," and don't intrude. Be available as others invite you into the group.

■ Distinguish between the "good guys" and the "bad guys." Identify the positive staff members and join their team. Avoid the complaining, negative teachers. When you walk into the teacher's lounge and hear a teaching colleague criticizing the principal or ridiculing a student, walk the other way!

■ Be a role model for students. Yes, students may need friends, but you're more than that—you're their teacher. Have well-prepared lessons, be fair and consistent, and provide a positive learning environment.

"The excitement of teaching is embodied in hard work, meeting challenges, and accomplishing goals."

■ Be professional—look the part and act the part. Work on your wardrobe. Weed out the casual, informal clothes that make you look like a college—or high school—student. Exude an aura of dependability and professionalism.

■ Accept the fact that you're the expert! Remember, you *are* the teacher. Parents and students look to you as the one with all the answers. Don't let them down!

■ Be open, yet sensitive, in dealing with parents. Whenever you talk to a mom or a dad about

one of their children, you are talking about an extension of their very beings. Understand that they may be very sensitive and may react emotionally about little Johnny or Susie. Be clear and concise, but tactful and kind.

■ Watch what you say and where you say it. Be honest and open, but sensitive to the informal culture of the school. Don't criticize the school secretary to an aide who may be her best friend. Don't complain about a student in the faculty lounge. Don't talk about school problems in the grocery store.

MEET THE CHALLENGE   New teachers face the challenges of discipline and classroom management, motivation of students, assessment of students' needs and abilities, heavy teaching loads, insufficient preparation time, and building appropriate relationships with fellow teachers, administrators, and parents. However, beginning teachers often have the most difficulty adjusting to the emotional rigors—the politics and etiquette—of the job. Remember:

■ Focus on the positive; avoid the negative.
■ Teaching can be lonely; find a friend.
■ Be patient—wisdom takes time to acquire.
■ Learn to love teaching!
■ Be the best you can be!

The job of teaching is an incredibly challenging one. You will need to give a total commitment to your role as a teacher. But don't confuse something that's difficult with something that's negative. The excitement of teaching is embodied in hard work, meeting challenges, and accomplishing goals.

As time passes (and with help from others), you will learn to work more efficiently and figure out easier and better ways to do those things that at first seemed so difficult. You will have mastered the school's formal and informal structures!

Accept the challenge—be your best—and you'll find that you will be appreciated, respected, and perhaps even loved! You are a teacher—there is no better or more rewarding career!

(Source: Mary Lee Howe in American Association for Employment in Education, *1995 Job Search Handbook for Educators,* Evanston, IL: Association for School, College and University Staffing, Inc., p. 31. Used with permission.)

SIX STRATEGIES FOR A SUCCESSFUL FIRST YEAR OF TEACHING

It has been said that teaching is a lot like skydiving—it's not something that you can ease into! While you will certainly be your students' "real" teacher from the very first day of class, you are not jumping in unprepared. You have studied all the theories, practiced the methods in student teaching, and now it's time to apply everything in your own classroom. The following six strategies are reminders to guide you through a productive and successful first year.

ACCEPT TODAY'S STUDENTS, ASSESSING THEIR PRIOR INTERESTS AND KNOWLEDGE   Your students are products of today's world. Their homes and communities may be very different from the one in which you grew up. Accepting all students who enter the classroom is the first step in teaching them. Getting to know your students at the beginning of the year is crucial. What are their interests and hobbies? What do they do during their free time? Icebreakers include asking about their favorite foods, TV programs, or songs.

Assess your students' study skills as well as their knowledge about subject matter. If, for example, they don't possess outlining skills, belittling your students or their previous teachers will not help them to improve their skills. Rather, teach the outlining skills as you introduce your first unit on history. If they all studied dinosaurs last year, how interested will they be this year? Remember that each student is an individual, and allow for individual differences within your class.

REACH OUT TO PARENTS, COLLEAGUES, ADMINISTRATORS, AND OTHER PROFESSIONALS   Teaching is too important to do alone, isolated in your classroom. Reach out to others for help and support, beginning with your students' parents. Introduce yourself to the parents as early as possible and make sure that your initial phone calls to parents are positive ones. Keep parents informed about your classes by sending out newsletters. When it's time for parent conferences, parents should already know who you are and some specifics about the classroom. Keep your principal informed, too, with copies of the same newsletters. While it's true that teachers work in a "sea of students," there are other adults in your building. Network with them! Many new teachers are paired with veterans in mentoring programs. If you are paired with a mentor, make the most of the opportunity by finding time to meet together and ask lots of questions.

Professional organizations provide wonderful resources and attending a conference may be just what you need to rejuvenate yourself during the bleak winter months. A nearby college or university may also offer weekend or after-school seminars. Call some friends from your last education course and get together for coffee and a discussion of the concerns and joys of your first year of teaching.

ORGANIZE, PREPARE, REORGANIZE, AND PREPARE AGAIN
There is no such thing as being overprepared. Even if you forget all the steps in a lesson plan, remember to make a plan of some sort with an introduction, a body, and a conclusion. Keep all of your plans in a file system where you can find them next year.

Organize your recordkeeping because accurate attendance records and documented grades are important. Organize your classroom so that it is user-friendly. A table by the door is a good place for students to pick up their graded papers and any other handouts they need for your class. Students can use another table to turn in papers and find past assignments. Have an assignment on the board and let students know that they will always accomplish something in your class.

PLAN FOR CLASSROOM MANAGEMENT   Investing time at the beginning of the year to teach the expected routines and behaviors of the classroom will prove rewarding throughout the year. Your classroom management plan should have rules, consequences, and positive motivators. Do remember that you are the one who will enforce the rules! Rules should be few in number—no more than four or five—and they should be posted, with copies sent home to parents. While every teacher has to be firm and fair, we have to be humane as well. Have reasonable consequences and get back-up support for major infractions. A teacher's stare and voice are keys to good management. Walking around the room and being in close proximity to students can stop many small problems.

Today's students need guidelines. A classroom management plan sets these guidelines so that students can go about the business of learning. Classroom management works when the students know that their teacher is respectful of them and serious about the learning process.

TEACH WITH A VARIETY OF STRATEGIES When you first approach the curriculum, don't ask, "How can I teach this material?" Rather, ask, "How can the students learn this material?" Students learn in many ways—reading, writing, discussing, experimenting, peer teaching, practicing, drawing, acting, interviewing, and presenting. Include these activities in your lesson plans and keep the students engaged.

Take advantage of other teachers in your district and team up with them to teach some units. Invite outside experts into your classroom. Use technology in the classroom.

Above all, don't forget to ask the students themselves how they learn best. Often the best strategy is not to attempt to teach everything, but rather to get the students interested so that they want to continue to learn about the subject.

BALANCE THE MANY ROLES YOU WILL PLAY AS A TEACHER Balancing the many roles of a teacher can be very stressful. In order to have the energy to teach, you will need to take care of yourself with a healthy lifestyle that includes diet, exercise, and relaxation. It is even more important to take the time to reflect upon your teaching and your role in the teaching profession.

Successful teachers develop a philosophy for what they do and why they do it. A philosophy for teaching can be as straightforward as "I teach to help the children," or "I teach to share my love of this subject." Your philosophy of teaching will guide you to a successful first year and a successful career in the teaching profession.

(Source: Mary C. Clement, 1997, American Association for Employment in Education, *1997 Job Search Handbook,* Evanston, IL: Association for School, College, and University Staffing, Inc., p. 37. Used with permission.)

DIMENSIONS OF CLASSROOM ORGANIZATION AND MANAGEMENT

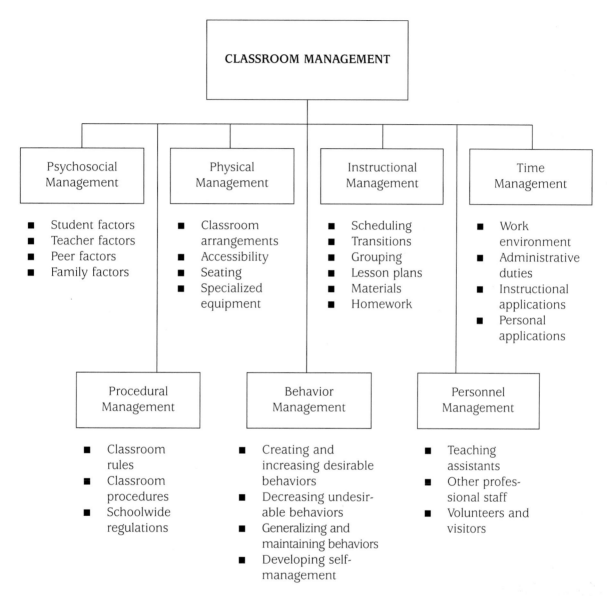

CLASSROOM MANAGEMENT

Psychosocial Management
- Student factors
- Teacher factors
- Peer factors
- Family factors

Physical Management
- Classroom arrangements
- Accessibility
- Seating
- Specialized equipment

Instructional Management
- Scheduling
- Transitions
- Grouping
- Lesson plans
- Materials
- Homework

Time Management
- Work environment
- Administrative duties
- Instructional applications
- Personal applications

Procedural Management
- Classroom rules
- Classroom procedures
- Schoolwide regulations

Behavior Management
- Creating and increasing desirable behaviors
- Decreasing undesirable behaviors
- Generalizing and maintaining behaviors
- Developing self-management

Personnel Management
- Teaching assistants
- Other professional staff
- Volunteers and visitors

(Source: Tom E. C. Smith, Edward A. Polloway, James R. Patton, Carol A. Dowdy (1995). *Teaching Students with Special Needs in Inclusive Settings.* Allyn and Bacon, p. 352. Used with permission.)

PARENT RESOURCE CENTERS

PROGRAM/ADDRESS	STATE	PHONE
Native American Parental Assistance Program P.O. Box 366	San Jacinto, CA 92383	909-654-2781
Colorado Parent Information & Resource Ctr 1445 Market St. Suite 220	Denver, CO 80202	303-820-5631
Greater Washington Urban League 3501 14th St, NW	Wash, DC 20010	202-265-8200
Florida Center for Parental Involvement 7406 Dixon Ave.	Tampa, FL 33604	813-229-3179
Parental Training Resource Assistance Ctr P.O. Box 1726	Albany, GA 31702-1726	912-888-0999
Parents & Children Together 1475 Linapuni Street, Rm 117 A	Honolulu, HI 96819	808-841-6177
Iowa Parent Resource Ctr 1025 Penkridge Dr.	Iowa City, IA 52246	319-354-5606
Parental Assistance Program 203 High St.	Flemingsburg, KY 41041	606-845-0081
Family Resource Project P.O. Box 2067	Augusta, ME 04338-2067	207-582-2504
Parenting Resource & Support Partnership 332 W. Edmonston Dr.	Rockville, MD 20852	301-294-4959
Mass. Parent Training & Empowerment Project MIT Building 20, Room 129	Cambridge, MA 02139	617-253-7093
Families United for Success 272 East 8th Street, Suite B	Holland, MI 49423	616-396-7566
Families & Schools Together (FAST) Forward 4826 Chicago Ave., South	Minneapolis, MN 55417	612-827-2966
Missouri Partnership for Parenting Assistance 300 S. Broadway	St. Louis, MO 83102	314-421-1970
Center for Healthy Families 3196 S. Maryland Parkway #307	Las Vegas, NV 89109	702-731-8373
Building Family Strengths P.O. Box 1422	Concord, NH 03302-1422	603-224-7005
Prevent Child Abuse–New Jersey 35 Halsey Street, Suite 300	Newark, NJ 07102-3031	201-643-3710

PROGRAM/ADDRESS	STATE	PHONE
CONNECTIONS P.O. Box 545	Geneseo, NY 14454	716-245-5681
Parents in Partnership Project P.O. Box 16	Davidson, NC 28036	704-892-1321
Ohio Parent Information Ctr. 4837 Ward St.	Cincinnati, OH 45227	513-272-0273
Parents As Partners in Education 4801 N. Classen, Suite 200	Oklahoma City, OK 73118	405-840-1359
S.W. Penn. Parental Assistance Center Project 22 West High St.	Waynesburg, PA 15370	412-852-2893
Black Hills Parent Resource Network P.O. Box 218	Sturgis, SD 57785	605-347-4467
Parents First 421 Great Circle Road, Suite 104	Nashville, TN 37228	615-255-4982
Family Focus Project 8401 Shoal Creek Blvd.	Austin, TX 78757	512-454-3706
Vermont Family Resource Project P.O. Box 646	Middlebury, VT 05753	802-388-3171
Children's Home Society of Washington 201 South 34th St.	Seattle, WA 98408	206-472-3355
Parents Plus P.O. Box 452	Menasha, WI 54952-0452	414-729-1787

Source: U.S. Department of Education. (March 1996). *Community Update,* p. 4.

PROGRAM CONTACTS FOR FAMILY-SCHOOL-COMMUNITY PARTNERSHIPS

Head Start Literacy Program:
Tizziana Fusco Weber
Manager, Community Relations
United Technologies Corporation
United Technologies Building
Hartford, CT 06101
(203) 728-7000

Hispanic Mother/Daughter Program:
Dr. Norma Guerra
University of Texas—San Antonio
San Antonio, TX 78285
(210) 691-4120

San Diego City Schools:
Jeana Preston
Parent Involvement Specialist
Rm 2121—Education Center
4100 Normal St.
San Diego, CA 92103
(619) 293-8560

Pittsburgh Public Schools:
Public Affairs
Pittsburgh Public Schools
341 S. Bellefield Ave.
Pittsburgh, PA 15213
(412) 622-3615
foulds@oberon.pps.pgh.pa.us

TIPS:
Publications Office
Center on Families, Communities,
Schools and Children's Learning
Johns Hopkins University
3505 North Charles St.
Baltimore, MD 21218
(410) 516-8800

Natchez-Adams School District Parent Center:
Judy H. Sturdivant, Chapter I Coordinator
Chapter 1 Parent Center
Natchez-Adams School District
P.O. Box 1188
Natchez, MS 39121
(601) 445-2819

Robert E. Lee High School:
Carlton Tucker, Principal
Robert E. Lee High School
6529 Beverly Hill
Houston, TX 77057
(713) 782-7310

Transparent School Model:
Jerold Bauch, Director
Betty Phillips Center for Parenthood Education
Box 81
Peabody College of Vanderbilt University
Nashville, TN 37203
(615) 322-8080

Katy Elementary School:
Nancy Dickson Stiles, Principal
5726 Sixth St.
Katy, TX 77493
(713) 391-4761

Sarah Scott Middle School:
Sandra Kelley, Principal
2000 South 9th St.
Terre Haute, IN 47802
(812) 462-4381

Kettering Middle School:
Marian White-Hood, Principal
65 Herrington Dr.
Upper Marlboro, MD 20772
(301) 808-4060

Booker T. Washington Elementary School:
Arnetta Rodgers, Principal
606 E. Grove St.
Champaign, IL 61820
(217) 351-3901

Source: The National Education Goals Report: Executive Summary: Improving Education Through Family-School-Community Partnerships, 1995 National Goals Panel.

CURRICULAR AND INSTRUCTIONAL RESOURCES

SELECTED RESOURCES FOR SERVICE LEARNING

BOOKS

150 Ways Teens Can Make a Difference: A Handbook for Action. M. Salzman and T. Relagies. Princeton, NJ: Peterson's Guides, Inc., 1991.

Building Support for Service Learning. Palo Alto, CA: Service Learning 2000 Center, 1996. (Available from The Service Learning 2000 Center, 50 Embarcadero Road, Palo Alto, CA 94301, 415-322-7271; E-mail: sl2000@forsythe.stanford.edu.)

High School Service-Learning Guide. Baltimore: Maryland State Department of Education, 1993. (Available from the Maryland Student Service Alliance, Maryland Department of Education, 200 W. Baltimore Street, Baltimore, MD 21201-2595, 410-767-0356.)

How to Establish a High School Service Learning Program. Judith T. Witmer and Carolyn S. Anderson. Alexandria, VA: Association for Supervision and Curriculum Development, 1994.

Learning by Giving: K–8 Service-Learning Curriculum Guide. R. Cairn. St. Paul, MN: National Youth Leadership Council, April 1993.

Learning Through Service: Ideas from the Field, 1994. Palo Alto, CA: Service Learning 2000 Center, 1995. (Available from The Service Learning 2000 Center, 50 Embarcadero Road, Palo Alto, CA 94301, 415-322-7271; E-mail: sl2000@forsythe. stanford.edu.)

Struggling to Learn Better: Portraits of Three High School Service Learning Programs. Palo Alto, CA: Service Learning 2000 Center, 1995. (Available from The Service Learning 2000 Center, 50 Embarcadero Road, Palo Alto, CA 94301, 415-322-7271.)

ORGANIZATIONS AND OTHER RESOURCES

National Service Learning Cooperative Clearinghouse
R460 Vo/Tech Building
1954 Buford Avenue
St. Paul, MN 55108
800-808-SERVE
E-mail: serve@maroon.tc.umn.edu
www.nicsl.coled.umn.edu

Association for Experiential Education
2305 Canyon Boulevard
Suite 100
Boulder, CO 80302
303-492-1411
E-mail: mikal@aee.org
www.ag.arizona.edu/ ~ rchamber./aee

National Helper's Network
245 5th Avenue
Suite 1705
New York, NY 10016
E-mail: helpnet@igc.apc.org

National Society for Experiential Education
3509 Haworth Drive
Suite 207
Raleigh, NC 27609
919-787-3263
E-mail: nsee@datasolv.com
www.tripod.com//nsee

National Youth Leadership Council
1910 West County Road B.
St. Paul, MN 55113-1337
800-366-6952
E-mail: NYLCUSA@aol.com

Service Learning 2000 Center
50 Embarcadero Road
Palo Alto, CA 94301
415-322-7271
E-mail: sl2000@forsythe.stanford.edu

Youth Service America
1101 15th Street, N.W.
Suite 200
Washington, DC 20005
E-mail: info@ysa.org
www.servenet.org

SELECTED RESOURCES FOR INCLUDING EXCEPTIONAL LEARNERS

Adapting Curriculum and Instruction in Inclusive Classrooms: A Teacher's Desk Reference. (Available from Institute for Study of Developmental Disabilities, 2853 E. 10th St., Bloomington, IN 47408-2601, 812-855-6508.)

Creating Schools for All Our Students: What 12 Schools Have to Say (Publication #P5064). (Available from Council for Exceptional Children, Dept. K50170, 1920 Association Drive, Reston, VA 20191, 800-CEC-READ.)

Inclusive Classrooms from A to Z and *I Can Learn! Strategies and Activities for Gray-Area Children.* Gretchen Goodman. (Available from Crystal Springs Books, 10 Sharon Rd., P.O. Box 500, Peterborough, NH 03458-0500, 800-321-0401.)

Educational Care: A System for Understanding and Helping Children with Learning Problems at Home and in Schools. Mel Levine. (Available from Educators Publishing Service, 31 Smith Place, Cambridge, MA 02138, 800-225-5750.)

Taming the Dragons: Real Help for Real School Problems. Susan Setley. (Available from Starfish Publishing Co., 5621 Delmar Blvd., Suite 110, St. Louis, MO 63112-2660, 314-367-9611.)

Teaching Kids with Learning Difficulties in the Regular Classroom. Susan Winebrenner. (Available from Free Spirit Publishing, 400 1st Ave. North, Suite 616, Minneapolis, MN 55401, 800-735-7323.)

BOOKS FOR TEACHERS ON MAINSTREAMING AND INCLUSION

Cooperative Learning Activities and Strategies for Inclusion: Celebrating Diversity in the Classroom. J. W. Putnam. Baltimore, MD: Paul Brookes, 1994.

Curriculum Considerations In Inclusive Schools. W. Stainback and S. Stainback (eds.). Baltimore, MD: Brookes Publishing Co., 1992.

Including Students with Special Needs: A Practical Guide for Classroom Teachers. M. Friend and W. Bursuck. Boston: Allyn and Bacon, 1996.

Inclusion: A Guide for Educators. S. Stainback and W. Stainback (eds.). Baltimore, MD: Paul Brookes, 1996.

Support Networks for Inclusive Schooling: Interdependent Integrated Education. W. Stainback and S. Stainback (eds.). Baltimore, MD: Paul Brookes, 1990.

Teaching Girls and Boys With Disabilities: Inclusion in the Classroom. Women's Education Equity Act Resource Center. (Available from WEEA Equity Resource Center, Education Development Center, Inc., 55 Chapel Street, Suite 200, Newton, MA 02158-1060, 800-225-3088; World Wide Web Site: http://www.edc.org/CEEC/WEEA1996.)

Teaching Mainstreamed, Diverse, and At-Risk Students in the General Education Classroom. S. Vaughn, C. S. Bos, and J. S. Schumm. Boston: Allyn and Bacon, 1997.

Teaching Students in Inclusive Settings: From Theory to Practice. D. F. Bradley, M. E. King-Sears, and D. Tessier-Switlick. Boston: Allyn and Bacon, 1997.

Teaching Students with Special Needs in Inclusive Settings, 2nd. ed. T. E. C. Smith, E. A. Polloway, J. R. Patton, and C. A. Dowdy. Boston: Allyn and Bacon, 1998.

Winners All: A Call for Inclusive Schools. (Available from the National Association of State Boards of Education Study Group on Special Education; NASBE, 1012 Cameron St., Alexandria, VA 22314, 703-684-4000.)

ORGANIZATIONS

The Churchill Center. Marsha Kessler, Churchill Center, 22 E. 95th St., New York, NY 10128, 212-722-7226.

Council for Exceptional Children (CEC). CEC, 1920 Association Drive, Reston, VA 20191, 800-641-7824; E-mail: cec@cec.sped.org   World Wide Web site: www.cec.sped.org.

The National Center on Educational Restructuring and Inclusion (NCERI). NCERI, City University of New York, 33 W. 42nd St., New York, NY 10036, 212-642-2656.

SELECTED RESOURCES FOR TEACHING STUDENTS AT RISK

ORGANIZATIONS

American Red Cross
431 18th Street NW
Washington, DC 20006
(703) 206-6750
www.redcross.org

Has produced several publications on AIDS. For sample copies, contact your local office or write AIDS Education Office.

Center for Successful Child Development
4848 South State Street
Chicago, IL 60609
(312) 373-8680

Child and Family Policy Center
218 6th Avenue
Suite 1021
Des Moines, IA 50309-4006
(515) 280-9027
hn2228@handsnet.org

Especially state policy on collaborating to meet children's needs.

Children's Defense Fund
25 E Street, NW
Washington, DC 20001
(202) 628-8787
cdfinfo@childrensdefense.org
www.childrensdefense.org

Improving the quality of schools and building parent and community support for achievement.

The Family Resource Coalition
200 South Michigan Avenue
Chicago, IL 60604
(312) 341-0900
hn4860@handsnet.org

Particularly good on ways to build support and resources that empower families and enhance the capacities of parents.

Foundation for Child Development
345 E. 46th Street
Suite 700
New York, NY 10017
(212) 697-3150
hn5863@connectinc.com

Institute for Educational Leadership, et al.
1001 Connecticut Avenue, NW
Suite 310
Washington, DC 20036-5541
(202) 822-8405
fax (202) 872-4050
bryants@iel.org
www.iel.org

National Coalition for an Urban Children's Agenda
c/o National Assoc. of State Boards of Education
Attn: Tom Schultz
1012 Cameron Street
Alexandria, VA 22314
(703) 684-4000
boards@nasbe.org
www.nasbe.org

Collaborative interagency models of service delivery.

National Coalition of Hispanic Health and Human Services Organizations
1501 16th Street NW
Washington, DC 20036
(202) 387-5000
cossmho@cossmho.org

Assists those needing AIDS information in Spanish.

National Collaboration for Youth
1319 F Street, NW
Suite 601
Washington, DC 20004
(202) 347-2080
www.nassembly.org/nonprofit

National Community Education Association
3929 Old Lee Highway, Suite 91A
Fairfax, VA 22030
(703) 359-8973
ncea@ncea.com

Good resource on ways to get broad-based community involvement to increase academic achievement and improve school climate.

National Education Association

NEA Communications
1201 16th Street NW
Washington, DC 20036
(202) 833-4000
neatoday@aol.com
www.nea.org

Published guide for members, titled "The Facts About AIDS." Write for NEA AIDS Booklet.

National Network of Runaway and Youth Services

1319 F Street, NW
Suite 401
Washington, DC 20004
(202) 783-7949

Networking Project for People with Disabilities

YWCA of New York
610 Lexington Avenue
New York, NY 10022
(212) 755-4500

Outward Bound USA

Route 9D, R2 Box 280
Garrison, NY 10524
(800) 243-8520
www.outwardbound.org

Parent Aide Support Service

Nebraska Dept. of Social Services
1050 N Street
Lincoln, NE 68508
(402) 471-7000

Parents as Teachers

10176 Corporate Square Drive
Suite 230
St. Louis, MO 63132
(314) 432-4330
patnc.patnc.org
www.patnc.org

Search Institute

700 South 3rd Street
Suite 210
Minneapolis, MN 55415
(800) 888-7828

BOOKS AND RELATED RESOURCES ON TEACHING STUDENTS AT RISK

101 Ways to Develop Student Self-Esteem and Responsibility. Jack Canfield and Frank Siccone. Boston: Allyn and Bacon, 1995.

The Accelerated Schools Resource Guide. Wendy S. Hopfenberg, Henry M. Levin, Christopher Chase, S. Georgia Christensen, Melanie Moore, Pilar Soler, Ilse Brunner, Beth Keller, and Gloria Rodriguez. San Francisco: Jossey-Bass Publishers, 1993.

"Addressing Race, Ethnicity and Culture in the Classroom," Deborah A. Byrnes. In *Common Bonds: Anti-Bias Teaching in a Diverse Society,* 2nd ed. Deborah A. Byrnes and Gary Kiger (eds.). Wheaton, MD: Association for Childhood Education International, 1996.

Beyond Discipline: From Compliance to Community. Alfie Kohn. Alexandria, VA: Association for Supervision and Curriculum Development, 1996.

"Class Differences: Economic Inequality in the Classroom," Ellen Davidson and Nancy Schniedewind. In *Common Bonds: Anti-Bias Teaching in a Diverse Society,* 2nd ed. Deborah A. Byrnes and Gary Kiger (eds.). Wheaton, MD: Association for Childhood Education International, 1996.

Closing the Achievement Gap: A Vision for Changing Beliefs and Practices. Belinda Williams (ed.). Alexandria, VA: Association for Supervision and Curriculum Development, 1996.

Cooperative Learning, Cooperative Lives: A Sourcebook of Learning Activities for Building A Peaceful New World. Nancy Schniedewind and Ellen Davidson. Dubuque, Iowa: W. C. Brown, 1987.

Hope at Last for At-Risk Youth. R. D. Barr and W. H. Parrett. Boston: Allyn and Bacon, 1995.

Multiple Intelligences in the Classroom. Thomas Armstrong. Alexandria, VA: Association for Supervision and Curriculum Development, 1994.

Open Minds to Equality: Learning Activities to Promote Race, Sex, Class and Age Equity, 2nd ed. Nancy Schniedewind and Ellen Davidson. Englewood Cliffs, NJ: Prentice Hall, 1996.

The New Circles of Learning: Cooperation in the Classroom and School. David W. Johnson, Roger T. Johnson, and Edythe J. Holubec. Alexandria, VA: Association for Supervision and Curriculum Development, 1994.

Reducing School Violence Through Conflict Resolution. David W. Johnson and Roger T. Johnson. Alexandria, VA: Association for Supervision and Curriculum Development, 1995.

Students at Risk. H. Lee Manning and Leroy G. Baruth. Boston: Allyn and Bacon, 1995.

Talk It Out: Conflict Resolution in the Elementary Classroom. Barbara Porro. Alexandria, VA: Association for Supervision and Curriculum Development, 1996.

Teaching and Learning through Multiple Intelligences. L. Campbell, B. Campbell, and D. Dickinson. Boston: Allyn and Bacon, 1996.

SELECTED RESOURCES FOR ACHIEVING GENDER EQUITY

BOOKS AND REPORTS

Achieving Gender Equity: Strategies for the Classroom. Hogan. Boston, Allyn and Bacon, 1995.

Anti-Bias Curriculum: Tools for Empowering Young Children. Louise Derman-Sparks and the ABC Task Force. Washington, DC: National Association for the Education of Young Children, 1989.

Creating a Gender-Fair Multicultural Curriculum. American Association of University Women. An AAUW Issue Brief, 1992. (Available from AAUW, 1111 16th Street, NW, Washington, DC 20036, 202-785-7700.)

Gender/Ethnic Expectations and Student Achievement (GESA): Teacher Handbook. D. A. Grayson and M. D. Martin, 1996. (Available from Gray Mill Publications, 31630 Railroad Canyon, Canyon Lake, CA, 92587.)

Gender Equity for Educators, Parents, and Community. Women's Equity for Educators Publishing Center, 1995.

"Gender Equity in the Classroom," Beverly Hardcastle Stanford. In *Common Bonds: Anti-bias Teaching in a Diverse Society* (2nd ed.), Deborah Byrnes and Gary Kiger (eds.).Washington, DC: Association for Childhood Education International, 1996.

Gender Issues in Education. H. Grossman and S. H. Grossman. Boston: Allyn and Bacon, 1994.

Growing Smart: What's Working for Girls in Schools. American Association of University Women (AAUW) report, researched by Sunny Hansen, Joyce Walker, and Barbara Flom, 1995. (Available from AAUW, 1111 16th Street, NW, Washington, DC 20036, 202-785-7700.)

SELECTED CURRICULAR RESOURCES

A-Gay-Yah: A Gender Equity Curriculum for Grades 6–12. Developed by the American Indian Resource Center, 1992. (Available from Women's Education Equity Act Equity Resource Center, Education Development Center, Inc., 55 Chapel Street, Suite 200, Newton, MA 02158-1060.)

Add-Ventures for Girls: Building Math Confidence. Margaret Franklin, 1990. (Available from WEEA Equity Resource Center, Education Development Center, Inc., 55 Chapel Street, Suite 200, Newton, MA 02158-1060.)

Math and Science for the Coed Classroom. P. B. Campbell and J. N. Storo, 1996. (Set of four pamphlets available from WEEA Equity Resource Center, Education Development Center, 55 Chapel Street, Suite 200, Newton, MA 02158-1060, 800-225-3088.)

Options for Girls: A Door to the Future. 1992. (Available from Foundation for Women's Resources, Pro-Ed, 3500 Jefferson, Suite 210, Austin, TX 78731. E-mail: fwravs1@onr.com; Internet: http://www.womensresources.com.)

OTHER RESOURCES

Education Equity Concepts. 114 East 32nd Street, Suite 701, New York, NY 10016, 212-725-1803; E-mail: 75507.1306@compuserve.

EQUALS programs. Lawrence Hall of Science, University of California, Berkeley, CA 94720, 510-642-1823; E-mail: equals@uclink.berkeley.edu; Internet: http://equals.lhs.berkeley.edu.

FAMILY MATH. Lawrence Hall of Science, University of California, Berkeley, CA 94720.

National Women's History Project. 7738 Bell Road, Windsor, CA 95492-8518, 707-838-6000; E-mail: nwhp@aol.com; Internet: http://www.nwhp.org.

Women's Educational Equity Act Resource Center. WEEA Equity Resource Center; Education Development Center, Inc., 55 Chapel Street, Suite 200, Newton, MA 02158-1060, 800-225-3088. World Wide Web Site: http://www.edc.org/CEEC/WEEA.

SELECTED RESOURCES
FOR MULTICULTURAL EDUCATION

BOOKS FOR TEACHERS

Affirming Diversity: The Sociopolitical Context of Multicultural Education. Sonia Nieto. White Plains, NY: Longman, 1996.

Celebrating Diversity: Building Self-Esteem in Today's Multicultural Classroom. Frank Siccone. Boston: Allyn and Bacon, 1994.

Common Bonds: Anti-Bias Teaching in a Diverse Society (2nd ed.). Deborah Byrnes and Gary Kiger (eds.). Washington, DC: Association for Childhood Education International, 1996.

The Dreamkeepers: Successful Teachers of African American Children. G. Ladson-Billings. San Francisco: Jossey-Bass Publishers, 1994.

Making Schooling Multicultural: Campus and Classroom. Carl A. Grant and Mary Louise Gomez. Englewood Cliffs, NJ: Prentice Hall, 1996.

Multicultural Education: Issues and Perspectives (3rd ed.). James A. Banks and Cherry A. McGee Banks (eds.). Boston: Allyn and Bacon, 1997.

Multicultural Education of Children and Adolescents (2nd ed.). M. Lee Manning and Leroy Baruth. Boston: Allyn and Bacon, 1996.

Not Only English: Affirming America's Multilingual Heritage. H. A. Daniels (ed.). Urbana, IL: National Council of Teachers of English, 1990.

Teaching Strategies for Ethnic Studies (6th ed.). James A. Banks. Boston: Allyn and Bacon, 1997.

Transforming the Curriculum: Ethnic Studies and Women Studies. Johnella E. Butler and John C. Walter (eds.). Albany, NY: State University of New York Press, 1990.

CURRICULAR RESOURCES

Anti-Bias Curriculum: Tools for Empowering Young Children. Louise Derman-Sparks and the A.B.C. Task Force. Washington, DC: National Association for the Education of Young Children, 1989.

Creating a Gender-Fair Multicultural Curriculum. American Association of University Women. An AAUW Issue Brief, 1992. (Available from AAUW, 1111 16th Street, NW, Washington, DC 20036, 202-785-7700.)

Multicultural Leader. Quarterly newsletter published by the Educational Materials and Services Center, 144 Railroad Avenue, Suite 107, Edmonds, WA 98020. Provides news on current theory, research, and teaching materials on race and ethnicity, gender, social class, and exceptionality.

Multicultural Teaching: A Handbook of Activities, Information and Resources (4th ed.). P. L. Tiedt and I. M. Tiedt. Boston: Allyn and Bacon, 1995.

Open Minds to Equality: A Sourcebook of Learning Activities to Promote Race, Sex, Class and Age Equity. Nancy Schniedewind and Ellen Davidson. Englewood Cliffs, NJ: Prentice Hall, 1983.

"Teacher They Called Me a _____!": Confronting Prejudice and Discrimination in the Classroom. Deborah A. Byrnes. New York: Anti-Defamation League of B'Nai B'rith, 1995.

Teaching Tolerance. Journal mailed twice a year at no charge to educators. Published by the Southern Poverty Law Center, which founded Teaching Tolerance in 1991 to provide teachers with resources and ideas to help promote harmony in the classroom. The Law Center is a nonprofit legal and educational foundation located at 400 Washington Ave., Montgomery, AL 36104.

FREE CURRICULUM MATERIALS

For free curriculum materials, consult the *Educators' Index of Free Materials,* an index published annually by

Educators Progress Service, Inc.
214 Center Street
Randolph, WI 53956
(414) 326-3126

As there is a rapid turnover in the availability of free materials, consult the most recent edition of the index (most college libraries subscribe to the index). In the following list, the numbers of free materials are given in parentheses.

Administration
    Board of Education (2)
    Superintendents and Principals (10)
Fine Arts
    Music Education (3)
Health and Physical Education
    Health Education (583)
    Nutrition Instruction (103)
    Physical Education and Recreation (77)
    Safety and First Aid (16)
Language Arts
    Reading, Writing, Spelling, and Literature (17)
    Television and Radio (6)
Science and Mathematics
    Earth-Space Science (16)
    Environmental Education
        Conservation (14)
        Forestry (1)
        General (34)
    General Science (52)
    Life Sciences (29)
    Mathematics (9)
    Physical Science (4)
Social Studies
    Citizenship (108)
    Economics (77)
    Geography
        United States and Territories (63)
        Various Other Countries (122)
    History (42)

    Sociology (76)
    World Affairs (29)
Special Areas
    Cocurricular Activities (15)
    Consumer Education (92)
    Driver Education (9)
    Guidance (148)
    Special Education (57)
    Transportation (6)
Vocational Education
    Agriculture
        Animal Husbandry (40)
        Crops and Soils (5)
        Farm Management (2)
    Home Economics Education
        Clothing Instruction (3)
        Cooking Instruction (47)
        Family Life Education (12)
        Home Management (19)
    Industrial Education (57)
Visual and Audiovisual Aids
    Charts, Pictures, and Posters (36)
    Exhibits (20)
    Magazines and Newsletters (66)
    Maps (6)

(Source: *Educators Index of Free Materials,* 105th ed, Mary Parent (ed). Randolph, WI: Educators Progress Service, Inc., 1996, p. ix.)

RESOURCES FOR EDUCATIONAL TECHNOLOGY

BOOKS ON INTEGRATING EDUCATIONAL TECHNOLOGY FOR TEACHERS

Creating Videos for School Use. W. J. Valmont. Boston: Allyn and Bacon, 1995.

Computers in the Classroom: How Teachers and Students Are Using Technology to Transform Learning. Andrea R. Gooden, Author. Fred Silverman, Ed. Jossey-Bass Publishers and Apple Press, 1996.

Computers in Education, 3rd ed. Paul F. Merrill, K. Hammons, B. R. Vincent, P. L. Reynolds, and L. Christensen. Boston: Allyn and Bacon, 1996.

Educational Computing: Learning with Tomorrow's Technologies. 2nd ed. C. D. Maddux, D. L. Johnson, and J. W. Willis. Boston: Allyn and Bacon, 1997.

The Educator's Guide to Hypercard and Hypertalk, 2nd ed. George H. Culp and G. Morgan Watkins. Boston: Allyn and Bacon, 1995.

Internet Adventures: Step-by-Step Guide for Finding and Using Educational Resources, Version 1.2. Cynthia Leshin. Boston: Allyn and Bacon, 1997.

Internet (and More) for Kids. Barbara Kurshan and Deneen Frazier. Alameda, CA: Sybex, 1994.

Internet Yellow Pages. Indianapolis, IN: New Riders Publishing, 1996.

The Internet for Teachers. Bard Williams (ed.). Foster City, CA: IDG Books, 1995.

Multimedia in the Classroom. P. W. Agnew, A. S. Kellerman, and J. Meyer. Boston: Allyn and Bacon, 1996.

Multimedia Magic: Exploring the Power of Multimedia Production. Arnie H. Abrams. Boston: Allyn and Bacon, 1996.

Teaching with Technology. Peter Desberg and Farah Fisher. Boston: Allyn and Bacon, 1995.

Teachers, Computers, and Curriculum: Microcomputers in the Classroom, 2nd ed. Paul G. Geisert and Mynga K. Futrell. Boston: Allyn and Bacon, 1995.

Technology for Teaching and Learning of Science. Karen E. Reynolds and Roberta H. Barba. Boston: Allyn and Bacon, 1997.

Using Interactive Video in Education. P. Semrau and B. Boyer. Boston: Allyn and Bacon, 1994.

Using a Microcomputer in the Classroom, 3rd ed. Gary G. Bitter, Ruth Camuse, and Vicki L. Durbin. Boston, Allyn and Bacon, 1993.

Welcome to the Internet: From Mystery to Master. Tom Badgett and Corey Sandler. New York: MIS Press, 1995.

World Wide Web for Teachers: An Interactive Guide. Ralph Cafolla, Dan Kauffman, and Richard H. Knee. Boston: Allyn and Bacon, 1997.

Young Children and Computers: A World of Discovery. Susan W. Haugland and June L. Wright. Boston: Allyn and Bacon, 1997.

SAMPLER OF ON-LINE RESOURCES FOR EDUCATORS

Association for Educational Communications and Technology (AECT)
sherylk@aect.org
http://www.aect.org/
Information on copyright laws, new products and trends, and conferences

AT&T Learning Network
(800) 809-1097
hearingnet@attmail.com
http://www.att.com/learning_network
K–12 curriculum-based multimedia Learning Circles

Big Sky Telegraph
franko@bigsky.dillon.mt.us
Rural distance learning and professional development resources for educators

Challenger Center for Space Science Education
www.challenger.org
Network for science education teleconferencing

Commercial Collaborative Learning Services
http://edweb.cnidr.org/comcoll.html
Directory of on-line collaborative learning projects and subscription information

Computer as Learning Partner
clp@obelisk.berkeley.edu
http://www.clp.berkeley.edu/CLP.html
Research on middle school science instruction

Computer Learning Foundation (CLF)
http://www.computerlearning.org
Resource guides and strategies for using computers in the classroom

Cyber-School Magazine
www.cyberschoolmag.com
Articles for teachers and students on diverse topics and links to more than 1,000 learning sites

EdWeb K–12 Resource Guide
http://edweb.cnidr.org/k12.html

Federal and State Operated Servers
http://edweb.cnidr.org:90/k12.html
http://edweb.cnidr.org/gopherwww.gov.html
http://edweb.cnidr.org/statenets.html
Directories of federal and state government networks and on-line educational resources

> **The AskERIC Virtual Library**
> gopher://ericir.syr.edu
> Federal government information server for education

> **California Department of Education Goldmine**
> gopher://goldmine.cde.ca.gov

> **CK:P—The Common Knowledge: Pittsburgh Gopher**
> gopher://gopher.pps.pgh.pa.us

> **The Community Learning Network (Ministry of Education, British Columbia)**
> gopher://cln.etc.bc.ca
> http://cln.etc.ba.ca

> **ESU #16 Gopher (Nebraska's K–12 Information Network)**
> gopher://esu16.esu16.k12.ne.us

> **Florida Department of Education Gopher**
> gopher://gopher.firn.edu/11/doe

> **IDEAnet (Indiana Department of Education Network)**
> gopher://ideanet.doe.state.edu

> **InforMNs (Minnesota's Teacher Network)**
> gopher://informns.k12.mn.us
> http://informns.k12.mn.us

Maryland Department of Education
gopher://sailor.lib.md.us/11/GovInfo/.md/.agency/.exec/.educ

Massachusetts Department of Education Gophers
gopher://rcnvms.rcn.mass.gov
gopher://gopher.mass.edu

MDEnet (Michigan Department of Education Gopher)
gopher://gopher.mde.state.mi.us

NASA Education Sites
http://quest.arc.nasa.gov
http://k12mac.larc.nasa.gov
http://www.nas.nasa.gov/HPCC/K12/edures.html
http://www.lerc.nasa.gov/Other_Groups/K–12/K–12_homepage.html

National Science Foundation
gopher://stis.nsf.gov
http://stis.nsf.gov

NYSERNet (New York's Education Server)
gopher://nysernet.org
http://nysernet.org

Ohio Education Computer Network K–12 Gopher
gopher://nwoca7.nwoca.ohio.gov

Oregon On-Line
gopher://gopher.state.or.us/

OSPI Math, Science, and Technology Server (Washington State's Office of Superintendent of Public Instruction)
http://164.116.16.10/html_docs/HomePage.html

OTPAD (New York State Education Department)
gopher://unix5.nysed.gov" > gopher://unix5.nysed.gov" > gopher://unix5.nysed.gov

TENET (Texas Educational Network)
gopher://gopher.tenet.edu

TIESnet (Technology and Information Educational Services of Minnesota)
gopher://tiesnet.ties.k12.mn.us
http://tiesnet.ties.k12.mn.us

"Upena Hawaii" (Hawaii Department of Education's National and International Network Services for Distance Education)
gopher://kalama.doe.hawaii.edu
http://kalama.doe.hawaii.edu

U.S. Education Department/ Office of Educational Research and Instruction
gopher://gopher.ed.gov

Vermont Educational Telecommunications Consortium Gopher
gopher://vetc.vsc.edu

WEdNet (Washington Education Network)
gopher://sitka.wsipc.wednet.edu/

WisDPI (Wisconsin Department of Public Instruction)
gopher://badger.state.wi.us/11/agencies/dpi
http://badger.state.wi.us:70/0h/agencies/dpi/www/dpi_home.htm

FrEdMail
arogers@bonita.cerf.fred.org
Information and idea exchange and peer assistance among teachers and students worldwide

The Globe Program
www.globe.gov
3,000 K–12 science classes collecting environmental data around the world

Incredible Art Department
www.in.net/`kenroar/
Teachers post lesson ideas and student art

Institute for the Transfer of Technology to Education (ITTE)
cwilliams@nsba.org
www.nsba.org.itte
Technology leadership consortium of the National School Boards Association

International Education and Resource Network (I*EARN)
http://www.igc.apc.org/iearn/
Provides internet links among teachers and students worldwide

International Society for Technology in Education (ISTE)
http://www.isteonline.uoregon.edu
Information on improving education through computer-based technology

K–12 Technology
craig@cvumail.cvu.cssd.k12.vt.us
http://www.cvu.cssd.k12.vt.us/K12TECH/K12TECH.html
Guide for K–12 schools seeking to come onto the Web

National Geographic Kids Network
(800) 368-2728
National Geographic Society science and geography curriculum for grades 4–6

Public Broadcasting Service (PBS)
K12@pbs.org
www.pbs.org
Schedule of public television programming for classroom use in all subjects and grade levels

Satellite Educational Resources Consortium (SERC)
serc@serc.org
www.scsn.net/users/serc
Alliance of state departments of education and networks providing for-credit courses via satellite

Teachers Network
www.teachnet.org
Searchable database of classroom projects and bulletin board for teachers

Turner Educational Services
http://www.turner.com/tesi/
Directory of educational services and products of Turner Broadcasting

Web 66
WebMaster@web66.coled.umn.edu
http://web66.coled.umn.edu/
Strategies for integrating the Web into the K–12 curriculum

SOFTWARE EVALUATION CRITERIA

1. *Educational content and value:* Is the content accurate? Clearly presented? Appropriate for the intended audience? Free of stereotypes? Important? Does the program seem to achieve its objectives? Is it easily integrated with classwork?

2. *Mode of instruction:* What is the program intended to teach: concepts, principles, skills, visualization, and/or problem solving? Is the appropriate form of instruction or are the appropriate classroom aids (such as simulation, tutorial, drill and practice, visualization materials, problem-solving materials) being used?

3. *Technical features:* Did you have any technical problems with the program? Is the layout visually attractive? Are graphics, color, and sound used effectively to enhance instruction? Could you modify the program?

4. *Ease of use:* Are the instructions clear? Can students operate the program easily? Control the pace? Review the instructions? End the program? How is inappropriate input handled?

5. *Motivation:* Does the program hold students' interest? Do students want to use it again? Does the program vary when repeated?

6. *Feedback:* Is the feedback positive and constructive? Appropriate for the grade level? Immediate? Varied? Does it provide help or an explanation?

7. *Record keeping:* Are students' records stored on disk for later retrieval? What information is stored? For how many students? Is the record-keeping system easy to use? Is it reasonably secure?

8. *Documentation:* Are the written instructions clear? Well organized? Comprehensive? Are the objectives, prerequisites, and intended audience specified?

9. *Summary and recommendations:* What are the program's strengths? What are its weaknesses? Does it take advantage of the computer's capabilities? Does it involve the learner in the learning process? How does it compare with others with similar objectives? Would you buy and use it?

(Source: Janice L. Flake, C. Edwin McClintock, and Sandra Turner, *Fundamentals of Computer Education,* Belmont, CA: Wadsworth, 1990, pp. 286–288.)

GUIDELINES FOR OFF-AIR RECORDINGS

Though not enacted into law, Congress suggested the following guidelines for off-air recordings made by nonprofit educational institutions.

1. A broadcast program may be recorded off-air simultaneously with the broadcast transmission (including a simultaneous cable retransmission) and retained by a nonprofit educational institution for up to forty-five calendar days from the date of recording. After forty-five days have elapsed, the off-air recordings must be erased or destroyed. Broadcast programs are television programs transmitted by television stations for general reception without charge.

2. Off-air recordings may be used once by individual teachers in the course of relevant teaching activities and repeated only once, when instructional reinforcement is necessary, during the first ten consecutive school days of the forty-five calendar days. The relevant teaching activities may take place in a single classroom, a single building, on a single campus, or in the homes of students receiving formalized home instruction. School days do not include days when school is not in session (e.g., weekends, holidays, vacation periods, examination periods, or other scheduled interruptions).

3. Off-air recordings may be made only at the request of, and used by, individual teachers; they

may not be regularly recorded in anticipation of requests. No broadcast program may be recorded off-air more than once at the request of the same teacher, regardless of the number of times the program may be rebroadcast.

4. A limited number of copies may be reproduced from each off-air recording to meet the legitimate needs of teachers under these guidelines. Each additional copy is subject to all of the provisions governing the original recording.

5. After the first ten consecutive days, the recordings may be used up to the end of the forty-five calendar day retention period for teacher evaluation purposes only; that is, to determine whether or not to include the broadcast program in the teaching curriculum. The recordings may not be used for student exhibition or any other nonevaluation purpose without authorization.

6. Off-air recordings need not be used in their entirety, but the recorded programs may not be altered from their original content. The recordings may not be physically or electronically combined or merged to constitute teaching anthologies or compilations.

7. All copies of off-air recordings must include the copyright notice on the broadcast program as recorded.

8. Educational institutions are expected to establish appropriate control procedures to maintain the integrity of these guidelines.

(Source: 127 *Congressional Record,* E4750-52 [daily ed., Oct. 14, 1981], as presented in Robert J. Shoop and Dennis R. Dunklee, *School Law for the Principal: A Handbook for Practitioners,* Boston: Allyn and Bacon, 1992, pp. 239–240.)

PROFESSIONAL RESOURCES FOR TEACHERS

THE NATIONAL EDUCATION GOALS

GOAL 1

By the year 2000, all children in America will start school ready to learn.

Objectives

- All disadvantaged and disabled children will have access to high-quality and developmentally appropriate preschool programs that help prepare children for school.
- Every parent in America will be a child's first teacher and devote time each day to helping his or her preschool child learn; parents will have access to the training and support they need.
- Children will receive the nutrition and health care needed to arrive at school with healthy minds and bodies, and the number of low-birth-weight babies will be significantly reduced through enhanced prenatal health systems.

GOAL 2

By the year 2000, the high school graduation rate will increase to at least 90 percent.

Objectives

- The nation must dramatically reduce its dropout rate, and 75 percent of those students who do drop out will successfully complete a high school degree or its equivalent.
- The gap in high school graduation rates between American students from minority backgrounds and their nonminority counterparts will be eliminated.

GOAL 3

By the year 2000, American students will leave grades four, eight, and twelve having demonstrated competency in challenging subject matter, including English, mathematics, science, history, and geography; and every school in America will ensure that all students learn to use their minds well, so they may be prepared for responsible citizenship, further learning, and productive employment in our modern economy.

Objectives

- The academic performance of elementary and secondary students will increase significantly in every quartile, and the distribution of minority students in each level will more closely reflect the student population as a whole.
- The percentage of students who demonstrate the ability to reason, solve problems, apply knowledge, and write and communicate effectively will increase substantially.
- All students will be involved in activities that promote and demonstrate good citizenship, community service, and personal responsibility.
- The percentage of students who are competent in more than one language will substantially increase.
- All students will be knowledgeable about the diverse cultural heritage of this nation and about the world community.

GOAL 4

By the year 2000, the nation's teaching force will have access to programs for the continued improvement of their professional skills and the opportunity to acquire the knowledge and skills needed to instruct and prepare all American students for the next century.

GOAL 5

By the year 2000, U.S. students will be first in the world in science and mathematics achievement.

Objectives

- Math and science education will be strengthened throughout the system especially in the early grades.
- The number of teachers with a substantive background in mathematics and science will increase by 50 percent.
- The number of U.S. undergraduates and graduate students, especially women and minorities, who complete degrees in mathematics, science, and engineering will increase significantly.

GOAL 6

By the year 2000, every adult American will be literate and will possess the knowledge and skills necessary to compete in a global economy and exercise the rights and responsibilities of citizenship.

Objectives
- Every major American business will be involved in strengthening the connection between education and work.
- All workers will have the opportunity to acquire the knowledge and skills, from basic to highly technical, needed to adapt to emerging new technologies, work methods, and markets through public and private educational, vocational, technical, workplace, or other programs.
- The number of quality programs, including those at libraries, that are designed to serve more effectively the needs of the growing number of part-time and mid-career students will increase substantially.
- The proportion of college graduates who demonstrate an advanced ability to think critically, communicate effectively, and solve problems will increase substantially.

GOAL 7
By the year 2000, every school in the United States will be free of drugs, violence, and the unauthorized presence of firearms and alcohol and will offer a disciplined environment conducive to learning.

Objectives
- Every school will implement a firm and fair policy on use, possession, and distribution of drugs and alcohol.
- Parents, businesses, governmental and community organizations will work together to ensure the rights of students to study in a safe and secure environment that is free of drugs and crime, and that schools provide a healthy environment and are a safe haven for all children.

- Every local educational agency will develop and implement a policy to ensure that all schools are free of violence and the unauthorized presence of weapons.
- Every local educational agency will develop a sequential, comprehensive kindergarten through twelfth grade drug and alcohol prevention education program.
- Drug and alcohol curriculum should be taught as an integral part of sequential, comprehensive health education.
- Community-based teams should be organized to provide students and teachers with needed support.
- Every school should work to eliminate sexual harassment.

GOAL 8
By the year 2000, every school will promote partnerships that will increase parental involvement and participation in promoting the social, emotional, and academic growth of children.

Objectives
- Every state will develop policies to assist local schools and local educational agencies to establish programs for increasing partnerships that respond to the varying needs of parents and the home, including parents of children who are disadvantaged or bilingual, or parents of children with disabilities.
- Every school will actively engage parents and families in a partnership that supports the academic work of children at home and shared educational decision making at school.
- Parents and families will help to ensure that schools are adequately supported and will hold schools and teachers to high standards of accountability.

THE NATIONAL EDUCATION GOALS PANEL

The National Education Goals Panel is a unique bipartisan body of federal and state officials created in July 1990 to assess state and national progress toward achieving the National Education Goals. With the passage by Congress of the 1994 *Goals 2000: Educate America Act,* the Goals Panel became a fully independent executive branch agency charged with

monitoring and speeding progress toward the eight national Education Goals. Panel members include eight governors, four members of Congress, four state legislators, the U.S. Secretary of Education, and the President's Domestic Policy Advisor. (Contact: 1255 22nd Street, NW, Suite 502, Washington, DC 20037, (202) 632-0952, Fax (202) 632-0957)

RESOURCES AVAILABLE FROM THE NATIONAL EDUCATION GOALS PANEL

The 1995 National Education Goals Report: Core Report, Volume 1: National Data, and *Volume 2: State Data.* This *Executive Summary* is part of a set of four documents that include national and state data on various indicators measuring progress toward meeting the Goals.

The Community Action Toolkit. Created to help answer the question, "What can I do at the local level?" The *Toolkit* offers an array of materials and information to help communities build broad-based support and participation in the democratic process of setting and achieving local education goals.

Inventory of Academic Standards-Related Activities. This inventory explores the work of twenty-six organizations in promoting and strengthening the movement toward the development of state academic standards and performance assessments.

ELECTRONIC INFORMATION RESOURCES

CD-ROM. Annual reports are available on CD-ROM for users of both IBM and Macintosh computers.

The CD-ROM will permit users to create customized Goals reports—enabling users to view, search (by state, Goal, or indicator), copy and print any portion of the Report, as well as allow the user to edit text.

GOAL LINE. Through the Coalition for Goals 2000, the Goals Panel has created a customized area on GOAL LINE, the Coalition's education reform on-line network. GOAL LINE was created to increase the scale and pace of grassroots education reform by enabling education activities to share information and effective programs with others.

Daily Report Card. Through the *Daily Report Card,* an on-line education newsletter, the Goals Panel supports the distribution of information on how state and local education reforms are progressing nationwide to help communities find ways to meet the National Education Goals.

NATIONAL STANDARDS PROJECTS IN THE CONTENT AREAS

ARTS

Music Educators National Conference
1806 Robert Fulton Drive
Reston, VA 22091
(703) 860-4000 or Fax (703) 860-4826.

In coordination with the American Alliance for Theater and Education, the National Art Education Association, and the National Dance Association.

CITIZENSHIP AND CIVICS

Center of Civic Education
5146 Douglas Fir Road
Calabasas, CA 91302-1467
(818) 591-9321
http://www.primenet.com/ ~ cce/stds.html

GEOGRAPHY

National Council of Geographic Education
Geography Standards Project
1600 M Street, NW—Suite 2611
Washington, DC 20036

In coordination with the Association of American Geographers, the National Geographic Society, and the American Geographical Society. For information contact the National Council for Geographic Education at 412/357-6290.

HISTORY

National Center for History in the Schools at UCLA
231 Moore Hall, 405 Hilgard Avenue
Los Angeles, CA 90024
http://www.sscnet.ucla.edu/nchg
UCLA Bookzone (310) 206-0788

MATHEMATICS

The National Council of Teachers of Mathematics
1906 Association Drive
Reston, VA 20091-1593
(703) 620-9840 or FAX (703) 476-2970.
inforcentral@nctm.org

ENGLISH, LANGUAGE ARTS

The Center for the Study of Reading
174 Children's Research Center
51 Gerty Drive
Champaign, IL 61820
IRA (800) 336-7323

In coordination with The National Council of Teachers of English (NCTE) and the International Reading Association (IRA).

FOREIGN LANGUAGE

American Council on the Teaching of Foreign Language, Inc.
6 Executive Plaza
Yonkers, NY 10701-6801
(914) 963-8830 or FAX (914) 963-1275.

In coordination with the American Association of Teachers of French, the American Association of Teachers of German, and the American Association of Teachers of Spanish and Portuguese.

SCIENCE

National Academy of Sciences
National Research Council
2101 Constitution Avenue, NW
Washington, DC 20418
(202) 334-1399 or FAX (202) 334-3159.

In coordination with the American Association for the Advancement of Science, the American Association of Physics Teachers, the American Chemical Society, the Council of State Science Supervisors, the Earth Science Coalition, and the National Association of Biology Teachers.

PHYSICAL EDUCATION

National Association for Sports and Physical Education
1900 Association Drive
Reston, VA 22091

NEA CODE OF ETHICS FOR TEACHERS

PREAMBLE

The educator, believing in the worth and dignity of each human being, recognizes the supreme importance of the pursuit of truth, devotion to excellence, and the nurture of democratic principles. Essential to these goals is the protection of freedom to learn and to teach and the guarantee of equal educational opportunity for all. The educator accepts the responsibility to adhere to the highest ethical standards.

The educator recognizes the magnitude of the responsibility inherent in the teaching process. The desire for the respect and confidence of one's colleagues, of students, of parents, and of the members of the community provides the incentive to attain and maintain the highest possible degree of ethical conduct. The *Code of Ethics of the Education Profession* indicates the aspiration of all educators and provides standards by which to judge conduct.

The remedies specified by the NEA and/or its affiliates for the violation of any provision of this code shall be exclusive and no such provision shall be enforceable in any form other than one specifically designated by the NEA or its affiliates.

PRINCIPLE I

Commitment of the Student

The educator strives to help each student realize his or her potential as a worthy and effective member of society. The educator therefore works to stimulate the spirit of inquiry, the acquisition of knowledge and understanding, and the thoughtful formulation of worthy goals.

In fulfillment of the obligation to the student, the educator:

1. Shall not unreasonably restrain the student from independent action in the pursuit of learning

2. Shall not unreasonably deny the student access to varying points of view
3. Shall not deliberately suppress or distort subject matter relevant to the student's progress
4. Shall make reasonable effort to protect the student from conditions harmful to learning or to health and safety
5. Shall not intentionally expose the student to embarrassment or disparagement
6. Shall not on the basis of race, color, creed, sex, national origin, marital status, political or religious beliefs, family, social or cultural background, or sexual orientation unfairly:
   a) Exclude any student from participation in any program
   b) Deny benefits to any student
   c) Grant any advantage to any student
7. Shall not use professional relationships with students for private advantage
8. Shall not disclose information about students obtained in the course of professional service, unless disclosure serves a compelling professional purpose or is required by law

PRINCIPLE II

Commitment to the Profession

The education profession is vested by the public with a trust and responsibility requiring the highest ideals of professional service.

In the belief that the quality of the services of the education profession directly influences the nation and its citizens, the educator shall exert every effort to raise professional standards, to promote a climate that encourages the exercise of professional judgment, to achieve conditions that attract persons worthy of the trust to careers in education, and to assist in preventing the practice of the profession by unqualified persons.

In fulfillment of the obligation to the profession, the educator:

1. Shall not in an application for a professional position deliberately make a false statement or fail to disclose a material fact related to competency and qualifications
2. Shall not misrepresent his/her professional qualifications
3. Shall not assist any entry into the profession of a person known to be unqualified in respect to character, education, or other relevant attribute
4. Shall not knowingly make a false statement concerning the qualifications of a candidate for a professional position
5. Shall not assist a noneducator in the unauthorized practice of teaching
6. Shall not disclose information about colleagues obtained in the course of professional service unless disclosure serves a compelling professional purpose or is required by law
7. Shall not knowingly make false or malicious statements about a colleague
8. Shall not accept any gratuity, gift, or favor that might impair or appear to influence professional decisions or actions

(Source: *Code of Ethics of the Education Profession,* adopted by the NEA Representative Assembly, 1975. The National Education Association, Washington, D.C. Used with permission.)

SAMPLER OF PROFESSIONAL ORGANIZATIONS FOR TEACHERS

American Alliance for Health, Physical Education, Recreation and Dance (AAHPERD)

1900 Association Drive
Reston, VA 22091
(703) 476-3400
Fax (703) 476-9527
info@aahperd.org
www.aahperd.org

Students and educators in physical education, dance, health, athletics, safety education, recreation, and outdoor education. Purpose is to improve its fields of education at all levels through such services as consultation, periodicals and special publications, leadership development, determination of standards, and research. **Publications:** *AAHPERD Update; Health Education; Journal of Physical Education, Recreation and Dance; Leisure Today; News Kit on Programs for the Aging; Research Quarterly.*

American Alliance of Teachers of French (AATF)
57 E. Armory Avenue
Champaign, IL 61820
(217) 333-2842
Fax (217) 333-2842

Teachers of French in public and private elementary and secondary schools, colleges, and universities. Maintains Pedadgogical Aids Bureau, conducts annual French contest in elementary and secondary schools, awards scholarships to teachers for study in France, maintains placement bureau and a pen pal agency. **Publications:** *AATF National Bulletin, French Review.*

American Association of Teachers of German (AATG)
112 Haddontowne Court, No. 104
Cherry Hill, NJ 08034
(609) 795-5553
Fax (609) 795-9398
73740.3231@compuserve.com
www.stolaf.edu/stolaf/depts/german/aatg/index.html

Teachers of German at all levels. Offers in-service teacher-training workshops and awards and scholarships to outstanding high school students and teachers of German. **Publications:** *American Association of Teachers of German—Newsletter, Die Unterrichtspraxis: For the Teaching of German, German Quarterly.*

American Association of Teachers of Spanish and Portuguese (Hispanic) (AATSP)
University of Northern Colorado
Gunter Hall
Greeley, CO 80636
(970) 351-1090
lsandste@bentley.univnorthco.edu

Teachers of Spanish and Portuguese languages and literatures and others interested in Hispanic culture. Operates placement bureau and maintains pen pal registry. Sponsors honor society, Sociedad Honoraria Hispanica and National Spanish Examinations for secondary school students. **Publication:** *Hispania.*

American Classical League (Language) (ACL)
Miami University
Oxford, OH 45056
(513) 529-7741
Fax (513) 529-7742
americanclassicalleague@muohio.edu

Teachers of classical languages in high schools and colleges. To promote the teaching of Latin and other classical languages. Maintains placement service, teaching materials, and resource center. **Publications:** *Classical Outlook, Prima* (handbook for elementary school teachers).

American Council on the Teaching of Foreign Languages (ACTFL)
6 Executive Plaza
Yonkers, NY 10701-6801
(914) 963-8830
Fax (914) 963-1275
http://www.Thomson.com.actfl/home.html

Individuals interested in the teaching of classical and modern foreign languages in schools and colleges. Operates materials center, conducts seminars and workshops, and presents awards. **Publications:** *ACTFL Newsletter, Foreign Language Annals* (professional journal covering teaching methods and educational research).

American Federation of Teachers (Education) (AFT)
555 New Jersey Avenue NW
Washington, DC 20001
(202) 879-4400
(800) 242-5465
http://www.aft.org

Works with teachers and other educational employees at the state and local level in organizing, collective bargaining, research, educational issues, and public relations. Conducts research in areas such as educational reform, bilingual education, teacher certification, and evaluation. Represents members' concerns through legislative action; offers technical assistance. Operates Education for Democracy Project. **Publications:** *American Educator, American Teacher, On Campus, Public Service Reporter,* and others.

Association for Childhood Education International (ACEI)
11501 Georgia Avenue, Suite 315
Wheaton, MD 20902
(301) 942-2443
(800) 423-3563
aceihq@aol.com
http:www.udel.edu/bateman/acei

Teachers, parents, and other caregivers in thirty-one countries interested in promoting good educational practices for children from infancy through early adolescence. Conducts workshops and travel/study tours abroad, bestows awards, conducts research and educational programs, maintains speakers bureau. **Publications:** *ACEI Exchange, Childhood Education, Journal of Research in Childhood Education.*

Association for Supervision and Curriculum Development (ASCD)

1250 N. Pitt Street
Alexandria, VA 22314-1403
(703) 549-9110
Fax (703) 549-3891
member@ascd.org
http://www.ascd.org/

Professional organization of supervisors, curriculum coordinators and directors, consultants, professors of education, classroom teachers, principals, superintendents, parents, and others interested in school improvement at all levels of education. Provides professional development experiences and training in curriculum and supervision; provides Research Information Service. **Publications:** *ASCD Update, Curriculum and Supervision.*

Council for Exceptional Children (Special Education) (CEC)

1920 Association Drive
Reston, VA 22091-1589
(703) 620-3660
cec@sped.org
www.cec.sped.org

Teachers, school administrators, teacher educators, and others with a direct or indirect concern for the education of the disabled and gifted. Provides information to teachers, parents, and others concerning the education of exceptional children. Maintains 63,000 volume library. Operates the ERIC Clearinghouse on Handicapped and Gifted Children. **Publications:** *Exceptional Child Education Resources, Exceptional Children, Teaching Exceptional Children.*

Foundation for Exceptional Children (Special Education) (FEC)

1920 Association Drive
Reston, VA 22091
(703) 620-1054

Institutions, agencies, educators, parents, and persons concerned with the education and personal welfare of gifted or disabled children. Established to further the educational, vocational, social, and personal needs of the disabled child or youth and the neglected educational needs of the gifted. **Publication:** *Foundation for Exceptional Children—Focus.*

International Reading Association (IRA)

800 Barksdale Road
P.O. Box 8139
Newark, DE 19714-8139
(302) 731-1600
Fax (302) 731-1057
73314.1411@compuserve.com
http://www.reading.org

Teachers, reading specialists, consultants, administrators, supervisors, researchers, psychologists, librarians, and parents interested in promoting literacy. Seeks to improve the quality of reading instruction at all educational levels; stimulate and promote the lifetime reading habit and an awareness of the impact of reading; encourage the development of every reader's proficiency to the highest possible level. Disseminates information pertaining to research on reading. **Publications:** *Desktop Reference to the International Reading Association, Journal of Reading, Reading Teacher, Reading Today.*

Music Teachers National Association (MTNA)

617 Vine Street, Suite 1432
Cincinnati, OH 45202
(513) 421-1420
Fax (513) 421-2503
mtnaadmin@aol.com
www.mtna.com

Professional society of music teachers in studios, conservatories, music schools, and public and private schools, colleges, and universities; undergraduate and graduate music students. Seeks to raise the level of musical performance, understanding, and instruction. **Publications:** *American Music Teacher Magazine, Music Teachers National Association—Directory of Nationally Certified Teachers.*

National Art Education Association (Arts) (NAEA)

1916 Association Drive
Reston, VA 22091-1590
(703) 860-8000
Fax (703) 860-2960
naea@dgs.dgsys.com
www.naea-reston.org

Teachers of art at elementary, secondary, and college levels; colleges, libraries, museums, and other educational institutions. Studies problems of teaching art; encourages research and experimentation. Serves as clearinghouse for information on art education programs, materials, and methods of instruction. Maintains placement services and library on art education. **Publications:** *Art Education, Studies in Art Education.*

National Association for Bilingual Education (Bilingualism) (NABE)

1220 L Street NW
Suite 605
Washington, DC 20005-4018
(202) 898-1829
Fax (202) 789-2866
nabe@nabe.org

Educators, administrators, paraprofessionals, community and laypeople, and students. Purposes are to recognize, promote, publicize bilingual education. Seeks to increase public understanding of the importance of language and culture. Utilizes and develops student proficiency and ensures equal opportunities in bilingual education for language-minority students. Works to preserve and expand the nation's linguistic resources. Educates language-minority parents in public policy decisions. Promotes research in language education, linguistics, and multicultural education. Coordinates development of professional standards. **Publications:** *Annual Conference Journal, Journal, Newsletter.*

National Association of Biology Teachers (NABT)

11250 Roger Bacon Drive, No. 19
Reston, VA 22090
(703) 471-1134
nabter@aol.com
www.nabt.org

Professional society of biology and life science teachers and teacher educators at all educational levels. Works to achieve scientific literacy among citizens. Promotes professional growth and development; fosters regional activities for biology teachers; confronts issues involving biology, society, and the future; provides a national voice for the profession. **Publications:** *American Biology Teacher, National Association of Biology Teachers—News and Views,* and others.

National Association for the Education of Young Children (Childhood Education) (NAEYC)

1509 16th Street NW
Washington, DC 20036
(202) 232-8777
(800) 424-2460
Fax (202) 328-1846
naeyc@org/naeyc
www.naeyc.org/naeyc

Teachers and directors of preschool and primary schools, kindergartens, childcare centers, cooperatives, church schools, and groups having similar programs for young children. Open to all individuals interested in serving and acting on behalf of the needs and rights of young children, with primary focus on the provision of educational services and resources. Offers voluntary accreditation for early childhood schools and centers through the National Academy of Early Childhood Programs. **Publications:** *Early Childhood Research Quarterly, Young Children.*

National Association for Gifted Children (NAGC)

1707 L Street NW
Suite 550
Washington, DC 20036
(202) 785-4268
www.nagc.org

Teachers, university personnel, administrators, and parents. To advance interest in programs for the gifted. Seeks to further education of the gifted and to enhance their potential creativity. Distributes information to teachers and parents on the development of the gifted child; sponsors annual convention to provide training in curriculum planning, program evaluation, and parenting and guidance relevant to gifted children. Maintains speakers' bureau. **Publication:** *Gifted Child Quarterly.*

National Association for Trade and Industrial Education (NATIE)

P.O. Box 1665
Leesburg, VA 22075
(703) 777-1740

Educators in trade and industrial education. Works for the promotion, development, and improvement of trade and industrial education. Supports instructional programs for members to prepare for job instruction, apprentice training, adult retraining, and special training for industry. **Publications:** *NATIE News Notes, State Supervisors/ Consultants of Trade and Industrial Education,* and others.

National Business Education Association (NBEA)
1914 Association Drive
Reston, VA 22091
(703) 860-8300
www.nbea.org/nbea.html

Teachers of business subjects in secondary and post-secondary schools and colleges; administrators and research workers in business education; businesspersons interested in business education; teachers in educational institutions training business teachers. **Publication:** *Business Education Forum.*

National Council for the Social Studies (NCSS)
3501 Newark Street, NW
Washington, DC 20016
(202) 966-7840
Fax (202) 966-2061
ncss@ncss.org
www.ncss.org

Teachers of elementary and secondary social studies, including instructors of civics, geography, history, economics, political science, psychology, sociology, and anthropology. **Publications:** *Social Education, The Social Studies Professional, Social Studies and the Young Learner, Theory and Research in Social Education.*

National Council of Teachers of English (NCTE)
1111 West Kenyon Road
Urbana, IL 61801
(217) 328-3870
Fax (217) 328-9645
www.ncte.org

Teachers of English at all school levels. Works to increase the effectiveness of instruction in English language and literature. Presents achievement awards for writing to high school juniors and students in the eighth grade, and awards for high school literary magazines. Provides information and aids for teachers involved in formulating objectives, writing and evaluating curriculum guides, and planning in-service programs for teacher education. **Publications:** *English Education, English Journal, Language Arts, Research in the Teaching of English,* and others.

National Council of Teachers of Mathematics (NCTM)
1906 Association Drive
Reston, VA 22091-1593
(703) 620-9840
Fax (703) 476-2970
infocentra@nctm.org
www.nctm.org

Teachers of mathematics in grades K–12, two-year colleges, and teacher educators. **Publications:** *Arithmetic Teacher, Journal for Research in Mathematics Education, Mathematics Teacher, National Council of Teachers of Mathematics—Yearbook,* and others.

National Education Association (NEA)
1201 16th Street, NW
Washington, DC 20036
(202) 833-4000
http://www.nea.org

Professional organization and union of elementary and secondary school teachers, college and university professors, administrators, principals, counselors, and others concerned with education. **Publications:** *NEA Today, Thought and Action,* and others.

National Science Teachers Association (NSTA)
1840 Wilson Blvd.
Arlington, VA 22201-3000
(703) 243-7100
Fax (703) 243-7177

Teachers seeking to foster excellence in science teaching. Studies students and how they learn, the curriculum of science, the teacher and his/her preparation, the procedures used in classroom and laboratory, the facilities for teaching science, and the evaluation procedures used. Affiliated with: American Association for the Advancement of Science. **Publications:** *Journal of College Science Teaching, Quantum, Science and Children, Science Scope, The Science Teacher.*

Phi Delta Kappa (Education)
8th and Union
P.O. Box 789
Bloomington, IN 47402-0789
(812) 339-1156
(800) 766-1156
Fax (812) 339-0018
headquarters@pdkintl.org
www.pdkintl.org

Professional, honorary, and recognition fraternity—education. To enhance quality education through research and leadership activities. Conducts seminars and workshops. **Publications:** *Phi Delta Kappan,* and others.

Pi Lambda Theta (Education)

4101 E. 3rd Street
P.O. Box 6626
Bloomington, IN 47407-6626
(812) 339-3411
members@pilambda.org
www.pilambda.org

Honor and professional association—education. Presents biennial awards. Sponsors comparative education tours and educational conferences. **Publication:** *Educational Horizons.*

Reading Is Fundamental (RIF)

600 Maryland Avenue, SW, Suite 800
Washington, DC 20024
(202) 287-3220
Fax (202) 287-3196
http://www.si.edu/rif

Volunteer groups composed of community leaders, educators, librarians, parents, and service club members who sponsor local grass roots reading motivation programs serving 3,000,000 children nationwide. Purpose is to involve youngsters, preschool to high school age, in reading activities aimed at showing that reading is fun. Provides services to parents to help them encourage reading in the home. **Publication:** *RIF Newsletter.*

Speech Communication Association (SCA)

5105 Backlick Road, Bldg. E
Annandale, VA 22003
(703) 750-0533
Fax (703) 914-9471

Elementary, secondary, college, and university teachers, speech clinicians, media specialists, communication consultants, students, theater directors, and others. To promote study, criticism, research, teaching, and application of the artistic, humanistic, and scientific principles of communication, particularly speech communication. Sponsors the publication of scholarly volumes in speech. Conducts international debate tours in the U.S. and abroad. Maintains placement service. **Publications:** *Communication Education, Speech Communication Teacher, Text and Performance Quarterly,* and others.

Teachers of English to Speakers of Other Languages (TESOL)

1600 Cameron Street, Suite 300
Alexandria, VA 22314-2751
(703) 836-0774
Fax (703) 836-7864
tesol@tesol.edu
www.tesol.edu

School, college, and adult education teachers who teach English as a second or foreign language. Aims to improve the teaching of English as a second or foreign language by promoting research, disseminating information, developing guidelines and promoting certification, and serving as a clearinghouse for the field. Offers placement service. **Publications:** *Directory of Professional Preparation, TESOL Journal, TESOL Quarterly,* and others.

For complete information on professional organizations, see Sandra Jaszczak (ed.), *Encyclopedia of Associations,* 1, (1996) Gale Research, Inc.

EDUCATION PERIODICALS AND PUBLICATIONS

Academic Computing

Action in Teacher Education

Adolescence

American Biology Teacher

American Educational Research Journal

American Educator: The Professional Journal of the American Federation of Teachers

American Journal of Education

American School Board Journal

Arithmetic Teacher

Art Education

Bilingual Review

Black Scholar

Business Education Forum

Career Development for Exceptional Individuals

Career Development Quarterly

Child Abuse and Neglect: The International Journal

Child Development

Child Study Journal

Child Welfare

Childhood Education

Children Today

Children's Literature in Education

Classroom Computer Learning

Clearing House

Communication Education

Comparative Education

Computers and Education

Computers and the Humanities

Computers in the Schools

Computing Teacher

Contemporary Education

Curriculum and Teaching

Early Childhood Research Quarterly

Education and Computing

Education and Urban Society

Educational Forum

Educational Horizons

Educational Leadership

Educational Record

Educational Research

Educational Research Quarterly

Educational Researcher

Educational Review

Educational Technology

Educational Theory

Electronic Learning

Elementary School Journal

English Education

English Journal

English Language Teaching Journal (ETL Journal)

Equity and Choice

Equity and Excellence

Exceptional Children

Focus on Exceptional Children

Focus on Learning Problems in Mathematics

Forum for Reading

Geographical Education

Gifted Child Quarterly

Gifted Child Today

Gifted Education International

Harvard Educational Review

Health Education

Health Education Quarterly

High School Journal

History and Social Science Teacher

History Teacher

Home Economic Research Journal

Industrial Education

Instructor

International Journal of Early Childhood

International Journal of Educational Research

Journal for Research in Mathematics Education

Journal for Vocational Special Needs Education

Journal of Adolescence

Journal of Alcohol and Drug Education

Journal of American Indian Education

Journal of Black Studies

Journal of Classroom Interaction

Journal of Computer-Assisted Learning

Journal of Computer-Based Instruction

Journal of Computers in Mathematics and Science Teaching

Journal of Curriculum and Supervision

Journal of Curriculum Studies

Journal of Developmental Education

Journal of Drug Education

Journal of Early Intervention

Journal of Education

Journal of Educational Computing Research

Journal of Educational Research

Journal of Environmental Education

Journal of Home Economics

Journal of Humanistic Education and Development

Journal of Learning Disabilities

Journal of Negro Education

Journal of Physical Education, Recreation, and Dance

Journal of Reading

Journal of Reading Behavior

Journal of Research in Childhood Education

Journal of Research in Computing in Education

Journal of Research in Music Education

Journal of Research in Reading

Journal of Research in Science Teaching

Journal of Rural and Small Schools

Journal of Social Studies Research

Journal of Special Education

Journal of Teacher Education

Journal of Teaching in Physical Education

Journal of Youth and Adolescence

Kappa Delta Pi Record

Language Arts

Language, Speech, and Hearing Services in Schools

Learning

Learning Disabilities Focus

Learning Disabilities Research

Learning Disability Quarterly

Mathematics and Computer Education

Mathematics Teacher

Music Educators Journal

NABE: The Journal for the National Association for Bilingual Education

NASSP Bulletin

Negro Educational Review

New Directions for Child Development

New Directions for Teaching and Learning

Peabody Journal of Education

Phi Delta Kappan

Physical Educator

Physics Teacher

Preventing School Failure

Programmed Learning and Educational Technology

Psychology in the Schools

PTA Today

Reading Horizons

Reading Improvement

Reading Research and Instruction

Reading Research Quarterly

Reading Teacher

Remedial and Special Education

Research in Rural Education

Research in the Teaching of English

Review of Educational Research

Rural Educator

School Arts

School Science and Mathematics

Science and Children

Science Education

Science Teacher

Social Studies and the Young Learner

Social Studies Journal

Social Studies Professional

Sociology of Education

Studies in Art Education

Teacher Magazine

Teachers College Record

Teaching Exceptional Children

TESOL Quarterly

T.H.E. Journal (Technological Horizons in Education)

Theory and Research in Social Education

Theory into Practice

Topics in Early Childhood Special Education

Urban Education

Vocational Education Journal

Young Children

Youth and Society

EDUCATIONAL RESOURCES INFORMATION CENTER (ERIC) CLEARINGHOUSES

U.S. Department of Education
National Library of Education
Office of Educational Research and Improvement (OERI)
555 New Jersey Avenue NW
Washington, DC 20208-5720
(202) 219-2221
E-mail: eric@inet.ed.gov
URL: http://www.ed.gov

Adult, Career, and Vocational Education
The Ohio State University
1900 Kenny Road
Columbus, OH 43210-1090
(614) 292-4353
(800) 848-4815
Fax: (614) 292-1260
E-mail: ericacve@magnus.acs.ohio-state.edu
URL: http://www.osu.edu/units/education/cete/ericave/index.html

Assessment and Evaluation
The Catholic University of America
210 O'Boyle Hall
Washington, DC 20064-4035
(202) 673-3811
(800) GO4-ERIC
Fax: (202) 319-6692
E-mail: eric_ae@cua.edu
Gopher: gopher.cua.edu, Special Resources
URL: http://www.cua.edu/www/eric_ae

Community Colleges
University of California at Los Angeles
3051 Moore Hall
P.O. Box 951521
Los Angeles, CA 90095-1521
(310) 825-3931
(800) 832-8256
Fax: (310) 206-8095
E-mail: ericcc@ucla.edu
URL: http://www.gseis.ucla.edu/ERIC/eric.html

Counselling and Student Services

School of Education
University of North Carolina at Greensboro
1000 Spring Garden Street
Greensboro, NC 27412-5001
(910) 334-4114
(800) 414-9769
Fax: (910) 334-4116
E-mail: ericcas2@dewey.uncg.edu
URL: http://www.uncg.edu/ ~ ericcas2

Disabilities and Gifted Education

The Council for Exceptional Children
1920 Association Drive
Reston, VA 20191-1589
(703) 264-9474
(800) 328-0272
TTY: (703) 264-9449
Fax: (703) 620-2521
E-mail: ericec@cec.sped.org
URL: http://www.cec.sped.org/ericec.html

Educational Management

5207 University of Oregon
1787 Agate Street
Eugene, OR 97403-5207
(541) 346-1684
(800) 438-8841
Fax: (541) 346-2334
E-mail: ppiele@oregon.uoregon.edu
URL: http://darkwing.uoregon.edu/
   ~ ericcem/home.html

Elementary and Early Childhood Education

University of Illinois at Urbana—Champaign
805 West Pennsylvania Avenue
Urbana, IL 61801-4897
(217) 333-1386
(800) 583-4135
Fax: (217) 333-3767
E-mail: ericeece@uiuc.edu
Gopher: ericps.ed.uiuc.edu
URL: http://ericps.ed.uiuc.edu/ericeece.html
NPIN URL: http://ericps.ed.uiuc.edu/npin/npinhome.
   html (National Parent Information Network)

Higher Education

The George Washington University
One Dupont Circle, NW, Suite 630
Washington, DC 20036-1183
(202) 296-2597
(800) 773-3742
Fax: (202) 452-1844
E-mail: eriche@inet.ed.gov

Information & Technology

Syracuse University
4–194 Center for Science and Technology
Syracuse, NY 13244-4100
(315) 443-3640
(800) 464-9107
Fax: (315) 443-5448
E-mail: eric@ericir.syr.edu; askeric@ericir.syr.edu
Gopher: ericir.syr.edu
URL AskERIC: http://ericir.syr.edu
URL ERIC/IT: http://ericir.syr.edu/ithome

Languages and Linguistics

Center for Applied Linguistics
1118 22nd Street, NW
Washington, DC 20037-0037
(202) 429-9292
(800) 276-9834
Fax: (202) 659-5641
E-mail: eric@cal.org
URL: http://www.cal.org/ericll

Reading, English, and Communication

Indiana University
Smith Research Center
2805 East 10th Street, Suite 150
Bloomington, IN 47408-2698
(812) 855-5847
(800) 759-4723
Fax: (812) 855-4220
E-mail: ericcs@indiana.edu
Gopher: gopher.indiana.edu
URL: http://www.indiana.edu/ ~ eric_rec

Rural Education and Small Schools

Appalachia Educational Laboratory
1031 Quarrier Street
P.O. Box 1348
Charleston, WV 25325-1348
(304) 347-0400
(800) 624-9120
TTY: (304) 347-0401
Fax: (304) 347-0487
E-mail: lanhamb@ael.org
URL: http://www.ael.org/erichp.html

Science, Mathematics, and Environmental Education

The Ohio State University
1929 Kenny Road
Columbus, OH 43210-1080
(614) 292-6717
(800) 276-0462
Fax: (614) 292-0263
E-mail: ericse@osu.edu
Gopher: gopher.ericse.ohio-state.edu
URL: http://www.ericse.org

Social Studies/Social Science Education

Indiana University
Social Studies Development Center
2805 East 10th Street, Suite 120
Bloomington, IN 47408-2698
(812) 855-3838
(800) 266-3815
Fax: (812) 855-0455
E-mail: ericso@indiana.edu
URL: http://www.indiana.edu/~ssdc/eric-chess.html

Teaching and Teacher Education

American Association of Colleges for Teacher Education
One Dupont Circle, NW, Suite 610
Washington, DC 20036-1186
(202) 293-2450
(800) 822-9229
Fax: (202) 457-8095
E-mail: ericsp@inet.ed.gov
URL: http://www.ericsp.org

Urban Education

Teachers College, Columbia University
Institute for Urban and Minority Education
Main Hall, Room 303, Box 40
New York, NY 10027-6696
(212) 678-3433
(800) 601-4868
Fax: (212) 678-4012
E-mail: eric-cue@columbia.edu
URL: http://eric-web.tc.columbia.edu

ADJUNCT CLEARINGHOUSES

Child Care

National Child Care Information Center
301 Maple Avenue West, Suite 602
Vienna, VA 22180
(800) 616-2242
Fax: (800) 716-2242
E-mail: agoldstein@acf.dhhs.gov
URL: http://ericps.ed.uiuc.edu/nccic/nccichome.html

Clinical Schools

American Association of Colleges for Teacher Education
One Dupont Circle, NW, Suite 610
Washington, DC 20036-1186
(202) 293-2450
(800) 822-9229
Fax: (202) 457-8095
E-mail: iabdlha@inet.ed.gov
URL: http://www.ericsp.org

Consumer Education

National Institute for Consumer Education
207 Rackham Building
Eastern Michigan University
Ypsilanti, MI 48197-2237
(313) 487-2292
Fax: (313) 487-7153
E-mail: NICE@emu.vax.emich.edu
URL: http://www.emich.edu/public/coe/nice/nice.html

Entrepreneurship Education

Center for Entrepreneurial Leadership
Ewing Marion Kauffman Foundation
4900 Oak Street
Kansas City, MO 64112-2776
(816) 932-1000
(888) 423-5233
Fax: (310) 206-8095
E-mail: celcee@ucla.edu
URL: http://www.celcee.edu

ESL Literacy Education

Center for Applied Linguistics
1118 22nd Street, NW
Washington, DC 20037-0037
(202) 429-9292, Extension 200
Fax: (202) 659-5641
E-mail: ncle@cal.org
URL: http://www.cal.org/cal/html/ncle.html

International Civic Education

Social Studies Development Center
Indiana University
2805 East Tenth Street, Suite 120
Bloomington, IN 47408
(812) 855-3838
(800) 266-3815
Fax: (812) 855-0455
E-mail: patrick@indiana.edu

Law-Related Education
Social Studies Development Center
Indiana University
2805 East Tenth Street, Suite 120
Bloomington, IN 47408
(812) 855-3838
(800) 266-3815
Fax: (812) 855-0455
E-mail: ericso@indiana.edu
URL: http://www.indiana.edu/~ssdc/lre.html

Service Learning
University of Minnesota
College of Education and Human Development
1954 Bufford Avenue, Room R-290, VoTech Building
St. Paul, MN 55108
(612) 625-6276
(800) 808-SERV
Fax: (612) 625-6277
E-mail: serv@maroon.tc.umn.edu
Gopher: gopher.nicsl.coled.umn.edu
URL: http://www.nicsl.coled.umn.edu

Test Collection
Educational Testing Service
Princeton, NJ 08541
(609) 734-5737
Fax: (609) 683-7186
E-mail: mhalpern@ets.org
Gopher: gopher.cua.edu, Special Resources
URL: http://www.cua.edu/www/eric_ae/testcol.html

SUPPORT COMPONENTS

Access ERIC
1600 Research Boulevard, 5F
Rockville, MD 20850-3172
(301) 251-5789
(800) LET-ERIC
Fax: (301) 309-2084
E-mail: acceric@inet.ed.gov
Gopher: aspensys.com, Education and Training Division
URL: http://www.aspensys.com/eric

ERIC Document Reproduction Service (EDRS)
7420 Fullerton Road, Suite 110
Springfield, VA 22153-2852
(703) 440-1400
(800) 443-ERIC
Fax: (703) 440-1408
E-mail:edrs@inet.ed.gov
Gopher: erds.com
URL: http://edrs.com

ERIC Processing and Reference Facility
Computer Sciences Corporation
1100 West Street, 2nd Floor
Laurel, MD 20707-3598
(301) 497-4080
(800) 799-ERIC
Fax: (301) 953-0263
E-mail: ericfac@inet.ed.gov
URL: http://ericfac.piccard.csc.com

DEPARTMENT OF EDUCATION REGIONAL ASSISTANCE CENTERS

Region 1: Connecticut, Maine, Massachusetts, New Hampshire, Rhode Island, Vermont
New England Comprehensive Center at Education
   Development Center, Newton, MA
(800) 332-0226
E-mail: viviang@edc.org
World Wide Web: site under construction

Region 2: New York state
New York Technical Assistance Center, New York City
(800) 469-8224
E-mail:millrla@is2nyu.edu
World Wide Web: http://www.nyu.edu/education/
   MetroCenter/

Region 3: Delaware, District of Columbia, Maryland, New Jersey, Ohio, Pennsylvania
Region III Comprehensive Assistance Center,
Arlington, VA
(800) 925-3223
E-mail: r3cc@ceee.gwu.edu
World Wide Web (site under construction):
   http://www.gwu.edu~r3cc

Region 4: Kentucky, North Carolina, South Carolina, Tennessee, Virginia, West Virginia
Region 4 Comprehensive Technical Assistance Center,
Charleston WV
(800) 624-9120
E-mail: aelinfo@ael.org
World Wide Web: http://www.ael.org

Region 5: Alabama, Arkansas, Georgia, Louisiana, Mississippi
Southeast Comprehensive Assistance Center
Metairie, LA
(800) 644-8671
E-mail: htran@sedl.org
World Wide Web: http://www.sedl.org/

Region 6: Iowa, Michigan, Minnesota, North Dakota, South Dakota, Wisconsin
Comprehensive Regional Assistance Center—
   Region VI, Madison, WI
(608) 263-4220
E-mail: mcoyne@macc.wisc.edu
World Wide Web: http://www.wcer.wisc.edu

Region 7: Illinois, Indiana, Kansas, Missouri, Nebraska, Oklahoma
Region VII Comprehensive Assistance Center,
Norman, OK
(800) 228-1766
E-mail: regionVII@ou.edu
World Wide Web: http://tel.occe.uoknor.edu/
   comp/comp.html

Region 8: Texas
Support for Texas Academic Renewal Center,
San Antonio, TX
(210) 684-8180
E-mail: acortez@txdirect.net
World Wide Web: http://www.csn.net/RMC/star

Region 9: Arizona, Colorado, New Mexico, Nevada, Utah
Southwest Comprehensive Regional Assistance Center,
Albuquerque, NM
(800) 247-4269
E-mail: swcc@cesdp.nmhu.edu
World Wide Web: http://www.nmhu.edu/cesdp

Region 10: Idaho, Montana, Oregon, Washington state, Wyoming
Northwest Regional Educational Laboratory,
Portland, OR
(800) 547-6339
E-mail: info@NWREL.org
World Wide Web: http://www.NWREL.org

Region 11: Northern California
Far West Laboratory for Educational Research,
San Francisco, CA
(800) 645-3276
E-mail: tross@wested.org
World Wide Web: http://www.wested.org

Region 12: Southern California
Southern California Comprehensive Regional
   Assistance Center, Downey, CA
(310) 922-6343
E-mail: mothner_henry@lacoe.edu
World Wide Web: http://SCCAC.lacoe.edu

Region 13: Alaska
Alaska Comprehensive Regional Assistance Center,
Juneau, AK
(907) 586-6806
E-mail: akrac@ptialaska.net
World Wide Web (site under construction):
   http://www.jun.alask.edu/akrac

Region 14: Florida, Puerto Rico, Virgin Islands
Region 14 Comprehensive Center, Tucker, GA
(800) 241-3865
E-mail: thensley@ets.org
World Wide Web: http://www.ets.org

Region 15: American Samoa, Federated States of Micronesia, Commonwealth of the Northern Mariana Islands, Guam, Hawaii, Republic of the Marshall Islands, Republic of Palau
Pacific Region Educational Laboratory, Honolulu, HI
(808) 533-6000
E-mail: askprel@prel.hawaii.edu
World Wide Web: http://www.prel.hawaii.edu

(Source: *Education Week*, May 29, 1996 p. 23.)

SELECTED NATIONAL EDUCATIONAL RESEARCH AND IMPROVEMENT CENTERS (OERI)

Center on Achievement in School Mathematics and Science
Wisconsin Center for Education Research, School
   of Education
University of Wisconsin—Madison
1025 Johnson Street
Madison, WI 53706
(608) 263-3605
Contact: Thomas A. Romberg
OERI Monitor: Carole Lacampagne (202) 219-2064,
National Institute on Student Achievement, Curriculum, and Assessment

Center for Research on Cultural Diversity and Second Language Learning
The Regents of the University of California
The University of California
1156 High Street
Santa Cruz, CA 95064
(408) 459-4114
Contact: Karen F. Reinaro
OERI Monitor: René Gonzalez (202) 219-2220,
National Institute on the Education of At-Risk Students

Center to Enhance Early Development of Learning
University of North Carolina—Chapel Hill
Frank Porter Graham Child Development Center
CB #4100
Chapel Hill, NC 27599-4100
(919) 966-4250
Contact: Don Bailey
OERI Monitor: Naomi Karp (202) 219-1586,
National Institute on Early Childhood Development
and Education

Center for Research on Evaluation, Standards, and Student Testing (CRESST)
University of California, Los Angeles
Graduate School of Education
1339 Moore Hall
405 Hilgard Avenue
Los Angeles, CA 90024
(310) 206-1530
Contacts: Eva L. Baker and Robert Linn
OERI Monitor: David Sweet (202) 219-1748,
National Institute on Student Achievement, Curriculum, and Assessment

Center for Research on the Education of Students Placed At Risk (CRESPAR)
Johns Hopkins University, CSOS
3505 North Charles Street
Baltimore, MD 21218
(410) 516-8800
   and
Howard University
Department of Psychology
Washington, DC 20059
(202) 806-8484
Contacts: Beverly Cole-Henderson (Howard) or
John H. Hollifield (John Hopkins)
OERI Co-monitors: René Gonzalez (202) 219-2220
and Debra Hillinger (202) 219-2024, National Institute on the Education of At-Risk Students

Center on Families, Communities, Schools, and Children's Learning
Boston University
605 Commonwealth Avenue
Boston, MA 02215
(617) 353-3309
Fax: (617) 353-8444
Co-directors: Don Davies and Joyce Epstein
OERI Center Monitor: Patricia Lines (202) 219-2223

Center on the Gifted and Talented
University of Connecticut
362 Fairfield Road U-7
Storrs, CT 06269-2007
(203) 486-2900
Contact: Joseph S. Renzulli
OERI Monitor: Beverly E. Coleman (202) 213-2260,
National Institute on the Education of At-Risk Students

Center on Improving Student Learning and Achievement in English
The Research Foundation of State University
   of New York
University of Albany, SUNY
Office for Research—AD 218
1400 Washington Avenue
Albany, NY 12222
(518) 442-3510
Contact: Judith Langer
OERI Monitor: Rita Foy (202) 219-2027
National Institute on Student Achievement, Curriculum, and Assessment

Center on Increasing the Effectiveness of State and Local Education Reform Efforts
Consortium for Policy Research in Education (CPRE)
Graduate School of Education
University of Pennsylvania
3440 Market Street, Suite 560
Philadelphia, PA 19104-3325
(215) 573-0700, ext. 224
Contact: Susan Fuhrman
OERI Monitor: James Fox (202) 219-2234,
National Institute on Educational Governance,
Finance, Policymaking, and Management

Reading Research Center
University of Georgia
318 Aderhold
Athens, GA 30602-7125
(706) 542-3678
Contact: Donna Alvermann
OERI Monitor: Anne Sweet (202) 219-2079,
National Institute on Student Achievement, Curriculum, and Assessment

Center for Research on Teacher Learning
Michigan State University
116 Erickson Hall
East Lansing, MI 48824-1034
(517) 355-9302
Fax: (517) 336-2795
Co-directors: Robert Floden and Williamson McDiarmid
OERI Center Monitor: Joyce Murphy (202) 219-2039

Center for Technology in Education
Educational Development Center, Inc.
610 West 112th Street
New York, NY 10025
(212) 875-4560
Fax: (212) 875-4760
Director: Jan Hawkins
OERI Center Monitor: Ram Singh (202) 219-2021

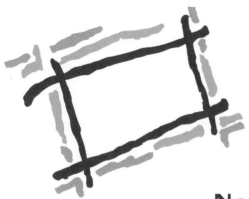

Name Index

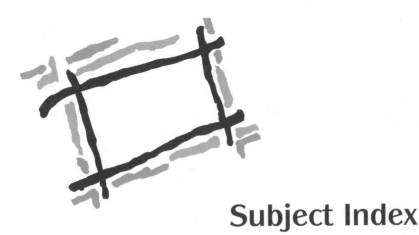

Subject Index

College Online, 60
Collegiality, 430, 431
Colonial curriculum
    religious objective and, 71
Commission on the Reorganization of Secondary
        Education, 81
Committee of Fifteen, The, 360
Committee of Ten, The, 360
Common School Journal, The, 78
Common schools, state-supported, 77–78
Community as resource, 451
Community-based partnerships, 450
Comparative education, 457–461
Compensatory education program, 124
Competency and effectiveness of teachers, 24–25
Compulsory education, 73–74
    historical effects on teaching profession, 79–82
Computer-assisted instruction (*see also* Technology in ed-
        ucation), 330–331
Computer revolution, 402–403
Computer software, copyright laws and, 217–218
Computers, 402–403
    on-line education resources, 56, 60, 94, 128, 162, 196,
        272–273, 306, 342, 376, 408, 434, 440, 474–475
Concerned Black Men, 451
Concrete operations stage (*see* Cognitive development)
Constructive assertiveness, 324, 325–326
Constructivism, 153–155, 332
Contingent teaching, 332
Contracts (*see* Teachers contracts)
Cooperative learning, 317–318
Copyright Act, 215, 217
Copyright laws, 215–218
    extended to cyberspace, 218
Core curriculum, 363
Cornfield v. Consolidated High School District No. 230, 224
Corporal punishment, 227–228
Corporate-education partnerships, 193, 451–452
Co-teaching, 436–437
Council of Chief State School Officers, 180
Creativity of teaching, 27
Credentials file, 420
Cross-age tutoring, 333
Culture of classroom, 310–314
Cultural identity, 239
Cultural literacy, 142
Cultural pluralism, 239
Culture, American, 238–242
Current Index to Journals in Education, 94
Curricular and Instructional Resources, 539–545
Curriculum, 346–351
    arts, position of, 371–372
    based on Great Books, 89–90, 143
    content, 350
    core, 363
    diversity in, 89
    excellence, concern with, 362
    explicit, 347
    focus of planning, 351
    hidden, 347

influences on, 355–364
inquiry-based, 362–363
integrated, 352, 354
national, 461
null, 348
outcome-based, 363–364
perennialist, 143
performance-based, 363–364
physical education and, 372–373
planners of, 354
reform, 87–88, 357–358, 397–399, 401
relevancy-based, 89, 363
state-mandated, 209–210
student-centered, 352
subject-centered, 352
teacher reform and, 397–399, 401
trends and issues in, 364–374
vocational goals, 358–360, 373–375
whole-language approach to, 364–366
Curriculum, national, 461
*Curriculum and Evaluation Standards for School Mathemat-
        ics* (National Council of Teachers of Mathematics),
        366–367
Curtis v. School Committee of Falmouth, 231
Cyberspace, impact on education, 464–466

Dailey v. Los Angeles Unified School District, 213
Dame schools, 72
Dare the School Build a New Social Order? (Counts), 113
Davis v. Meek, 226
Death-at-an-Early-Age (Kozol), 87
Deductive thinking (*see* Logic)
Democracy and Social Ethics (Addams), 81
Democratic classroom, 322
Demographic Look at Tomorrow, A (Hodgkinson), 248
Departmentalization, 109
Department of Defense overseas dependents schools, 182
Department of education, state, 179
Desegregation, 87, 249
Developmental, stages of, 276–285
Developmental Bilingual Elementary Education Discus-
        sion List, 273
Developmental stresses
    of adolescence, 283
    of childhood, 282
Direct instruction, 328
Discipline
    assertive, 326
    Eighth Amendment and, 228
    prevention of problems, 322–323
Discovery learning, 332
Dismissal, 205
Distance learning, 45
District of Columbia v. Doe, 213
Diversity, 238–270
    in curricula, 89
    in families, 117
    rewards related to, 5–6
Doe v. Renfrow, 224
Dress codes, 220–221

Reader Feedback

We would sincerely appreciate your suggestions for improving this book. Please respond briefly to the following questions and return this form to Allyn & Bacon, 160 Gould St., Needham Heights, MA 02194-2310. Thank you.

Please tell us your overall impression of the text.

	Excellent	Good	Fair	Poor
Was it written in a clear and understandable style?	_____	_____	_____	_____
Were difficult concepts explained?	_____	_____	_____	_____
How would you rate the photos and illustrations?	_____	_____	_____	_____
How does this text compare with texts you are using in other education courses?	_____	_____	_____	_____

1. What were the most useful features of this book?

2. What were the least useful features?

3. What topics should be added or enlarged?

4. What changes would you recommend in the book?

5. Other comments.